ASCENT
CENTER FOR TECHNICAL KNOWLEDGE

Autodesk® Revit® 2018
Structure Fundamentals

Student Guide
Imperial - 1st Edition

AUTODESK.
Authorized Publisher

CONTINUING EDUCATION
AIA

ASCENT - Center for Technical Knowledge®
Autodesk® Revit® 2018
Structure Fundamentals
Imperial - 1st Edition

Prepared and produced by:

ASCENT Center for Technical Knowledge
630 Peter Jefferson Parkway, Suite 175
Charlottesville, VA 22911

866-527-2368
www.ASCENTed.com

Lead Contributor: Martha Hollowell

ASCENT - Center for Technical Knowledge is a division of Rand Worldwide, Inc., providing custom developed knowledge products and services for leading engineering software applications. ASCENT is focused on specializing in the creation of education programs that incorporate the best of classroom learning and technology-based training offerings.

We welcome any comments you may have regarding this student guide, or any of our products. To contact us please email: feedback@ASCENTed.com.

Contents

Preface

To take full advantage of Building Information Modeling, the *Autodesk® Revit® 2018: Structure Fundamentals* student guide has been designed to teach the concepts and principles from building design through construction documentation using the Autodesk® Revit® 2018 Structure software. This student guide is intended to introduce students to the user interface and the basic building components of the software that makes it a powerful and flexible structural modeling tool. The goal is to familiarize you with the tools required to create, modify, analyze, and document the parametric model.

Topics Covered

- Introduction to the Autodesk Revit software

- Basic drawing and editing tools

- Setting up levels and grids

- Working with views

- Starting a structural project based on a linked architectural model

- Adding structural columns and walls

- Adding foundations and structural slabs

- Structural reinforcement

- Beams, trusses, and framing systems

- Analytical models and placing loads

- Project practices to reinforce learning

- Construction documents

- Annotating construction documents

- Detailing

- Scheduling

Note on Software Setup

This student guide assumes a standard installation of the software using the default preferences during installation. Lectures and practices use the standard software templates and default options for the Content Libraries.

Students and Educators can Access Free Autodesk Software and Resources

Autodesk challenges you to get started with free educational licenses for professional software and creativity apps used by millions of architects, engineers, designers, and hobbyists today. Bring Autodesk software into your classroom, studio, or workshop to learn, teach, and explore real-world design challenges the way professionals do.

Get started today - register at the Autodesk Education Community and download one of the many Autodesk software applications available.

Visit www.autodesk.com/joinedu/

Note: Free products are subject to the terms and conditions of the end-user license and services agreement that accompanies the software. The software is for personal use for education purposes and is not intended for classroom or lab use.

Lead Contributor: Martha Hollowell

Martha incorporates her passion for architecture and education into all her projects, including the student guides she creates on Autodesk Revit for Architecture, MEP, and Structure. She started working with AutoCAD in the early 1990's, adding AutoCAD Architecture and Autodesk Revit as they came along.

After receiving a B.Sc. in Architecture from the University of Virginia, she worked in the architectural department of the Colonial Williamsburg Foundation and later in private practice, consulting with firms setting up AutoCAD in their offices.

Martha has over 20 years' experience as a trainer and instructional designer. She is skilled in leading individuals and small groups to understand and build on their potential. Martha is trained in Instructional Design and has achieved the Autodesk Certified Instructor (ACI) and Autodesk Certified Professional designations for Revit Architecture.

Martha Hollowell has been the Lead Contributor for *Autodesk Revit Structure Fundamentals* since 2008.

In this Guide

The following images highlight some of the features that can be found in this Student Guide.

Practice Files

To download the practice files for this student guide, use the following steps:

1. Type the URL shown below into the address bar of your Internet browser. The URL must be typed **exactly as shown**. If you are using an ASCENT ebook, you can click on the link to download the file.

2. Press <Enter> to download the .ZIP file that contains the Practice Files.

3. Once the download is complete, unzip the file to a local folder. The unzipped file contains an .EXE file.

4. Double-click on the .EXE file and follow the instructions to automatically install the Practice Files on the C:\ drive of your computer.

Do not change the location in which the Practice Files folder is installed. Doing so can cause errors when completing the practices in this student guide.

ftp://ftp.ascented.com/cware/xxxxxxxx.zip

FTP link for practice files

Practice Files

The Practice Files page tells you how to download and install the practice files that are provided with this student guide.

Chapter 1

Getting Started

In this chapter you learn how to start the AutoCAD® software, become familiar with the basic layout of the AutoCAD screen, how to access commands, use your pointing device, and understand the AutoCAD Cartesian workspace. You also learn how to open an existing drawing, view a drawing by zooming and panning, and save your work in the AutoCAD software.

Learning Objectives in this Chapter

- Launch the AutoCAD software and complete a basic initial setup of the drawing environment.
- Identify the basic layout and features of AutoCAD interface including the Ribbon, Drawing Window, and Application Menu.
- Locate commands and launch them using the Ribbon, shortcut menus, Application Menu, and Quick Access Toolbar.
- Locate points in the AutoCAD Cartesian workspace.
- Open and close existing drawings and navigate to file locations.
- Move around a drawing using the mouse, the **Zoom** and **Pan** commands, and the Navigation Bar.
- Save drawings in various formats and set the automatic save options using the **Save** commands.

Learning Objectives for the chapter

Chapters

Each chapter begins with a brief introduction and a list of the chapter's Learning Objectives.

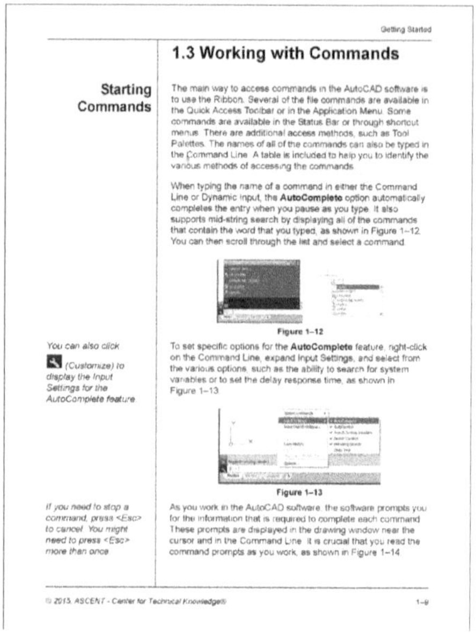

Getting Started

1.3 Working with Commands

Starting Commands

The main way to access commands in the AutoCAD software is to use the Ribbon. Several of the file commands are available in the Quick Access Toolbar or in the Application Menu. Some commands are available in the Status Bar or through shortcut menus. There are additional access methods, such as Tool Palettes. The names of all of the commands can also be typed in the Command Line. A table is included to help you to identify the various methods of accessing the commands.

When typing the name of a command in either the Command Line or Dynamic Input, the **AutoComplete** option automatically completes the entry when you pause as you type. It also supports mid-string search by displaying all of the commands that contain the word that you typed, as shown in Figure 1–12. You can then scroll through the list and select a command.

Figure 1–12

You can also click (Customize) to display the Input Settings for the AutoComplete feature.

To set specific options for the **AutoComplete** feature, right-click on the Command Line, expand Input Settings, and select from the various options, such as the ability to search for system variables or to set the delay response time, as shown in Figure 1–13.

Figure 1–13

If you need to stop a command, press <Esc> to cancel. You might need to press <Esc> more than once.

As you work in the AutoCAD software, the software prompts you for the information that is required to complete each command. These prompts are displayed in the drawing window near the cursor and in the Command Line. It is crucial that you read the command prompts as you work, as shown in Figure 1–14.

© 2015, ASCENT - Center for Technical Knowledge® 1–9

Side notes

Side notes are hints or additional information for the current topic.

Instructional Content

Each chapter is split into a series of sections of instructional content on specific topics. These lectures include the descriptions, step-by-step procedures, figures, hints, and information you need to achieve the chapter's Learning Objectives.

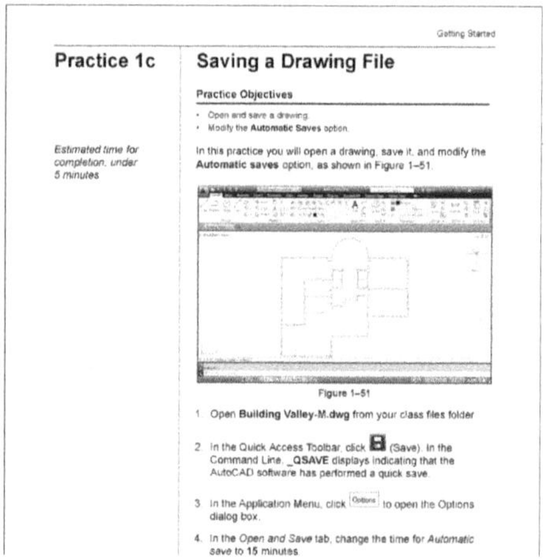

Getting Started

Practice 1c Saving a Drawing File

Practice Objectives

- Open and save a drawing.
- Modify the **Automatic Saves** option.

Estimated time for completion: under 5 minutes

In this practice you will open a drawing, save it, and modify the **Automatic saves** option, as shown in Figure 1–51.

Figure 1–51

1. Open **Building Valley-M.dwg** from your class files folder.
2. In the Quick Access Toolbar, click (Save). In the Command Line, **_QSAVE** displays indicating that the AutoCAD software has performed a quick save.
3. In the Application Menu, click Options to open the Options dialog box.
4. In the *Open and Save* tab, change the time for *Automatic save* to **15** minutes.

Practice Objectives

Practices

Practices enable you to use the software to perform a hands-on review of a topic.

Some practices require you to use prepared practice files, which can be downloaded from the link found on the Practice Files page.

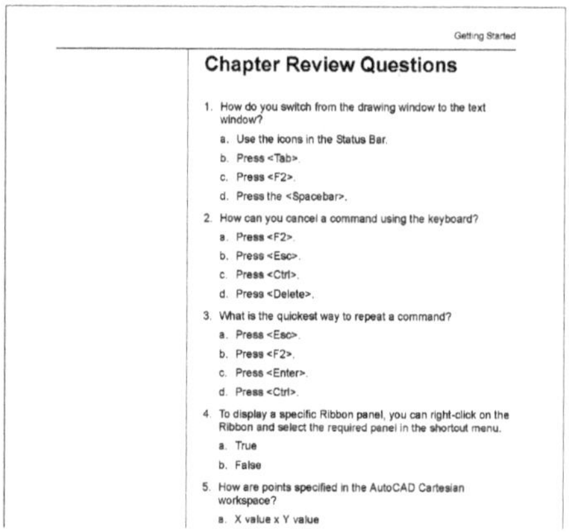

Getting Started

Chapter Review Questions

1. How do you switch from the drawing window to the text window?
   a. Use the icons in the Status Bar.
   b. Press <Tab>.
   c. Press <F2>.
   d. Press the <Spacebar>.
2. How can you cancel a command using the keyboard?
   a. Press <F2>.
   b. Press <Esc>.
   c. Press <Ctrl>.
   d. Press <Delete>.
3. What is the quickest way to repeat a command?
   a. Press <Esc>.
   b. Press <F2>.
   c. Press <Enter>.
   d. Press <Ctrl>.
4. To display a specific Ribbon panel, you can right-click on the Ribbon and select the required panel in the shortcut menu.
   a. True
   b. False
5. How are points specified in the AutoCAD Cartesian workspace?
   a. X value x Y value

Chapter Review Questions

Chapter review questions, located at the end of each chapter, enable you to review the key concepts and learning objectives of the chapter.

Command Summary

The Command Summary is located at the end of each chapter. It contains a list of the software commands that are used throughout the chapter, and provides information on where the command is found in the software.

Autodesk Certification Exam Appendix

This appendix includes a list of the topics and objectives for the Autodesk Certification exams, and the chapter and section in which the relevant content can be found.

Icons in this Student Guide

The following icons are used to help you quickly and easily find helpful information.

New in 2018	Indicates items that are new in the Autodesk Revit 2018 software.
Enhanced in 2018	Indicates items that have been enhanced in the Autodesk Revit 2018 software.

Practice Files

To download the practice files for this student guide, use the following steps:

1. Type the URL shown below into the address bar of your Internet browser. The URL must be typed **exactly as shown**. If you are using an ASCENT ebook, you can click on the link to download the file.

Address bar

http://www.ASCENTed.com/getfile?id=salticidae

File   Edit   View   Favorites   Tools   Help

2. Press <Enter> to download the .ZIP file that contains the Practice Files.

3. Once the download is complete, unzip the file to a local folder. The unzipped file contains an .EXE file.

4. Double-click on the .EXE file and follow the instructions to automatically install the Practice Files on the C:\ drive of your computer.

   Do not change the location in which the Practice Files folder is installed. Doing so can cause errors when completing the practices in this student guide.

http://www.ASCENTed.com/getfile?id=salticidae

Stay Informed!

Interested in receiving information about upcoming promotional offers, educational events, invitations to complimentary webcasts, and discounts? If so, please visit:

www.ASCENTed.com/updates/

Help us improve our product by completing the following survey:

www.ASCENTed.com/feedback

You can also contact us at: *feedback@ASCENTed.com*

Introduction to BIM and Autodesk Revit

Building Information Modeling (BIM) and the Autodesk® Revit® software work hand in hand to help you create smart, 3D models that are useful at all stages in the building process. Understanding the software interface and terminology enhances your ability to create powerful models and move around in the various views of the model.

Learning Objectives in this Chapter

- Describe the concept and workflow of Building Information Modeling in relation to the Autodesk Revit software.
- Navigate the graphic user interface, including the ribbon (where most of the tools are found), the Properties palette (where you make modifications to element information), and the Project Browser (where you can open various views of the model).
- Open existing projects and start new projects using templates.
- Use viewing commands to move around the model in 2D and 3D views.

1.1 BIM and Autodesk Revit

Building Information Modeling (BIM) is an approach to the entire building life cycle, including design, construction, and facilities management. The BIM process supports the ability to coordinate, update, and share design data with team members across disciplines.

The Autodesk Revit software is a true BIM product. It enables you to create complete 3D building models (as shown on the left in Figure 1–1) that provide considerable information reported through construction documents, and enables you to share these models with other programs for more extensive analysis.

The Autodesk® Revit® software includes tools for architectural, mechanical, electrical, plumbing, and structural design.

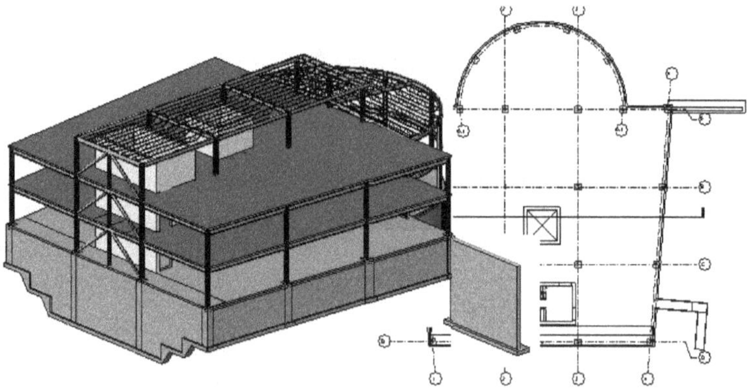

Figure 1–1

The Autodesk Revit software is considered a Parametric Building Modeler:

- *Parametric:* A relationship is established between building elements: when one element changes, other related elements change as well. For example, if you add an element in a plan view, it also displays in all of the other views.

- *Building:* The software is designed for working with buildings and the surrounding landscape, as opposed to gears or highways.

- *Modeler:* A project is built in a single file based on the 3D building model, as shown on the left in Figure 1–1. All views, such as plans (as shown on the right in Figure 1–1), elevations, sections, details, construction documents, and reports are generated based on the model.

- It is important that everyone who is collaborating on a project works in the same version and build of the software.

Workflow and BIM

BIM has changed the process of how a building is planned, budgeted, designed, constructed, and (in some cases) operated and maintained.

In the traditional design process, construction documents are created independently, typically including plans, sections, elevations, details, and notes. Sometimes, a separate 3D model is created in addition to these documents. Changes made in one document, such as the addition of a light fixture in a plan, have to be coordinated with the rest of the documents and schedules in the set, as shown in Figure 1–2.

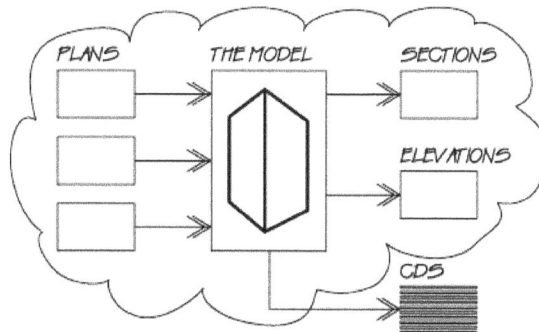

Figure 1–2

In BIM, the design process revolves around the model, as shown in Figure 1–3. Plans, elevations, and sections are simply 2D versions of the 3D model, while and schedules are a report of the information stored in the model. Changes made in one view automatically update in all views and related schedules. Even Construction Documents update automatically with callout tags in sync with the sheet numbers. This is called bidirectional associativity.

By creating complete models and associated views of those models, the Autodesk Revit software takes much of the tediousness out of producing a building design.

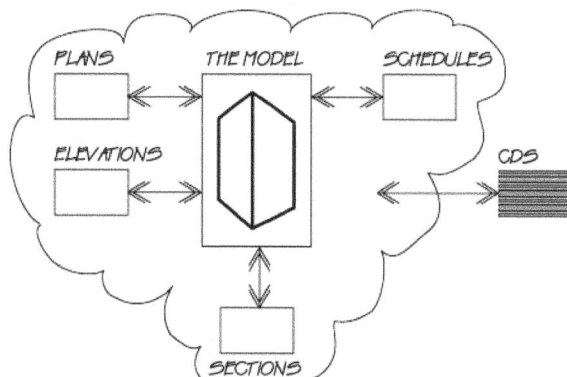

Figure 1–3

Revit Terms

When working in the Autodesk Revit software, it is important to know the typical terms used to describe items. Views and reports display information about the elements that form a project. There are three types of elements: Model, Datum, and View-specific, as shown in Figure 1–4 and described below:

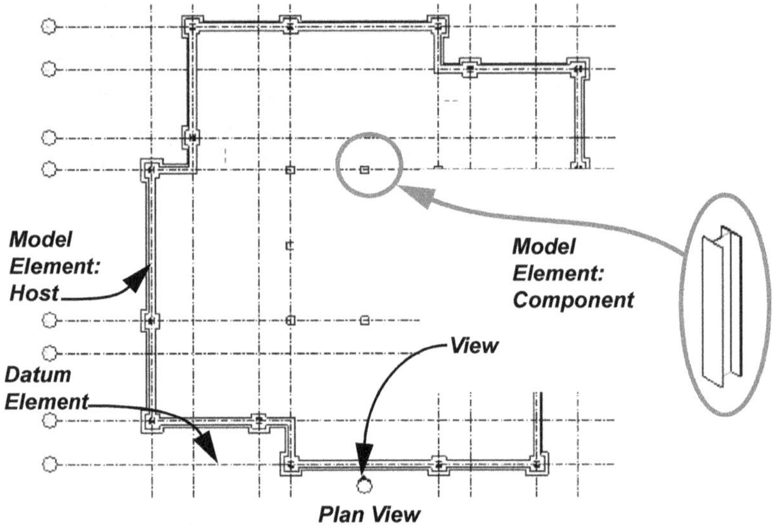

Plan View

Figure 1–4

Views	Enable you to display and manipulate the model. For example, you can view and work in floor plans, ceiling plans, elevations, sections, schedules, and 3D views. You can change a design from any view. All views are stored in the project.
Reports	Reports, including schedules, gather information from the building model element that can be presented in the construction documents or used for analysis.
Model Elements	Include all parts of a building such as walls, floors, roofs, ceilings, doors, windows, plumbing fixtures, lighting fixtures, mechanical equipment, columns, beams, furniture, plants and many more. • Host elements support other categories of elements. • Hosted elements must be attached to a host element. • Standalone elements do not require hosts.
Datum Elements	Define the project context such as the levels for the floors and other vertical distances, column grids, and reference planes.
View-specific Elements	Only display in the view in which they are placed. The view scale controls their size. These include annotation elements such as dimensions, text, tags, and symbols as well as detail elements such as detail lines, filled regions, and 2D detail components.

- Autodesk Revit elements are "smart": the software recognizes them as walls, columns, plants, ducts, or lighting fixtures. This means that the information stored in their properties automatically updates in schedules, which ensures that views and reports are coordinated across an entire project, and are generated from a single model.

Revit and Construction Documents

In the traditional workflow, the most time-consuming part of the project is the construction documents. With BIM, the base views of those documents (i.e., plans, elevations, sections, and schedules) are produced automatically and update as the model is updated, saving hours of work. The views are then placed on sheets that form the construction document set.

For example, a floor plan is duplicated. Then, in the new view, all but the required categories of elements are hidden or set to halftone and annotations are added. The plan is then placed on a sheet, as shown in Figure 1–5.

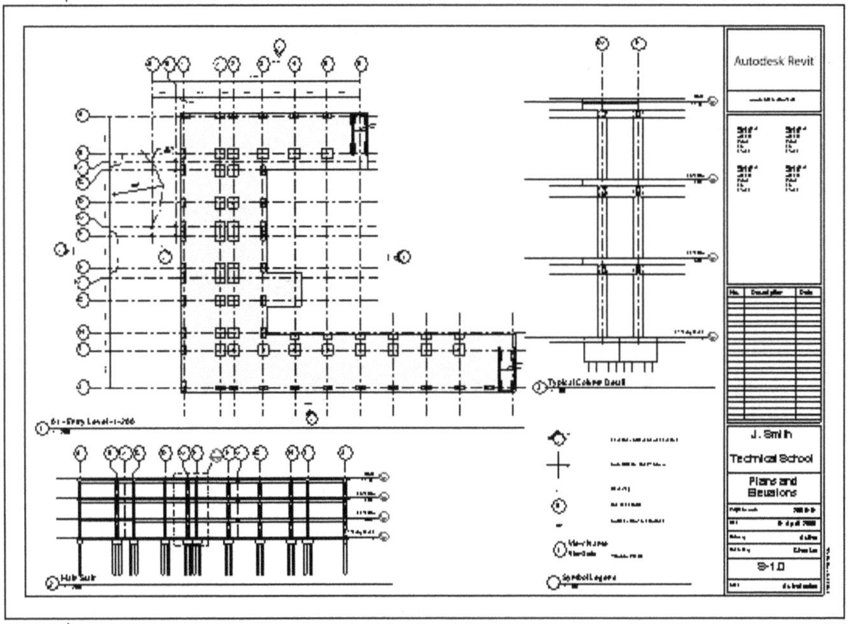

Figure 1–5

- Work can continue on a view and is automatically updated on the sheet.

- Annotating views in the preliminary design phase is often not required. You might be able to wait until you are further along in the project.

1.2 Overview of the Interface

The Autodesk Revit interface is designed for intuitive and efficient access to commands and views. It includes the ribbon, Quick Access Toolbar, Navigation Bar, and Status Bar, which are common to most of the Autodesk® software. It also includes tools that are specific to the Autodesk Revit software, including the Properties Palette, Project Browser, and View Control Bar. The interface is shown in Figure 1–6.

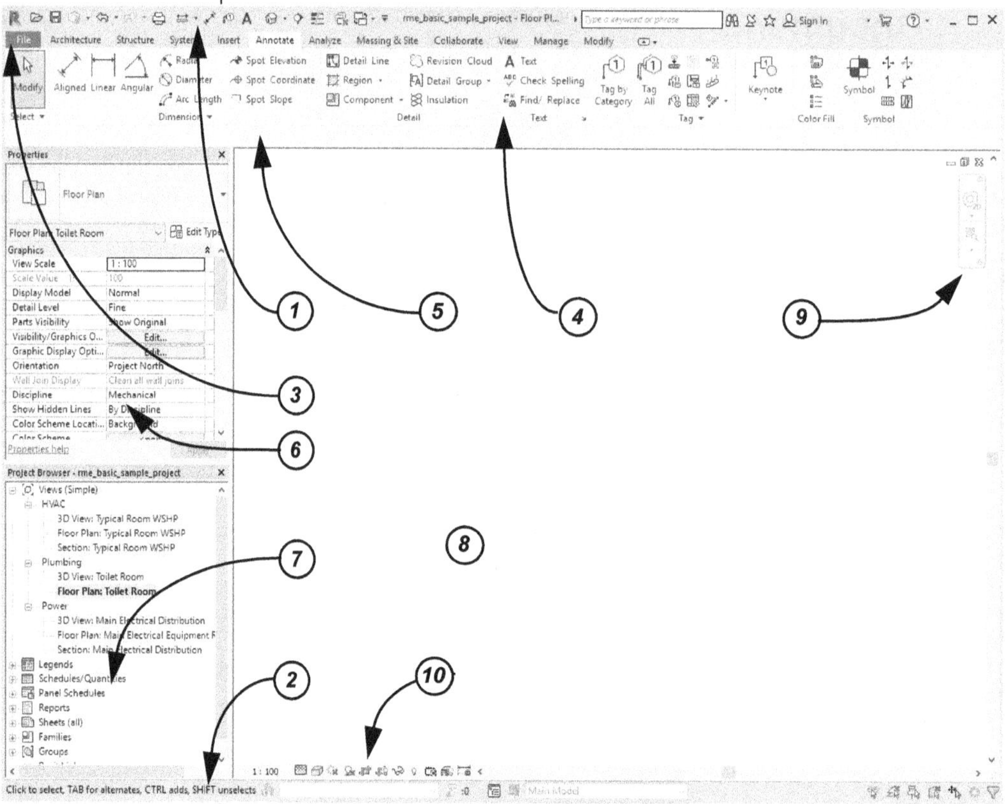

Figure 1–6

1. Quick Access Toolbar	6. Properties Palette
2. Status Bar	7. Project Browser
3. File tab	8. View Window
4. Ribbon	9. Navigation Bar
5. Options Bar	10. View Control Bar

1. Quick Access Toolbar

Enhanced
in 2018

The Quick Access Toolbar (shown in Figure 1–7) includes commonly used commands, such as **Open**, **Save**, **Undo**, **Redo,** and **Print**. It also includes frequently used annotation tools, including Measuring tools, **Aligned Dimension**, **Tag by Category**, and **Text**. Viewing tools, including several different 3D Views and **Sections**, are also easily accessed here.

Figure 1–7

Hint: Customizing the Quick Access Toolbar

Right-click on the Quick Access Toolbar to change the docked location of the toolbar to be above or below the ribbon, or to add, relocate, or remove tools on the toolbar. You can also right-click on a tool in the ribbon and select **Add to Quick Access Toolbar**, as shown in Figure 1–8.

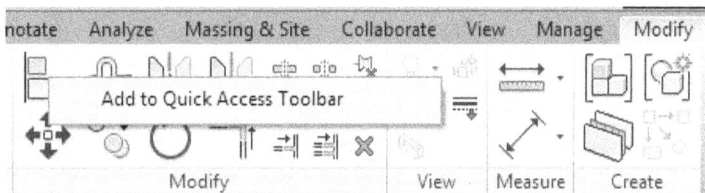

Figure 1–8

The top toolbar also hosts the InfoCenter (as shown in Figure 1–9) which includes a search field to find help on the web as well as access to the Communication Center, Autodesk A360 sign-in, the Autodesk App Store, and other help options.

Click here to collapse the search field to save screen space.

Figure 1–9

2. Status Bar

The Status Bar provides information about the current process, such as the next step for a command, as shown in Figure 1–10.

Click to enter wall start point.

Enter wall end point. (SZ) to close loop. Space flips orientation.

Figure 1–10

- Other options in the Status Bar are related to Worksets and Design Options (advanced tools) as well as selection methods and filters.

Hint: Shortcut Menus

Shortcut menus help you to work smoothly and efficiently by enabling you to quickly access required commands. These menus provide access to basic viewing commands, recently used commands, and the available Browsers, as shown in Figure 1–11. Additional options vary depending on the element or command that you are using.

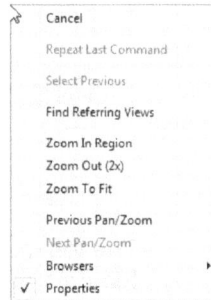

Cancel

Repeat Last Command

Select Previous

Find Referring Views

Zoom In Region
Zoom Out (2x)
Zoom To Fit

Previous Pan/Zoom
Next Pan/Zoom
Browsers   ▶
✓ Properties

Figure 1–11

3.File Tab

The *File* tab of the ribbon provides access to file commands, settings, and documents, as shown in Figure 1–12. Hover the cursor over a command to display a list of additional tools.

If you click the primary icon, rather than the arrow, it starts the default command.

Figure 1–12

- To display a list of recently used documents, click

  (Recent Documents). The documents can be reordered as shown in Figure 1–13.

Click (Pin) next to a document name to keep it available.

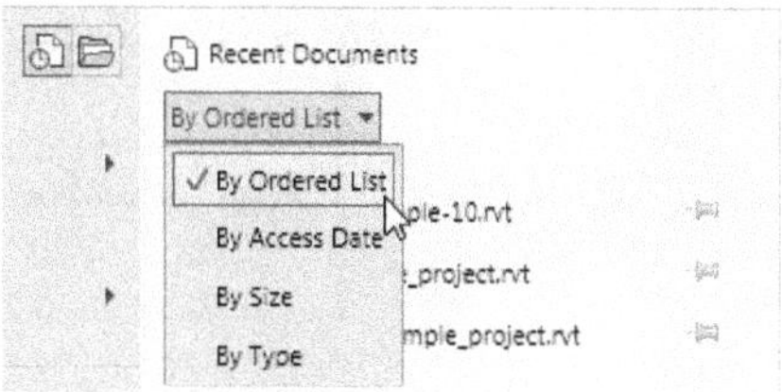

Figure 1–13

You can use the Open Documents list to change between views.

- To display a list of open documents and views, click

  (Open Documents). The list displays the documents and views that are open, as shown in Figure 1–14.

	Open Documents
	Project1 - Elevation: East
	Project1 - Floor Plan: Level 1
	BHM-Office-Grids-10 - Reflected Ceiling Plan: First Floor
	BHM-Office-Grids-10 - Floor Plan: First Floor
	BHM-Office-Grids-10 - Elevation: North

Figure 1–14

- Click (Close) to close the current project.

- At the bottom of the menu, click **Options** to open the Options dialog box or click **Exit Revit** to exit the software.

4. Ribbon

The ribbon contains tools in a series of tabs and panels as shown in Figure 1–15. Selecting a tab displays a group of related panels. The panels contain a variety of tools, grouped by task.

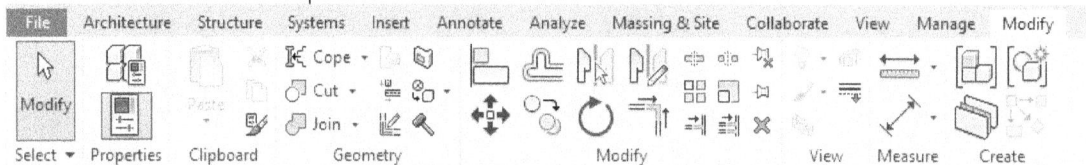

Figure 1–15

When you start a command that creates new elements or you select an element, the ribbon displays the *Modify | contextual* tab. This contains general editing commands and command specific tools, as shown in Figure 1–16.

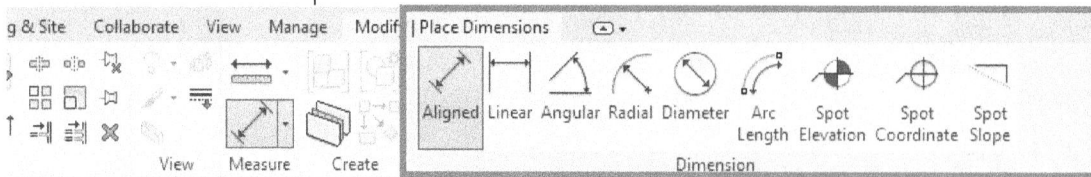

Contextual tab

Figure 1–16

- When you hover over a tool on the ribbon, tooltips display the tool's name and a short description. If you continue hovering over the tool, a graphic displays (and sometimes a video), as shown in Figure 1–17.

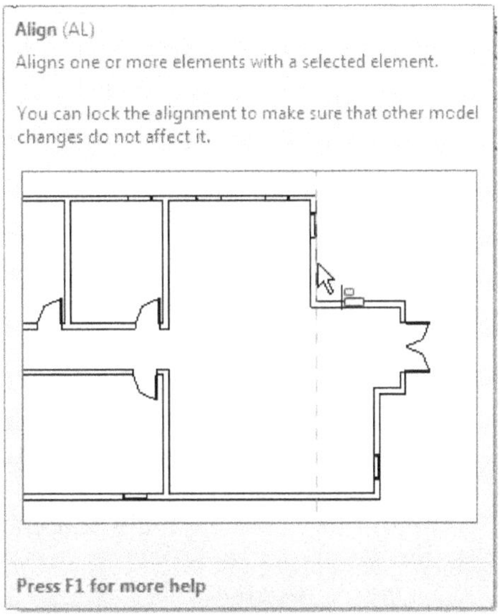

Align (AL)

Aligns one or more elements with a selected element.

You can lock the alignment to make sure that other model changes do not affect it.

Press F1 for more help

Figure 1–17

- Many commands have shortcut keys. For example, type **AL** for **Align** or **MV** for **Move**. They are listed next to the name of the command in the tooltips. Do not press <Enter> when typing shortcuts.

- To arrange the order in which the ribbon tabs are displayed, select the tab, hold <Ctrl>, and drag it to a new location. The location is remembered when you restart the software.

- Any panel can be dragged by its title into the view window to become a floating panel. Click the **Return Panels to Ribbon** button (as shown in Figure 1–18) to reposition the panel in the ribbon.

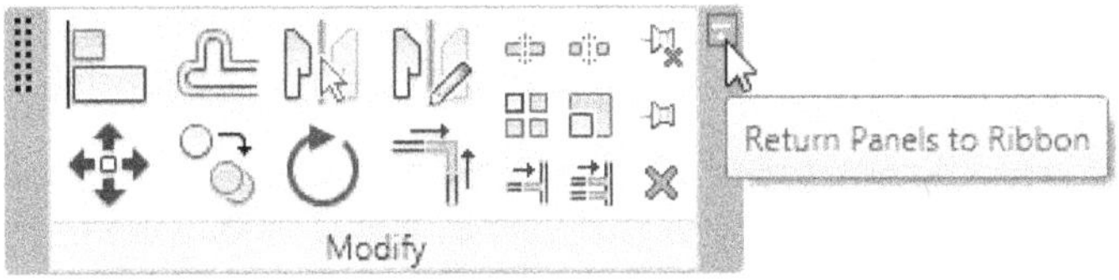

Return Panels to Ribbon

Modify

Figure 1–18

> **Hint: You are always in a command when using the Autodesk Revit software.**
>
> When you are finished working with a tool, you typically default back to the **Modify** command. To end a command, use one of the following methods:
>
> - In any tab on the ribbon, click 🔖 (Modify).
> - Press <Esc> once or twice to revert to **Modify**.
> - Right-click and select **Cancel...** once or twice.
> - Start another command.

5. Options Bar

The Options Bar displays options that are related to the selected command or element. For example, when the **Rotate** command is active it displays options for rotating the selected elements, as shown at the top in Figure 1–19. When the **Place Dimensions** command is active it displays dimension related options, as shown at the bottom in Figure 1–19.

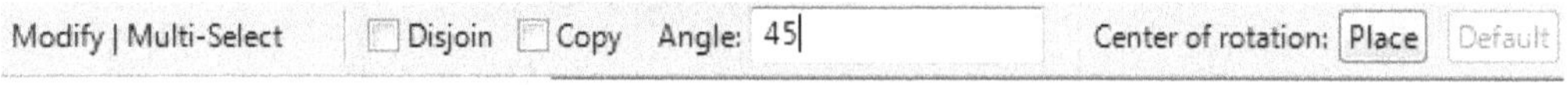

| Modify | Multi-Select | ☐ Disjoin ☐ Copy Angle: 45 | Center of rotation: | Place | Default |

Options Bar for Rotate Command

Modify | Place Dimensions   Wall centerline ▾   Pick: Individual Reference ▾   Options

Options Bar for Dimension Command

Figure 1–19

6. Properties Palette

The Properties palette includes the Type Selector, which enables you to choose the size or style of the element you are adding or modifying. This palette is also where you make changes to information (parameters) about elements or views, as shown in Figure 1–20. There are two types of properties:

- **Instance Properties** are set for the individual element(s) you are creating or modifying.

- **Type Properties** control options for all elements of the same type. If you modify these parameter values, all elements of the selected type change.

The Properties palette is usually kept open while working on a project to easily permit changes at any time. If it does not display, in the Modify tab>Properties panel

click (Properties) or type PP.

Type Selector

Filter drop-down

Instance Properties

Access to Type Properties

Figure 1–20

Some parameters are only available when you are editing an element. They are grayed out when unavailable.

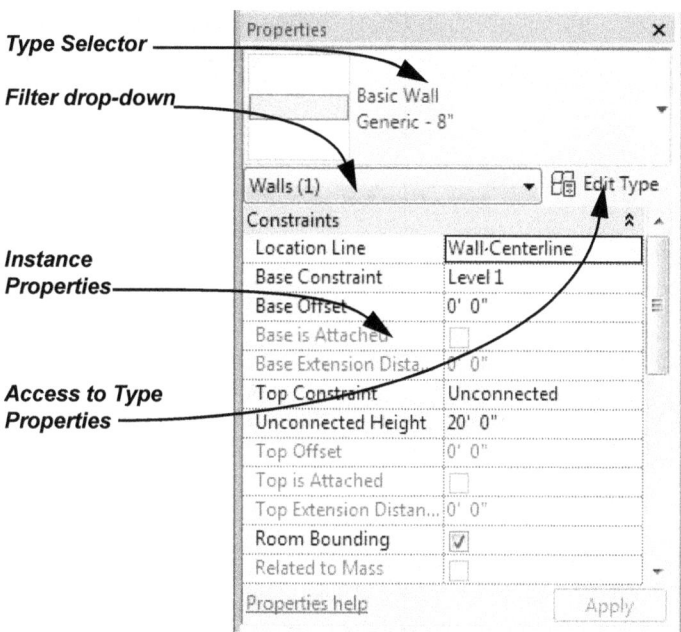

- Options for the current view display if the **Modify** command is active, but you have not selected an element.

- If a command or element is selected, the options for the associated element display.

- You can save the changes by either moving the cursor off of the palette, or by pressing <Enter>, or by clicking **Apply**.

- When you start a command or select an element, you can set the element type in the Type Selector, as shown in Figure 1–21.

You can limit what shows in the drop-down list by typing in the search box.

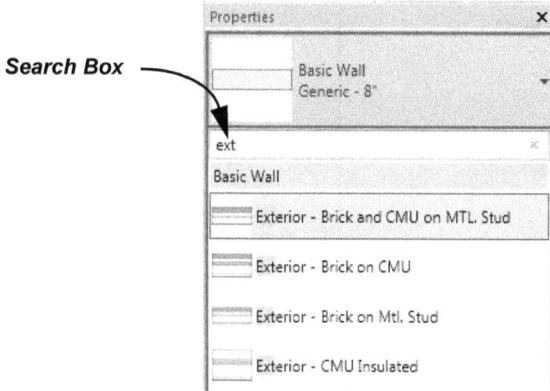

Search Box

Figure 1–21

- When multiple elements are selected, you can filter the type of elements that display using the drop-down list, as shown in Figure 1–22.

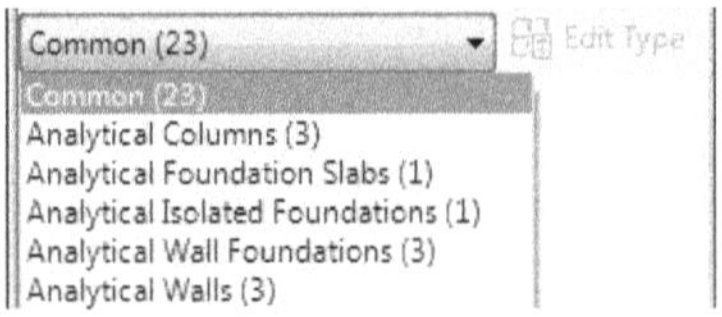

Figure 1–22

- The Properties palette can be placed on a second monitor, or floated, resized, and docked on top of the Project Browser or other dockable palettes, as shown in Figure 1–23. Click the tab to display its associated panel.

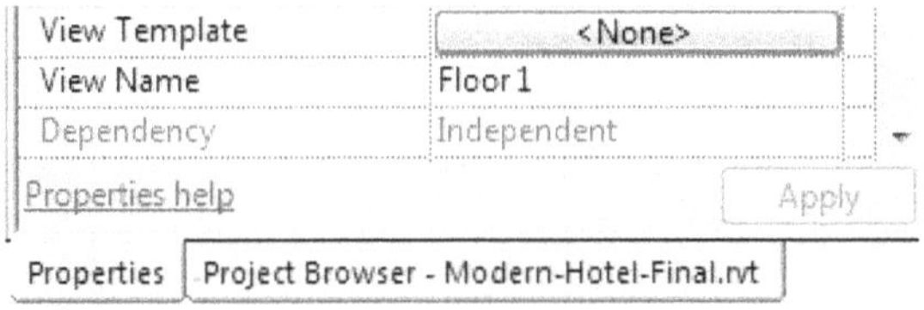

Figure 1–23

7. Project Browser

The Project Browser lists the views that can be opened in the project, as shown in Figure 1–24. This includes all views of the model in which you are working and any additional views that you create, such as floor plans, ceiling plans, 3D views, elevations, sections, etc. It also includes views of schedules, legends, sheets (for plotting), groups, and Autodesk Revit Links.

The Project Browser displays the name of the active project.

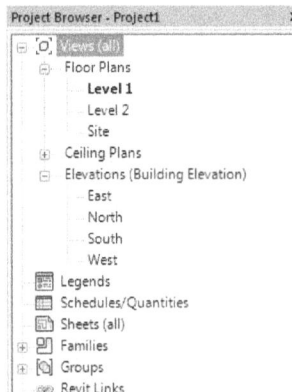

Figure 1–24

- Double-click on an item in the list to open the associated view.

- To display the views associated with a view type, click ⊞ (Expand) next to the section name. To hide the views in the section, click ⊟ (Contract).

- Right-click on a view and select **Rename** or press <F2> to rename a view in the Project Browser.

- If you no longer need a view, you can remove it. Right-click on its name in the Project Browser and select **Delete**.

- The Project Browser can be floated, resized, docked on top of the Properties palette, and customized. If the Properties palette and the Project Browser are docked on top of each other, use the appropriate tab to display the required panel.

How To: Search the Project Browser

1. In the Project Browser, right-click on the top level Views node as shown in Figure 1–25.

Project Browser - Project1   ✕

⊟ ◻ Views (all)
  ⊟ Fl   Browser Organization...
               Search...
        Site

Figure 1–25

2. In the Search in Project Browser dialog box, type the words that you want to find (as shown in Figure 1–26), and click **Next**.
3. In the Project Browser, the first instance of that search displays as shown in Figure 1–27.

Search in Project Browser   ✕

Find: Analytical

   [Next]   [Previous]   [Close]
   ☐ Match case

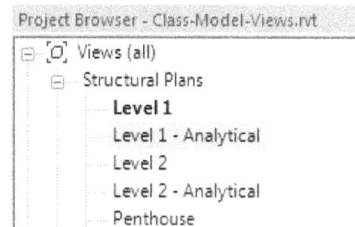

Project Browser - Class-Model-Views.rvt

⊟ ◻ Views (all)
  ⊟ Structural Plans
       Level 1
       Level 1 - Analytical
       Level 2
       Level 2 - Analytical
       Penthouse

Figure 1–26   **Figure 1–27**

4. Continue using **Next** and **Previous** to move through the list.
5. Click **Close** when you are done.

8. View Window

Each view of a project opens in its own window. Each view displays a Navigation Bar (for quick access to viewing tools) and the View Control Bar, as shown in Figure 1–28.

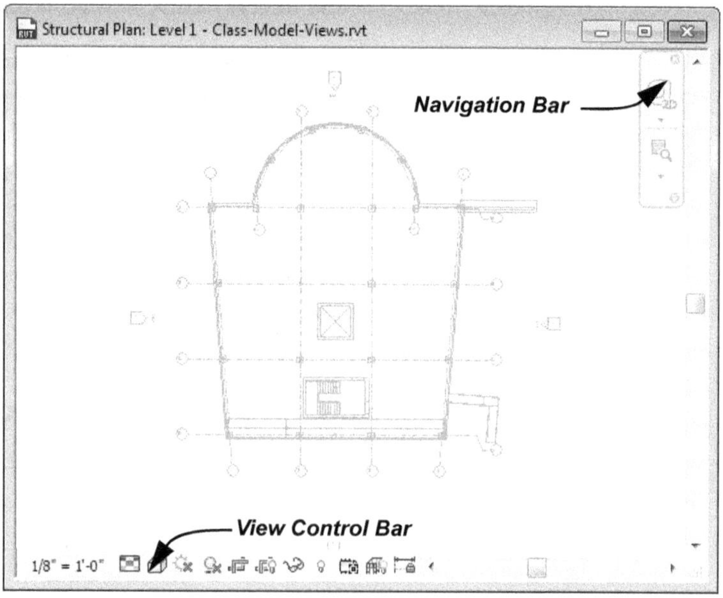

In 3D views you can also use the ViewCube to rotate the view.

Figure 1–28

- To cycle through multiple views you can use several different methods:
    - Press <Ctrl>+<Tab>
    - Select the view in the Project Browser
    - In the Quick Access Toolbar or *View* tab>Windows panel, expand 🗔 (Switch Windows) and select the view from the list.

- You can Tile or Cascade views. In the *View* tab>Windows panel, click 🗗 (Cascade Windows) or 🗗 (Tile Windows). You can also type the shortcuts **WC** to cascade the windows or **WT** to tile the windows.

9. Navigation Bar

The Navigation Bar enables you to access various viewing commands, as shown in Figure 1–29.

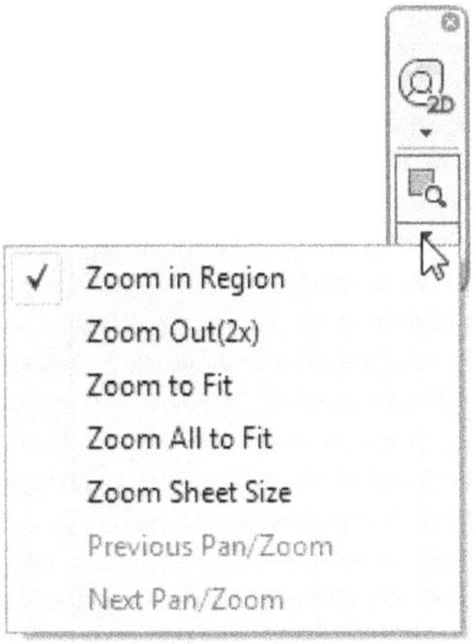

Figure 1–29

10. View Control Bar

The number of options in the View Control Bar change when you are in a 3D view.

The View Control Bar (shown in Figure 1–30), displays at the bottom of each view window. It controls aspects of that view, such as the scale and detail level. It also includes tools that display parts of the view and hide or isolate elements in the view.

Figure 1–30

1.3 Starting Projects

File operations to open existing files, create new files from a template, and save files in the Autodesk Revit software are found in the *File* tab, as shown in Figure 1–31.

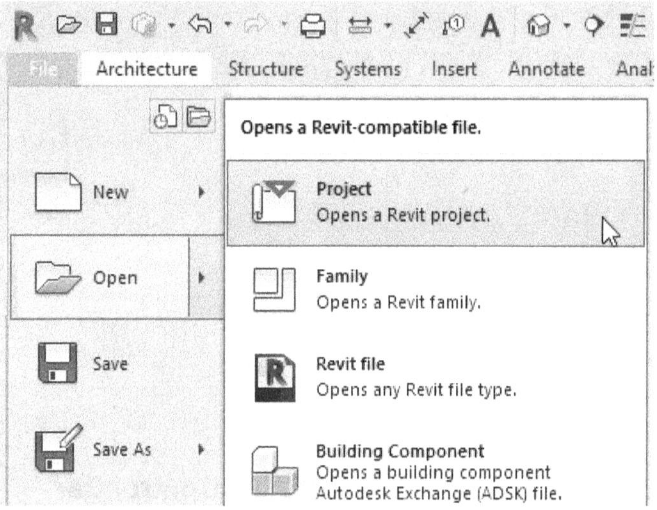

Figure 1–31

There are three main file formats:

- **Project files (.rvt):** These are where you do the majority of your work in the building model by adding elements, creating views, annotating views, and setting up printable sheets. They are initially based on template files.

- **Family files (.rfa):** These are separate components that can be inserted in a project. They include elements that can stand alone (e.g., a table or piece of mechanical equipment) or are items that are hosted in other elements (e.g., a door in a wall or a lighting fixture in a ceiling). Title block and Annotation Symbol files are special types of family files.

- **Template files (.rte):** These are the base files for any new project or family. They are designed to hold standard information and settings for creating new project files. The software includes several templates for various types of projects. You can also create custom templates.

Opening Projects

To open an existing project, in the Quick Access Toolbar or *File* tab click 📂 (Open), or press <Ctrl>+<O>. The Open dialog box opens (as shown in Figure 1–32), in which you can navigate to the required folder and select a project file.

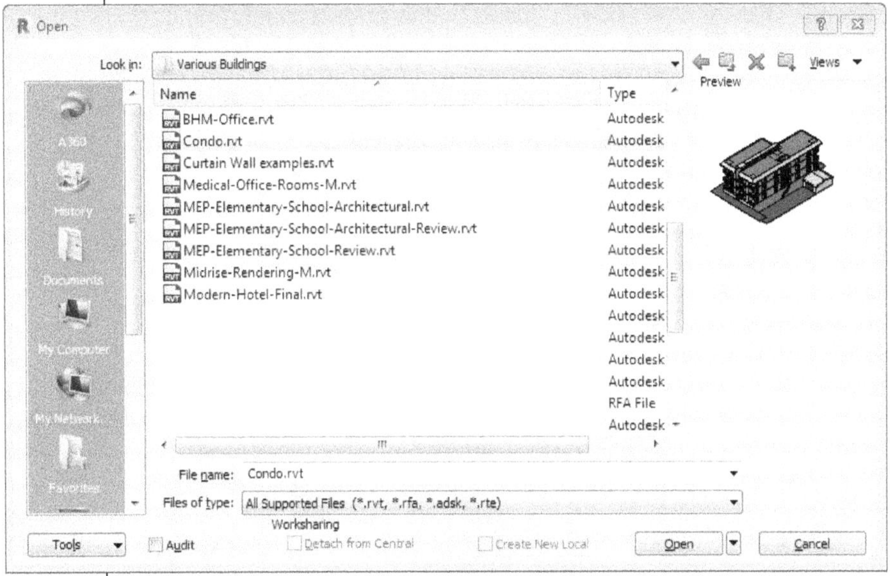

Figure 1–32

- When you first open the Autodesk Revit software, the Startup Screen displays, showing lists of recently used projects and family files as shown in Figure 1–33. This screen also displays if you close all projects.

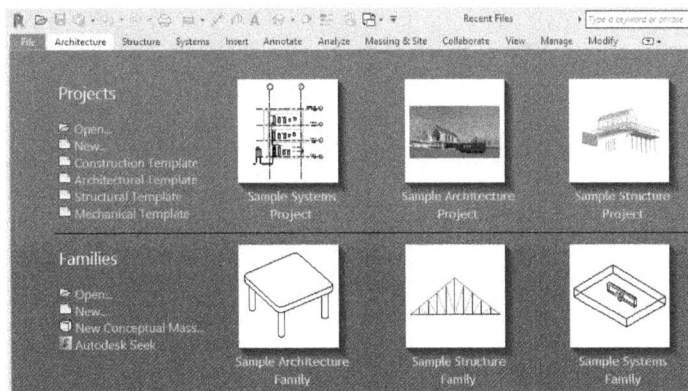

Figure 1–33

- You can select the picture of a recently opened project or use one of the options on the left to open or start a new project using the default templates.

Hint: Opening Workset-Related Files

Worksets are used when the project becomes large enough for multiple people to work on it at the same time. At this point, the project manager creates a central file with multiple worksets (such as element interiors, building shell, and site) that are used by the project team members.

When you open a workset related file it creates a new local file on your computer as shown in Figure 1–34. Do not work in the main central file.

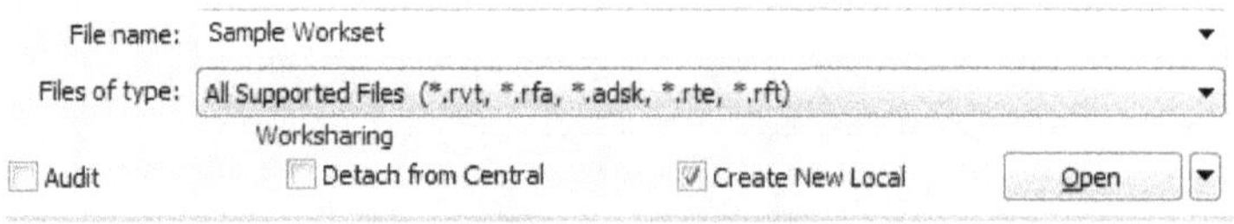

| File name: | Sample Workset | ▼ |
| Files of type: | All Supported Files (*.rvt, *.rfa, *.adsk, *.rte, *.rft) | ▼ |

Worksharing

☐ Audit   ☐ Detach from Central   ☑ Create New Local   Open ▼

Figure 1–34

• For more information on establishing and using Worksets, refer to the *Autodesk Revit: Collaboration Tools* student guide.

• It is very important that everyone working on a project uses the same software release. You can open files created in earlier versions of the software in comparison to your own, but you cannot open files created in newer versions of the software.

• When you open a file created in an earlier version, the Model Upgrade dialog box (shown in Figure 1–35) indicates the release of a file and the release to which it will be upgraded. If required, you can cancel the upgrade before it completes.

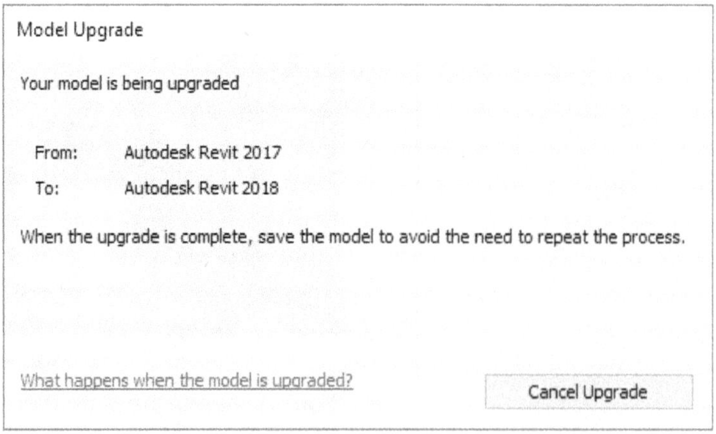

Model Upgrade

Your model is being upgraded

From: Autodesk Revit 2017

To: Autodesk Revit 2018

When the upgrade is complete, save the model to avoid the need to repeat the process.

What happens when the model is upgraded?   Cancel Upgrade

Figure 1–35

Starting New Projects

New projects are based on a template file. The template file includes preset levels, views, and some families, such as wall styles and text styles. Check with your BIM Manager about which template you need to use for your projects. Your company might have more than one based on the types of building that you are designing.

How To: Start a New Project

1. In the *File* tab, expand ⬜ (New) and click ⬜ (Project) (as shown in Figure 1–36), or press <Ctrl>+<N>.

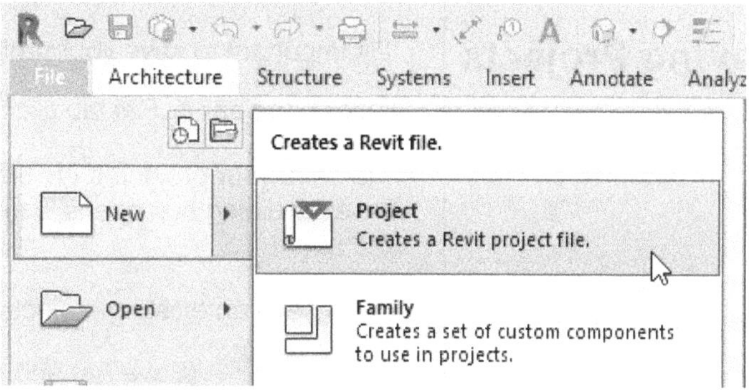

Figure 1–36

2. In the New Project dialog box (shown in Figure 1–37), select the template that you want to use and click **OK**.

The list of Template files is set in the Options dialog box in the File Locations pane. It might vary depending on the installed product and company standards.

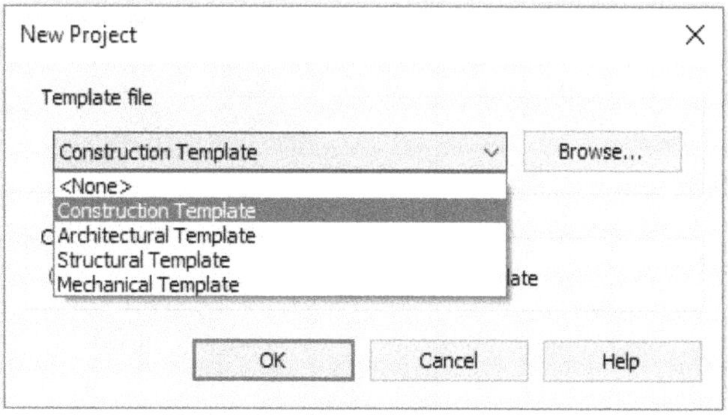

Figure 1–37

- You can select from a list of templates if they have been set up by your BIM Manager.

- You can add ▢ (New) to the Quick Access Toolbar. At the end of the Quick Access Toolbar, click ▾ (Customize Quick Access Toolbar) and select **New**, as shown in Figure 1–38.

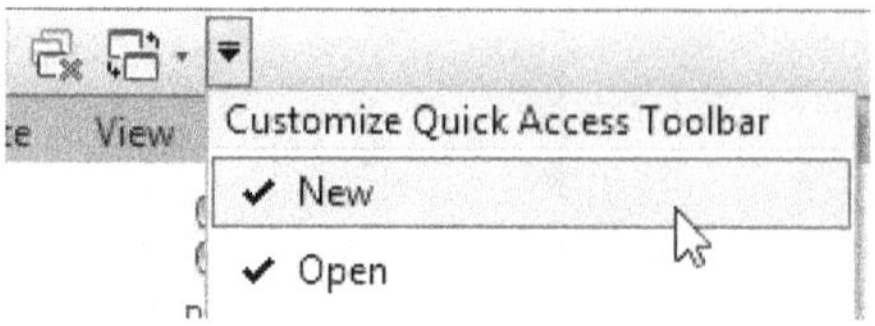

Figure 1–38

Saving Projects

It is important to save your projects frequently. In the Quick Access Toolbar or *File* tab click 🖫 (Save), or press <Ctrl>+<S> to save your project. If the project has not yet been saved, the Save As dialog box opens, where you can specify a file location and name.

- To save an existing project with a new name, in the *File* tab, expand 🖫 (Save As) and click 🗋 (Project).

- If you have not saved in a set amount of time, the software opens the Project Not Saved Recently alert box, as shown in Figure 1–39. Select **Save the project**. If you want to set reminder intervals or not save at this time, select the other options.

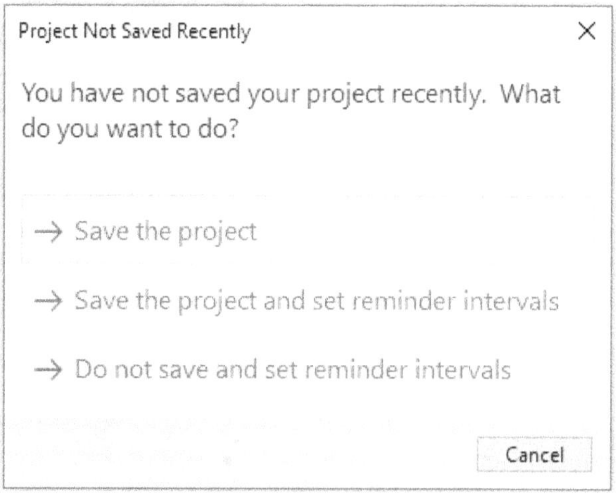

Figure 1–39

- You can set the *Save Reminder interval* to **15** or **30 minutes**, **1**, **2**, or **4 hours**, or to have **No reminders** display. In the *File* tab, click **Options** to open the Options dialog box. In the left pane, select **General** and set the interval as shown in Figure 1–40.

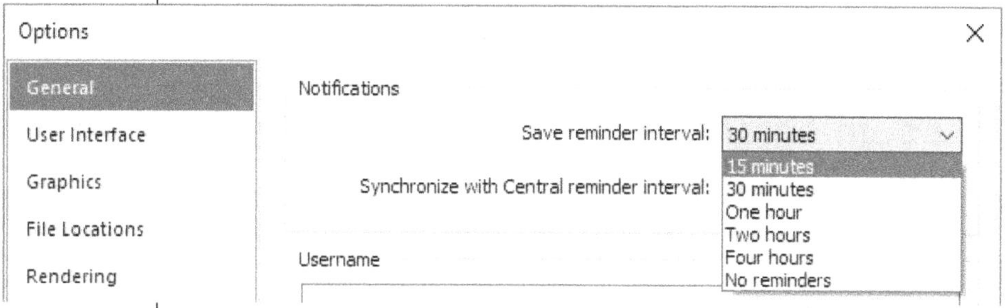

Figure 1–40

Saving Backup Copies

By default, the software saves a backup copy of a project file when you save the project. Backup copies are numbered incrementally (e.g., **My Project.0001.rvt**, **My Project.0002.rvt**, etc.) and are saved in the same folder as the original file. In the Save As dialog box, click **Options...** to control how many backup copies are saved. The default number is three backups. If you exceed this number, the software deletes the oldest backup file.

> **Hint: Saving Workset-Related Projects**
>
> If you use worksets in your project, you need to save the project locally and to the central file. It is recommended to save the local file frequently, just like any other file, and save to the central file every hour or so.
>
> To synchronize your changes with the main file, in the Quick Access Toolbar expand (Synchronize and Modify Settings) and click (Synchronize Now). After you save to the central file, save the file locally again.
>
> At the end of the day, or when you are finished with the current session, use (Synchronize and Modify Settings) to relinquish the files you have been working on to the central file.

- The maximum number of backups for workset-enabled files is set to 20 by default.

1.4 Viewing Commands

Viewing commands are crucial to working efficiently in most drawing and modeling programs and the Autodesk Revit software is no exception. Once in a view, you can use the Zoom controls to navigate in it. You can zoom in and out and pan in any view. There are also special tools for viewing in 3D.

Zooming and Panning

Using The Mouse to Zoom and Pan

Use the mouse wheel (shown in Figure 1–41) as the main method of moving around the models.

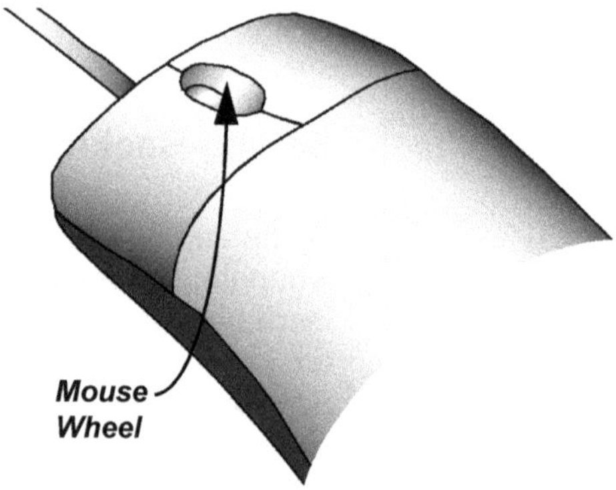

Mouse Wheel

Figure 1–41

- Scroll the wheel on the mouse up to zoom in and down to zoom out.
- Hold the wheel and move the mouse to pan.
- Double-click on the wheel to zoom to the extents of the view.
- In a 3D view, hold <Shift> and the mouse wheel and move the mouse to rotate around the model.
- When you save a model and exit the software, the pan and zoom location of each view is remembered. This is especially important for complex models.

Zoom Controls

A number of additional zoom methods enable you to control the screen display. **Zoom** and **Pan** can be performed at any time while using other commands.

- You can access the **Zoom** commands in the Navigation Bar in the upper right corner of the view (as shown in Figure 1–42). You can also access them from most shortcut menus and by typing the shortcut commands.

*(2D Wheel) provides cursor-specific access to **Zoom** and **Pan**.*

✓	Zoom in Region
	Zoom Out(2x)
	Zoom to Fit
	Zoom All to Fit
	Zoom Sheet Size
	Previous Pan/Zoom
	Next Pan/Zoom

Figure 1–42

Zoom Commands

	Zoom In Region (ZR)	Zooms into a region that you define. Drag the cursor or select two points to define the rectangular area you want to zoom into. This is the default command.
	Zoom Out(2x) (ZO)	Zooms out to half the current magnification around the center of the elements.
	Zoom To Fit (ZF or ZE)	Zooms out so that the entire contents of the project only display on the screen in the current view.
	Zoom All To Fit (ZA)	Zooms out so that the entire contents of the project display on the screen in all open views.
	Zoom Sheet Size (ZS)	Zooms in or out in relation to the sheet size.
N/A	**Previous Pan/Zoom (ZP)**	Steps back one **Zoom** command.
N/A	**Next Pan/Zoom**	Steps forward one **Zoom** command if you have done a **Previous Pan/Zoom**.

Viewing in 3D

Even if you started a project entirely in plan views, you can quickly create 3D views of the model, as shown in Figure 1–43. There are two types of 3D views: isometric views created by the **Default 3D View** command and perspective views created by the **Camera** command.

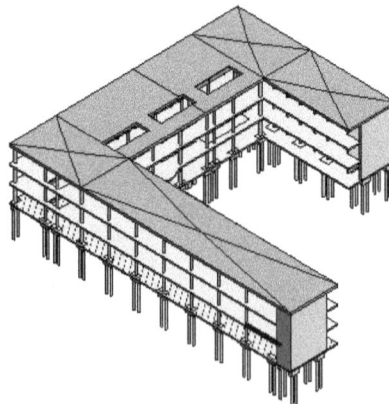

Figure 1–43

Enhanced in 2018

Working in 3D views helps you visualize the project and position some of the elements correctly. You can create and modify elements in both isometric and perspective 3D views, just as you can in plan views.

- Once you have created a 3D view, you can save it and easily return to it.

How To: Create and Save a 3D Isometric View

1. In the Quick Access Toolbar or *View* tab>Create panel, click

   (Default 3D View). The default 3D Southeast isometric view opens, as shown in Figure 1–44.

You can spin the view to a different angle using the mouse wheel or the middle button of a three-button mouse. Hold <Shift> as you press the wheel or middle button and drag the cursor.

Figure 1–44

2. Modify the view to display the building from other directions.

3. In the Project Browser, right-click on the {3D} view and select **Rename...**
4. Type a new name in the Rename View dialog box, as shown in Figure 1–45, and click **OK**.

All types of views can be renamed.

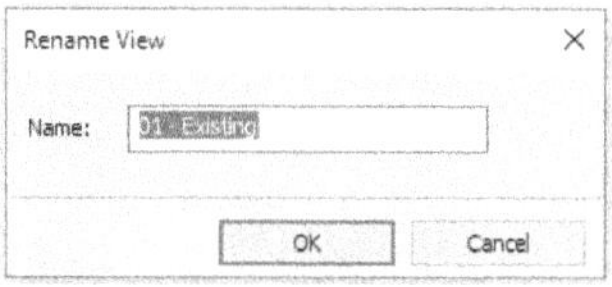

Rename View ×

Name: 01 - Existing

OK   Cancel

Figure 1–45

- When changes to the default 3D view are saved and you start another default 3D view, it displays the Southeast isometric view once again. If you modified the default 3D view but did not save it to a new name, the **Default 3D View** command opens the view in the last orientation you specified.

How To: Create a Perspective View

1. Switch to a Floor Plan view.
2. In the Quick Access Toolbar or *View* tab>Create panel,

   expand 🏠 (Default 3D View) and click 📷 (Camera).
3. Place the camera on the view.
4. Point the camera in the direction in which you want it to shoot by placing the target on the view, as shown in Figure 1–46.

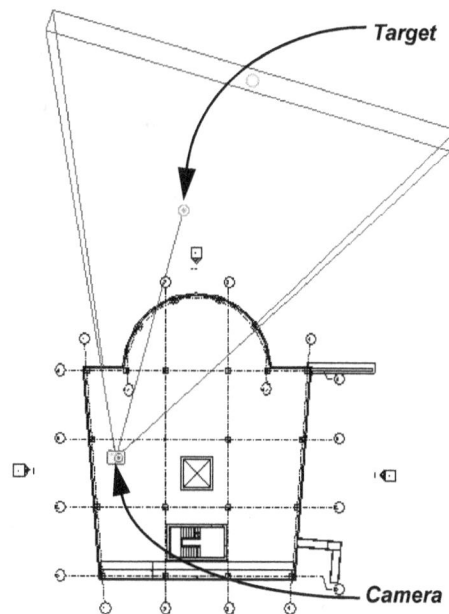

Target

Camera

Figure 1–46

A new view is displayed, as shown in Figure 1–47.

Figure 1–47

Use the round controls to modify the display size of the view and press <Shift> + the mouse wheel to change the view.

5. In the Properties palette scroll down and adjust the *Eye Elevation* and *Target Elevation* as required.

- If the view becomes distorted, reset the target so that it is centered in the boundary of the view (called the crop region).

  In the *Modify | Cameras* tab>Camera panel, click (Reset Target).

- You can further modify a view by adding shadows. In the

  View Control Bar, toggle (Shadows Off) and (Shadows On). Shadows display in any model view, not just in the 3D views.

Visual Styles

Any view can have a visual style applied. The **Visual Style** options found in the View Control Bar (as shown in Figure 1–48), specify the shading of the building model. These options apply to plan, elevation, section, and 3D views.

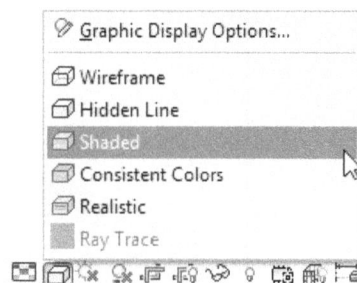

Figure 1–48

- ⬚ (Wireframe) displays the lines and edges that make up elements, but hides the surfaces. This can be useful when you are dealing with complex intersections.

- ⬚ (Hidden Line) displays the lines, edges, and surfaces of the elements, but it does not display any colors. This is the most common visual style to use while working on a design.

- ⬚ (Shaded) and ⬚ (Consistent Colors) give you a sense of the materials, including transparent glass. An example that uses Consistent Colors is shown in Figure 1–49.

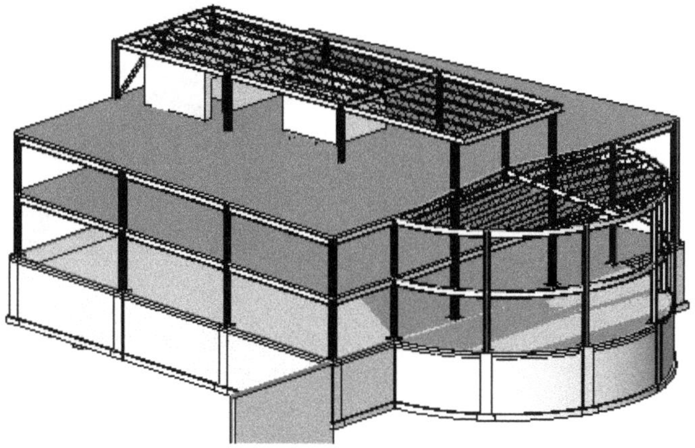

Figure 1–49

- ⬚ (Realistic) displays what is shown when you render the view, including RPC (Rich Photorealistic Content) components and artificial lights. It takes a lot of computer power to execute this visual style. Therefore, it is better to use the other visual styles most of the time as you are working.

- ⬚ (Ray Trace) is useful if you have created a 3D view that you want to render. It gradually moves from draft resolution to photorealistic. You can stop the process at any time.

Hint: Rendering

Rendering is a powerful tool which enables you to display a photorealistic view of the model you are working on, such as the example shown in Figure 1–50. This can be used to help clients and designers to understand a building's design in better detail.

Figure 1–50

- In the View Control Bar, click 🐷 (Show Rendering Dialog) to set up the options. **Show Rendering Dialog** is only available in 3D views.

Practice 1a

Open and Review a Project

Practice Objectives

- Navigate the graphic user interface.
- Manipulate 2D and 3D views by zooming and panning.
- Create 3D Isometric and Perspective views.
- Set the Visual Style of a view.

Estimated time for completion: 15 minutes

In this practice you will open a project file and view each of the various areas in the interface. You will investigate elements, commands, and their options. You will also open views through the Project Browser and view the model in 3D, as shown in Figure 1–51.

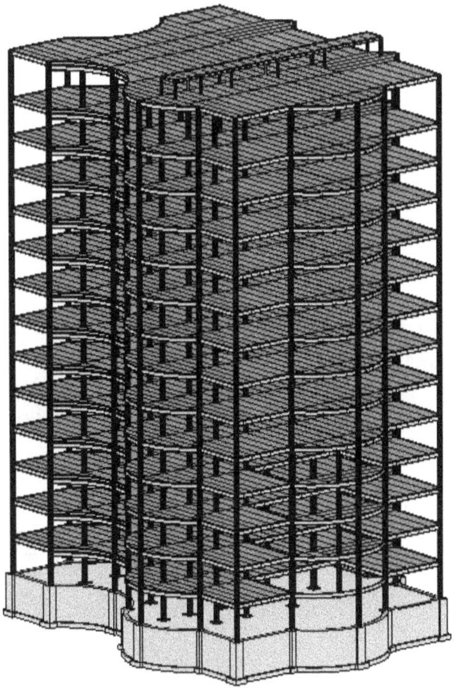

Figure 1–51

- This is a version of the main project you will work on throughout the student guide.

Task 1 - Explore the interface.

1. In the *File* tab, expand 🗁 (Open) and click 🗂 (Project).

---

2. In the Open dialog box, navigate to the practice files folder and select **Syracuse-Suites.rvt**.

3. Click **Open**. The 3D view of the building opens in the view window.

4. In the Project Browser, double-click on the **Structural Plans: 00 GROUND FLOOR** view. It opens a plan with the Visual Style set to **Wireframe** so that the footings and foundation walls display, although there is a slab over them.

If the Project Browser and Properties palette are docked over each other, use the Project Browser tab at the bottom to display it.

5. In the View Control toolbar, change the *Visual Style* to **Hidden Line**. The lines that are hidden in the view display as dashed, as shown in Figure 1–52.

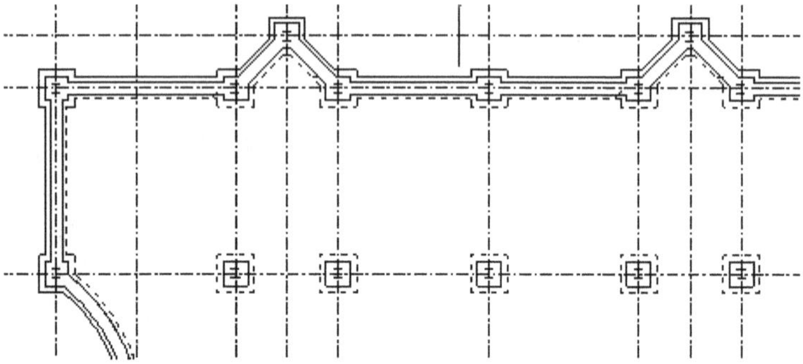

Figure 1–52

6. In the Project Browser, double-click on the **Structural Plans: T.O. FOOTING** view. The strip footings and spread footings display as continuous lines because they are not obscured by a slab, as shown in Figure 1–53.

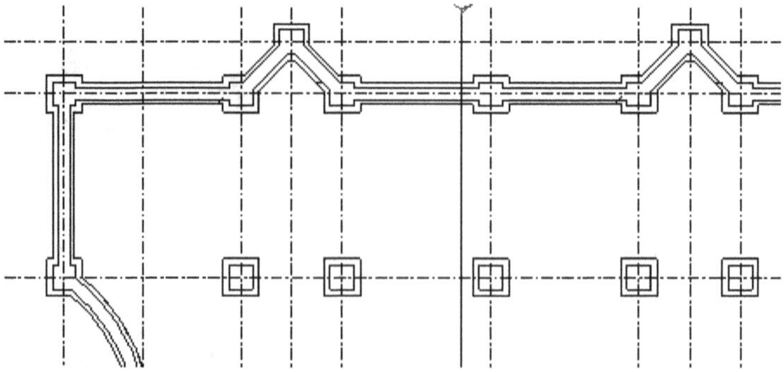

Figure 1–53

7. Zoom in on one corner of the building. The foundation walls are in-filled with the appropriate concrete hatch, as shown in Figure 1–54.

Figure 1–54

8. Double-click the mouse wheel or type **ZE** to zoom to the extents of the view. (**ZA** zooms to the extents of all of the opened view windows). Find the section marker that extends vertically along the model as shown in Figure 1–55.

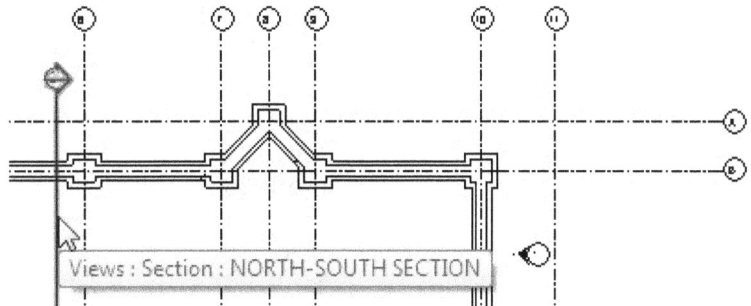

Views : Section : NORTH-SOUTH SECTION

Figure 1–55

9. Double-click on the section head to open the **NORTH-SOUTH SECTION** view.

10. In the Project Browser, navigate to the *Sections (Building Section)* category. The **NORTH-SOUTH SECTION** view name is bold. You can navigate through your model by double-clicking on the element in the Project Browser, or by using the graphical view elements in the model.

11. In the section view, zoom in on the area in which the callout has been placed as shown in Figure 1–56. Double-click on the callout-head to open the **TYPICAL EDGE DETAIL** view.

Views : Section : TYPICAL EDGE DETAIL

Figure 1–56

12. In the **TYPICAL EDGE DETAIL** view, select the floor, as shown in Figure 1–57.

Figure 1–57

13. This is a full 3D floor element. You can edit it using the tools shown in the *Modify | Floors* contextual tab, as shown in Figure 1–58.

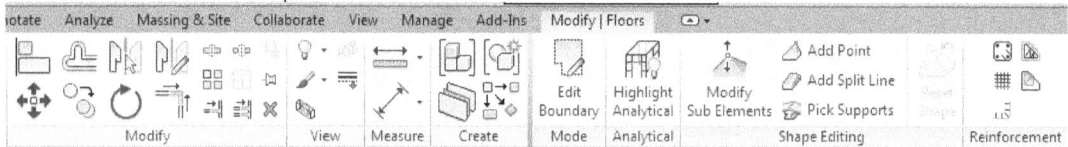

Figure 1–58

14. The Properties palette displays the Instance Parameters for the element, as shown in Figure 1–59.

Any changes made here are applied to the selected element only.

Figure 1–59

15. In Properties, click ⊞ (Edit Type) to access the Type Parameters in the Type Properties dialog box, as shown in Figure 1–60.

Any changes made here to the element are applied to all its other instances in the project.

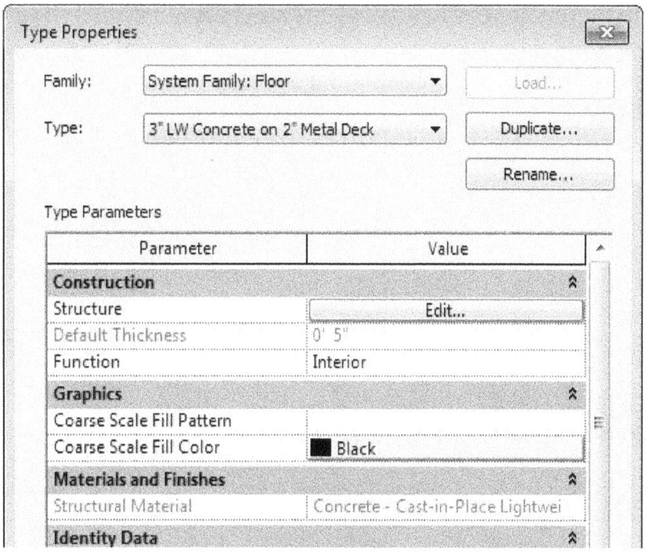

Figure 1–60

16. Click **Cancel** to close the Type Properties dialog box.

17. Press <Esc> or click in empty space to clear the selection.

18. Select one of the bolted connections. This is a detail component (2D element). The *Modify | Detail Items* contextual tab displays the modifying options specific to this element as shown in Figure 1–61.

Figure 1–61

19. Press <Esc> to clear the selection.

Task 2 - Work with Multiple views and 3D views.

---

1. In the **Section: TYPICAL EGE DETAIL** view, double-click on the **01 FIRST FLOOR** datum mark, as shown in Figure 1–62. This opens the **Structural Plans: 01 FIRST FLOOR** view.

01 FIRST FLOOR
15' - 0"

Goto the floor plan that corresponds to this level

Figure 1–62

2. In the Quick Access Toolbar, expand (Switch Windows). The growing list of opened windows displays as shown in Figure 1–63. This can quickly become a management issue once the model size increases.

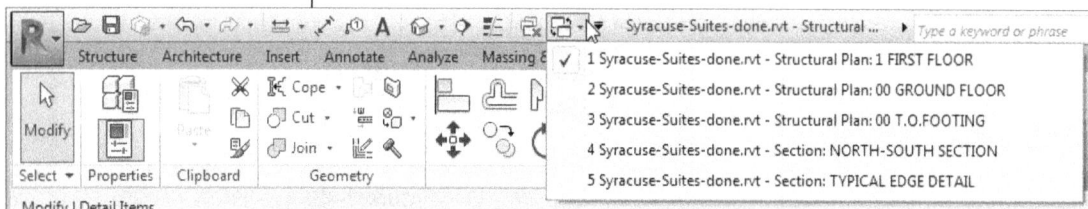

Syracuse-Suites-done.rvt - Structural ...

✓ 1 Syracuse-Suites-done.rvt - Structural Plan: 1 FIRST FLOOR
2 Syracuse-Suites-done.rvt - Structural Plan: 00 GROUND FLOOR
3 Syracuse-Suites-done.rvt - Structural Plan: 00 T.O.FOOTING
4 Syracuse-Suites-done.rvt - Section: NORTH-SOUTH SECTION
5 Syracuse-Suites-done.rvt - Section: TYPICAL EDGE DETAIL

Figure 1–63

3. In the Quick Access Toolbar, click ⬚ (Close Hidden Windows) so that only the current window remains open.

4. In the *View* tab>Create panel or the Quick Access Toolbar, click ⬚ (3D View).

5. Type **WT** to tile the windows.

6. Type **ZA** to zoom extents in both windows, as shown in Figure 1–64. This view configuration is useful when placing elements in a model.

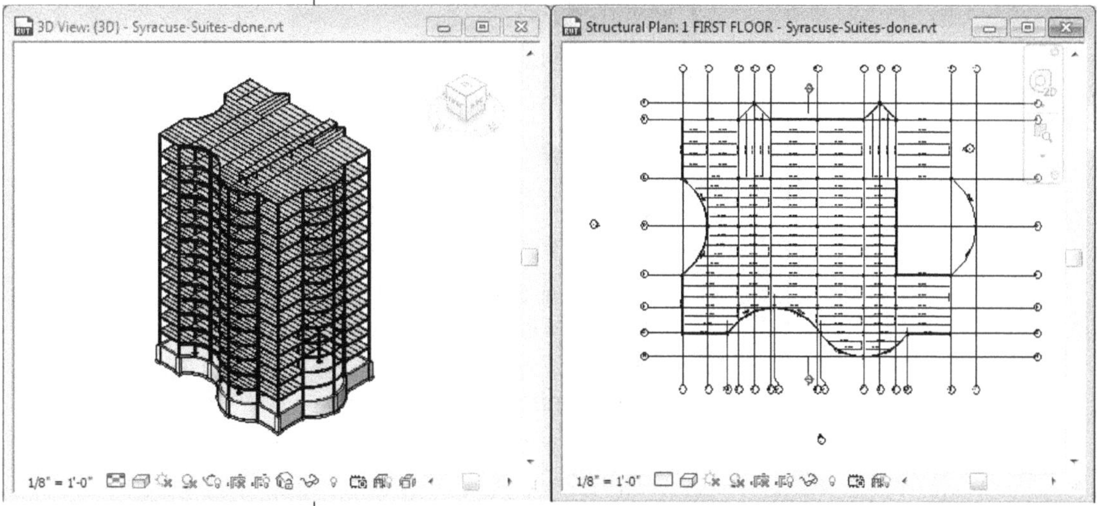

Figure 1–64

7. Click inside the 3D view window.

8. Press and hold <Shift> and then press and hold the wheel on the mouse. Move the mouse to dynamically view the 3D model. You can also navigate in 3D using the ViewCube in the upper right corner of the view.

9. In the upper right corner of the view, click ⊠ (Close) to close the 3D view. (This also works when many views are open.)

10. Expand the Application Menu and click ⬚ (Close) to exit the project. Do not save changes.

Chapter Review Questions

1. When you create a project in the Autodesk Revit software, do you work in 3D (as shown on the left in Figure 1–65) or 2D (as shown on the right in Figure 1–65)?

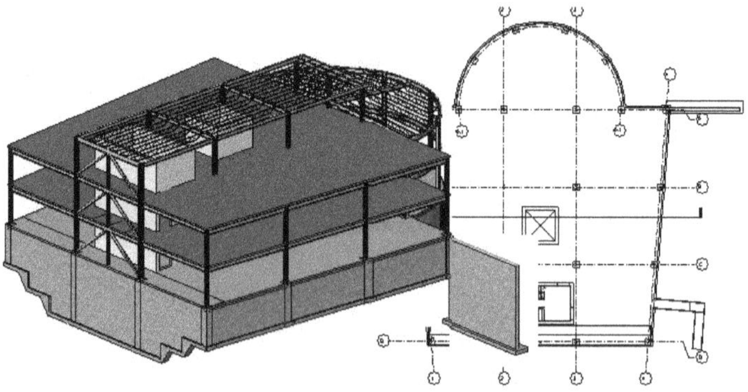

Figure 1–65

   a. You work in 2D in plan views and in 3D in non-plan views.

   b. You work in 3D almost all of the time, even when you are using what looks like a flat view.

   c. You work in 2D or 3D depending on how you toggle the 2D/3D control.

   d. You work in 2D in plan and section views and in 3D in isometric views.

2. What is the purpose of the Project Browser?

   a. It enables you to browse through the building project, similar to a walk through.

   b. It is the interface for managing all of the files that are required to create the complete architectural model of the building.

   c. It manages multiple Autodesk Revit projects as an alternative to using Windows Explorer.

   d. It is used to access and manage the views of the project.

3. Which part(s) of the interface changes according to the command you are using? (Select all that apply.)

   a. Ribbon

   b. View Control Bar

   c. Options Bar

   d. Properties Palette

4. The difference between Type Properties and Properties (the ribbon location is shown in Figure 1–66) is...

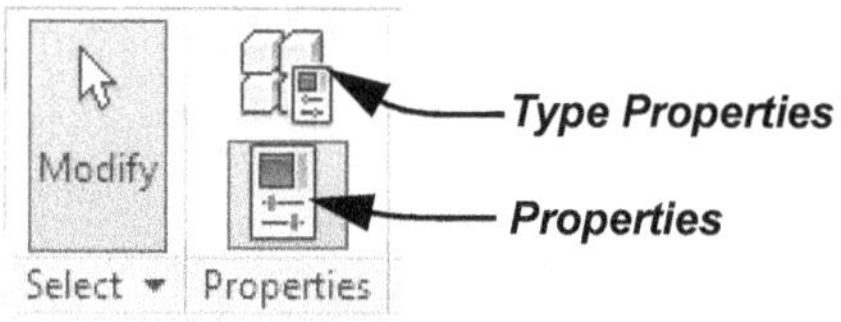

Figure 1–66

a. Properties stores parameters that apply to the selected individual element(s). Type Properties stores parameters that impact every element of the same type in the project.

b. Properties stores the location parameters of an element. Type Properties stores the size and identity parameters of an element.

c. Properties only stores parameters of the view. Type Properties stores parameters of model components.

5. When you start a new project, how do you specify the base information in the new file?

a. Transfer the base information from an existing project.

b. Select the right template for the task.

c. The Autodesk Revit software automatically extracts the base information from imported or linked file(s).

6. What is the main difference between a view made using

(Default 3D View) and a view made using (Camera)?

a. Use Default **3D View** for exterior views and **Camera** for interiors.

b. **Default 3D View** creates a static image and a **Camera** view is live and always updated.

c. **Default 3D View** is isometric and a **Camera** view is perspective.

d. **Default 3D View** is used for the overall building and a **Camera** view is used for looking in tight spaces.

Command Summary

Button	Command	Location
General Tools		
	Modify	• **Ribbon:** All tabs>Select panel • **Shortcut:** MD
	New	• **Quick Access Toolbar** (Optional) • *File* **tab** • **Shortcut:** <Ctrl>+<N>
	Open	• **Quick Access Toolbar** • *File* **tab** • **Shortcut:** <Ctrl>+<O>
	Open Documents	• *File* **tab**
	Properties	• **Ribbon:** *Modify* tab>Properties panel • **Shortcut:** PP
	Recent Documents	• *File* **tab**
	Save	• **Quick Access Toolbar** • *File* **tab** • **Shortcut:** <Ctrl>+<S>
	Synchronize and Modify Settings	• **Quick Access Toolbar**
	Synchronize Now/	• **Quick Access Toolbar**>expand Synchronize and Modify Settings
	Type Properties	• **Ribbon:** *Modify* tab>Properties panel • **Properties palette**
Viewing Tools		
	Camera	• **Quick Access Toolbar**> Expand Default 3D View • **Ribbon:** *View* tab>Create panel> expand Default 3D View
	Default 3D View	• **Quick Access Toolbar** • **Ribbon:** *View* tab>Create panel
	Home	• **ViewCube**
N/A	**Next Pan/Zoom**	• **Navigation Bar** • **Shortcut Menu**
N/A	**Previous Pan/Zoom**	• **Navigation Bar** • **Shortcut Menu** • **Shortcut:** ZP
	Shadows On/Off	• **View Control Bar**

	Show Rendering Dialog/ Render	• **View Control Bar** • **Ribbon:** *View* tab>Graphics panel • **Shortcut:** RR
	Zoom All to Fit	• **Navigation Bar** • **Shortcut:** ZA
	Zoom in Region	• **Navigation Bar** • **Shortcut Menu** • **Shortcut:** ZR
	Zoom Out (2x)	• **Navigation Bar** • **Shortcut Menu** • **Shortcut:** ZO
	Zoom Sheet Size	• **Navigation Bar** • **Shortcut:** ZS
	Zoom to Fit	• **Navigation Bar** • **Shortcut Menu** • **Shortcut:** ZF, ZE
Visual Styles		
	Consistent Colors	• **View Control Bar:**
	Hidden Line	• **View Control Bar** • **Shortcut:** HL
	Ray Trace	• **View Control Bar:**
	Realistic	• **View Control Bar**
	Shaded	• **View Control Bar** • **Shortcut:** SD
	Wireframe	• **View Control Bar** • **Shortcut:** WF

Basic Sketching and Modify Tools

Basic sketching, selecting, and modifying tools are the foundation of working with all types of elements in the Autodesk® Revit® software. Using these tools with drawing aids helps you to place and modify elements to create accurate building models.

Learning Objectives in this Chapter

- Sketch linear elements such as walls, beams, and pipes.
- Ease the placement of elements by incorporating drawing aids, such as alignment lines, temporary dimensions, permanent dimensions, and snaps.
- Place Reference Planes as temporary guide lines.
- Use techniques to select and filter groups of elements.
- Modify elements using a contextual tab, Properties, temporary dimensions, and controls.
- Move, copy, rotate, and mirror elements and create array copies in linear and radial patterns.
- Align, trim, and extend elements with the edges of other elements.
- Split linear elements anywhere along their length.
- Offset elements to create duplicates a specific distance away from the original.

2.1 Using General Sketching Tools

When you start a command, the contextual tab on the ribbon, the Options Bar, and the Properties palette enable you to set up features for each new element you are placing in the project. As you are working, several features called *drawing aids* display, as shown in Figure 2–1. They help you to create designs quickly and accurately.

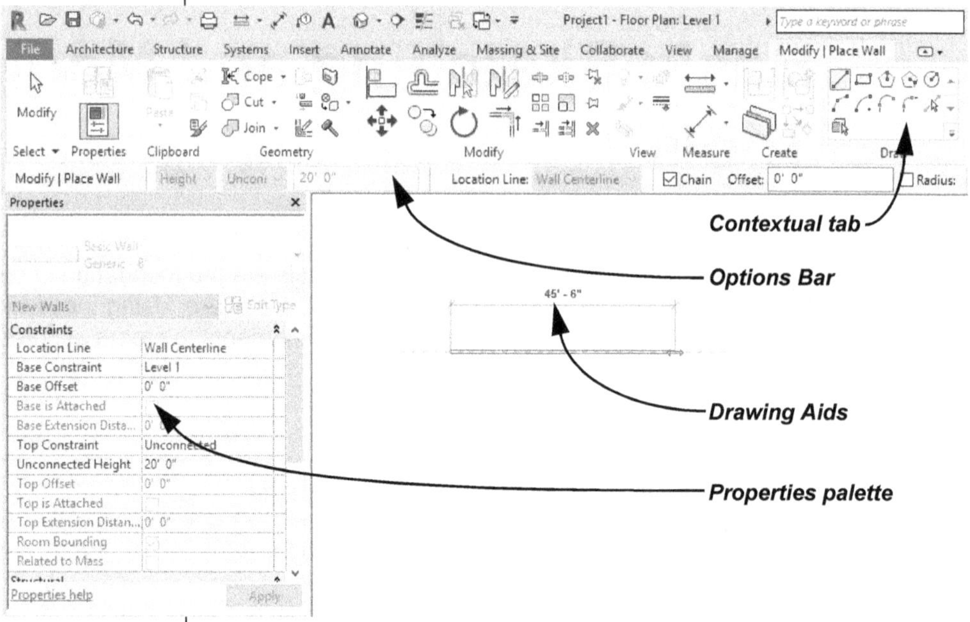

Figure 2–1

- in Autodesk Revit, you are most frequently creating 3D model elements rather than 2D sketches. These tools work with both 3D and 2D elements in the software.

Draw Tools

Many linear elements (such as walls, beams, ducts, pipes, and conduits) are modeled using the tools on the contextual tab on the *Draw* panel, as shown for walls in Figure 2–1. Other elements (such as floors, ceilings, roofs, and slabs) have boundaries that are sketched using many of the same tools. Draw tools are also used when you create details or schematic drawings.

Two methods are available:

The exact tools vary according to the element being modeled.

- *Draw* the element using a geometric form
- *Pick* an existing element (such as a line, face, or wall) as the basis for the new element's geometry and position.

How To: Create Linear Elements

1. Start the command you want to use.
2. In the contextual tab>Draw panel, as shown in Figure 2–2, select a drawing tool.
3. Select points to define the elements.

You can change from one Draw tool shape to another in the middle of a command.

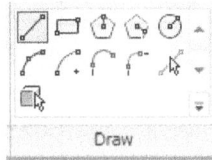

Figure 2–2

4. Finish the command using one of the standard methods:

- Click   (Modify).
- Press <Esc> twice.
- Start another command.

Draw Options

When you are in Drawing mode, several options display in the Options Bar, as shown in Figure 2–3.

Different options display according to the type of element that is selected or the command that is active.

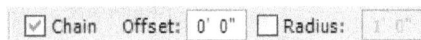

Figure 2–3

- **Chain**: Controls how many segments are created in one process. If this option is not selected, the **Line** and **Arc** tools only create one segment at a time. If it is selected, you can continue adding segments until you press <Esc> or select the command again.

- **Offset**: Enables you to enter values so you can create linear elements at a specified distance from the selected points or element.

- **Radius**: Enables you to enter values when using a radial tool or to add a radius to the corners of linear elements as you sketch them.

Draw Tools

	Line	Draws a straight line defined by the first and last points. If Chain is enabled, you can continue selecting end points for multiple segments.
	Rectangle	Draws a rectangle defined by two opposing corner points. You can adjust the dimensions after selecting both points.
	Inscribed Polygon	Draws a polygon inscribed in a hypothetical circle with the number of sides specified in the Options Bar.
	Circumscribed Polygon	Draws a polygon circumscribed around a hypothetical circle with the number of sides specified in the Options Bar.
	Circle	Draws a circle defined by a center point and radius.
	Start-End-Radius Arc	Draws a curve defined by a start, end, and radius of the arc. The outside dimension shown is the included angle of the arc. The inside dimension is the radius.
	Center-ends Arc	Draws a curve defined by a center, radius, and included angle. The selected point of the radius also defines the start point of the arc.
	Tangent End Arc	Draws a curve tangent to another element. Select an end point for the first point, but do not select the intersection of two or more elements. Then select a second point based on the included angle of the arc.
	Fillet Arc	Draws a curve defined by two other elements and a radius. Because it is difficult to select the correct radius by clicking, this command automatically moves to edit mode. Select the dimension and then modify the radius of the fillet.
	Spline	Draws a spline curve based on selected points. The curve does not actually touch the points (Model and Detail Lines only).
	Ellipse	Draws an ellipse from a primary and secondary axis (Model and Detail Lines only).
	Partial Ellipse	Draws only one side of the ellipse, like an arc. A partial ellipse also has a primary and secondary axis (Model and Detail Lines only).

Pick Tools

⚲	**Pick Lines**	Use this option to select existing linear elements in the project. This is useful when you start the project from an imported 2D drawing.
▤	**Pick Face**	Use this option to select the face of a 3D massing element (walls and 3D views only).
⬚	**Pick Walls**	Use this option to select an existing wall in the project to be the basis for a new sketch line (floors, ceilings, etc.).

Drawing Aids

As soon as you start sketching or placing elements, three drawing aids display, as shown in Figure 2–4:

- Alignment lines

- Temporary dimensions

- Snaps

These aids are available with most modeling and many modification commands.

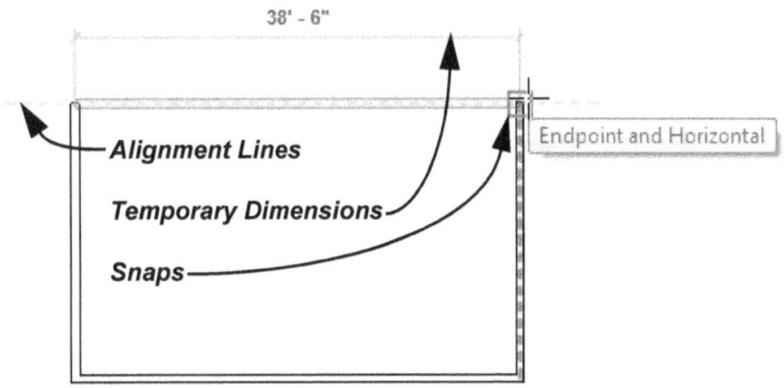

Figure 2–4

Alignment lines display as soon as you select your first point. They help keep lines horizontal, vertical, or at a specified angle. They also line up with the implied intersections of walls and other elements.

- Hold <Shift> to force the alignments to be orthogonal (90 degree angles only).

Temporary dimensions display to help place elements at the correct length, angle and location.

- You can type in the dimension and then move the cursor until you see the dimension you want, or you can place the element and then modify the dimension as required.

- The length and angle increments shown vary depending on how far in or out the view is zoomed.

- For Imperial measurements (feet and inches), the software uses a default of feet. For example, when you type **4** and press <Enter>, it assumes 4'-0". For a distance such as 4'-6", you can type any of the following: **4'-6"**, **4'6**, **4-6**, or **4 6** (the numbers separated by a space). To indicate distances less than one foot, type the inch mark (") after the distance, or enter **0**, a space, and then the distance.

Hint: Temporary Dimensions and Permanent Dimensions

Temporary dimensions disappear as soon as you finish adding elements. If you want to make them permanent, select the control shown in Figure 2–5.

32' - 0"

Make this temporary dimension permanent

Figure 2–5

Snaps are key points that help you reference existing elements to exact points when modeling, as shown in Figure 2–6.

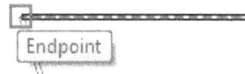

Endpoint

Figure 2–6

- When you move the cursor over an element, the snap symbol displays. Each snap location type displays with a different symbol.

Hint: Snap Settings and Overrides

In the *Manage* tab>Settings panel, click 🧲 (Snaps) to open the Snaps dialog box, which is shown in Figure 2–7. The Snaps dialog box enables you to set which snap points are active, and set the dimension increments displayed for temporary dimensions (both linear and angular).

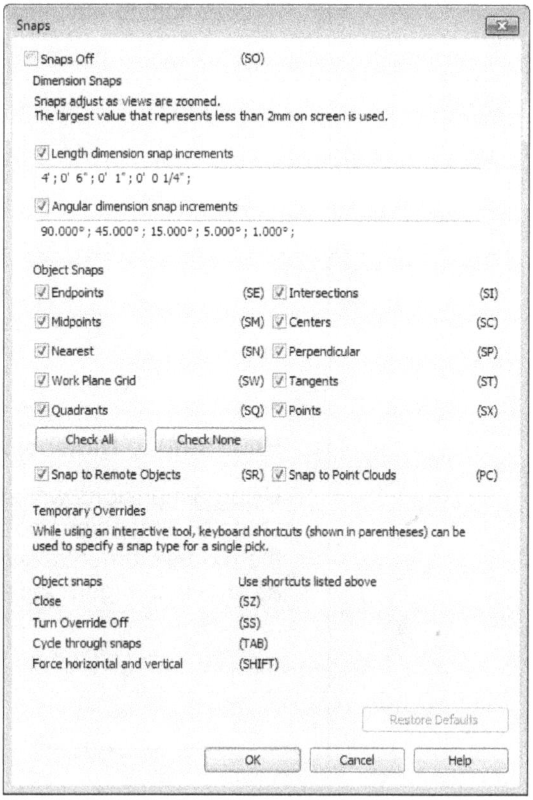

Figure 2–7

- Keyboard shortcuts for each snap can be used to override the automatic snapping. Temporary overrides only affect a single pick, but can be very helpful when there are snaps nearby other than the one you want to use.

Using Dimensions as Drawing Aids

Dimensions are a critical part of construction documents that can also help you create the elements in your model. There are a variety of dimension types, but the most useful is **Aligned Dimension** with the *Individual References* option.

How To: Add Aligned Dimensions to Individual References

1. In the Quick Access Toolbar or the *Modify* tab>Measure panel, click ⤢ (Aligned Dimension), or type **DI**.
2. Select the elements in order.
3. To position the dimension string, click a point at the location where you want it to display, ensuring that the string is not overlapping anything else, as shown in Figure 2–8.

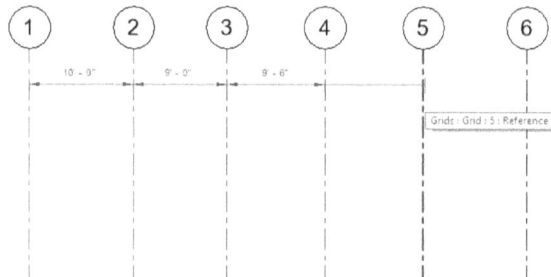

Figure 2–8

Hint: Setting Dimensions Equal

Using dimensions while you are modeling enables you to set a string of dimensions so that they are equal. Doing this updates the model elements, such as the location of windows in a wall, as shown in Figure 2–9.

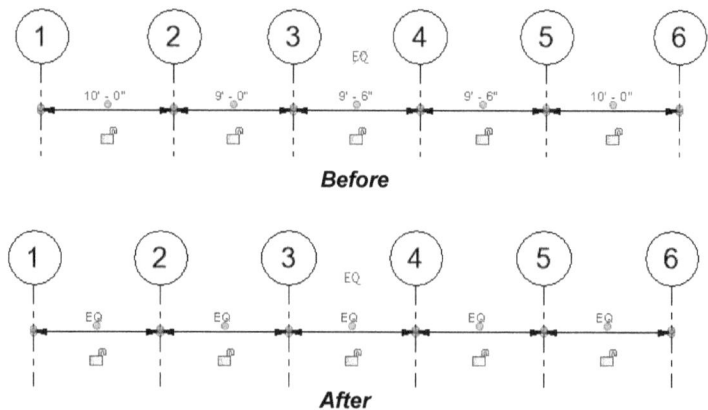

Before

After

Figure 2–9

Reference Planes

As you develop designs in the Autodesk Revit software, there are times when you need lines to help you define certain locations. You can sketch reference planes (displayed as dashed green lines) and snap to them whenever you need to line up elements. For the example shown in Figure 2–10, the lighting fixtures in the reflected ceiling plan are placed using reference planes.

- To insert a reference plane, in the *Architecture, Structure,* or *Systems* tab>Work Plane panel, click ✎ (Ref Plane) or type **RP**.

Reference planes do not display in 3D views.

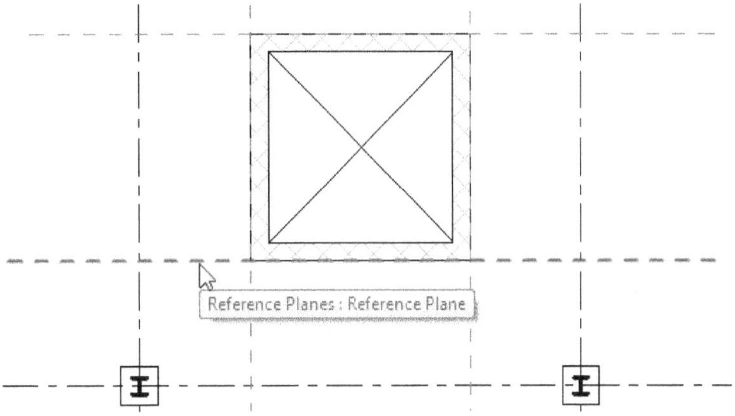

Figure 2–10

- Reference planes display in associated views because they are infinite planes, and not just lines.

- You can name Reference planes by clicking on **<Click to name>** and typing in the text box, as shown in Figure 2–11.

Figure 2–11

- If you sketch a reference pane in Sketch Mode (used with floors and similar elements), it does not display once the sketch is finished.

- Reference planes can have different line styles if they have been defined in the project. In Properties, select a style from the Subcategory list.

2.2 Editing Elements

Building design projects typically involve extensive changes to the model. The Autodesk Revit software was designed to make such changes quickly and efficiently. You can change an element using the following methods, as shown in Figure 2–12:

- Type Selector enables you to specify a different type. This is frequently used to change the size and/or style of the elements.

- Properties enables you to modify the information (parameters) associated with the selected elements.

- The contextual tab in the ribbon contains the Modify commands and element-specific tools.

- Temporary dimensions enable you to change the element's dimensions or position.

- Controls enable you to drag, flip, lock, and rotate the element.

- Shape handles (not shown) enable you to drag elements to modify their height or length.

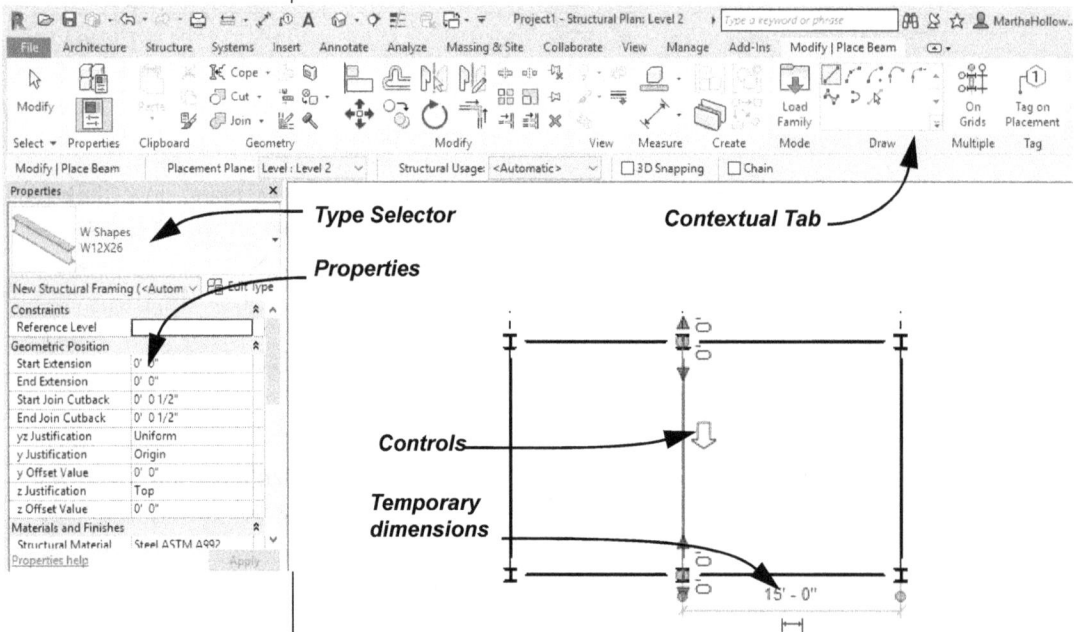

Figure 2–12

- To delete an element, select it and press <Delete>, right-click and select **Delete**, or in the Modify panel, click ✖ (Delete).

Working with Controls and Shape Handles

When you select an element, various controls and shape handles display depending on the element and view. For example, in plan view you can use controls to drag the ends of a wall and change its orientation. You can also drag the wall ends in a 3D view, and you can also use the arrow shape handles to change the height of the wall, as shown in Figure 2–13

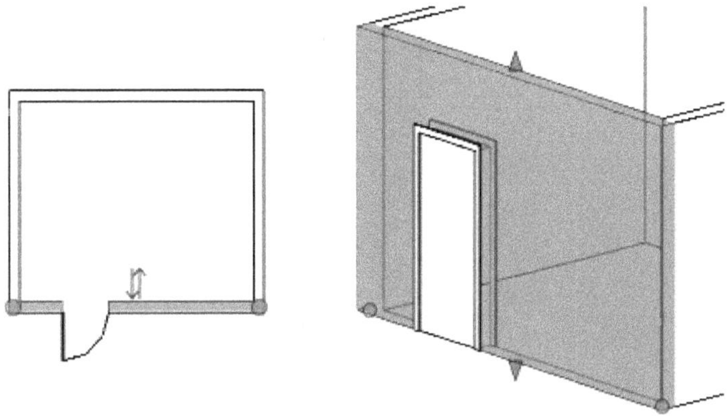

Figure 2–13

- If you hover the cursor over the control or shape handle, a tool tip displays showing its function.

Hint: Editing Temporary Dimensions

Temporary dimensions automatically link to the closest wall. To change this, drag the *Witness Line* control (as shown in Figure 2–14) to connect to a new reference. You can also click on the control to toggle between justifications in the wall.

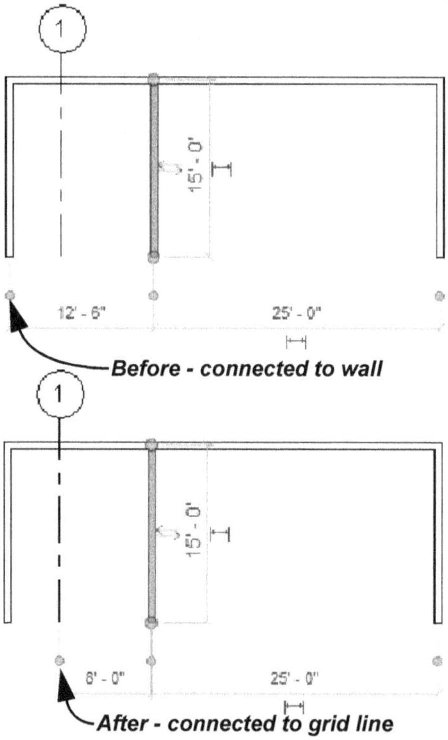
1
15' - 0'
12' - 6"
25' - 0"
Before - connected to wall
1
15' - 0'
8' - 0"
25' - 0"
After - connected to grid line

Figure 2–14

- The new location of a temporary dimension for an element is remembered as long as you are in the same session of the software.

Selecting Multiple Elements

- Once you have selected at least one element, hold <Ctrl> and select another item to add it to a selection set.

- To remove an element from a selection set, hold <Shift> and select the element.

- If you click and drag the cursor to *window* around elements, you have two selection options, as shown in Figure 2–15. If you drag from left to right, you only select the elements completely inside the window. If you drag from right to left, you select elements both inside and crossing the window.

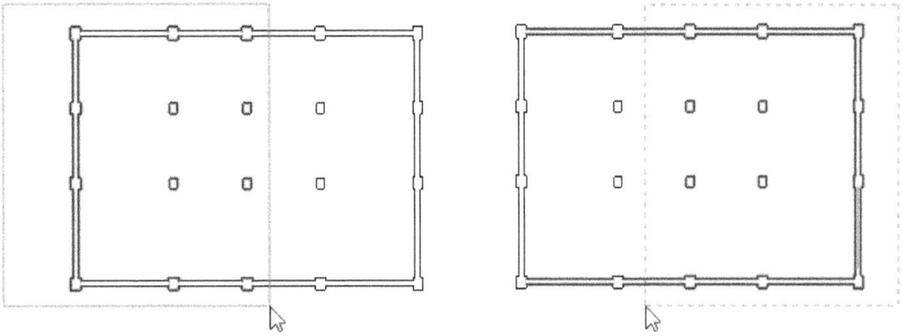

Window: Left to Right   *Crossing: Right to Left*

Figure 2–15

- If several elements are on or near each other, press <Tab> to cycle through them before you click. If there are elements that might be linked to each other, such as walls that are connected, pressing <Tab> selects the chain of elements.

- Press <Ctrl>+<Left Arrow> to reselect the previous selection set. You can also right-click in the view window with nothing selected and select **Select Previous**.

- To select all elements of a specific type, right-click on an element and select **Select All Instances>Visible in View** or **In Entire Project**, as shown in Figure 2–16.

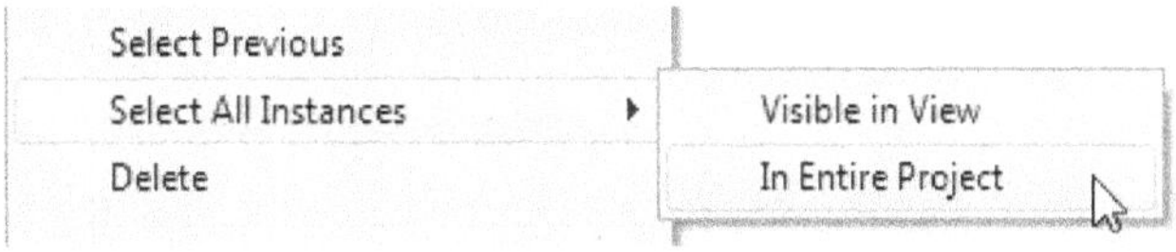

Select Previous	
Select All Instances ▶	Visible in View
Delete	In Entire Project

Figure 2–16

Hint: Measuring Tools

When modifying a model, it is useful to know the distance between elements. This can be done with temporary dimensions, or more frequently, by using the measuring tools found in the Quick Access Toolbar or on the *Modify* tab> Measure panel, as shown in Figure 2–17.

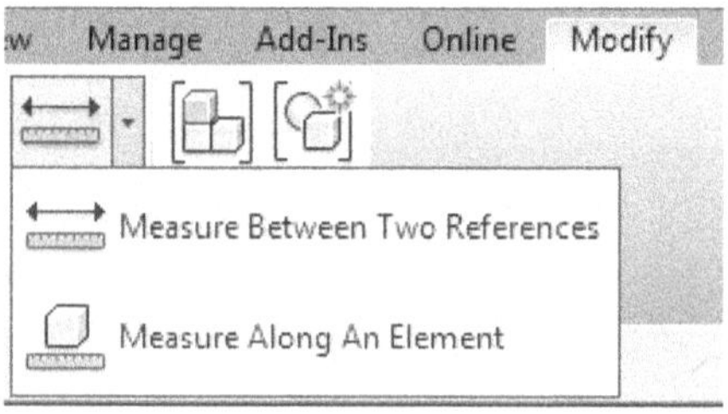

Figure 2–17

- ⟷ (Measure Between Two References) - Select two elements and the measurement displays.

- ▱ (Measure Along An Element) - Select the edge of a linear element and the total length displays. Use <Tab> to select other elements and then click to measure along all of them, as shown in Figure 2–18.

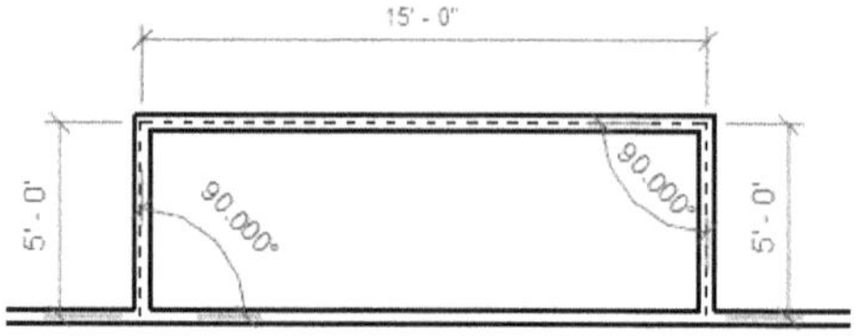

Figure 2–18

- References include any snap point, wall lines, or other parts of elements (such as door center lines).

Filtering Selection Sets

When multiple element categories are selected, the *Multi-Select* contextual tab opens in the ribbon. This gives you access to all of the Modify tools, and the **Filter** command. The **Filter** command enables you to specify the types of elements to select. For example, you might only want to select columns, as shown in Figure 2–19.

Figure 2–19

How To: Filter a Selection Set

1. Select everything in the required area.
2. in the *Modify | Multi-Select* tab>Selection panel, or in the Status Bar, click ⌷ (Filter). The Filter dialog box opens, as shown in Figure 2–20.

The Filter dialog box displays all types of elements in the original selection.

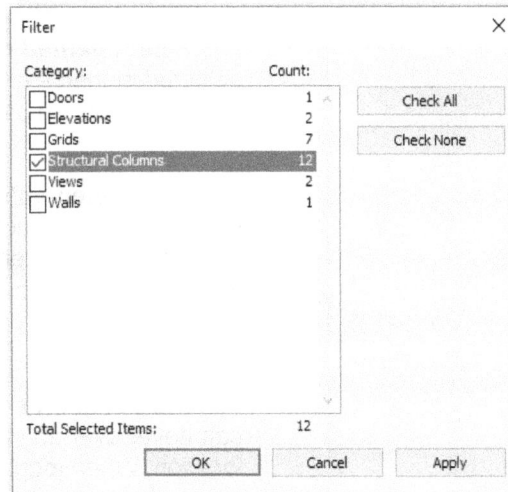

Figure 2–20

3. Click **Check None** to clear all of the options or **Check All** to select all of the options. You can also select or clear individual categories as required.

4. Click **OK**. The selection set is now limited to the elements you specified.

- The number of elements selected displays on the right end of the status bar and in the Properties palette.

- Clicking **Filter** in the Status Bar also opens the Filter dialog box.

Hint: Selection Options

You can control how the software selects specific elements in a project by toggling Selection Options on and off on the Status Bar, as shown in Figure 2–21. Alternatively, in any tab on the ribbon, expand the Select panel's title and select the option.

Figure 2–21

- **Select links:** When toggled on, you can selected linked CAD drawings or Autodesk Revit models. When it is toggled off you cannot select them when using **Modify** or **Move**.

- **Select underlay elements:** When toggled on, you can select underlay elements. When toggled off, you cannot select them when using **Modify** or **Move**.

- **Select pinned elements:** When toggled on, you can selected pinned elements. When toggled off, you cannot select them when using **Modify** or **Move**.

- **Select elements by face:** When toggled on you can select elements (such as the floors or walls in an elevation) by selecting the interior face or selecting an edge. When toggled off, you can only select elements by selecting an edge.

- **Drag elements on selection:** When toggled on, you can hover over an element, select it, and drag it to a new location. When toggled off, the Crossing or Box select mode starts when you press and drag, even if you are on top of an element. Once elements have been selected they can still be dragged to a new location.

Practice 2a

Sketch and Edit Elements

Practice Objective

- Use sketch tools and drawing aids.

Estimated time for completion: 10 minutes

In this practice you will use a variety of ways to select elements, use the Filter dialog box to only select one type of element, select only elements of one type in the view, and use the Type Selector to change the type. You will then modify element locations using temporary dimensions as shown in Figure 2–22.

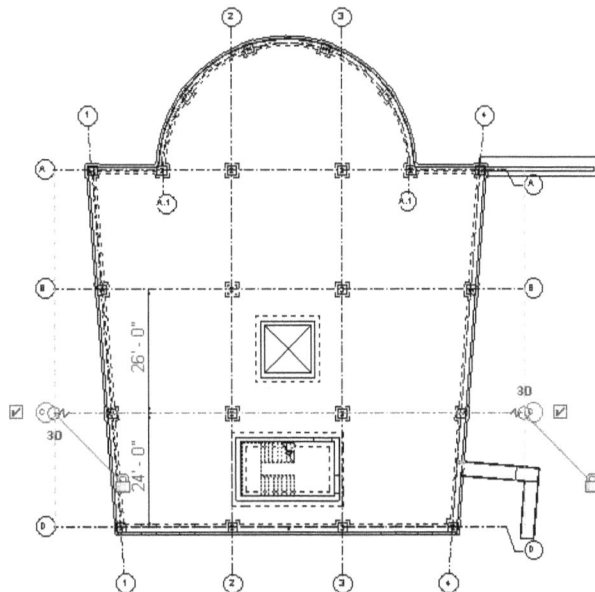

Figure 2–22

Task 1 - Select elements.

1. Open the project **Practice-Model-Select.rvt**.

2. Select a point just outside the upper left corner of the building.

3. Hold the mouse button and drag a window toward the lower right corner, as shown in Figure 2–23.

Figure 2–23

4. Select a second point. All of the elements inside the window are selected and those outside the window are not selected. Press <Esc>.

5. Select two points from just outside the upper right corner of the building to the lower left corner, as shown in Figure 2–24. All of the elements inside and touching the window are selected.

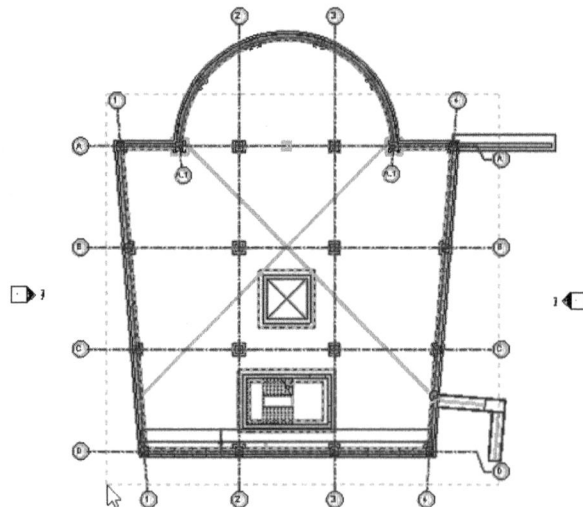

Figure 2–24

6. In the Status Bar, click ▼ (Filter).

7. In the Filter dialog box shown in Figure 2–25, review the selected element categories.

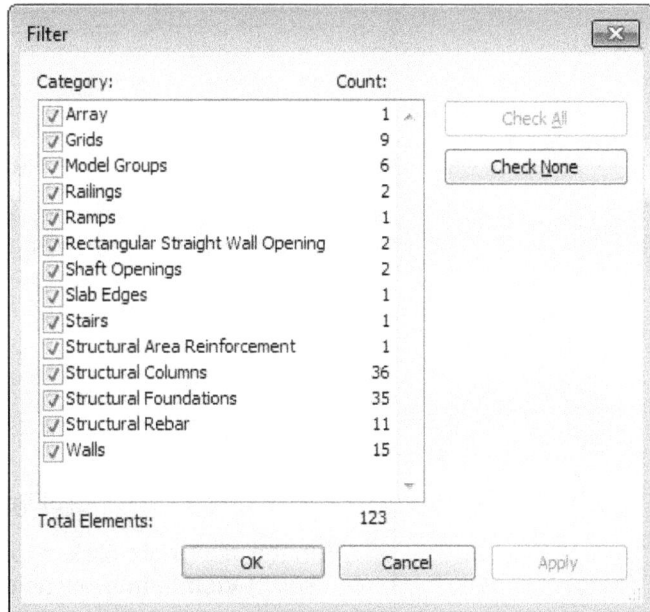

Category:	Count:
☑ Array	1
☑ Grids	9
☑ Model Groups	6
☑ Railings	2
☑ Ramps	1
☑ Rectangular Straight Wall Opening	2
☑ Shaft Openings	2
☑ Slab Edges	1
☑ Stairs	1
☑ Structural Area Reinforcement	1
☑ Structural Columns	36
☑ Structural Foundations	35
☑ Structural Rebar	11
☑ Walls	15

Total Elements: 123

Figure 2–25

8. Click **Check None**.

9. Select only the Structural Columns category and click **OK**.

10. The total number of Structural Columns in the selection set displays in the Status Bar as shown in Figure 2–26.

Figure 2–26

11. In Properties, the display indicates that multiple Families are selected.

12. Click in empty space to clear the selection.

13. Zoom in on the lower left corner of the building and select one Structural Column as shown in Figure 2–27.

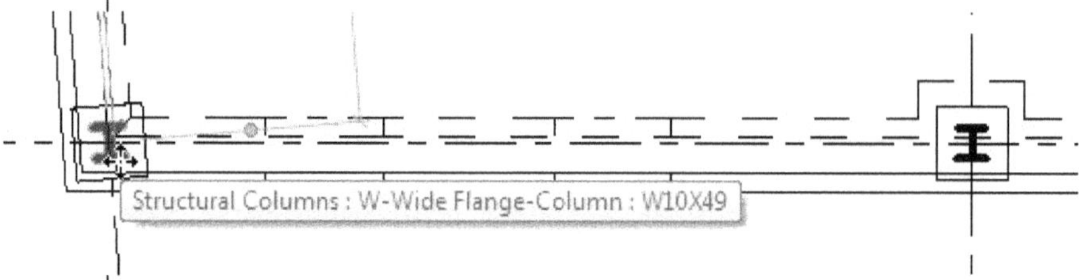

Structural Columns : W-Wide Flange-Column : W10X49

Figure 2–27

14. In the Type Selector, the column name and type are displayed as shown in Figure 2–28.

Properties

W-Wide Flange-Column
W10X49

Structural Columns (1)   Edit Type

Figure 2–28

15. In the view, right-click, expand **Select All Instances**, and select **Visible in View** as shown in Figure 2–29.

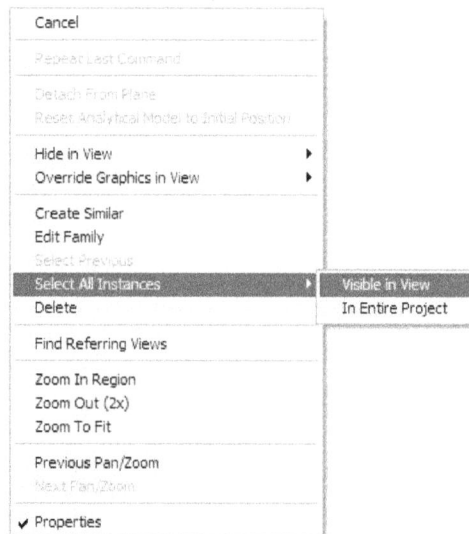

Cancel

Repeat Last Command

Detach From Plane
Reset Analytical Model to Initial Position

Hide in View   ▶
Override Graphics in View   ▶

Create Similar
Edit Family
Select Previous

Select All Instances   ▶   Visible in View
Delete   In Entire Project

Find Referring Views

Zoom In Region
Zoom Out (2x)
Zoom To Fit

Previous Pan/Zoom
Next Pan/Zoom

✓ Properties

Figure 2–29

16. The total number of this type of column displays in the Status Bar by Filter and in Properties.

17. In the Type Selector, select **W-Wide Flange-Column: W12x40**, as shown in Figure 2–30.

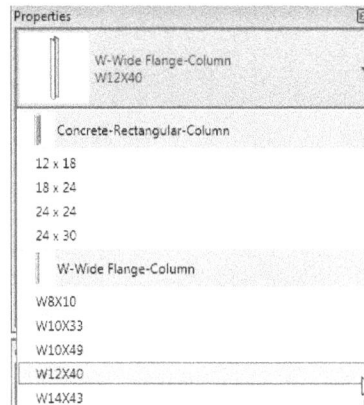

Figure 2–30

18. The view regenerates and the selected columns are updated to the new type. Press <Esc> to release the selection set.

Task 2 - Using temporary dimensions.

---

1. Zoom out to see the entire building.

2. Select Grid C.

3. If the temporary dimensions are not displayed, in the Options Bar, click **Activate Dimensions**.

4. The temporary dimensions are automatically connected to the closest structural elements.

5. Use the **Move Witness Line** controls on the temporary dimensions and move them to the nearest grid lines as shown in Figure 2–31.

Figure 2–31

6. Click ⛶ (Make this temporary dimension line permanent).

7. Click in empty space to release the selection. The new dimensions are now part of the view.

8. Select Grid C again.

9. Click **Activate Dimensions**, if required.

10. Select the lower dimension text and change it to **24'-0"** as shown in Figure 2–32. Press <Enter>.

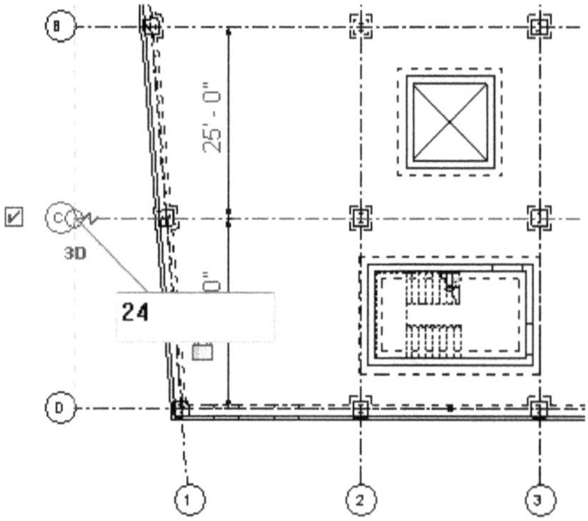

Figure 2–32

11. The model regenerates and the percentage of completion is displayed in the Status Bar as shown in Figure 2–33. This change is being made to the grid and throughout the model, wherever elements touch the grid.

Figure 2–33

12. Save and close the project.

2.3 Working with Basic Modify Tools

The Autodesk Revit software contains controls and temporary dimensions that enable you to edit elements. Additional modifying tools can be used with individual elements or any selection of elements. They are found in the *Modify* tab>Modify panel, as shown in Figure 2–34, and in contextual tabs.

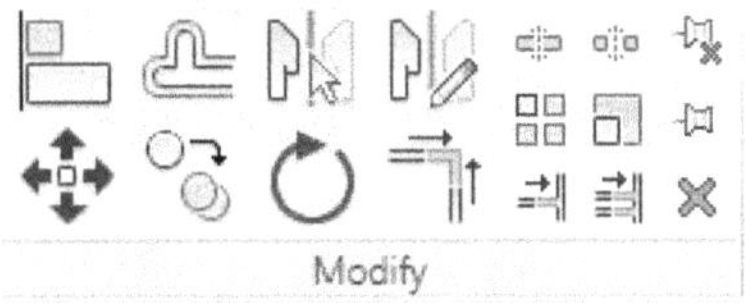

Figure 2–34

- The **Move**, **Copy**, **Rotate**, **Mirror**, and **Array** commands are covered in this topic. Other tools are covered later.

- For most modify commands, you can either select the elements and start the command, or start the command, select the elements, and press <Enter> to finish the selection and move to the next step in the command.

Moving and Copying Elements

The **Move** and **Copy** commands enable you to select the element(s) and move or copy them from one place to another. You can use alignment lines, temporary dimensions, and snaps to help place the elements, as shown in Figure 2–35.

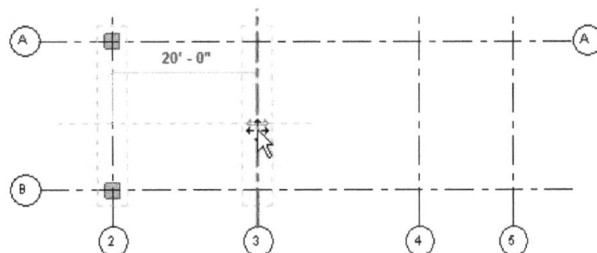

Figure 2–35

Hint: Nudge

Nudge enables you to move an element in short increments. When an element is selected, you can press one of the four arrow keys to move the element in that direction. The distance the element moves depends on how far in or out you are zoomed.

*You can also use the shortcut for **Move, MV** or for **Copy, CO**.*

How To: Move or Copy Elements

1. Select the elements you want to move or copy.
2. In the Modify panel, click ✛ (Move) or ⟲ (Copy). A boundary box displays around the selected elements.
3. Select a move start point on or near the element.
4. Select a second point. Use alignment lines and temporary dimensions to help place the elements.
5. When you are finished, you can start another modify command using the elements that remain selected, or switch back to **Modify** to end the command.

- If you start the **Move** command and hold <Ctrl>, the elements are copied.

Move/Copy Elements Options

The **Move** and **Copy** commands have several options that display in the Options Bar, as shown in Figure 2–36.

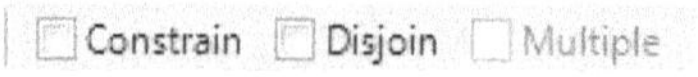

☐ Constrain ☐ Disjoin ☐ Multiple

Figure 2–36

Constrain	Restricts the movement of the cursor to horizontal or vertical, or along the axis of an item that is at an angle. This keeps you from selecting a point at an angle by mistake. **Constrain** is off by default.
Disjoin (Move only)	Breaks any connections between the elements being moved and other elements. If **Disjoin** is on, the elements move separately. If it is off, the connected elements also move or stretch. **Disjoin** is off by default.
Multiple (Copy only)	Enables you to make multiple copies of one selection. **Multiple** is off by default.

- These commands only work in the current view, not between views or projects. To copy between views or projects, In the *Modify* tab>Clipboard panel use ⬜ (Copy to Clipboard), ✂ (Cut to the Clipboard) and ⬜ (Paste from Clipboard).

Hint: Pinning Elements

If you do not want elements to be moved, you can pin them in place, as shown in Figure 2–37. Select the elements and in the

Modify tab, in the Modify panel, click <img> (Pin). Pinned elements can be copied, but not moved. If you try to delete a pinned element, a warning dialog displays reminding you that you must unpin the element before the command can be started.

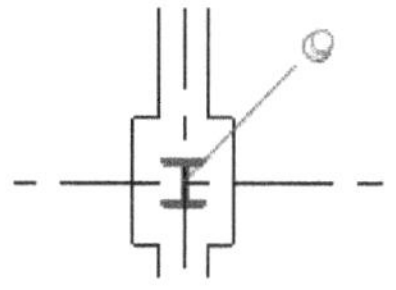

Figure 2–37

Select the element and click <img> (Unpin) or type the shortcut **UP** to free it.

Rotating Elements

The **Rotate** command enables you to rotate selected elements around a center point or origin. You can use alignment lines, temporary dimensions, and snaps to help specify the center of rotation and the angle. You can also create copies of the element as it is being rotated.

How To: Rotate Elements

1. Select the element(s) you want to rotate.

2. In the Modify panel, click ○ (Rotate) or type the shortcut **RO**.

*To start the **Rotate** command with a prompt to select the center of rotation, select the elements first and type **R3**.*

3. The center of rotation is automatically set to the center of the element or group of elements, as shown on the top in Figure 2–38. To change the center of rotation (as shown on the bottom in Figure 2–38), use the following:

   - Drag the ⟳ (Center of Rotation) control to a new point.
   - In the Options Bar, next to **Center of rotation**, click **Place** and use snaps to move it to a new location.
   - Press <Spacebar> to select the center of rotation and click to move it to a new location.

Figure 2–38

4. In the Options Bar, specify if you want to make a Copy (select **Copy**), type an angle in the *Angle* field (as shown in Figure 2–39), and press <Enter>. You can also specify the angle on screen using temporary dimensions.

Figure 2–39

5. The rotated element(s) remain highlighted, enabling you to start another command using the same selection, or click

   (Modify) to finish.

- The **Disjoin** option breaks any connections between the elements being rotated and other elements. If **Disjoin** is on (selected), the elements rotate separately. If it is off (cleared), the connected elements also move or stretch, as shown in Figure 2–40. **Disjoin** is toggled off by default.

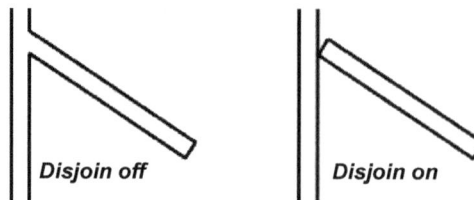

Disjoin off   *Disjoin on*

Figure 2–40

Mirroring Elements

The **Mirror** command enables you to mirror elements about an axis defined by a selected element, as shown in Figure 2–41, or by selected points.

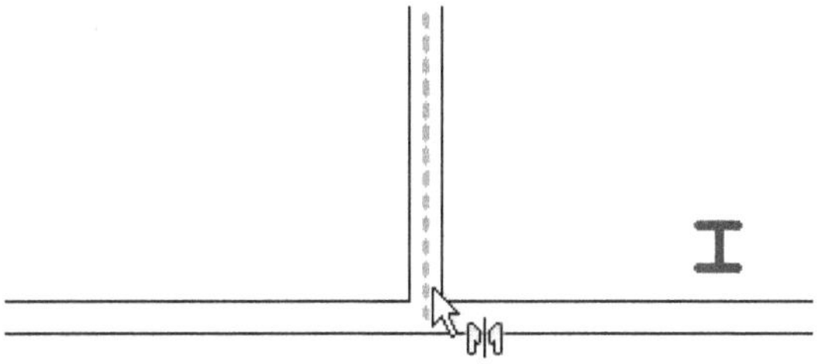

Figure 2–41

How To: Mirror Elements

1. Select the element(s) to mirror.
2. In the Modify panel, select the method you want to use:

   - Click (Mirror - Pick Axis) or type the shortcut **MM**. This prompts you to select an element as the **Axis of Reflection** (mirror line).

   - Click (Mirror - Draw Axis) or type the shortcut **DM**. This prompts you to select two points to define the axis about which the elements mirror.

3. The new mirrored element(s) remain highlighted, enabling you to start another command, or return to **Modify** to finish.

- By default, the original elements that were mirrored remain. To delete the original elements, clear the **Copy** option in the Options Bar.

Hint: Scale

The Autodesk Revit software is designed with full-size elements. Therefore, not much should be scaled. For example, scaling a wall increases its length but does not impact the width, which is set by the wall type. However, you can use

(Scale) in reference planes, images, and imported files from other programs.

Creating Linear and Radial Arrays

The **Array** command creates multiple copies of selected elements in a linear or radial pattern, as shown in Figure 2–42. For example, you can array a row of columns to create a row of evenly spaced columns on a grid, or array a row of parking spaces. The arrayed elements can be grouped or placed as separate elements.

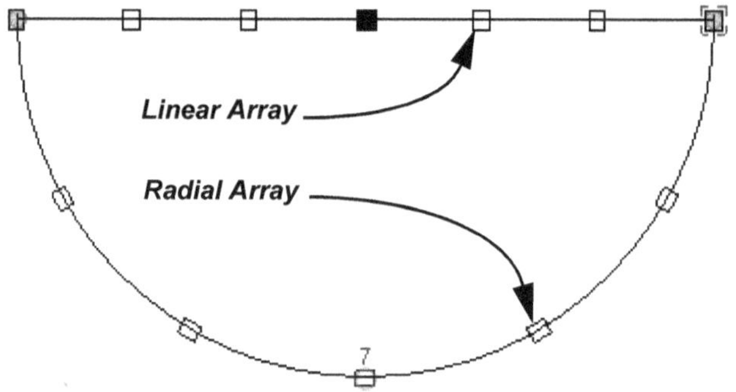

A linear array creates a straight line pattern of elements, while a radial array creates a circular pattern around a center point.

Figure 2–42

How To: Create a Linear Array

1. Select the element(s) to array.
2. In the Modify panel, click ▫▫ (Array) or type the shortcut **AR**.
3. In the Options Bar, click ⬒ (Linear).
4. Specify the other options as required.
5. Select a start point and an end point to set the spacing and direction of the array. The array is displayed.
6. If **Group and Associate** is selected, you are prompted again for the number of items, as shown in Figure 2–43. Type a new number or click on the screen to finish the command.

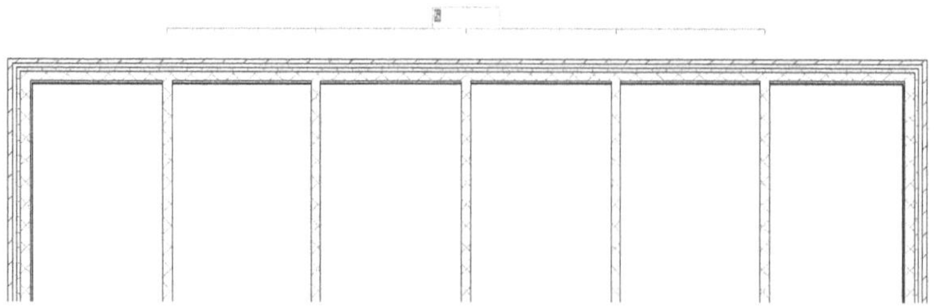

Figure 2–43

- To make a linear array in two directions, you need to array one direction first, select the arrayed elements, and then array them again in the other direction.

Array Options

In the Options Bar, set up the **Array** options for **Linear Array** (top of Figure 2–44) or **Radial Array** (bottom of Figure 2–44).

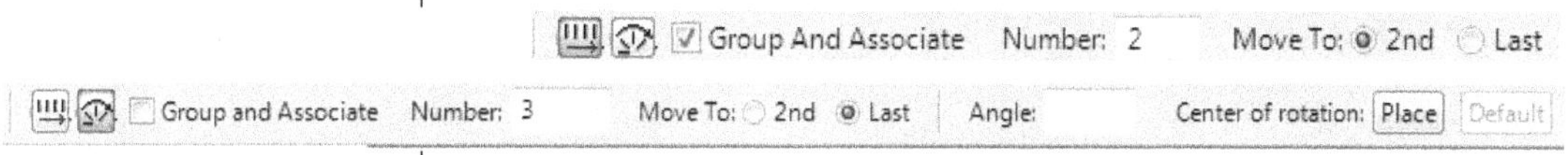

☑ Group And Associate   Number: 2   Move To: ◉ 2nd ○ Last

☐ Group and Associate   Number: 3   Move To: ○ 2nd ◉ Last | Angle: Center of rotation: Place | Default

Figure 2–44

Group and Associate	Creates an array group element out of all arrayed elements. Groups can be selected by selecting any elements in the group.
Number	Specifies how many instances you want in the array.
Move To:	**2nd** specifies the distance or angle between the center points of the two elements. **Last** specifies the overall distance or angle of the entire array.
Constrain	Restricts the direction of the array to only vertical or horizontal (Linear only).
Angle	Specifies the angle (Radial only).
Center of rotation	Specifies a location for the origin about which the elements rotate (Radial only).

How To: Create a Radial Array

1. Select the element(s) to array.

2. In the Modify panel, click ⊞ (Array).

3. In the Options Bar, click ⟁ (Radial).

4. Drag ↻ (Center of Rotation) or use **Place** to the move the center of rotation to the appropriate location, as shown in Figure 2–45.

Remember to set the
Center of Rotation
control first, because it is easy to forget to move it before specifying the angle.

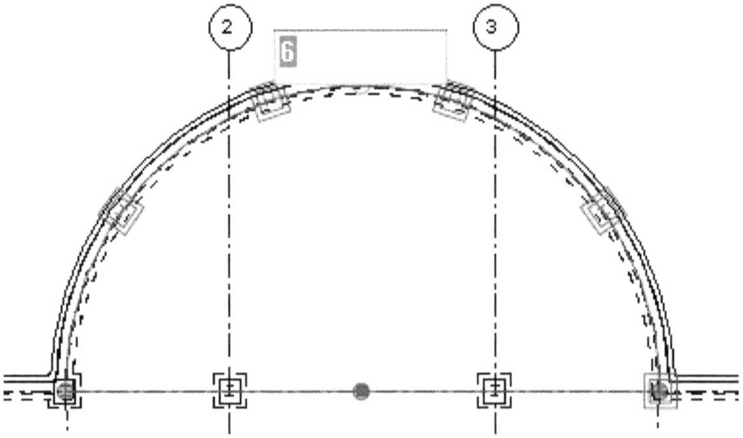

Figure 2–45

5. Specify the other options as required.
6. In the Options Bar, type an angle and press <Enter>, or specify the rotation angle by selecting points on the screen.

Modifying Array Groups

When you select an element in an array that has been grouped, you can change the number of instances in the array, as shown in Figure 2–46. For radial arrays you can also modify the distance to the center.

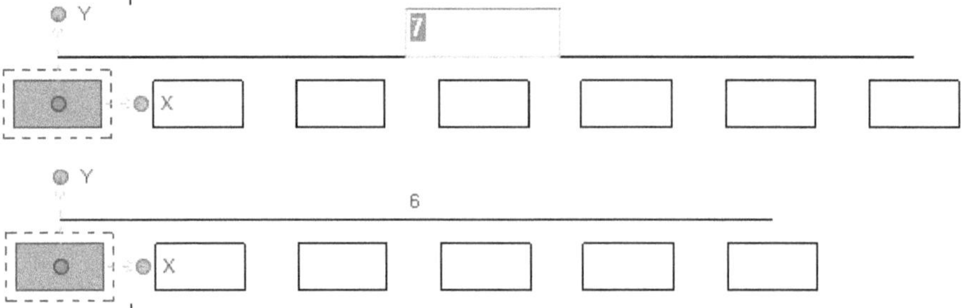

Figure 2–46

• Dashed lines surround the element(s) in a group, and the XY control lets you move the origin point of the group

If you move one of the elements in the array group, the other elements move in response based on the distance and/or angle, as shown in Figure 2–47.

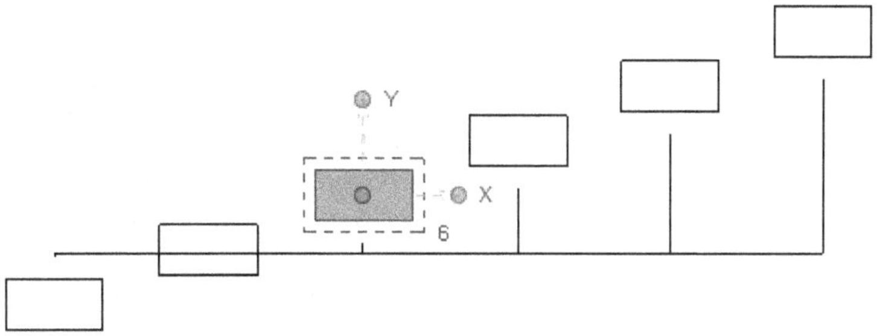

Figure 2–47

*   To remove the array constraint on the group, select all of the elements in the array group and, in the *Modify* contextual tab>Group panel, click (Ungroup).

*   If you select an individual element in an array and click (Ungroup), the element you selected is removed from the array, while the rest of the elements remain in the array group.

*   You can use (Filter) to ensure that you are selecting only **Model Groups**.

Practice 2b

Work with Basic Modify Tools

Practice Objective

- Use basic modify tools such as Move, Copy, Rotate, and Array.

Estimated time for completion: 10 minutes

In this practice you will use **Move** and **Copy** to create a column grid with columns using existing elements in a project. You will then rotate one of the grid lines and the columns along that grid line and mirror the new grid lines to create the opposite part of the building. Finally you will array a set of columns around an arc, and create a grid line of the array as shown in Figure 2–48.

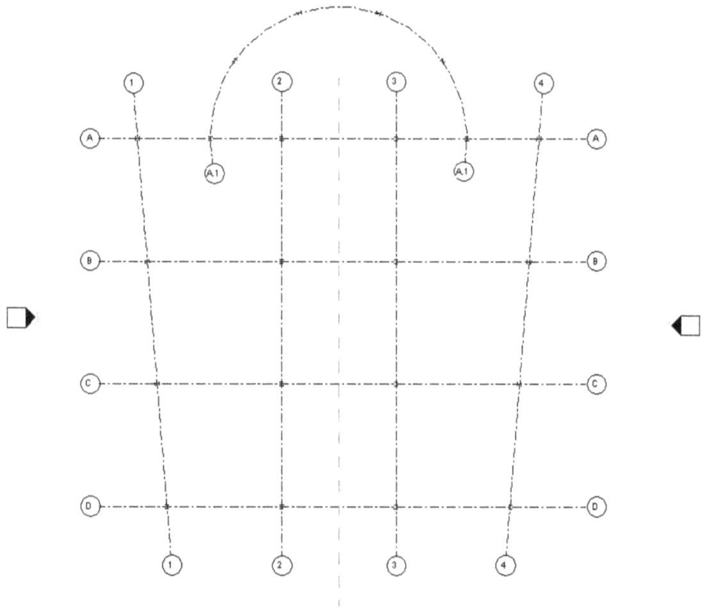

Figure 2–48

Task 1 - Move and copy elements.

1. Open the project **Practice-Model-Editing.rvt**.

2. Select Grid A and the structural column that is at the intersection. (**Hint:** hold <Ctrl> to select more than one element.)

3. In the *Modify | Multi-Select* tab>Modify panel, click
   (Copy).

4. In the Options Bar, select **Multiple**, as shown in Figure 2–49.

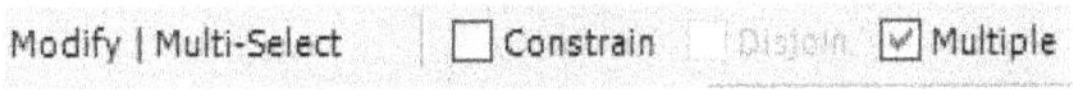

Modify | Multi-Select   ☐ Constrain   Disjoin ☑ Multiple

Figure 2–49

5. Pick a point anywhere along the grid line for the start point.

6. Move the cursor down below the grid line and type **24'**. Create two more copies which are 24'-0" apart for a total of four horizontal grid lines.

7. Click ⌖ (Modify) to exit the command.

8. Select Grid 1 and the four columns along Grid 1. Copy the elements to the right at a distance of **24'-0"** until you have a total of four vertical grid lines with the associated columns.

   Click ⌖ (Modify) to exit the command.

9. Renumber the grid lines as shown in Figure 2–50.

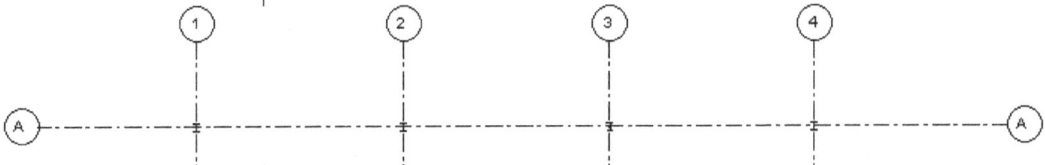

Figure 2–50

10. Zoom in on column **A1**.

11. Select the column (but not the grid line). In the *Modify* tab> Modify panel, click ⬥ (Move) and move it **6'-0"** to the left as shown in Figure 2–51.

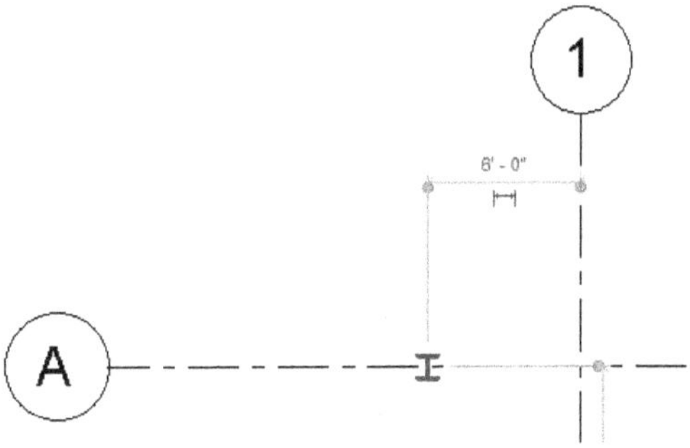

1

A

6' - 0"

Figure 2–51

12. Save the project.

Task 2 - Rotate elements.

1. Select Grid 1.

2. In the *Modify | Grids* tab>Modify panel, click ↻ (Rotate).

3. In the Options Bar, click **Place** and select the midpoint of column **D1** as the center of rotation.

4. To start rotating, select the intersection of grid lines **A1**.

5. To finish rotating, select the midpoint of the column you moved earlier as shown in Figure 2–52.

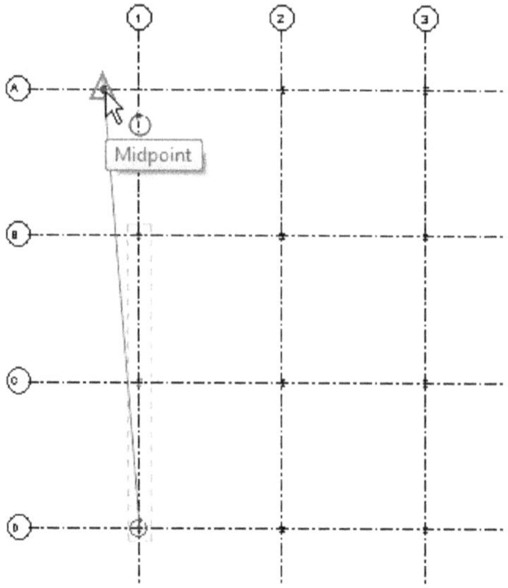

Figure 2–52

6. Zoom in on column **A1**.

7. Select column **A1** and click ↻ (Rotate). The center point is in the correct location.

8. For the start angle, select a point to the right along Grid A as shown in Figure 2–53.

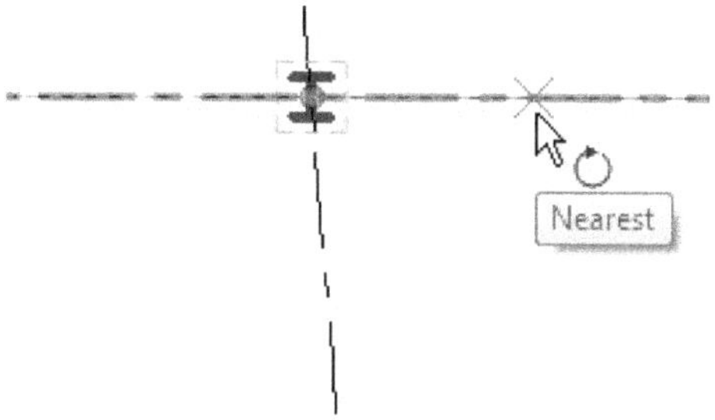

Figure 2–53

9. For the second angle, select a point along Grid 1, as shown on the left in Figure 2–54. The column is now rotated perpendicular to the angle of Grid 1 as shown on the right in Figure 2–54.

Figure 2–54

10. Repeat the process for the rest of the columns along Grid 1.

11. Save the project.

Task 3 - Mirror elements.
---

1. Delete Grid 4 and its columns. You are going to mirror Grid 1 and its columns to this place.

2. In the *Structure* tab>Work Plane panel, click ✏ (Ref Plane).

3. In the *Modify | Place Reference Plane* tab>Draw panel, click ✏ (Line).

4. Draw a vertical line between Grid 2 and Grid 3 and use temporary dimensions to set the distances from each grid to **12'-0"** as shown in Figure 2–55, and click (Modify) to end.

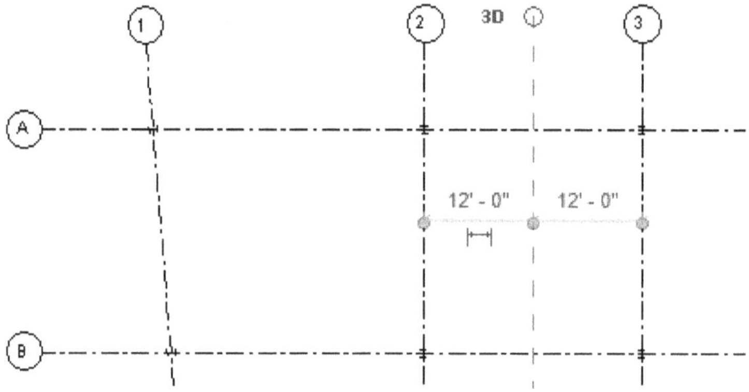

Figure 2–55

5. Select Grid 1 and all of the columns in the grid. (To select multiple elements, draw a window around the group or hold <Ctrl> as you select.)

6. In the *Modify | Multi-Select* tab>Modify panel, click (Pick Mirror Axis).

7. Select the vertical reference plane that you created earlier as shown in Figure 2–56. Renumber the new grid line to **4**.

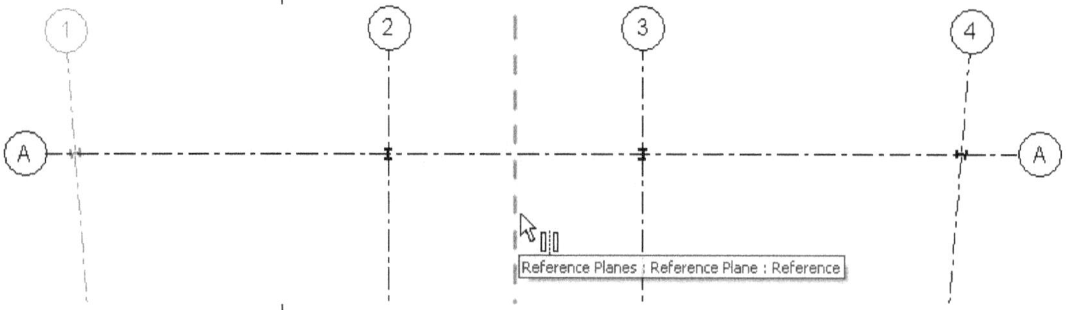

Figure 2–56

8. Save the project.

Task 4 - Array elements.

1. Select column **A3**. Click ⌾ (Copy) and copy column A3 to the right by **15'-0"**. The new column is selected.

2. In the *Modify | Structural Columns* tab>Modify panel, click ▦ (Array).

3. A Warning box opens. This issue is corrected in later steps. Click **OK**.

4. In the Options Bar, click ⟳ (Radial), select **Group and Associate**, set the *Number* to **8**, and set *Move to:* to **Last**.

5. Relocate the center of the array by dragging ⟳ to the intersection of the vertical ref plane and Grid 1 as shown in Figure 2–57.

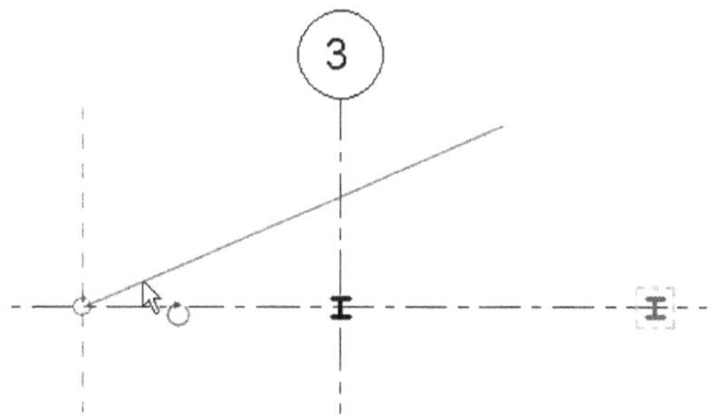

Figure 2–57

6. In the Options Bar, set the *Angle* to **180** and press <Enter>. The new columns display along the arc with the number still selected as shown in Figure 2–58.

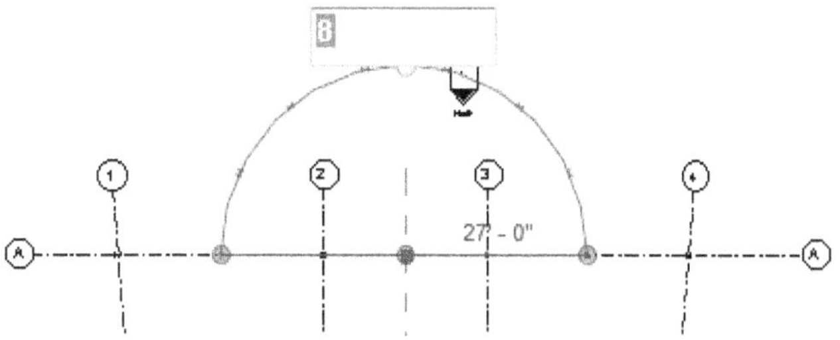

Figure 2–58

7. Change the number to **6**.

8. Click in empty space to release the selection.

9. Move the elevation marker out of the way.

10. In the *Structure* tab>Datum panel, click ⌗ (Grid).

11. In the Draw panel, click ⬈ (Pick Lines).

12. Move the cursor over the area of the array as shown in Figure 2–59. When an arc displays, select it.

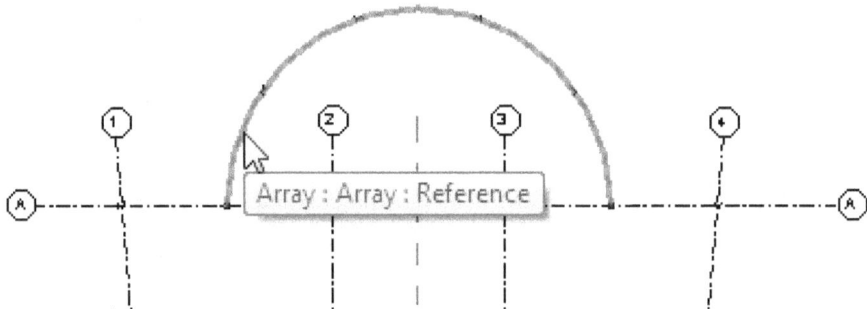

Figure 2–59

13. Click ⬈ (Modify).

14. Drag the grid bubbles down past the columns and rename the new grid **A.1** as shown in Figure 2–60.

Figure 2–60

15. Save the project.

2.4 Working with Additional Modify Tools

As you work on a project, some additional tools on the *Modify* tab>Modify panel, as shown in Figure 2–61, can help you with placing, modifying, and constraining elements. **Align** can be used with a variety of elements, while **Split Element**, **Trim/Extend**, and **Offset** can only be used with linear elements.

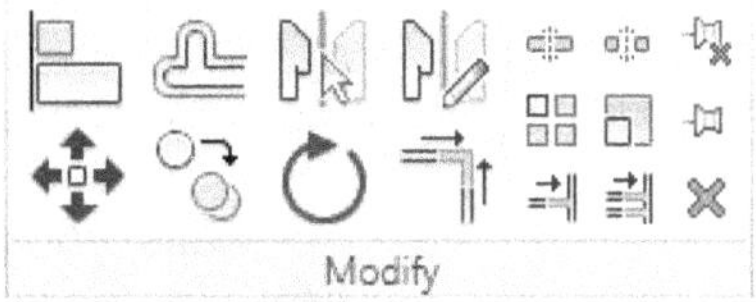

Figure 2–61

Aligning Elements

The **Align** command enables you to line up one element with another, as shown in Figure 2–62. Most Autodesk Revit elements can be aligned. For example, you can line up the tops of windows with the top of a door, or line up furniture with a wall.

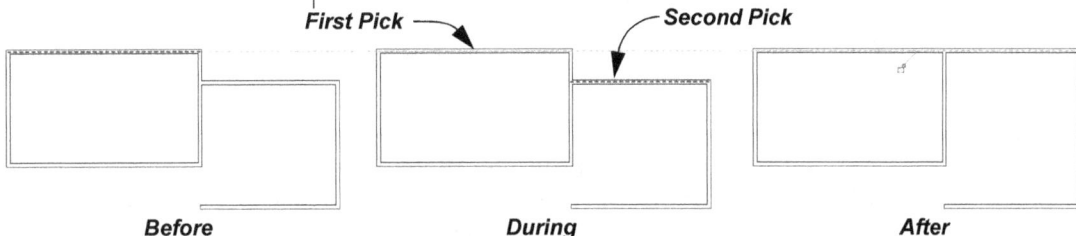

First Pick   Second Pick

Before   *During*   *After*

Figure 2–62

How To: Align Elements

1. In the *Modify* tab>Modify panel, click ⬜ (Align).
2. Select a line or point on the element that is going to remain stationary. For walls, press <Tab> to select the correct wall face.
3. Select a line or point on the element to be aligned. The second element moves into alignment with the first one.

- The **Align** command works in all model views, including parallel and perspective 3D views.

- You can lock alignments so that the elements move together if either one is moved. Once you have created the alignment, a padlock is displayed. Click on the padlock to lock it, as shown in Figure 2–63.

Locking elements enlarges the size of the project file, so use this option carefully.

Figure 2–63

- Select **Multiple Alignment** to select multiple elements to align with the first element. You can also hold <Ctrl> to make multiple alignments.

- For walls, you can specify if you want the command to prefer **Wall centerlines**, **Wall faces**, **Center of core**, or **Faces of core**, as shown in Figure 2–64. The core refers to the structural members of a wall as opposed to facing materials, such as sheet rock.

Figure 2–64

Splitting Linear Elements

The **Split Element** command enables you to break a linear element at a specific point. You can use alignment lines, snaps, and temporary dimensions to help place the split point. After you have split the linear element, you can use other editing commands to modify the two parts, or change the type of one part, as shown with walls in Figure 2–65.

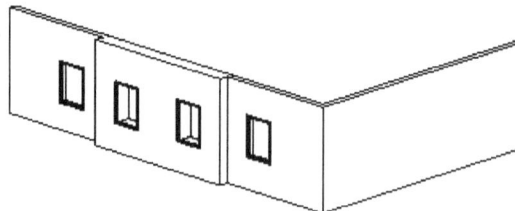

You can split walls in plan, elevation or 3D views.

Figure 2–65

Enhanced in 2018

- The **Split Element** command works with structural columns and framing elements. The command respects connections, justifications, and other settings.

How To: Split Linear Elements

1. In the *Modify* tab>Modify panel, click ⊕ (Split Element) or type the shortcut **SL**.
2. In the Options Bar, select or clear the **Delete Inner Segment** option.
3. Move the cursor to the point you want to split and select the point.
4. Repeat for any additional split locations.
5. Modify the elements that were split, as required.

• The **Delete Inner Segment** option is used when you select two split points along a linear element. When the option is selected, the segment between the two split points is automatically removed.

• An additional option, ⊕ (Split with Gap), splits the linear element at the point you select (as shown in Figure 2–66), but also creates a *Joint Gap* specified in the Options Bar.

This command is typically used with structural precast slabs.

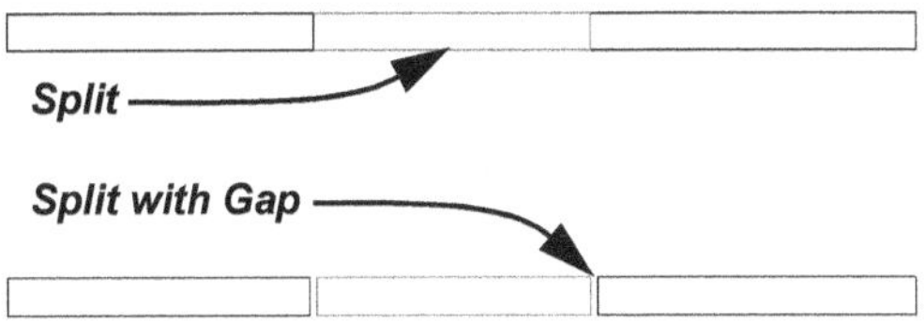

Figure 2–66

Trimming and Extending

There are three trim/extend methods that you can use with linear elements: **Trim/Extend to Corner**, **Trim/Extend Single Element**, and **Trim/Extend Multiple Elements**.

• When selecting elements to trim, click the part of the element that you want to keep. The opposite part of the line is then trimmed.

How To: Trim/Extend to Corner

1. In the *Modify* tab>Modify panel, click ⃗ (Trim/Extend to Corner) or type the shortcut **TR**.
2. Select the first linear element on the side you want to keep.

3. Select the second linear element on the side you want to keep, as shown in Figure 2–67.

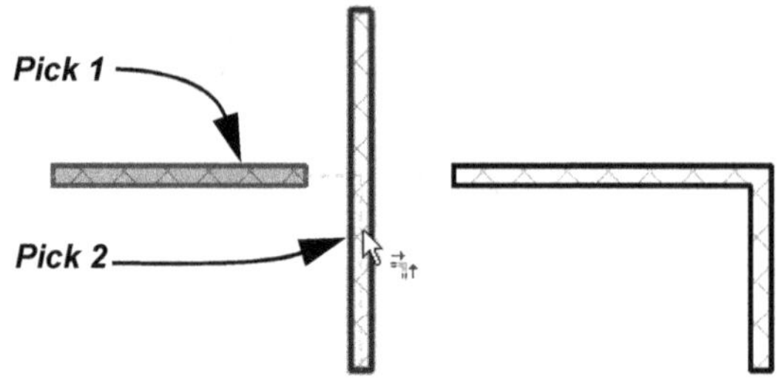

Figure 2–67

How To: Trim/Extend a Single Element

1. In the *Modify* tab>Modify panel, click ⇥‖ (Trim/Extend Single Element).
2. Select the cutting or boundary edge.
3. Select the linear element to be trimmed or extended, as shown in Figure 2–68.

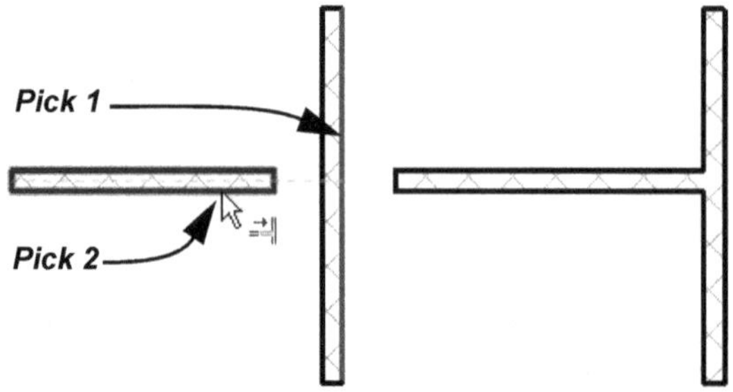

Figure 2–68

How To: Trim/Extend Multiple Elements

1. In the *Modify* tab>Modify panel, click ⇥‖ (Trim/Extend Multiple Elements).
2. Select the cutting or boundary edge.
3. Select the linear elements that you want to trim or extend by selecting one at a time, or by using a crossing window, as shown in Figure 2–69. For trimming, select the side you want to keep.

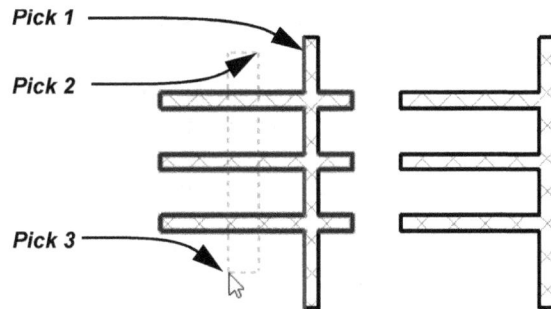

Figure 2–69

- You can click in an empty space to clear the selection and select another cutting edge or boundary.

Offsetting Elements

The **Offset** command is an easy way of creating parallel copies of linear elements at a specified distance, as shown in Figure 2–70. Walls, beams, braces, and lines are among the elements that can be offset.

Figure 2–70

- If you offset a wall that has a door or window embedded in it, the elements are copied with the offset wall.

The offset distance can be set by typing the distance (**Numerical** method shown in Figure 2–71) or by selecting points on the screen (**Graphical** method).

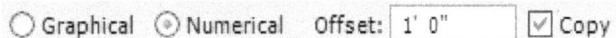

Figure 2–71

How To: Offset using the Numerical Method

*The **Copy** option (which is on by default) makes a copy of the element being offset. If this option is not selected, the **Offset** command moves the element the set offset distance.*

1. In the *Modify* tab>Modify panel, click ⬒ (Offset) or type the shortcut **OF**.
2. In the Options Bar, select the **Numerical** option.
3. In the Options Bar, type the required distance in the *Offset* field.
4. Move the cursor over the element you want to offset. A dashed line previews the offset location. Move the cursor to flip the sides, as required.
5. Click to create the offset.
6. Repeat Steps 4 and 5 to offset other elements by the same distance, or to change the distance for another offset.

- With the **Numerical** option, you can select multiple connected linear elements for offsetting. Hover the cursor over an element and press <Tab> until the other related elements are highlighted. Select the element to offset all of the elements at the same time.

How To: Offset using the Graphical Method

1. Start the **Offset** command.
2. In the Options Bar, select **Graphical**.
3. Select the linear element to offset.
4. Select two points that define the distance of the offset and which side to apply it. You can type an override in the temporary dimension for the second point.

- Most linear elements connected at a corner automatically trim or extend to meet at the offset distance, as shown in Figure 2–72.

Figure 2–72

Practice 2c

Work with Additional Modify Tools

Practice Objective

- Align, Split, Trim/Extend, and Offset elements.

Estimated time for completion: 10 minutes

In this practice you will use **Split** and **Trim** to clean up existing walls in a project. You will then offset the entire foundation from the centerline, as shown in Figure 2–73, where it can support an architectural brick facade.

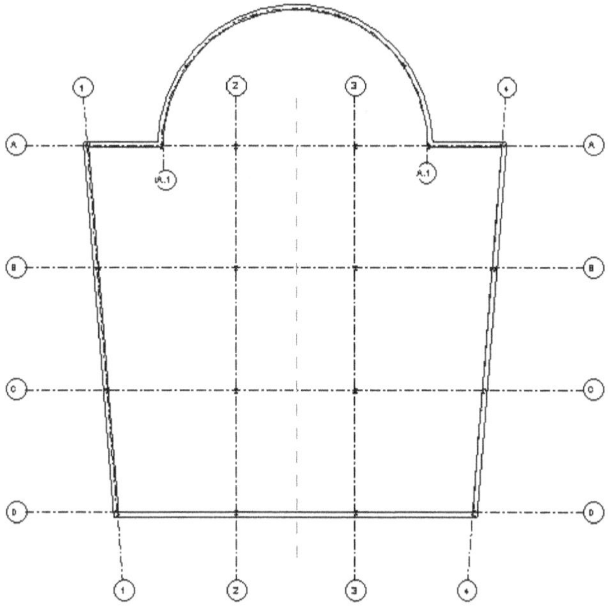

Figure 2–73

Task 1 - Split and trim elements.

1. Open the project **Practice-Model-Modify.rvt**.

2. Select the horizontal foundation wall on Grid line A.

3. In the *Modify | Walls* tab>Modify panel, click ⊏⊐ (Split Element).

4. Select the intersection of the reference plane and the foundation wall along Student Guide A as shown in Figure 2–74.

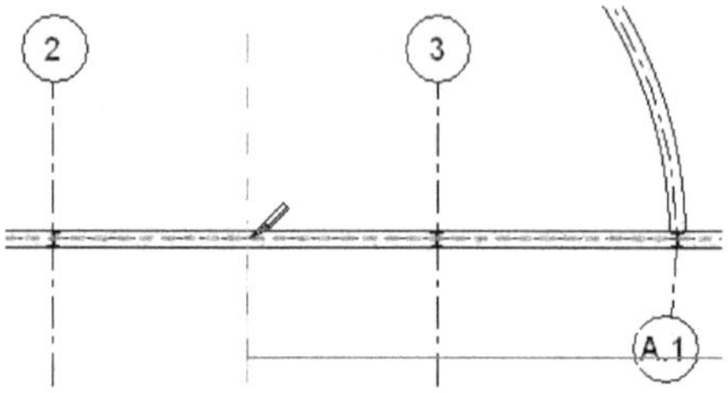

Figure 2–74

5. In the *Modify* tab>Modify panel, click ⇉ᵢ̈ (Trim/Extend to Corner).

6. Select the horizontal wall as shown in Figure 2–75. Remember to select the side of the wall that you want to keep.

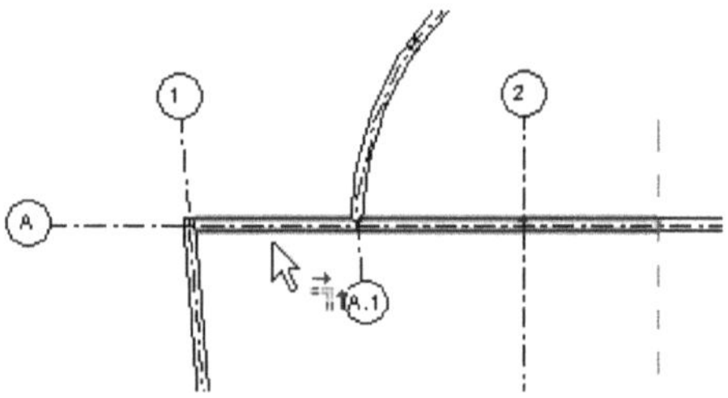

Figure 2–75

7. Select the curved wall. The walls are trimmed as shown in Figure 2–76.

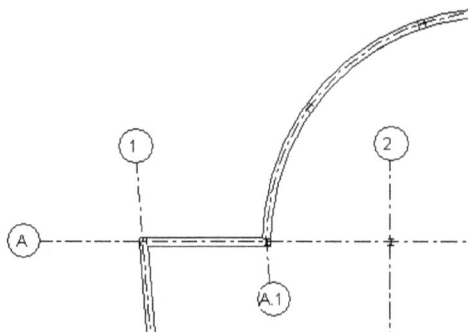

Figure 2–76

8. If the Reset analytical model warning opens, close it.

9. Repeat the process on the other end.

Task 2 - Offset elements.

1. In the *Modify* tab>Edit panel, click ⬚ (Offset).

2. In the Options Bar, select **Numerical**, set the *Offset* to **4"**, and clear the **Copy** option as shown in Figure 2–77.

○ Graphical ⊙ Numerical   Offset: | 0' 4" | ☐ Copy

Figure 2–77

3. Hover the cursor over one of the foundation walls but do not select the wall. The blue alignment line should display on the inside of the wall but outside of the student guide line.

4. Press <Tab>. All of the foundation walls are selected as shown in Figure 2–78.

Chain of walls or lines

A.1

Figure 2–78

5. Once all of the walls are highlighted and the blue alignment line displays on the outside of the grid line, select a point. The foundation is offset from the grid line as shown in Figure 2–79.

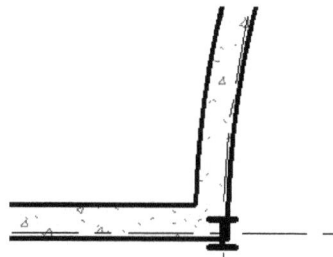

Figure 2–79

6. Press <Esc> to finish the command.

7. Save and close the model.

Chapter Review Questions

1. What is the purpose of an alignment line?

   a. Displays when the new element you are placing or modeling is aligned with the grid system.

   b. Indicates that the new element you are placing or modeling is aligned with an existing object.

   c. Displays when the new element you are placing or modeling is aligned with a selected tracking point.

   d. Indicates that the new element is aligned with true north rather than project north.

2. When you are modeling (not editing) a linear element, how do you edit the temporary dimension, as that shown in Figure 2–80?

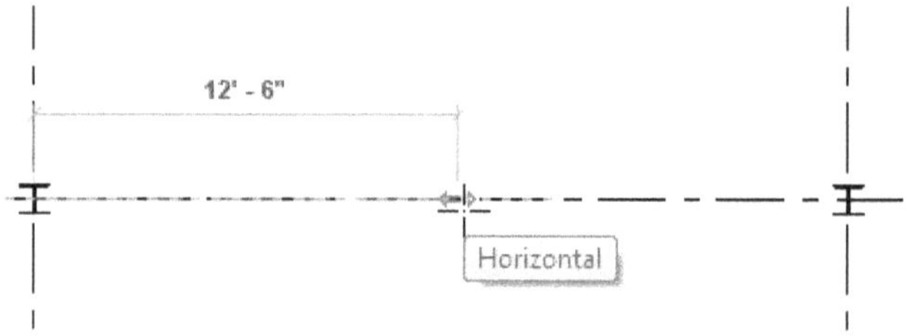

Figure 2–80

   a. Select the temporary dimension and enter a new value.

   b. Type a new value and press <Enter>.

   c. Type a new value in the Distance/Length box in the Options Bar and press <Enter>.

3. How do you select all structural column types, but no other elements in a view?

   a. In the Project Browser, select the *Structural Column* category.

   b. Select one structural column, right-click and select **Select All Instances>Visible in View**.

   c. Select all of the objects in the view and use ▽ (Filter) to clear the other categories.

   d. Select one structural column, and click ▵ (Select Multiple) in the ribbon.

4. What are the two methods for starting ⊹ (Move) or

   ⊙ (Copy)?

   a. Start the command first and then select the objects, or select the objects and then start the command.

   b. Start the command from the *Modify* tab, or select the object and then select **Move** or **Copy** from the shortcut menu.

   c. Start the command from the *Modify* tab, or select the objects and select **Auto-Move**.

   d. Use the **Move/Copy** command or **Cut/Copy** and **Paste** using the Clipboard.

5. Where do you change the wall type for a selected wall, as shown in Figure 2–81?

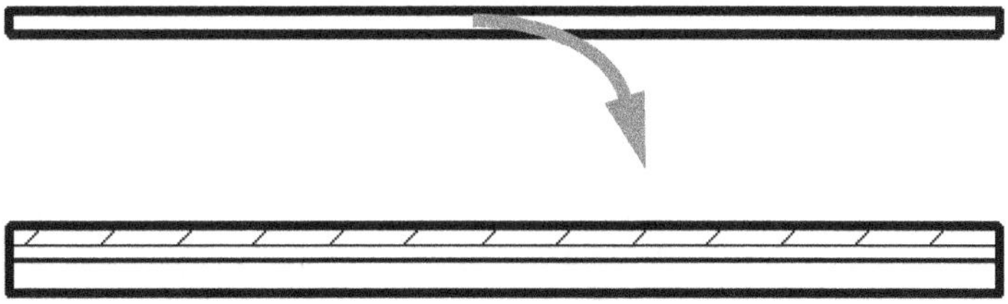

Figure 2–81

   a. In the *Modify | Walls* tab>Properties panel, click ⊞ (Type Properties) and select a new wall type in the dialog box.

   b. In the Options Bar, click **Change Element Type**.

   c. Select the dynamic control next to the selected wall and select a new type in the drop-down list.

   d. In Properties, select a new type in the Type Selector drop-down list.

6. Both ⟳ (Rotate) and ⊞ (Array) with ◲ (Radial) have a center of rotation that defaults to the center of the element or group of elements you have selected. How do you move the center of rotation to another point as shown in Figure 2–82? (Select all that apply.)

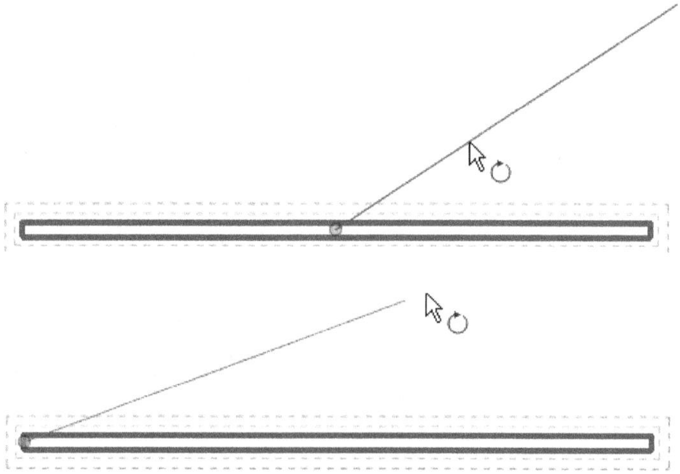

Figure 2–82

a. Select the center of rotation and drag it to a new location.

b. In the Options Bar, click **Place** and select the new point.

c. In the *Modify* tab>Placement panel, click ⊘ (Center) and select the new point.

d. Right-click and select **Snap Overrides>Centers** and select the new point.

7. Which command would you use to remove part of a wall?

a. ⊹ (Split Element)

b. ⊯ (Wall Joins)

c. ⬠ (Cut Geometry)

d. ⚒ (Demolish)

8. Which of the following are ways in which you can create additional parallel walls, as shown in Figure 2–83? (Select all that apply.)

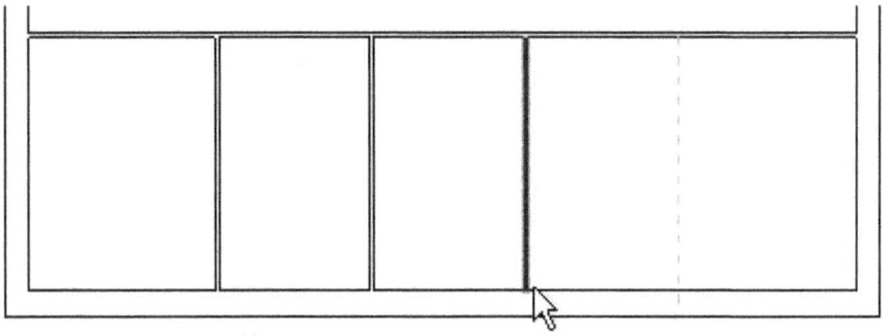

Figure 2–83

a. Select an existing wall, right-click and select **Create Offset**.

b. Use the **Offset** tool in the *Modify* tab.

c. Select an existing wall, hold <Ctrl> and drag the wall to a new location.

d. Use the **Wall** tool and set an offset in the Options Bar.

9. Which command do you use if you want two walls that are not touching to come together, as shown in Figure 2–84?

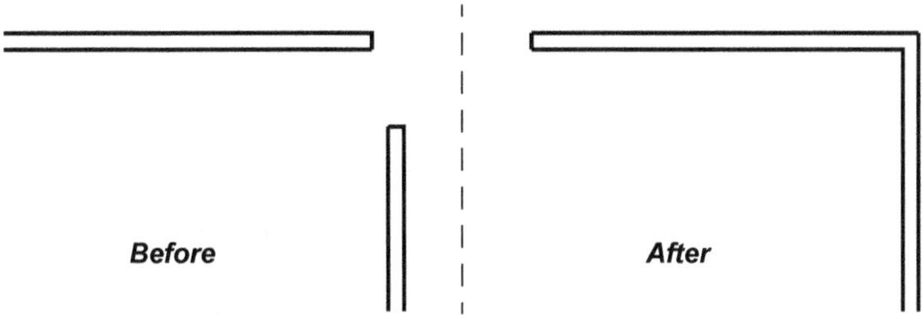

Before   *After*

Figure 2–84

a. (Edit Wall Joins)

b. (Trim/Extend to Corner)

c. (Join Geometry)

d. (Edit Profile)

Command Summary

Button	Command	Location
Draw Tools		
	Center-ends Arc	• **Ribbon:** *Modify	(various linear elements)* tab>Draw panel
	Circle	• **Ribbon:** *Modify	(various linear elements)* tab>Draw panel
	Circumscribed Polygon	• **Ribbon:** *Modify	(various linear elements)* tab>Draw panel
	Ellipse	• **Ribbon:** *Modify	Place Lines, Place Detail Lines, and various boundary sketches*>Draw panel
	Ellipse Arc	• **Ribbon:** *Modify	Place Lines, Place Detail Lines, and various boundary sketches*>Draw panel
	Fillet Arc	• **Ribbon:** *Modify	(various linear elements)* tab>Draw panel
	Inscribed Polygon	• **Ribbon:** *Modify	(various linear elements)* tab>Draw panel
	Line	• **Ribbon:** *Modify	(various linear elements)* tab>Draw panel
	Pick Faces	• **Ribbon:** *Modify	Place Wall*> Draw panel
	Pick Lines	• **Ribbon:** *Modify	(various linear elements)* tab>Draw panel
	Pick Walls	• **Ribbon:** *Modify	(various boundary sketches)*>Draw panel
	Rectangle	• **Ribbon:** *Modify	(various linear elements)* tab>Draw panel
	Spline	• **Ribbon:** *Modify	Place Lines, Place Detail Lines, and various boundary sketches*>Draw panel
	Start-End-Radius Arc	• **Ribbon:** *Modify	(various linear elements)* tab>Draw panel
	Tangent End Arc	• **Ribbon:** *Modify	(various linear elements)* tab>Draw panel
Modify Tools		
	Align	• **Ribbon:** *Modify* tab>Modify panel • **Shortcut:** AL
	Array	• **Ribbon:** *Modify* tab>Modify panel • **Shortcut:** AR
	Copy	• **Ribbon:** *Modify* tab>Modify panel • **Shortcut:** CO

	Copy to Clipboard	• **Ribbon:** *Modify* tab>Clipboard panel • **Shortcut:** <Ctrl>+<C>
	Delete	• **Ribbon:** *Modify* tab>Modify panel • **Shortcut:** DE
	Mirror - Draw Axis	• **Ribbon:** *Modify* tab>Modify panel • **Shortcut:** DM
	Mirror - Pick Axis	• **Ribbon:** *Modify* tab>Modify panel • **Shortcut:** MM
	Move	• **Ribbon:** *Modify* tab>Modify panel • **Shortcut:** MV
	Offset	• **Ribbon:** *Modify* tab>Modify panel • **Shortcut:** OF
	Paste	• **Ribbon:** *Modify* tab>Clipboard panel • **Shortcut:** <Ctrl>+<V>
	Pin	• **Ribbon:** *Modify* tab>Modify panel • **Shortcut:** PN
	Rotate	• **Ribbon:** *Modify* tab>Modify panel • **Shortcut:** RO
	Scale	• **Ribbon:** *Modify* tab>Modify panel • **Shortcut:** RE
	Split Element	• **Ribbon:** *Modify* tab>Modify panel • **Shortcut:** SL
	Split with Gap	• **Ribbon:** *Modify* tab>Modify panel
	Trim/Extend Multiple Elements	• **Ribbon:** *Modify* tab>Modify panel
	Trim/Extend Single Element	• **Ribbon:** *Modify* tab>Modify panel
	Trim/Extend to Corner	• **Ribbon:** *Modify* tab>Modify panel • **Shortcut:** TR
	Unpin	• **Ribbon:** *Modify* tab>Modify panel • **Shortcut:** UP
Select Tools		
	Drag elements on selection	• **Ribbon:** All tabs>Expanded Select panel • **Status Bar**
	Filter	• **Ribbon:** *Modify* | *Multi-Select* tab>Filter panel • **Status Bar**
	Select Elements By Face	• **Ribbon:** All tabs>Expanded Select panel • **Status Bar**

	Select Links	• **Ribbon:** All tabs>Expanded Select panel
		• **Status Bar**
	Select Pinned Elements	• **Ribbon:** All tabs>Expanded Select panel
		• **Status Bar**
	Select Underlay Elements	• **Ribbon:** All tabs>Expanded Select panel
		• **Status Bar**

Additional Tools

	Aligned Dimension	• **Ribbon:** *Modify* tab>Measure panel
		• Quick Access Toolbar
	Detail Line	• **Ribbon:** *Annotate* tab>Detail panel
		• **Shortcut:** DL
	Model Line	• **Ribbon:** *Architectural* tab>Model panel
		• **Shortcut:** LI
	Reference Plane	• **Ribbon:** *Architecture/Structure/ Systems* tab> Work Plane panel

Starting Structural Projects

Structural projects are typically started after an architectural project is underway, and need to use information provided by the architect as the base for the project. You can link CAD drawings or Autodesk® Revit® models and then build the structural model around them, copying and monitoring the required information from the architectural model into the structural project.

Learning Objectives in this Chapter

- Link or import CAD files to use as a basis for developing a design.
- Link Revit models into the project so that you can design the structural project.
- Add levels to define floor to floor heights and other vertical references.
- Copy and monitor elements from linked Revit models so that you know when changes have been made.
- Run Coordination Reviews to identify changes between the current project and any linked models.

3.1 Linking and Importing CAD Files

CAD files can be imported or linked into an Autodesk Revit structural project. As an example, a designer might lay out a floor plan using the standard 2D AutoCAD® software, and you need to incorporate that information into your structural model. In addition, many renovation projects start with existing 2D drawings. Instead of redrawing from scratch, link or import the CAD file (as shown in Figure 3–1) and trace over it in the Autodesk Revit software.

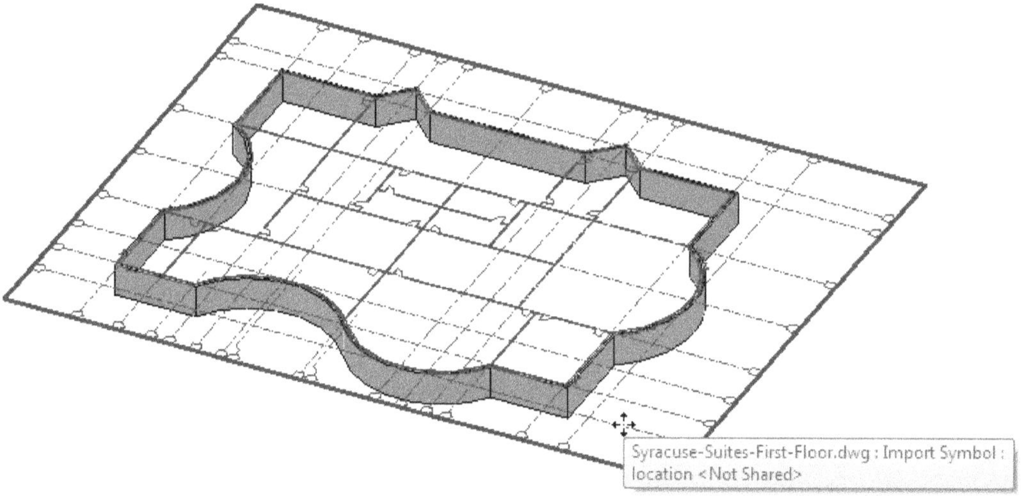

Syracuse-Suites-First-Floor.dwg : Import Symbol : location <Not Shared>

Figure 3–1

* CAD files that can be linked or imported include AutoCAD .DWG and .DXF, Microstation .DGN, ACIS .SAT, and Sketchup .SKP files.

Linking vs. Importing

* **Linked files:** Become part of the project, but are still connected to the original file. Use them if you expect the original file to change. The link is automatically updated when you open the project.

* **Imported files:** Become part of the project and are not connected to the original file. Use them if you know that the original file is not going to change.

How To: Link or Import a CAD File

1. Open the view into which you want to link or import the file.
   - For a 2D file, this should be a 2D view. For a 3D file, open a 3D view.

2. In the *Insert* tab>Link panel, click [CAD] (Link CAD), or in the *Insert* tab>Import panel, click [CAD] (Import CAD).

3. In the Link CAD Formats or Import CAD Formats dialog box (shown in Figure 3–2), select the file that you want to import.

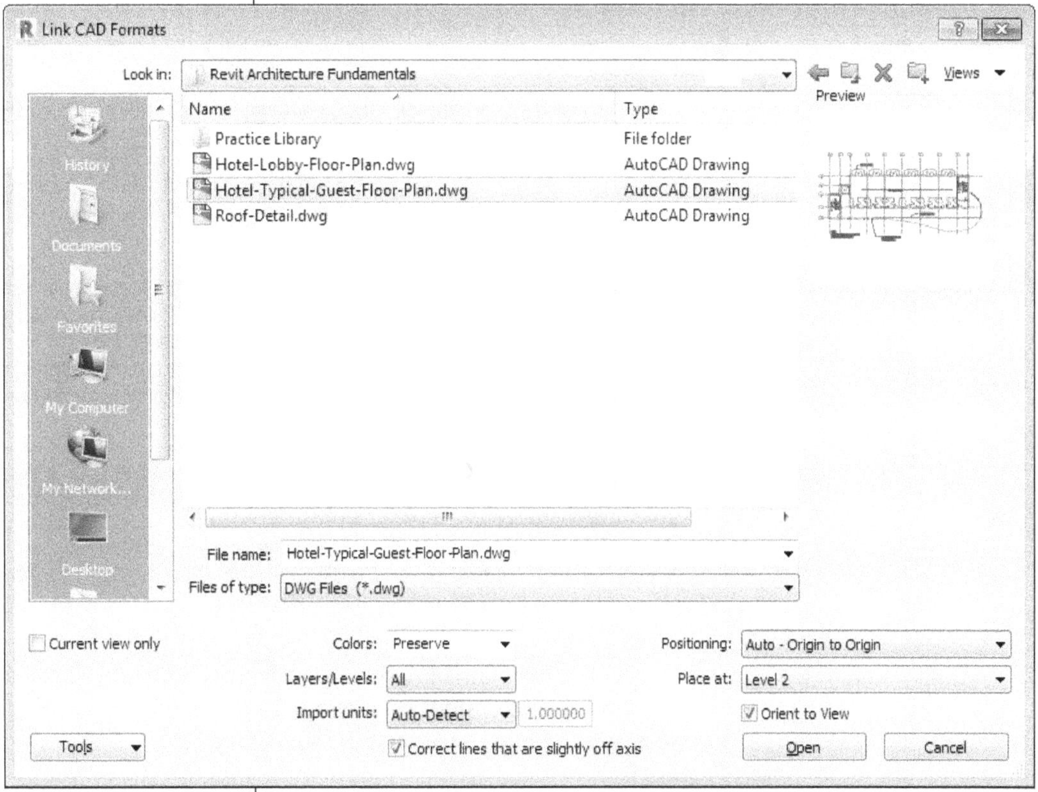

Figure 3–2

- The dialog boxes for Link CAD Formats and Import CAD Formats are the same.
- Select a file format in the **Files of Type** drop-down list to limit the files that are displayed.

4. Set the other options as outlined below.

5. Click **Open**.

Link and Import Options

Current view only	Determine whether the CAD file is placed in every view, or only in the current view. This is especially useful if you are working with a 2D floor plan that you only need to have in one view.
Colors	Specify the color settings. Typical Autodesk Revit projects are mainly black and white. However, other software frequently uses color. You can **Invert** the original colors, **Preserve** them, or change everything to **Black and White**.
Layers / Levels	Indicates which CAD layers are going to be brought into the model. Select how you want layers/levels to be imported: **All**, **Visible**, or **Specify**. • Layers are in .DWG files, while levels are in .DGN files.
Import units	Select the units of the original file, as required. **Auto-Detect** works in most cases.
Correct Lines...	If lines in a CAD file are off axis by less than 0.1 degree selecting this option straightens them. It is selected by default.
Positioning	Specify how you want the imported file to be positioned in the current project: **Auto-Center to Center**, **Auto-Origin to Origin**, **Manual-Origin**, **Manual-Base Point**, or **Manual-Center**. The default position is **Auto-Origin to Origin**. If linking the file, **Auto-By Shared Coordinates** is also available.
Place at	Select a level in which to place the imported file. If you selected **Current view only**, this option is grayed out.
Orient to View	Select this option if the view you are working in is set to True North (and is different from Project North) so that the CAD file is aligned to True North.

• When a file is positioned **Auto-Origin to Origin**, it is pinned in place and cannot be moved. To move the file, click on the pin to unpin it, as shown in Figure 3–3.

To pin a file that is not automatically pinned, select it and in the Modify tab>Modify panel, click ⊶ (Pin).

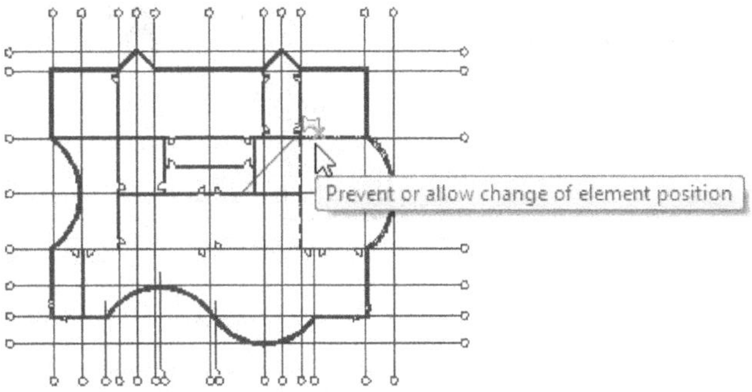

Figure 3–3

Setting an Imported or Linked File to Halftone

To see the difference between new elements and the linked or imported file, you can set the file to Halftone, as shown in Figure 3–4.

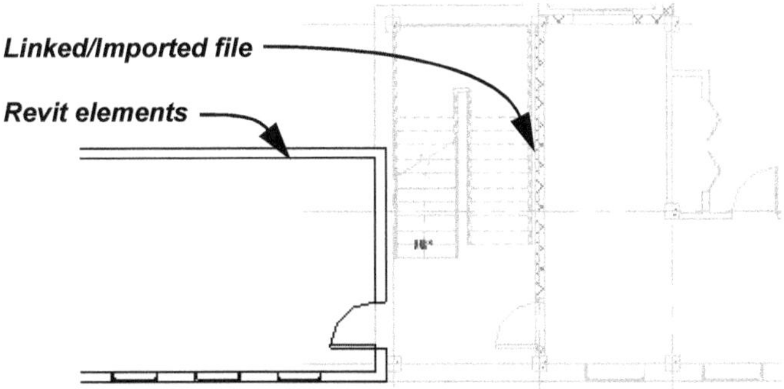

Linked/Imported file

Revit elements

Figure 3–4

How To: Set an Element Halftone

1. Select the imported file.
2. Right-click and select **Override Graphics in View>By Element...**.
3. In the View Specific Element Graphics dialog box, select **Halftone**, as shown in Figure 3–5.

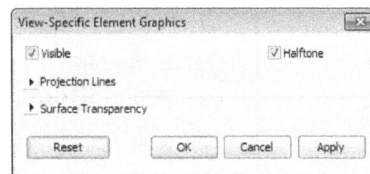

Figure 3–5

4. Click **OK**.

Practice 3a

Estimated time for completion: 5 minutes

Start a CAD-based Structural Project

Practice Objective

- Link a 2D DWG file into a new project.

In this practice you will link an AutoCAD (.DWG) file as the base floor plan for a project, move elevation markers in the current project to match the footprint of the building, and modify the visibility graphics of the linked file so that it displays in halftone, as shown in Figure 3–6.

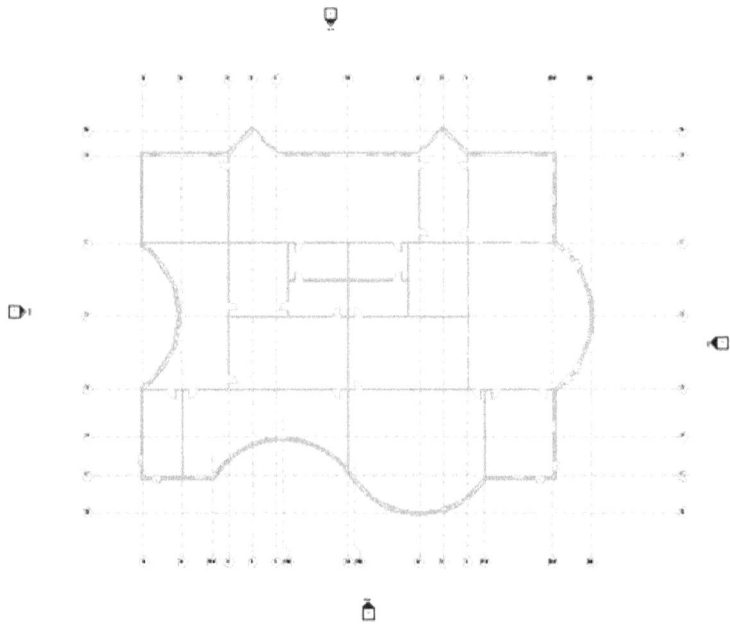

Figure 3–6

Task 1 - Link an AutoCAD file.

1. In the Application Menu, click ⬜ (New).

2. In the New Project dialog box, *Template File* drop-down list, select **Structural Template** and click **OK**.

3. In the Project Browser, open the **Structural Plans: Level 1** view. (The default structural template automatically opens in Level 2. You are importing the **Level 1** floor plan from the AutoCAD file and therefore need to open that view).

4. In the *Insert* tab>Link panel, click 🔲 (Link CAD).

5. In the Link CAD Formats dialog box, navigate to your practice files folder and select but do not open **Syracuse-Suites-First-Floor.dwg**.

6. Set or verify the options as follows:

   • Select **Current view only**.
   • *Colors:* **Black and White**
   • *Layers:* **All**
   • *Import Units:* **Auto-Detect**
   • *Positioning:* **Auto-Origin-to-Origin**

7. Click **Open**.

8. Zoom to the extents of the view. (Hint: Type **ZE** or double-click on the mouse wheel.)

9. Move the Building Elevation markers so that they are on the outside of the imported file as shown in Figure 3–7. Select both parts of the elevation markers.

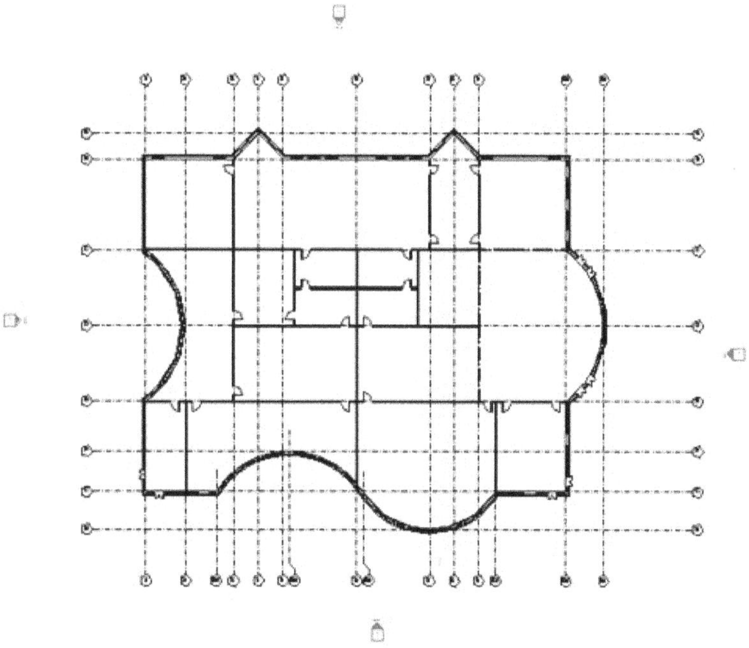

Figure 3–7

10. Right-click on the linked file (also called an import symbol) and select **Override Graphics in View>By Element**.

11. In the View-Specific Element Graphics dialog box, select **Halftone** as shown in Figure 3–8.

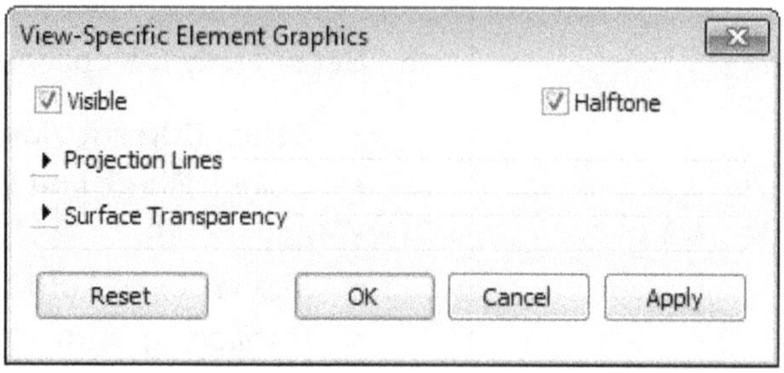

View-Specific Element Graphics	
☑ Visible	☑ Halftone
▸ Projection Lines	
▸ Surface Transparency	
Reset	OK	Cancel	Apply

Figure 3–8

12. Click **OK**.

13. Click away from the linked file to release the selection.

14. In the Quick Access Toolbar click ⬦ (Default 3D View). No linked file displays because you linked it only into the Level 1 view.

15. Return to the **Structural Plans: Level 1** view.

16. Save the model as **Syracuse-Suites-CAD.rvt** and close the project.

3.2 Linking in Revit Models

You can link Autodesk Revit architectural or engineering models directly into a structural project. When the model is linked into the structural project, it only displays structural related elements by default, such as floors, columns, and walls. An example is shown in Figure 3–9.

A linked model automatically updates when the original file is changed.

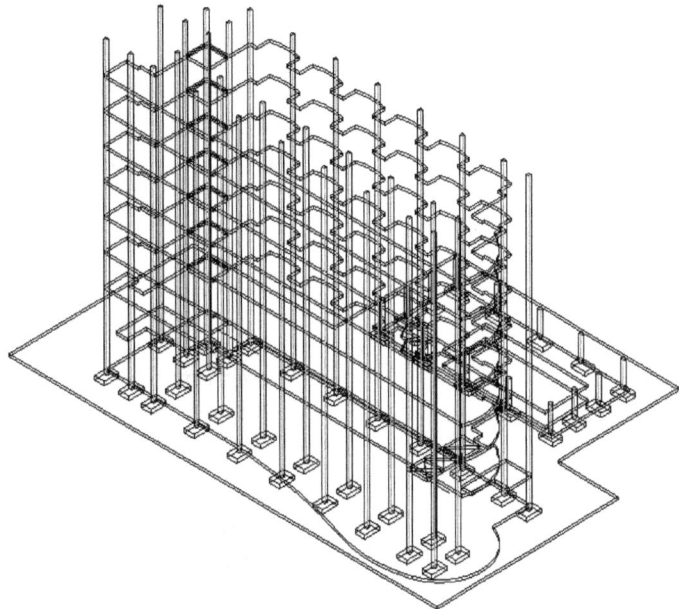

Architectural model linked into a structural project.

Figure 3–9

- Architectural, structural, and MEP models created in the Autodesk Revit software can be linked to each other as long as they are from the same release cycle.

- When you use linked models, clashes between disciplines can be detected and information can be passed between disciplines.

> **Hint: Views and Disciplines**
>
> When using a structural template, most of the views are set to display only structural elements. To display the architectural information (or that of another discipline) in Properties, change the *Discipline* of the view.

How To: Add a Linked Model to a Host Project

1. In the *Insert* tab>Link panel, click ![Link Revit icon] (Link Revit).
2. In the Import/Link RVT dialog box, select the file that you want to link. Before opening the file, set the *Positioning*, as shown in Figure 3–10.

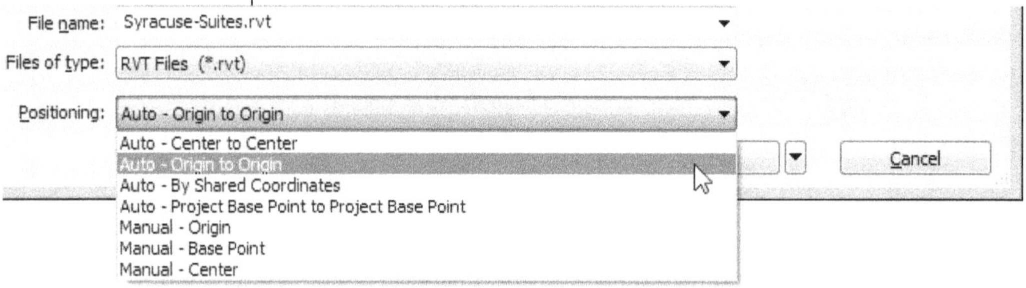

File name:	Syracuse-Suites.rvt
Files of type:	RVT Files (*.rvt)
Positioning:	Auto - Origin to Origin

Auto - Center to Center
Auto - Origin to Origin
Auto - By Shared Coordinates
Auto - Project Base Point to Project Base Point
Manual - Origin
Manual - Base Point
Manual - Center

Cancel

Figure 3–10

3. Click **Open**.
4. Depending on how you decide to position the file, it is automatically placed in the project or you can manually place it with the cursor.

• As the links are loading, do not click on the screen or click any buttons. The more links present in a project, the longer it takes to load.

Hint: Preventing Linked Model from being moved

Once a linked model is in the correct location, you can lock it in place to ensure that it does not get moved by mistake, or prevent the linked model from being selected.

- To toggle off the ability to select links, in the Status Bar, click 🔾 (Select Links).

- To pin the linked model in place, select it and in the *Modify* tab>Modify panel, click 📌 (Pin).

- To prevent pinned elements from being selected, in the Status Bar, click 📌 (Select Pinned Elements).

- To toggle off the ability to select links, in the Status Bar, click 🔾 (Select Links).

If a linked file is moved, you can reposition it to the Project Base Point or Internal Origin. Right-click on it and select the option as shown in Figure 3–11.

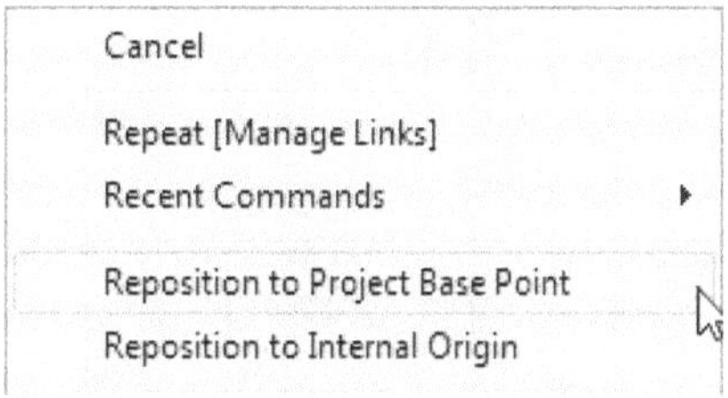

Cancel
Repeat [Manage Links]
Recent Commands ▸
Reposition to Project Base Point
Reposition to Internal Origin

Figure 3–11

Multiple Copies of Linked Models

Copied instances of a linked model are typically used when creating a master project with the same building placed in multiple locations, such as a university campus with six identical student residence halls.

- Linked models can be moved, copied, rotated, arrayed, and mirrored. There is only one linked model, and any copies are additional instances of the link.

- Copies are numbered automatically. You can change their names in Properties when the instance is selected.

- When you have placed a link in a project, you can drag and drop additional copies of the link into the project from the Project Browser>**Revit Links** node, as shown in Figure 3–12.

Revit Links
    Warehouse Layout.rvt

Figure 3–12

Managing Links

The Manage Links dialog box (shown in Figure 3–13) enables you to reload, unload, add, and remove links, and also provides access to set other options. To open the Manage Links dialog box, in the *Insert* tab>Link, panel click 🖵 (Manage Links), or select the link and, in the *Modify | RVT Links* tab>Link panel, click 🖵 (Manage Links).

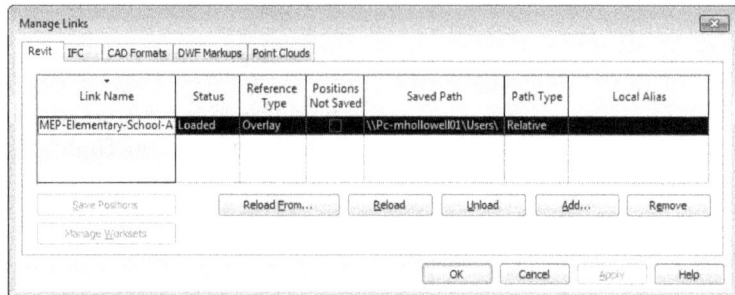

Figure 3–13

The options available in the Manage Links dialog box include the following:

*Reload is also available in the Project Browser. Expand the Revit Links node. Right-click on the Revit Link and select **Reload** or **Reload From...***

- **Reload From:** Opens the Add Link dialog box, which enables you to select the file you want to reload. Use this if the linked file location or name has changed.

- **Reload:** Reloads the file without additional prompts.

- **Unload:** Unloads the file so that it the link is kept, but the file is not displayed or calculated in the project. Use **Reload** to restore it.

- **Add:** Opens the Import/Link RVT dialog box which enables you to link additional models into the host project.

- **Remove:** Deletes the link from the file.

Links can be nested into one another. How a link responds when the host project is linked into another project depends on the option in the *Reference Type* column:

- **Overlay**: The nested linked model is not referenced in the new host project.

- **Attach:** The nested linked model displays in the new host project.

The option in the *Path Type* column controls how the location of the link is remembered:

- **Relative**
    - Searches the root folder of the current project.
    - If the file is moved, the software still searches for it.

- **Absolute**
    - Searches only the folder where the file was originally saved.
    - If the original file is moved, the software is not able to find it.

Other options control how the linked file interfaces with Worksets and Shared Positioning.

Hint: Visibility Graphics and Linked Files

When you open the Visibility/Graphics dialog box (type **VV** or **VG**), you can modify the graphic overrides for Revit links as shown in Figure 3–14. This can help you clean up the view, or assign a view to build on.

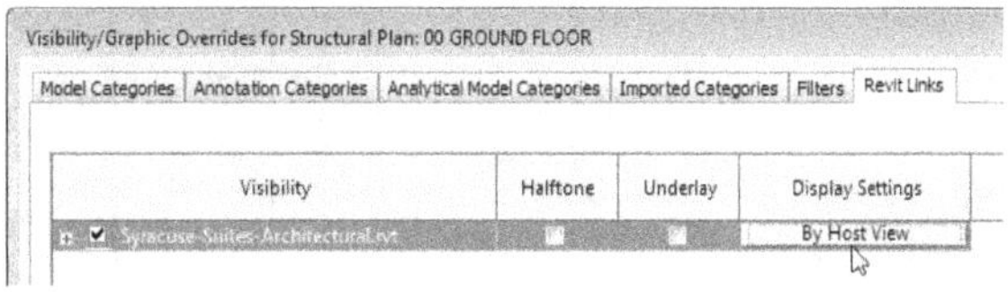

Figure 3–14

The *Display Settings* include:

- **By host view:** The display of the Revit link is based on the view properties of the current view in the host model.

- **By linked view:** The appearance of the Revit link is based on the view properties of the selected linked view and ignores the view properties of the current view.

- **Custom:** You can override all of the graphical elements.

Practice 3b | Start a Model-based Structural Project

Practice Objectives

- Start a new project from a template.
- Link an architectural model into a structural project.

Estimated time for completion: 5 minutes

In this practice you will link an architectural model created in Autodesk Revit into a new structural project and pin the linked model into place. You will then change view properties to a coordination view that shows both the structural and architectural features, as shown in Figure 3–15.

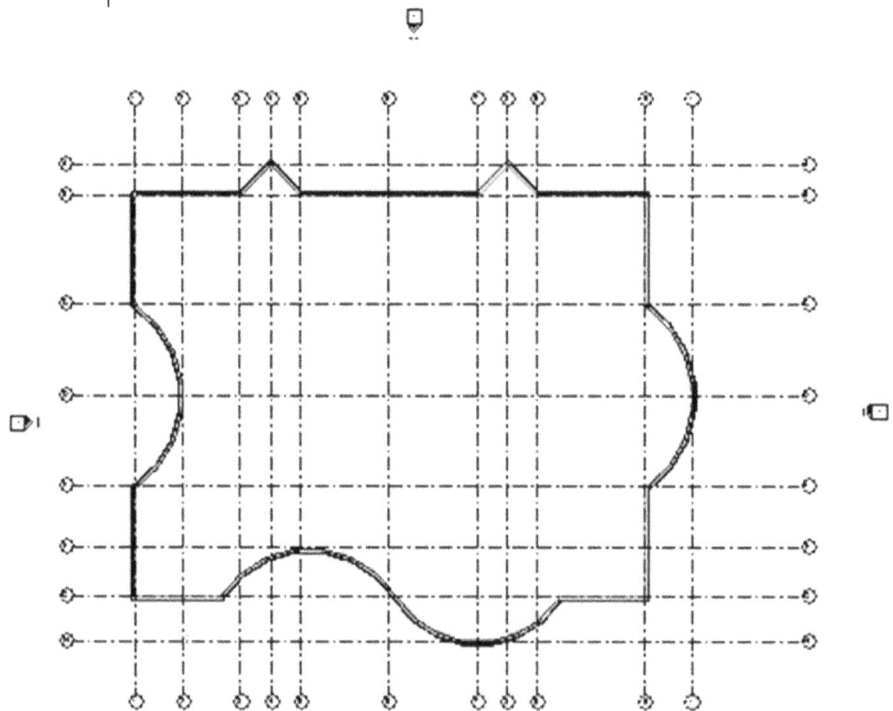

Figure 3–15

Task 1 - Link an architectural model into a structural project.

1. Start a new project based on the default structural template. The file automatically opens in the **Structural Plans: Level 2** view.

2. In the *Insert* tab>Link panel, click ![icon] (Link Revit).

3. In the Import/Link RVT dialog box, select the file **Syracuse-Suites-Architectural.rvt** in your practice files folder. Ensure that *Positioning: is set* to **Auto - Origin to Origin** and then click **Open**.

4. Select the linked model in the view (only gridlines display).

5. In the *Modify | RVT Links* tab>Modify panel, click ![pin icon] (Pin). This will ensure that the linked model will not be accidentally moved in the view.

6. Adjust the Building Elevation markers so that they are around the link, as shown in Figure 3–16.

Figure 3–16

Only the grids are currently displayed because the view is set to display structural elements only.

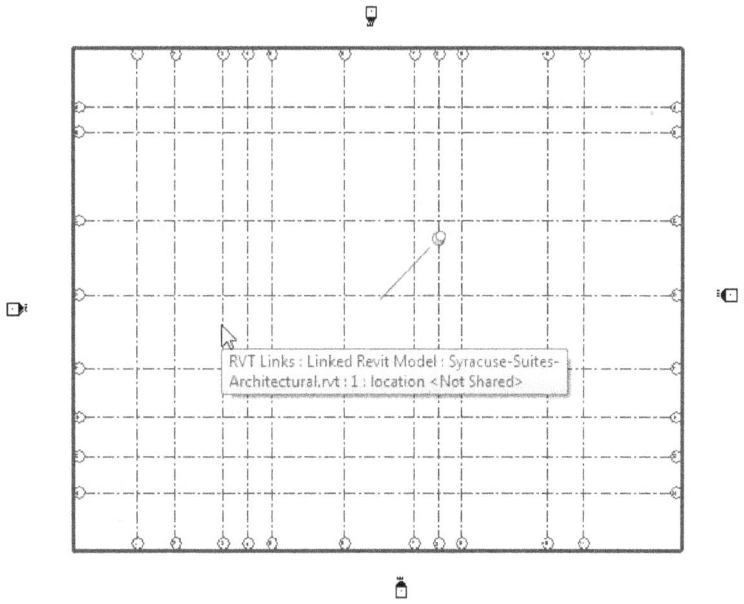

7. Zoom to fit the view (Hint: Type **ZF**.)

8. Ensure that you do not have anything selected so that the Structural Plan Properties of the new view are displayed.

9. In Properties, change the *Discipline* to **Coordination**, as shown in Figure 3–17.

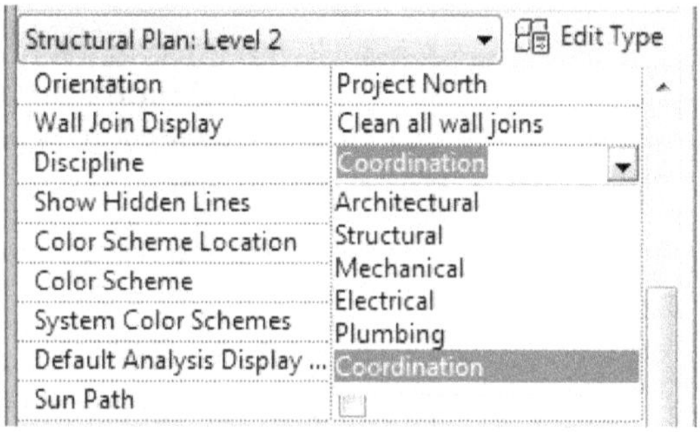

Figure 3–17

10. Click **Apply**. The architectural walls now display.

11. Save the project in your practice files folder as **Syracuse Suites-<your initials>.rvt**.

3.3 Setting Up Levels

Levels define stories and other vertical heights, as shown in Figure 3–18. The default structural template includes two levels, but you can define as many levels in a project as required. They can go down (for basements) as well as up.

Floor levels are frequently set by the architect and need to be copied and monitored into the structural model. You can also draw levels directly in a project, as required.

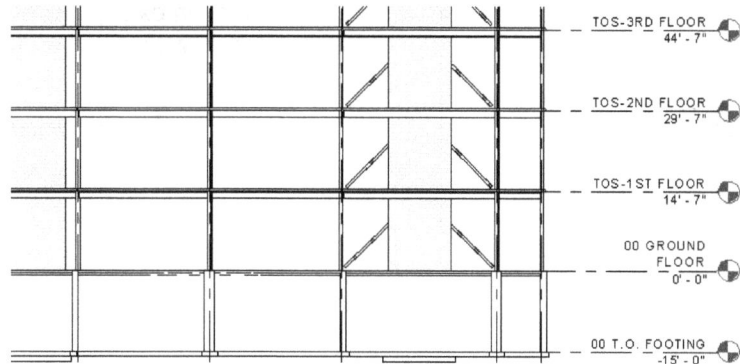

TOS-3RD FLOOR
44' - 7"

TOS-2ND FLOOR
29' - 7"

TOS-1ST FLOOR
14' - 7"

00 GROUND
FLOOR
0' - 0"

00 T.O. FOOTING
-15' - 0"

Figure 3–18

- You must be in an elevation or section view to define levels.

- Once you constrain an element to a level it moves with the level when the level is changed.

How To: Create Levels

1. Open an elevation or section view.

2. In the *Structure* tab>Datum panel, click (Level), or type **LL**.

3. In the Type Selector, set the Level Head type if required.

4. In the Options Bar, select or clear **Make Plan View** as required. You can also click **Plan View Types...** to select the types of views to create when you place the level.

5. In the *Modify | Place Level* tab>Draw panel, click:

   - (Line) to draw a level.

   - (Pick Lines) to select an element using an offset.

   Be careful when you use **Pick Lines** that you do not place levels on top of each other or other elements by mistake.

6. Continue adding levels as required.

- Level names are automatically incremented as you place them so it is helpful to name them in simply (i.e., Floor 1, Floor 2, etc., rather than First Floor, Second Floor, etc.). This also makes it easier to find the view in the Project Browser.

- A fast way to create multiple levels is to use the ⚲ (Pick Lines) option using an offset. In the Options Bar, specify an *Offset,* select an existing level, and then pick above or below to place the new level, as shown in Figure 3–19.

You specify above or below the offset by hovering the mouse on the required side.

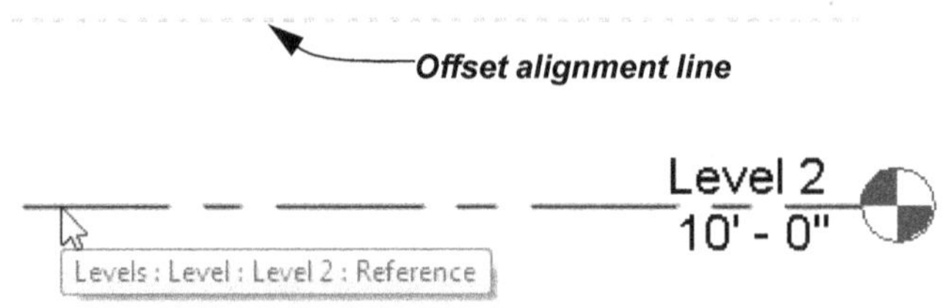

Offset alignment line

Level 2
10' - 0"

Levels : Level : Level 2 : Reference

Figure 3–19

- When using the ✏ (Line) option, alignments and temporary dimensions help you place the line correctly, as shown in Figure 3–20.

You can sketch the level lines from left to right or right to left depending on where you want the bubble. However, ensure that they are all sketched in the same direction.

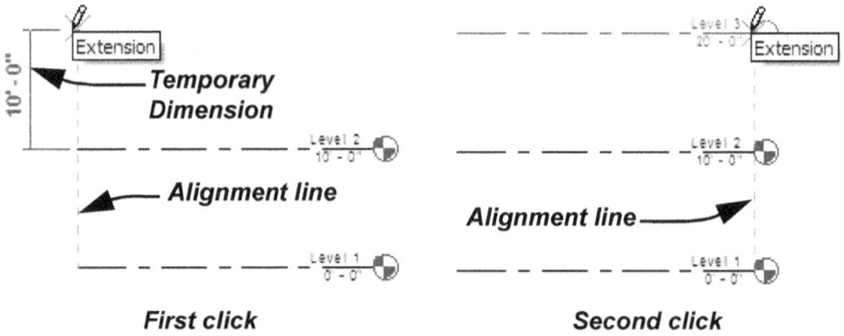

Extension

Temporary Dimension

Alignment line

First click

Alignment line

Extension

Second click

Figure 3–20

- You can also use ⟳ (Copy) to duplicate level lines. The level names are incremented but a plan view is not created.

Modifying Levels

You can change levels using standard controls and temporary dimensions, as shown in Figure 3–21. You can also make changes in the Properties palette.

Figure 3–21

- ☑ ☐ (Hide / Show Bubble) displays on either end of the level line and toggles the level head symbol and level information on or off.

- 2D 3D (Switch to 3d / 2d extents) controls whether any movement or adjustment to the level line is reflected in other views (3D) or only affects the current view (2D).

- ⌖ (Modify the level by dragging its model end) at each end of the line enables you to drag the level head to a new location.

- 🔒 🔓 (Create or remove a length or alignment constraint) controls whether the level is locked in alignment with the other levels. If it is locked and the level line is stretched, all of the other level lines stretch as well. If it is unlocked, the level line stretches independent of the other levels.

- Click ∿ (Add Elbow) to add a jog to the level line as shown in Figure 3–22. Drag the shape handles to new locations as required. This is a view-specific change.

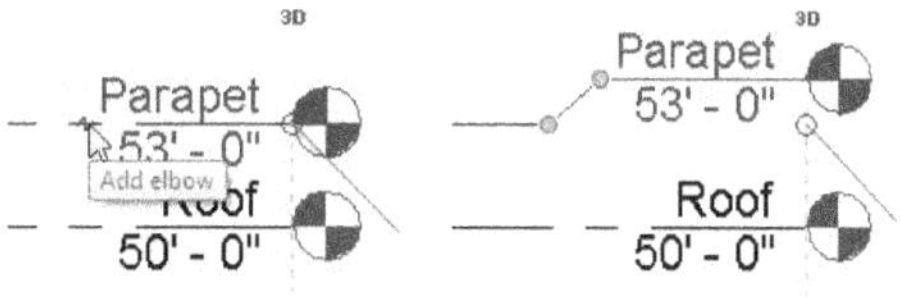

Before　　　　**After**

Figure 3–22

- To change the level name or elevation, double-click on the information next to the level head, or select the level and modify the *Name* or *Elevation* fields in Properties, as shown in Figure 3–23.

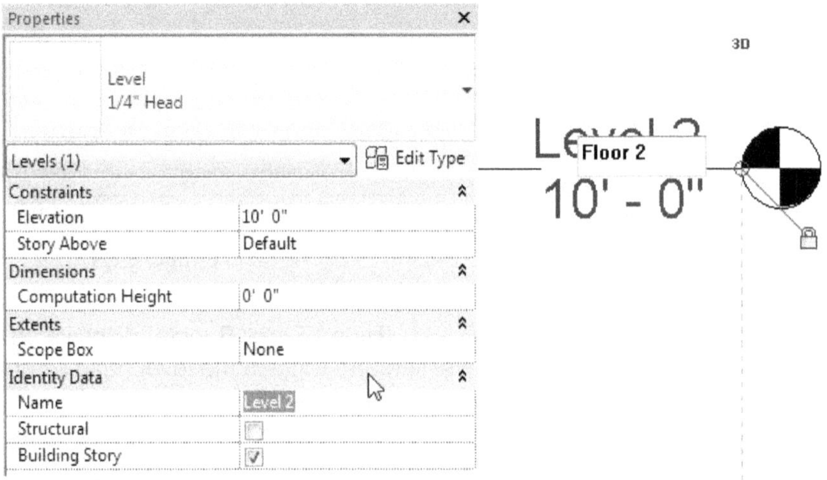

Figure 3–23

- When you rename a Level, an alert box opens, prompting you to rename the corresponding views as shown in Figure 3–24.

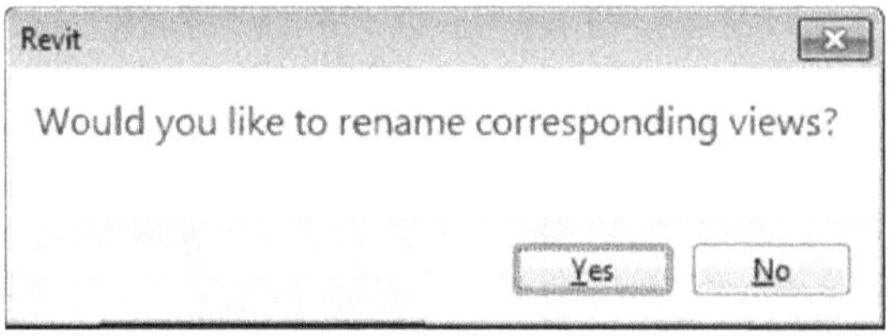

Figure 3–24

- The view is also renamed in the Project Browser.

Hint: Copying Levels and Grids from other projects

Levels and grid lines can be added by drawing over existing levels or grids in an imported or linked CAD file. It can also be copied and monitored from a linked Autodesk® Revit® file. Some projects might require both methods.

Creating Plan Views

By default, when you place a level, plan views for that level are automatically created. If **Make Plan View** was toggled off when adding the level, or if the level was copied, you can create plan views to match the levels.

- Level heads with views are blue and level heads without views are black, as shown in Figure 3–25.

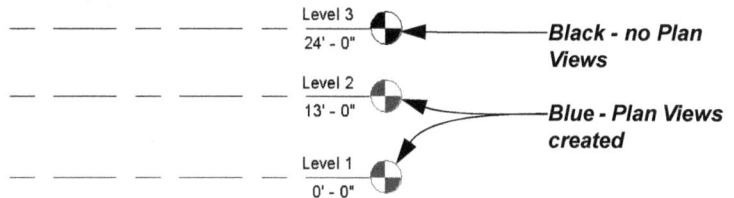

Figure 3–25

Typically, you do not need to create plan views for levels that specify data, such as the top of a foundation wall or the truss bearing height.

How To: Create Plan Views

1. In the *View* tab>Create panel, expand (Plan Views) and select the type of plan view you want to create, as shown on the left in Figure 3–26.
2. In the New Plan dialog box (shown on the right in Figure 3–26), select the levels for which you want to create plan views.

Hold <Ctrl> or <Shift> to select more than one level.

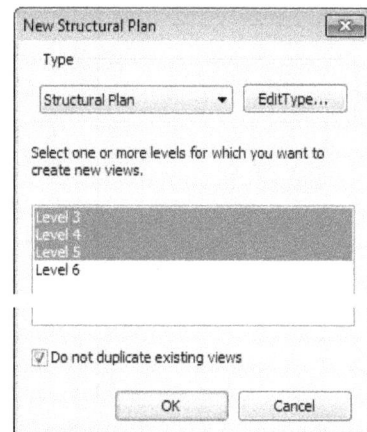

Figure 3–26

3. Click **OK**.

- When **Do not duplicate existing views** is selected, views without the selected plan type display in the list.

3.4 Copying and Monitoring Elements

Once a linked architectural model is in place, the next step is to copy and/or monitor elements that you need from the linked file into the structural project. These elements most often include grids, levels, columns, walls, and floors. A monitoring system keeps track of the copied elements and prompts for updates if something is changed. In the example shown in Figure 3–27, grids have been linked from an architectural model, and the ⊡ (Monitor) icon indicates the monitored elements.

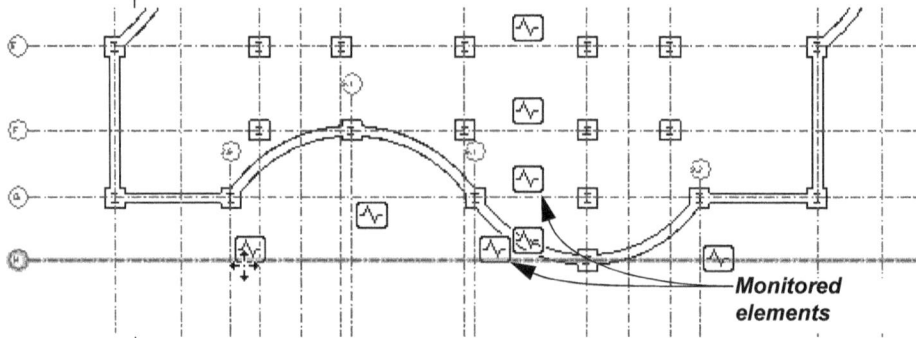

Figure 3–27

- **Copy** creates a duplicate of a selected element in the current project and monitors it to a selected element in the linked model or current project.

- **Monitor** compares two elements of the same type against each other, either from a linked model to the current project (as shown in Figure 3–28) or in the current project.

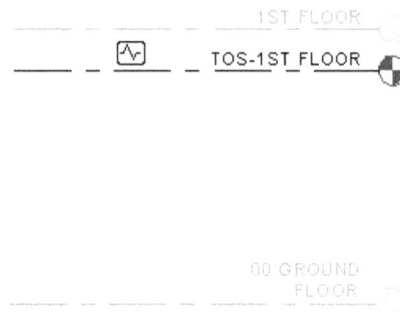

Figure 3–28

How To: Copy and Monitor Elements from a Linked File

1. In the *Collaborate* tab>Coordinate panel, expand 📷 (Copy/Monitor) and click 📄 (Select Link).
2. Select the link.
3. In the *Copy/Monitor* tab>Tools panel, click ⊙ (Copy) or 📷 (Monitor).
4. If copying from the linked file, select each element that you want to copy. Alternatively, use the **Multiple** option:
   - In the Options Bar, select **Multiple**, as shown in Figure 3–29.

   Copy/Monitor   ▽   ☑ Multiple   [Finish]   [Cancel]

   Figure 3–29

   - Hold <Ctrl> and select the elements that you want to copy into your model individually, or use a pick and drag window around multiple elements.
   - In the Options Bar, click **Finish**.

   If monitoring elements in the current project with elements in the linked model, first select the element in the current project, and then select the element in the linked model.

5. Click ✓ (Finish) to end the session of Copy/Monitor.

How To: Copy and Monitor Elements in the Current Project.

1. In the *Collaborate* tab>Coordinate panel, expand 📷 (Copy/Monitor) and click 📄 (Use Current Project).
2. In the *Copy/Monitor* tab>Tools panel, click ⊙ (Copy) or 📷 (Monitor).
3. Select the two elements you want to monitor.
4. Repeat the process for any additional elements.
5. Click ✓ (Finish) to end the command.

- The elements do not have to be at the same elevation or location for the software to monitor them.

Warnings about duplicated or renamed types might display.

Copy/Monitor Settings

Before starting the copy/monitor process, you can modify settings for the types of elements.

- In the *Copy/Monitor* tab>Tools panel, click ✐ (Options). In the Copy/Monitor Options dialog box, select the tab for the type of element that you want to copy: *Levels*, *Grids*, *Columns*, *Walls*, or *Floors*, as shown in Figure 3–30.

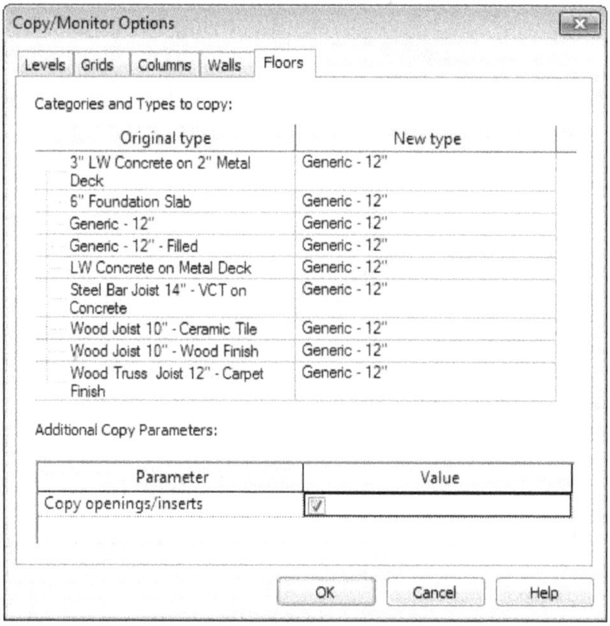

Tabs display for the categories that exist in the linked project.

Copy/Monitor Options		

Levels | Grids | Columns | Walls | **Floors**

Categories and Types to copy:

Original type	New type
3" LW Concrete on 2" Metal Deck	Generic - 12"
6" Foundation Slab	Generic - 12"
Generic - 12"	Generic - 12"
Generic - 12" - Filled	Generic - 12"
LW Concrete on Metal Deck	Generic - 12"
Steel Bar Joist 14" - VCT on Concrete	Generic - 12"
Wood Joist 10" - Ceramic Tile	Generic - 12"
Wood Joist 10" - Wood Finish	Generic - 12"
Wood Truss Joist 12" - Carpet Finish	Generic - 12"

Additional Copy Parameters:

Parameter	Value
Copy openings/inserts	☑

OK   Cancel   Help

Figure 3–30

Practice 3c

Copy and Monitor Elements

Practice Objective

- Copy and monitor elements from the linked model into the current project.

Estimated time for completion: 10 minutes

In this practice you will monitor an existing level and copy additional levels from a linked architectural model into the current structural project, as shown in Figure 3–31.

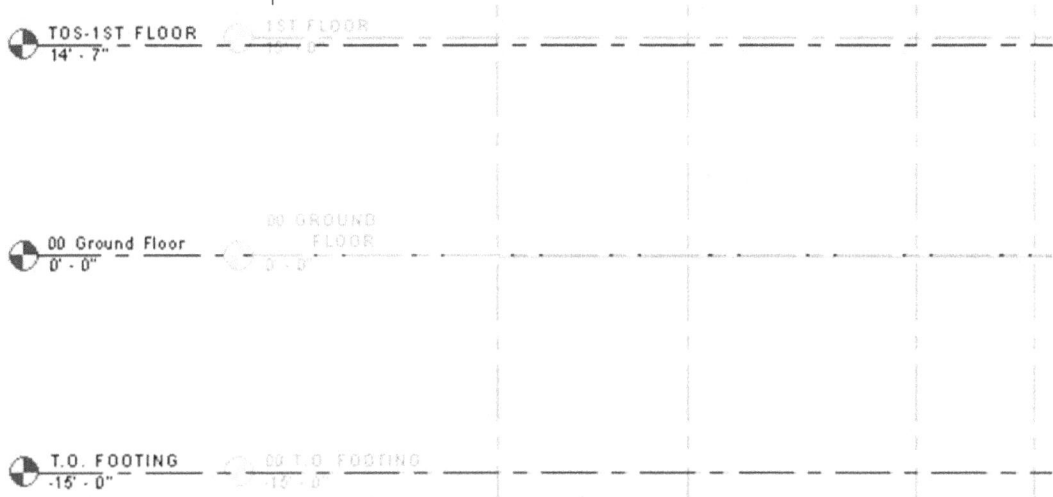

TOS-1ST FLOOR
14' - 7"

1ST FLOOR

00 Ground Floor
0' - 0"

00 GROUND FLOOR
0' - 0"

T.O. FOOTING
-15' - 0"

00 T.O FOOTING
-15' - 0"

Figure 3–31

Task 1 - Monitor elements in the active project with elements in the linked model.

1. Open the project **Syracuse-Suites-Monitor.rvt**.
   - If the linked file needs to be reloaded, in the Manage Links dialog box, click **Reload From**. Navigate to the practice folder, select **Syracuse-Suites-Architecture.rvt**, and click **Open**.

2. In the Project Browser, open the **Elevations (Building Elevation): South** view.

3. Select the link. There are two existing levels in the current project and a large number of levels in the linked model, as shown in Figure 3–32.

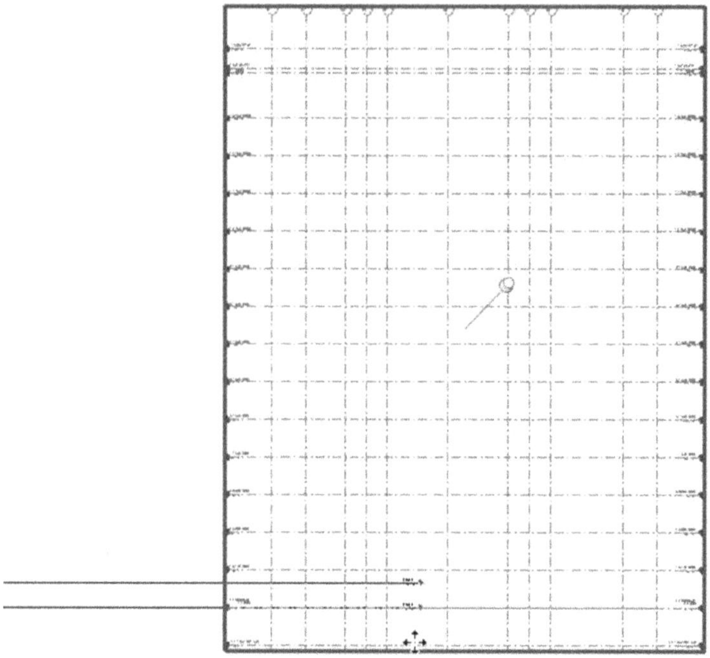

Figure 3–32

4. Right-click on the link and select **Override graphics in View>By Category**.

5. In the View-Specific Category Graphics dialog box, select **Halftone** and click **OK**.

6. Click ⌨ (Modify) and delete **Level 2**. A Warning dialog box opens as shown in Figure 3–33. Click **OK** to delete the corresponding views as they are not required in this project.

A later step creates new levels that are automatically named based on the linked model's levels.

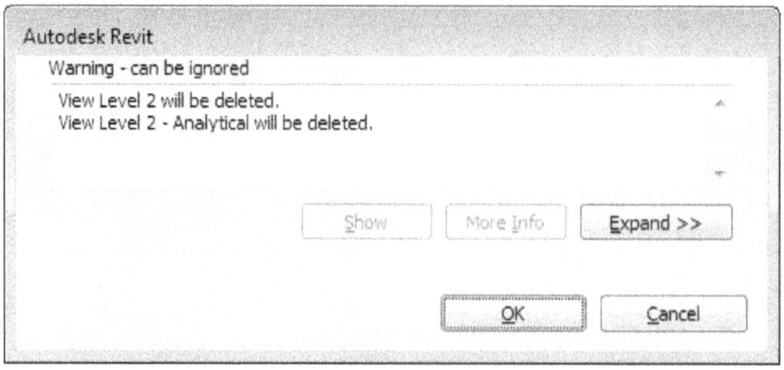

Autodesk Revit
Warning - can be ignored
View Level 2 will be deleted.
View Level 2 - Analytical will be deleted.

Show   More Info   Expand >>

OK   Cancel

Figure 3–33

7. Select **Level 1**. Use controls to make the level line in the host project longer than the level lines in the linked model so that you can see the difference., using the zoom and pan as required.

8. Click on the level name and rename the level to **00 GROUND FLOOR**, as shown in Figure 3–34.

Figure 3–34

9. When prompted, click **Yes** to rename the associated views.

10. In the Project Browser, the former **Level 1** view has been renamed **00 GROUND FLOOR**, as shown in Figure 3–35.

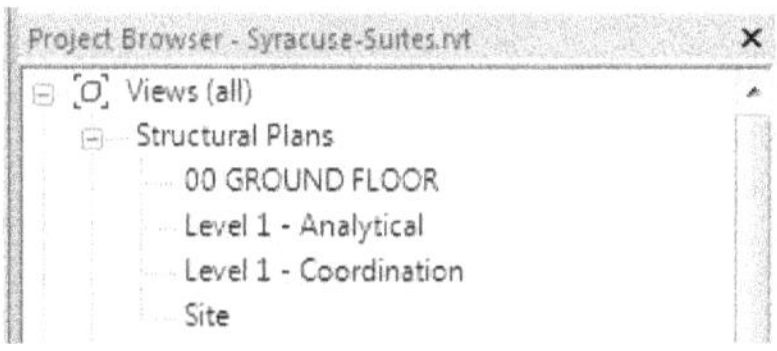

Figure 3–35

11. In the Project Browser, right-click on the other two Level 1 views and rename them **00 GROUND FLOOR – Analytical** and **00 GROUND FLOOR - Coordination**.

12. If you opened one or more of the structural plan views, close them and return to the South elevation view. (Hint: in the Quick Access Toolbar, click [icon] (Close Hidden Windows).

13. Save the project.

Task 2 - Copy and monitor levels.

1. In the *Collaborate* tab>Coordinate panel, expand [icon] (Copy/Monitor) and click [icon] (Select Link).

2. Select the linked model.

3. In the *Copy/Monitor* tab>Tools panel, click [icon] (Monitor).

4. Select level **00 GROUND FLOOR** in the current project and then the corresponding level in the linked model. The level is now monitored, as shown in Figure 3–36.

Figure 3–36

• You might need to zoom out to see the monitor icon.

5. In the *Copy/Monitor* tab>Tools panel, click (Options).

6. In the Copy/Monitor Options dialog box, select the *Levels* tab. Change *Reuse matching Levels* to **Reuse if Elements match exactly** as shown in Figure 3–37.

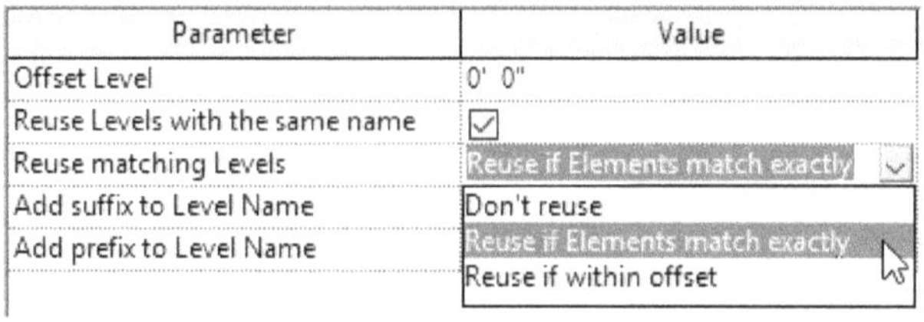

Parameter	Value
Offset Level	0' 0"
Reuse Levels with the same name	☑
Reuse matching Levels	Reuse if Elements match exactly ⌄
Add suffix to Level Name	Don't reuse
Add prefix to Level Name	Reuse if Elements match exactly
	Reuse if within offset

Figure 3–37

7. Click **OK**.

8. In the *Copy/Monitor* tab>Tools panel, click (Copy).

9. Select level **T.O. Footing**.

10. Close the Warning message about copies of the Grid Head being renamed. A replica of the level in the linked model is copied into the current project as shown in Figure 3–38.

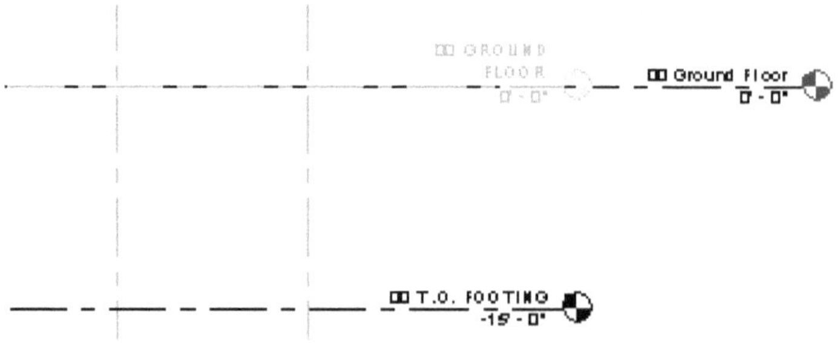

Figure 3–38

11. In the *Copy/Monitor* tab>Tools panel, click ✐ (Options).

12. In the Copy/Monitor Options dialog box select the *Levels* tab. Set the *Offset Level* to (negative) **-5"** and *Add prefix to Level Name* to **TOS-** as shown in Figure 3–39.

Parameter	Value
Offset Level	-0' 5"
Reuse Levels with the same name	☑
Reuse matching Levels	Reuse if Elements match exactly
Add suffix to Level Name	
Add prefix to Level Name	TOS-

Figure 3–39

13. Click **OK**.

14. In the *Copy/Monitor* tab>Tools panel, click ⃝ (Copy).

15. Select each of the levels for the 1st through 14th floors. ⟨Aᵥ⟩ (Monitor) displays at each Level line as it is placed.

16. In the Copy/Monitor panel, click ✓ (Finish).

17. New levels with the prefix TOS- are copied into the current project at **5"** below the level in the linked model, as shown in Figure 3–40.

Align the level head symbols so that you can see both the current and linked levels on each end.

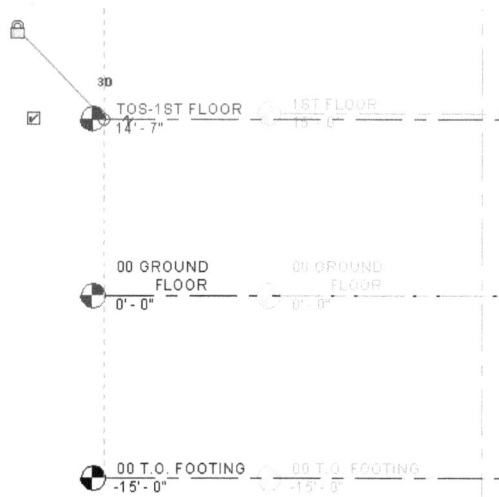

Figure 3–40

18. Zoom to fit the view (Type ZF) and save the project.

Task 3 - Set up views.

1. In the Project Browser, note that the floor plans of the new levels do not display, as shown in Figure 3–41.

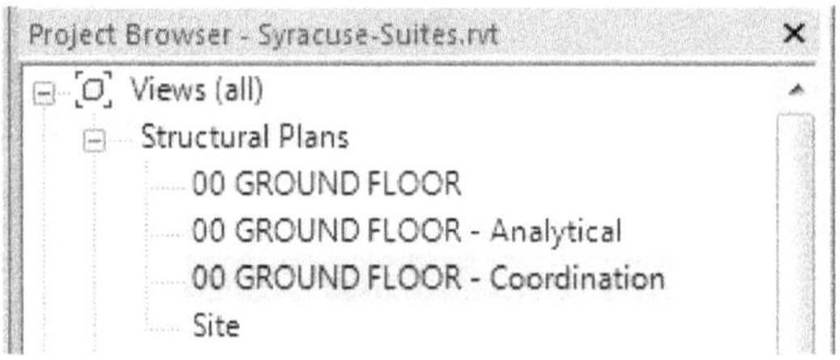

Project Browser - Syracuse-Suites.rvt ✕
- ⊡ 🗗 Views (all)
  - ⊟ Structural Plans
    - 00 GROUND FLOOR
    - 00 GROUND FLOOR - Analytical
    - 00 GROUND FLOOR - Coordination
    - Site

Figure 3–41

2. In the *View* tab>Create panel, expand 🗗 (Plan Views) and click 🖿 (Structural Plan).

3. In the New Structural Plan dialog box, select all of the levels, as shown in Figure 3–42, and click **OK**.

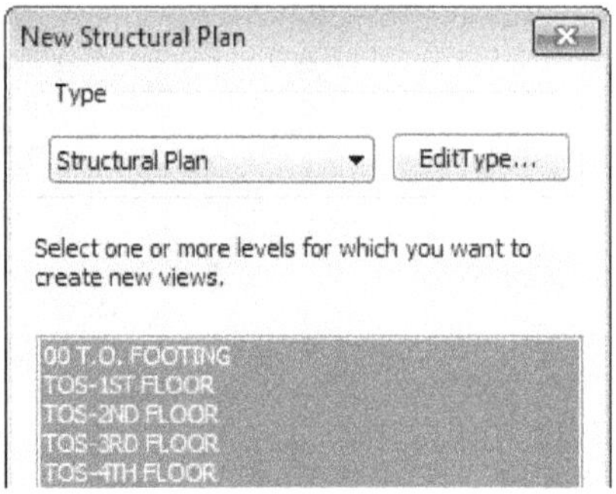

New Structural Plan

Type

Structural Plan ▼ EditType...

Select one or more levels for which you want to create new views.

00 T.O. FOOTING
TOS-1ST FLOOR
TOS-2ND FLOOR
TOS-3RD FLOOR
TOS-4TH FLOOR

Figure 3–42

4. The new views display in the Project Browser as shown in Figure 3–43. **TOS-14 ROOF** (the last plan created) is automatically opened.

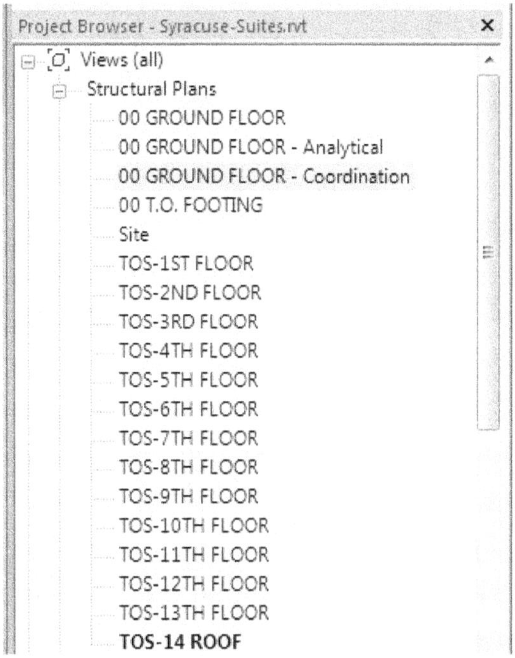

Figure 3–43

5. Open the **Elevations (Building Elevation): South** view.

6. Save and close the project.

3.5 Coordinating Linked Models

Monitoring elements identifies changes in the data as well as changes in placement. For example, if you move a grid line, a Coordination Monitor alert displays, as shown in Figure 3–44. You can run a Coordination Review to correct or accept these changes.

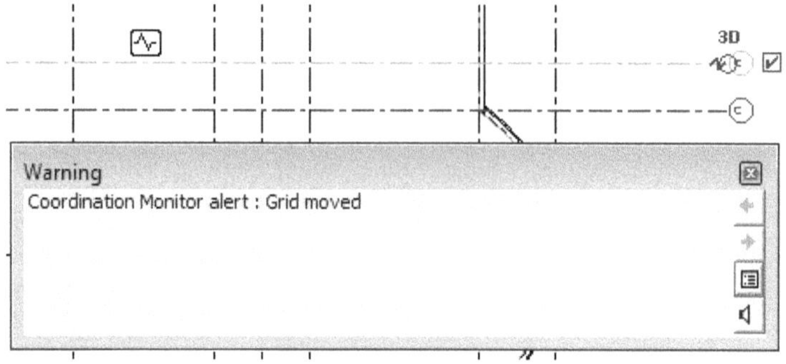

Figure 3–44

*   If you open a project with a linked file which contains elements that have been modified and monitored, the Warning shown in Figure 3–45 displays.

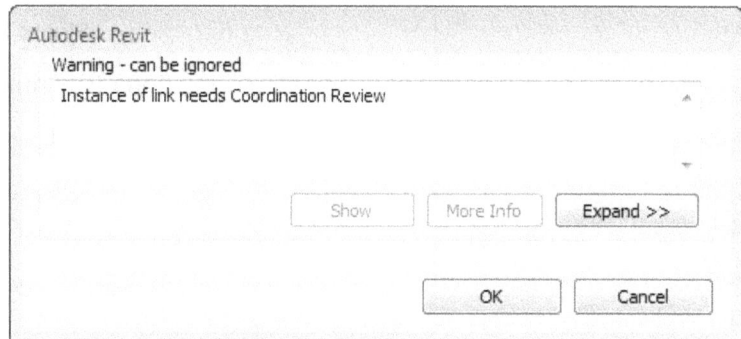

Figure 3–45

*   Warnings do not prevent you from making a change, but alert you that the element is monitored and needs further coordination.

*   If you no longer want an element to be monitored, select it and in the associated *Modify* tab>Monitor panel, click

    (Stop Monitoring).

How To: Run a Coordination Review

1. In the *Collaborate* tab>Coordinate panel, expand

   ![icon] (Coordination Review) and click ![icon] (Use Current

   Project) or ![icon] (Select Link). The Coordination Review dialog
   box lists any conflicts detected, as shown in Figure 3–46.

   - If there are no conflicts, the *Message* area is empty.

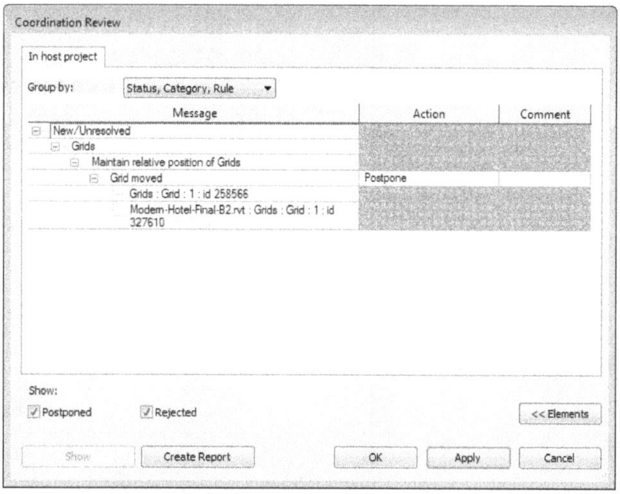

Figure 3–46

2. Use the Group by: drop-down list to group the information by
   Status, **Category**, and **Rule** in a variety of different ways.
   This is important if you have many elements to review.
3. Select an Action for each conflict related to the elements
   involved, as shown in Figure 3–47.

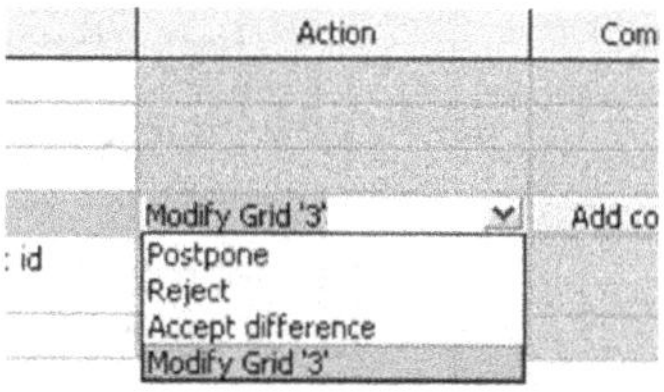

Figure 3–47

   - **Postpone** - Do nothing, but leave it to be handled later.
   - **Reject** - Do not accept the change. The change needs to
     be made in the other model.
   - **Accept Difference** - Make no change to the monitored
     element in the current project, but accept the change
     (such as a distance between the elements) in the monitor
     status.

- **Rename/Modify/Move** - Apply the change to the monitored element.
- Other options display when special cases occur. See the Autodesk Revit help files for more information.

4. Add a comment, click **Add comment** in the column to the right. This enables you to make a note about the change, such as the date of the modification
5. Select the element names or click **Show** to display any items in conflict. Clicking **Show** changes the view to center the elements in your screen. Selecting the name does not change the view.
6. Click **Create Report** to create an HTML report that you can share with other users, as shown in Figure 3–48.

Revit Coordination Report

In host project

New/Unresolved	Levels	Maintain Position	Level moved by 1' - 0"	Levels : Level : TOS-14 ROOF : id 518290 Syracuse-Suites-Architectural-TEST.rvt : Levels : Level : 14 ROOF : id 199895

Figure 3–48

Hint: Trouble Shooting

When working with various elements, Warnings (such as the one shown in Figure 3–49), display when something is wrong, but you can keep on working. In many cases you can close the dialog box and fix the issue or wait and do it later.

Warning	
Stair top end exceeds or cannot reach the top elevation of the stair. Add/remove risers at the top end or change top elevation settings in Stair instance properties.	

Figure 3–49

Sometimes Errors display where you must take action. These force you to stop and fix the situation.

When you select an element for which there has been a warning ⚠ (Show Related Warnings) displays in the ribbon. It opens a dialog box in which you can review the warning(s) related to the selected element. You can also display a list of all of the warnings in the project by clicking ⊞ (Review Warnings) in the *Manage* tab>Inquiry panel.

Practice 3d

Coordinate Linked Models

Practice Objectives

- Make a modification to an architectural model.
- Run a Coordination Review.

In this practice you will make a modification to the architectural model, and then open the structural project which prompts you of the change. You will then run a Coordination Review and update the structural project to match the change in the architectural model, as shown in Figure 3–50.

Estimated time for completion: 10 minutes

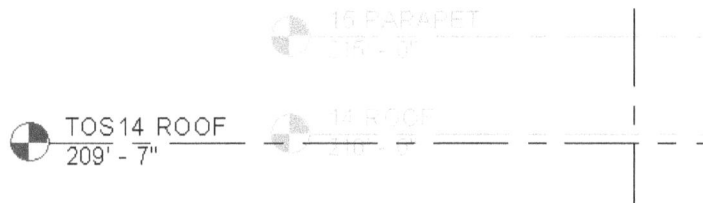

Figure 3–50

Task 1 - Modify the architectural model.

1. Open **Syracuse-Suites-Architectural.rvt** from the practice files folder.

2. Open the **Elevations (Building Elevation): SOUTH ELEVATION** view.

3. Zoom in on the upper levels of the building.

4. Double-click on the number below **14 ROOF** and change the height to **210'-0"**, as shown in Figure 3–51.

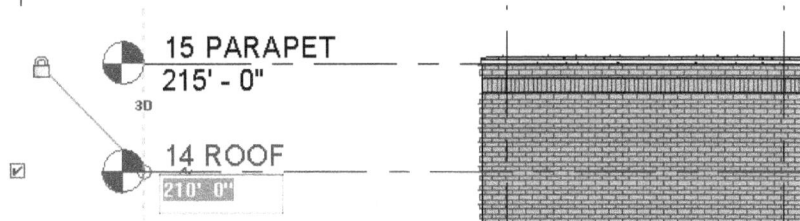

Figure 3–51

5. Save and close the model.

Task 2 - Coordinate the architectural and structural models.

1. Open **Syracuse Suites-Coordinate.rvt**.

2. A Warning dialog box displays and a warning that the linked file needs a Coordination Review, as shown in Figure 3–52.

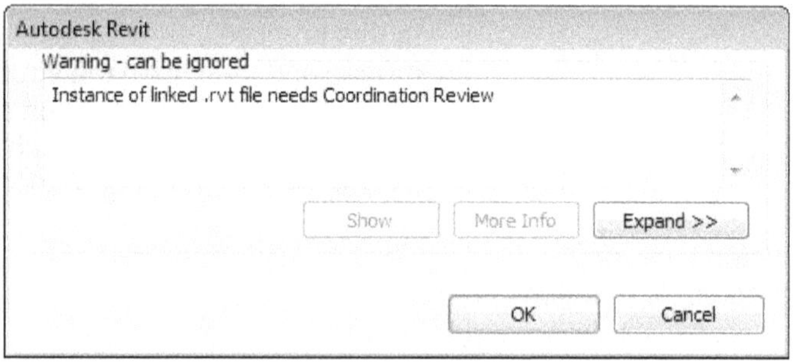

Figure 3–52

3. Click **OK**.

4. Select the linked model and in the *Modify RVT Links* tab> Monitor panel, click ⬚ (Coordination Review).

5. In the Coordination Review dialog box, expand the **Level moved** node. In the *Action* column, expand the drop-down list and select **Move Level 'TOS-14 ROOF',** as shown in Figure 3–53.

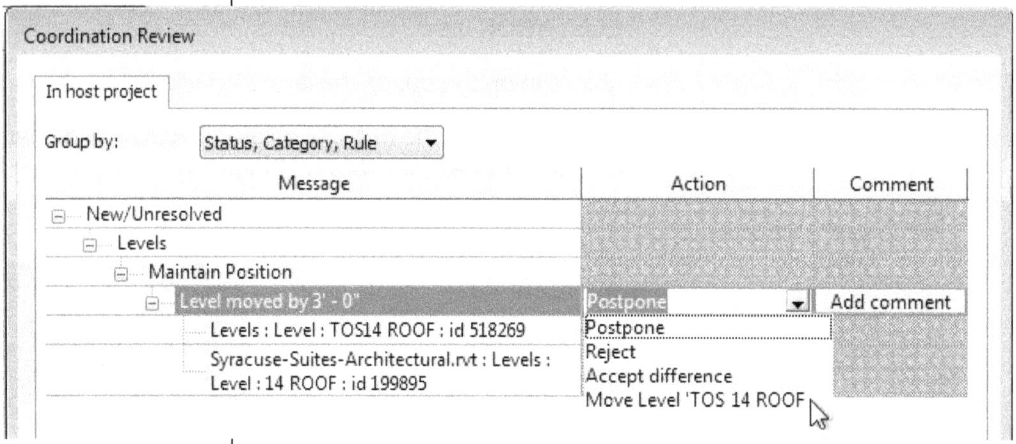

Figure 3–53

6. Click **OK**. The levels now reflect the change in both the linked model and the current model as shown in Figure 3–54.

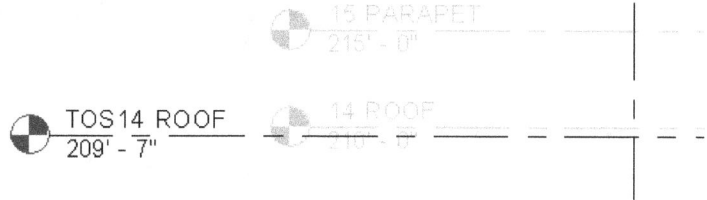

Figure 3–54

7. Zoom out to see the entire elevation.

8. Save and close the project.

Chapter Review Questions

1. When you import a CAD file into the Autodesk Revit software, as shown in Figure 3–55, it comes in as lines and text.

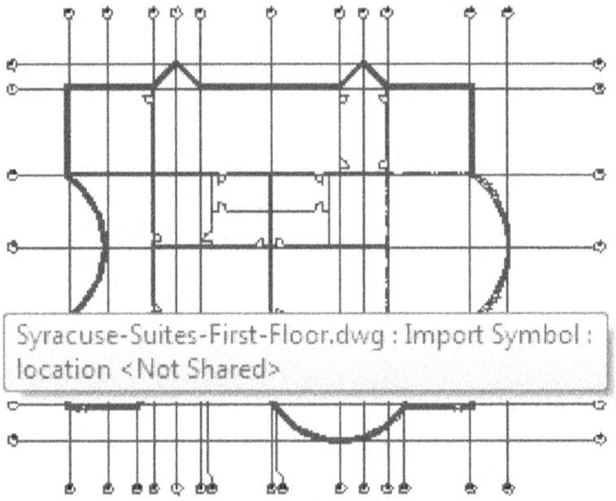

Figure 3–55

  a. True

  b. False

2. What type of view do you need to be in to add a level to your project?

  a. Any non-plan view.

  b. As this is done using a dialog box, the view does not matter.

  c. Any view except for 3D.

  d. Any section or elevation view.

3. Which of the following elements can be copied and monitored? (Select all that apply.)

  a. Grids

  b. Levels

  c. Beams

  d. Braces

4. On which of the following element types can a coordination review with the host project be performed?

   a. CAD link

   b. CAD import

   c. Revit link

   d. Revit import

5. When linking an architectural model into a structural project which of the positioning methods, as shown in Figure 3–56, keeps the model in the same place if the extents of the linked model changes in size?

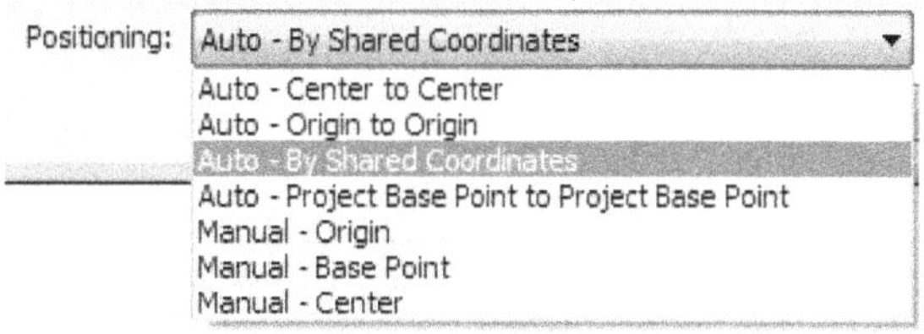

Positioning: Auto - By Shared Coordinates

Auto - Center to Center
Auto - Origin to Origin
Auto - By Shared Coordinates
Auto - Project Base Point to Project Base Point
Manual - Origin
Manual - Base Point
Manual - Center

Figure 3–56

   a. Auto - Center-to-Center

   b. Auto - Origin-to-Origin

   c. Manual - Basepoint

   d. Manual - Center

6. How many times can one project file be linked into another project?

   a. Once

   b. It is limited by the size of the link.

   c. As many as you want.

Command Summary

Button	Command	Location
General Tools		
	Level	• **Ribbon:** *Architecture* tab>Datum panel • **Shortcut:** LL
	Override By Category	• **Ribbon:** *Modify* tab>View panel, expand Override Graphics in View • **Shortcut Menu:** Override Graphics in View>By Category...
	Override By Element	• **Ribbon:** *Modify* tab>View panel, expand Override Graphics in View • **Shortcut Menu:** Override Graphics in View>By Element...
	Pin	• **Ribbon:** *Modify* tab>Modify Panel
	Select Links	• **Status Bar**
	Select Pinned Elements	• **Status Bar**
CAD Files		
	Import CAD	• **Ribbon:** *Insert* tab>Import panel
	Link CAD	• **Ribbon:** *Insert* tab>Link panel
Linked Revit Files		
	Coordination Review	• **Ribbon:** *Collaborate* tab>Coordinate panel
	Copy (from linked file)	• **Ribbon:** *Copy/Monitor* tab>Tools panel
	Copy/Monitor> Select Link	• **Ribbon:** *Collaborate* tab>Coordinate panel, expand Copy/Monitor
	Copy/Monitor> Use Current Project	• **Ribbon:** *Collaborate* tab>Coordinate panel, expand Copy/Monitor
	Link Revit	• **Ribbon:** *Insert* tab>Link panel
	Manage Links	• **Ribbon:** *Manage* tab>Manage Projects panel or *Insert* tab>Link panel
	Monitor	• **Ribbon:** *Copy/Monitor* tab>Tools panel
	Options (Copy/Monitor)	• **Ribbon:** *Copy/Monitor* tab>Tools panel

Working with Views

Views are the cornerstone of working with Autodesk® Revit® models as they enable you to see the model in both 2D and 3D. As you are working, you can duplicate and change views to display different information based on the same view of the model. Callouts, elevations, and sections are especially important views for construction documents.

Learning Objectives in this Chapter

- Change the way elements display in different views to show required information and set views for construction documents.
- Duplicate views so that you can modify the display as you are creating the model and for construction documents.
- Create callout views of parts of plans, sections, or elevations for detailing.
- Add building and interior elevations that can be used to demonstrate how a building will be built.
- Create building and wall sections to help you create the model and to include in construction documents.

4.1 Setting the View Display

Views are a powerful tool as they enable you to create multiple versions of a model without having to recreate building elements. For example, you can have views that are specifically used for working on the model, while other views are annotated and used for construction documents. Different disciplines can have different views that show only the features they require, as shown in Figure 4–1. Properties of a view are independent of the properties of other views.

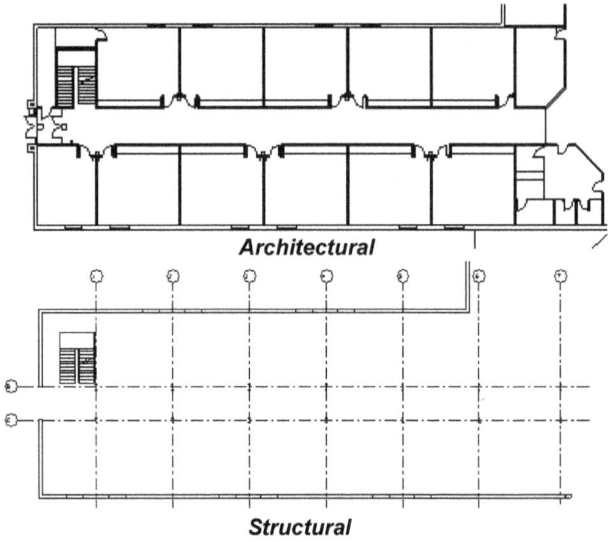

Architectural

Structural

Figure 4–1

The view display can be modified in the following locations:

- View Control Bar
- Properties
- Shortcut menu
- Visibility/Graphic Overrides dialog box

Hiding and Overriding Graphics

Two common ways to customize a view are to:

- Hide individual elements or categories

- Modify how graphics display for elements or categories (e.g., altering lineweight, color, or pattern)

An element is an individual item such as one wall in a view, while a category includes all instances of a selected element, such as all walls in a view.

For example, you can gray out all of the foundation elements by modifying the category in a Structural Plan, as shown in Figure 4–2.

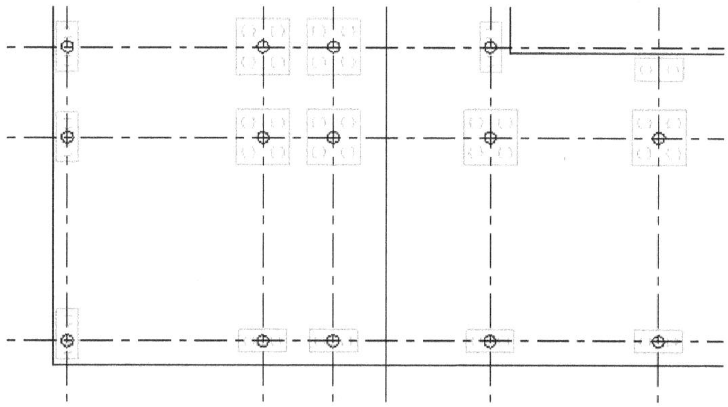

Figure 4–2

How To: Hide Elements or Categories in a view

1. Select the elements or categories you want to hide.
2. Right-click and select **Hide in View>Elements** or **Hide in View>Category**, as shown in Figure 4–3.
3. The elements or categories are hidden in current view only.

*A quick way to hide entire categories is to select an element(s) and type **VH**.*

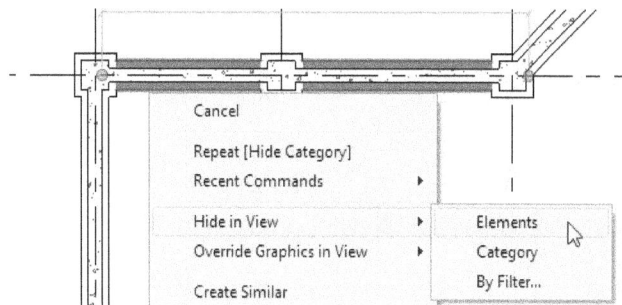

Figure 4–3

How To: Override Graphics of Elements or Categories in a View

1. Select the element(s) you want to modify.
2. Right-click and select **Override Graphics in View>By Element** or **By Category**. The View-Specific Element (or Category) Graphics dialog box opens, as shown in Figure 4–4.

The exact options in the dialog box vary depending on the type of elements selected.

Figure 4–4

3. Select the changes you want to make and click **OK**.

View-Specific Options

- Clearing the **Visible** option is the same as hiding the elements or categories.

- Selecting the **Halftone** option grays out the elements or categories.

- The options for Projection Lines, Surface Patterns, Cut Lines, and Cut Patterns include **Weight**, **Color**, and **Pattern**, as shown in Figure 4–4.

- **Surface Transparency** can be set by moving the slider bar, as shown in Figure 4–5.

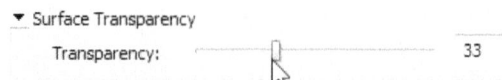

Figure 4–5

- The View-Specific Category dialog box includes **Open the Visibility Graphics dialog...**, which opens the full dialog box of options.

The Visibility/Graphic Overrides Dialog Box

The options in the Visibility/Graphic Overrides dialog box (shown in Figure 4–6) control how every category and sub-category of elements is displayed per view.

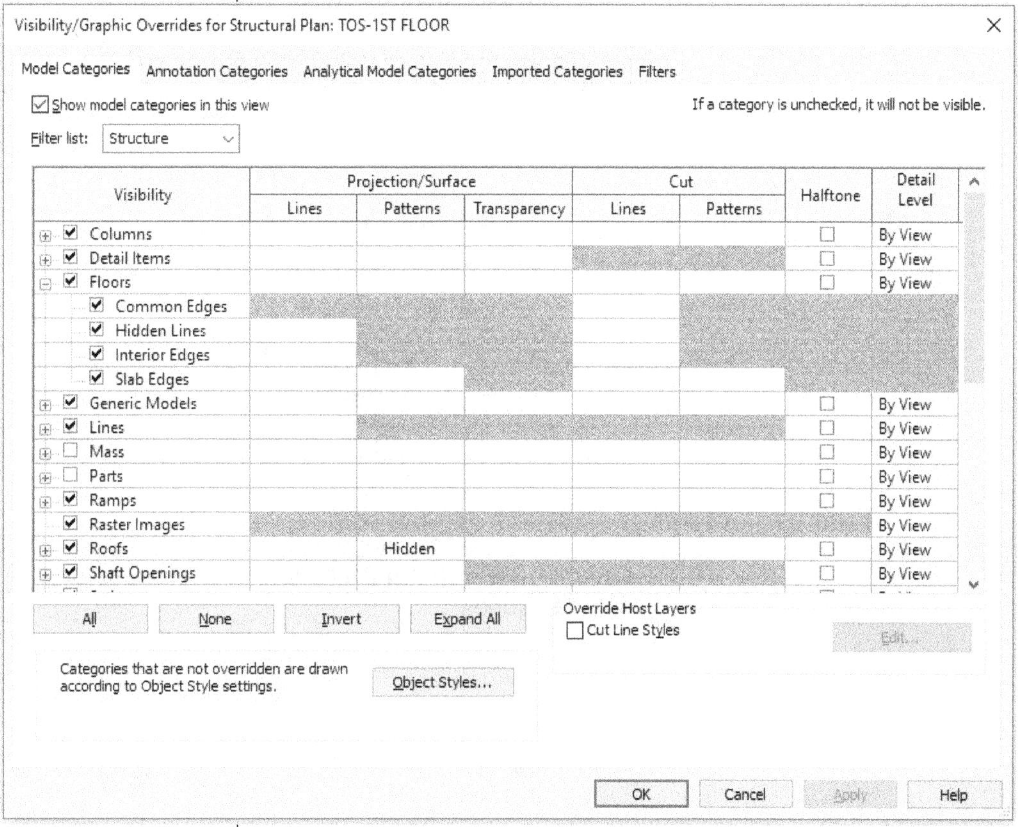

Figure 4–6

To open the Visibility/Graphic Overrides dialog box, type **VV** or **VG**. It is also available in Properties: in the *Graphics* area, beside *Visibility/Graphic Overrides*, click **Edit...**.

- The Visibility/Graphic Overrides are divided into *Model*, *Annotation*, *Analytical Model*, *Imported,* and *Filters* categories.

- Other categories might be available if specific data has been included in the project, including *Design Options*, *Linked Files*, and *Worksets*.

- To limit the number of categories showing in the dialog box select a discipline from the *Filter list,* as shown in Figure 4–7

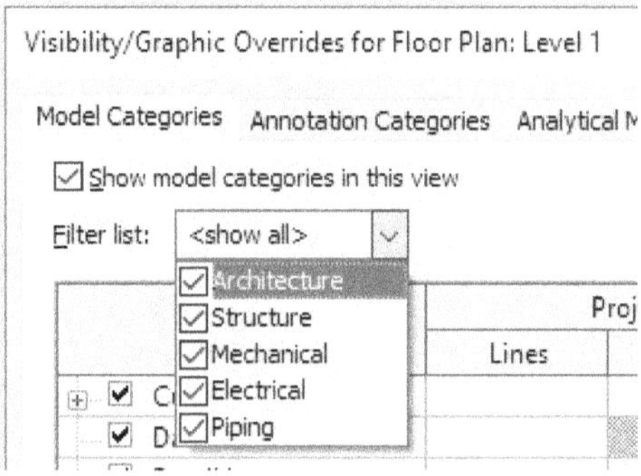

Figure 4–7

- To help you select categories, use the **All**, **None**, and **Invert** buttons. The **Expand All** button displays all of the sub-categories.

Hint: Restoring Hidden Elements or Categories

If you have hidden categories, you can display them using the Visibility/Graphic Overrides dialog box. To display hidden elements, however, you must temporarily reveal the elements first.

1. In the View Control Bar, click 🔲 (Reveal Hidden Elements). The border and all hidden elements are displayed in magenta, while visible elements in the view are grayed out, as shown in Figure 4–8.

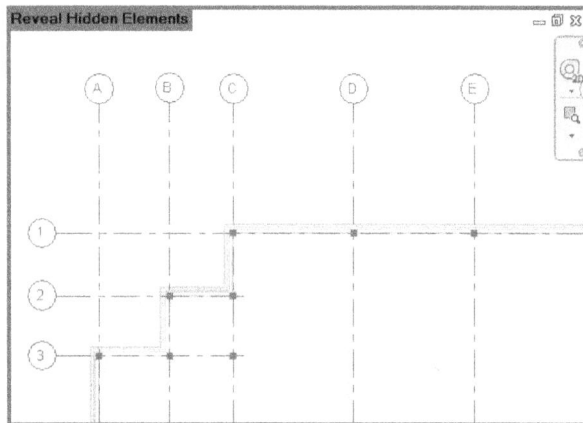

Figure 4–8

2. Select the hidden elements you want to restore, right-click, and select **Unhide in View>Elements** or **Unhide in View>Category**. Alternatively, in the *Modify |* contextual tab>Reveal Hidden Elements panel, click 🔲 (Unhide Element) or 🔲 (Unhide Category).

3. When you are finished, in the View Control Bar, click 🔲 (Close Reveal Hidden Elements) or, in the *Modify |* contextual tab>Reveal Hidden Elements panel click ☒ (Toggle Reveal Hidden Elements Mode).

View Properties

The most basic properties of a view are accessed using the View Control Bar, shown in Figure 4–9. These include the *Scale*, *Detail Level*, and *Visual Style* options. Additional options include temporary overrides and other advanced settings.

1/8" = 1'-0"   ☐ ⬠ ⁂ ☒ ⬚ ⬚ ⬚ ◌ ⬚ ⬚

Figure 4–9

Other modifications to views are available in Properties, as shown in Figure 4–10. These properties include *Underlays*, *View Range*, and *Crop Regions*.

The options in Properties vary according to the type of view. A plan view has different properties than a 3D view.

Properties	✕
▦ Structural Plan	▾

Structural Plan: TOS-1ST FLOOR ⌄	🔲 Edit Type
Display Model	Normal
Detail Level	Medium
Parts Visibility	Show Original
Visibility/Graphics O...	Edit...
Graphic Display Opt...	Edit...
Orientation	Project North
Wall Join Display	Clean all wall joins
Discipline	Structural
Show Hidden Lines	By Discipline
Color Scheme Locat...	Background
Color Scheme	<none>
System Color Sche...	Edit...
Default Analysis Dis...	None
Sun Path	☐
Properties help	Apply

Figure 4–10

Setting an Underlay

Setting an *Underlay* is helpful if you need to display elements on a different level, such as the basement plan shown with an underlay of the first floor plan in Figure 4–11. You can then use the elements to trace over or even copy to the current level of the view.

Underlays are only available in Floor Plan and Ceiling Plan views.

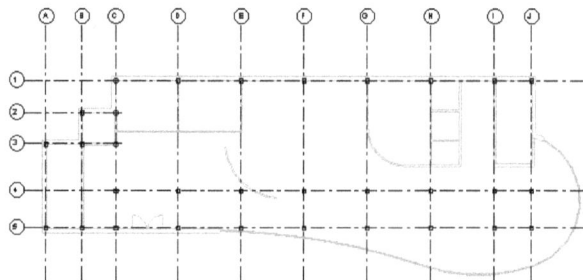

Figure 4–11

In Properties in the *Underlay* area, specify the *Range: Base Level* and the *Range: Top Level*. You can also specify the Underlay Orientation to **Look down** or **Look up** as shown in Figure 4–12.

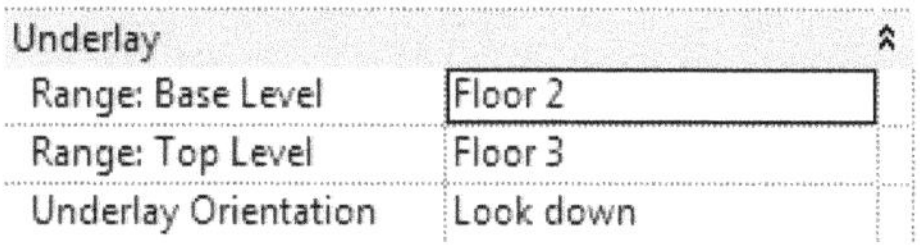

Underlay	☆
Range: Base Level	Floor 2
Range: Top Level	Floor 3
Underlay Orientation	Look down

Figure 4–12

- To prevent moving elements in the underlay by mistake, in the Select panel, expand the panel title, and clear **Select underlay elements**. You can also toggle this on/off using

  ⇶ (Select Underlay Elements) in the Status Bar.

How To: Set the View Range

1. In Properties, in the *Extents* area, beside *View Range*, select **Edit...** or type **VR**.
2. In the View Range dialog box, as shown in Figure 4–13, modify the Levels and Offsets for the *Primary Range* and *View Depth.*
   - Click **Show>>** to display the Sample View Range graphics and key to the various options.
3. Click **OK**.

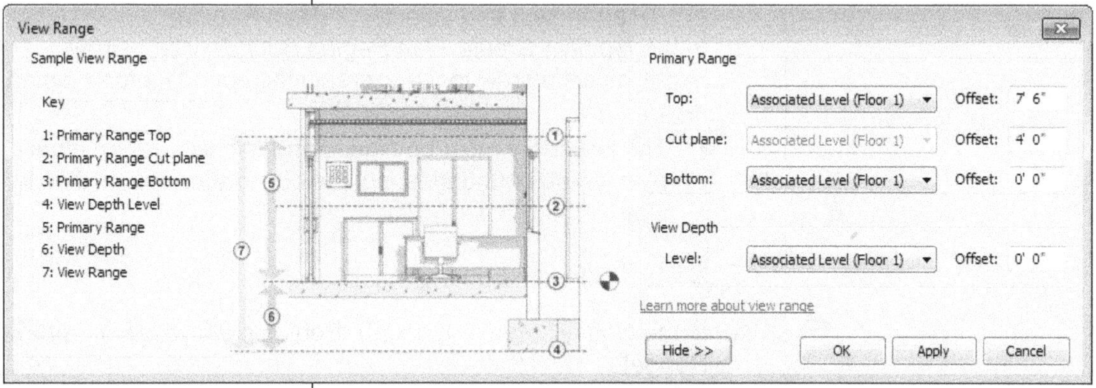

Figure 4–13

- If the settings used cannot be represented graphically, a warning displays stating the inconsistency.

Plan Regions

When you have a plan view with multiple levels of floors or ceilings, you can create plan regions that enable you to set a different view range for part of a view, as shown in Figure 4–14.

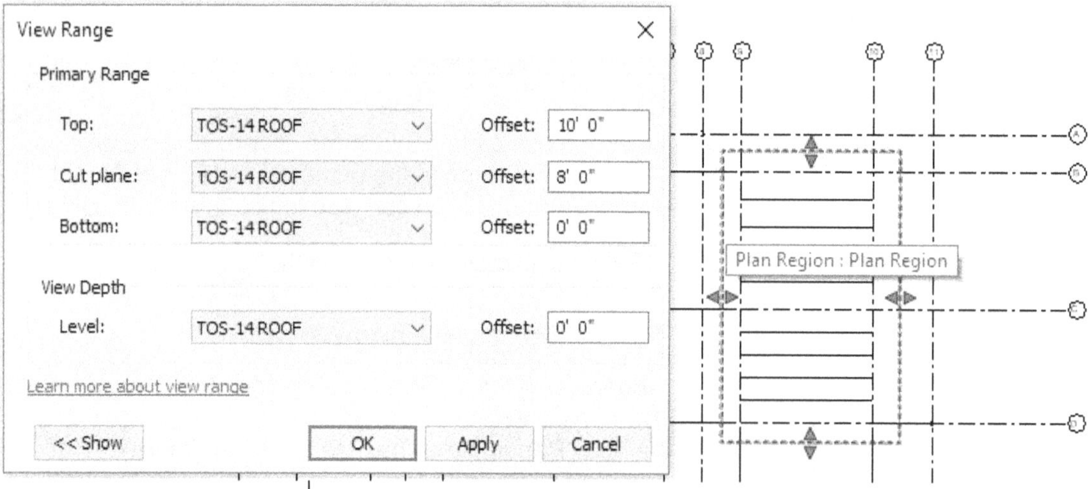

Figure 4–14

How To: Create Plan Regions

1. In a plan view, in the *View* tab>Create panel, expand

    (Plan Views) and select   (Plan Region).
2. In the *Modify | Create Plan Region Boundary* tab>Draw panel, select a draw tool and create the boundary for the plan region.

    - The boundary must be closed and cannot overlap other plan region boundaries, but the boundaries can be side by side.

3. Click   (Finish Edit Mode).

4. In the *Modify | Plan Region* tab>Region panel, click   (View Range).
5. In the View Range dialog box, specify the offsets for the plan region and click **OK**. The plan region is applied to the selected area.

    - Plan regions can be copied to the clipboard and then pasted into other plan views.

- You can use shape handles to resize plan region boundaries without having to edit the boundary.

- Plan Regions can be toggled on and off in the Visibility/ Graphic Overrides dialog box on the *Annotation Categories* tab. If they are displayed, the plan regions are included when printing and exporting.

Hint: Depth Clipping and Far Clipping

Depth Clipping, shown in Figure 4–15, is a viewing option which sets how sloped walls are displayed if the *View Range* of a plan is set to a limited view.

Far Clipping (shown in Figure 4–16) is available for section and elevation views.

Figure 4–15   Figure 4–16

- An additional Graphic Display Option enables you to specify *Depth Cueing*, so that items that are in the distance will be made lighter.

Crop Regions

Plans, sections, and elevations can all be modified by changing how much of the model is displayed in a view. One way to do this is to set the Crop Region. If there are dimensions, tags, or text near the required crop region, you can also use the Annotation Crop Region to include these, as shown in Figure 4–17.

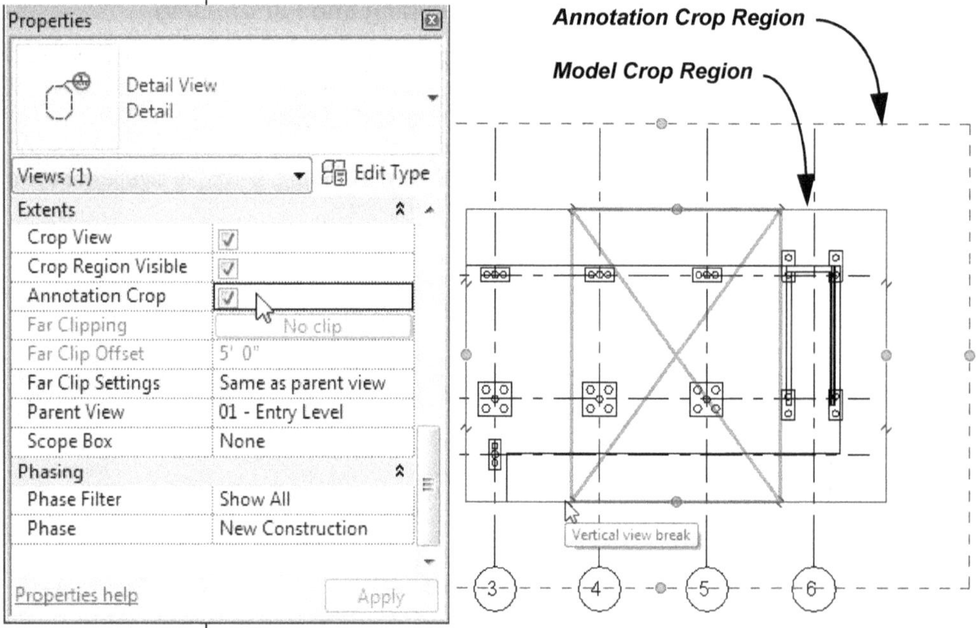

Figure 4–17

Zoom out if you do not see the crop region when you set it to be displayed.

- The crop region must be displayed to modify the size of the view. In the View Control Bar, click ⬚ (Show Crop Region) Alternatively, in Properties, in the *Extents* area, select **Crop Region Visible**. **Annotation Crop** is also available in this area.

- Resize the crop region using the ⊙ control on each side of the region.

Breaking the crop region is typically used with sections or details.

- Click ⤳ (Break Line) control to split the view into two regions, horizontally or vertically. Each part of the view can then be modified in size to display what is required and be moved independently.

- It is a best practice to hide a crop region before placing a view on a sheet. In the View Control Bar, click ⬚ (Hide Crop Region).

Using View Templates

A powerful way to use views effectively is to set up a view and then save it as a View Template. You can apply view templates to views individually, or though the Properties palette. Setting the View Template using the Properties palette helps to ensure that you do not accidentally modify the view while interacting with it.

How To: Create a View Template from a View

1. Set up a view, as required.
2. In the Project Browser, right-click on the view and select **Create View Template from View**.
3. In the New View Template dialog box, type in a name and then click **OK**.
4. The new view template is listed in the View Templates dialog box. Make any required modifications.
5. Click **OK**.

How To: Specify a View Template for a View

1. In the Project Browser, select the view or views to which you want to apply a view template.
2. In Properties, scroll down to the *Identity Data* section and click the button beside *View Template*.
3. In the Apply View Template dialog box, select the view template from the list, as shown in Figure 4–18.

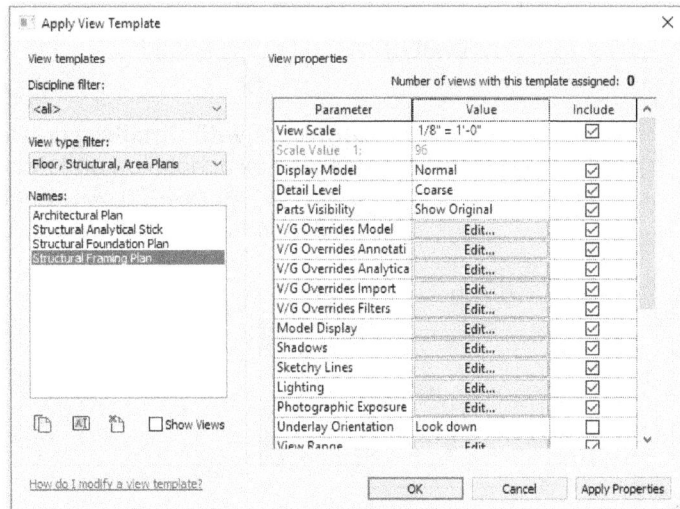

Figure 4–18

4. Click **OK**.

- In the View Control Bar, use ⌗ (Temporary View Properties) to temporarily apply a view template to a view.

4.2 Duplicating Views

Once you have created a model, you do not have to recreate the elements at different scales or copy them so that they can be used on more than one sheet. Instead, you can duplicate the required views and modify them to suit your needs.

Duplication Types

Duplicate creates a copy of the view that only includes the building elements, as shown in Figure 4–19. Annotation and detailing are not copied into the new view. Building model elements automatically change in all views, but view-specific changes made to the new view are not reflected in the original view.

Original *Duplicate*

Figure 4–19

Duplicate with Detailing creates a copy of the view and includes all annotation and detail elements (such as tags), as shown in Figure 4–20. Any annotation or view-specific elements created in the new view are not reflected in the original view.

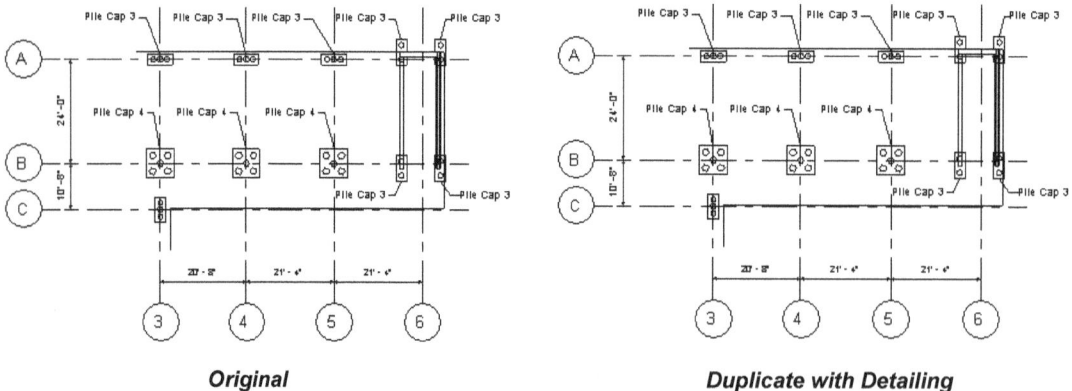

Original *Duplicate with Detailing*

Figure 4–20

Duplicate as a Dependent creates a copy of the view and links it to the original (parent) view, as shown in the Project Browser in Figure 4–21. View-specific changes made to the overall view, such as changing the *Scale*, are also reflected in the dependent (child) views and vice-versa.

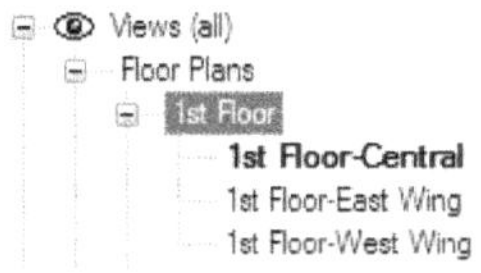

Figure 4–21

- Use dependent views when the building model is so large that you need to split the building onto separate sheets, while ensuring that the views are all same scale.

- If you want to separate a dependent view from the original view, right-click on the dependent view and select **Convert to independent view**.

How To: Create Duplicate Views

1. Open the view you want to duplicate.
2. In the *View* tab>Create panel, expand **Duplicate View** and select the type of duplicate view you want to create, as shown in Figure 4–22.

Most types of views can be duplicated.

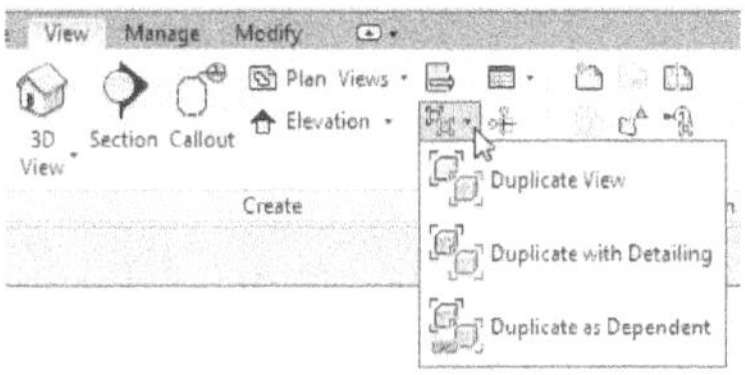

Figure 4–22

- Alternatively, you can right-click on a view in the Project Browser and select the type of duplicate that you want to use, as shown in Figure 4–23.

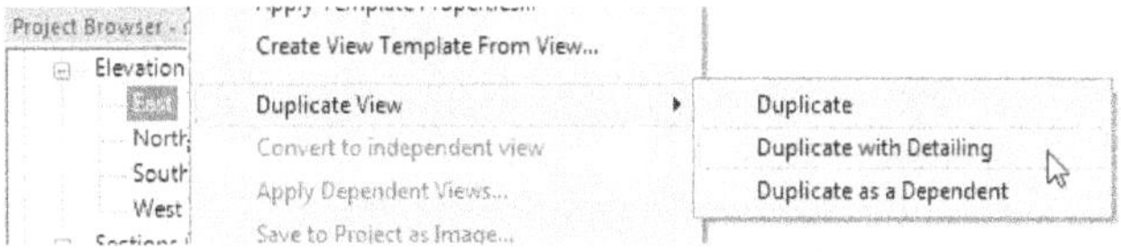

Figure 4–23

- To rename a view, right-click on the new view in the Project Browser and select **Rename**. In the Rename View dialog box, type in the new name, as shown in Figure 4–24.

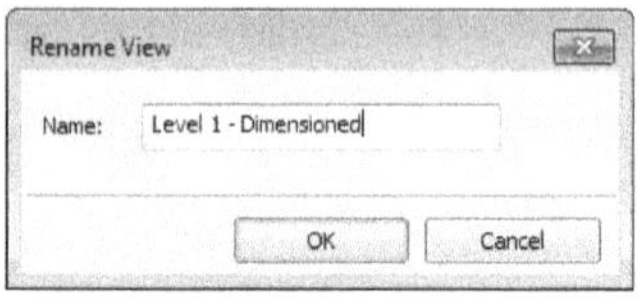

Figure 4–24

- You can also press <F2> to start the **Rename** command.

Practice 4a

Duplicate Views and Set the View Display

Practice Objectives

- Duplicate views.
- Change the view template.

Estimated time for completion: 10 minutes

In this practice you will create an analytical view by duplicating a view and then applying an analytical view template that sets the view display, as shown in Figure 4–25.

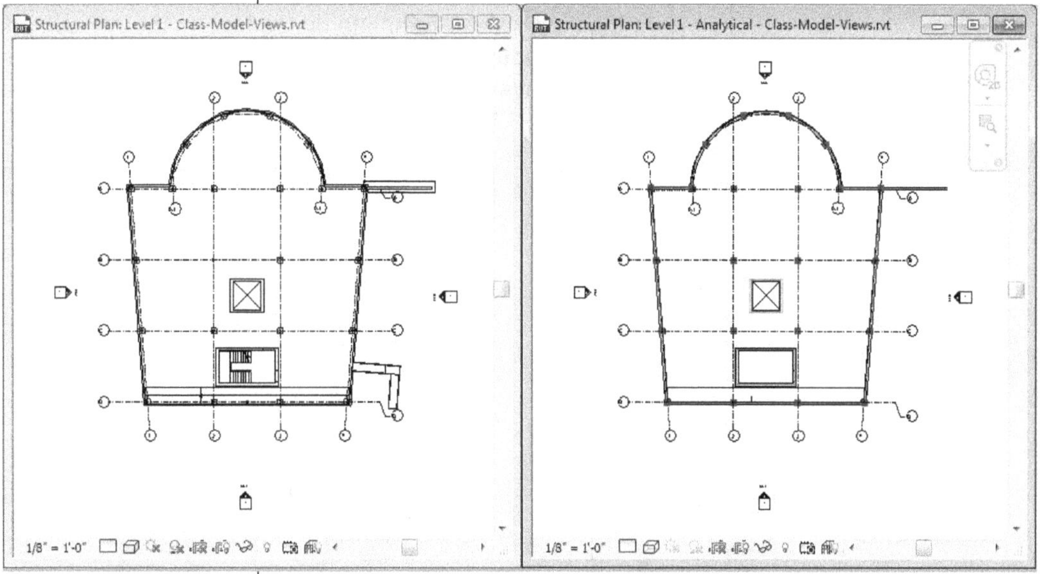

Figure 4–25

Task 1 - Duplicate views.

1. Open **Practice-Model-Views.rvt**.

2. Open the **Structural Plans**: **Level 2** view.

3. Open the **Structural Plans: Level 2 - Analytical** view to see the difference between the two views.

4. Close both of the **Level 2** views.

5. Right-click on **Level 1** and select **Duplicate View> Duplicate**.

6. In the Project Browser, right-click on the copy and rename it **Level 1 - Analytical**.

7. Verify that only the two **Level 1** views are open and tile them (Hint: type **WT**.)

8. Zoom each view so that you can see the entire building. (Hint: type **ZA**.)

9. In the Project Browser, select the new **Level 1 - Analytical** view. Right-click and select **Apply Template Properties...**

10. In the Apply View Template dialog box, in the *Names* area select **Structural Analytical Stick** and click **OK**. The new view displays with analytical indicators, as shown on the right in Figure 4–26.

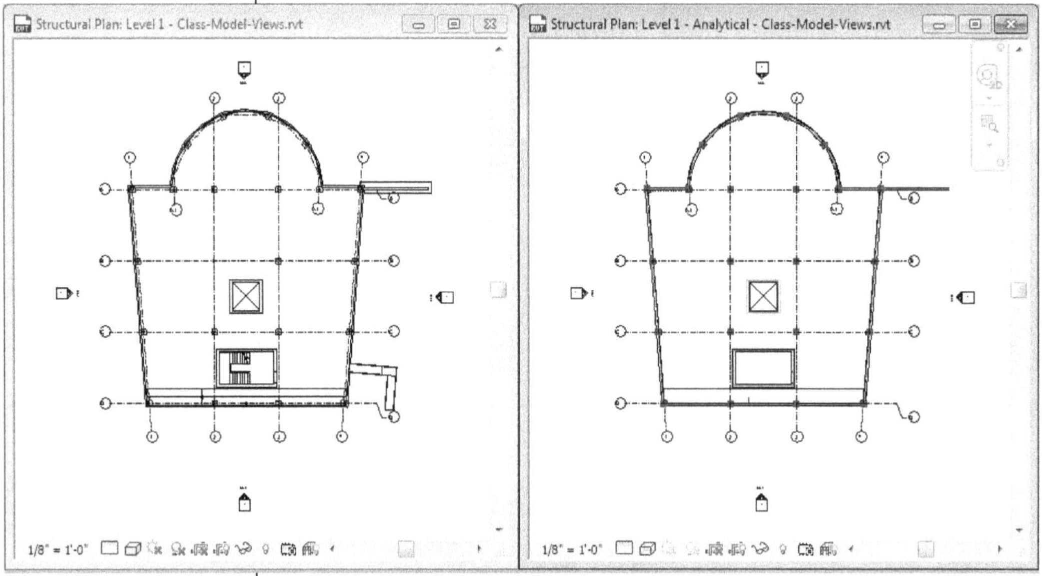

Figure 4–26

11. Close the analytical view and maximize the **Level 1** view window.

12. Save the project.

4.3 Adding Callout Views

Callouts are details of plan, elevation, or section views. When you place a callout in a view, as shown in Figure 4–27, it automatically creates a new view clipped to the boundary of the callout, as shown in Figure 4–28. If you change the size of the callout box in the original view, it automatically updates the callout view and vice-versa. You can create rectangular or sketched callout boundaries.

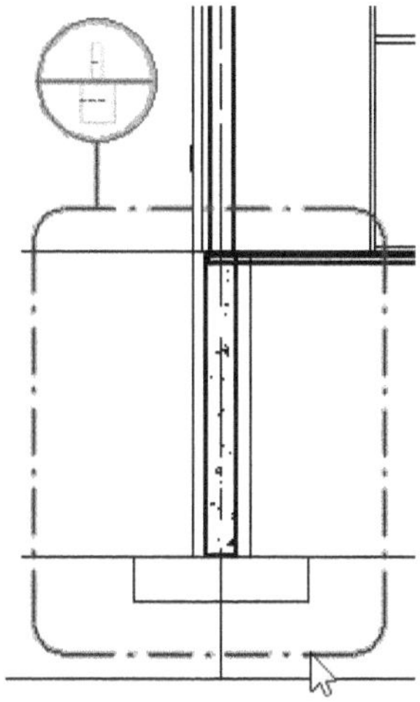

Callout in a view

Figure 4–27

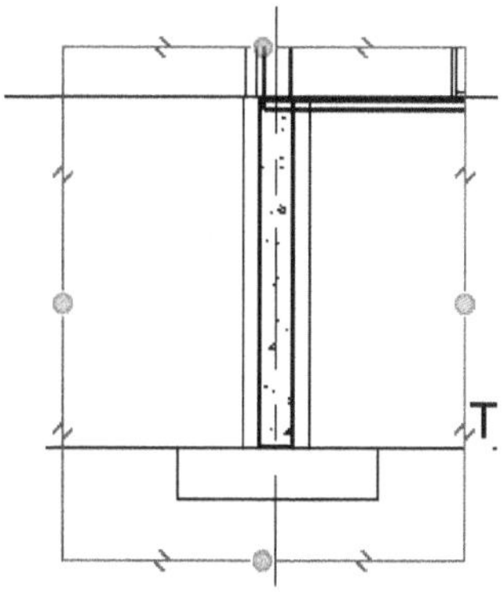

Callout view

Figure 4–28

How To: Create a Rectangular Callout

1. In the *View tab>Create panel,* click ⌀ **(Callout)**.
2. Select points for two opposite corners to define the callout box around the area you want to detail.
3. Select the callout and use the shape handles to modify the location of the bubble and any other edges that might need changing.
4. In the Project Browser, rename the callout.

How To: Create a Sketched Callout

1. In the *View tab>Create panel,* expand ⊙ (Callout), and click ✎ (Sketch).

2. Sketch the shape of the callout using the tools in the *Modify | Edit Profile* tab>Draw panel, as shown in Figure 4–29.

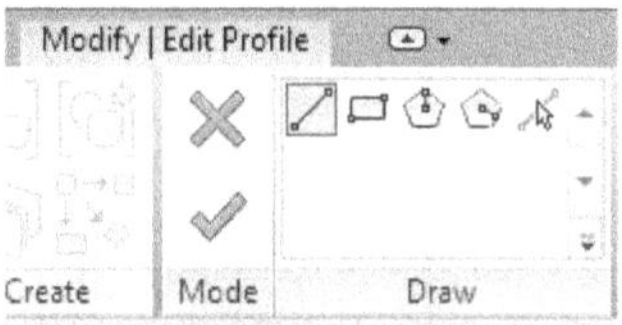

Figure 4–29

3. Click ✔ (Finish) to complete the boundary.
4. Select the callout and use the shape handles to modify the location of the bubble and any other edges that might need to be changed.
5. In the Project Browser, rename the callout

• To open the callout view, double-click on its name in the Project Browser or double-click on the callout bubble (verify that the callout itself is not selected before you double-click on it).

Modifying Callouts

The callout bubble displays numbers when the view is placed on a sheet.

In the original view where the callout is created, you can use the shape handles to modify the callout boundary and bubble location, as shown in Figure 4–30.

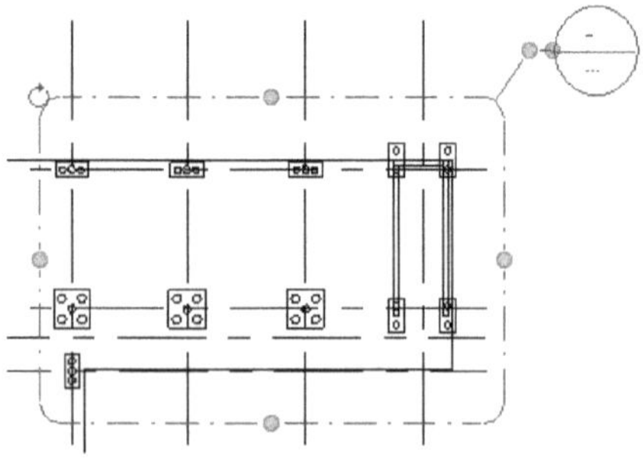

Figure 4–30

• You can rotate the callout box by dragging the ↺ (Rotate) control or by right-clicking on edge of callout and selecting **Rotate**.

In the callout view, you can modify the crop region with shape handles and view breaks, as shown in Figure 4–31.

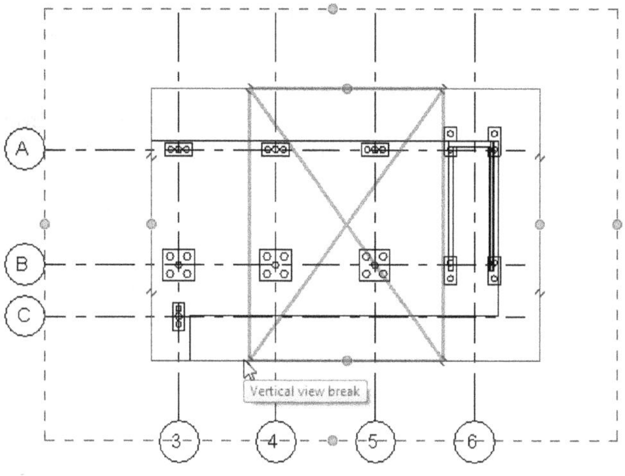

Figure 4–31

- If you want to edit the crop region to reshape the boundary of the view, select the crop region and, in the *Modify | Floor Plan* tab>Mode panel, click (Edit Crop).

- If you want to return a modified crop region to the original rectangular configuration, click (Reset Crop).

- You can also resize the crop region and the annotation crop region using the Crop Region Size dialog box as shown in Figure 4–32. In the *Modify | Floor Plan* tab>Crop panel, click (Size Crop) to open the dialog box.

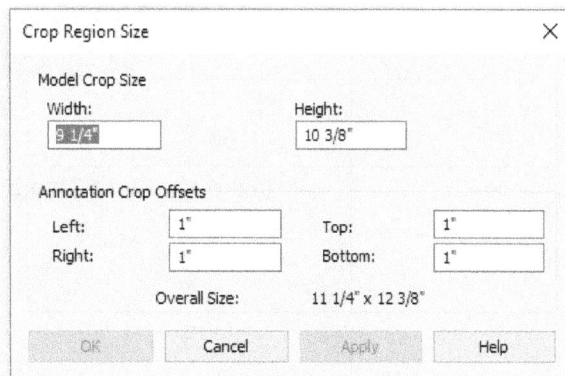

Figure 4–32

Practice 4b

Estimated time for completion: 5minutes

Add Callout Views

Practice Objective

- Create callouts.

In this practice you will create a callout view of the elevator pit walls, as shown in Figure 4–33.

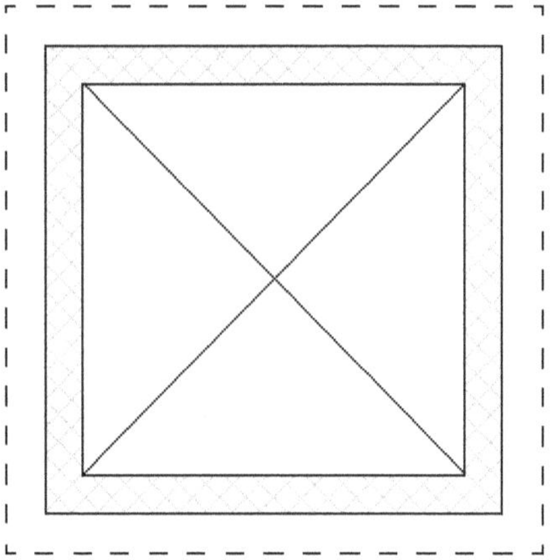

Figure 4–33

Task 1 - Add a callout view.

1. Open **Practice-Model-Callouts.rvt**.

2. Ensure that you are in the **Structural Plans: Level 1** view.

3. In the View Control Bar, check the *Scale* and *Detail Level* of the view, as shown in Figure 4–34.

1/8" = 1'-0"

Figure 4–34

4. In the *View* tab>Create panel, click (Callout).

5. Draw a callout box around the elevator pit walls, as shown in Figure 4–35. Move the callout bubble as required.

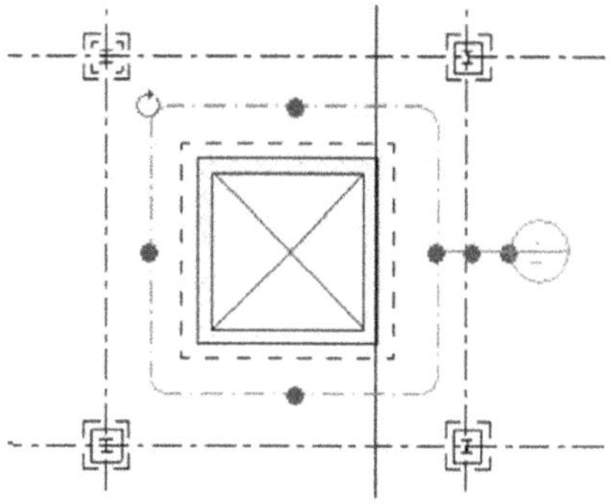

Figure 4–35

6. In the Project Browser, in the *Structural Plans* area, rename *Level 1- Callout* as **Elevator Pit Enlarged Plan**.

7. Open the view to display the callout.

8. In the View Control Bar, set the *Scale* to **1/4"=1'-0"** and the *Detail Level* to **Fine**.

9. In the View Control Bar, click 🗊 (Hide Crop Region).

10. Return to the **Level 1** view.

11. Save the project.

4.4 Creating Elevations and Sections

Elevations and sections are critical elements of construction documents and can assist you as you are working on a model. Any changes made in one of these views (such as the section in Figure 4–36), changes the entire model and any changes made to the project model are also displayed in the elevations and sections.

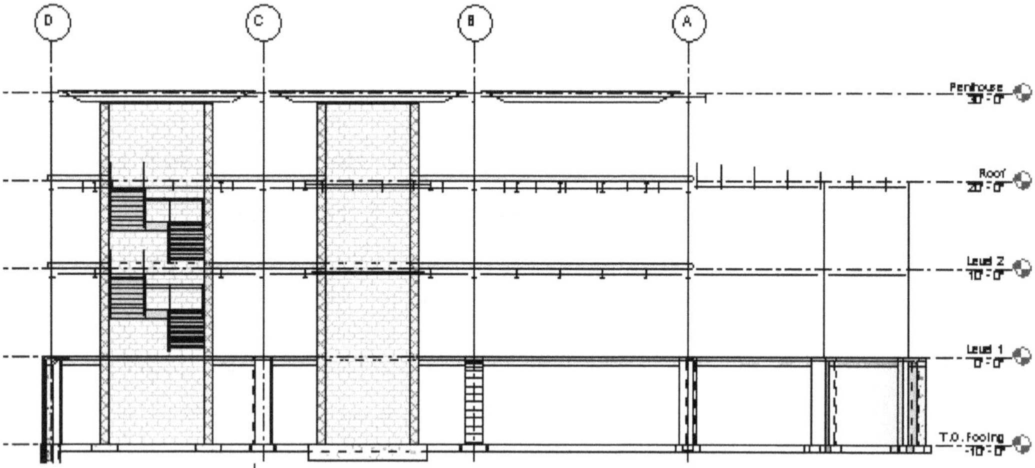

Figure 4–36

- In the Project Browser, elevations are separated by elevation type and sections are separated by section type as shown in Figure 4–37.

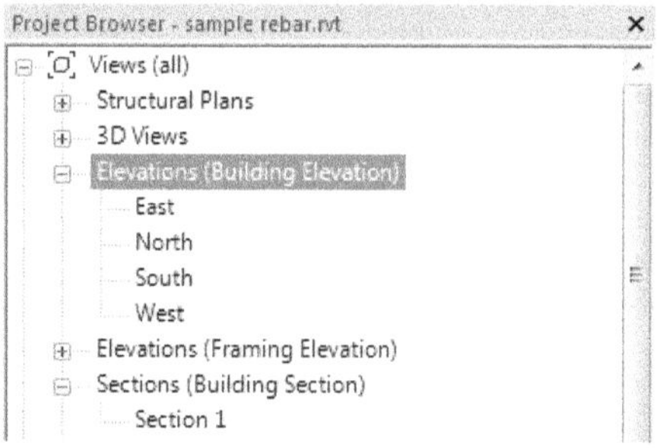

Figure 4–37

- To open an elevation or section view, double-click on the marker arrow or on its name in the Project Browser.

- To give the elevation or section a new name, right-click on it in the Project Browser and select **Rename...**

Elevations

Elevations are *face-on* views of the interiors and exteriors of a building. Four Exterior Elevation views are defined in the default template: **North**, **South**, **East**, and **West**. You can create additional building elevation views at other angles or framing elevation views, as shown in Figure 4–38.

When you add an elevation or section to a sheet, the detail and sheet number are automatically added to the view title.

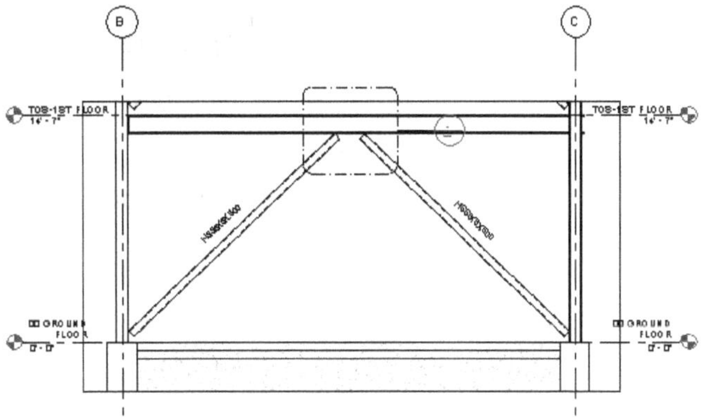

Figure 4–38

- Elevations must be created in plan views.

- A framing elevation is set up to only capture framing elements that are behind other model elements in an elevation of a single area in a building.

  - By default, the framing elevation snaps and sets the extents along the grid lines by using **Attach to Grid** in the Options Bar.

  - The most common use for a framing elevation is to generate braced frames and shear wall elevations.

How To: Create an Elevation

The software remembers the last elevation type used, so you can click the top button if you want to use the same elevation command.

1. In the *View* tab>Create panel, expand 🏠 (Elevation) and click 🏠 (Elevation).

2. In the Type Selector, select the elevation type. Two types come with the templates: **Building Elevation** and **Framing Elevation**.

3. Move the cursor near one of the walls that defines the elevation. The marker follows the angle of the wall.

4. Click to place the marker.

- The length, width, and height of an elevation are defined by the walls and ceiling/floor at which the elevation marker is pointing.

- When creating interior elevations, ensure that the floor or ceiling above is in place before creating the elevation or you will need to modify the elevation crop region so that the elevation markers do not show on all floors.

How To: Create Framing Elevations

1. Open a plan view.

2. In the *View* tab>Create panel, expand ⌂ (Elevation) and click ⟳ (Framing Elevation).

3. Hover the cursor over a grid line to display an elevation element, as shown in Figure 4–39. Click to add the marker.

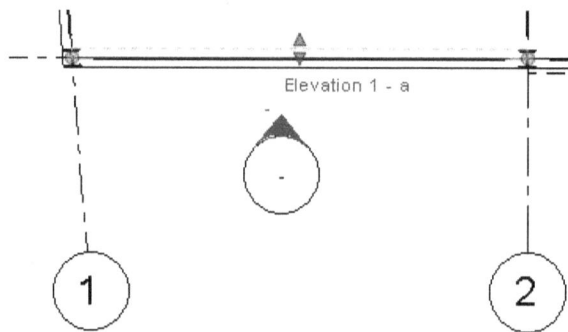

Figure 4–39

4. Click ⟲ (Modify) and select the marker. The extents focus on the bracing bay only. You can use the round segment handles to expand the length of the elevation, as required.

- Framing Elevations are listed in the Project Browser in the *Elevations (Framing Elevation)* area.

Sections

Sections are slices through a model. You can create a section through an entire building, as shown in Figure 4–40, or through one wall for a detail.

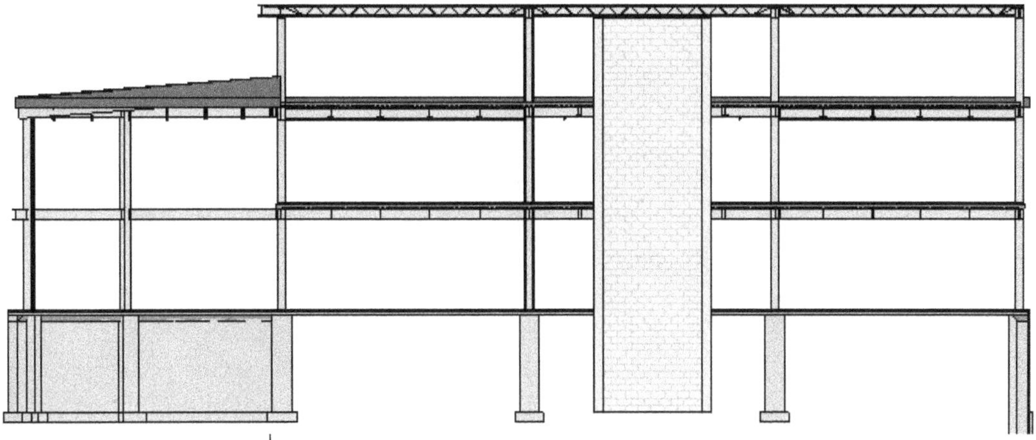

Figure 4–40

- Sections can be created in plan, elevation, and other section views.

How To: Create a Section

1. In the *View* tab>Create panel or in the Quick Access Toolbar, click ♀ (Section).

2. In the Type Selector, select **Section: Building Section** or **Section: Wall Section.** If you want a section in a Drafting view select **Detail View: Detail.**

3. In the view, select a point where you want to locate the bubble and arrowhead.

4. Select the other end point that describes the section.

5. The shape controls display. You can flip the arrow and change the size of the cutting plane, as well as the location of the bubble and flag.

Hint: Selection Box

You can modify a 3D view to display parts of a building, as shown in Figure 4–41.

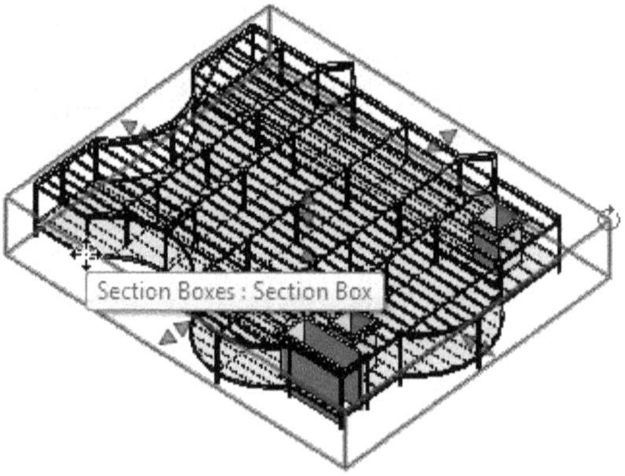

Figure 4–41

1. In a 3D view, select the elements you want to isolate. In the example shown in Figure 4–41, the front wall was selected.

2. In the *Modify* tab>View panel click 🔲 (Selection Box) or type **BX**.

3. The view is limited to a box around the selected item(s).

4. Use the controls of the Section Box to modify the size of the box to show exactly what you want.

• To toggle off a section box and restore the full model, in the view's Properties, in the *Extents* area, clear the check from **Section Box**.

Modifying Elevations and Sections

There are two parts to modifying elevations and sections:

- To modify the view (as shown in Figure 4–42), use the controls to modify the size or create view breaks.

- To modify the markers (as shown in Figure 4–43), use the controls to change the length and depth of elevations and sections. There are other specific type options as well.

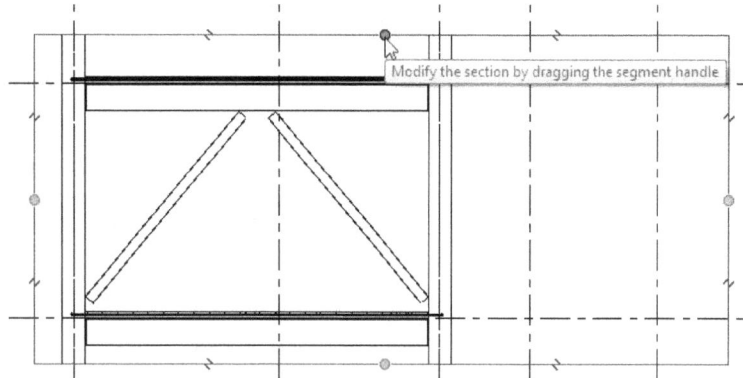

Modify the section by dragging the segment handle

Figure 4–42

Modify the section by dragging the segment handle

Figure 4–43

Modifying Elevation Markers

When you modify elevation markers, you can specify the length and depth of the clip plane, as shown in Figure 4–44.

- Select the arrowhead of the elevation marker (not the circle portion) to display the clip plane.

- Drag the round shape handles to lengthen or shorten the elevation.

- Drag the ▲▼ (Arrow) controls to adjust the depth of the elevation.

To display additional interior elevations from one marker, select the circle portion (not the arrowhead) and place a checkmark in the directions that you want to display, as shown in Figure 4–44.

Figure 4–44

- Use the ↺ (Rotate) control to angle the marker (i.e., for a room with angled walls).

Modifying Section Markers

When you modify section markers, various shape handles and controls enable you to modify a section, as shown in Figure 4–45.

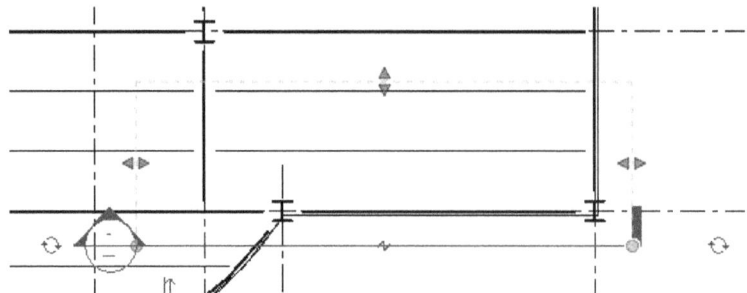

Figure 4–45

- Drag the ▲▼ (Arrow) controls to change the length and depth of the cut plane.

- Drag the circular controls at either end of the section line to change the location of the arrow or flag without changing the cut boundary.

- Click ⇆ (Flip) to change the direction of the arrowhead, which also flips the entire section.

- Click ↻ (Cycle Section Head/Tail) to switch between an arrowhead, flag, or nothing on each end of the section.

- Click ⇜ (Gaps in Segments) to create an opening in section lines, as shown in Figure 4–46. Select it again to restore the full section cut.

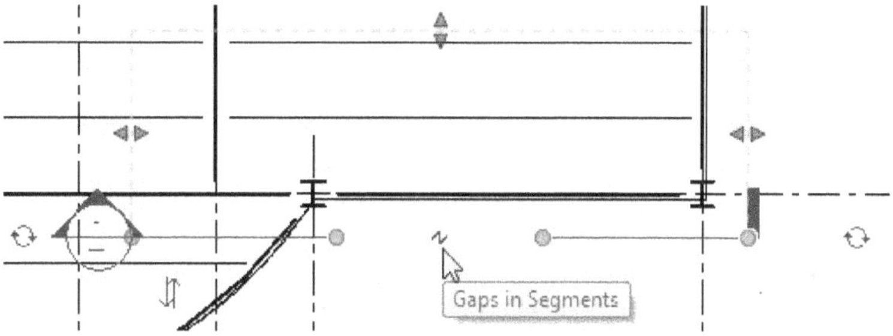

Figure 4–46

How To: Add a Jog to a Section Line

1. Select the section line you want to modify.

2. In the *Modify | Views* tab> Section panel, click ⬚ (Split Segment).

3. Select the point along the line where you want to create the split, as shown in Figure 4–47.

4. Specify the location of the split line, as shown in Figure 4–48.

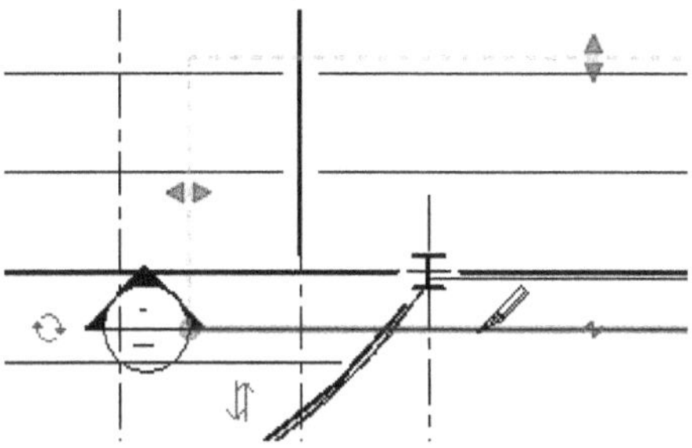

Figure 4–47

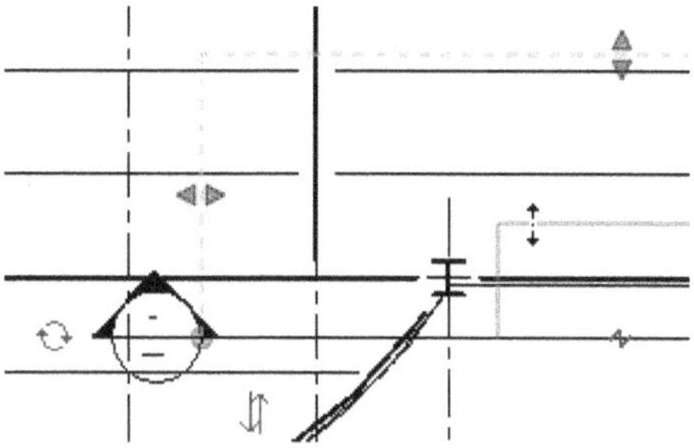

Figure 4–48

- If you need to adjust the location of any segment on the section line, modify it and drag the shape handles along each segment of the line, as shown in Figure 4–49.

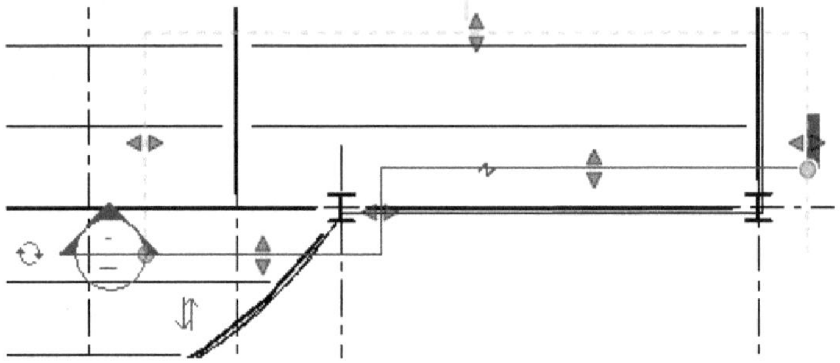

Figure 4–49

To bring a split section line back into place, use a shape handle to drag the jogged line until it is at the same level with the rest of the line.

Hint: Using Thin Lines

The software automatically applies line weights to views, as shown for a section on the left in Figure 4–50. If a line weight seems heavy or obscures your work on the elements, toggle off the line weights. In the Quick Access Toolbar or in the *View* tab>Graphics panel, click ▦ (Thin Lines) or type **TL**. The lines display with the same weight, as shown on the right in Figure 4–50.

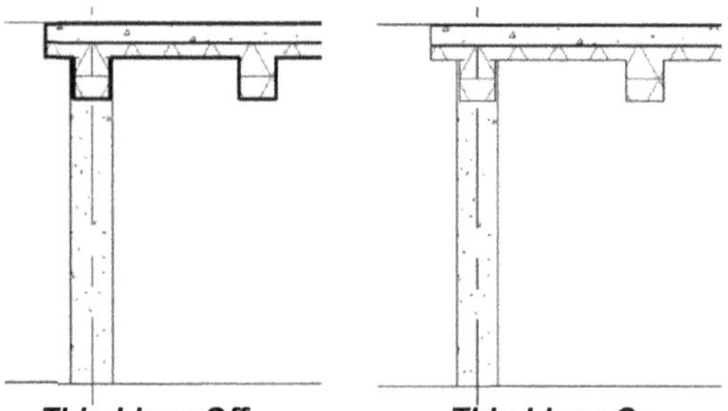

Thin Lines Off   *Thin Lines On*

Figure 4–50

- The Thin Line setting is remembered until you change it, even if you shut down and restart the software.

Practice 4c

Create Elevations and Sections

Practice Objectives

Estimated time for completion: 15 minutes

- Add building sections and wall sections.
- Add a framing elevation

In this practice you will add a Building Section and a Wall Section to an existing project. You will also add a Framing Elevation as shown in Figure 4–51.

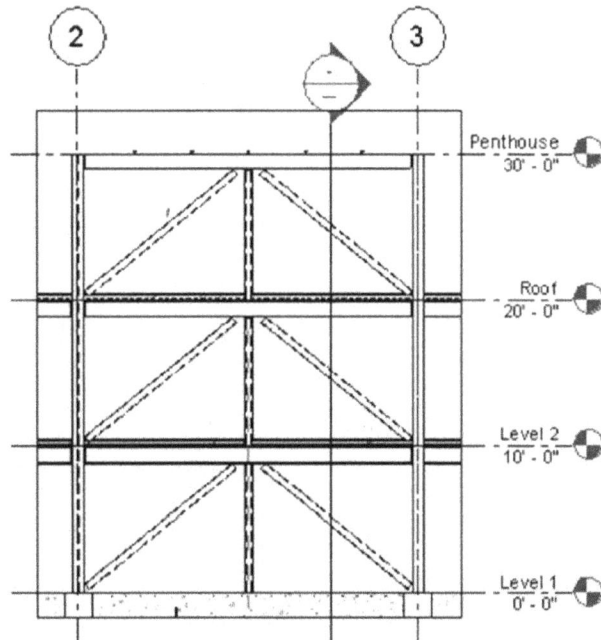

Figure 4–51

Task 1 - Create sections.

1. Open **Practice-Model-Sections.rvt**.

2. In the Project Browser, open the **Structural Plans: Level 1** view.

3. In the *View* tab>Create panel or in the Quick Access Toolbar, click ❯ (Section).

4. Place a vertical section offset slightly from the middle. Change the width of the section using the controls as shown in Figure 4–52.

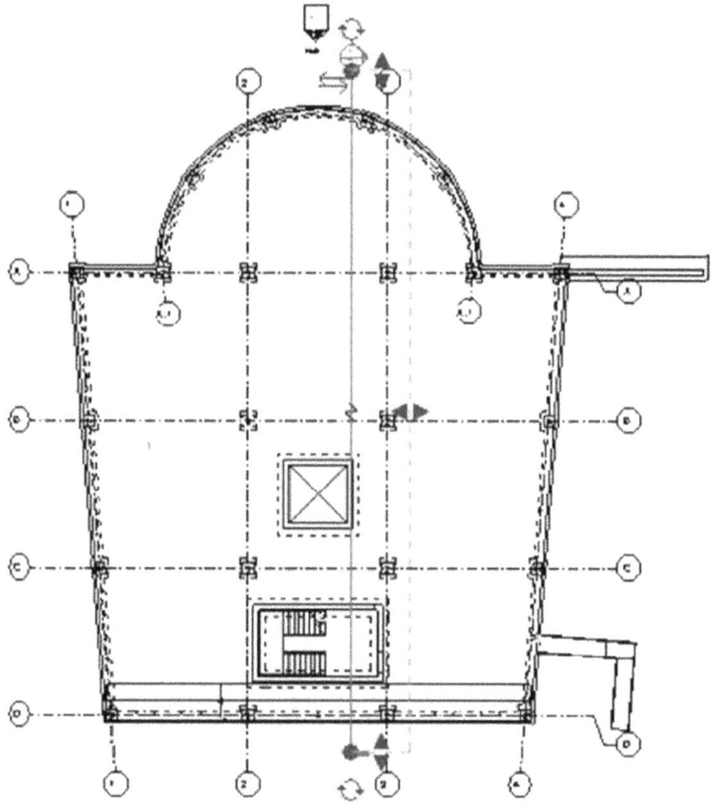

Figure 4–52

5. In the Project Browser, expand *Sections (Building Section)*. Right-click on the new section and rename it **Building Section**, as shown in Figure 4–53.

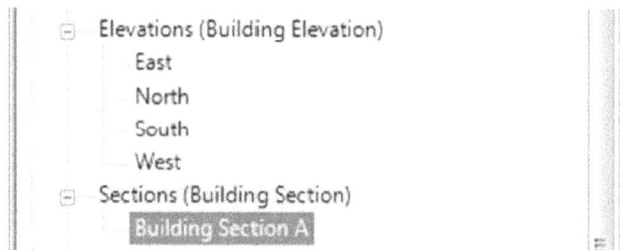

Figure 4–53

6. Open the new section by double-clicking on its name in the Project Browser. The entire Building displays as shown in Figure 4–54. Note that the view varies based on exactly where you placed the section.

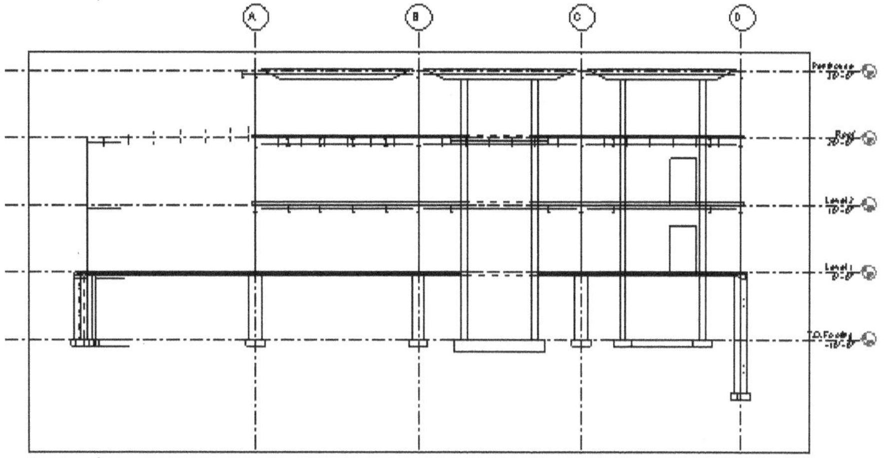

Figure 4–54

7. Select the crop region and use the controls to shorten the section so that the curved walls to the left do not display, as shown in Figure 4–55.

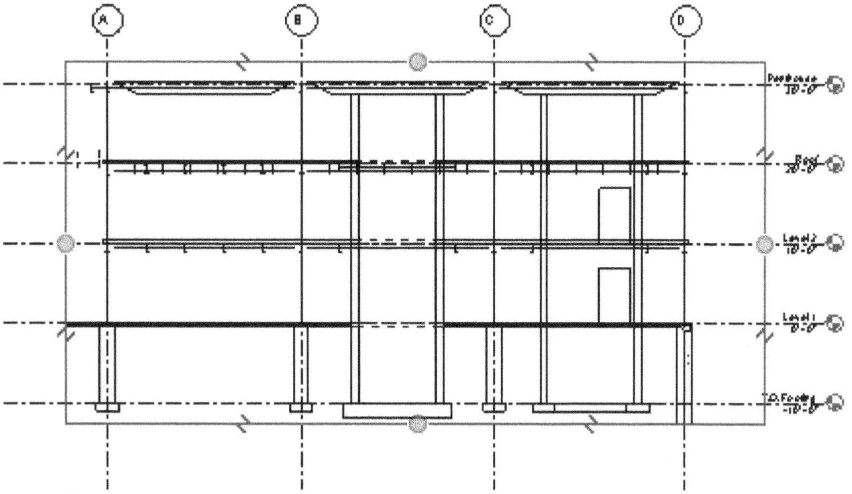

Figure 4–55

8. Return to the Level 1 view. The boundary of the section has changed as shown on the left in Figure 4–56. Use the circular control to move the section head down as shown on the right in Figure 4–56.

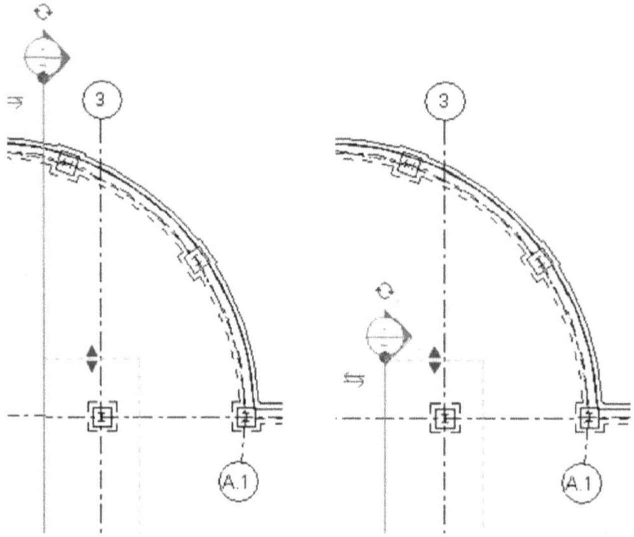

Boundary changed   **Section head moved**

Figure 4–56

9. Start the **Section** command again.

10. In the Type Selector, select **Section: Wall Section**.

11. Draw a short section through the wall as shown in Figure 4–57. Modify the section boundary so that it does not touch anything other than the wall.

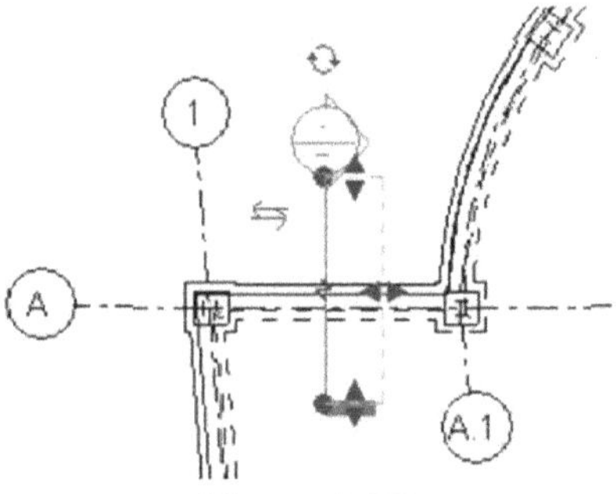

Figure 4–57

12. In the Project Browser, expand *Sections (Wall Section)* and rename the section as **Foundation Section**.

13. Open the new section view.

14. In the View Control Bar, change the *Scale* to **1/2"=1'-0"**.

15. By default, the section expands the entire height of the project. Use the controls to resize the section so that only the foundation displays as shown in Figure 4–58.

Figure 4–58

Task 2 - Add a framing elevation.

1. Open the **Structural Plans: Level 1** view.

2. Zoom in on the south wall of the building between columns 2 and 3.

3. In the *View* tab>Create panel, expand 🔺 (Elevation) and click ⌖ (Framing Elevation).

4. Hover the cursor over Grid D as shown in Figure 4–59. Pick a point when the elevation marker is on the outside of the building.

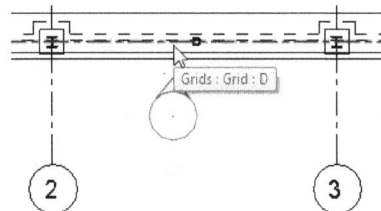

Figure 4–59

5. In the Project Browser, in the *Elevations (Framing Elevation)* area, rename the view as **Typical Bracing**.

6. Click on the pointer of the elevation marker. Expand the length of the elevation so that it is just on each side of the columns as shown in Figure 4–60.

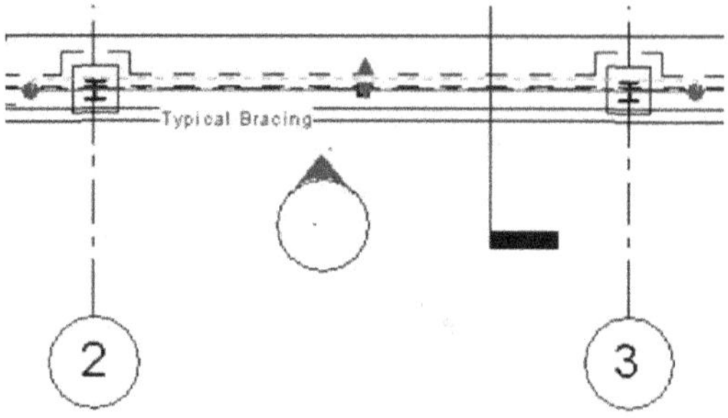

Figure 4–60

7. Open the framing elevation.

8. In the View Control Bar, change the *Detail Level* to ▧ (Fine).

9. Modify the size of the elevation to only display the bracing as shown in Figure 4–61.

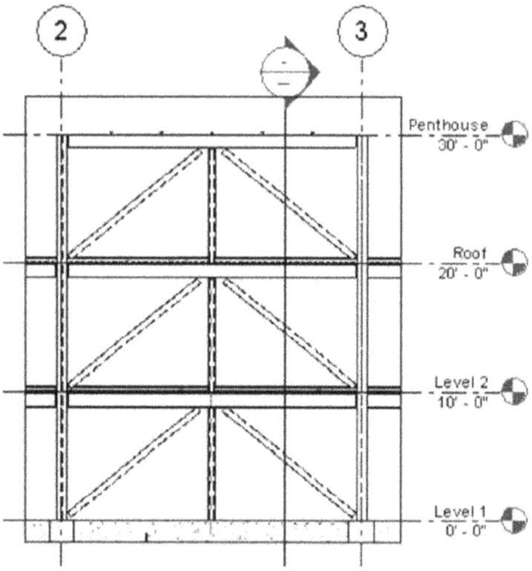

Figure 4–61

10. Return to the **Structural Plans: Level 1** view.

11. Zoom out to display the entire building.

12. In the Quick Access Toolbar, click ▭ (Close Hidden Windows).

13. Save the project.

Chapter Review Questions

1. Which of the following commands shown in Figure 4–62, creates a view that results in an independent view displaying the same model geometry and containing a copy of the annotation?

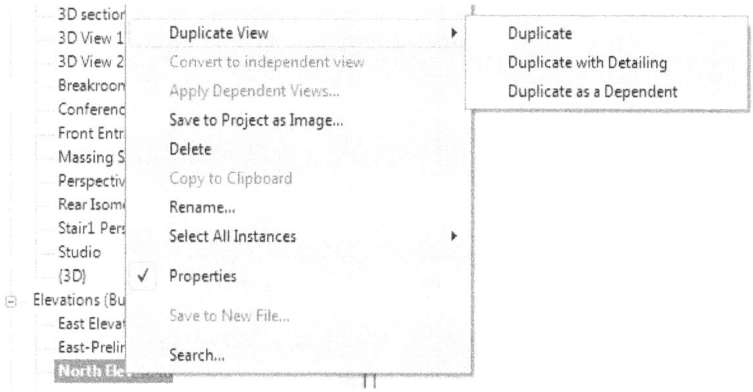

Figure 4–62

   a. Duplicate

   b. Duplicate with Detailing

   c. Duplicate as a Dependent

2. Which of the following is true about the Visibility Graphic Overrides dialog box?

   a. Changes made in the dialog box only affect the current view.

   b. It can only be used to toggle categories on and off.

   c. It can be used to toggle individual elements on and off.

   d. It can be used to change the color of individual elements.

3. The purpose of callouts is to create a...

   a. Boundary around part of the model that needs revising, similar to a revision cloud.

   b. View of part of the model for export to the AutoCAD® software for further detailing.

   c. View of part of the model that is linked to the main view from which it is taken.

   d. 2D view of part of the model.

4. You placed dimensions in a view and some of them display and others do not, as shown in Figure 4–63. You were expecting the view to display as shown in Figure 4–64. To display the missing dimensions, you need to modify the...

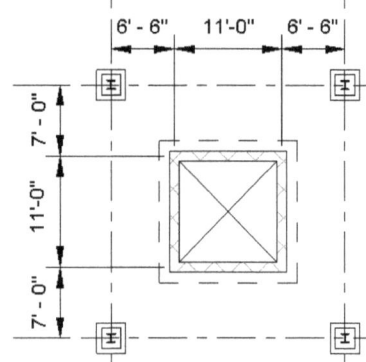

Figure 4–63   Figure 4–64

a. Dimension Settings

b. Dimension Type

c. Visibility Graphic Overrides

d. Annotation Crop Region

5. How do you create a jog in a building section, such as that shown in Figure 4–65?

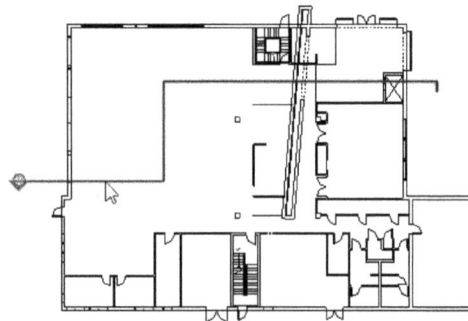

Figure 4–65

a. Use the **Split Element** tool in the *Modify* tab>Modify panel.

b. Select the building section and then click **Split Segment** in the contextual tab.

c. Select the building section and click the blue control in the middle of the section line.

d. Draw two separate sections, and use the **Section Jog** tool to combine them into a jogged section.

Command Summary

Button	Command	Location
Views		
	Elevation	• **Ribbon:** *View* tab>Create panel> expand Elevation
	Callout: Rectangle	• **Ribbon:** *View* tab>Create panel> expand Callout
	Callout: Sketch	• **Ribbon:** *View* tab>Create panel> expand Callout
	Duplicate	• **Ribbon:** *View* tab>Create panel> expand Duplicate View • **Right-click:** (*on a view in the Project Browser*) expand Duplicate View
	Duplicate as Dependent	• **Ribbon:** *View* tab>Create panel> expand Duplicate View • **Right-click:** (*on a view in the Project Browser*) expand Duplicate View
	Duplicate with Detailing	• **Ribbon:** *View* tab>Create panel> expand Duplicate View • **Right-click:** (*on a view in the Project Browser*) Duplicate View
	Framing Elevation	• **Ribbon:** *View* tab>Create panel> expand Elevation
	Plan Region	• **Ribbon:** *View* tab>Create panel> expand Plan Views
	Section	• **Ribbon:** *View* tab>Create panel • **Quick Access Toolbar**
	Split Segment	• **Ribbon:** (*when the elevation or section marker is selected*) *Modify	Views* tab>Section panel
Crop Views		
	Crop View	• **View Control Bar** • **View Properties:** Crop View (*check*)
	Do Not Crop View	• **View Control Bar** • **View Properties:** Crop View (*clear*)
	Edit Crop	• **Ribbon:** (*when the crop region of a callout, elevation, or section view is selected*) *Modify	Views* tab>Mode panel
	Hide Crop Region	• **View Control Bar** • **View Properties:** Crop Region Visible (*clear*)
	Reset Crop	• **Ribbon:** (*when the crop region of a callout, elevation or section view is selected*) *Modify	Views* tab>Mode panel

	Show Crop Region	• **View Control Bar** • **View Properties:** Crop Region Visible (*check*)
	Size Crop	• **Ribbon:** (*when the crop region of a callout, elevation or section view is selected*) Modify | Views tab>Mode panel

View Display

	Hide in View	• **Ribbon:** Modify tab>View Graphics panel>Hide>Elements *or* By Category • **Right-click:** (*when an element is selected*) Hide in View>Elements *or* Category
	Override Graphics in View	• **Ribbon:** Modify tab>View Graphics panel>Hide>Elements *or* By Category • **Right-click:** (*when an element is selected*) Override Graphics in View>By Element *or* By Category • **Shortcut:** (*category only*) VV or VG
	Reveal Hidden Elements	• **View Control Bar**
	Temporary Hide/Isolate	• **View Control Bar**
	Temporary View Properties	• **View Control Bar**

Structural Grids and Columns

Structural grids describe the pattern and location for structural columns. Once you have placed columns, you are able to build the rest of the structural design.

Learning Objectives in this Chapter

- Add structural grids to provide the location for structural columns.
- Add structural columns to the project as the first design consideration.

5.1 Adding Structural Grids

The structural grid indicates how to space the bays of a building and where to place columns, as shown in Figure 5–1. Any changes to the grid influences the elements that are referenced to them.

Figure 5–1

- Each line or arc in a grid is a separate entity and can be placed, moved, and modified individually.

- Grid and Level lines are very similar in how they are drawn and modified.

How To: Create a Structural Grid

1. In the *Structure* tab>Datum panel, click ⌗ (Grid) or type **GR**.
2. In the Type Selector, select the Grid type which controls the size of the bubble and the linestyle.
3. In the *Modify | Place Grid* tab>Draw panel (shown in Figure 5–2) select the method you want to use.

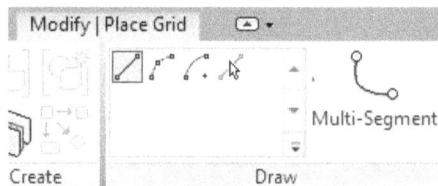

Figure 5–2

4. In the Options Bar, set the *Offset* if required.
5. Continue adding grid lines as required.

- Grids can be drawn at any angle, but you should ensure that all parallel grids are drawn in the same direction (i.e., from left to right, or from bottom to top).

- When using the Multi-Segment tool (shown in Figure 5–3), sketch the line and click ✔ (Finish Edit Mode) to complete it.

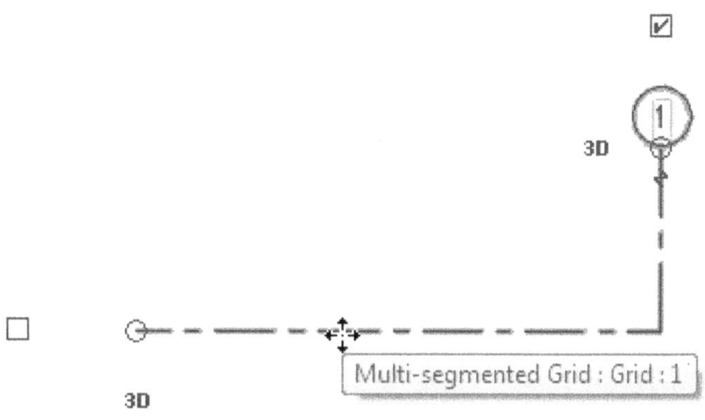

Figure 5–3

Modifying Grid Lines

Grid lines are very similar to Level lines. You can modify grid lines using controls, alignments, and temporary dimensions (as shown in Figure 5–4), or from the Properties palette and Type Selector.

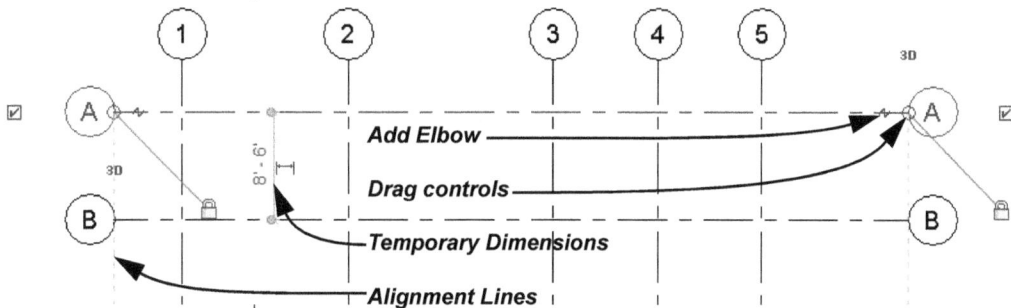

Figure 5–4

- To modify a grid number, double-click on the number in the bubble and type the new number. Grid numbers can be numbers, letters, or a combination of the two.

- Grid numbers increment automatically.

Hint: Propagating Datum Extents

If column grids do not display in a view, this might be due to adding a level after the grids were added. To display the grids in plan views, select the grids in a view in which they are displayed. In the *Modify | Grids* tab>Datum panel, click

(Propagate Extents). In the Propagate datum extents dialog box (shown in Figure 5–5), select the views to project the grid lines to.

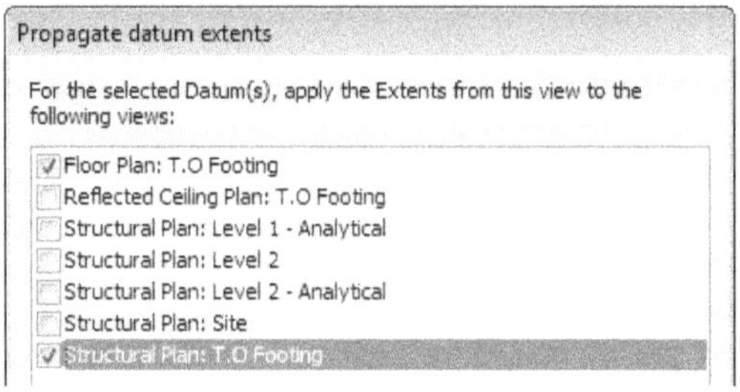

Propagate datum extents

For the selected Datum(s), apply the Extents from this view to the
following views:

☑ Floor Plan: T.O Footing
☐ Reflected Ceiling Plan: T.O Footing
☐ Structural Plan: Level 1 - Analytical
☐ Structural Plan: Level 2
☐ Structural Plan: Level 2 - Analytical
☐ Structural Plan: Site
☑ Structural Plan: T.O Footing

Figure 5–5

• This also works for levels.

• (Propagate Extents) is particularly useful to make Grids display the same in all views.

Practice 5a

Add Structural Grids

Practice Objectives

Estimated time for completion: 10 minutes

- Copy and monitor grid lines from a linked architectural model.
- Add additional structural grid lines.

In this practice you will copy and monitor grid lines from a linked architectural model. You will then add additional grid lines where curved walls need extra support, as shown in Figure 5–6.

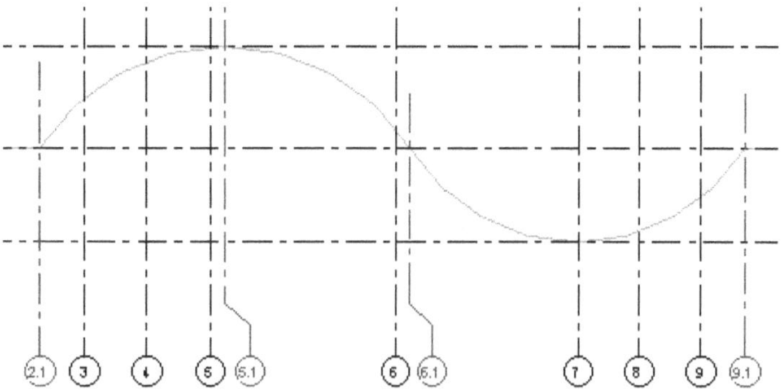

Figure 5–6

Task 1 - Copy and monitor grids.

1. Open the project **Syracuse-Suites-Grids.rvt**.

2. Open the **Structural Plans: 00 GROUND FLOOR** view.

3. Start the **Copy/Monitor** command and select the linked model.

4. In the *Copy/Monitor* tab>Tools panel, click (Copy).

5. In the Options Bar, select **Multiple**.

*In this case only the grids are available to copy into the project. If there were other elements, you could use the **Filter** command to limit the selection set.*

6. Select all of the grids. You can select them one by one (hold <Ctrl> as you do so) or use pick and drag from right to left to form a crossing window touching each one.

7. In the Options Bar, click **Finish**.

8. Close the Warning.

9. (Monitor) displays at each grid line, as shown in Figure 5–7.

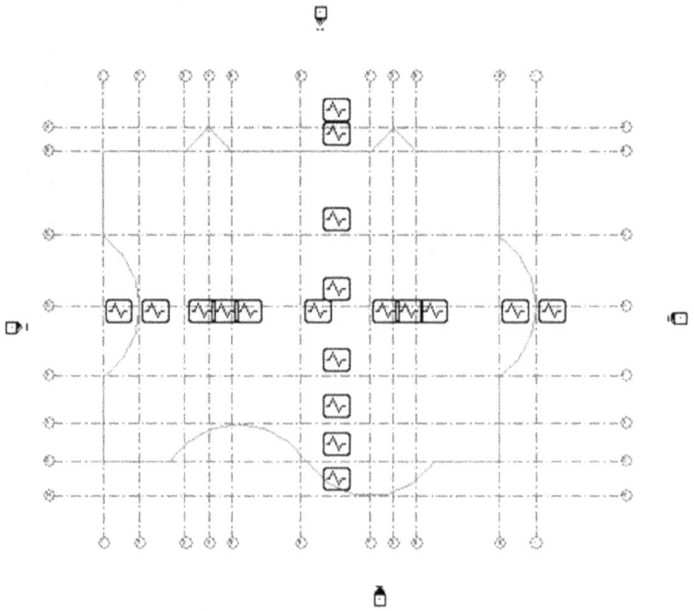

Figure 5–7

10. In the *Copy/Monitor* tab>Copy/Monitor panel, click

    (Finish).

11. Navigate through the different floor plans. The Grids have populated throughout each floor plan, as shown in Figure 5–8.

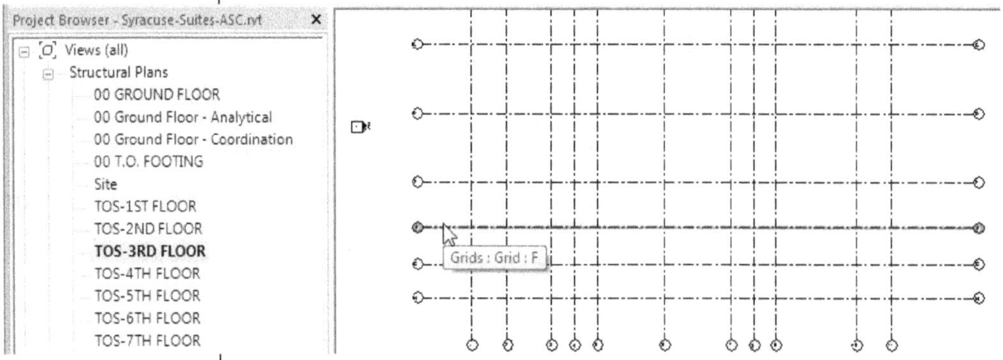

Figure 5–8

12. Open the **Structural Plans: 00 GROUND FLOOR** view.

13. Save the project.

Task 2 - Add grid lines at arc points.

1. In the **Structural Plans: 00 GROUND FLOOR** view, zoom in on the south side of the floor plan, where the green outline shows two curves (curtain wall locations). Additional grids need to be placed at the midpoints and end points of the arcs to support the curtain wall.

2. In the *Structure* tab>Datum panel, click ⌗ (Grid). In the *Modify | Place Grid* tab>Draw panel, verify that ✎ (Line) is selected.

3. Select the end point of the arc on **Grid G** between Grid 2 and Grid 3 and draw the vertical grid line, as shown in Figure 5–9.

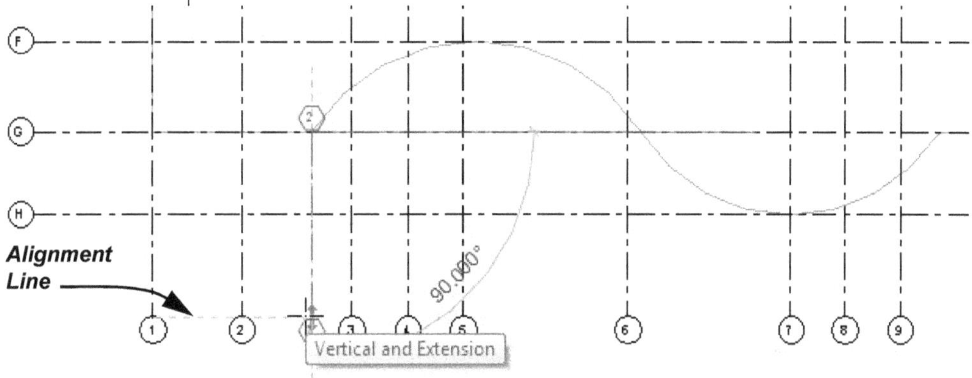

Figure 5–9

- Draw the grid line until the blue alignment line displays, as shown above in Figure 5–9. This ensures the new bubbles stay locked in line with the other bubbles.

4. Once the grid is in place, rename it to **2.1**. At the top end of the grid clear the check above the bubble to toggle it off. Then stretch the grid line up, as shown in Figure 5–10.

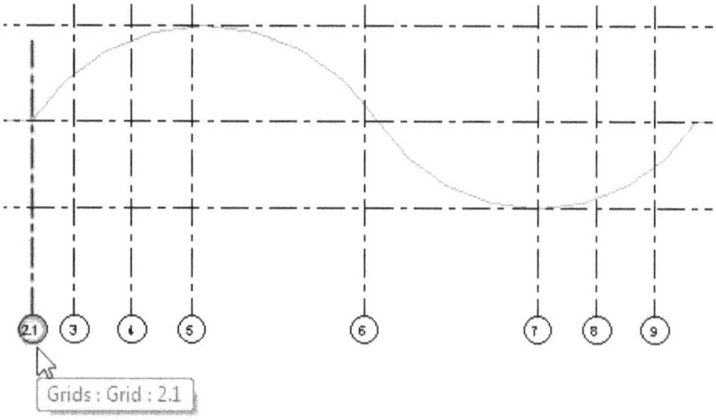

Figure 5–10

5. Draw another vertical grid line at the midpoint of the same arc, as shown in Figure 5–11. Rename the grid to **5.1**. Use (Add Elbow) to modify the bubble location.

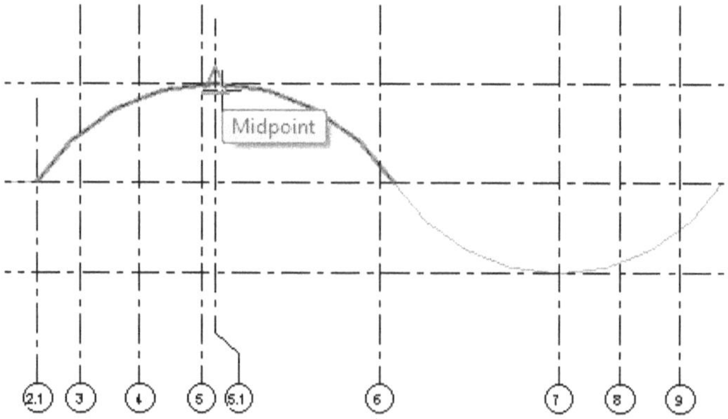

Figure 5–11

6. Add grid lines to the end points of the second arc, as shown in Figure 5–12. When you are finished, there should be four new grids: **2.1**, **5.1**, **6.1**, and **9.1**.

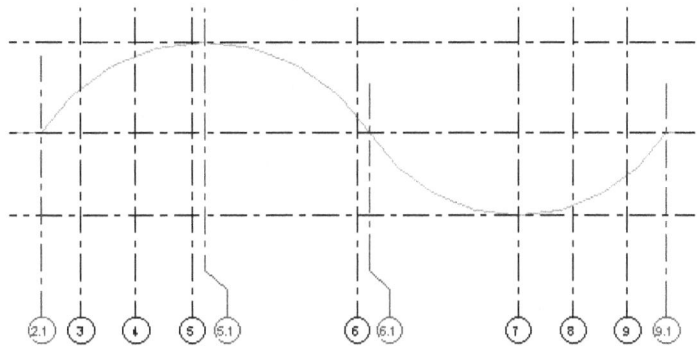

Figure 5–12

7. Clear the bubble and adjust the top ends of the grid lines to align them.

8. Zoom out to see the full layout.

9. Save the model.

5.2 Placing Structural Columns

Adding columns to a structural model is a straightforward process. The Autodesk® Revit® software has a deep library containing standard steel structural shapes, as well as concrete structural shapes as shown in Figure 5–13. The software also keeps analytical data stored for each column that can be read by analytical software programs (such as Robot Structural Analysis, ETABS, RISA, and RAM).

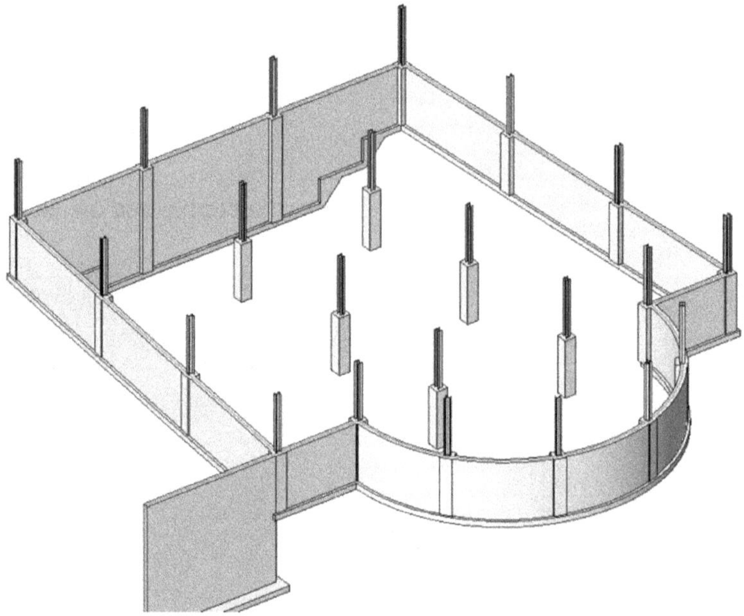

Structural columns can be copied and monitored from linked files.

Figure 5–13

How To: Place Structural Columns

1. In the *Structure* tab>Structure panel, click ⬚ (Column).
2. In the Type Selector, select a column type.

3. In the Options Bar (as shown in Figure 5–14), set the following information:

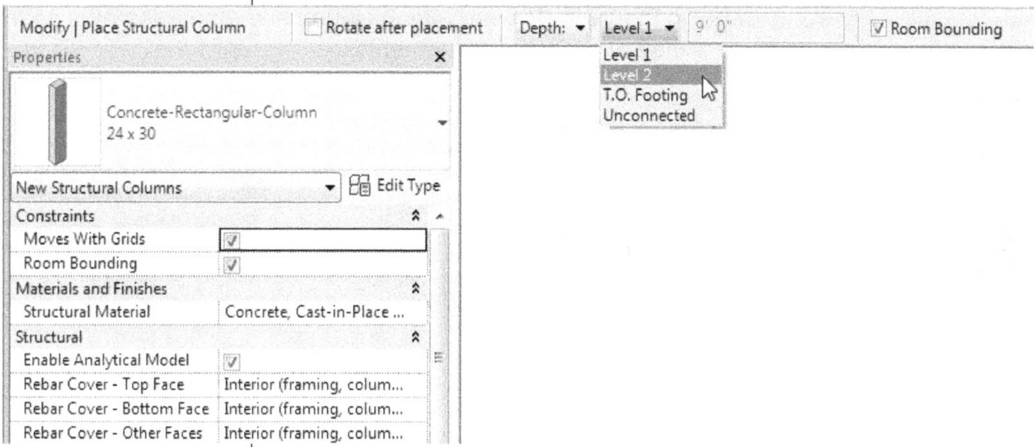

Figure 5–14

- *Depth* or *Height*: Architects typically draw columns from the bottom up.
- *Level/Unconnected:* Specify a level, or click **Unconnected**. If you select **Unconnected**, assign a distance.
- *Rotate after placement*: Enables you to place the column and then graphically select a rotation angle.
- *Room bounding*: (Concrete only) The column can be used to define the boundary of a room for area and volume calculations.

4. To place individual columns, click at the required location. Columns automatically snap to grid lines and walls.

To place multiple columns, in the *Modify | Place Structural Column* tab>Multiple panel, click:

- (At Columns) to place a structural column at the center of selected architectural columns. Select the architectural columns where you want the columns to be placed and then click (Finish.)

- (At Grids) to place structural columns at intersecting grids. Select the grid lines where you want the columns to be placed and then click (Finish.)

Use (Filter) to help you select only the architectural columns or grids for these options.

Slanted columns are covered later in this student guide.

Modifying Columns

When you select a column you can change its type by selecting a different one in the Type Selector. You can also change a variety of constraints and other options in Properties (as shown in Figure 5–15) and attach columns to other elements so that they move with the elements.

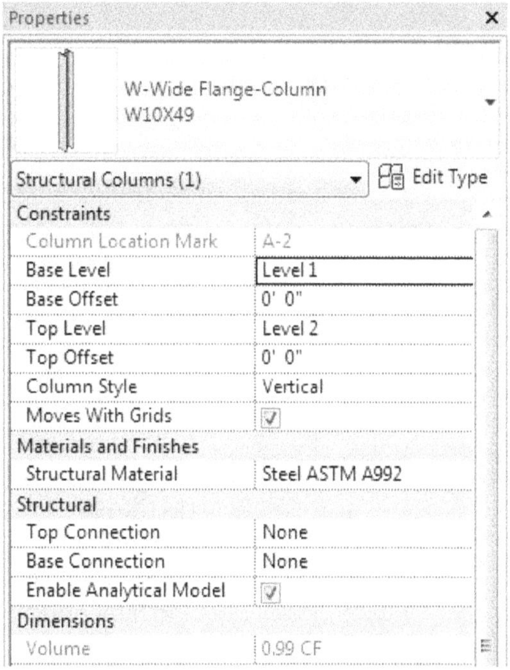

The location of columns on grids are included in the properties of the column. If the column is not on a grid it displays the distance from the closest grid intersection.

Figure 5–15

* Verify that **Moves with Grids** is toggled on. This ensures that when a grid line is moved, the columns connected to it move as well. This toggle is normally on by default, but it is good practice to check its status.

* When changing the top and base levels and offsets, you should make these changes in a logical order, as having a zero or negative height column results in an error message.

How To: Attach Columns to other elements

Attaching columns to other objects associates or constrains certain parameters, such as height.

1. Select a column or group of columns.
2. In the *Modify | Structural Columns* tab>Modify Column panel, click ⬚ (Attach Top/Base).

3. In the Options Bar, set *Attach Column* to **Top** or **Base** and set the *Attachment Style* (as shown in Figure 5–16), *Attachment Justification*, and *Offset from Attachment*.

Attach Column: ⦿ Top ◯ Base   Attachment Style: Cut Column ⌄   Attachment Justification: Minimum Intersection ▾   Offset From Attachment: 0' 0"
                            Cut Column
                            Cut Target
                            Do Not Cut

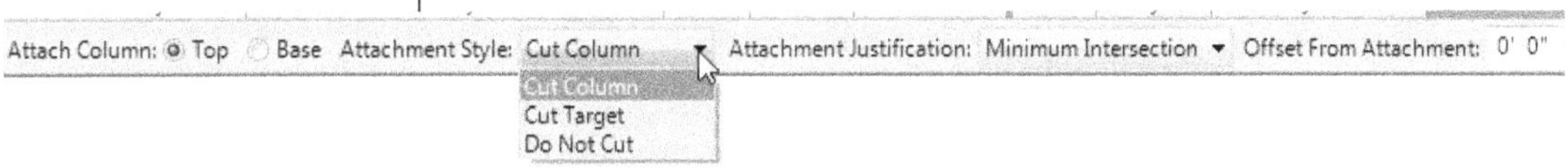

Figure 5–16

4. Select the floor, roof, footing, beam, reference plane, or level to which you want the column(s) attached.

   • If you what to detach a column that has been attached,

     select the column and click ⊡↓ (Detach Top/Base).

• You can use the **Attach Top/Base** command to attach structural columns to isolated foundations and footings. If the foundation height changes, the length of the column changes with it.

• When you are placing columns and the required structural column family or type is not listed, you can load additional families and add family types (sizes) from the library.

How To: Load Structural Column Types

1. Start the **Structural Column** command.
2. In the *Modify | Place Structural Column* tab>Mode panel, click

   ⬇ (Load Family).
3. In the Load Family dialog box, open the folder that contains the column families. In the default library, this is the *Structural Columns* folder as shown in Figure 5–17. Select the column material folder and then select the individual column type you want to use.

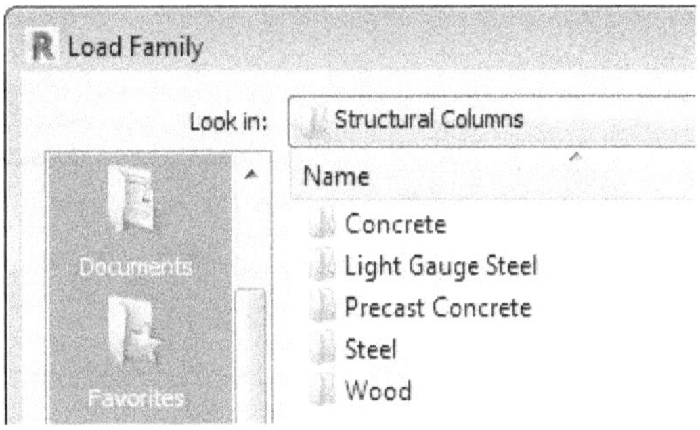

Figure 5–17

Hold <Ctrl> to select multiple families.

4. Navigate to the column family type that you want to use and click **Open**.
5. In the Specify Types dialog box, as shown in Figure 5–18, select a column size in the list and click **Open**.

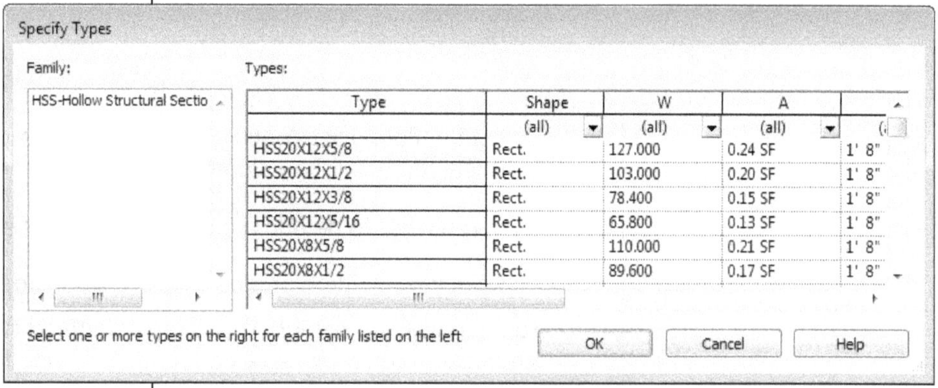

Type	Shape	W	A	
(all)	(all)	(all)	(all)	(;
HSS20X12X5/8	Rect.	127.000	0.24 SF	1' 8"
HSS20X12X1/2	Rect.	103.000	0.20 SF	1' 8"
HSS20X12X3/8	Rect.	78.400	0.15 SF	1' 8"
HSS20X12X5/16	Rect.	65.800	0.13 SF	1' 8"
HSS20X8X5/8	Rect.	110.000	0.21 SF	1' 8"
HSS20X8X1/2	Rect.	89.600	0.17 SF	1' 8"

Family: HSS-Hollow Structural Sectio

Select one or more types on the right for each family listed on the left

OK   Cancel   Help

Figure 5–18

- If the Family Already Exists dialog box opens, as shown in Figure 5–19, select **Overwrite the existing version** or select **Overwrite the existing version and its parameter values**.

*If you select **Overwrite the existing version** and overwrite the parameter values, any changes that you have made to any related families in the model are removed.*

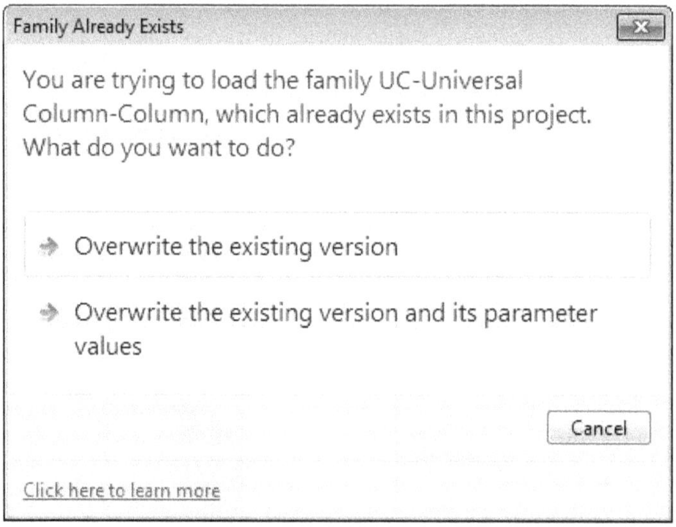

Family Already Exists

You are trying to load the family UC-Universal Column-Column, which already exists in this project. What do you want to do?

→ Overwrite the existing version

→ Overwrite the existing version and its parameter values

Cancel

Click here to learn more

Figure 5–19

Practice 5b

Place Structural Columns

Practice Objective

Estimated time for completion: 5 minutes

*   Place columns on grids.

In this practice you will place columns at the grid intersections. The completed practice is shown in 3D in Figure 5–20.

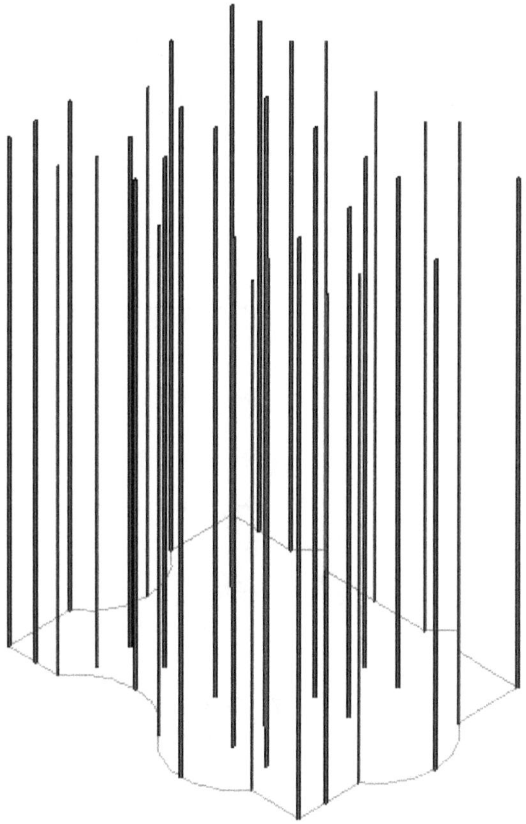

Figure 5–20

Task 1 - Add columns.

1. Open **Syracuse-Suites-Columns.rvt**.

2. Ensure that you are in the **Structural Plans: 00 GROUND FLOOR** view.

3. In the *Structure* tab>Structure panel, click ⬚ (Structural Column).

4. In the Type Selector, select **W-Wide flange-Column: W10x33**.

5. In the Options Bar, change *Depth* to **Height** and set the *Height* to **Level TOS-14 Roof**.

6. Place columns at the locations shown in Figure 5–21. (In some cases, it might be faster to place columns at the grid intersections and then delete any extra columns.)

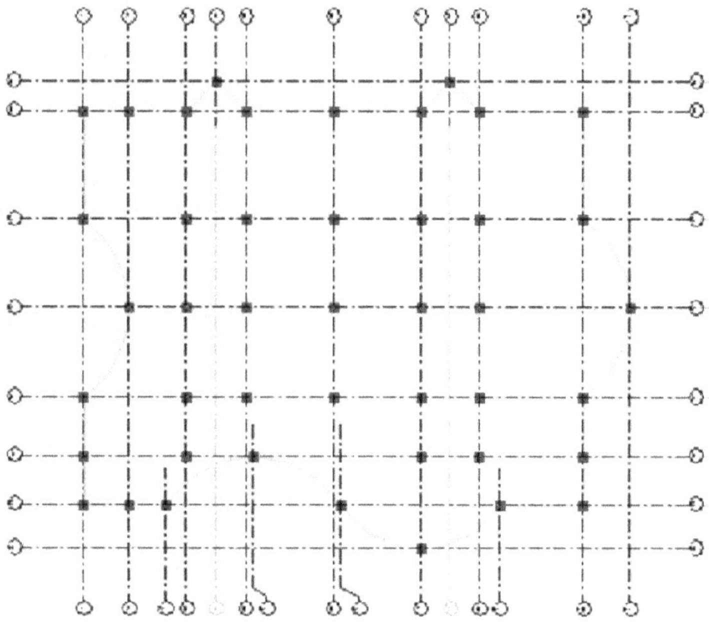

Figure 5–21

7. Open the **Default 3D** view to display the full height of the columns.

8. Save the project.

Chapter Review Questions

1. How do you line up grid lines that might be different lengths, as shown in Figure 5–22?

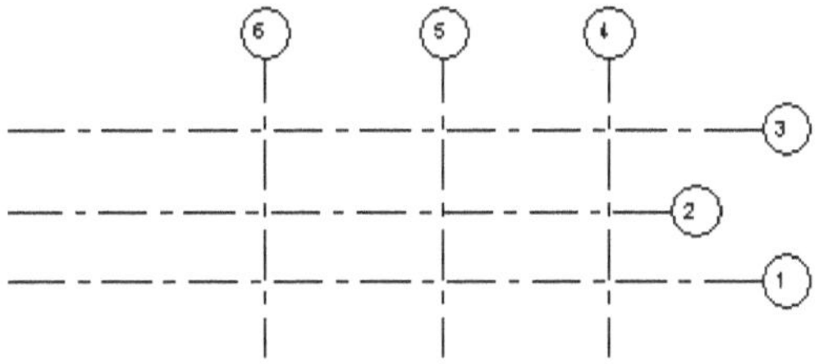

Figure 5–22

a. Use ⬚ (Trim/Extend Multiple Elements) to line them up with a common reference line.

b. Select the grid line and drag its model end to line up with the other grid lines.

c. Select the grid line, right-click and select **Auto-Align**.

d. In Properties, change the *Length* and then use ✛ (Move) to get them into position.

2. Where can columns be placed?

a. Columns can only be placed on grids.

b. Architectural columns can be placed anywhere, but structural columns can only be placed on grids.

c. Both types of columns can be placed wherever you want.

d. Grid-based column types must be placed on the grid, but free-standing column types can be placed anywhere.

3. How do you add additional column families to use in a project?

a. Import them.

b. Copy and Paste them from another file.

c. Draw them in the project.

d. Load them from the Library.

Command Summary

Button	Command	Location
Columns and Grids		
	At Columns	• **Ribbon:** *Modify | Place Structural Column* tab>Multiple panel
	At Grids	• **Ribbon:** *Modify | Place Structural Column* tab>Multiple panel
	Grid	• **Ribbon:** *Structure* tab>Datum panel> Grid • **Shortcut:** GR
	Structural Column	• **Ribbon:** *Structure* tab>Structural panel • **Shortcut:** CL
	Vertical Column	• **Ribbon:** *Modify | Place Structural Column* tab>Placement panel
Tools		
	Attach Top/Base	• **Ribbon:** *Modify | Structural Column* tab>Modify Column panel
	Detach Top/Base	• **Ribbon:** *Modify | Structural Column* tab>Modify Column panel

Chapter

6

Foundations

Foundations are frequently created using concrete walls, columns, and footings. Autodesk® Revit® includes standard tools for creating walls and columns in several different materials, as well as specific tools for adding wall and column footings.

Learning Objectives in this Chapter

- Create walls for that can be used in foundations.
- Add bearing and retaining wall footings under the walls.
- Create column types to be used as piers and pilasters.
- Place isolated footings under the columns.

6.1 Modeling Walls

Walls in the Autodesk Revit software are more than just two lines on a plan. They are complete 3D elements that store detailed information, including height, thickness, and materials. This means they are useful in both 2D and 3D views. Structural walls (as shown in Figure 6–1) are bearing walls that can act as Exterior, Foundation, Retaining, and Shaft walls.

Walls are not automatically reinforced. You must apply reinforcement as separate elements.

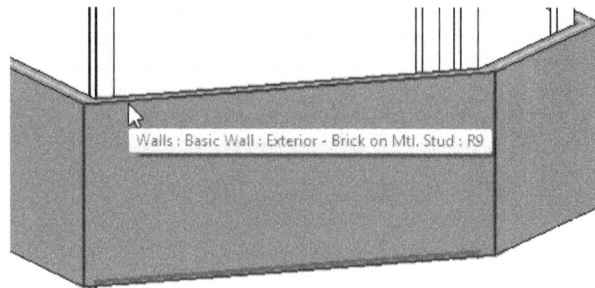

Walls : Basic Wall : Exterior - Brick on Mtl. Stud : R9

Figure 6–1

While some walls are made of only one material such as poured concrete other walls can be made of multiple layers such as block, air space, and brick all in one wall type. These compound walls can have different justifications as shown in Figure 6–2.

Wall Centerline

Core Centerline

Figure 6–2

The core is typically the structural part of the wall.

How To: Model a Wall

1. In the *Structure* tab>Structure panel, click ▭ (Wall: Structural).
   - Architectural walls (which are created with the **Wall: Architectural** command) are typically non-bearing walls, such as curtain walls and partitions. They do not display when the view *Discipline* is set to **Structural**.
2. In the Type Selector, select a wall type, as shown in Figure 6–3.

Figure 6–3

You can use the Search box to quickly find specific types of walls.

3. In the Options Bar (shown in Figure 6–4), specify the following information about the wall before you start drawing:

Figure 6–4

- **Depth:** Set the depth of a wall to either Unconnected (with a specified distance) or to a level. This command can also be set to **Height**.
- **Location Line:** Set the justification of the wall using the options shown in Figure 6–4.
- **Chain:** Enables you to draw multiple connected walls.
- **Offset:** Enables you to enter the distance at which a new wall is created from an existing element.
- **Radius:** Adds a curve of a specified radius to connected walls as you draw.
- **Join Status:** Select between **Allow**, which permits automatic wall joins, and **Disallow**, which prohibits the walls from cleaning up when they touch other walls.

4. In the *Modify | Place Wall* tab>Draw panel (shown in Figure 6–5), select one of the options to create the wall.

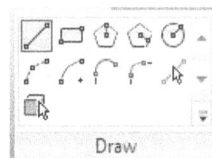

Figure 6–5

- Use alignment lines, temporary dimensions, and snaps to place the walls.

- When using the *Chain* option, press <Esc> to finish the string of walls and remain in the Wall command.
- As you are sketching, you can press <Spacebar> to flip the orientation of compound walls.

Modifying Walls

There are several methods of modifying walls, as shown in Figure 6–6. These methods include the following:

- Changing the type of wall using the Type Selector.

- Using controls and shape handles to modify the length and wall orientation.

- Using temporary and permanent dimensions to change the location or length of a wall in 2D and 3D.

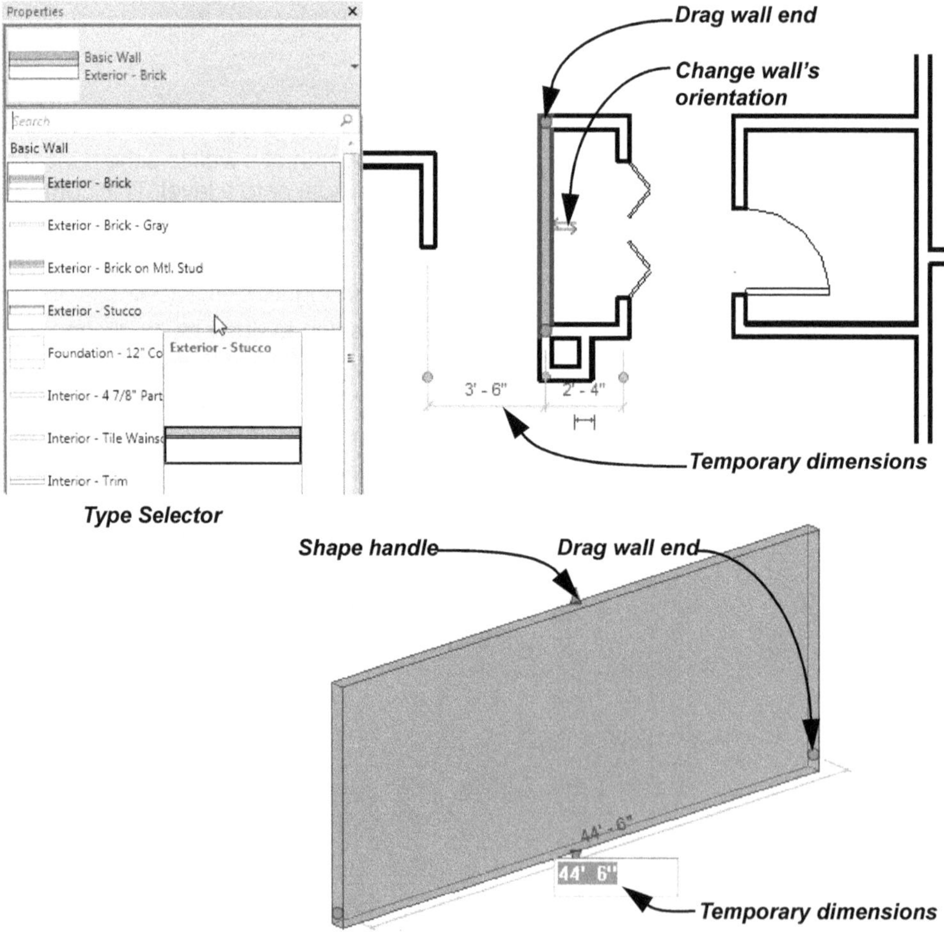

Type Selector

Drag wall end

Change wall's orientation

Temporary dimensions

Shape handle   *Drag wall end*

Temporary dimensions

Figure 6–6

- To display the hatching in the walls in plan views, in the View Control Bar, set the *Detail Level* to **Medium** or **Fine**, as shown in Figure 6–7.

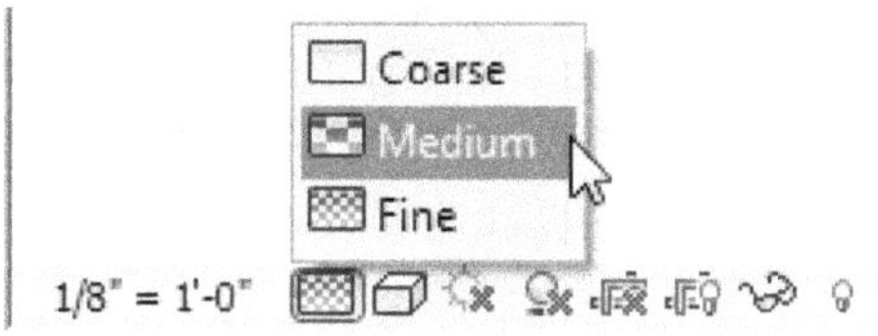

Figure 6–7

6.2 Adding Wall Footings

Wall footings for bearing and retaining are hosted by the walls. Once a footing is in place, you can add reinforcement, as shown in Figure 6–8. With the advantages of having a true foundation in place, you can accurately tag and schedule the footings.

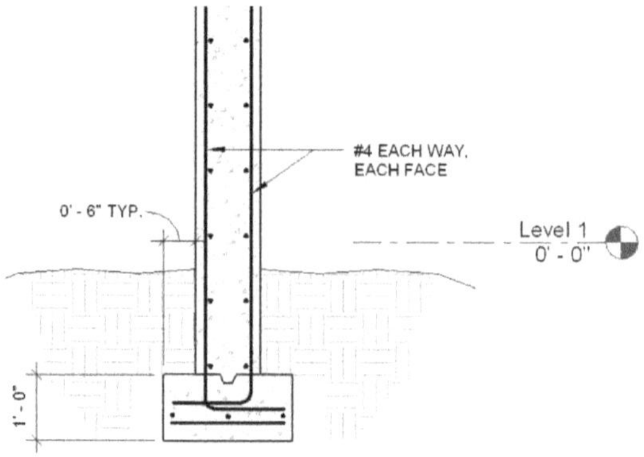

Figure 6–8

- You can apply two types of continuous footing systems, as shown in Figure 6–9:

  - **Retaining footings:** A footing with one side offset to accommodate additional lateral loads and reinforcement

  - **Bearing footings:** A footing with an equal distance on either side of the bearing wall.

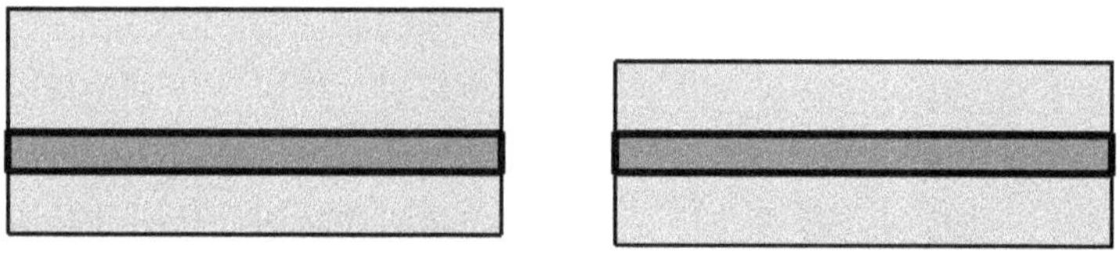

Retaining Footing   *Bearing Footing*

Figure 6–9

How To: Place a Bearing or Retaining Footing

Wall foundations can also be placed in 3D, section, and elevation views.

1. Create walls or use existing ones. A wall must be in place for this command to work.
2. Open a foundation plan and set it up so that the walls are displayed and you can select them.

3. In the *Structure* tab>Foundation panel, click ⬚ (Wall) to start the **Structural Foundations: Wall** command, or type **FT**.
4. In the Type Selector, select a type, as shown in Figure 6–10.

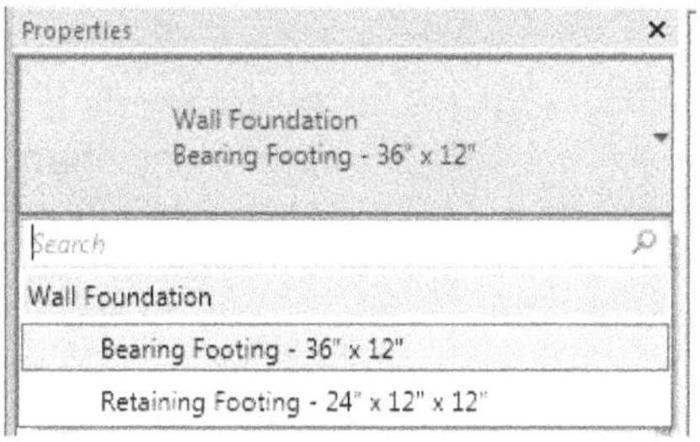

Figure 6–10

5. Select a wall, the footing is placed beneath the wall as shown in Figure 6–11.

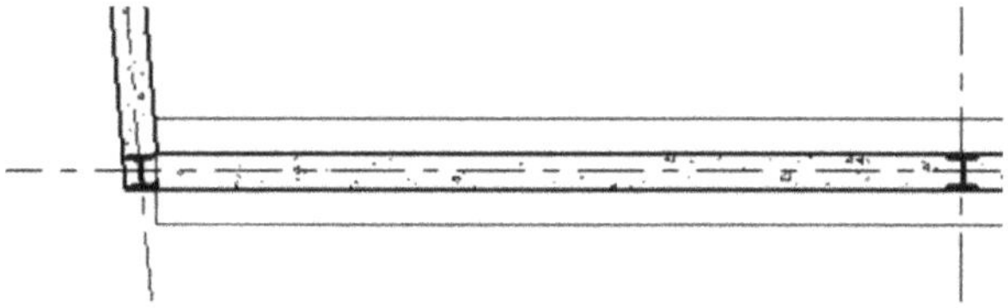

Figure 6–11

- To select multiple walls, hover over one wall and then press <Tab> to select all connected walls. Alternatively, in the *Modify | Place Wall Foundation* tab>Multiple panel,

  click ⬚ (Select Multiple). Select the walls using any selection method (they do not need to be connected) and

  click ✓ (Finish) to place the footings.
- You can flip retaining footings as shown in Figure 6–12.

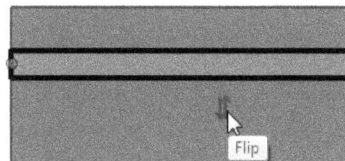

Figure 6–12

How To: Create a Footing Type

1. Select an existing foundation wall element or start the **Structural Foundation: Wall** command.
2. In the Type Selector, select a type similar to the type that you want to create and in Properties, click ⊞ (Edit Type).
3. In the Type Properties dialog box, click **Duplicate**.
4. In the Name dialog box, type a new name for the element.
5. Make any changes to the type properties, as required as shown in Figure 6–13.

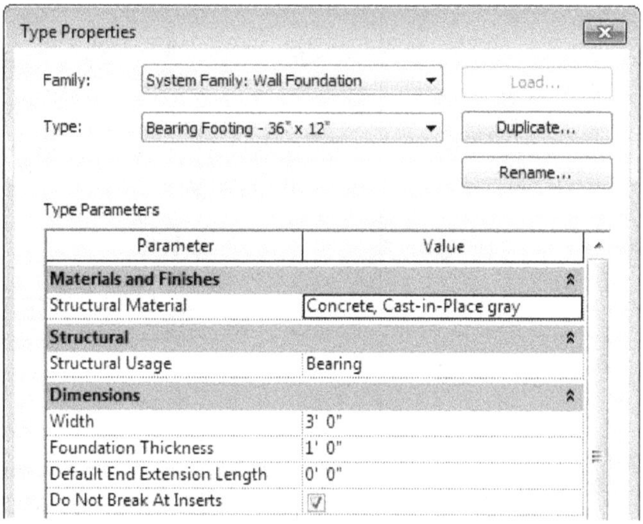

Figure 6–13

6. Click **OK** to close the dialog box.

• You can also create a new type through the Project Browser. Find an existing type in the *Families* area, right-click on the type and select **Duplicate**, as shown in Figure 6–14. The new footing is added to the list. Rename it and then double-click to open the Type Properties dialog box.

Figure 6–14

Wall Profiles and Footings

Footings are appended to the bottom of a wall, which means that any change to the base of the host wall influences the footing. This occurs for lateral movement and horizontal movement. For the example shown in Figure 6–15, when the wall profile changes based on a sloped site (as shown on the left), the footing breaks and follows the modified profile (as shown on the right). This is accomplished by editing the profile of the foundation wall.

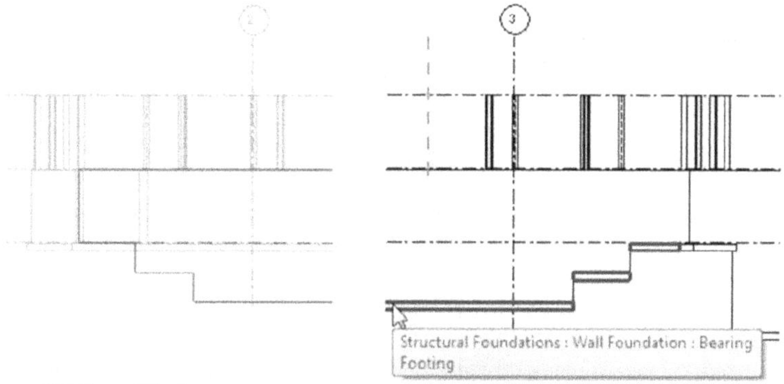

Wall profile in process   *Completed wall with footing*

Figure 6–15

How To: Edit the Profile of a Wall

1. Open an elevation or section view in which you can see the face of the wall that you want to edit.
2. Select the wall (by highlighting the wall boundary).
3. In the *Modify | Walls* tab>Mode panel, click   (Edit Profile). The wall is outlined in magenta indicating the profile of the wall.

4. In the *Modify | Walls>Edit Profile* tab>Draw panel, use the tools to modify the profile sketch of the wall, as shown on the left in Figure 6–16.

5. Once the profile is complete, click ✓ (Finish Edit Mode). The footing now follows the new profile, as shown on the right in Figure 6–16.

The sketch must form a continuous loop. Verify that the lines are clean without any gaps or overlaps. Use any of the tools in the Modify panel to clean up the sketch.

Modified sketch   **Finished Wall**

Figure 6–16

•   After you adjust the sketch you can add isolated footings to create the appropriate shape, as shown in Figure 6–17.

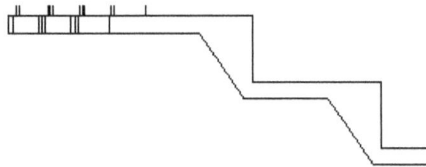

Figure 6–17

Hint: Materials

When you are creating some types, such a wall footings, one option is to set the *Structural Material*. In the Type Properties dialog box, in the *Materials and Finishes* area, click in the *Value* column and then click (Browse), shown in Figure 6–18.

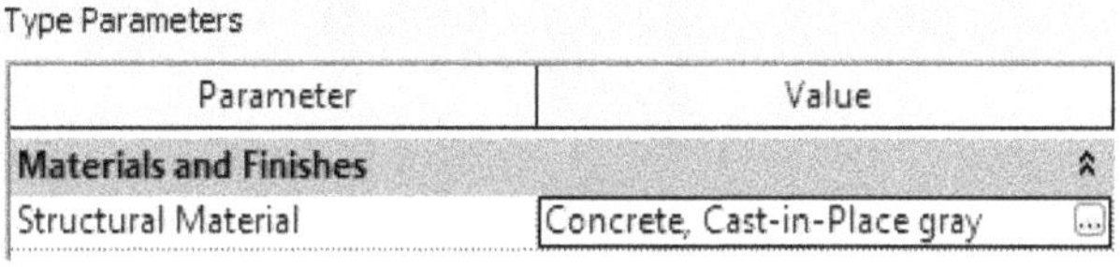
Type Parameters
Parameter
Value
Materials and Finishes
Structural Material
Concrete, Cast-in-Place gray

Figure 6–18

In the Material Browser (shown in Figure 6–19), specify the material you want to use and then click **OK.**

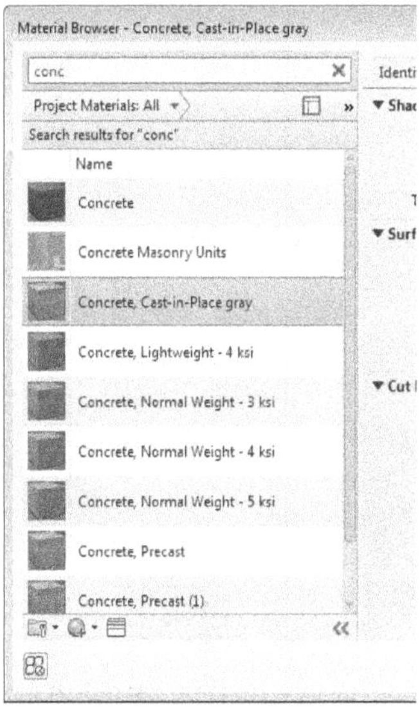
Material Browser - Concrete, Cast-in-Place gray
conc
Project Materials: All
Search results for "conc"
Name
Concrete
Concrete Masonry Units
Concrete, Cast-in-Place gray
Concrete, Lightweight - 4 ksi
Concrete, Normal Weight - 3 ksi
Concrete, Normal Weight - 4 ksi
Concrete, Normal Weight - 5 ksi
Concrete, Precast
Concrete, Precast (1)

Figure 6–19

Practice 6a

Estimated time for completion: 15 minutes

Model Walls and Wall Footings

Practice Objectives

- Place structural walls
- Create and apply wall footings.

In this practice you will model the perimeter foundation walls as shown in Figure 6–20.

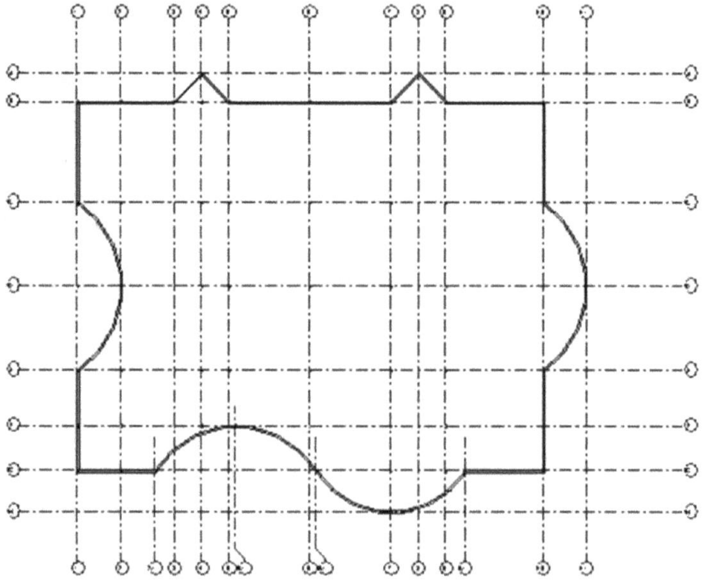

Figure 6–20

Task 1 - Add walls.

1. Open **Syracuse-Suites-Walls.rvt**.

2. Open the **Structural Plan: 00 GROUND FLOOR** view. (The green lines are the outline of the building.)

3. In the *Structure* tab>Structure panel, click ⬭ (Wall: Structural).

4. In the Type Selector, select **Basic Wall: Exterior - 8" Concrete**.

5. In the Options Bar, set the *Depth* to **T.O. FOOTING** and ensure that the *Location Line* is **Wall Centerline**.

6. In the *Modify | Place Structural Wall* tab>Draw panel, click

   ✏ (Line). In the Options Bar, ensure that **Chain** is selected.

7. Select the start point by snapping to the intersection at **Grid G1** as shown in Figure 6–21.

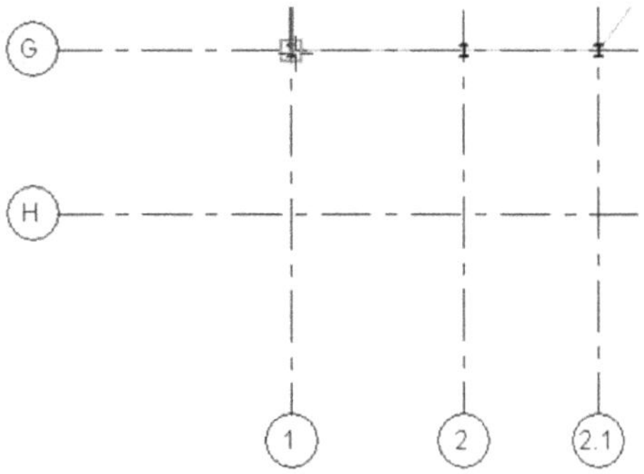

Figure 6–21

8. Draw the wall up to the intersection of **Grid E1**.

9. In the Draw panel, click ⌒ (Start-End-Radius Arc). Select the second point at **Grid C1** and then the third point anywhere along the green arc to specify the radius of the arc, as shown in Figure 6–22.

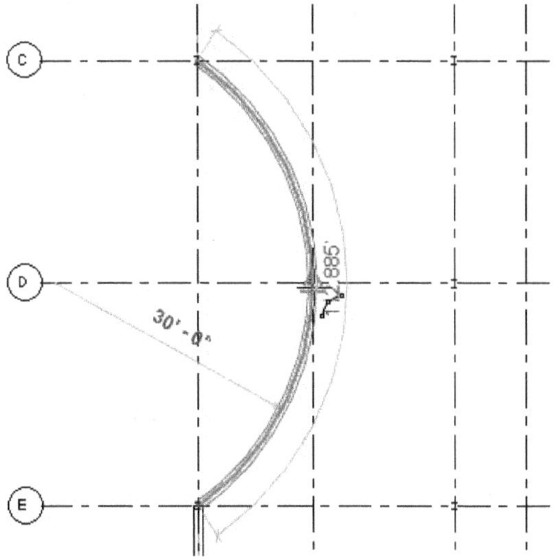

Figure 6–22

10. Click ✏ (Line) again and select the intersection of **Grid B1**.

11. Following the green outline, continue drawing walls all of the way around the perimeter as shown in Figure 6–23.

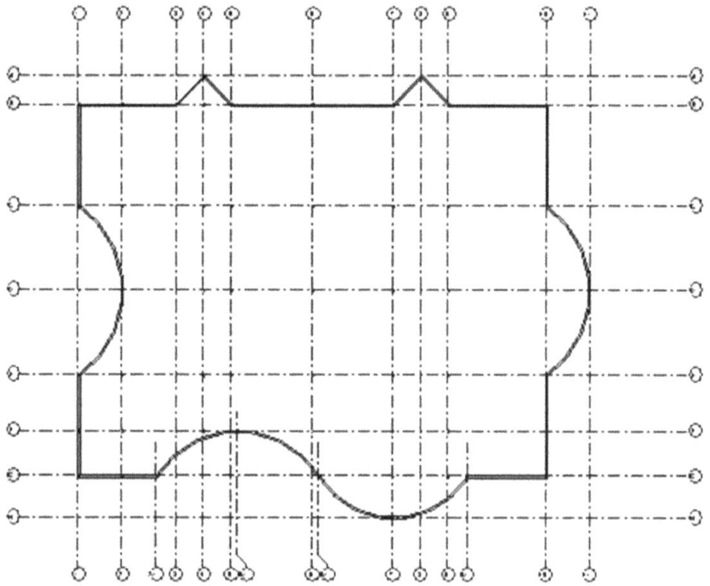

Figure 6–23

12. Save the project.

Task 2 - Create and apply wall footings.

1. Open the **Structural Plans: 000 FOUNDATION PLAN** view.

2. In the *Structure* tab>Foundation panel, click 🏗 (Wall) or type **FT**.

3. In the Type Selector, click 🗔 (Edit Type).

4. In the Type Properties dialog box, click **Duplicate...**

5. In the Name dialog box, type **Bearing Footing – 24" x 12"** and then click **OK**.

6. In the Type Properties dialog box, under *Dimensions*, set the *Width* to **2'-0"**, as shown in Figure 6–24.

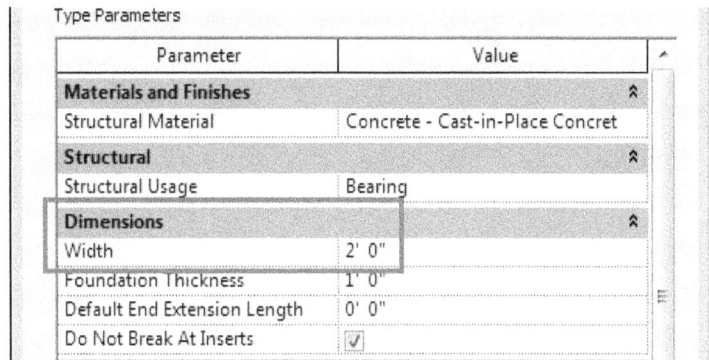

Type Parameters

Parameter	Value	
Materials and Finishes		⌃
Structural Material	Concrete - Cast-in-Place Concret	
Structural		⌃
Structural Usage	Bearing	
Dimensions		⌃
Width	2' 0"	
Foundation Thickness	1' 0"	
Default End Extension Length	0' 0"	≡
Do Not Break At Inserts	☑	

Figure 6–24

7. Click **OK**.

8. You are still in the **Wall Foundation** command. In the Type Selector, ensure that the new **Wall Foundation: Bearing Footing - 24" x 12"** is selected, as shown in Figure 6–25.

Properties ✕

Wall Foundation
Bearing Footing - 24" x 12" ▾

Search 🔎

Wall Foundation

Bearing Footing - 24" x 12"
Bearing Footing - 36" x 12"
Retaining Footing - 24" x 12" x 12"

Most Recently Used Types

Wall Foundation : Bearing Footing - 24" x 12"

Figure 6–25

9. Hover the cursor over one of the existing walls and press <Tab> to highlight the entire wall system. Click to select the walls. The footing is placed under the entire structure.

10. End the command.

11. In the Quick Access Toolbar, click (Default 3D View) to go to a 3D view and verify that the footing is placed correctly as shown in part in Figure 6–26.

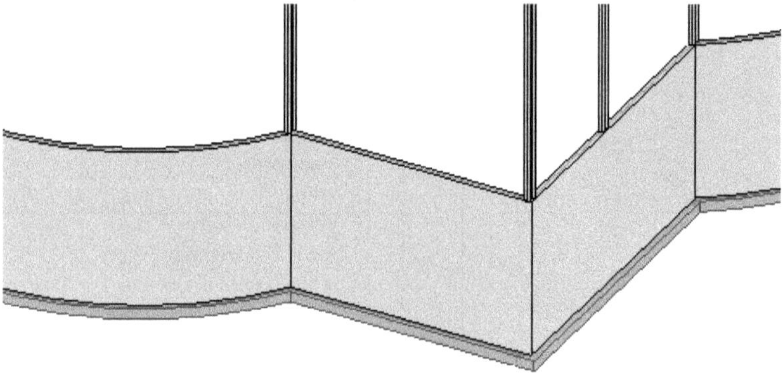

Figure 6–26

12. Save the project.

6.3 Creating Piers and Pilasters

The Autodesk Revit software does not have specific categories for piers and pilasters. If you need to create these elements, the best method is to use concrete columns as shown in Figure 6–27. You can then analyze them as part of the foundation system and independently schedule them from the main column schedule. A concrete column also automatically embeds itself into a concrete wall.

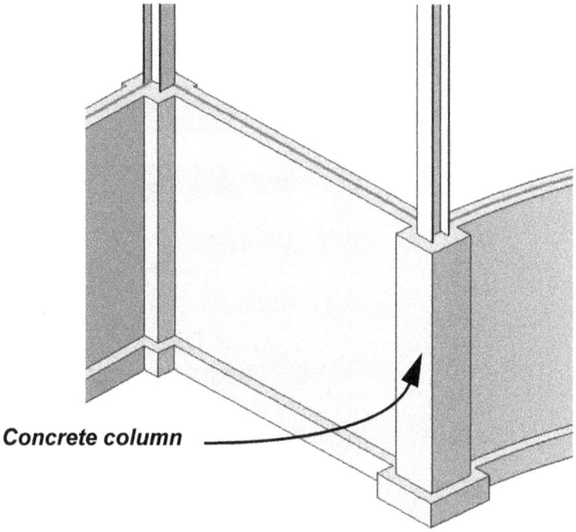

Concrete column

Figure 6–27

- Poured concrete columns can be created in many sizes. For typical rectangular, square, and round columns, it is easy to create custom sizes.

How To: Create a Custom Column Size

1. Open a plan view.

2. In the *Structure* tab>Structure panel, click ⬚ (Column).

3. In the Type Selector, select an existing column family type similar to the one you want to create, such as **Concrete-Rectangular-Column**.

4. In Properties, click 🗗 (Edit Type).

5. In the Type Properties dialog box, click **Duplicate**.

6. In the Name dialog box, type a name as shown in Figure 6–28.

Figure 6–28

7. Modify the dimensions as required. Enter the required values for *b* (base) and *h* (height), as shown in Figure 6–29.

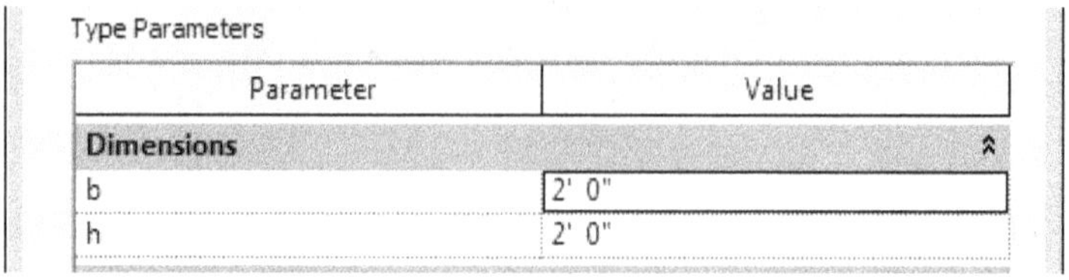

Parameter	Value
Dimensions	☆
b	2' 0"
h	2' 0"

Type Parameters

Figure 6–29

8. Click **OK**.
9. The new pier column can placed at the base of the existing steel columns, as shown in Figure 6–30.

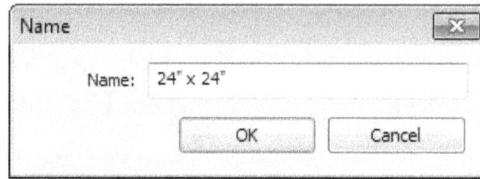

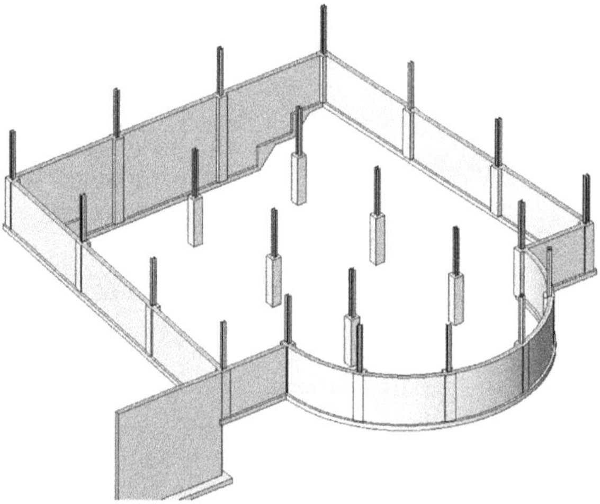

Figure 6–30

Hint: Temporary Hide/Isolate

You might want to temporarily hide elements from a view, modify the project, and then restore the elements. Instead of completely toggling the elements off, you can use

(Temporary Hide/Isolate) in the View Control Bar. The Temporary Hide/Isolate status is not saved with the project.

Select the elements you want to hide (make invisible) or isolate (keep displayed while all other elements are hidden) and click

(Temporary Hide/Isolate). Select the method you want to use, as shown in Figure 6–31.

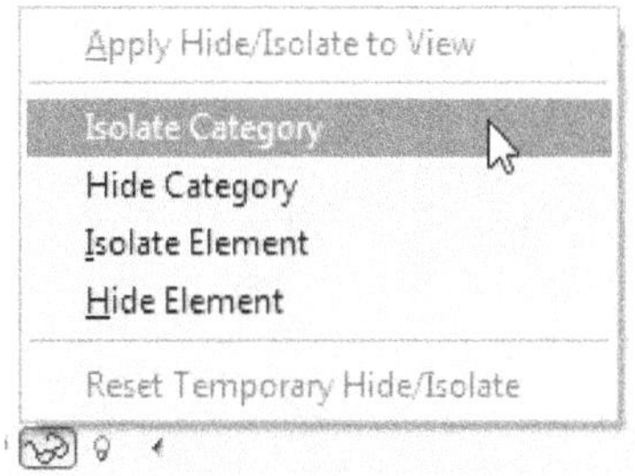

Figure 6–31

The elements or category are hidden or isolated. A cyan border displays around the view with a note in the upper left corner, as shown in Figure 6–32. It indicates that the view contains temporarily hidden or isolated elements.

Figure 6–32

- Click (Temporary Hide/Isolate) again and select **Reset Temporary Hide/Isolate** to restore the elements to the view.

- If you want to permanently hide the elements in the view, select **Apply Hide/Isolate to View**.

- Any elements that are temporarily hidden still print.

Practice 6b

Estimated time for completion: 10 minutes

The steel columns have been hidden in this view for clarity.

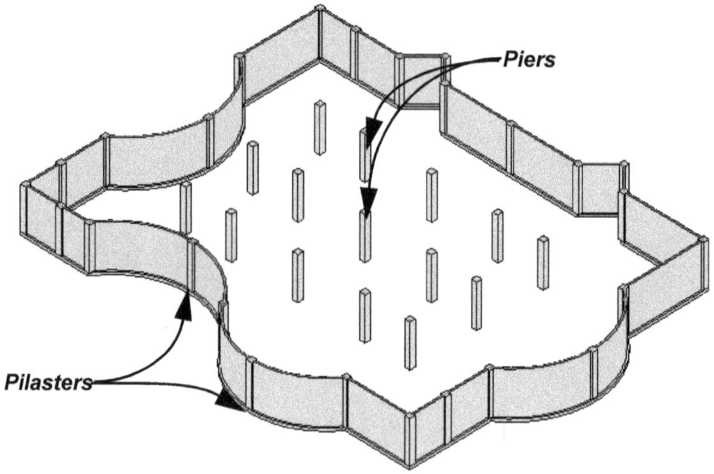

Create Piers and Pilasters

Practice Objectives

- Create a new column type.
- Add columns.

In this practice you will create a new column type and place piers and pilasters (types of columns). The resulting model is shown in Figure 6–33.

Figure 6–33

Task 1 - Create a new column type.

1. Open **Syracuse-Suites-Foundations.rvt**.

2. Open the **Structural Plans: 000 FOUNDATION PLAN** view.

3. In the *Structure* tab>Structure panel, click ⌷ (Column), or type **CL**.

4. In the Type Selector, select one of the **Concrete-Rectangular-Column** types.

5. In Properties, click ⛶ (Edit Type).

6. In the Type Properties dialog box, click **Duplicate**.

7. Rename the column to **24 x 24.** The family name,
   Concrete-Rectangular-Column is automatically applied to
   the name. Click **OK**.

8. In the Type Properties dialog box, change the dimensions for
   both *b* (base) and *h* (height) to **2'-0"**, as shown in
   Figure 6–34.

Type Parameters

Parameter	Value	
Structural		≈
Section Shape	Not Defined	
Dimensions		≈
b	2' 0"	
h	2' 0"	

Figure 6–34

9. Click **OK**.

10. Click 🖰 (Modify).

Task 2 - Place piers and pilasters.

---

1. Select one of the steel columns. In the View Control Bar,
   expand 🕲 (Temporary Hide/Isolate) and click **Isolate
   Category**, as shown in Figure 6–35. Only the columns
   display.

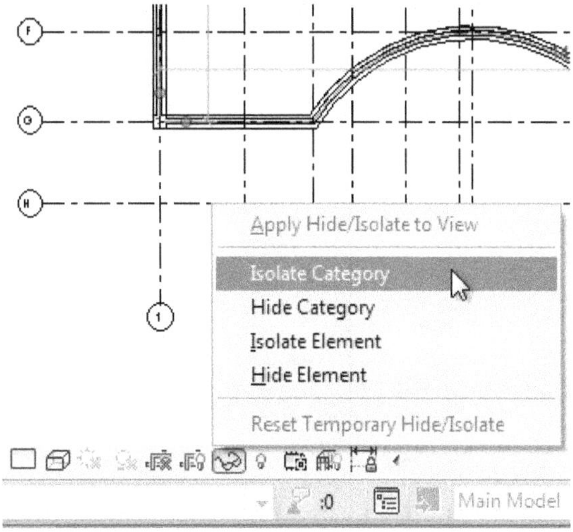

*This is one method that
can help you place the
columns. You can also
use **At Grids** and delete
the columns that you do
not need.*

Figure 6–35

---

2. In the *Structure* tab>Structure panel, click ▯ (Column), or type **CL**.

3. Ensure that **Concrete-Rectangular-Column: 24 x 24** is selected in the Type Selector.

4. In the Options Bar, set *Depth* to ***T.O. Footing***.

5. Place a concrete column at each existing steel column.

6. In the Quick Access Toolbar, click 🏠 (Default 3D View). and view the new column placement, as shown in Figure 6–36.

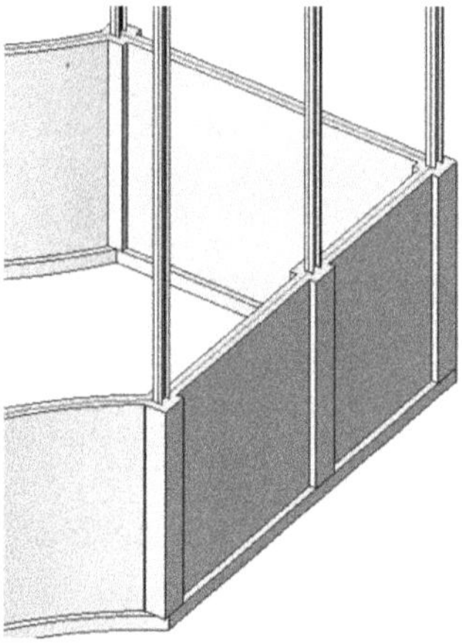

Figure 6–36

7. Save the project.

6.4 Adding Isolated Footings

Footings for columns (shown in Figure 6–37) are placed using the **Structural Foundation: Isolated** command. When you select a column, the footing automatically attaches to the bottom of the column. This is true even when the bottom of the column is on a lower level than the view you are working in.

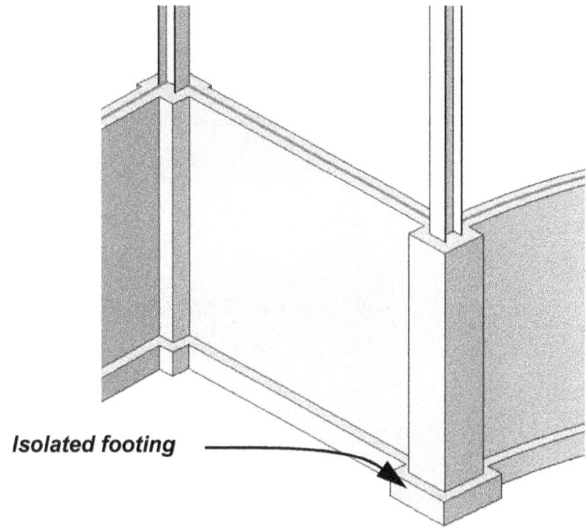

Isolated footing

Figure 6–37

How To: Place an Isolated Footing

1. Open a plan view, such as a **T.O. Footing** structural floor plan.

2. In the *Structure* tab>Foundation panel, click (Isolated) to start the **Structural Foundation: Isolated** command.
3. In the Type Selector, select a footing type.
4. In the view, click to place the individual footing as shown in Figure 6–38.

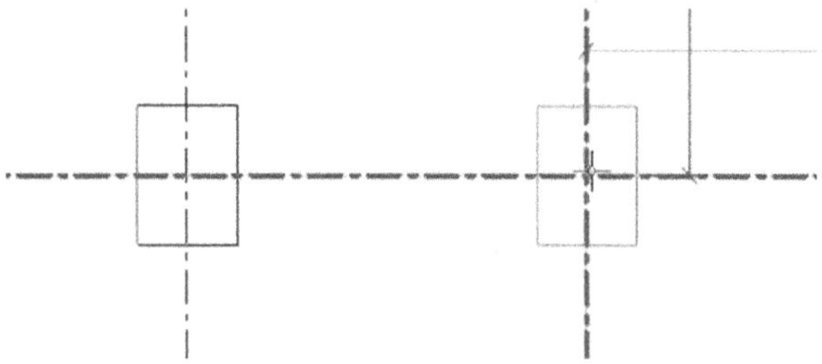

Figure 6–38

5. To add more than one footing at a time, in the *Modify | Place Isolated Foundation* tab>Multiple panel, select (At Grids) or (At Columns) and select the grids or columns.

- If the material of the wall footing and the material of the isolated footing are the same they automatically join, as shown in Figure 6–39.

Figure 6–39

Hint: Foundation Element Properties

Many element properties are automatically gathered from the location and size of the element in the model. These can be used in tags and schedules. For example, Host, Elevation at Top, and Elevation at Bottom are grayed out (as shown in Figure 6–40), because they are automatically generated and cannot be modified directly.

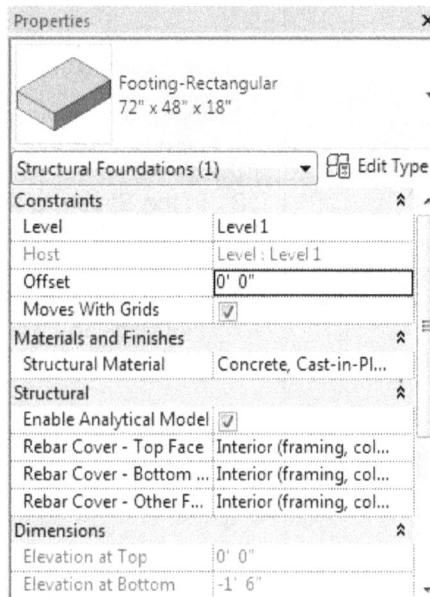

Figure 6–40

Working with Custom Families

Sometimes you need to work with a custom family that has parameters that you can manipulate to fit a specific situation. For example, to add the step footings shown in Figure 6–41 you need to insert an angled isolated footing and modify it to fit the exact size and location.

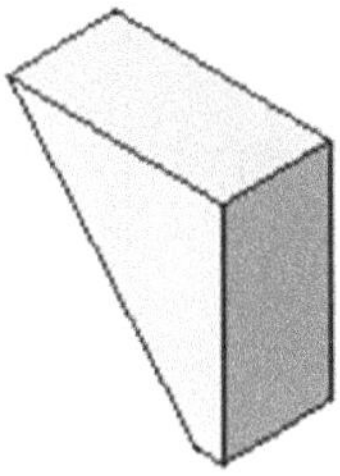

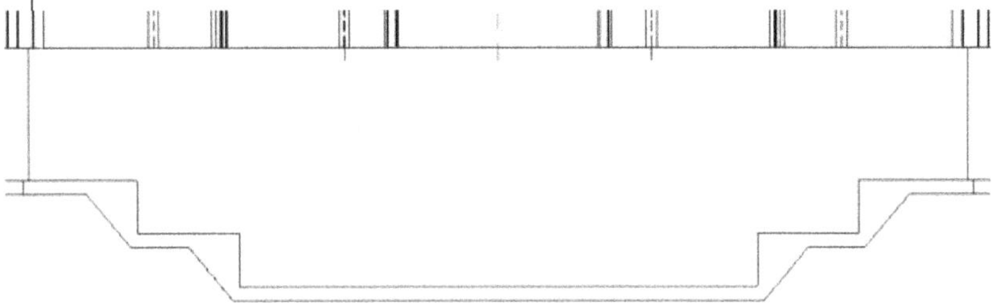

Figure 6–41

How To: Load, Insert, and Modify a Custom Footing

1. Open a plan view.

2. In the *Structure* tab>Foundation panel, click (Isolated) and in the *Modify | Place Isolated Foundation* tab>Mode panel, click (Load Family).

3. In the Load Family dialog box, find the footing family that you want to use and click **Open**.

4. Place the footing in the plan. It might not be in exactly the right place but you can modify it in other views.

5. Open an elevation or section view.

6. Move the footing to the correct location. As long as it is in line with another footing it automatically cleans up as shown in Figure 6–42.

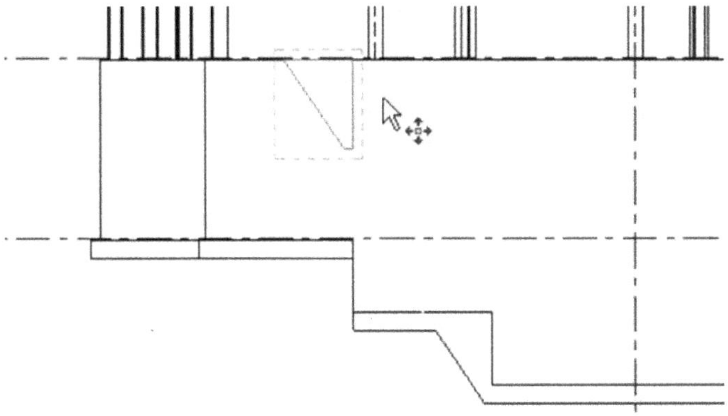

Figure 6–42

- Use (Align) to align footing with the footing already placed. When it is aligned, select the lock as shown in Figure 6–43 to ensure that if the elevation of the wall footing changes, the step footing also adjusts appropriately.

Figure 6–43

- Some custom families have sizing options in either Properties (per instance) or in the Type Properties as shown in Figure 6–44 so that you can create additional types in various sizes as required in the project.

Type Parameters

Parameter	
Dimensions	
Width	2' 0"
Height	5' 0"
Length	4' 0"
Bottom Extension	0' 6"
Identity Data	
Assembly Code	A1010100

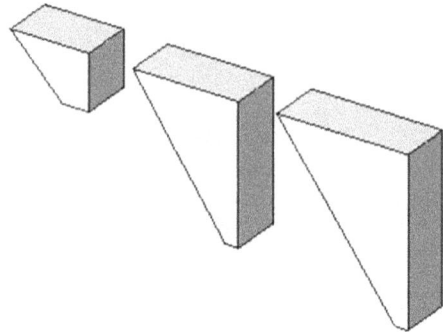

Figure 6–44

Practice 6c

Add Isolated Footings

Practice Objectives

- Place isolated footings.
- Modify a wall profile and add stepped footings.

Estimated time for completion: 15 minutes

In this practice you will create a new footing type and place isolated footings, as shown in Figure 6–45. You will also create a series of stepped footings by modifying a wall profile and adding custom footings.

The steel columns have been hidden in this view for clarity.

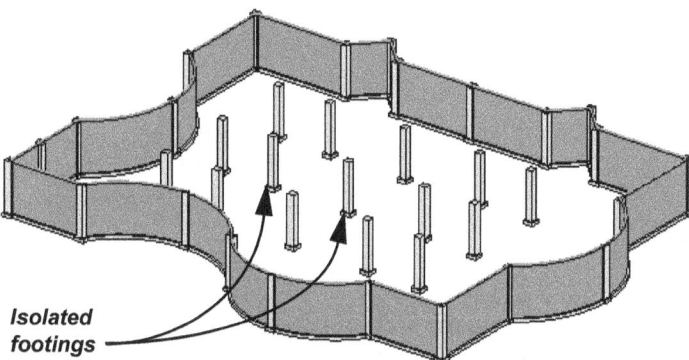

Isolated footings

Figure 6–45

Task 1 - Place isolated footings.

1. Open the project **Syracuse-Suites-Footings.rvt**.

2. Open the **Structural Plans: T.O. FOOTING** view.

3. In the *Structure* tab>Foundation panel, click ⬇ (Isolated).

4. In Properties, click 🔲 (Edit Type).

5. Duplicate the type and name it **36"x36"x12"**.

6. In the Type Properties dialog box, set the following, as shown in Figure 6–46:

- *Width*: **3'-0"**
- *Length*: **3'-0"**
- *Thickness*: **1'-0"**

Parameter	Value
Dimensions	⌃
Width	3' 0"
Length	3' 0"
Thickness	1' 0"

Type Parameters:

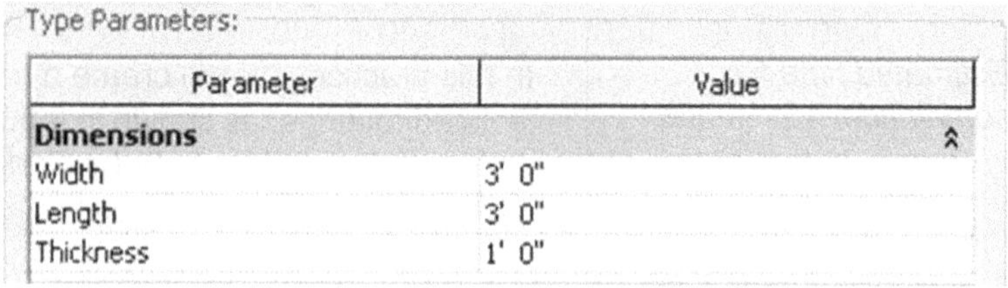

Figure 6–46

7. Click **OK**.

8. Zoom in and place the isolated footing underneath a pilaster. The isolated footing and wall footing automatically join together as shown in Figure 6–47.

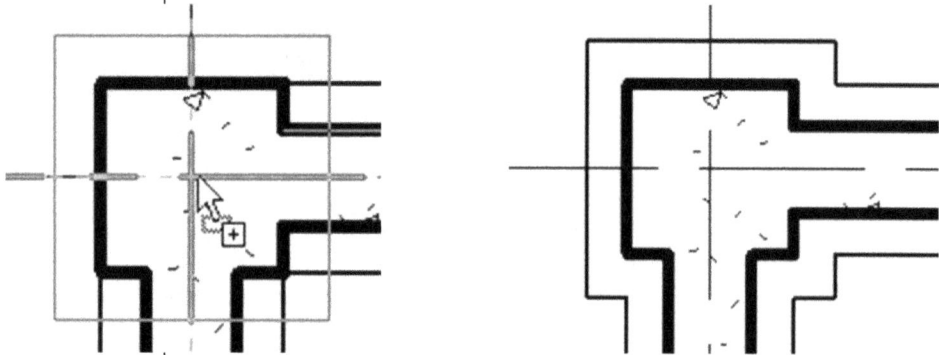

Figure 6–47

9. In the *Modify | Place Isolated Foundation* tab>Multiple panel, click ⬚ (At Columns). Use a pick window to select all of the columns and click ✓ (Finish).

10. Reopen the Default 3D view.

11. There should be an isolated footing under each pier and pilaster, as shown in Figure 6–48.

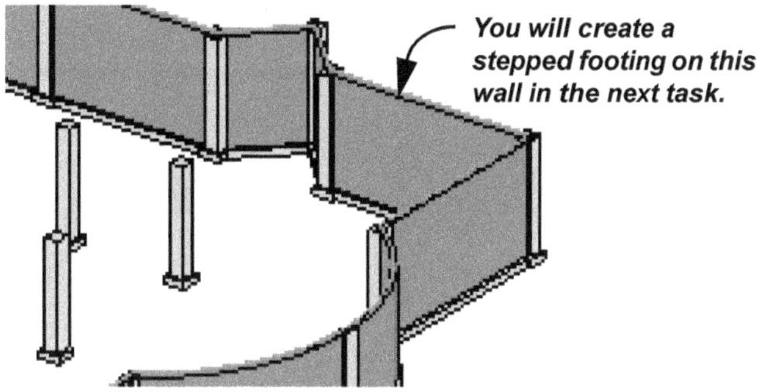

The steel columns were hidden in this figure for clarity.

You will create a stepped footing on this wall in the next task.

Figure 6–48

12. Save the project.

Task 2 - Modify the profile of a wall and add stepped footings.

---

1. Open the **Elevations (Building Elevation): North** view.

2. Zoom in on the left end of the foundation wall and select the wall shown in Figure 6–49

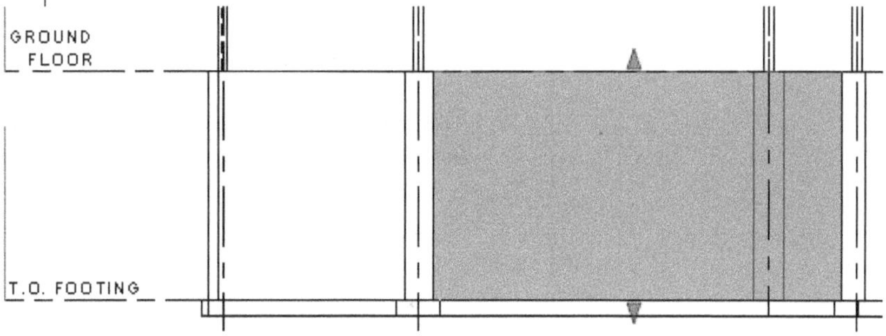

GROUND FLOOR

T.O. FOOTING

Figure 6–49

3. In the **Modify | Walls** tab>Mode panel, click (Edit Profile).

4. Use the Draw and Modify tools to add the stepped profile shown in Figure 6–50. The dimensions are for information only.

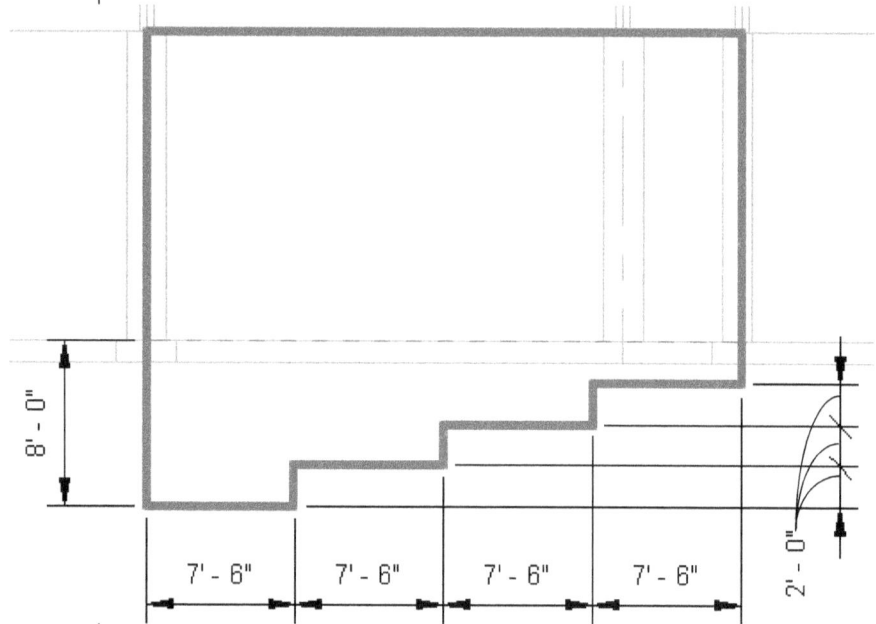

Figure 6–50

5. Click ✓ (Finish Edit Mode).

6. The profile is modified and the wall footings are modified along with it, as shown in Figure 6–51.

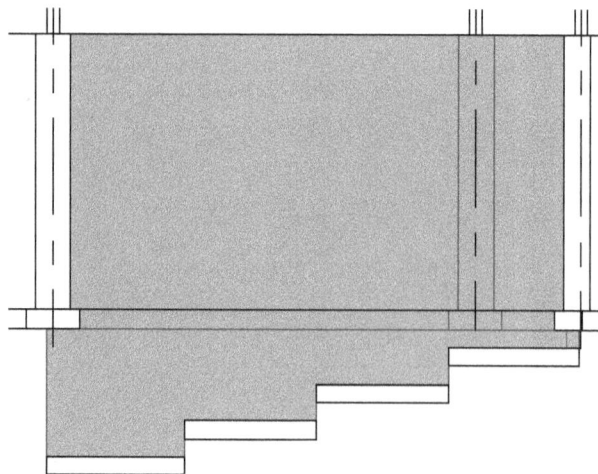

Figure 6–51

7. Open the Structural Plans: **T.O. Footing** view and zoom in on the upper right corner of the building. You should be able to see lines that show the steps of the footing below.

8. In the *Structure* tab>Foundation panel, click ⬇ (Isolated).

9. In the *Modify | Place Isolated Foundation* tab>Mode panel, click 🔲 (Load Family).

10. In the Load Family dialog box, navigate to the practice files folder and select **Angled-Footing.rfa**. Click **Open**.

11. In the Type Selector, select **Angled-Footing: 24" x 24" x 36"**.

12. Place three footings along the wall, similar to those shown in Figure 6–52.

The exact location does not matter at this time.

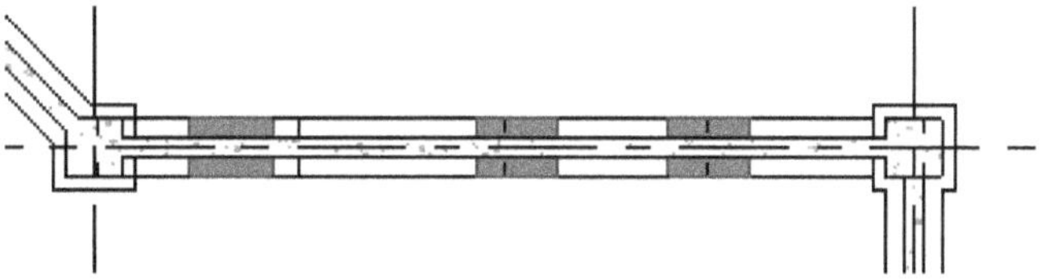

Figure 6–52

13. Return to the **North** elevation view. The three footings are still on the level where they were placed, as shown in Figure 6–53.

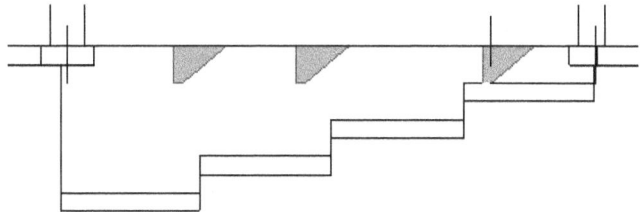

Figure 6–53

14. In the *Modify* tab>Modify panel, click 🔲 (Align) or type **AL**.

15. Align each Angled Footing to the wall footings, as shown in Figure 6–54.

Completed   *In Process*

Figure 6–54

16. View the new footings in 3D, as shown in Figure 6–55

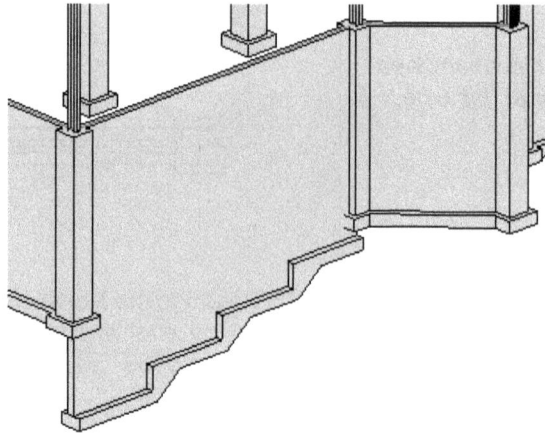

Figure 6–55

17. (Optional) Modify the nearby wall, columns, and footings to match up with the new stepped footings.

18. Save the project.

Chapter Review Questions

1. Which of the following are ways that you can create walls in a project? (Select all that apply.)

   a. Draw Lines

   b. Pick Lines

   c. Insert Lines

   d. Pick Face

2. Which command do you use to insert a pier or a pilaster such as those shown in Figure 6–56?

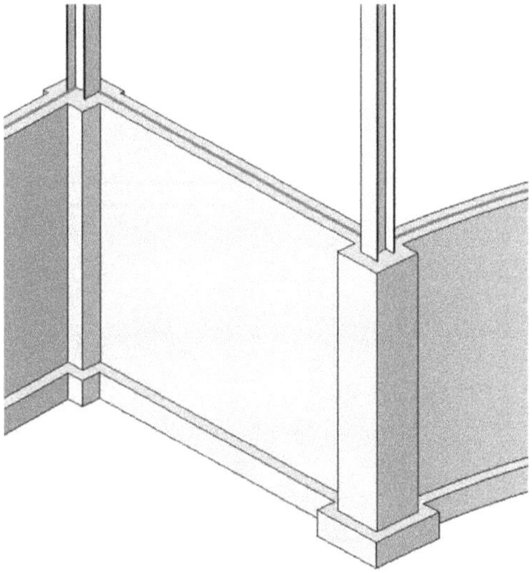

   Figure 6–56

   a. **Structural Pier**

   b. **Isolated Foundation**

   c. **Structural Column**

   d. **Isolated Column**

3. How do you create additional column sizes for column types already in the project?

   a. In Properties, duplicate an existing type and change the sizes.

   b. Start a new Autodesk Revit project and draw it there.

   c. Import additional sizes from another project.

   d. In the Library, load additional sizes from other families.

4. Which element is the host for an isolated footing?

    a. Column

    b. Wall

    c. Slab

    d. Floor

5. The (Structural Foundation: Wall) command requires a host wall to already be in place.

    a. True

    b. False

6. Which command do you use to add a custom footing type under a wall such as the ones shown in Figure 6–57?

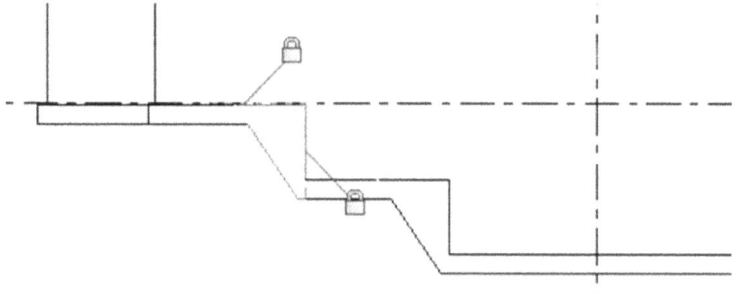

Figure 6–57

    a. **Component**

    b. **Structural Foundation: Isolated**

    c. **Structural Foundation: Wall**

    d. **Component: Structural Foundation**

Command Summary

Button	Command	Location
	Structural Foundation: Wall	• **Ribbon:** *Structure* tab>Foundation panel
	Structural Foundation: Isolated	• **Ribbon:** *Structure* tab>Foundation panel
	Wall: Structural	• **Ribbon:** *Structure* tab>Structure panel

Structural Framing

The skeleton of a building is its structural framing. Together, elements such as columns, beams, bracing, and trusses give buildings the stability they need. While the basic process of adding these elements to the project is simple, you also need to complete more complex tasks, such as manipulating connections (by setting bearing offsets, cantilevers, cut backs, and justifications), applying beam coping, and editing beam joins.

Learning Objectives in this Chapter

- Sketch individual beams for girders connecting columns and structural walls.
- Create Beam Systems of multiple similar sized beams spaced at equal intervals to speed up adding joists.
- Add Bracing to support the integrity of other framing members.
- Make changes to framing members so that the connections fit the exact situation.
- Add trusses to support long spans of open space.

7.1 Modeling Structural Framing

The Autodesk® Revit® software enables you to frame a building with wood, concrete, and steel framing and bracing, such as the steel example shown in Figure 7–1. You can add individual beams, as well as beam systems and bracing elements.

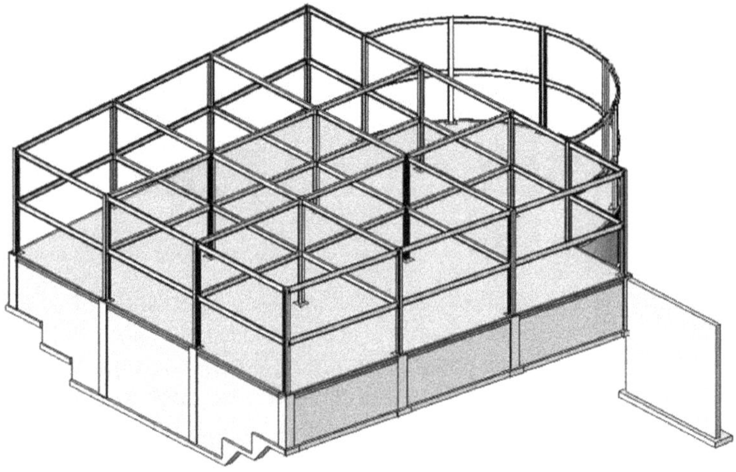

Figure 7–1

- Framing types include: **Concrete**, **Light Gauge Steel**, **Precast Concrete**, **Steel**, and **Wood**.

- In views set to a **Coarse** detail level, the software assigns a lineweight to the structural members based on their structural usage. For example, a Girder displays in a heavier lineweight than a Joist, while a Purlin displays with a dashed line. as shown in Figure 7–2.

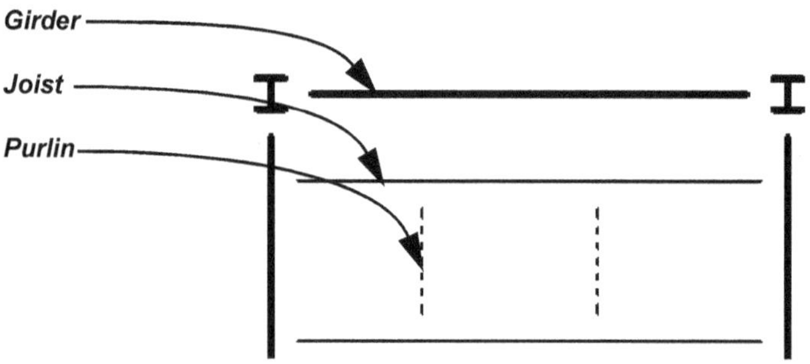

Girder ─
Joist ─
Purlin ─

Figure 7–2

How To: Add Beams

1. In the *Structure* tab>Structure panel, click ✏️ (Beam).
2. In the Type Selector, select a beam type.
3. In the Options Bar, specify the options, as shown in Figure 7–3 and described below.

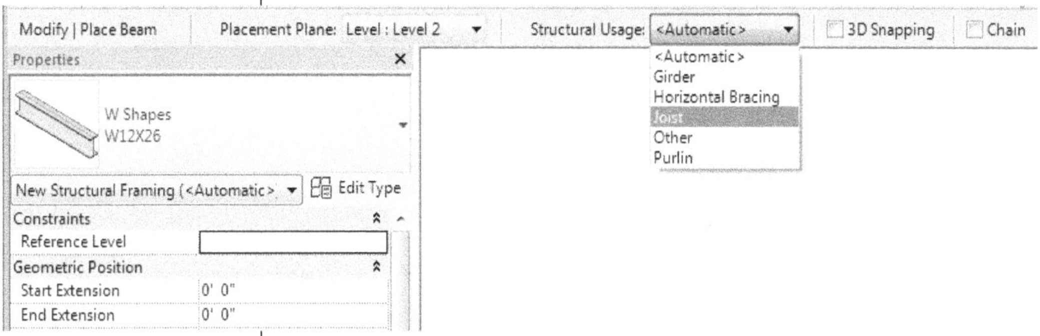

Figure 7–3

- *Placement Plane:* Defaults to the current level if you are in a plan view but can be modified to other levels.
- *Structural Usage:* Select a type (as shown in Figure 7–3), or accept the default of **<Automatic>**.
- **3D Snapping:** Select this if you want to draw a beam from one point to another at different heights.
- **Chain:** Select this if you want to draw a series of beams in a row. To stay in the command and start another chain, press <Esc> once.

4. For automatic tagging, in the *Modify | Place Beam* tab>Tag panel, click ⌐① (Tag on Placement).
5. In the *Modify | Place Beam* tab>Draw panel, use the Draw tools to draw the beams.

How To: Add Multiple Beams on Grid Lines

1. Start the **Beam** command and specify the type and other options, as outlined above.

2. In the *Modify | Place Beam* tab>Multiple panel, click ⠿ (On Grids).

3. Select the grids where you want to locate the beams. A beam is placed between each grid intersection, as shown in Figure 7–4. Hold <Ctrl> to select more than one grid, or use a pick and drag window to select multiple grids at one time.

Columns must be in place to support the beams for this to work.

Figure 7–4

4. In the *Modify | Place Beam>On Grid Line* tab>Multiple panel, click ✔ (Finish).

- Sometimes this can be the quickest way to add beams. If you need to use various sizes of beams, when you are finished, select those beams and make any changes in the Type Selector.

Beam Systems

Beam Systems are layouts of parallel beams placed between other beams, as shown in Figure 7–5. Typically used in joist layouts, beam systems can be set up to use either a fixed distance or number of beams.

- Beam systems can be created automatically with sufficient bounding elements (other beams). You can also sketch the boundary for a beam system.

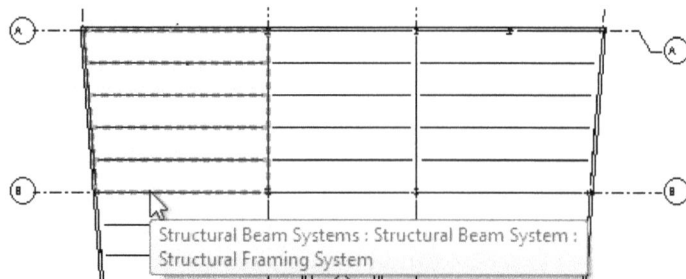

Structural Beam Systems : Structural Beam System : Structural Framing System

Figure 7–5

How To: Add Automatic Beam Systems

1. In the *Structure* tab>Structure panel, click ▥ (Beam System) or type **BS**.
2. The *Modify | Place Structural Beam System* tab>Beam System panel, click ▥ (Automatic Beam System).
3. When 🔲① (Tag on Placement) is selected, in the Options Bar, set the *Tag Style* as shown in Figure 7–6.
   - **Framing**: Tags each individual member.
   - **System**: Places one tag for the entire framing system.

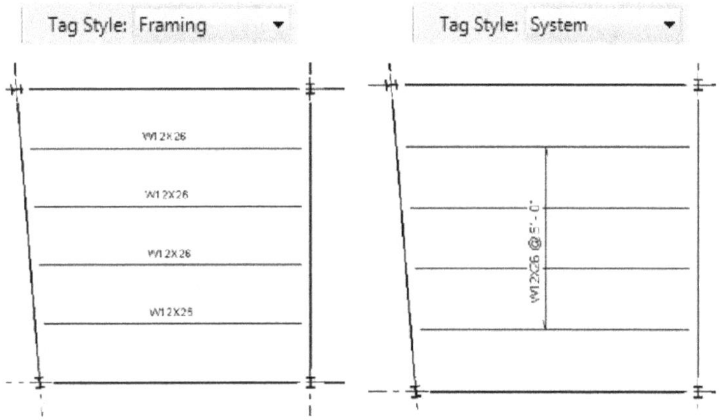

Figure 7–6

4. In the Options Bar (shown in Figure 7–7), set the *Beam Type*, *Justification*, and *Layout Rule*.

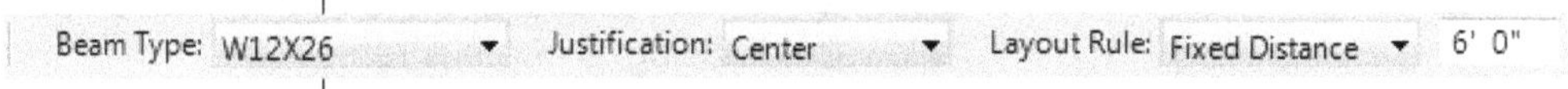

Figure 7–7

   - The *Layout Rules* include: **Clear Spacing**, **Fixed Distance**, **Fixed Number**, and **Maximum Spacing**. Set the required distance or number.
   - Make changes in Properties or in the Options Bar as required to establish the required beam system.

5. Move the cursor over an existing beam until the guide lines display in the correct area and direction, as shown vertically and horizontally in Figure 7–8. This can also identify angled lines.

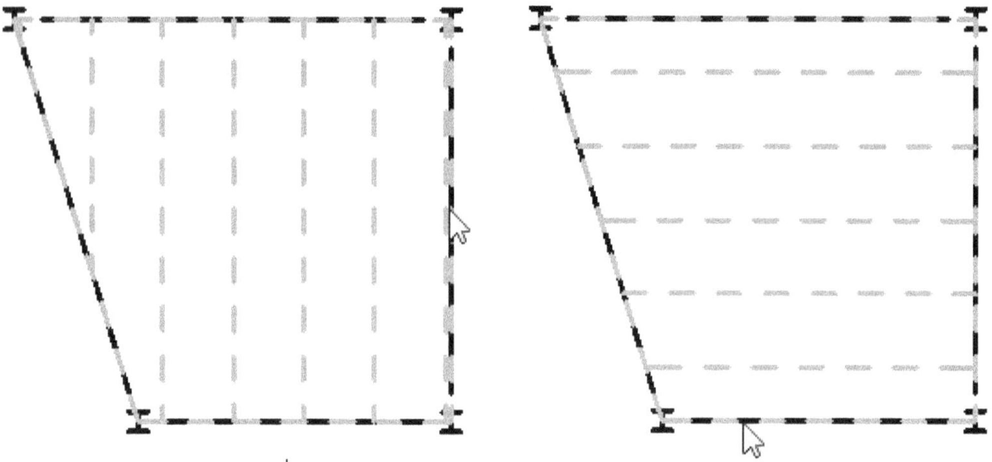

Figure 7–8

6. Select the existing beam to place the system.
7. Repeat this step in other bays as required.

*   The Beam System is one uniform group. You can change beam's type, spacing, and elevation in Properties or in the Options Bar.

*   If a grid line is moved, the beams automatically space themselves. If the bay increases beyond the minimum spacing, a beam is added. If the bay shrinks below the allowable spacing, a beam is removed.

*   If you need to change the system to individual beams, in the *Modify | Structural Beam Systems* tab>Beam System panel,

    click   (Remove Beam System). The individual beams remain but are no longer grouped together.

How To: Sketch a Beam System

1. In the *Structure* tab>Structure panel, click ⬚ (Beam System).
2. In the *Modify | Place Structural Beam System* tab>Beam System panel, click ⬚ (Sketch Beam System).
3. In the *Modify | Create Beam System Boundary* tab>Draw panel, click 📐 (Pick Supports) or use one of the other drawing tools.
4. In the Draw panel, click ╫╫ (Beam Direction) and select one of the sketch lines that runs as you want the system to run, as shown on the top horizontal beam in Figure 7–9.

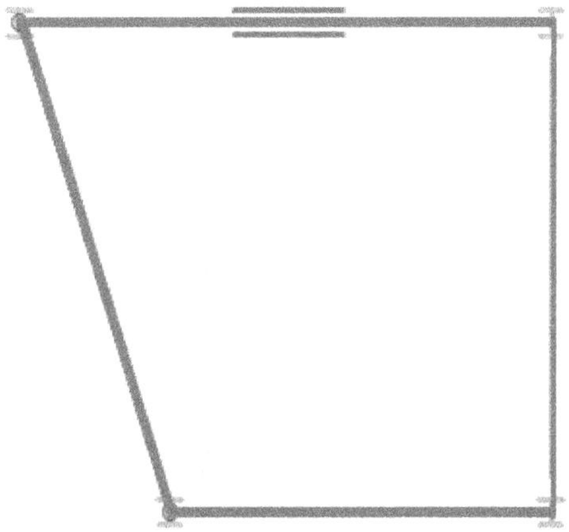

Figure 7–9

5. Clean up all of the corners so that there are no overlaps or gaps.
6. In the *Modify | Create Beam System Boundary* tab>Mode panel, click ✓ (Finish Edit Mode).
7. Make changes in Properties or in the Options Bar as required to establish the required beam system.

• To include an opening in a beam system, draw another opening inside the original sketched boundary.

Adding Bracing

Braces automatically attach to other structural elements, such as beams, columns, and walls. They recognize typical snap points such as the end point of a column and the middle of a beam, as shown in Figure 7–10.

Figure 7–10

- Bracing can be added in plan view or, more typically, in a framing elevation view.

How To: Add Bracing

1. Create and open a framing elevation.

2. In the *Structure* tab>Structure panel, click ⊠ (Brace).
3. In the Type Selector, select a brace type.
4. Pick two points for the end points of the brace.

   - Work from the centerline of all of framing members so that the analytical line extends into the adjacent framing, even though the graphical member stops at the edge of the column or beam, as shown in Figure 7–11.

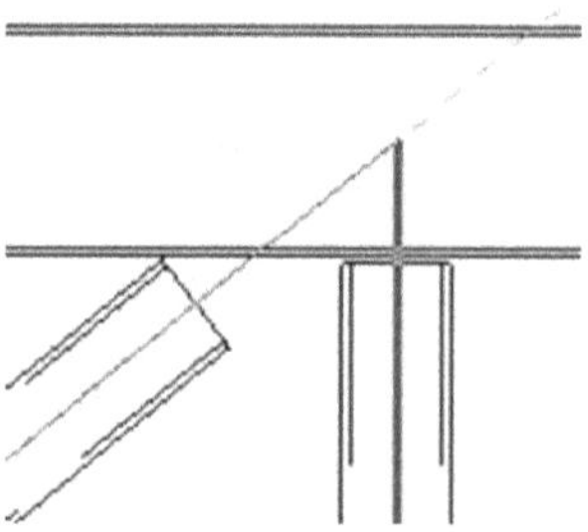

Figure 7–11

Cross Bracing Settings

In plan view, cross bracing needs to be displayed graphically, usually by hidden lines. The software has a separate setting that controls cross bracing as viewed in plan. These settings enable you to display bracing above, below, or both. The bracing can be displayed as parallel lines or as a line at an angle, as shown in Figure 7–12.

Parallel

Line with angle

Figure 7–12

- In the *Manage* tab>Settings panel, expand 🛠 (Structural Settings) and click 🛠 (Structural Settings). In the Structural Settings dialog box, *in the Symbolic Representation Settings* tab, select the **Brace Symbol** options, as shown in Figure 7–13.

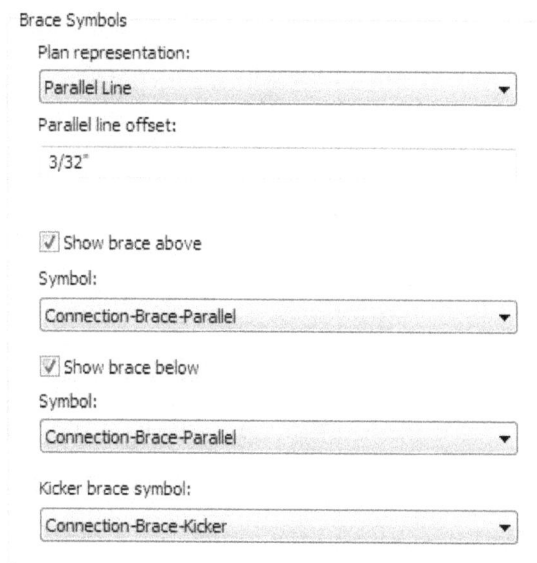

Brace Symbols

Plan representation:

Parallel Line ▼

Parallel line offset:

3/32"

☑ Show brace above

Symbol:

Connection-Brace-Parallel ▼

☑ Show brace below

Symbol:

Connection-Brace-Parallel ▼

Kicker brace symbol:

Connection-Brace-Kicker ▼

Figure 7–13

Hint: Copying Elements to Multiple Levels

Instead of drawing the same elements on each level, you can copy them to the clipboard and then paste them aligned to the other levels.

1. Select the required elements.
2. In the *Modify <contextual>* tab>Clipboard panel, click

   ⬚ (Copy to Clipboard).

3. In the *Modify* tab>Clipboard panel, expand ⬚ (Paste) and

   click ⬚ (Aligned to Selected Levels).
4. In the Select Levels dialog box, as shown in Figure 7–14, select the levels to which you want to copy the beams.

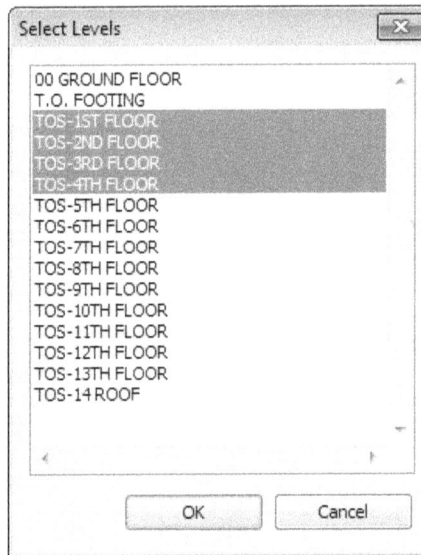

Select Levels

00 GROUND FLOOR
T.O. FOOTING
TOS-1ST FLOOR
TOS-2ND FLOOR
TOS-3RD FLOOR
TOS-4TH FLOOR
TOS-5TH FLOOR
TOS-6TH FLOOR
TOS-7TH FLOOR
TOS-8TH FLOOR
TOS-9TH FLOOR
TOS-10TH FLOOR
TOS-11TH FLOOR
TOS-12TH FLOOR
TOS-13TH FLOOR
TOS-14 ROOF

OK   Cancel

Figure 7–14

5. Click **OK**.

• This command is for copying model elements only. If you want to include tags or other annotation, use **Paste>Aligned to Selected Views**.

Practice 7a

Model Structural Framing

Practice Objectives

- Place beams and beam systems.
- Copy framing to additional levels.
- Create a framing elevation.
- Add bracing

Estimated time for completion: 20 minutes

In this practice you will add framing for one floor of a building (as shown in Figure 7–15), and then copy and paste the framing to the levels above. You will then add bracing to one part of the structure.

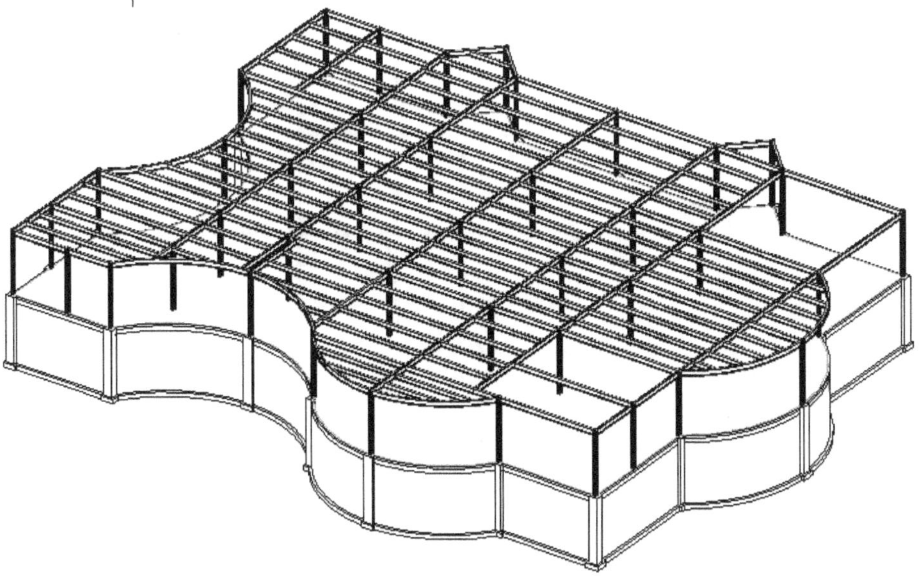

Figure 7–15

- This graphic is modified for clarity.

Task 1 - Place perimeter beams.

1. Open the project **Syracuse-Suites-Beams.rvt**.

2. Open the **Structural Plans: TOS-1ST FLOOR** view.

3. In Properties, in the *Underlay* area, set the *Range: Base Level* to **T.O. FOOTING** so that you can see the outline of the building.

4. In the View Control Bar set the *Detail Level* to ⊠ (Medium).

5. In the *Structure* tab>Structure panel, click ✏️ (Beam).

6. In the Type Selector, select **W-Wide-Flange: W14x30**.

7. Add framing between each column (and in some cases between beams), as shown in Figure 7–16. You can use a variety of techniques to place the beams.

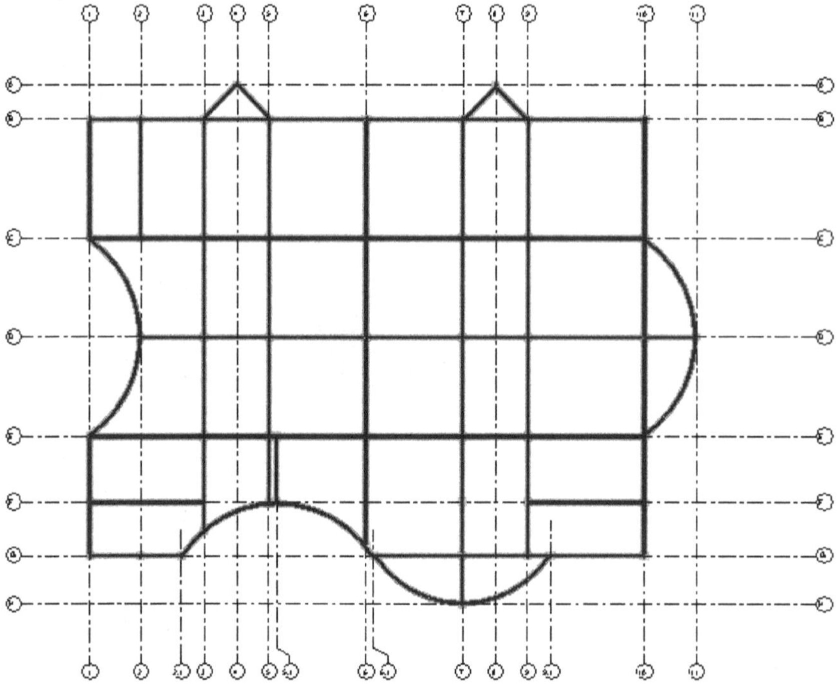

Figure 7–16

- If you use ⊹ (At Grids), ensure that you select the correct grids. You might need to delete beams that are not used.
- If you are sketching the beams, in the Options Bar, select **Chain** to keep the sketching active between picks. Press <Esc> once to end the chain but remain in the command.
- To place the curved beams. use either ⤢ (Pick Lines) or the ⌐ (Start-End-Radius Arc) tool
- Use ⊹ (Split Element) to break each curved beam into two beams at the midpoint.

8. Save the project.

Task 2 - Create Beam Systems.

1. In the *Structure* tab>Structure panel, click ▦ (Beam System).

2. In the *Modify | Place Structural Beam System* tab, verify that ▦ (Automatic Beam System) is selected.

3. In the Tag panel, click ⌐① (Tag on Placement) to toggle it off.

4. In the Options Bar, set the following:

   - *Beam Type:* **W12x26**
   - *Layout Rule:* **Maximum Spacing of 6'-0"**

5. Click inside each bay, ensuring that the beams are running in a West-East direction. Exclude the bays shown in Figure 7–17.

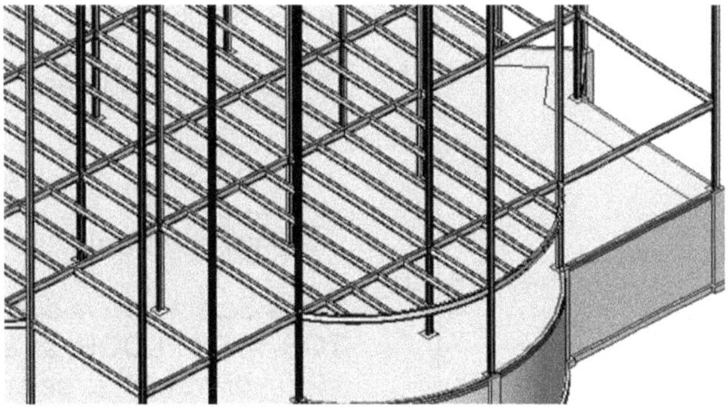

Figure 7–17

6. Use ▦ (Sketch Beam System) for any bays that cannot be applied automatically.

   - In Properties, in the *Identity Data* area, set *Tag new members in view* to **None**.

7. Once all of the framing is in place end the command.

8. Save the project.

Task 3 - Copy the framing to the other levels.

1. Use a crossing window to select **everything** on the first floor.

2. In the Status Bar, click ▽ (Filter).

3. In the Filter dialog box, clear the **Structural Columns** category as shown in Figure 7–18. If elements other than framing are displayed, clear those categories as well.

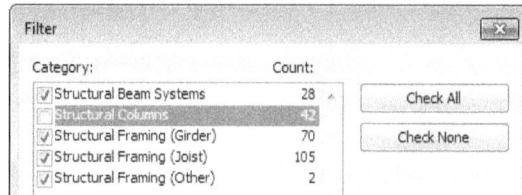

Filter		
Category:	Count:	
☑ Structural Beam Systems	28	Check All
☐ Structural Columns	42	
☑ Structural Framing (Girder)	70	Check None
☑ Structural Framing (Joist)	105	
☑ Structural Framing (Other)	2	

Figure 7–18

4. Click **OK**.

5. In the *Modify | Multi-Select* tab>Clipboard panel, click 📋 (Copy to Clipboard).

6. In the Clipboard panel, expand 📋 (Paste) and click 📑 (Aligned to Selected Levels).

7. In the Select Levels dialog box, select **TOS-2ND FLOOR** to **TOS-13TH FLOOR**, as shown in Figure 7–19. (Hint: Hold <Ctrl> or <Shift> to select multiple levels.)

Select Levels

```
00 GROUND FLOOR
T.O. FOOTING
TOS-1ST FLOOR
TOS-2ND FLOOR
TOS-3RD FLOOR
TOS-4TH FLOOR
TOS-5TH FLOOR
TOS-6TH FLOOR
TOS-7TH FLOOR
TOS-8TH FLOOR
TOS-9TH FLOOR
TOS-10TH FLOOR
TOS-11TH FLOOR
TOS-12TH FLOOR
TOS-13TH FLOOR
TOS-14 ROOF
```

OK   Cancel

Figure 7–19

8. Click **OK**. This will take some time to process.

9. Open the **Structural Plans: TOS-13TH FLOOR** view.

10. Only the Girder beams of each bay are required on the roof level. With a crossing window, select everything and filter out everything but **Structural Framing (Girder)**.

11. Press <Ctrl> + **C** (the **Copy to Clipboard** shortcut).

12. In the Clipboard panel, expand 📋 (Paste) and click 📋 (Aligned to Selected Levels).

13. In the Select Levels dialog box, select **TOS-14 ROOF** and click **OK**.

14. Open a 3D view to see the full model, as shown in Figure 7–20.

This graphic is shown at the Coarse detail level for clarity.

Figure 7–20

15. Save the project.

Task 4 - Create a framing elevation.

1. Open the **TOS-1st FLOOR** structural plan view.

2. In the *View* tab>Create panel, expand ⌖ (Elevation) and click ⌖ (Framing Elevation).

3. Select the beam along **Grid 1** between **Grid B** and **Grid C**, as shown in Figure 7–21.

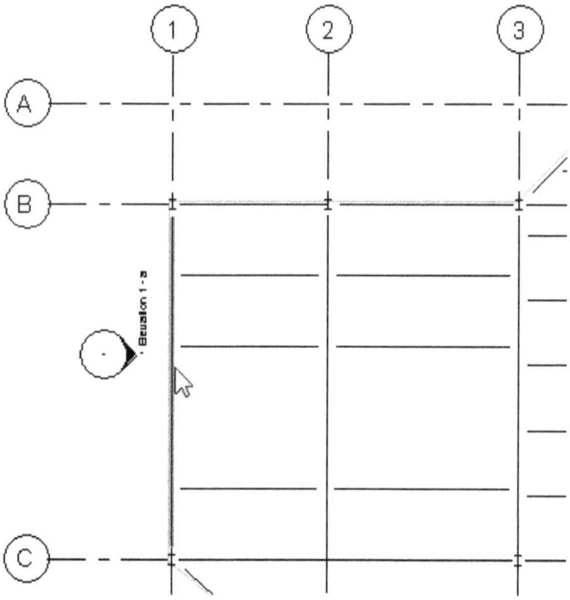

Figure 7–21

4. In the Project Browser, expand *Elevations (Framing Elevation)* and rename Elevation 1 – a as **West Bracing**.

5. Open the elevation.

6. Move the crop region to display the columns.

7. In the View Control Bar, set the *Detail Level* to ▨ (Fine).

8. Zoom in to display the **00 GROUND FLOOR** and **TOS-1ST FLOOR** level heads.

9. Save the project.

Task 5 - Add bracing.

1. In the *Structure* tab>Structure panel, click ⊠ (Brace).

2. In the Type Selector, select **HSS Hollow Structural Section: HSS6X6X.500**.

3. Draw from the centerline of the base of the column on the left to the midpoint of the beam located on the 1st Floor, as shown in Figure 7–22. Repeat this step on the other side.

2nd point *4th point*

1st point *3rd point*

Figure 7–22

4. Click ⌖ (Modify) and select the two new braces.

5. Copy and paste aligned the braces from the Ground to the 12th TOS Floor levels.

6. Zoom up to the top level.

7. Select the top two braces, if required.

8. Drag the circular control up to the beam above it, as shown in Figure 7–23.

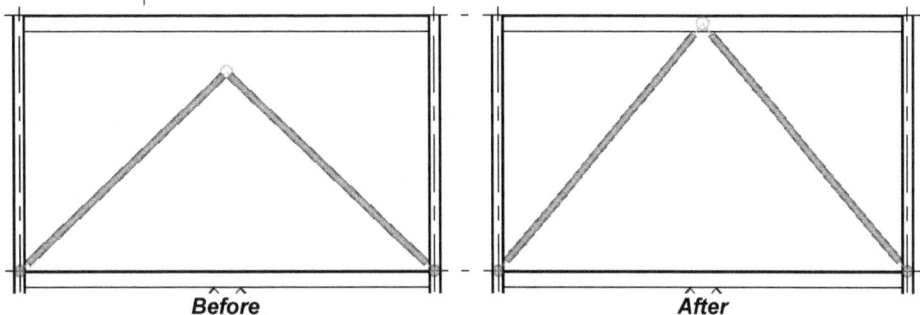

Before *After*

Figure 7–23

9. Zoom out to see the entire framing elevation.

10. Save the project.

7.2 Modifying Structural Framing

The default connections of columns, beams, and braces might need to be modified to suit specific situations, such as when the beams are offset from their associated level, or cantilevered beyond a framing member. Modifications can be made by using graphical controls and shape handles, the Properties, or special tools found on the *Modify | Structural Framing* tab, as shown in Figure 7–24.

Figure 7–24

- The *Detail Level* of a view impacts the way in which framing members display, as shown in Figure 7–25. Some editing tools only work in a Medium or Fine detail view.

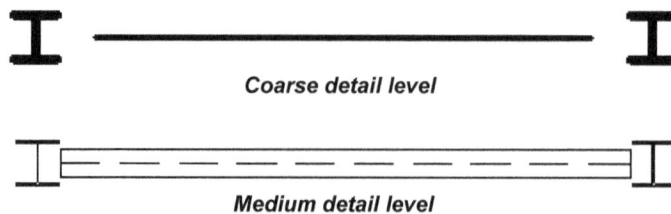

Coarse detail level

Medium detail level

Figure 7–25

- The Location Line can be used as a visual reference, as shown in Figure 7–26. In the Visibility/Graphics dialog box, in the *Model Categories* tab, expand **Structural Framing** and select **Location Line**.

- Additionally, you can view structural connections using Analytical Lines, as shown in Figure 7–27. In the View Control Bar, click 🔲 (Show/Hide Analytical Model) to toggle this on and off.

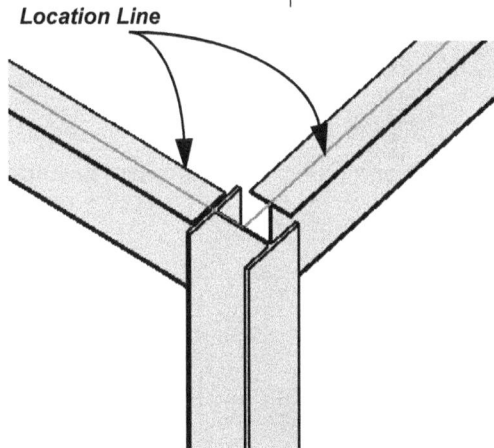

Figure 7–26

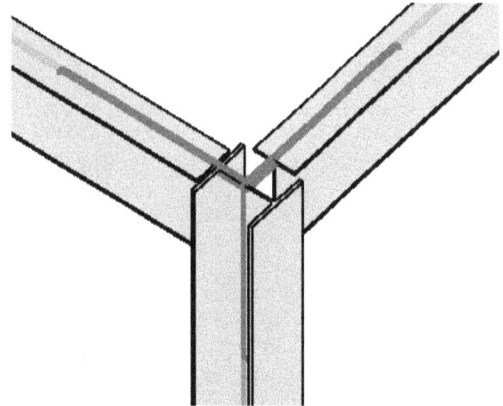

Figure 7–27

- When you draw framing members, the start/end orientation is based on the first and second points picked. In some modification instances it is important to know the start point verses the end point. In the analytical model, the start point is green and the end point is red, as shown in Figure 7–28.

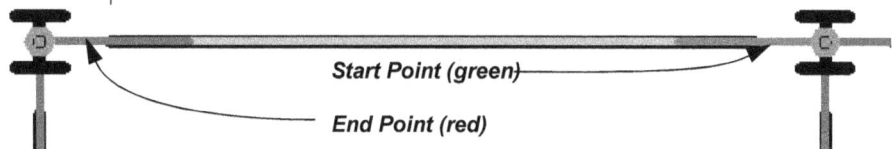

Start Point (green)

End Point (red)

Figure 7–28

- To flip the start and end points, in a 3D view, right-click on the member and select **Flip Structural Framing ends.**

Sloping and Offsetting Beams

Beams can be modified to slope or offset from the level where they are placed. This can be done by using the *Start/End Level Offset* control, as shown on the left in Figure 7–29, or in Properties, as shown on the right in Figure 7–29.

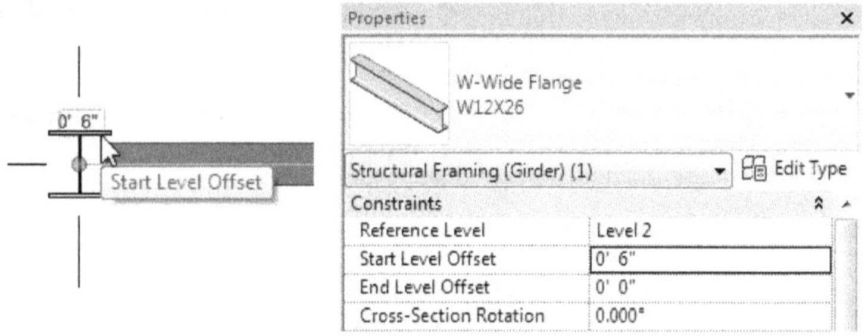

Figure 7–29

- Setting the offset at only one end slopes the beam as shown in Figure 7–30.

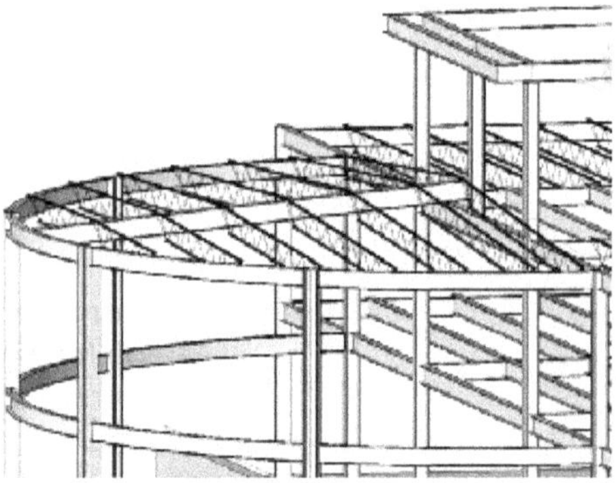

Figure 7–30

- The **Cross-Section Rotation** option rotates the beam along its axis at the angle specified in Properties.

Hint: Using 3D Snapping

When you draw beams, you can toggle on **3D Snapping** and then snap to other beams or structural walls of different heights. You can also do this with beam systems when you use the Automatic Beam System method. On the left in Figure 7–31, the **3D** and **Walls Define Slope** options are selected, while on the right, they are not.

Figure 7–31

- Setting the **Start/End Level Offset** the same at each end raises or lowers the entire beam. For example, when Wide Flange Beams are supporting Open Web Steel Joists (as shown in Figure 7–32), you need to offset that increment based on the specific joist's seat.

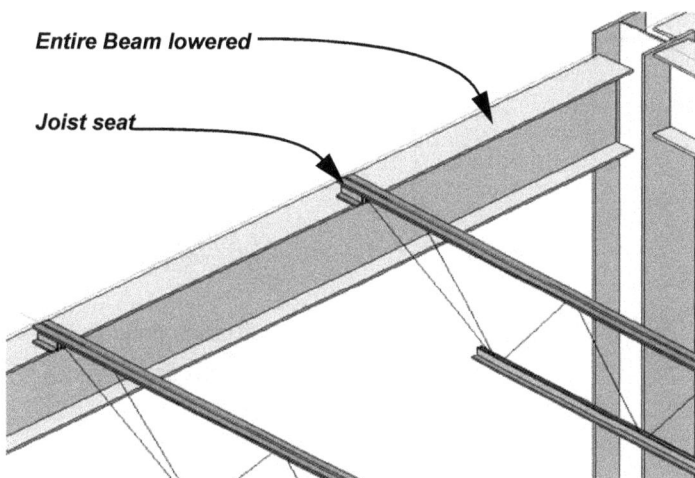

Entire Beam lowered

Joist seat

Figure 7–32

Adding Beam Cantilevers and Cutbacks

Use this method to extend joists for a fascia system, or in any situation in which a roof or slab extends past the main structure.

It is common to need a joist extension that cantilevers a bearing member. In the example shown in Figure 7–33, the joist seat needs to extend past the beam it bears on to frame into a cantilevered ridge beam. By modifying the individual joists, you can extend either end to meet the requirements.

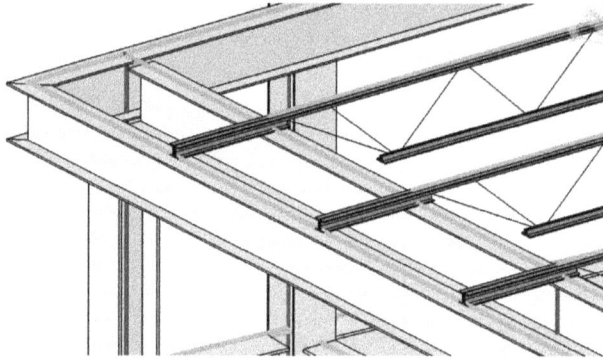

Figure 7–33

To cantilever or cutback a beam that is joined to other structural elements, use the shape handles to drag it to a new location, or set the *Start/End Join Cutback* in Properties, as shown in Figure 7–34,

Figure 7–34

* The Cutbacks only displays if the *Detail Level* is set to ▣ (Medium) or ▦ (Fine).

To cantilever a beam when the beam is not joined to other elements, you can use the **Drag Structural Framing Component End** shape handle (as shown in Figure 7–35), or in Properties set the *Start* or *End Extension.*

Figure 7–35

- When working with Beam Systems you first need to unpin the individual beam you want to work with. Select it and click the

  (Prevent or allow change of element position) icon.

Hint: Structural Connections

Structural connections can be added to framing joins to share in-depth information about the join with the contractor and fabricator. One generic connection (as shown in Figure 7–36) comes with Autodesk Revit. Others may be available with 3rd party add-ins.

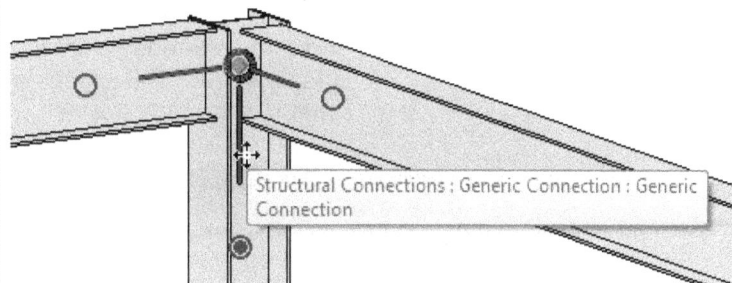

Figure 7–36

- In the *Structure* tab>Connection panel click

  (Connection). Then, hold <Ctrl> and select the structural elements assigned to the connection. Press <Enter> to apply the connection.

Changing the Cutback

You can select more than one element to adjust as long as they are connected to the same reference.

Another way to modify the join connection of structural framing is to change the cutback from the connected element. For example, the default cutback of the column shown in Figure 7–37 is the bounding box of the column, not the vertical support. You can change the reference to a more appropriate part of the framing.

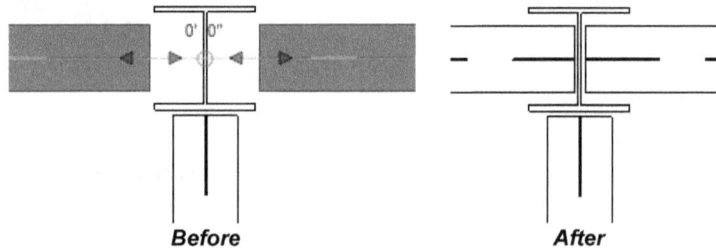

Before   *After*

Figure 7–37

- You can changing the reference in 2D and 3D views if the *Display Level* is set to **Medium** or **Fine**.

How To: Adjust the Cutback of Structural Framing

1. Select the structural framing member you want to modify.
2. In the *Modify | Structural Framing* tab>Join Tools panel, click

    ▓ (Change Reference).
3. Select the reference point for alignment, as shown on the left in Figure 7–38. This can be another beam, a structural column, or a structural wall.

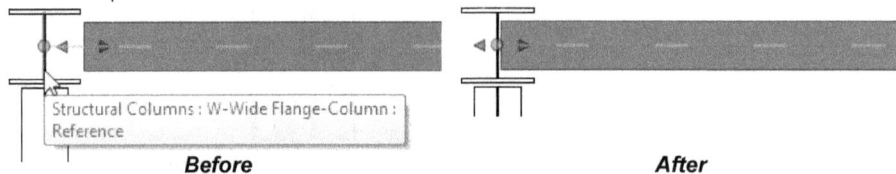

Structural Columns : W-Wide Flange-Column : Reference

Before   *After*

Figure 7–38

4. The end of the framing, the member moves to the new reference location, as shown on the right in Figure 7–38.
5. In Properties modify the *Start Join Cutback* or *End Join Cutback* distance as required.

- To return the beam end to its default setback position, click

    ▓ (Change Reference) again, and then select the bounding box (dashed lines) of the other element

Changing Justifications

Another modification you can make to beams is to change their justification. You can set the horizontal (y) and vertical (z) justification points to one of nine different points, such as **Origin Left**, shown in Figure 7–39. The Location Line remains in place, with the framing element moved to the new justification. You can also change the offset from the justification point in either the **y** (left to right), or **z** (top to bottom) directions. Both of these options can be modified either graphically or through Properties.

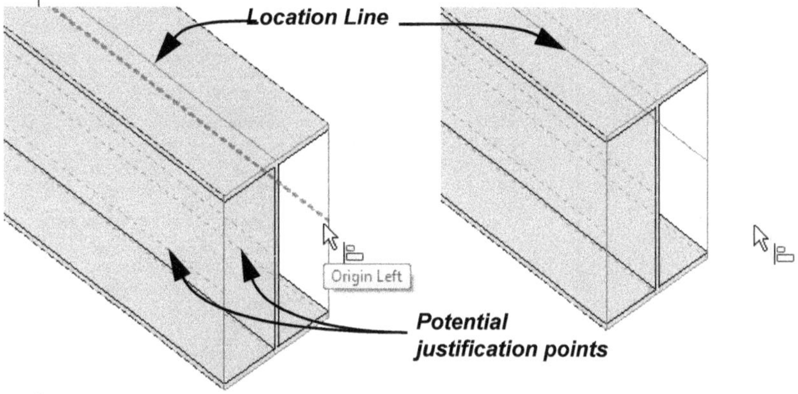

Figure 7–39

How To: Set the Justification of Framing Elements Graphically

1. Select the beam you want to modify.
2. in the *Modify | Structural Framing* tab>Justification panel, click ⊥ (Justification Points), or type **JP**.
3. Select the Justification points you want to use, as shown in Figure 7–40.

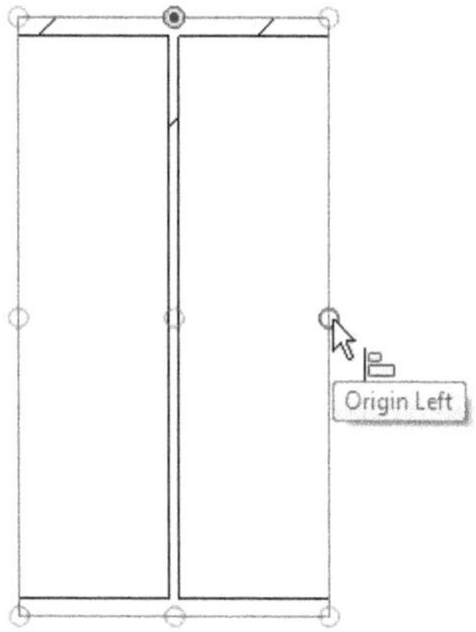

Figure 7–40

- The location line does not change, but the framing element repositions to the selected justification point.

- You can also modify the Justification points using the *y Justification* and *z* Justification parameters in Properties, as shown in Figure 7–41.

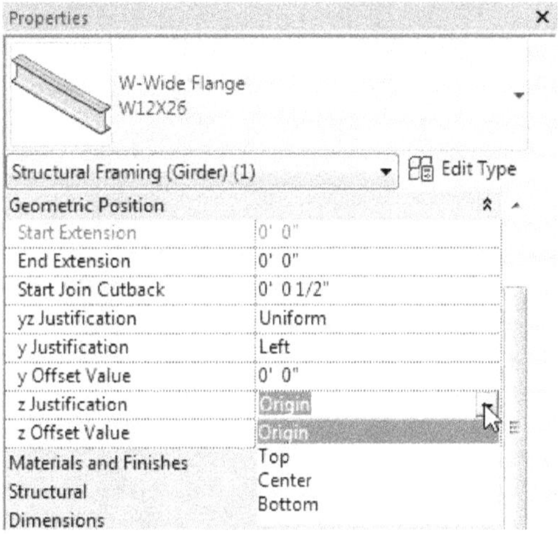

Figure 7–41

How To: Change the Justification Offset Graphically

1. Select the structural framing element.
2. In the *Modify | Structural Framing* tab>Justification panel:
   - Modify the horizontal offset and distance by clicking

     ⌐Ⅱ (y Offset), or type **JY**.
   - Modify the vertical offset and distance by clicking

     ⌐Ⅱ (z Offset), or type **JZ**.
3. Select the offset start point and then the offset end point.

- You can also modify the offset values in Properties by using the *y Offset Value* and *z Offset Value*.

- The *yz Justification* can be set to **Uniform** (where the same justification offset is applied to both ends) or **Independent** (where the justification offset can be different for each end). When this is selected you can set both the *Start y (or z) Offset Value* and the *End y (or z) Offset Values* in Properties, as shown in Figure 7–42.

Geometric Position		⋩
Start Extension	0' 0"	
End Extension	0' 0"	
yz Justification	Independent	
Start y Justification	Origin	
Start y Offset Value	0' 0"	
Start z Justification	Top	
Start z Offset Value	0' 0"	
End y Justification	Origin	
End y Offset Value	0' 0"	
End z Justification	Top	
End z Offset Value	0' 0"	

Figure 7–42

Hint: Viewing Justifications

At the Coarse Detail Level, when you select the beam, the justification line is displayed, as shown in Figure 7–43.

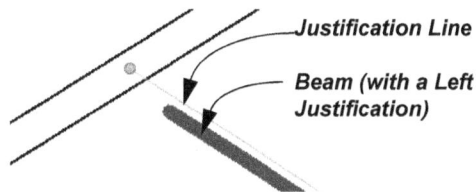

Figure 7–43

When working in the Medium (or Fine) Detail Level, along with toggling on the Location Line in Visibility/Graphics it can help to display the analytical model, as shown in Figure 7–44. In the View Control Bar, click (Show Analytical Model).

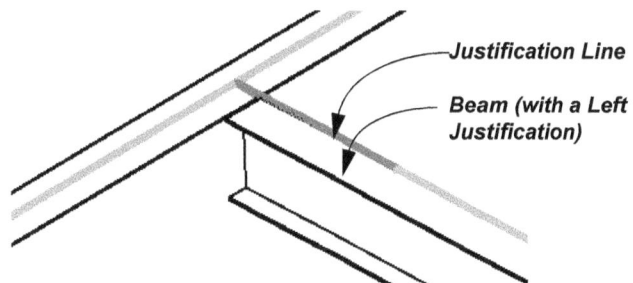

Figure 7–44

Attaching a Column to a Beam

The columns that support the cantilever can be attached to the bottom of the framing member, as shown in Figure 7–45. This removes the need to estimate the actual bearing depth of the framing member, and ensures that the column always remains connected to the beam.

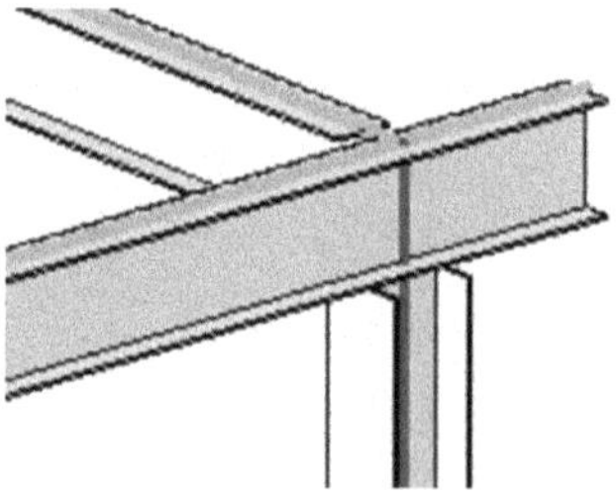

Figure 7–45

How To: Attach a Column to the Bottom of a Beam

1. Select a column.
2. In the *Modify Structural Columns* tab>Modify Column panel, click ⬛ (Attach Top/Base).
3. In the Options Bar, set the options as required. If you need to add a bearing plate, set the *Offset from Attachment* value.
4. Select the beam that the column will attach to.

- You can also use this command to attach the base of a beam to structural footings. When the footing moves in height, the length of the column resizes to match.

Applying Beam Coping

When one beam connects with another beam you might need to modify the connection. In the example shown in Figure 7–46, the lower joist-bearing beam runs into the perimeter beam. This is a coping situation.

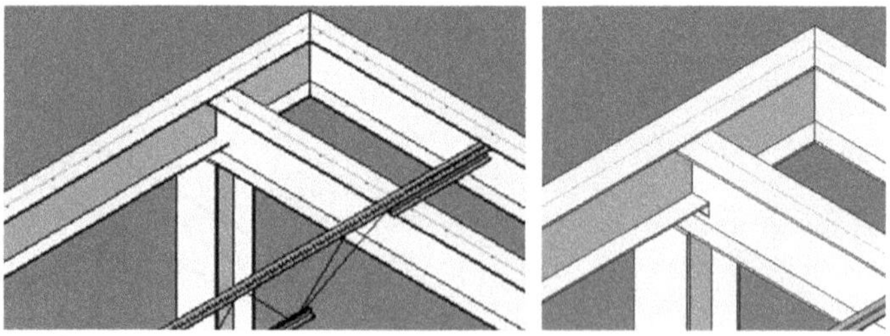

Figure 7–46

How To: Cope Beams

1. Open a 3D view, section, or detail view.
2. Zoom in to a beam to beam (or beam to column) connection.

3. In the *Modify* tab>Geometry panel, expand ⅃ᴄ (Cope) and

   select ⅃ᴄ (Apply Coping).
4. Select the beam to be coped first followed by the column/beam from which to cut. The cope is then completed.

   - You can change the *Coping Distance* setting in Properties.

Editing Beam Joins

When you add beams to a project there is a default layout to the beam joins. However, you might need to override the joins. You can do this by using **Change Beam Status**, as shown in Figure 7–47.

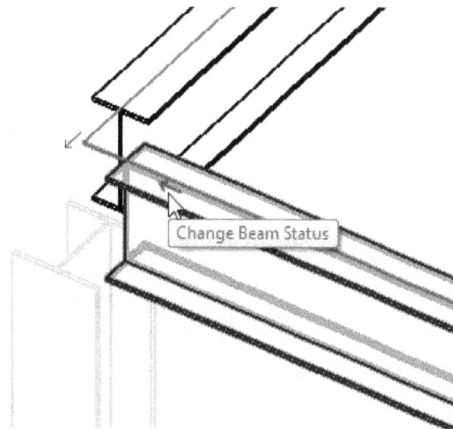

Figure 7–47

How To: Edit Beam Joins

1. In the *Modify* tab>Geometry panel, click ▀ (Beam/Column Joins). The work area switches to **Sketch** mode.

   - Only the beams and/or columns that can be changed are highlighted.
   - You cannot use this tool on beams that are attached to vertical columns.

2. In the Options Bar, specify the types of beams that you want to work with as shown in Figure 7–48.

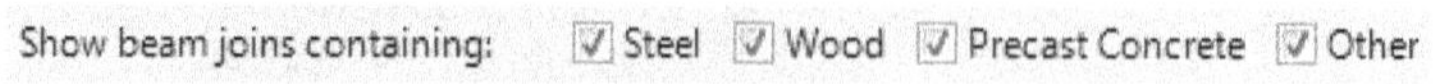

Show beam joins containing: ☑ Steel ☑ Wood ☑ Precast Concrete ☑ Other

Figure 7–48

3. Click the **Change Beam Status** control to toggle the join.

4. Click (Beam/Column Joins) again to toggle the command off.

 • If you are mitering a corner, you can lock the miter as shown in Figure 7–49.

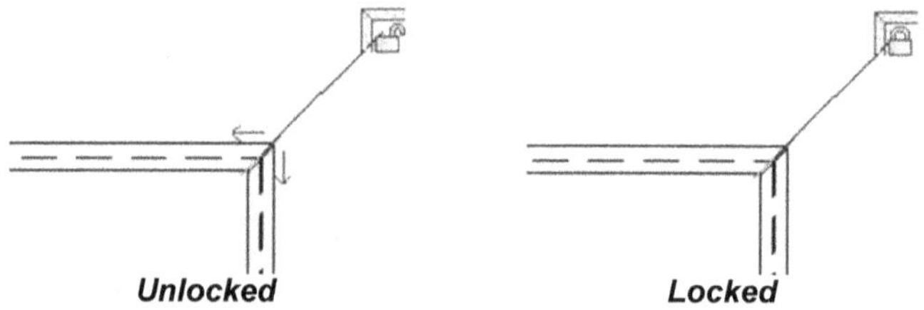

Unlocked   *Locked*

Figure 7–49

Hint: Join Status

You can modify the *Join Status* of structural framing to position framing that butts against a wall or other beams. Right-click on the join control (the circle), select **Disallow Join** (as shown on the left in Figure 7–50), and make the required modifications. Click **Allow Join** to rejoin the elements.

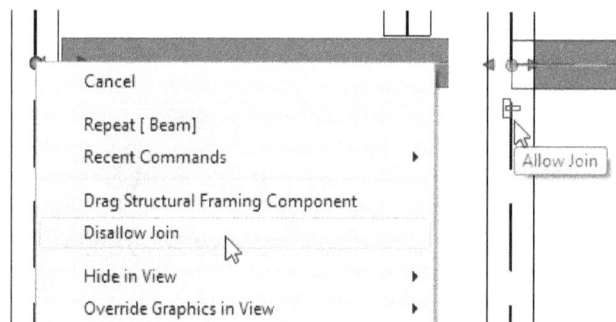

Figure 7–50

 • *Join Status* is field that can be used in schedules. You can modify the status in the schedule.

Practice 7b | Modify Structural Framing

Practice Objectives

- Modify beam level offsets.
- Sketch Beam Systems.

Estimated time for completion: 20 minutes

In this practice you will modify beam level offsets for correct joist bearing and add beam systems using the automatic method where you can and sketch beam systems in areas where they cannot be automatically placed, as shown in Figure 7–51.

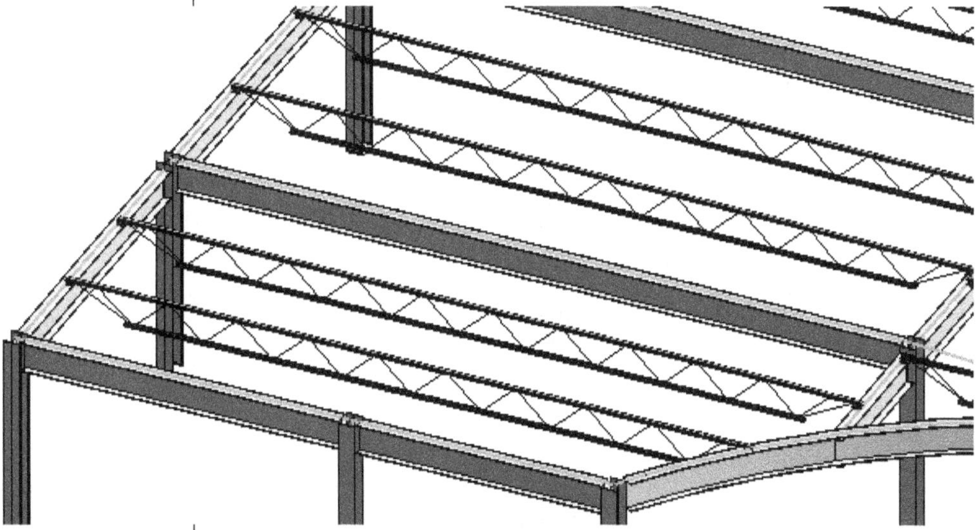

Figure 7–51

Task 1 - Modify beam level offsets.

1. Open **Syracuse-Suites-Framing.rvt**.

2. Open the **Structural Plans: TOS-14 ROOF** view.

3. Hide the grids.

4. For this level you need to lower the perimeter beams of each bay in the North-South direction for the joist bearing. Select all of the vertical beams in the plan, excluding the beams along the far right, as shown in Figure 7–52.

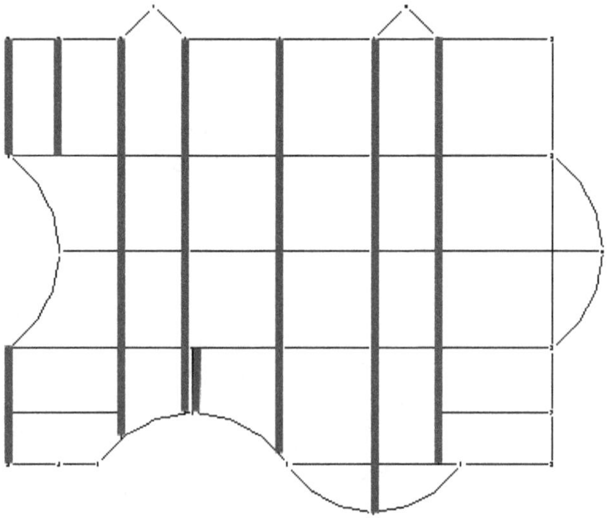

If you selected bracing element, you need to filter them out.

Figure 7–52

5. In Properties, change the *Start Level* and *End Level Offsets* to (negative) **-2 1/2"**.

6. Click **Apply**.

7. Open a 3D view and zoom in on one of the top floor intersections. The North-South girders should be displayed below the East-West girders as shown in Figure 7–53.

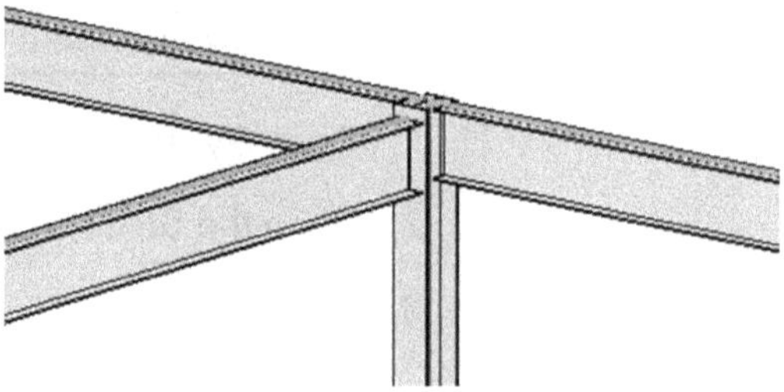

Figure 7–53

8. Save the project.

Task 2 - Sketch beam systems.

1. Switch to **Structural Plans: TOS-14 ROOF** view.

2. In the *Insert* tab>Load from Library panel, click 📥 (Load Family).

3. In the Load Family dialog box, browse to the *Structural Framing>Steel* folder, select **K-Series Bar Joist-Rod Web.rfa**, and click **Open**.

4. In the Specify Types dialog box, select **16K7** from the list and click **OK**.

5. In the *Structure* tab>Structure panel, click ▦ (Beam System). In the Options Bar and Properties, set the following parameters:
   - *Beam Type:* **16K7**
   - *Layout Rule:* **Maximum Spacing**
   - *Maximum Spacing:* **6'-0"**

6. Hover the cursor over the lower left girder as shown in Figure 7–54. The Beam System does not stop at the boundary of the other girders as expected because of the lower bearing offset. Do not select the beam.

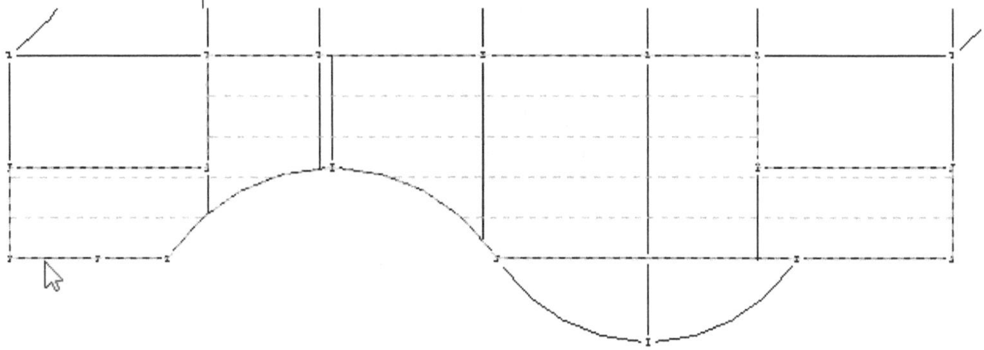

Figure 7–54

7. In the *Modify | Place Structural Beam System* tab>Beam System panel, click ▦ (Sketch Beam System).

8. In Properties, In the *Identity Data* section, change *Tag new members* in view to **None**.

9. In the *Modify | Place Beam System Boundary* tab>Draw panel, click ⬚ (Pick Supports).

10. Draw a boundary with the beam direction running **West** to **East** as shown in Figure 7–55. Use ⬚ (Trim) to clean up overlapping lines.

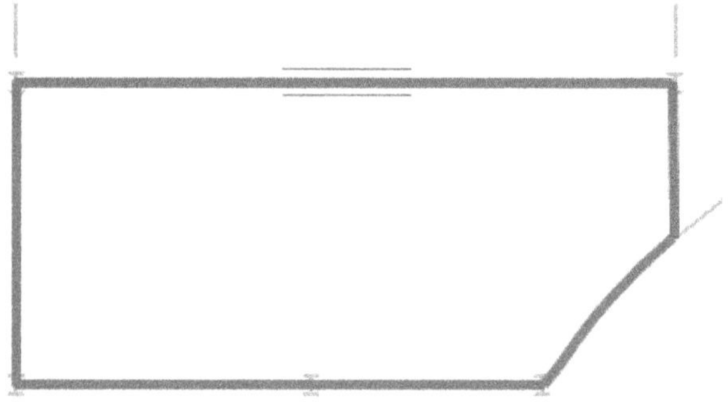

Figure 7–55

11. In the Mode panel, click ✓ (Finish Edit Mode).

12. Repeat this procedure for the rest of the bays, as shown in Figure 7–56.

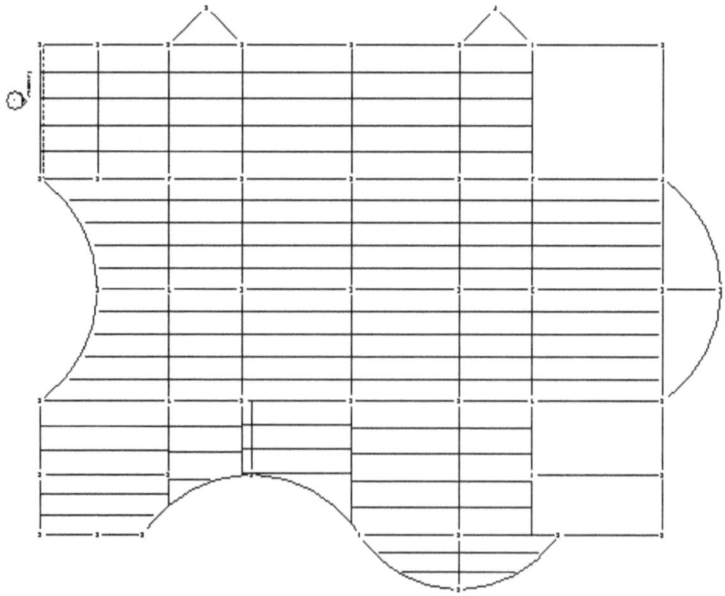

Figure 7–56

- Use ⬚ (Automatic Beam System) where you can. If you have trouble placing the joists because of the bearing offset, use ⬚ (Sketch Beam System).
- If the error shown in Figure 7–57 opens, the space for the joist might be too small to be created by the **Beam System** command. Click **Delete Type**. You can add a beam separately as required.

Errors such as this occur, so you should not neglect potential problems. They are an important part of using the BIM model process.

Autodesk Revit Structure
Error - cannot be ignored

Can't make type "K-Series Bar Joist-Rod Web : 16K7".

Show   More Info   Expand >>

Delete Type   OK   Cancel

Figure 7–57

13. Save the project.

7.3 Adding Trusses

A truss can be added to a project using the same basic method as placing a beam. Trusses are typically comprised of one or more triangular sections, as shown in Figure 7–58. These sections are constructed with structural members whose ends are connected at joints, which are referred to as nodes. As various forces act on these nodes, the triangular shape provides structural stability to prevent bending.

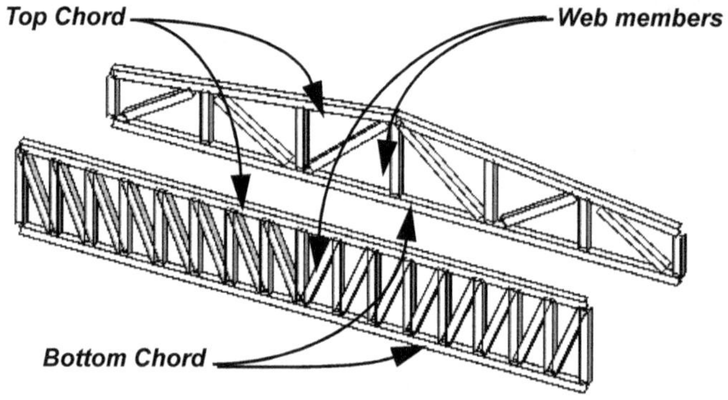

Figure 7–58

Truss elements include:

- **Bottom Chord**, the lower horizontal member.
- **Top Chord**, the upper horizontal member.
- **Web**, the series of structural framing elements that stabilize the truss.

The **Top** and **Bottom Chords** fulfill the same function as a beam's top and bottom flanges. The **Web** takes the place of the beam's continuous plate.

How To: Add Trusses

1. In the *Structure* tab>Structure panel click ▧ (Structural Trusses).
2. In the Type Selector, select the type of truss you want to use

   - Click 🗇 (Load Family) and navigate to the *Structural Trusses* folder to add families to the project.

3. In the *Modify | Place Truss* tab>Draw panel, click ╱ (Line) or ⟋ (Pick Lines) and add the trusses to the project.

Attaching Trusses to Roofs

Trusses can be attached to roofs or floor slabs. They can also follow the slope of the roof and automatically extend to fit, as shown in Figure 7–59.

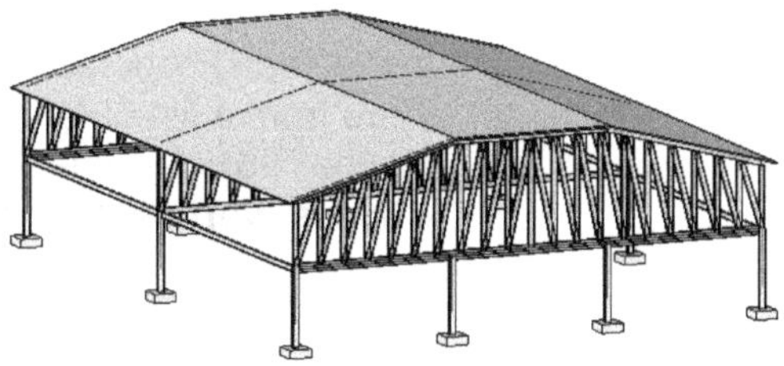

Figure 7–59

How To: Attach Trusses to Roofs

1. In the *Modify | Structural Trusses* tab>Modify Truss panel, click ⬚↑ (Attach Top/Bottom).
2. In the Options Bar, set *Attach Trusses* to **Top** or **Bottom**.
3. Select the roof or floor element. The truss attaches to the element and follows the angle or slope, as shown in Figure 7–60.

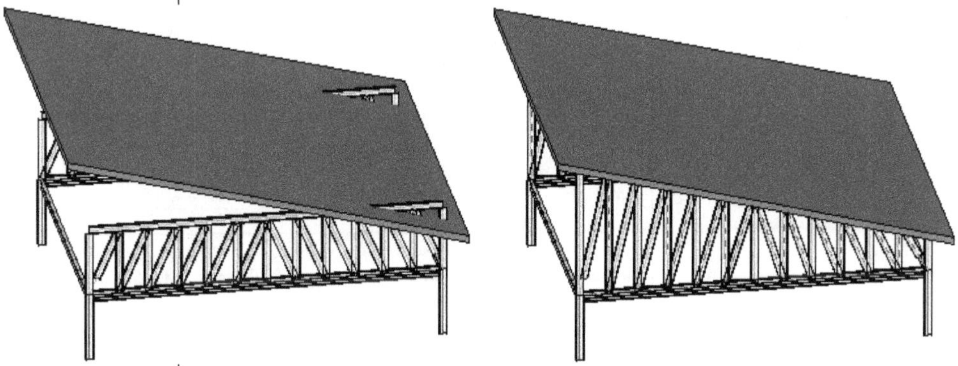

Figure 7–60

- The top chord must be one continuous line in the family. If it is broken into segments, attaching it might not work properly.

- Verify that the bottom chord is specified as the bearing chord in the element properties of the truss. This ensures that the roof loads are carried throughout the truss appropriately.

- If the roof/floor slab does not cover the length of the truss, an error message opens and you might have to detach the truss.

Setting Framing Types in Trusses

When truss families are created they can include structural framing members for the chords and webs. However, they often just use default members. Therefore, you need to specify the precise framing types you want to use in the project.

In the Type Properties dialog box, select the **Structural Framing Type** from a list of families loaded into the project, as shown in Figure 7–61. Set the *Structural Framing Type* for the **Top Chords**, **Vertical Webs**, **Diagonal Webs**, and **Bottom Chords**.

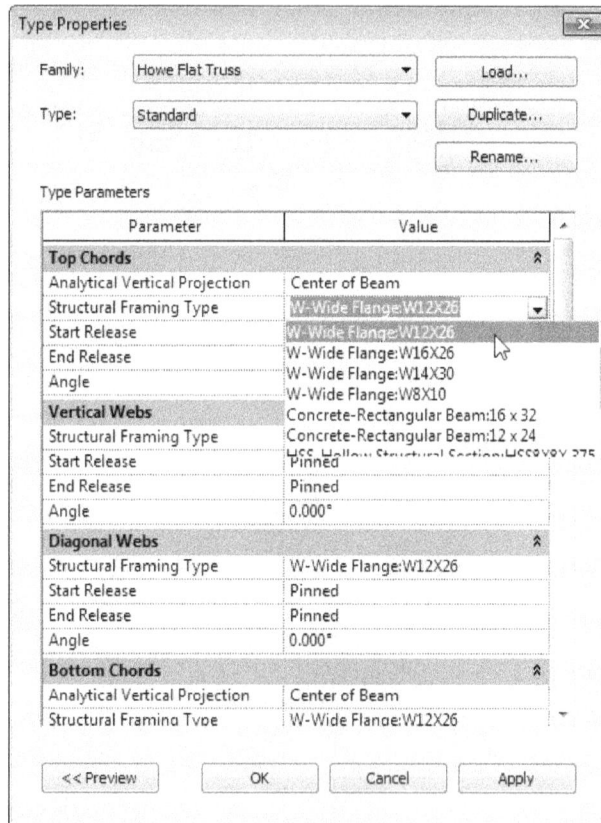

Figure 7–61

- To select an entire truss, ensure that the dashed lines are displayed, as shown on the left in Figure 7–62. To select one element of the truss, press <Tab> until the element that you want to select is highlighted, as shown on the right in Figure 7–62.

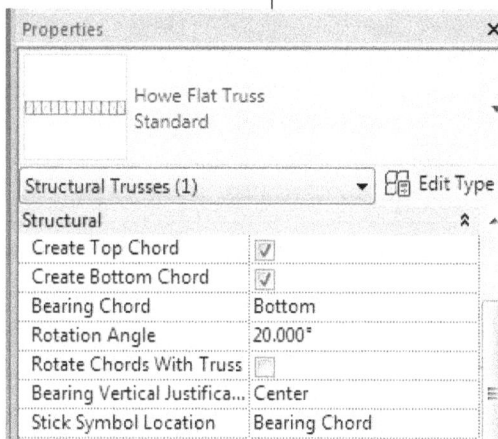

Structural Framing : W-Wide Flange : W12X26

Figure 7–62

- Individual Truss members are pinned to the truss framework. If you want to modify one of these you need to click

  🔘 (Prevent or allow change of element position) to unpin only that member.

- You can rotate Trusses. and specify if the chords rotate with the truss. In Properties, type in a *Rotation Angle* and select or clear *Rotate Chords with Truss,* as shown in Figure 7–63.

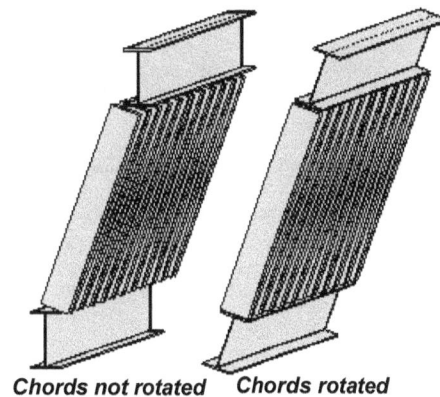

Properties ✕

Howe Flat Truss
Standard

Structural Trusses (1)   ▾ 🔲 Edit Type

Structural   ⌃
Create Top Chord	☑
Create Bottom Chord	☑
Bearing Chord	Bottom
Rotation Angle	20.000°
Rotate Chords With Truss	☐
Bearing Vertical Justifica...	Center
Stick Symbol Location	Bearing Chord

Chords not rotated   *Chords rotated*

Figure 7–63

Practice 7c | Add Trusses

Practice Objectives

- Set up a truss type.
- Add trusses to a project.
- Attach trusses to a roof.

Estimated time for completion: 10 minutes

In this practice you will setup a truss using specific structural framing types for the chords and webs. You will then draw a truss and array it across an open span. Finally, you will attach the trusses to an existing roof element, as shown in Figure 7–64.

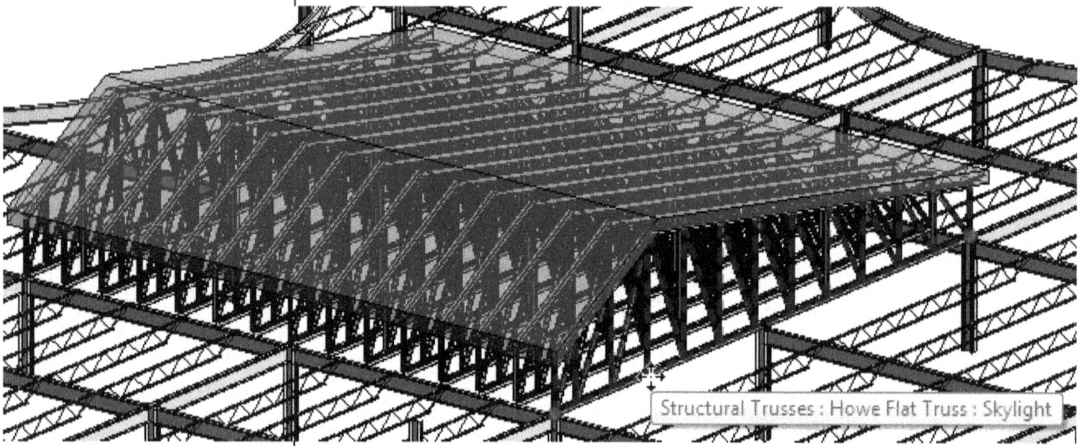

Structural Trusses : Howe Flat Truss : Skylight

Figure 7–64

Task 1 - Set up a Truss Type

1. Open **Syracuse-Suites-Trusses.rvt**.

2. Start the ✍ (Beam) command and investigate the available structural framing elements, shown in Figure 7–65. There are two sizes of LL-Double-Angles, but you need an additional, smaller size.

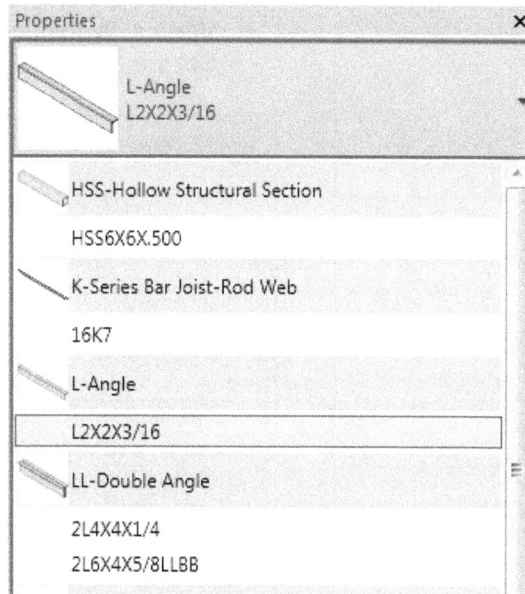

Figure 7–65

3. In the *Insert* tab>Load from Library panel, click 📥 (Load Family).

4. In the Load Family dialog box, navigate to the *Structural Framing>Steel* folder and select **LL-Double Angle.rfa**. Click **Open**.

5. In the Specify Types dialog box, select **2L3X2-1/2X1/2LLBB** and click **OK**.

6. When the Family Already Exists dialog box displays, select **Overwrite the existing version and its parameter values**.

7. In the *Structure* tab>Structure panel, click ⋀⋀⋀ (Truss).

8. In the Type Selector, select **Howe Flat Truss: Standard** and click 🗒 (Edit Type).

9. In the Type Properties dialog box, click **Duplicate**.

10. In the Name dialog box, type **Skylight**, and click **OK**.

11. In the Type Properties dialog box, set the following properties as shown in Figure 7–66:

- **Top Cords** and **Bottom Chords:**
  Set the *Structural Framing Type* to **2L6X4X5/8LLBB**.
- **Vertical Webs** and **Diagonal Webs:**
  Set the *Structural Framing Type* to **2L3X2-1/2X1/2LLBB**.

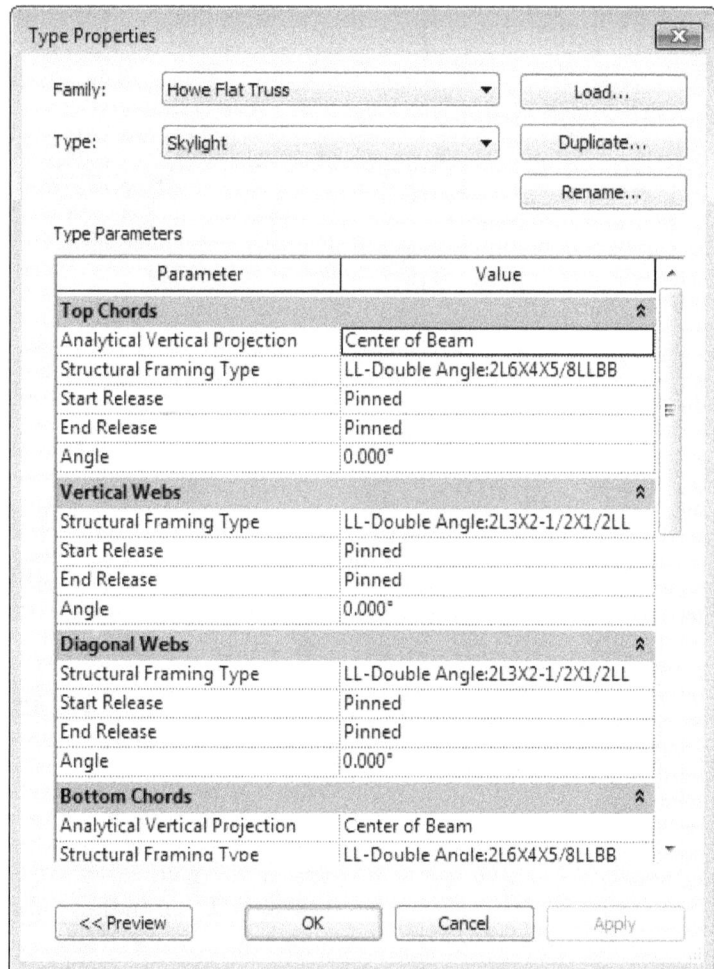

Figure 7–66

12. Click **OK**.

13. Save the project.

Task 2 - Add Trusses.

1. Open the **Structural Plans: TOS-14 ROOF** view. Some of the structural framing has been removed in this plan to make way for a large skylight, as shown in Figure 7–67.

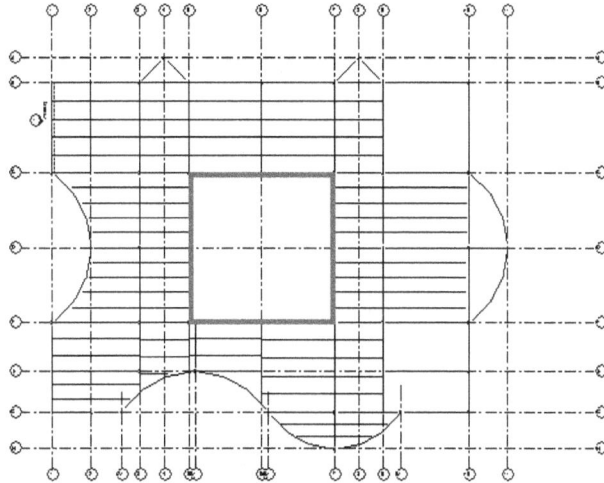

Figure 7–67

2. Start the ▨ (Truss) command.

3. In the Type Selector, verify that the **Howe Flat Truss: Skylight** is selected.

4. In Properties, set the *Bearing Chord* to **Bottom** and the *Truss Height* to **4'-0"**.

5. Draw the first truss, as shown in Figure 7–68.

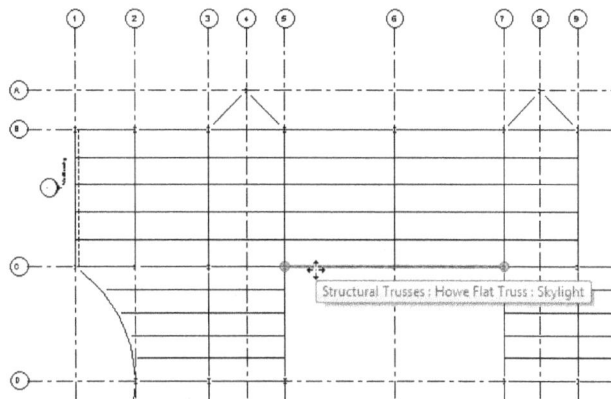

Structural Trusses : Howe Flat Truss : Skylight

Figure 7–68

6. Click ⌖ (Modify) and select the new truss.

7. In the *Modify | Structural Trusses* tab>Modify panel, click ⊞ (Array).

8. In the Options Bar, ensure that ᴍ (Linear) is selected and **Group and Associate** is cleared. Set the *Number* to **15** and the *Move To:* to **Last**.

9. To specify the length of the array, click on **Grid C** and then on **Grid E**.

10. Open the **3D Views: Roof and Skylight** view to see the trusses, as shown in Figure 7–69.

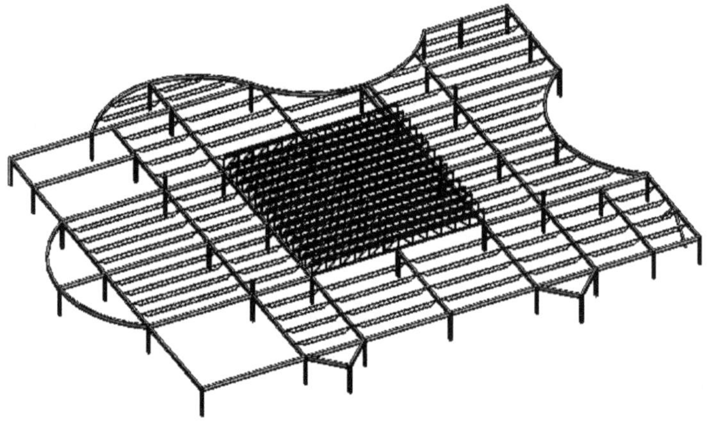

Figure 7–69

11. Save the project.

Task 3 - Attach the Trusses to a Roof.

1. Open the Visibility Graphic Overrides dialog box and toggle on **Roofs**. An existing roof (referencing the location of the skylight) displays.

2. In the Quick Access Toolbar, click ⬚ (Close Hidden Windows) so that only the 3D view displays.

3. Open the **Elevations (Building Elevations): East** and **South** views.

4. Type **WT** to tile the three views and **ZA** so that they are all zoomed out fully.

5. Zoom in on the skylight roof in the two elevation views, similar to that shown in Figure 7–70.

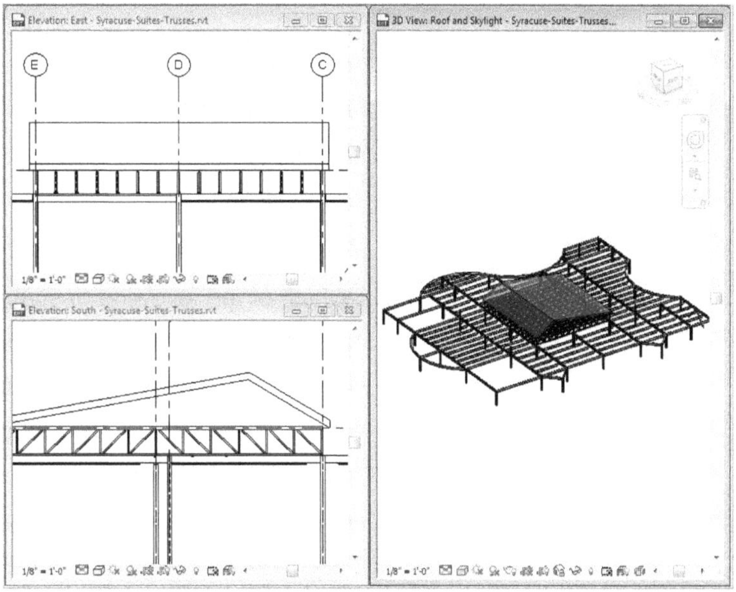

Figure 7–70

6. In the **Elevation: East** view, use a crossing window to select all of the trusses and other overlapping elements and then filter out everything but the trusses.

7. In the *Modify | Structural Trusses* tab>Modify Truss panel, click (Attach Top/Bottom).

8. Select the roof. Allow time for it all to process until the trusses expand to touch the roof, as shown in Figure 7–71.

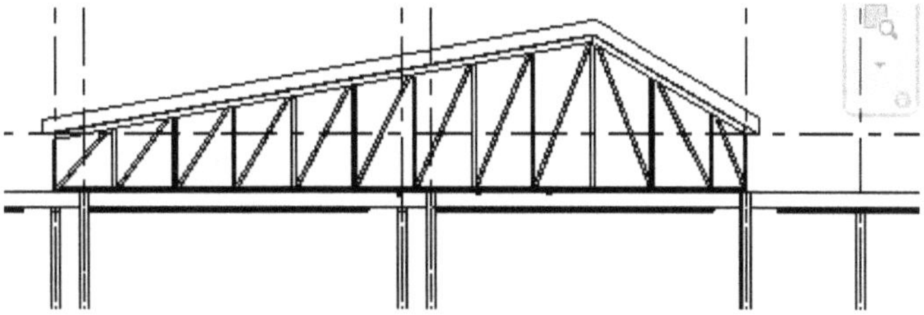

Figure 7–71

9. Expand the **3D View: Roof and Skyligh**t view to fit the window.

10. Save the project.

Chapter Review Questions

1. When placing a beam, which of the following is NOT an option?

   a. Structural Usage

   b. Placement Plane

   c. 3D Snapping

   d. At Columns

2. Which of the following describes a Beam System?

   a. Parallel beams grouped together after they are placed.

   b. Parallel beams placed at the same time.

   c. All beams in a bay grouped together after they are placed.

   d. All beams in a bay placed at the same time.

3. In a plan view, which of the following changes the display to show the stick symbol for beams, as shown in Figure 7–72?

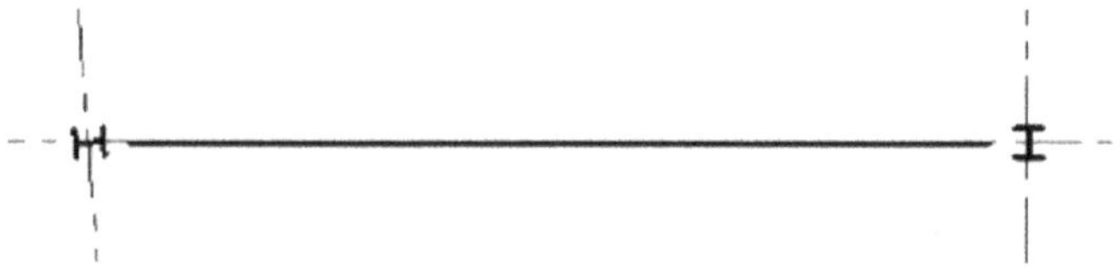

Figure 7–72

   a. Detail Level: Coarse

   b. Detail Level: Medium

   c. Visual Style: Wireframe

   d. Visual Style: Hidden

4. How do you create sloped beams such as those shown in Figure 7–73?

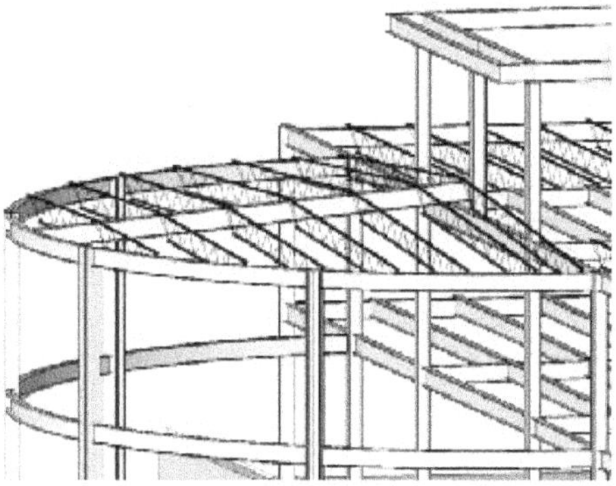

Figure 7–73

a. Specify the Slope before you start drawing the beam.

b. Specify the Start/End Level Offset before you start drawing the beam.

c. Change the Slope after you have drawn the beam.

d. Change the Start/End Level Offset after you have drawn the beam.

5. Where do you assign the structural member types and sizes for the components of a truss, such as that shown in Figure 7–74? (Select all that apply.)

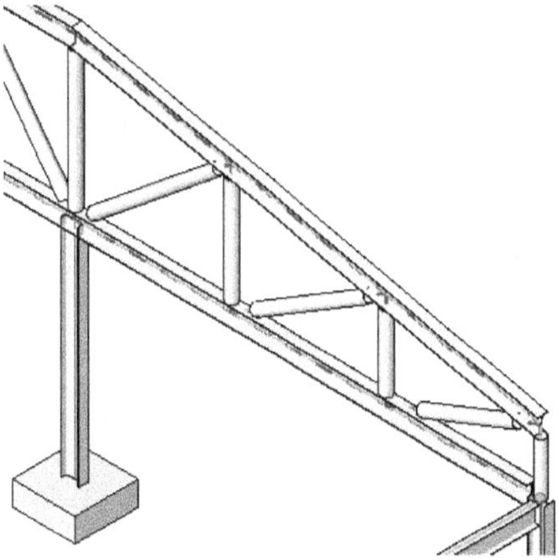

Figure 7–74

a. In Family Types

b. In Properties

c. In Type Properties

d. In the Options Bar

Command Summary

Button	Command	Location
Clipboard		
	Copy to Clipboard	• **Ribbon:** *Modify* tab>Clipboard panel • **Shortcut:** <Ctr>+C
	Paste	• **Ribbon:** *Modify* tab>Clipboard panel • **Shortcut:** <Ctr>+<V>
	(Paste) Aligned to Selected Levels	• **Ribbon:** *Modify* tab>Clipboard panel
	(Paste) Aligned to Selected View	• **Ribbon:** *Modify* tab>Clipboard panel
Structural Framing Elements		
	Beam	• **Ribbon:** *Structure* tab>Structure panel
	Beam System	• **Ribbon:** *Structure* tab>Structure panel
	Brace	• **Ribbon:** *Structure* tab>Structure panel • **Shortcut:** BR
	Structural Trusses	• **Ribbon:** *Structure* tab>Structure panel
Structural Framing Modification		
	Apply Coping	• **Ribbon:** *Modify* tab>Geometry panel, expand Cope
	Attach Top/Base	• **Ribbon:** *Modify	Structural Columns>* Modify Column panel
	Attach Top/Bottom	• **Ribbon:** *Modify	Structural Trusses>* Modify Truss panel
	Beam/Column Joins	• **Ribbon:** *Modify* tab>Geometry panel
	Change Reference	• **Ribbon:** *Modify	Structural Framing>* Join Tools panel
	Connection	• **Ribbon:** *Structure* tab>Connection panel
	Detach Top/Base	• **Ribbon:** *Modify	Structural Columns>* Modify Column panel
	Detach Top/Bottom	• **Ribbon:** *Modify	Structural Trusses>* Modify Truss panel
	Justification Points	• **Ribbon:** *Modify	Structural Framing>* Justification panel • **Shortcut:** JP

	Offset	• **Ribbon:** *Modify	Structural Framing>* Justification panel	
	y Offset	• **Ribbon:** *Modify	Structural Framing>* Justification panel • **Shortcut:** JY	
	z Offset	• **Ribbon:** *Modify	Structural Framing>* Justification panel • **Shortcut:** JZ	

Adding Structural Slabs

Structural slabs can be used for foundation slabs (slab on grade), floors, and roofs. Slab edges can be added to foundation slabs and floors to provide additional stability. For multi-story buildings, you can cut holes in the slabs either individually, or by creating a shaft that passes through several slabs.

Learning Objectives in this Chapter

- Create slabs for foundations, structural floors, and roofs.
- Add slab edges for stability along each side of the slab.
- Create shaft openings that pass through multiple levels for elevators and stairwells.

8.1 Modeling Structural Slabs

Floors, some roofs, and foundation slabs (shown in Figure 8–1) are created using similar tools. Slabs are created by sketching a boundary and then applying options such as **Span Direction** and **Slope**. After you create a structural slab, you can add and modify the slab edges.

The term slab in this topic applies to structural foundation slabs, floors, and roofs.

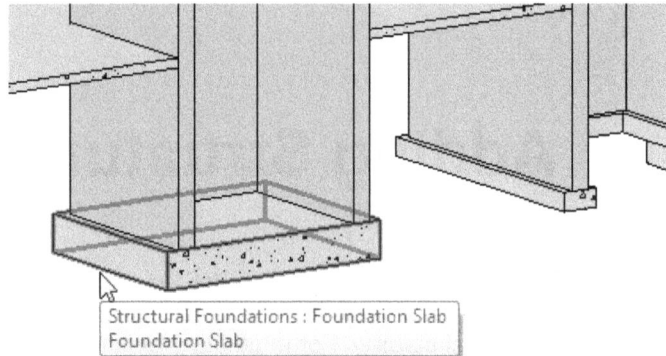

Structural Foundations : Foundation Slab
Foundation Slab

Figure 8–1

How To: Place a Structural Slab for Foundations or Floors

1. In the *Structure* tab>Foundation panel, click ⬭ (Slab) or in the *Structure* tab>Structure panel, click ⌒ (Floor: Structural) or type **SB**.
2. In the Type Selector, select the slab or floor type you want to use.
3. In Properties, set any other options you might need
4. In the *Modify | Create Floor Boundary* tab>Draw panel, use one of the following options to create a closed boundary:

   - Use the Draw tools, such as ⁄ (Line) or ⬉ (Pick Lines) when the slab is not defined by walls or other structural elements.

   - Use ⬚ (Pick Walls) when walls define the perimeter

   - Use ⬚ (Pick Supports) and select structural walls or beams if support beams have already been placed in the project.

Boundaries created by **Pick Walls** *and* **Pick Supports** *ensure that the slab adjusts if the footprint of the building changes.*

5. Click 🔲 (Span Direction) to modify the direction for floor spans. It comes in automatically when you place the first boundary line, as shown in Figure 8–2.

6. ↔ (Flip) switches the inside/outside status of the boundary location if you have a wall selected, as shown in Figure 8–2.

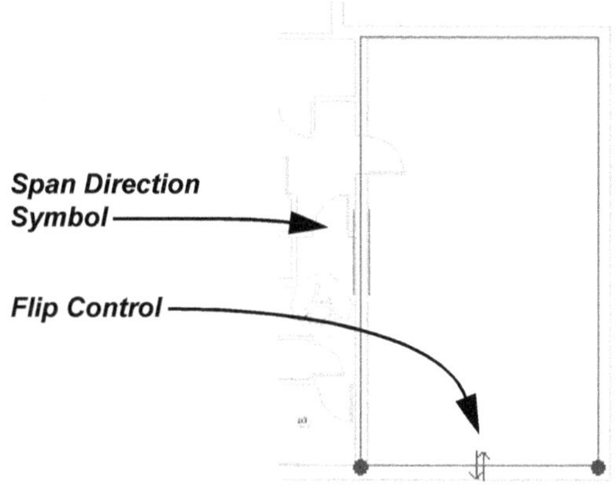

Span Direction Symbol ————

Flip Control ————

Figure 8–2

7. In the *Modify | Create Floor Boundary* tab>Mode panel, click

   ✓ (Finish Edit Mode).

• While placing the slab boundary, you can set an offset in the Options Bar, which places the sketched line at a distance offset from a selected wall or another sketched line.

• If you are using 🔲 (Pick Walls), the **Extend into wall (to core)** option is also available in the Options Bar. Use this if you want the slab to cut into the wall. For example, the slab would cut through the gypsum wall board and the air space but would stop at a core layer such as CMU.

• If you select one of the boundary sketches, you can also set **Cantilevers** for *Concrete* or *Steel*, as shown in Figure 8–3.

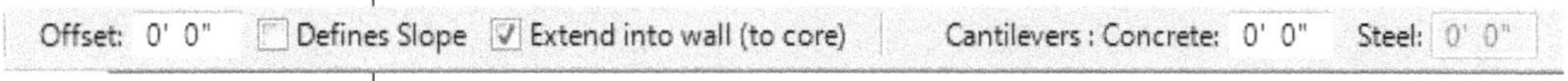

Offset: 0' 0" ☐ Defines Slope ☑ Extend into wall (to core)   Cantilevers : Concrete: 0' 0"   Steel: 0' 0"

Figure 8–3

- Each line that defines the perimeter of the slab has its own set of properties. This is because different sides of the building can have different slab edge conditions. Setting a cantilever can control the detail as shown in Figure 8–4.

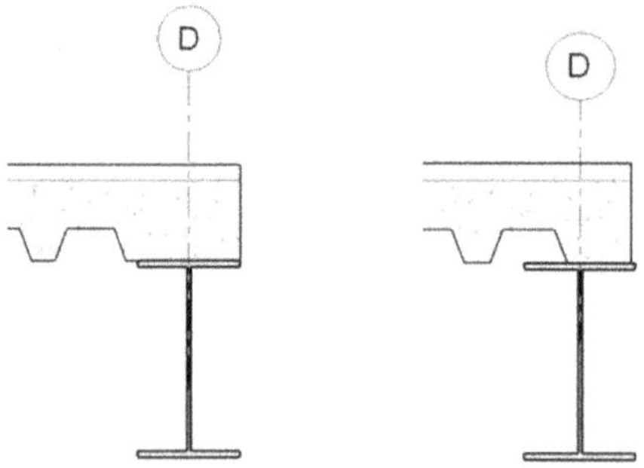

Figure 8–4

- If you specify a cantilever, such as the example shown in Figure 8–5, both the magenta line for the sketch and the black line for the actual slab edge display. This affects how the decking is terminated.

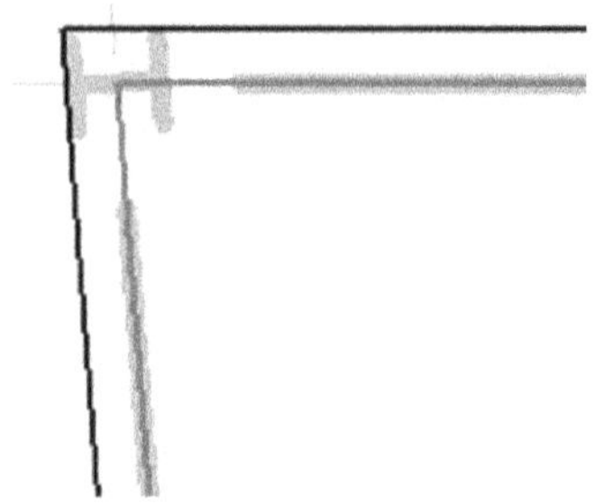

Figure 8–5

- This does not add a pour stop or edge angle. You can do so after you finish the sketch.

- To create an opening inside the sketch, create a separate closed loop inside the first sketch, as shown in Figure 8–6.

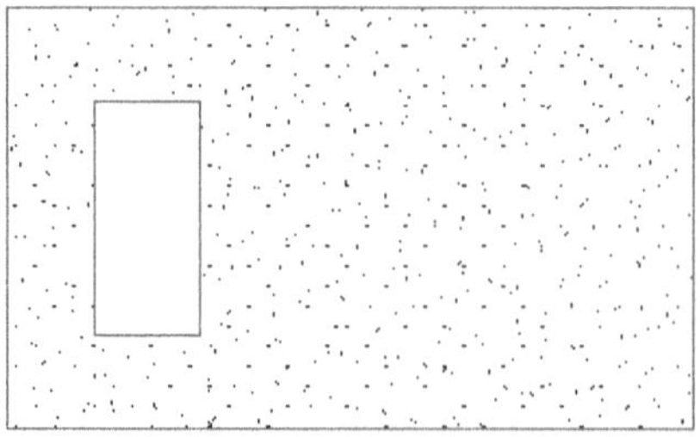

Figure 8–6

- If you create a floor on an upper level, an alert box displays asking if you want the walls below to be attached to the underside of the floor and its level. If you have a variety of wall heights, it is better to click **No** and attach the walls separately.

- Another alert box might open, as shown in Figure 8–7. You can automatically join the geometry now or later.

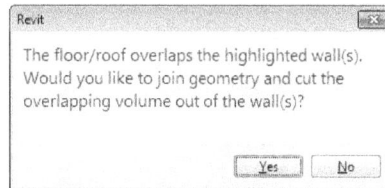

Figure 8–7

- If the *Visual Style* is set to ⬭ (Hidden Line), the slab hides any lines that are underneath it, usually displaying as a dashed line, as shown in Figure 8–8.

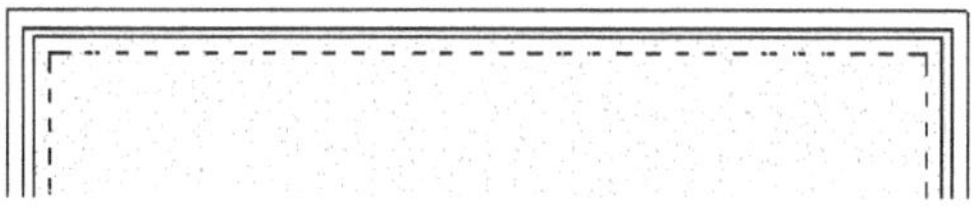

Figure 8–8

How To: Place a Roof Slab

Structural floor elements are occasionally used in place of roof elements.

1. In the *Architecture* tab>Build panel, expand ⬐ (Roof) and click ⬐ (Roof by Footprint)
2. In the Type Selector, select the roof type you want to use.
3. In the *Modify | Create Roof Footprint* tab>Draw panel, use the following options to create a closed boundary:

   - Use the Draw tools, such as ⟋ (Line), ⬨ (Pick Lines), or ⬓ (Pick Walls) when walls define the perimeter

4. In the Options Bar, set the slope and overhang options. Clear the **Define slope** option and set *Overhang* to **0** for a flat roof, as shown in Figure 8–9.

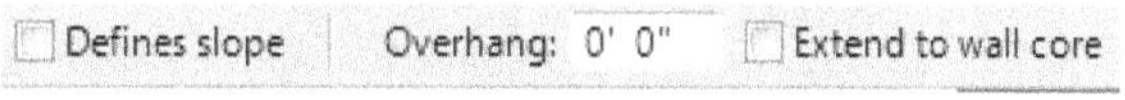

Figure 8–9

5. Click ✓ (Finish Edit Mode).

Modifying Slabs

You can change a slab to a different type in the Type Selector. In Properties, you can modify parameters including the *Height Offset From Level*, as shown for a structural floor in Figure 8–10. When you have a slab selected, you can also edit the boundaries.

The slab type controls the thickness of a slab.

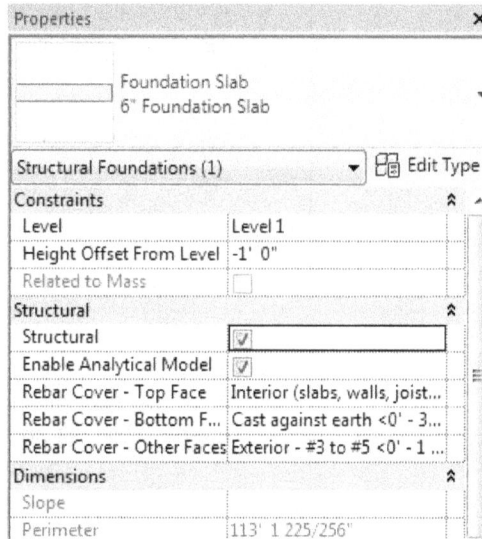

Figure 8–10

Many of the parameters in Properties are used in schedules, including Elevation at Top (Bottom) and Elevation at Top (Bottom) Core for multi-layered floors.

How To: Modify the Slab Sketch

1. Select a slab. You might need to highlight an element near the slab and press <Tab> until the type displays in the Status Bar or in a tooltip, as shown in Figure 8–11.

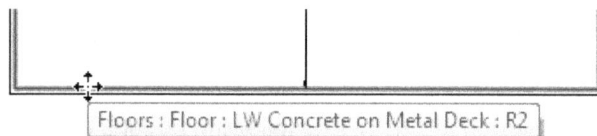

Floors : Floor : LW Concrete on Metal Deck : R2

Figure 8–11

2. In the *Modify contextual* tab>Mode panel, click (Edit Boundary). You are placed in sketch mode.
3. Modify the sketch lines by using the draw tools, controls, and other modify tools.

4. Click (Finish Edit Mode).

- Double-click on a slab to move directly to editing the boundary.

- Sketches can be edited in plan and 3D views, but not in elevations. If you try to edit a sketch in an elevation view, you are prompted to select another view for editing.

> **Hint: Selecting Slab Faces**
>
> If it is difficult to select the slab edges, toggle on ⬚ (Select elements by face). This enables you to select the slab face in addition to the edges. This is also helpful to use when selecting walls in elevation or section views.

Slab Edges

Cutting a section through the objects you want to join helps to display them more clearly.

You can add elements to a foundation slab or structural floor for a haunched or thickened slab edge, as shown in Figure 8–12. Once the slab edge is in place it needs to be joined to the slab or structural floor.

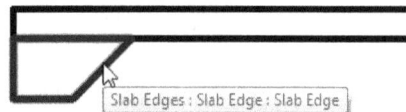

Figure 8–12

- Slab edges cannot be applied to roof elements.

How To: Place a Slab Edge

1. Open a 3D view showing the slab.
2. In the *Structure* tab>Foundation panel, expand ◇ (Slab) or in the *Structure* tab>Structure panel, expand ⌒ (Floor) and click ◇ (Floor: Slab Edge).
3. In the Type Selector, select the slab edge type.
4. Select the edges of the slab or floor where you want to apply the slab edge as shown in Figure 8–13. You can press <Tab> to highlight and select all sides of the slab.

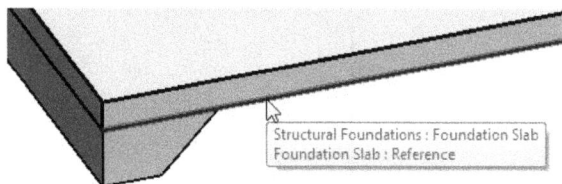

Figure 8–13

Joining Geometry

Join Geometry is a versatile command used to clean up intersections. The elements remain separate, but the intersections are cleaned up. It can be used with many types of elements including slabs, floors, walls, and roofs. A typical use is to connect slab edges with the slab, as shown in the section views in Figure 8–14.

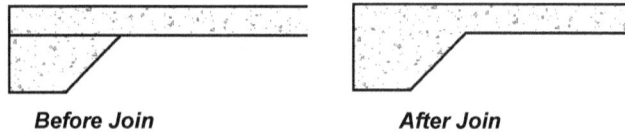

Before Join   *After Join*

Figure 8–14

If the material is not exactly the same, a thin line still separates the elements.

- Joining geometry makes two separate elements display as one, but they can still be modified individually after being joined.

How To: Join Geometry

1. In the *Modify* tab>Geometry panel, expand (Join) and click (Join Geometry).
2. Select the elements to join.

- If you toggle on the **Multiple Join** option in the Options Bar, you can select several elements to join to the first selection.

- To remove the join, expand (Join), click (Unjoin Geometry), and select the elements to unjoin.

Practice 8a

Model Structural Slabs

Estimated time for completion: 25 minutes

Practice Objectives

- Add a slab with an edge.
- Add structural floors.

In this practice you will create slab foundations at the base of elevator shafts and add a slab edge to them. You will also create a floor slab and then copy and modify the type to create the rest of the floors and roof deck, as shown in Figure 8–15.

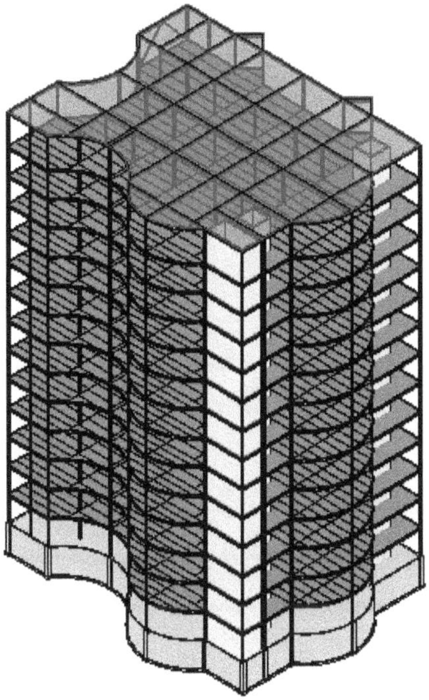

Figure 8–15

- This practice file contains additional wall elements.

Task 1 - Add slab foundations for elevator shafts.

1. Open **Syracuse-Suites-Slabs.rvt**.

2. Open the **Structural Plans: T.O. FOOTING** view.

3. Zoom into the lower right corner of the building where the section marker is.

4. In the *Structure* tab>Foundation panel click ⬭ (Slab).

5. In the Type Selector, select **Foundation Slab: 12"
   Foundation Slab.**

6. In the Options Bar, set the *Offset* to **2'-0"** and in the *Modify |
   Create Floor Boundary* tab>Draw panel, click ▨ (Pick
   Walls).

7. Click on each wall to create a boundary line, as shown in
   Figure 8–16.

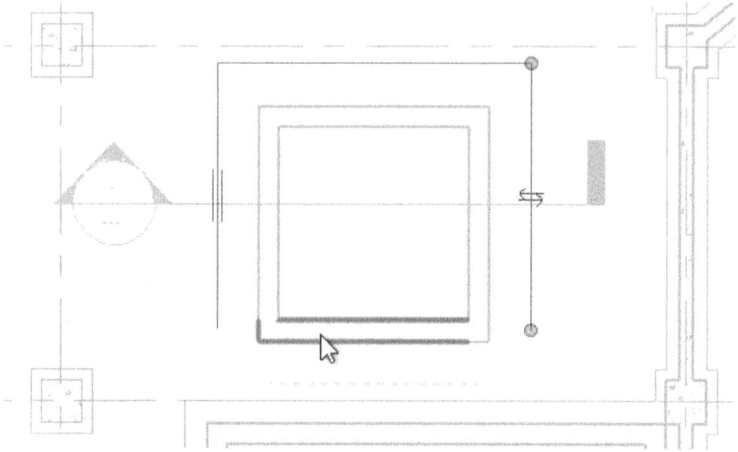

Figure 8–16

8. Click ✔ (Finish Edit Mode).

9. Click ▷ (Modify) and select the **Foundation Span
   Direction** symbol, which is automatically added when you
   finish the sketch. Delete the symbol in this view (it can be
   added again in a working document view).

10. Save the project.

Task 2 - Add a slab edge to the slab.

---

1. Open the default 3D view.

2. In the View Control Bar, click ⬚ (Hide Analytical Model) if
   required. Once complete, the tooltip displays **Show
   Analytical Model**.

3. Select at least one beam, beam system, column, and wall. in the View Control Bar, expand ✎ (Temporary Hide/Isolate) and select **Hide Category**. Hide any other elements that might be in the way of seeing just the slabs, such as rebar.

4. In the View Control Bar, set the Visual Style to ▱ (Consistent Colors).

5. Use the ViewCube to rotate the model so the you are viewing the bottom of the slab, as shown in Figure 8–17. (Hint: In the ViewCube, click the corner at the intersection of the **FRONT**, **RIGHT**, and **BOTTOM** planes.)

Figure 8–17

6. Zoom in on the slab.

7. In the *Structure* tab>Foundation panel, expand ▱ (Slab) and click ▱ (Floor: Slab Edge).

8. Select the four bottom edges of the slab, as shown in Figure 8–18. Rotate the view as required to see each edge.

If you add a slab edge in a plan view, the software selects the top edge of the slab rather than the bottom.

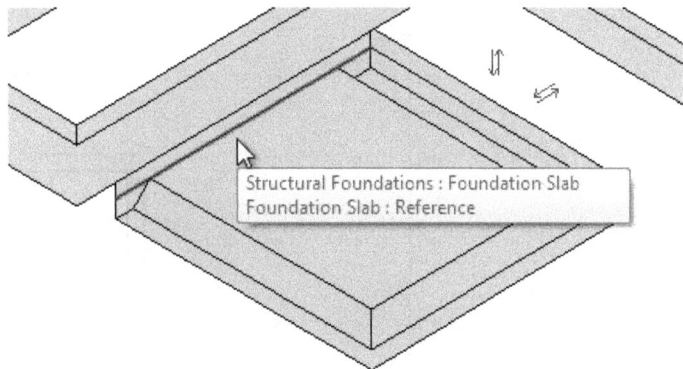

Structural Foundations : Foundation Slab
Foundation Slab : Reference

Figure 8–18

9. Click ⬚ (Modify).

10. In the *Modify* tab>Geometry panel, click ⬡ (Join). Select the foundation and then the thickened slab edge. You only need to select one segment of the edge as it one element.

11. Return the view to viewing from the top. (**Hint:** In the ViewCube click the corner at the intersection of the **TOP**, **FRONT**, and **RIGHT** planes.)

12. In the View Control Bar, expand ⬡ (Temporary Hide/Isolate) and select **Reset Temporary Hide/Isolate**.

13. Switch back to the **Structural Plans: T.O. FOOTING** view.

14. Double-click on the arrow of the section through the slab. The geometry should look similar to that shown in Figure 8–19.

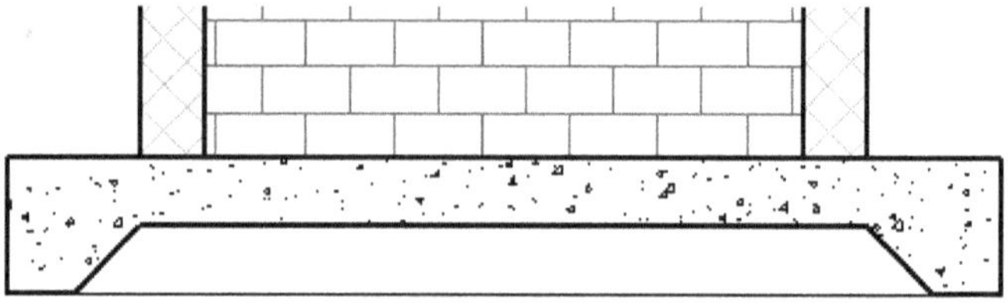

Figure 8–19

15. Return to the **Structural Plans: T.O. Footing** view.

16. Select the slab and slab edges. Copy the edges from the upper left corner of the elevator shaft wall to the other elevator shaft wall, as shown in Figure 8–20.

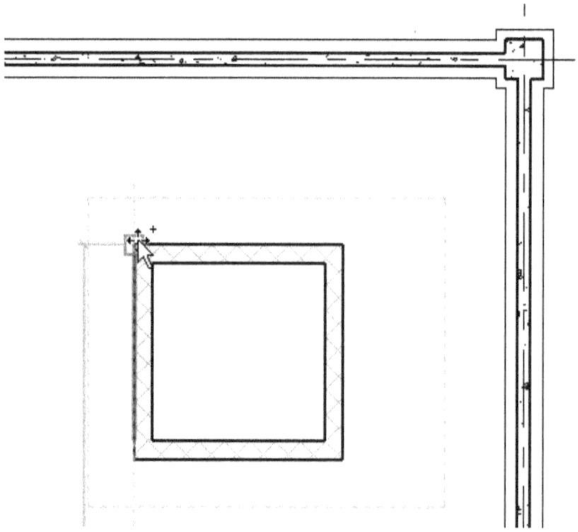

Figure 8–20

17. Click away from the elements to clear the selection.

18. Save the project.

Task 3 - Add a structural floor to the ground floor Level.

1. Open the **Structural Plans: 00 GROUND FLOOR** view.

2. In the *Structure* tab>Structure panel, click 〰 (Floor: Structural).

3. In the Type Selector, select **Floor: 6" Concrete**, and in Properties set the *Height Offset From Level* to **0'-0"**

4. In the *Modify | Create Floor Boundary* tab>Draw panel, click 🖫 (Pick Walls), if it is not already selected

5. In the Options Bar, set the *Offset* to **0'-0"** and clear the check from **Extend into wall (to core)**.

6. Hover over one of the perimeter walls and press <Tab> to select all of the walls, as shown in Figure 8–21.

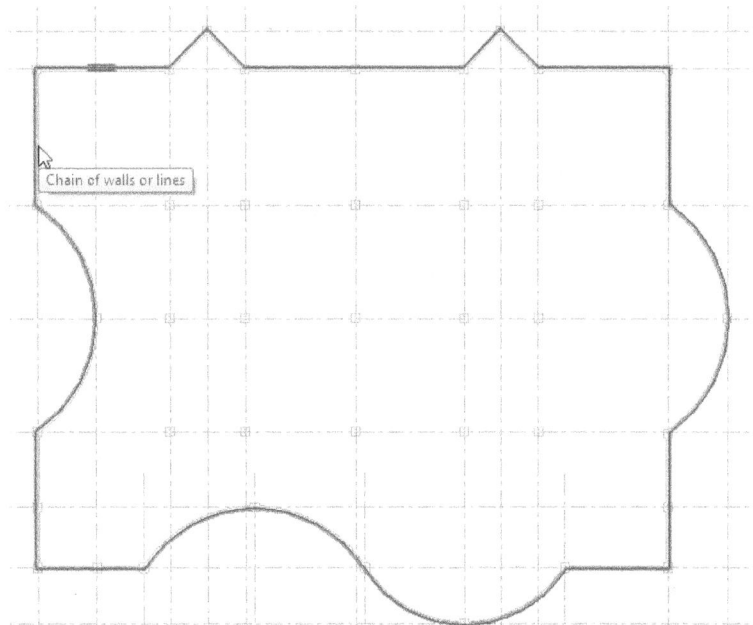

Chain of walls or lines

Figure 8–21

7. Ensure the cursor is on the outside of the wall as shown in Figure 8–22. Click to accept the selection.

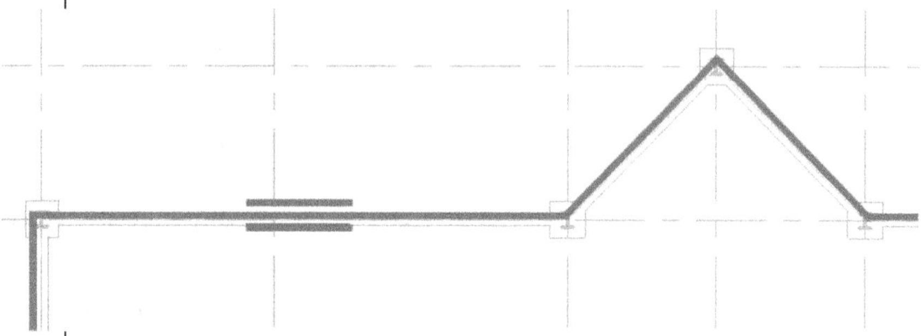

Figure 8–22

8. In the Mode panel, click ✓ (Finish Edit Mode).

9. When prompted for the walls to go up to the floor's level and attach to its bottom, click **Yes**.

10. Clear the selection of the new floor element.

11. Zoom out and save the project.

Task 4 - Add floor slabs to the rest of the floors.

---

1. Open the default 3D view and reorient the view to see the new floor slab. Select the slab.

2. In the *Modify | Floors* tab>Clipboard panel, click ▢ (Copy to Clipboard).

3. In the same panel expand ▢ (Paste) and click ▣ (Aligned to Selected Levels).

4. In the Select Levels dialog box, select **TOS-1ST FLOOR** and click **OK**.

5. With the copied floor still selected, in the Type Selector, change the floor type to **Floor: 3" LW Concrete on 2" Metal Deck**.

6. In Properties, under *Constraints*, change the *Height Offset From Level* to **5"**. to leave room for the steel structure below the slab. Click **Apply**.

7. Using **Copy to the Clipboard** and **Paste Aligned to Selected Levels**, copy the metal deck floor to the rest of the floors, from **TOS-2ND FLOOR** up to **TOS-14 ROOF**.

8. Zoom out to see the entire building. The top slab is still selected. In the Type Selector, change it to **Floor: 1 1/2" Metal Roof Deck** as shown in Figure 8–23.

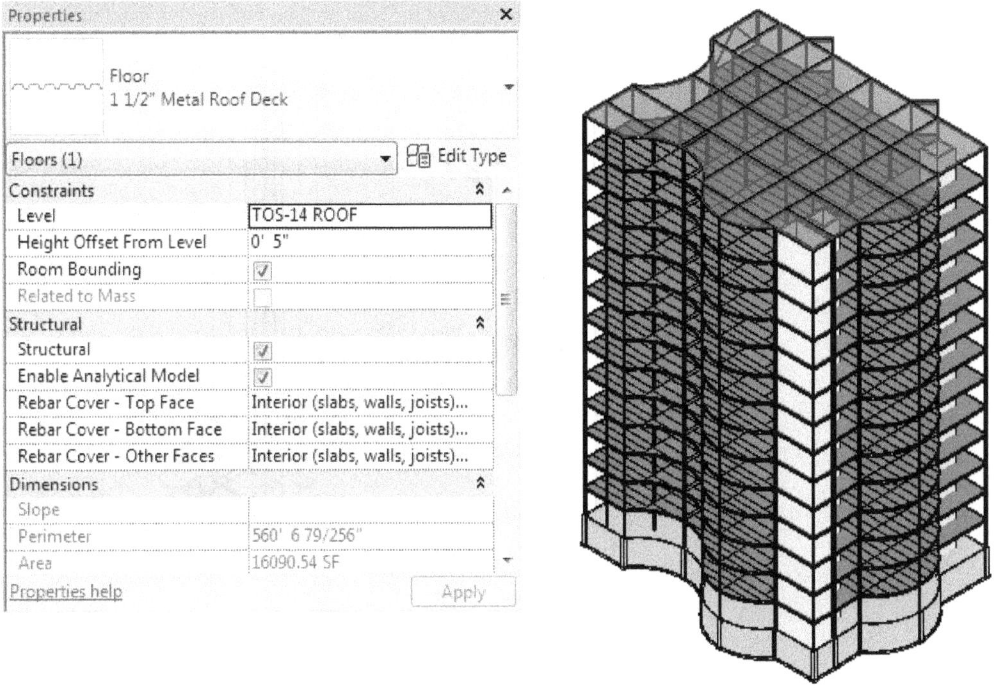

Figure 8–23

9. Clear the selection of the roof.

10. Save the project.

Task 5 - Add a Slab Edge to the ground floor.

---

1. Zoom in on the ground floor slab.

2. Change the *Visual Style* to ⬚ (Wireframe).

3. In the *Structure* tab>Foundation panel, expand ⬚ (Slab) and click ⬚ (Floor: Slab Edge).

4. Hover over the bottom edge of the ground floor slab and press <Tab> to select the entire chain of lines.

5. Click to place the slab edge. It is placed around the entire edge of the slab, as shown in Figure 8–24.

   • Slab edges are copied with the slab. Since it isn't required on the upper floors, add it after copying up at least one floor.)

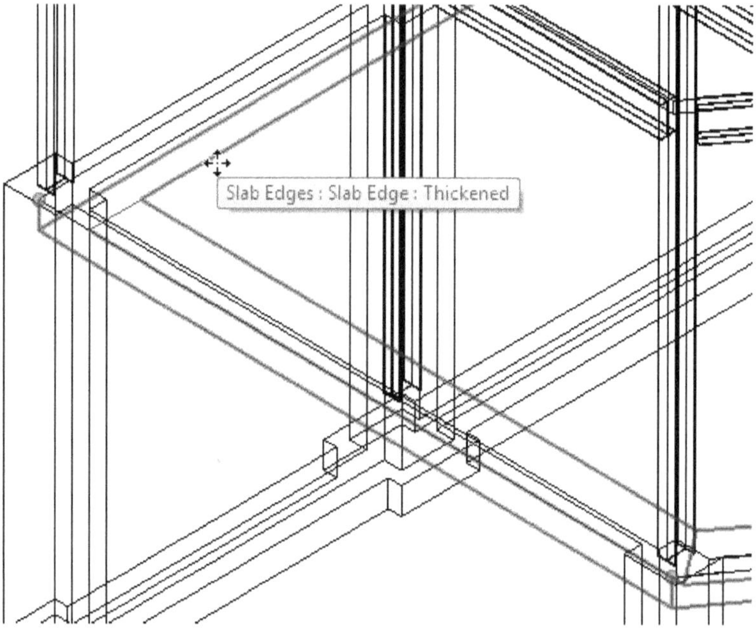

Figure 8–24

6. Zoom out (**Hint:** Type **ZE**) to see the overall 3D view of the model and return the *Visual Style* to ⬜ (Consistent Colors).

7. Save the project.

8.2 Creating Shaft Openings

Shaft openings are designed to create a void in the structure through which only beams, framing, and other structural components can pass. Floors, roofs, and slabs are cut away from these areas, as shown in Figure 8–25. If the geometry of the shaft opening changes, the slab openings are automatically updated.

Shaft Openings only cut floors, roofs, and ceilings. They do not cut walls, beams, or other objects.

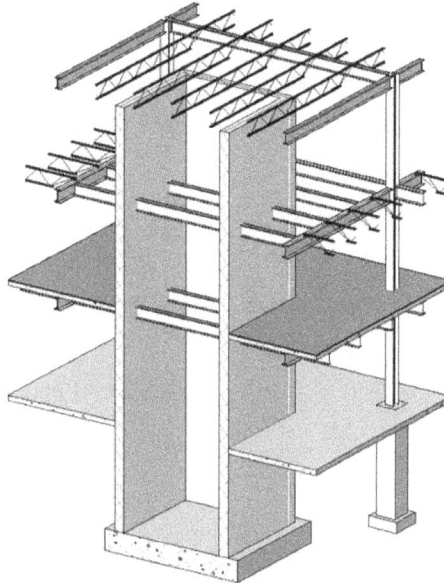

Figure 8–25

How To: Create a Shaft Opening

1. In the *Structure* tab>Opening panel, click (Shaft Opening).
2. In the *Modify | Create Shaft Opening Sketch* tab>Draw panel,

   click (Boundary Line) and draw a line to define the opening.

3. In the Draw panel, click (Symbolic Line) and add lines that show the opening symbol in plan view.
4. In Properties, set the following:
   - *Base and Top Constraint*
   - *Base and Top Offset* or *Unconnected Height*

5. Click ✓ (Finish Edit Mode) to create the opening.

- When using ⬚ (Pick Walls) or other drawing tools to define the perimeter of the opening, you can select the flip arrow to flip the lines to the outside, as shown in Figure 8–26.

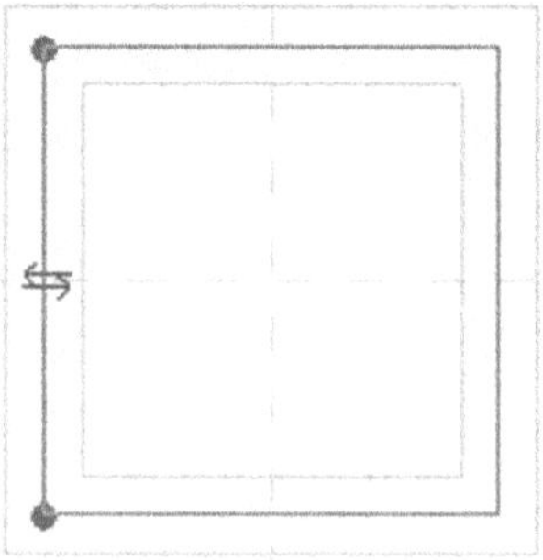

Figure 8–26

- A Shaft Opening element can include symbolic lines that repeat on each level, displaying the shaft in a plan view.

6. Shafts are a separate element from the floor, roof, ceiling, or wall, and can be deleted without selecting a host element.

Practice 8b

Estimated time for completion: 10 minutes

Create Shaft Openings

Practice Objective

- Create shaft openings.

In this practice you will add shaft openings in the two elevator shafts and the stairwell, as shown in Figure 8–27.

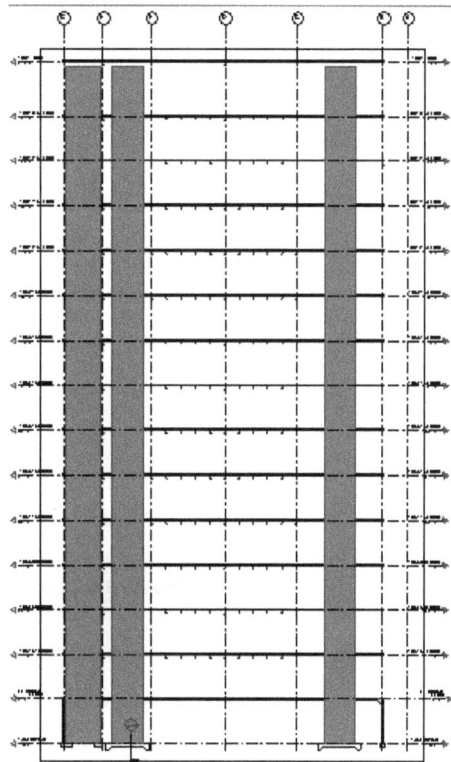

Figure 8–27

Task 1 - Add shaft openings.

1. Open **Syracuse-Suites-Shafts.rvt**

2. Open the **Structural Plans: T.O. FOOTING** view. and zoom in on the stairwell.

3. In the *Structure* tab>Opening panel, click ⊞ (Shaft).

---

4. In the *Modify | Create Shaft Opening Sketch* tab>Draw panel, ensure that ⌐ (Boundary Line) is highlighted, and click ▣ (Pick Walls).

5. Select the exterior face of the masonry walls around the stairwell (select one wall and press <Tab> to select the chain of walls). If required, select the flip arrow to flip the lines to the exterior, as shown in Figure 8–28.

Figure 8–28

6. In the *Draw* panel, click ▣ (Symbolic Line).

7. Using ✎ (Line), draw an **X** in the opening, as shown in Figure 8–29.

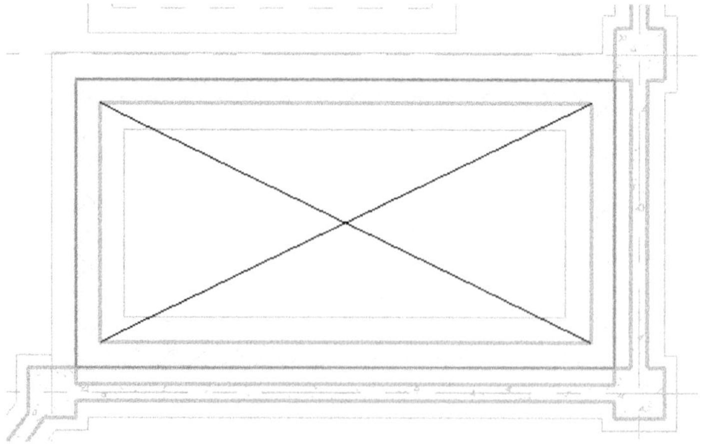

Figure 8–29

8. In the Mode panel, click ✔ (Finish Edit Mode).

9. Repeat the procedure for the two elevator shafts. Ensure that the shaft openings are aligned with the outside faces of the shaft walls.

10. Zoom to fit the view and save the project.

Task 2 - Modify the Shaft Properties

---

1. Create a building section through the three shafts limiting the width of the section so that it does not display the entire building.

2. Open the section view. The shafts do not display, but you can hover over one of them near the base of the footing and select it. The shaft only extends through one set of floors, as shown in Figure 8–30.

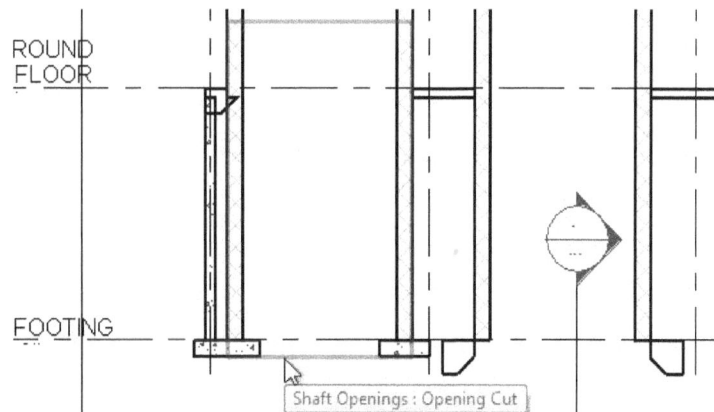

Figure 8–30

3. Hold <Ctrl> and select the other two shafts.

4. In Properties, set the following parameters:

- *Base Constraint:* **T.O. FOOTING**
- *Base Offset:* **1"**
- *Top Constraint:* **Up to level: TOS-14TH ROOF**
- *Top Offset:* (negative) **-1' 3"**

5. Zoom out to see that the shafts now expand from the top of the footing to just below the roof.

6. Clear the selection of the elements and save the project.

Setting the base offset prevents the void from cutting the foundation

Chapter Review Questions

1. When creating a slab, which of the following Draw Tools used to create a boundary automatically updates the slab boundary if the other elements are changed? (Select all that apply.)

   a. ╱ (Line)

   b. ⬚ (Pick Lines)

   c. ▦ (Pick Walls)

   d. ▦ (Pick Supports)

2. Foundation slabs often have slab edges as shown in a section in Figure 8–31. Which of the following is true of slab edges.

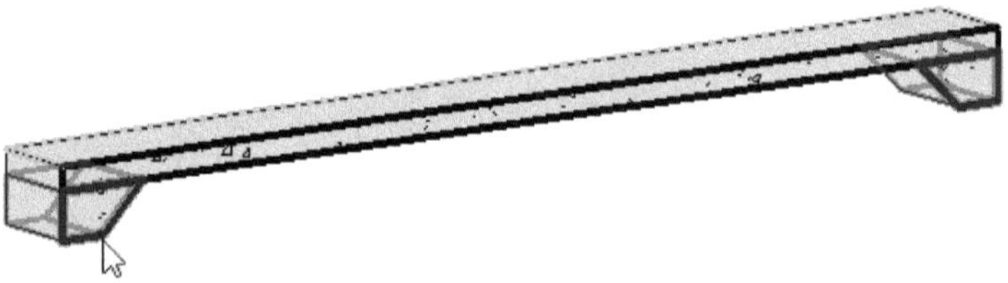

Figure 8–31

   a. They come in automatically when you draw the slab.

   b. You can add them by selecting **Slab Edge** in the Options Bar.

   c. You need to add them with the separate **Slab Edge** command.

   d. You can add them by modifying the *Type Properties* of the slab.

3. Which of the following elements cannot be cut by a shaft opening such as those shown in Figure 8–32?

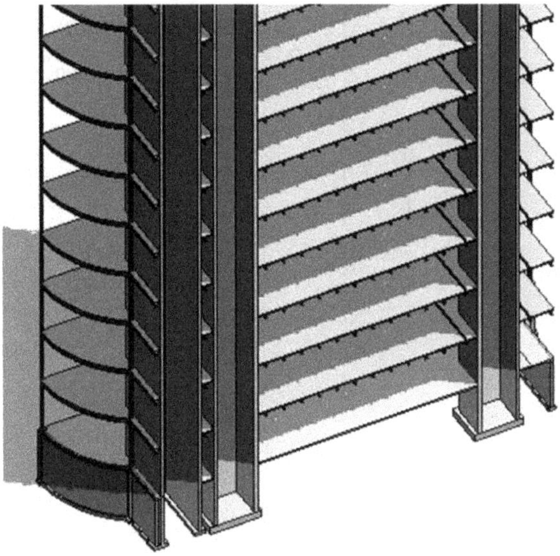

Figure 8–32

   a. Roofs

   b. Floors

   c. Ceilings

   d. Beams

4. Which tool would you use to set or modify the direction of metal decking in a structural floor?

   a. Boundary Line

   b. Slope Arrow

   c. Span Direction

   d. Pick Supports

Command Summary

Button	Command	Location
	Floor: Slab Edge	• **Ribbon:** *Structure* tab>Foundation panel, expand Slab
	Floor: Structural	• **Ribbon:** *Structure* tab>Structure panel, expand Floor • **Shortcut:** SB
	Roof by Footprint	• **Ribbon:** *Architecture* tab>Build panel, expand Roof
	Shaft	• **Ribbon:** *Structure* tab>Opening panel
	Structural Foundation: Slab	• **Ribbon:** *Structure* tab>Foundation panel, expand Slab

Structural Reinforcement

Adding reinforcement is an important part of the process when designing concrete structures. One of the primary methods of adding reinforcement is rebar, which comes in many possible sizes and shapes. You can add rebar types individually, in an area, along a path, and using fabric reinforcement sheets.

Learning Objectives in this Chapter

- Examine the types of elements that can have reinforcement added to them.
- Set the reinforcement settings.
- Place existing rebar shapes and sketch custom shapes for single or multi-planer rebar.
- Modify rebar by using controls, properties, and other modification tools.
- Place area and path reinforcement in walls or floors.
- Add fabric reinforcement.

9.1 Structural Reinforcement

The Autodesk® Revit® software provides tools for modeling reinforcement in concrete and structural elements, as shown in Figure 9–1. Rebar components are attached to host elements, such as concrete or pre-cast concrete beams, columns, or foundations.

Walls, structural floors, and slab edges can also be valid hosts as long as they have a structural usage and contain a concrete layer.

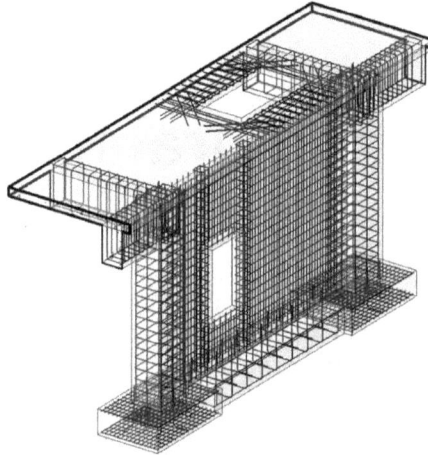

Figure 9–1

You can place reinforcements using the following element types:

• Structural Framing	• Structural Columns
• Structural Foundations	• Walls
• Structural Floors	• Structural Connections
• Foundation Slabs	• Wall Foundations
• Slab Edges	• Imported concrete elements from SAT files or InfraWorks

New in **2018**

- Rebar can be placed in free form concrete elements, such as curved columns and slabs.

Before you add rebar to a project, there are two groups of settings you can establish.

- *Rebar Cover Settings* control the acceptable distance from the element's face, so that when you add rebar to a host you are limited to that setting.
- *Reinforcement Settings* indicate the reinforcement elements display and how to annotate the reinforcement using custom symbols and tags.

Setting the Rebar Cover Depth

Rebar cover settings can differ depending on the project's soil or regional conditions and other issues. Although the software has default settings, they can be changed or additional cover settings can be created when required. As you place reinforcement, the cover depth displays with dashed lines as shown in Figure 9–2.

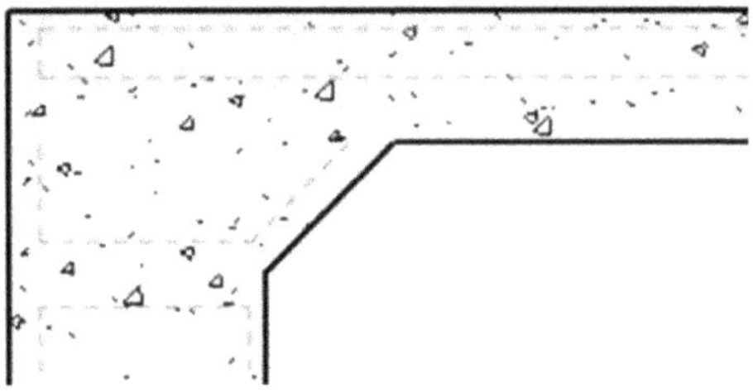

Figure 9–2

- Each structural element has preset cover settings. You can customize the settings by element or by the individual faces in an element.

How To: Add a Rebar Cover Setting

1. In the *Structure* tab> Reinforcement panel, expand the panel title and click [icon] (Rebar Cover Settings).
2. In the Rebar Cover Settings dialog box, click **Add** to create a new cover setting, or select an existing setting and click **Duplicate**.
3. A new setting is added as shown in Figure 9–3. Rename the Description as required for the purpose of the setting and set the *Setting* clearance.

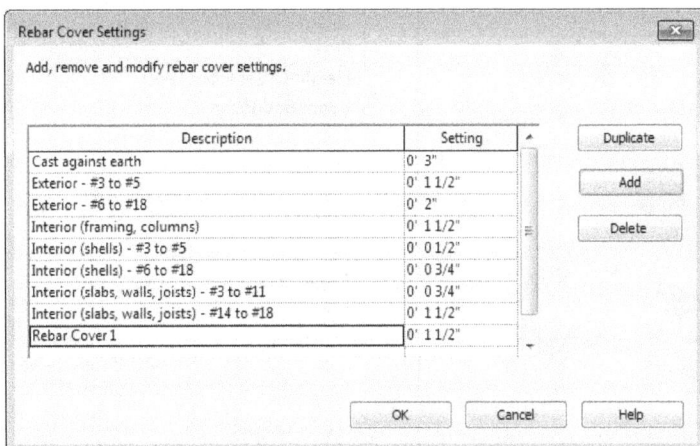

Figure 9–3

4. Click **OK**.

How To: Edit the Rebar Cover

1. In the *Structure* tab>Reinforcement panel, click (Cover).
2. In Options, select (Pick Elements) or (Pick Faces).
3. Select an element or the face of an element.
4. In the Options Bar, select the cover settings for this specific object as shown in Figure 9–4.

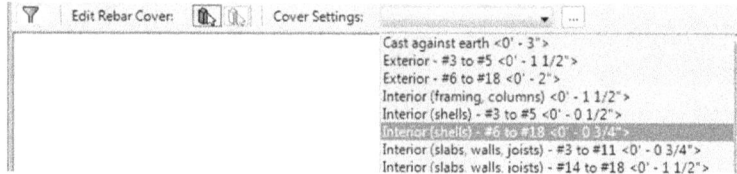

Edit Rebar Cover:
Cover Settings:
Cast against earth <0' - 3">
Exterior - #3 to #5 <0' - 1 1/2">
Exterior - #6 to #18 <0' - 2">
Interior (framing, columns) <0' - 1 1/2">
Interior (shells) - #3 to #5 <0' - 0 1/2">
Interior (shells) - #6 to #18 <0' - 0 3/4">
Interior (slabs, walls, joists) - #3 to #11 <0' - 0 3/4">
Interior (slabs, walls, joists) - #14 to #18 <0' - 1 1/2">

Figure 9–4

- For more options, click (Browse) to open the Rebar Cover Settings dialog box in which you can add a new cover restraint.
- Cover settings can also be modified in Properties when a rebar host element is selected, as shown in Figure 9–5. This only modifies the selected element.

Properties
Floor
6" Concrete
Floors (1)
Edit Type
Constraints
Level
Level 2
Height Offset From Level
0' 0"
Room Bounding
Related to Mass
Structural
Structural
Enable Analytical Model
Rebar Cover - Top Face
Interior (slabs, walls, joists)...
Rebar Cover - Bottom Face
Interior (slabs, walls, joists)...
Rebar Cover - Other Faces
) - #3 to #11 <0' - 0 3/4">
Dimensions
Slope
Perimeter
Properties help
Project Browser - Project1
Exterior - #3 to #5 <0' - 1 1/2">
Exterior - #6 to #18 <0' - 2">
Interior (framing, columns) <0' - 1 1/2">
Interior (shells) - #3 to #5 <0' - 0 1/2">
Interior (shells) - #6 to #18 <0' - 0 3/4">
Interior (slabs, walls, joists) - #3 to #11 <0' - 0 3/4">

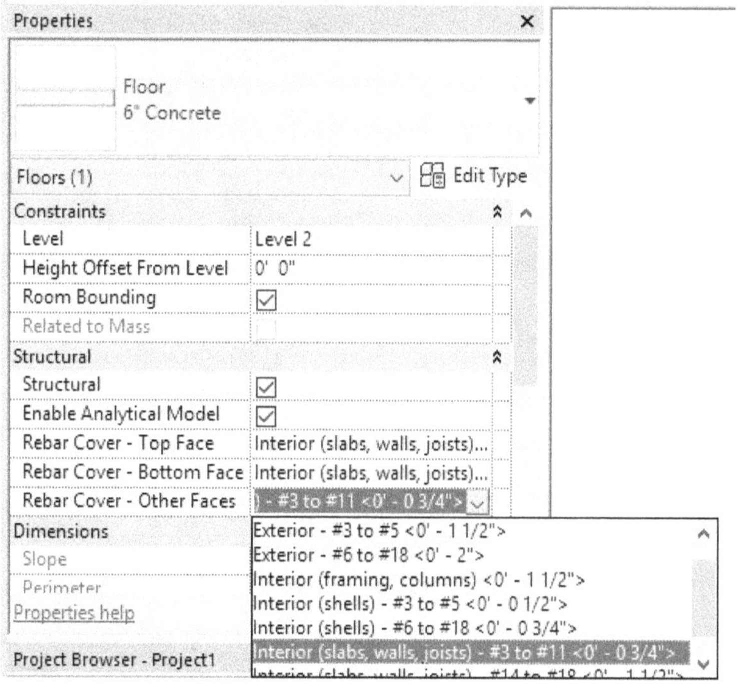

Figure 9–5

Reinforcement Settings

Using Reinforcement Settings, you can specify the structural rebar hosting of area/path reinforcement and annotate the area/path reinforcement region using custom symbols and tags.

*   In the *Structure* tab> Reinforcement panel, expand the panel title and click ✏ (Reinforcement Settings).

General Pane

In the *General* pane, as shown in Figure 9–6, you can determine how area and path reinforcements work in their host elements of floors and walls as well as if hooks are included in rebar shapes. Both of these are on by default in new projects. If you are using couplers to define end treatments then select **Include end treatments in Rebar Shape definition**. This option is off by default.

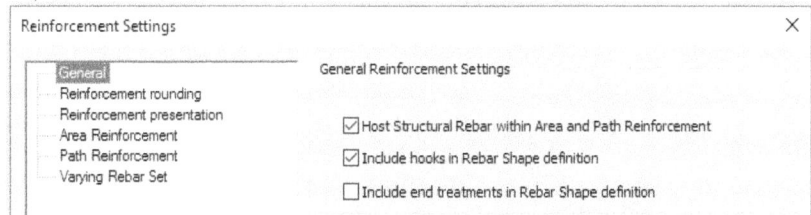

Figure 9–6

*   These options must be set before you place any rebar in a project.

*   The first time you place rebar an alert box displays noting which settings are selected as shown in Figure 9–7.

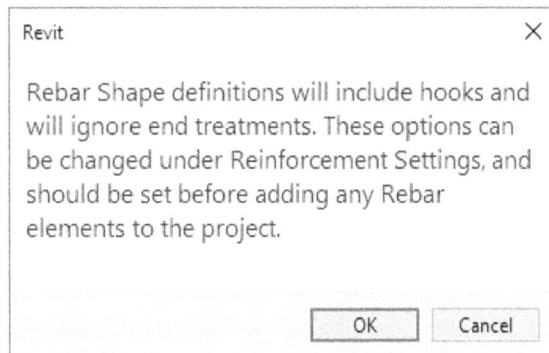

Figure 9–7

When **Host Structural Rebar with Area and Path Reinforcement** is selected, the structural rebar elements display in the floor or wall, as shown on the left in Figure 9–8. When this option is cleared, the structural rebar elements do not display in the floor or wall, as shown on the right in Figure 9–8, but you can annotate the area/path reinforcement region using custom symbols and tags.

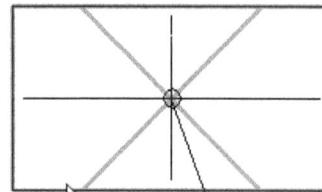

Structural Rebar : Rebar Bar : #4

Rebar hosted

Structural Area Reinforcement : Structural Area Reinforcement : Structural Area Reinforcement 1

Rebar not hosted

Figure 9–8

When **Include hooks in Rebar Shape definition** is selected, any added hooks are included in standard rebar shapes. This minimizes the number of custom shapes in a project. When this option is cleared, adding hooks to a shape creates additional shapes.

Reinforcement Rounding Pane

In the *Reinforcement rounding* pane (shown in Figure 9–9), you can specify and set up the rounding method (i.e., Nearest, Up, or Down), and the amount of rounding for Structural Rebar and Structural Fabric Reinforcement. This overrides Project Units rounding for these elements.

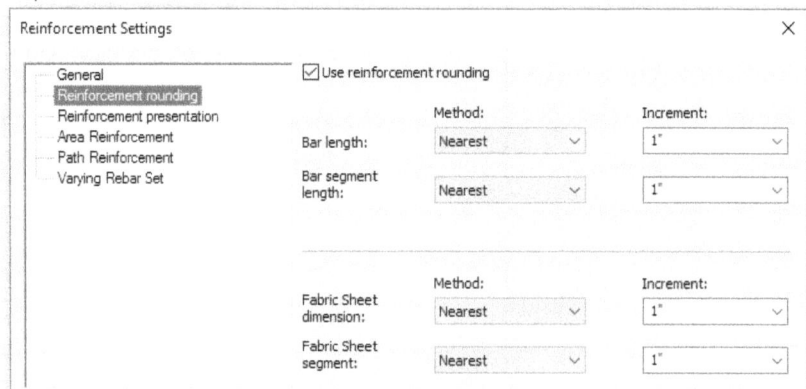

Figure 9–9

Reinforcement Presentation Pane

In the *Reinforcement presentation* pane you can specify how Rebar Sets display in views and sections, as shown in Figure 9–10.

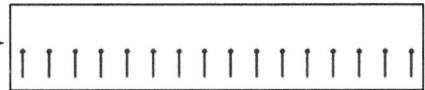

Figure 9–10

Area and Path Reinforcement Panes

In the *Area Reinforcement* or *Path Reinforcement* panes, specify the values (abbreviations) used in tags. For example, for **Area Reinforcements**, you might want to change the *Value* for Slab Top - Major Direction and Slab Top - Minor Direction to **Slab Top**, as shown in Figure 9–11.

Reinforcement Settings   ✕

	Setting	Value
General	Slab Top - Major Direction	Slab Top
Reinforcement rounding	Slab Top - Minor Direction	Slab Top
Reinforcement presentation	Slab Bottom - Major Direction	(B)
Area Reinforcement	Slab Bottom - Minor Direction	(B)
Path Reinforcement	Wall Interior - Major Direction	(I)
Varying Rebar Set	Wall Interior - Minor Direction	(I)
	Wall Exterior - Major Direction	(E)
	Wall Exterior - Minor Direction	(E)
	Each Way	E.W.
	Each Face	E.F.

Figure 9–11

Varying Rebar Set

In the Varying Rebar Set pane (shown in Figure 9–12), you can specify the numbering method for the rebar set of different lengths.

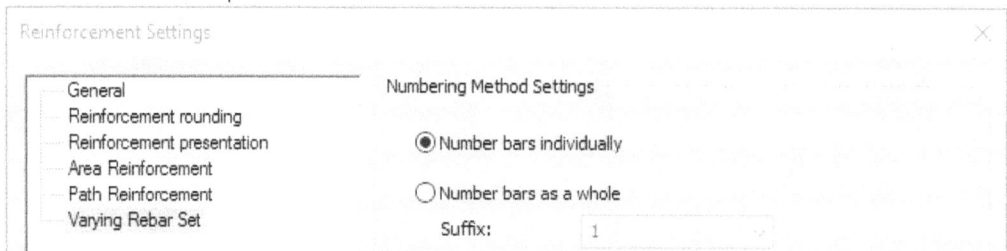

Reinforcement Settings   ✕

General
Reinforcement rounding
Reinforcement presentation
Area Reinforcement
Path Reinforcement
Varying Rebar Set

Numbering Method Settings

◉ Number bars individually

◯ Number bars as a whole

Suffix: 1

Figure 9–12

- **Number bars Individually:** Each rebar in the set is assigned a different number, though similar rebar will be matched throughout the project.

- **Number bars as a whole:** Each rebar in the set is assigned the same number with additional suffix numbers.

Hint: Rebar Visibility

By default, rebar automatically displays in section views, but not in other views. If you want to display rebar in other views, such as the 3D view shown in Figure 9–13, set the **View Visibility States** of the rebar.

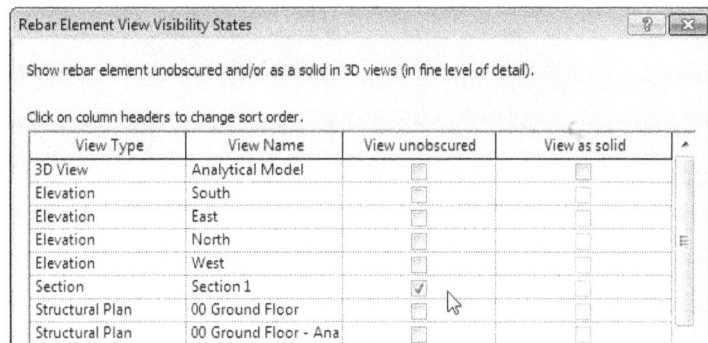

Structural Rebar : Rebar Bar : #4

Figure 9–13

How To: Set the Rebar Visibility

1. In a section view, select the rebar in a structural element.
2. In Properties, in the *Graphics* area, beside *View Visibility States*, click **Edit...**.
3. In the Rebar Element View Visibility States dialog box, as shown in Figure 9–14, you can set where and in which views to display the reinforcement in your model.

Rebar Element View Visibility States

Show rebar element unobscured and/or as a solid in 3D views (in fine level of detail).

Click on column headers to change sort order.

View Type	View Name	View unobscured	View as solid
3D View	Analytical Model		
Elevation	South		
Elevation	East		
Elevation	North		
Elevation	West		
Section	Section 1	✓	
Structural Plan	00 Ground Floor		
Structural Plan	00 Ground Floor - Ana		

Figure 9–14

9.2 Adding Rebar

As you start reinforcing structural walls, columns, slabs, and framing, you can add rebar shapes directly into the host elements. You can place existing rebar shapes either parallel to the work plane (or cover) or perpendicular to the cover. You can also draw a custom sketch as shown in Figure 9–15.

You typically work in a wall section as you place the rebar, but rebar can be added in any 2D view.

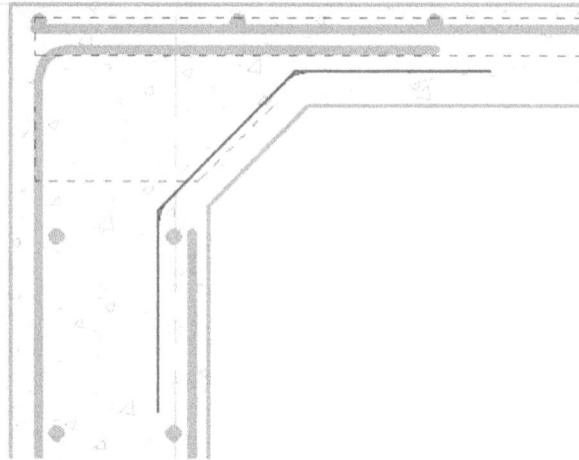

Figure 9–15

- The Rebar tools are available in the *Structure* tab> Reinforcement panel and (when a host element is selected) in the *Modify |* contextual tab>Reinforcement panel.

- When you start the rebar command, the *Modify | Place Rebar* tab displays. Depending on the size and shape of your screen you may not see the information in the panels. Hover over the arrow at the bottom to display the full panel, as shown in Figure 9–16.

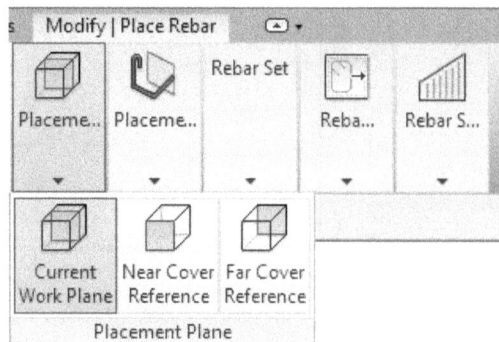

Figure 9–16

How To: Place Rebar

1. In the *Structure* tab>Reinforcement panel, click ⬚ (Rebar).
2. In the Options Bar or Rebar Shape Browser, select a Rebar Shape, as shown in Figure 9–17. You can also select the type in the Type Selector.

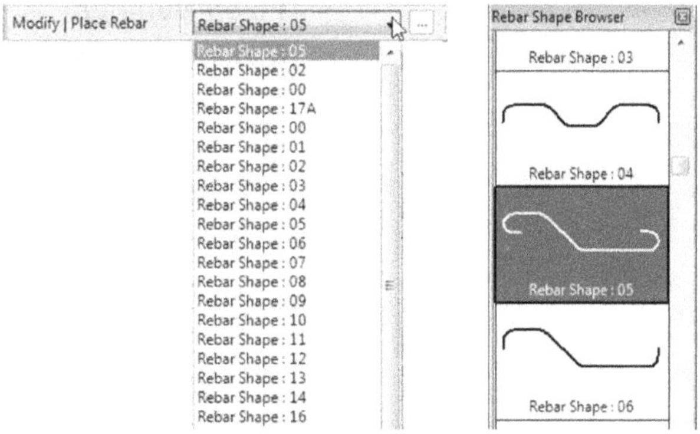

If the Rebar Shape Browser does not display, in the Options Bar, click ⬚ (Browse).

Figure 9–17

- In the *Modify | Place Rebar* tab>Family panel, click

  ⬚ (Load Shapes) to load additional rebar family types.

3. In the *Modify | Place Rebar* tab>Placement Plane panel select the placement location:

⬚	Current Work Plane	Places rebar on the active work plane in the view.
⬚	Near Cover Reference	Places rebar on the closest cover reference parallel to the view.
⬚	Far Cover Reference	Places rebar on the furthest cover reference parallel to the view.

4. In the *Modify | Place Rebar* tab>Placement Orientation panel, select the placement type:

⬚	Parallel to Work Plane	Places rebar parallel to the established work plane and in the cover references.
⬚	Parallel to Cover	Places rebar parallel to the nearest cover reference and perpendicular to the work plane.
⬚	Perpendicular to Cover	Places rebar perpendicular to the work plane and perpendicular to the nearest cover reference.

5. In the *Modify | Place Rebar* tab>Rebar Set panel, (shown in Figure 9–18) or in the *Rebar Set* area of Properties (shown in Figure 9–19), specify the *Layout Rule* and then set up the corresponding *Quantity* and *Spacing* as required. *Layout Rule* options include:

    *   **Single**
    *   **Fixed Number**
    *   **Maximum Space**
    *   **Number with Spacing**
    *   **Minimum Clear Spacing**

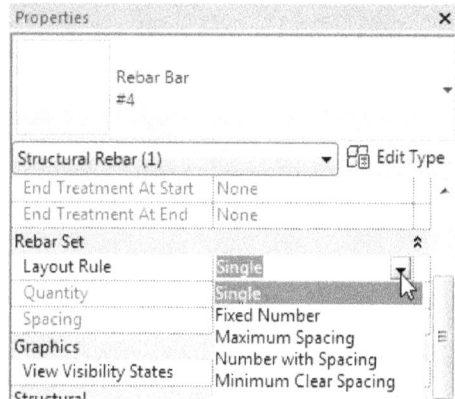

| Figure 9–18 | Figure 9–19 |

6. Hover the cursor over the element that you want to reinforce as shown in Figure 9–20. Click to place it when it is in the required position.

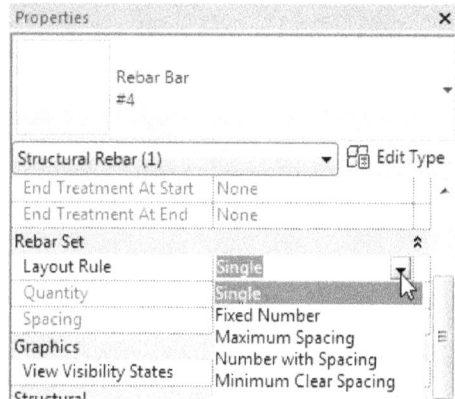

Figure 9–20

*   The dashed lines indicate the maximum cover settings of the element.
*   Press <Spacebar> to flip or rotate the rebar element before it is placed.
*   Press <Shift> to place the rebar parallel to any host face.

Hint: Constraining Rebar to Other Rebar

To help you place rebar more precisely, you can constrain rebar to nearby shapes. When you move the original rebar, all the constrained elements move as well, as shown in Figure 9–21.

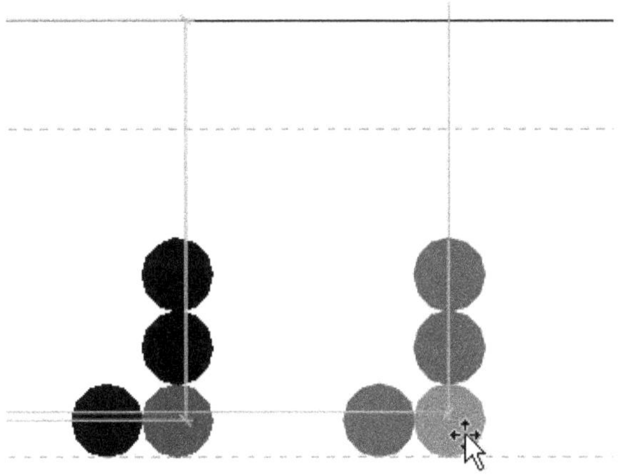

Figure 9–21

- In the *Modify | Place Rebar* tab> Rebar Constraints panel, click ⬚ (Constrained Placement). Then, move the cursor close to the other rebar and click when you see it snap to the preferred constrain.

- Once the rebar is placed, you can select it and use the temporary dimensions to change the location. This breaks the constraint.

- This tool only works when placing single rebar.

Sketching Rebar Shapes

At times, the standard rebar shapes are not exactly what is required. In these cases, you can sketch a new shape as shown in Figure 9–22.

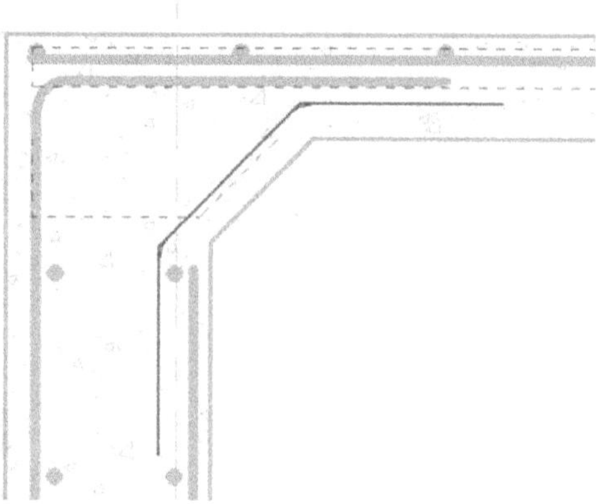

Figure 9–22

- When sketching rebar, you are not restricted to the rebar cover settings.

How To: Place a Rebar Shape by Sketch

1. Start the **Rebar** command.
2. In the *Modify | Place Rebar* tab>Placement Methods panel,

   click (Sketch Rebar).
3. Select the host for the rebar (unless it is already selected).
4. To draw the sketch, use the tools in the *Modify | Create Rebar Sketch* tab>Draw panel, as shown in Figure 9–23.

Figure 9–23

5. Click (Finish Edit Mode).

- The new Rebar Shape displays in the Shape Browser. To change the shape name, in the Project Browser, expand the *Families>Structural Rebar>Rebar Shape* node, right-click on the shape name and select **Rename**.

Multi-planar Rebar

When you are sketching rebar you can also create multi-planar reinforcement. The rebar shape is sketched in 2D and then duplicated and connected by a segment, as shown in Figure 9–24.

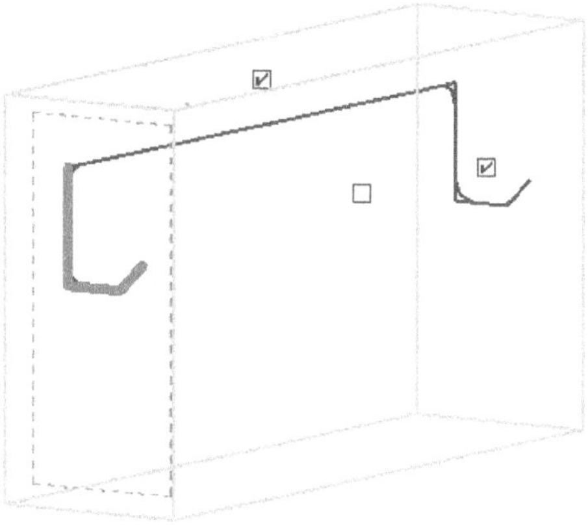

Figure 9–24

How To: Sketch Multi-planar Rebar

1. Start the **Rebar** command with the **Sketch Rebar** option.
2. In the *Modify | Create Rebar Sketch* tab> Reinforcement panel, click ⌐ (Multi-planar).
3. Draw the rebar sketch in the 2D view. It automatically displays in any open 3D views, as shown in Figure 9–25.

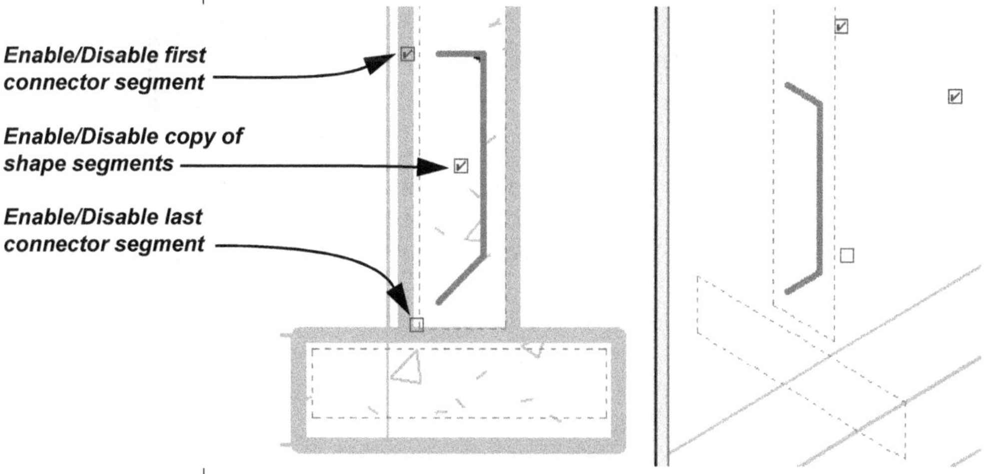

Enable/Disable first connector segment

Enable/Disable copy of shape segments

Enable/Disable last connector segment

Figure 9–25

4. Select the appropriate check boxes on the sketch.

5. In the Type Selector, select the Rebar bar size and in Properties, set other information.

6. Click ✓ (Finish Edit Mode). The rebar is added to the length of the element as shown in Figure 9–26.

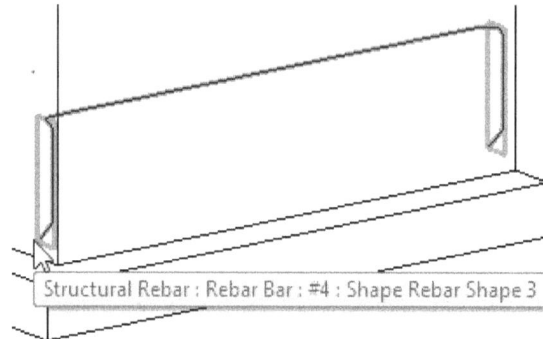

Structural Rebar : Rebar Bar : #4 : Shape Rebar Shape 3

Figure 9–26

• You can modify the multi-planar rebar shape using the drag controls, as shown in Figure 9–27. Alternatively, in the

   Modify | Structural Rebar tab>Mode panel, click 📝 (Edit Sketch).

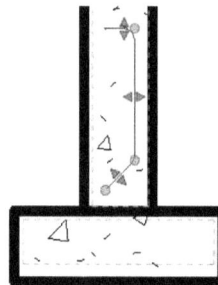

Figure 9–27

• When placing rebar, if you select a multi-planar rebar type in the Rebar Shape Browser, select a *Placement Perspective*, as shown in Figure 9–28, before you add it to the host.

Figure 9–28

9.3 Modifying Rebar

You can make additional changes to the rebar once it is placed. For example, select the rebar and use the shape handles to move it into place, as shown in Figure 9–29. Rebar that is perpendicular to the work plane also has temporary dimensions.

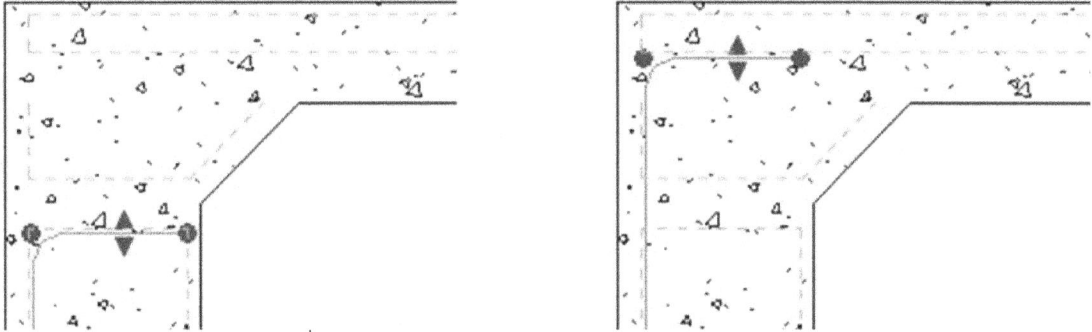

Figure 9–29

- To quickly select multiple instances of related rebar, select one, right-click, and select **Select All Rebar in Host**.

- You can use other modify tools to place rebar, such as **Move**, **Copy**, and **Mirror**.

When you select existing rebar in a model a number of tools display in the *Modify | Structural Rebar* tab, as shown in Figure 9–30. You can create or modify rebar sets, pick a new host for the rebar, edit the constraints of the rebar, apply rebar couplers, and specify a variable length rebar set type.

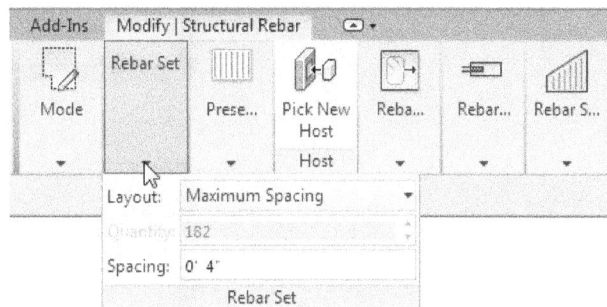

Figure 9–30

- Rebar Couplers can be added to the end or between lengths of rebar. They are used when you take the model to the next level of detail.

Hint: Rebar Set Visibility

When you select a rebar set, you can specify how that set displays. The default presentation style is set in the Reinforcement Settings dialog box, but you can change each rebar set individually.

Select a rebar set and in the *Modify | Structural Rebar* tab> Presentation panel, choose the presentation style, as shown in Figure 9–31.

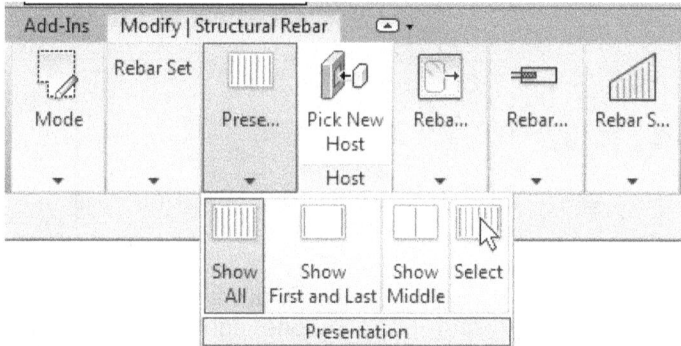

Figure 9–31

* You can also chose to display each end of a rebar set using check boxes, as shown in Figure 9–32.

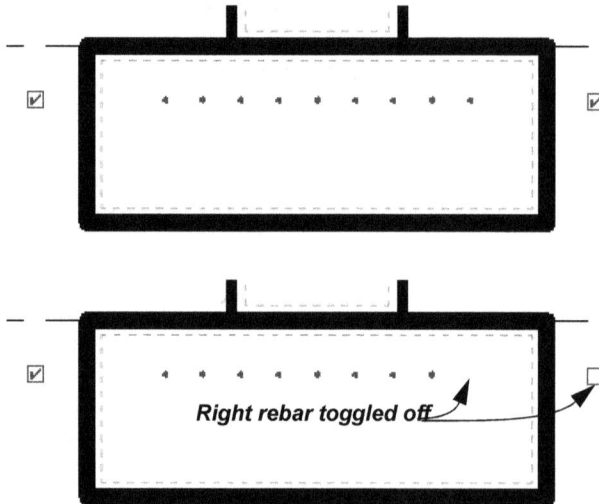

Right rebar toggled off

Figure 9–32

How To: Pick a New Host

1. To change the element that supports rebar. Select the rebar and, in the *Modify | Structural Rebar* tab>Host panel, click

   📂⁰ (Pick New Host).
2. Select the new host element.

For example, in Figure 9–33, the rebar is hosted by the wall on the left and by the slab on the right. You can see the difference in the constraints.

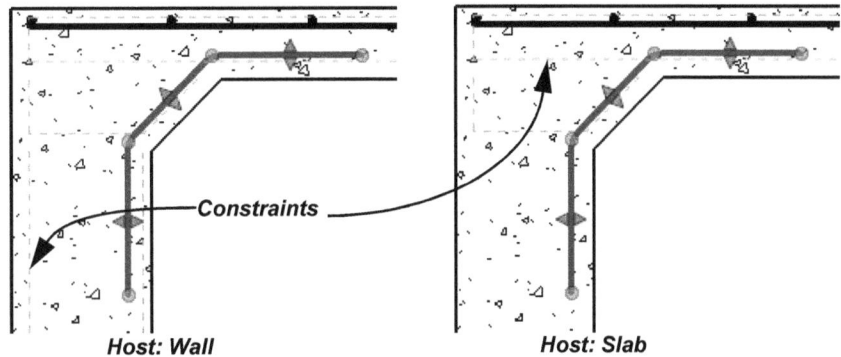

Figure 9–33

Hint: Thin Lines

If you have trouble viewing the reinforcement because of the thickness of the lines (as shown on the left in Figure 9–34), you can change the view to only display a single line weight, as shown on the right in Figure 9–34. In the Quick Access Toolbar,

click ☰ (Thin Lines) to toggle back and forth between the two view types.

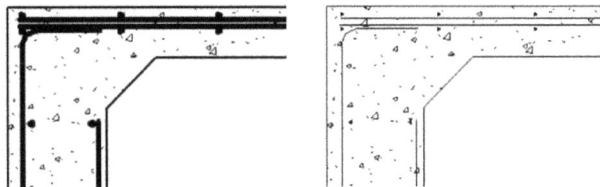

Figure 9–34

• The look of rebar in a view is also controlled by the Detail Level. **Coarse** displays 1-line representation, while **Medium** and **Fine** displays the actual size of the rebar.

How To: Edit Rebar Constraints

1. To graphically override the nearby constraints, select the rebar you want to modify.
2. In the *Modify* | *Structural Rebar* tab>Rebar Constraints panel, click ⬚ (Edit Constraints). The element and reference are highlighted in orange.
3. Using the temporary dimension, type in a new distance, as shown in Figure 9–35.

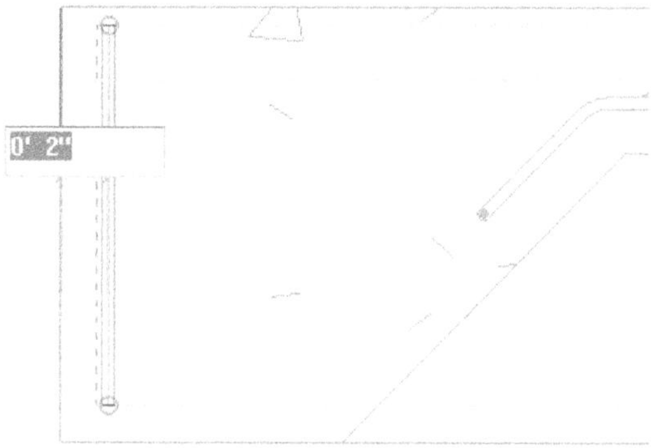

Figure 9–35

4. Click ✓ (Finish)

- If additional constraint references are available, they are highlighted in blue. Click on the blue reference to switch to that dimension.

New in 2018

- You can edit rebar constraints in 3D views.

How To: Add Varying Rebar Sets

Enhanced in 2018

1. To have rebar follow the angle of a host element, set up the rebar following standard processes as shown for a wall in Figure 9–36. Varying rebar sets can be placed in curved and free form elements.

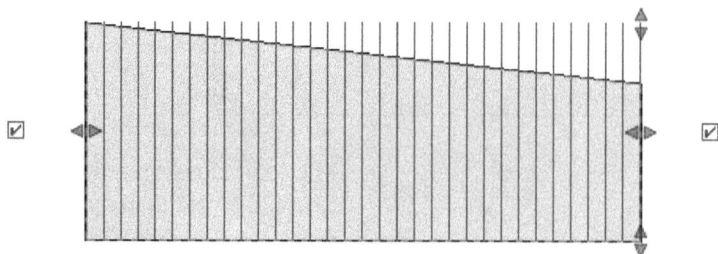

Figure 9–36

2. In the *Modify | Structural Rebar* tab> Rebar Set Type panel, click ▨ (Varying Rebar Set). The rebar now follows the edge as shown in Figure 9–37. This tool is an on/off toggle.

Figure 9–37

3. Use the arrow-like shape handles to resize the rebar to fit the element if required, as shown in Figure 9–38.

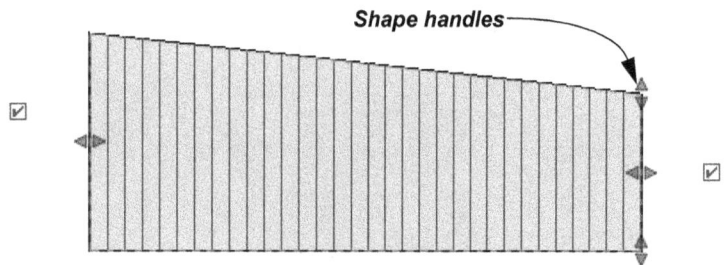

Figure 9–38

Practice 9a | # Add Rebar

Practice Objectives

- Add individual rebar elements.
- Create a repeating layout of rebar.
- Sketch a rebar design.

Estimated time for completion: 15 minutes

In this practice you will add individual rebar to a wall in a foundation section using premade shapes, and then modify the exact location and size using controls. You will then change the layout to create rebar sets. You will also sketch a new rebar shape, as shown in Figure 9–39.

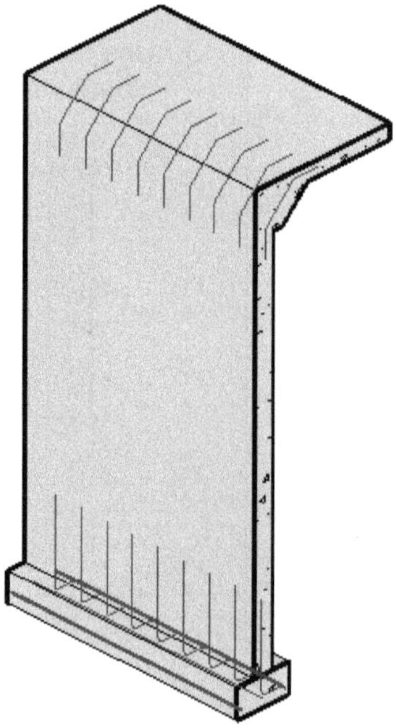

Figure 9–39

Task 1 - Create a Foundation Wall Section.

1. Open **Syracuse-Suites-Rebar.rvt**.

2. Open the Structural Plans: **00 GROUND FLOOR** view.

3. In the Quick Access Toolbar, click ♀ (Section).

4. In the Type Selector, select **Wall Section**.

5. Draw the section shown in Figure 9–40.

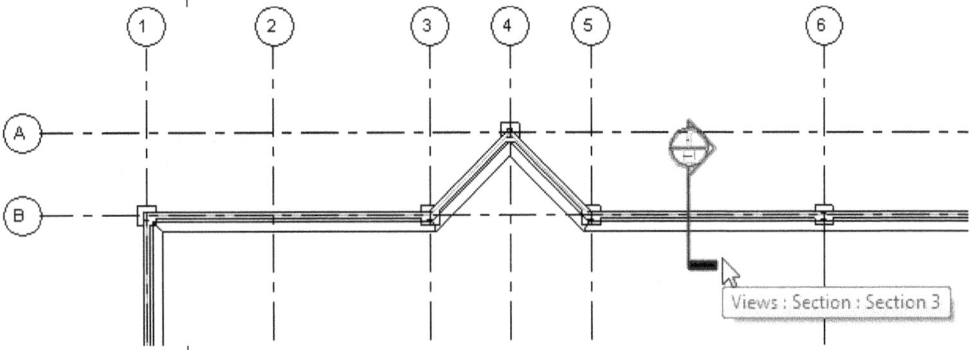

Figure 9–40

6. In the Project Browser, in the **Sections (Wall Section)** node, right-click on the new wall section view and rename it **Typical Foundation Wall Section**.

7. Open the view and resize the crop region so that it only displays the foundation.

8. In the View Control Bar change the *Scale* to **1/4"=1'-0"**, the *Detail Level* to ⊠ (Medium), and toggle off the crop region.

9. Hide the **Grid** and **Levels**.

10. In the *Modify* tab> Geometry panel, click ⬚ (Join Geometry) and select the wall and the slab edge, as shown in Figure 9–41.

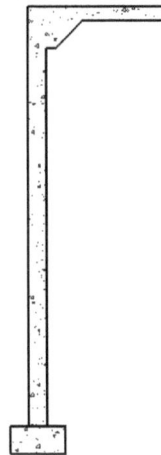

Figure 9–41

11. Save the project.

Task 2 - Add Rebar.

1. Continue working in the wall section and zoom in on the footing.

2. In the *Structure* tab>Reinforcement panel, click ⬚ (Rebar). If an alert about Hooks included in Rebar Shapes comes up, click **OK**.

3. In the *Modify | Place Rebar* tab>Placement Plane verify that ⬚ (Current Work Plane) is selected.

4. In the *Modify | Place Rebar* tab>Placement Orientation panel, click ⬚ (Parallel to Work Plane).

5. In the Rebar Shape Browser, select **Rebar Shape: 17A**.

6. Add the rebar shape to the footing, as shown in Figure 9–42.

The rebar shape fits exactly within the preset constraints.

Figure 9–42

7. Press <Esc> after the rebar is placed and then select the rebar.

8. Use the handles and controls to modify the shape so that it extends into the wall, as shown in Figure 9–43.

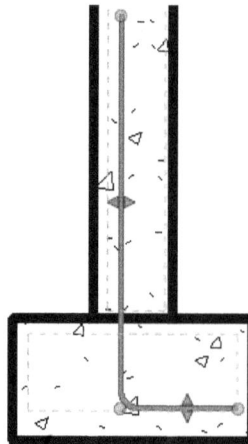

Figure 9–43

9. In the *Structure* tab>Reinforcement panel, click ⬚ (Rebar).

10. In the *Modify | Place Rebar* tab>Placement Orientation panel, click ▧ (Perpendicular to Cover).

11. In the Rebar Set panel, change the *Layout* to **Fixed Number** and *Quantity* to **3**.

12. Add **Rebar Shape: 00** to the bottom left face of the footing. Three copies are placed, as shown in Figure 9–44.

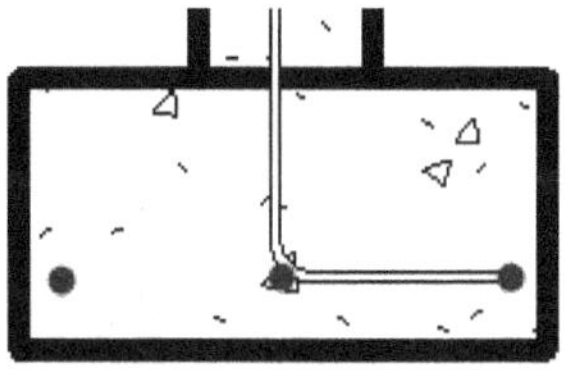

Figure 9–44

13. Click **Modify**. Then, select and move the L-shaped rebar above the dowels of the continuous footing, as shown in Figure 9–45.

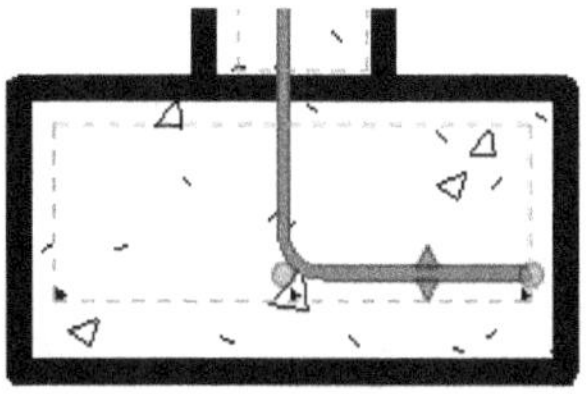

Figure 9–45

14. With the L-shaped rebar still selected, in the *Modify | Structural Rebar* tab>Rebar Set panel, change the *Layout* to **Maximum Spacing** and *Spacing* to **1'-0"**, as shown in Figure 9–46.

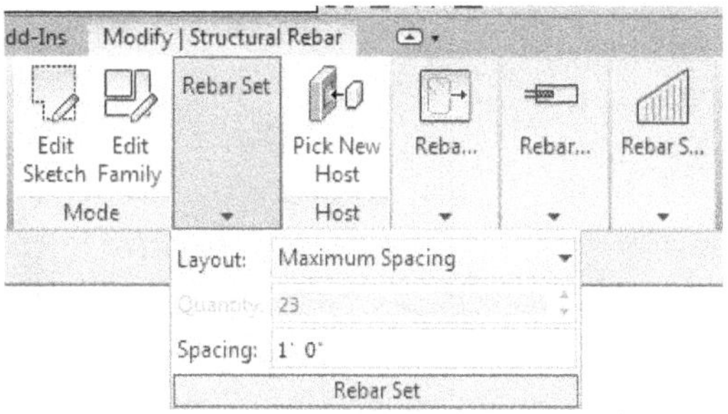

Figure 9–46

15. Save the project.

Task 3 - Sketch individual rebar.

1. Pan up to the slab and slab edge.

2. In the *Structure* tab>Reinforcement panel, click ⬚ (Rebar).

3. In the *Modify | Place Rebar* tab>Placement Methods panel, click ✎ (Sketch Rebar).

4. The cursor displays as a target ⊕ and the software prompts you to pick a host for the rebar. Select the wall.

   • Although most of this dowel is outside the wall, selecting the wall ensures that the dowels are only along this specific wall. If you had selected the slab, the dowels would have spaced themselves to the other side of the building, regardless of the wall underneath them.

5. Use the **Draw** tools to sketch the dowel similar to the one shown in Figure 9–47.

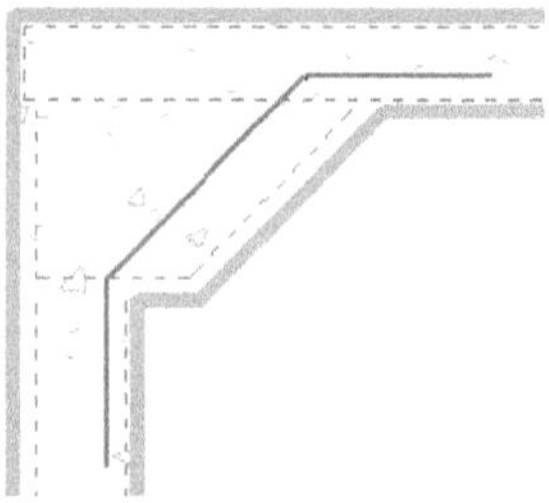

Figure 9–47

6. In the *Modify | Create Rebar Sketch* tab>Mode panel, click

   ✔ (Finish Edit Mode). A dowel is created with the new Rebar Shape in the Rebar Browser, as shown in Figure 9–48.

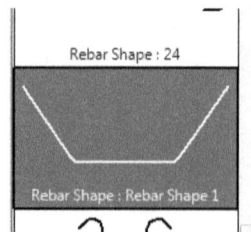

The picture might vary depending on how you drew the shape.

Figure 9–48

7. Click **Modify** and select the new dowel. Use the controls on the ends and the shape handles on the midpoint of the bar to make smaller adjustments.

8. In the Rebar Set panel, set *Layout* to **Maximum Spacing** and *Spacing* to **1'-0"**.

9. Save the project.

Task 4 - Create a 3D Section view.

1. In the Quick Access Toolbar, click 🏠 (Default 3D View).

2. Right-click on the ViewCube and select **Orient to View> Sections>Section: Typical Foundation Wall Section.**

3. Rotate the view and hide the section box, as shown in Figure 9–49.

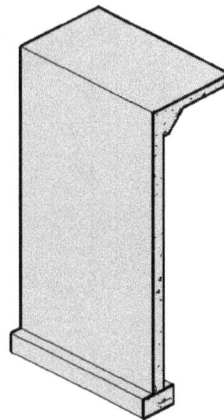

Figure 9–49

4. In the Project Browser, in the 3D Views node, rename the view to *3D Foundation*.

5. Window around everything and select it. You can see the rebar. Using ▽ (Filter) select only the Structural Rebar.

6. In Properties, next to *View Visibility States,* click **Edit....**

7. In the Rebar Element View Visibility States dialog box, beside the **3D Foundation** view name, select **View unobscured** and **View as solid** and click **OK**

8. In Properties click **Apply** or move the cursor into the view. The rebar sets now display in the view.

9. In the View Control Bar, set the *Detail Level* to ▨ (Fine).

10. Save the project.

9.4 Reinforcing Walls, Floors, and Slabs

There are three types of reinforcement that can be used with walls, floors, and slabs. Area Reinforcement places evenly spaced rebar in structural walls and floors according to a boundary you specify, as shown on the wall in Figure 9–50. Path Reinforcement enables you to specify reinforcing that bends from the slab into the bearing wall, as shown on the floor in Figure 9–50. Fabric Reinforcement places sheets of reinforcing wires within a boundary you specify.

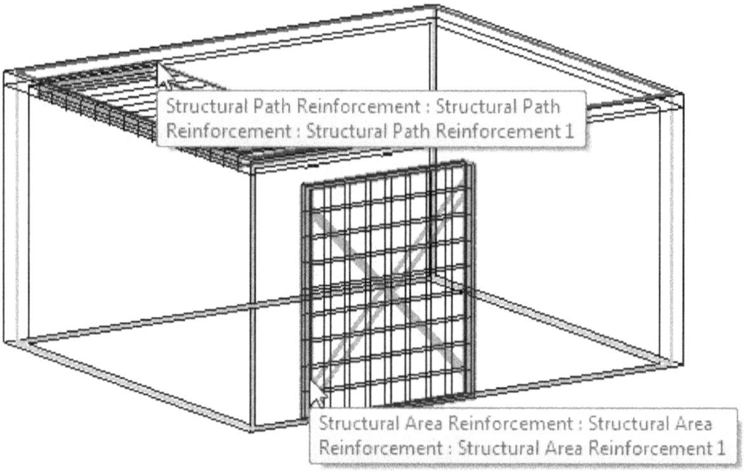

Figure 9–50

- Area, Path, and Fabric Reinforcement can be edited by modifying the sketch, by changing parameters in Properties, and by removing the entire system. Area and Path Reinforcement systems can also be removed but they retain the individual rebar. You can change how these display in views.

Area Reinforcement

Area reinforcement can be placed in 3D, plan, elevation, or section views depending on the element you are reinforcing.

When creating an **Area Reinforcement**, you sketch a boundary, as shown in Figure 9–51, and then set up the spacing and layers in Properties.

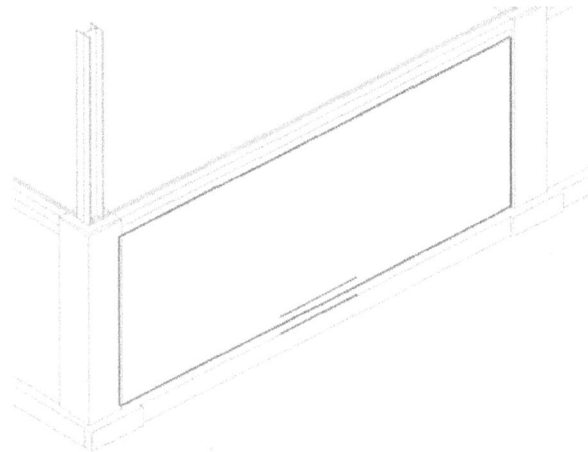

Figure 9–51

How To: Add Area Reinforcement

1. In the *Structure* tab>Reinforcement panel, click ⊞ (Area), select a structural floor or a wall or select a floor or wall and, in the *Modify |* contextual tab>Reinforcement panel, click

   ⊞ (Area).
2. In Properties, modify the parameters as required for the layout, as shown in Figure 9–52, and rebar size and spacing.

Scroll down to see the rebar sizing and spacing.

Structural Area Reinforcement	▼ ⊞ Edit Type
Construction	⚥
Layout Rule	Maximum Spacing
Additional Exterior Cover Offset	0' 0"
Additional Interior Cover Offset	0' 0"
Graphics	⚥
View Visibility States	Edit...
Structural	⚥
Reinforcement Volume	0.00 in³
Layers	⚥
Exterior Major Direction	☑
Exterior Major Bar Type	#4
Exterior Major Hook Type	None

Figure 9–52

3. Click **Apply**.

*Note that locking
sketches to elements
increases the size of the
model. You should only
do this if it is more
efficient in the long run.*

4. In the *Modify | Create Reinforcement Boundary* tab>Draw panel, click (Pick Lines) or one of the other draw tools.

- If you are using **Pick Lines**, you can lock the lines to the elements you pick. When you select an edge a padlock symbol displays. Select it to lock the area reinforcement boundary to the wall or slab edge perimeter so that any changes made to the wall or slab automatically update the area reinforcement as well.

- If you select **Lock** in the Options Bar, each sketch line is locked to the selected edge. This only works with **Pick Lines**.

- The boundary must be a closed loop without any overlapping lines. Use the **Modify** tools if required.

5. Click (Finish Edit Mode). The reinforcement displays either as just the symbol, as shown in Figure 9–53, or displays the rebar depending on how the view is set.

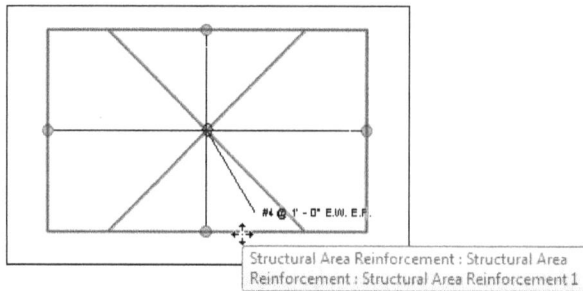

Figure 9–53

- When drawing the boundary, the first line you select displays a set of double lines indicating the major direction, as shown in Figure 9–54. To change it, in the *Modify | Structural Area Reinforcement>Edit Boundary* tab>Draw panel, click

  (Major Direction) and select or draw the edge that defines the direction for the major bars.

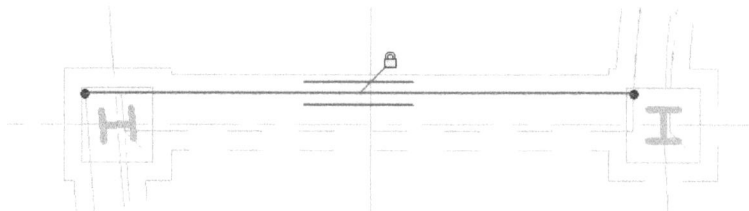

Figure 9–54

Hint: Displaying Area and Path Reinforcement

When you first place area or path reinforcement, a box displays at the boundary of the elements. By default, the rebar does not display, but it can be displayed when the Visual Style is set to ⬜ (Wireframe) or if you modify the View Visibility State of the rebar element in Properties, as shown in Figure 9–55.

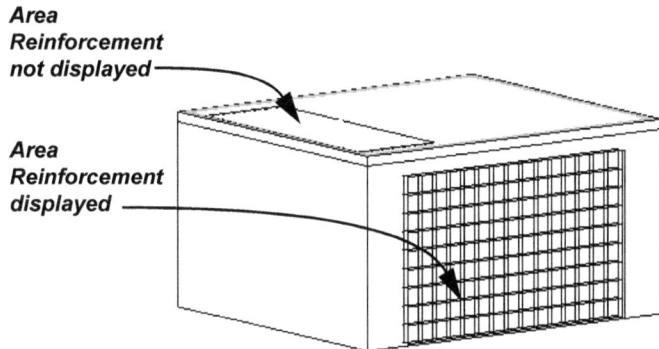

Area Reinforcement not displayed

Area Reinforcement displayed

Figure 9–55

Path Reinforcement

In some cases, additional reinforcement is required along the length of some edges to prevent curling and other issues. Path Reinforcement creates reinforcing that bends from the slab into the bearing wall, but is only extended into the slab at a specified distance, as shown in Figure 9–56. This is also handy for the foundation design of pre-engineered metal structures, where the pilasters and other elements need to be pinned back to the slab.

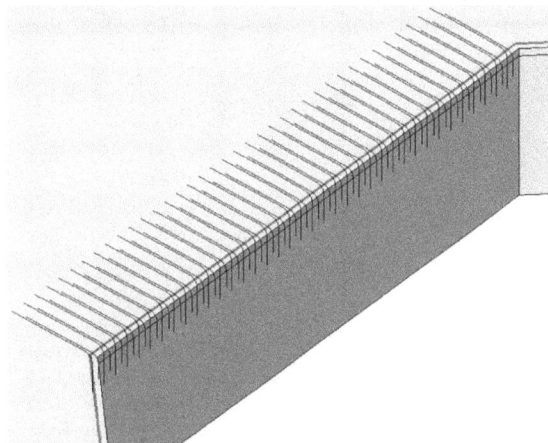

Figure 9–56

How To: Add Path Reinforcement

1. In the *Structure* tab>Reinforcement panel, click ⊔⅃ (Path Reinforcement).
2. Select the structural floor or wall.
3. In the *Modify | Create Reinforcement Path* tab>Draw panel, use the Draw tools to place a single line specifying an open path, as shown in Figure 9–57.

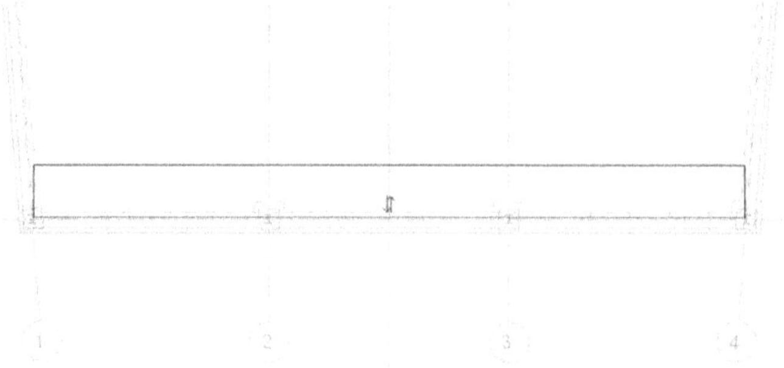

Figure 9–57

4. Click ⟷ (Flip) as required, to set the placement of the path.
5. In Properties, as shown in Figure 9–58, modify the parameters as required.

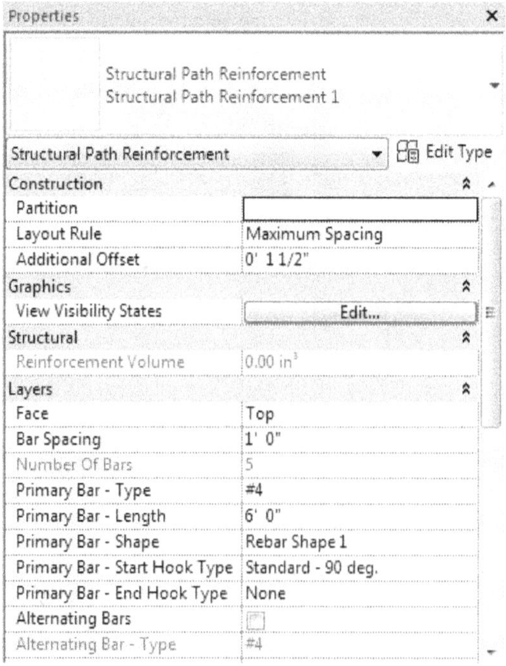

Figure 9–58

6. In the Mode panel, click ✓ (Finish Edit Mode). The Reinforcement is added as shown in Figure 9–59.

Figure 9–59

Fabric Reinforcement

The Structural Fabric Area tool sketches the boundary of a fabric area to populate with fabric sheets, as shown in Figure 9–60. Fabric Reinforcement is made up of 2 element types, Fabric Wire and Fabric Sheets. The Fabric Wire is used to define the reinforcing wire which is used to create the Fabric Sheets. You can also add individual fabric sheets.

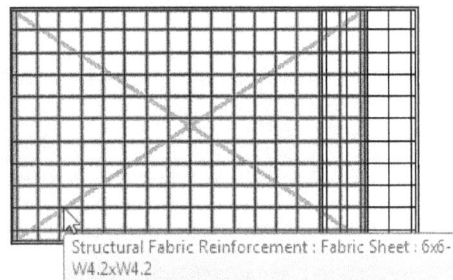

Figure 9–60

*   Fabric Reinforcement can be hosted in structural floors, foundation slabs, and structural walls.

How To: Add a Single Fabric Sheet

1. In the *Structure* tab>Reinforcement panel (or if you have already selected an element, in the *Modify | contextual* tab),

    click 📄 (Fabric Sheet).
2. In the Type Selector specify the type of sheet you want to use.
3. In Properties specify the *Location* (**Top** or **Bottom**), and other settings.

4. Click to place the sheet where you want it. (It must be in a concrete host, such as a wall or floor.)
5. The command remains active and you can place additional sheets, as shown in Figure 9–61.

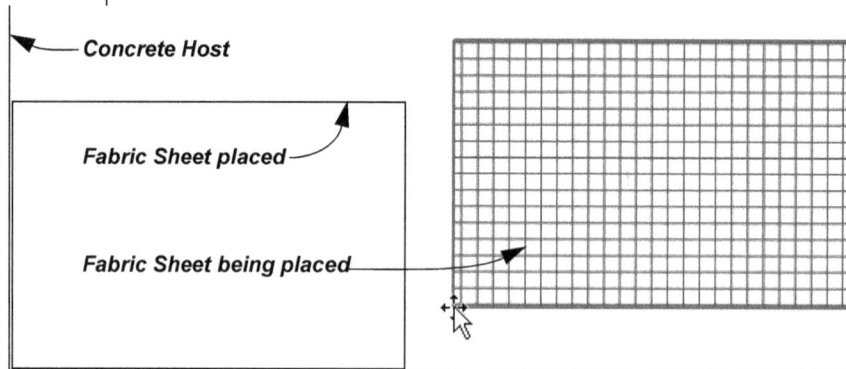

Concrete Host

Fabric Sheet placed

Fabric Sheet being placed

Figure 9–61

6. End the command.

How To: Add a Bent Fabric Sheet

1. Open a view perpendicular to the work plane, such as a section.

2. Start the (Fabric Sheet) command.
3. In the *Modify | Place Fabric Sheet* tab> Mode panel, click

   (Bend Sketch)
4. Select the host for the bent fabric sheet.
5. Using the tools in the *Modify | Create Bend Profile* tab, sketch a profile such as the one shown in Figure 9–62.

Figure 9–62

6. Click ✓ (Finish). The fabric sheet is bent following the sketch, as shown in Figure 9–63.

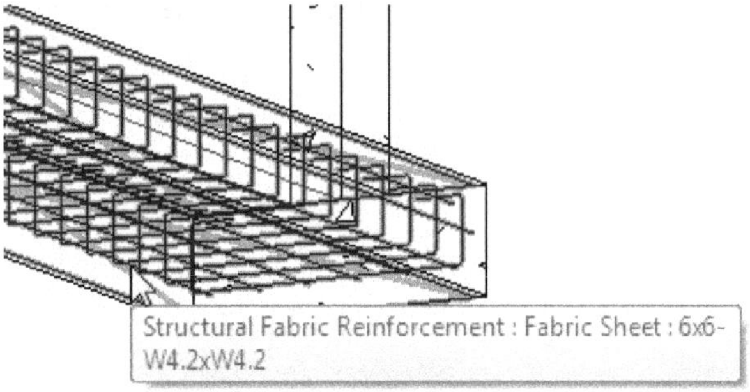

Structural Fabric Reinforcement : Fabric Sheet : 6x6-W4.2xW4.2

Figure 9–63

How To: Add Fabric Area Reinforcement

1. In the *Structure* tab>Reinforcement panel (or in the *Modify | contextual* tab if you have already selected an element), click

   ⬛ (Fabric Area).

2. Select the structural wall, floor, or slab if you did not select it already.

3. In the *Modify | Create Fabric Boundary* tab>Draw panel, use the Draw tools to define the closed boundary.

   • Use ⬚ (Pick lines) and lock the boundary to the host element so that it automatically updates if the host is changed.

   • The set of double lines indicates the major direction. To change it, in the *Modify | Create Fabric Boundary* tab>

   Draw panel, click ⠿ (Major Direction) and select one of the other lines to set the direction of the reinforcement.

4. The preview graphics displays the full size of the sheets as delivered to the construction site, as shown in Figure 9–64. Use the check boxes and Properties to obtain the required fabric sheet layout.

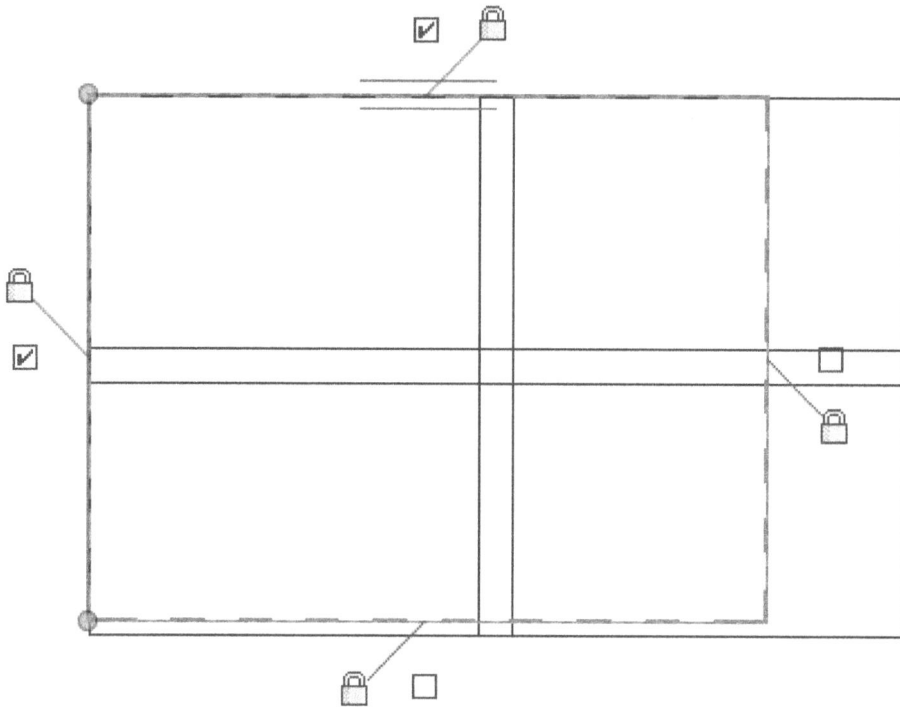

Figure 9–64

- The check boxes at each edge determine the start point of the Fabric sheet layout and its direction. The start point is defined by at least 2 selected check boxes on the rectangular edges, as shown in Figure 9–64. Select additional check boxes to determine the fabric sheet alignment.

5. In Properties, as shown in Figure 9–65, modify the parameters as required for the *Fabric Sheet, Location, Lap Splice Position, Major* and *Minor lap Splice Length*, etc.

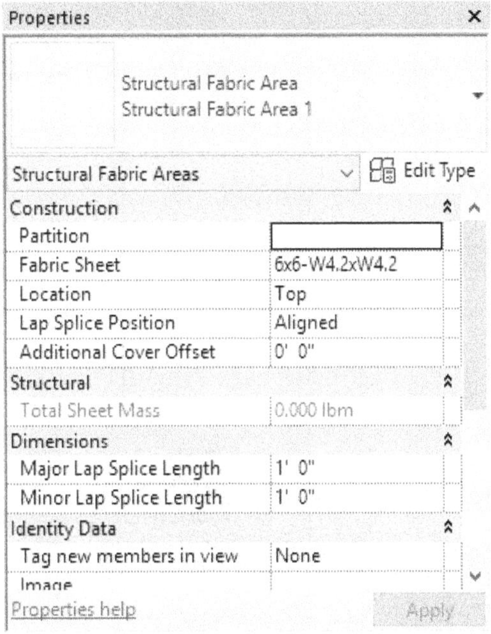

Figure 9–65

6. Click ✓ (Finish Edit Mode) and the fabric reinforcement is added to the element with the specified overlaps, as shown in Figure 9–66.

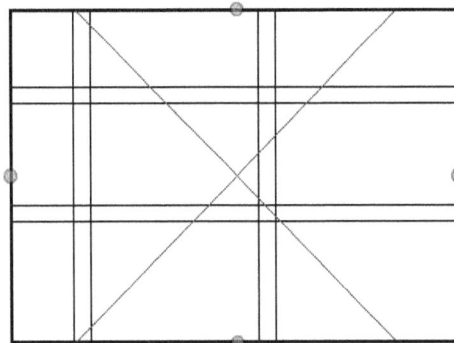

Figure 9–66

- If you want to change the way the fabric sheets overlap, modify the *Lap Splice Position* in Properties. For example, the sheets shown in Figure 9–67 are set to **Major Half-way Stagger**. The *Major* and *Minor Lap Splice Lengths* can also be modified.

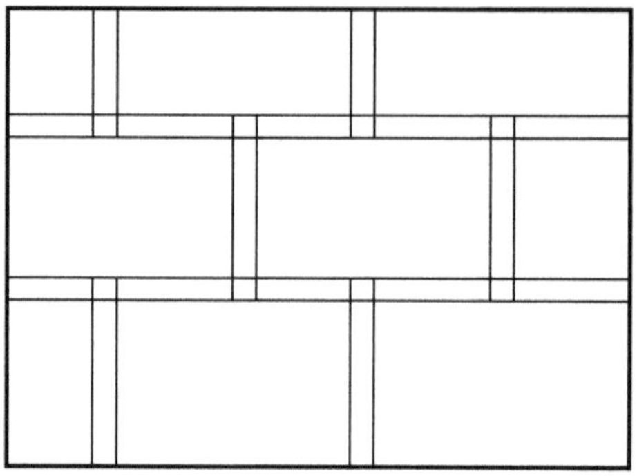

Figure 9–67

- To place symbols and tags automatically, in Properties, under *Identity Data*, select a view from the Tag new members in view drop-down list, as shown in Figure 9–68.

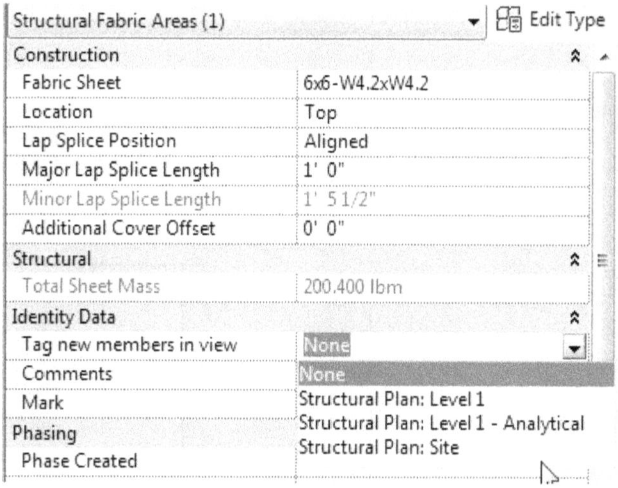

Structural Fabric Areas (1)	⯆ Edit Type
Construction	⌃
Fabric Sheet	6x6-W4.2xW4.2
Location	Top
Lap Splice Position	Aligned
Major Lap Splice Length	1' 0"
Minor Lap Splice Length	1' 5 1/2"
Additional Cover Offset	0' 0"
Structural	⌃
Total Sheet Mass	200.400 lbm
Identity Data	⌃
Tag new members in view	None ⯆
Comments	None
Mark	Structural Plan: Level 1
Phasing	Structural Plan: Level 1 - Analytical
Phase Created	Structural Plan: Site

Figure 9–68

- Only views that are parallel to the placement plane are listed in the drop-down list. Using this parameter also defines the view to place new symbols and tags if the fabric area changes size during regeneration.

Modifying Area, Path, & Fabric Reinforcement

As with most elements in Autodesk Revit software, there are a variety of ways to modify area, path, and fabric reinforcement including editing the boundary or path, using shape handles, and changing the properties, as shown in Figure 9–69. You can also delete entire systems or break the systems down into individual rebar elements or sheets.

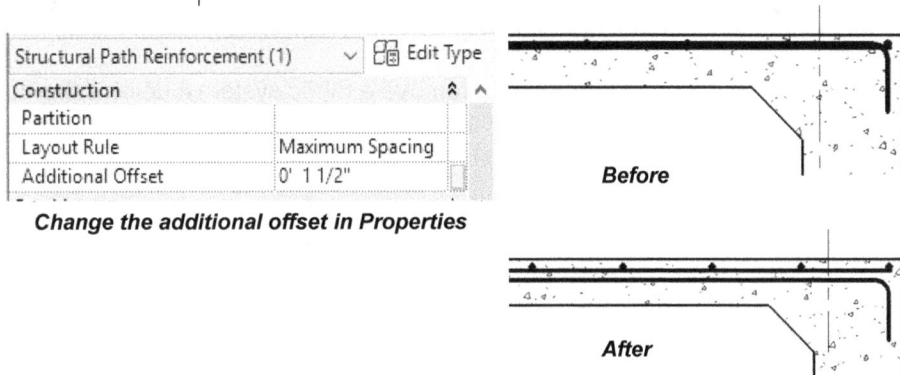

Change the additional offset in Properties

Before

After

Figure 9–69

- To quickly select multiple instances of related rebar or fabric, select one, right-click and select **Select All Rebar in Host** or **Select All Fabric in Host**.

- When you select the area, path, or fabric area reinforcement you can adjust the boundary by stretching the shape handles, as shown in Figure 9–70.

Path

Area

Fabric

Figure 9–70

- When you have the reinforcement selected you can use the related 🖎 (Edit) tool found in the Mode panel. This opens the sketch mode where you can use the draw tools to change the boundary or path.

- If you want to remove the reinforcement completely, ensure that you select the boundary of the system and then delete it.

- If you want to keep the individual rebar elements but drop the system, click ▦ (Remove Area System), ⊞ (Remove Path System), or ◸ (Remove Fabric System) in the respective *Modify* tabs.

- When you remove a fabric system it deletes the boundary and leaves the full size of all of the sheets, as shown on the right in Figure 9–71.

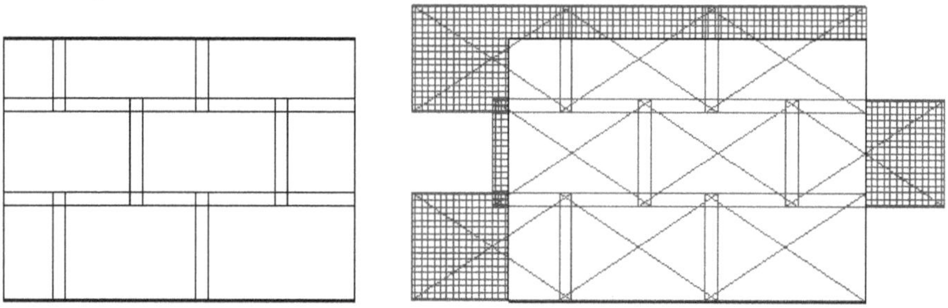

Fabric System before   **Fabric System after**

Figure 9–71

- When the area or path system is removed, the individual bars create standard joins to the hosting elements. In some cases this can cause these bars to shift slightly. This is much more evident if Stirrup/Tie bars are in close proximity to the hosted bars.

- When the system is removed, the associated tags, symbols, and dimensions are also removed.

- It can help to view reinforcement in a section view. For example, in path reinforcement you can check the hook direction and modify it if required with the **Toggle Hook Orientation** control, as shown in Figure 9–72.

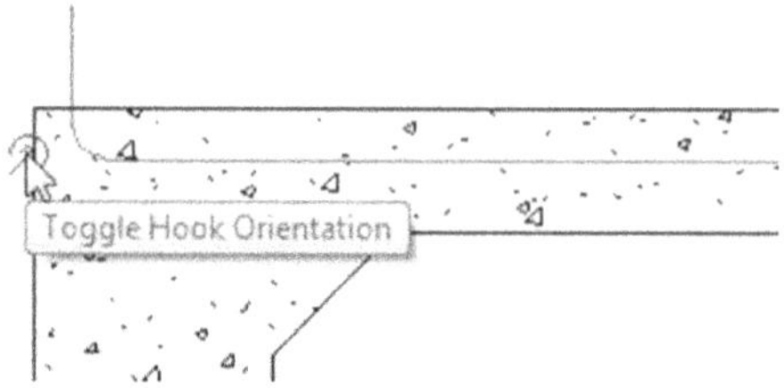

Toggle Hook Orientation

Figure 9–72

- You can also modify the other hook information in Properties. For example, you can change the **Primary Bar-Start Hook Type** as shown in Figure 9–73.

Structural Path Reinforcement (1)		Edit Type
Bar Spacing	1' 0"	
Number Of Bars	16	
Primary Bar - Type	#4	
Primary Bar - Length	5' 0"	
Primary Bar - Start Hook ...	Stirrup/Tie - 135 deg.	
Primary Bar - End Hook T...	None	
Primary Bar - Hook Orien...	Standard - 90 deg.	
Alternating Bars	Standard - 180 deg.	
Alternating Bar - Type	Stirrup/Tie - 90 deg.	
Alternating Bar - Length	Stirrup/Tie - 135 deg.	
Alternating Bar - Offset	Stirrup/Tie Seismic - 135 deg.	

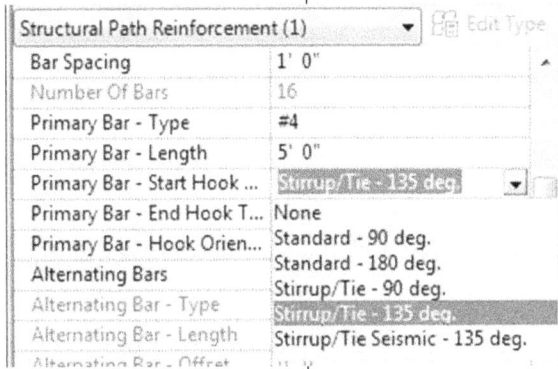

Figure 9–73

Practice 9b

| Reinforce Structural Elements

Practice Objective

Estimated time for completion: 15 minutes

- Add area, path, and fabric reinforcement.

In this practice you will apply area and path reinforcement to a slab. You will also add area reinforcement to a wall and fabric reinforcement, as shown in Figure 9–74.

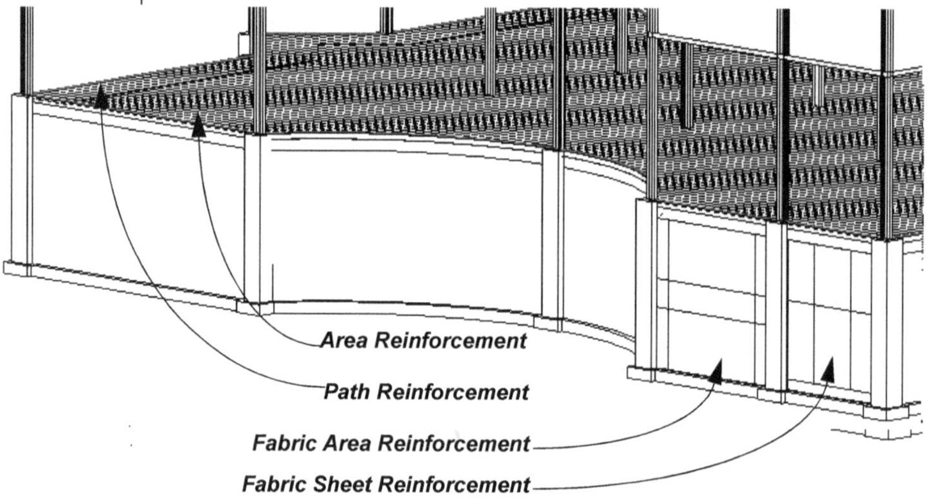

Area Reinforcement

Path Reinforcement

Fabric Area Reinforcement

Fabric Sheet Reinforcement

Figure 9–74

Task 1 - Apply area reinforcement.

1. Open **Syracuse-Suites-Reinforcing.rvt**.

2. In the **Structural Plans: 00 GROUND FLOOR** view, change the *Visual Style* to ⬛ (Hidden Line).

3. Select the structural floor by clicking on an edge. You can use <Tab> to cycle through elements.

4. In the View Control Bar, expand 🐛 (Temporary Hide/ Isolate) and select **Isolate Element**. This makes it easier for you to work specifically with the slab outline only.

5. In the *Modify | Floors* tab>Reinforcement panel, click ⊞ (Area Reinforcement).

6. In Properties, under *Layers,* clear the **Bottom Major Direction** and **Bottom Minor Direction** parameters.

7. In the *Modify | Create Reinforcement Boundary* tab>Draw panel, click ⬥ (Pick Lines).

8. In the Options Bar, select **Lock**. This ensures that, if the floor slab is modified, the boundary of the area reinforcement will update to match.

Hint: Hover over one line and press <Tab> so that all the connected lines highlight.

9. Select the outside edges of the slab and the outlines of the elevator and stairwell. Verify that the magenta sketch lines do not overlap, do not have any gaps, and form a closed loop on the outside and around each opening.

10. In the *Modify | Create Reinforcement Boundary* tab>Draw panel, click ⫼ (Major Direction) and select a horizontal line.

11. In the Mode panel, click ✓ (Finish Edit Mode). The area reinforcement symbol and tag display as shown in Figure 9–75.

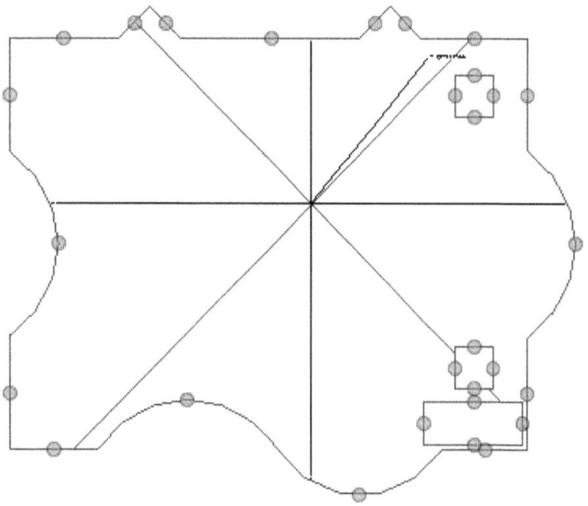

Figure 9–75

12. With the area reinforcement element still selected, in Properties, next to *View Visibility States*, click **Edit...**.

13. In the Rebar Element View Visibility States dialog box, for *Structural Plan: 00 GROUND FLOOR*, select **View unobscured,** as shown in Figure 9–76. Click **OK**.

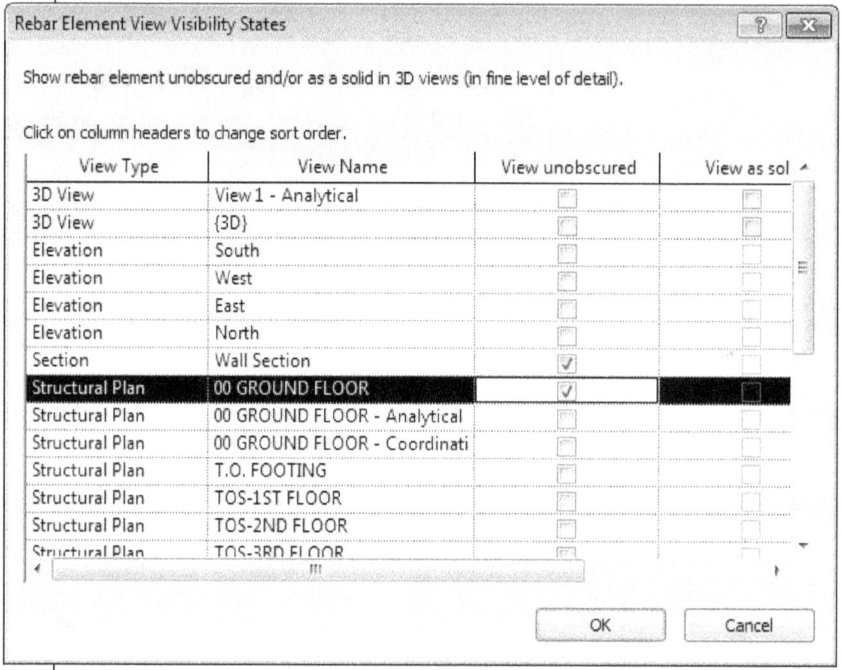

Rebar Element View Visibility States

Show rebar element unobscured and/or as a solid in 3D views (in fine level of detail).

Click on column headers to change sort order.

View Type	View Name	View unobscured	View as sol
3D View	View 1 - Analytical	☐	☐
3D View	{3D}	☐	☐
Elevation	South	☐	☐
Elevation	West	☐	☐
Elevation	East	☐	☐
Elevation	North	☐	☐
Section	Wall Section	☑	
Structural Plan	00 GROUND FLOOR	☑	☐
Structural Plan	00 GROUND FLOOR - Analytical	☐	☐
Structural Plan	00 GROUND FLOOR - Coordinati	☐	☐
Structural Plan	T.O. FOOTING	☐	☐
Structural Plan	TOS-1ST FLOOR	☐	☐
Structural Plan	TOS-2ND FLOOR	☐	☐
Structural Plan	TOS-3RD FLOOR	☐	☐

OK   Cancel

Figure 9–76

14. Press <Esc> so that the area reinforcement is not selected. Then highlight the elements. Each rebar displays individually as shown in Figure 9–77.

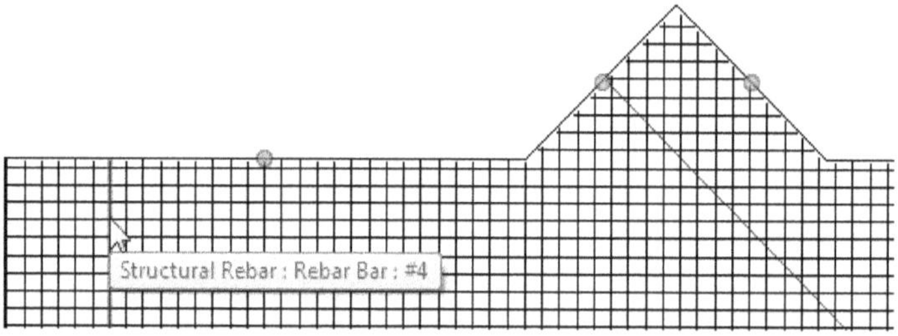

Structural Rebar : Rebar Bar : #4

Figure 9–77

15. Select one of the rebar elements and identify its properties. Most of the parameters are automatically assigned by the area reinforcement element but you can change the *Schedule Mark* and *View Visibility States*.

16. Select the entire area reinforcement element. Edit *View Visibility States* and clear the plan view. The view displays just the outline.

17. Open the **Sections (Wall Section): Typical Foundation Wall Section** view. The area reinforcement displays in the section as shown in Figure 9–78. The rebar and area reinforcement elements can be selected separately.

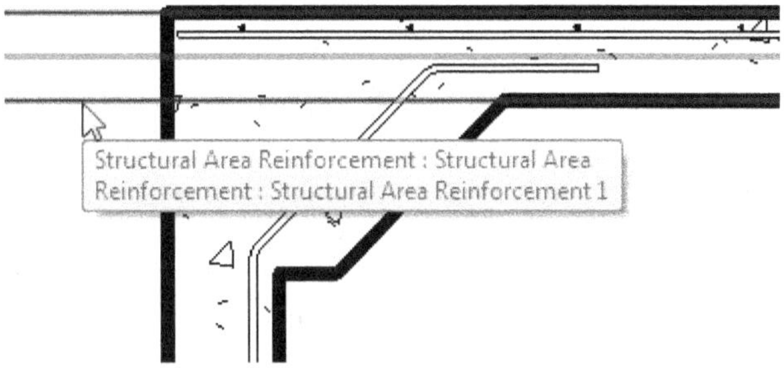

Figure 9–78

18. Save the project.

Task 2 - Apply path reinforcement.

1. Switch back to the **Structural Plans: 00 GROUND FLOOR** view with only the floor displaying.

2. In the *Structure* tab>Reinforcement panel, click ⌐³ (Path) and select the floor.

3. In Properties, set the *Additional Offset* to **1 1/2"** and the *Primary Bar - Shape* to **Rebar Shape 1**, as shown in Figure 9–79. Ensure that the *Alternating Bars* is toggled off.

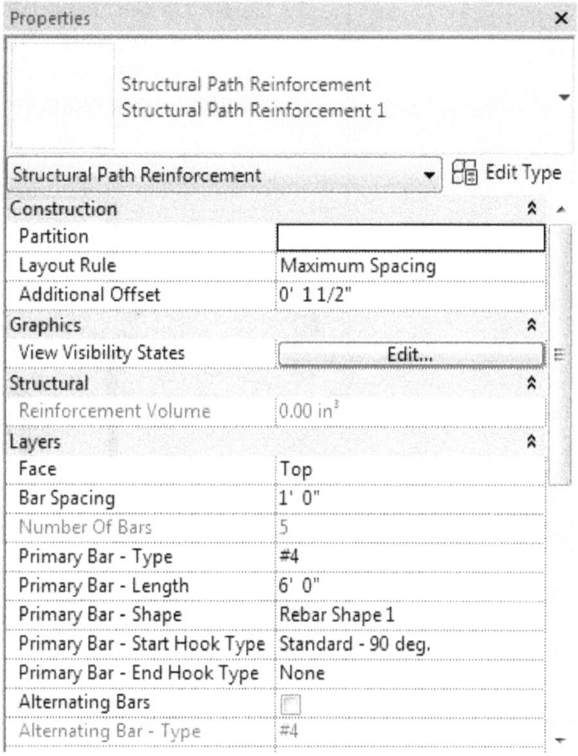

Figure 9–79

4. Using the tools in the Draw panel, draw a single line path along the north wall. Flip the path reinforcement, if required, so that it is set to the inside, as shown in Figure 9–80.

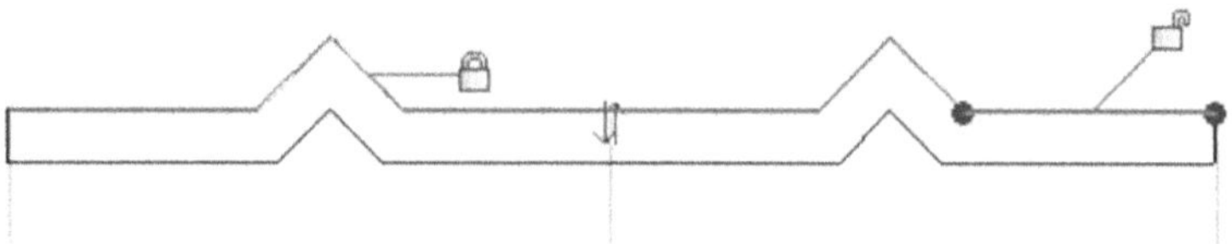

Figure 9–80

5. In the Mode panel, click ✓ (Finish Edit Mode).

6. In the View Control Bar, click ➹ (Temporary Hide/Isolate) and select **Reset Temporary Hide Isolate**.

7. Open the **Sections (Wall Section): Typical Foundation Wall Section** view. The path reinforcement displays in the section as shown in Figure 9–81.

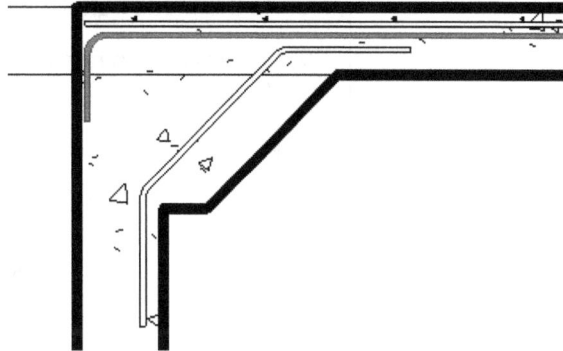

Figure 9–81

8. Save the project.

Task 3 - Reinforce walls.

1. In the **Typical Foundation Wall Section** view, select the wall.

2. Open the **Elevations (Building Elevation): North** view and zoom in on the selected foundation wall. Do not isolate the element because you need to see the other elements to draw the correct boundary.

3. In the *Modify | Walls* tab>Reinforcement panel, click

   ▦ (Area).

4. Draw the boundary between the piers and set the *Major Direction* to the vertical sketch line to the left, as shown in Figure 9–82. Use the **Trim** command to clean up the corners. Remember that there cannot be any gaps or overlapping lines.

Chain of walls or lines

Figure 9–82

5. In Properties, ensure that both the *Interior* and *Exterior Major* and *Minor* spacing is set to **1'-0"**.

6. In the Mode panel, click ✔ (Finish Edit Mode).

7. The new area reinforcement is added, as shown in Figure 9–83.

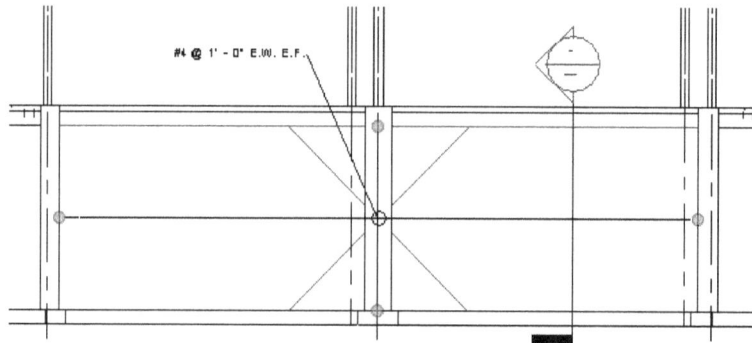

Figure 9–83

8. Save the project.

Task 4 - Fabric Area and Sheet Reinforcement.

1. Open **Elevations (Building Elevation): West** view.

2. Zoom in to the lower right corner of the building and select the wall as shown in Figure 9–84.

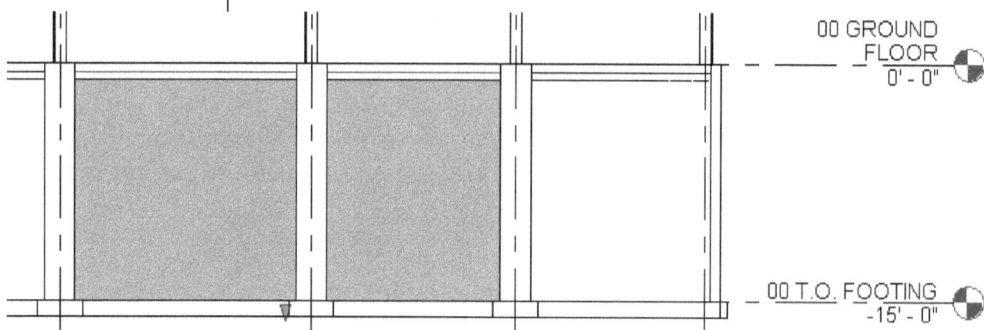

Figure 9–84

3. In the *Modify | Walls* tab>Reinforcement panel, click ▨ (Fabric Area).

4. When prompted, do not load the Structural Fabric Reinforcement Symbols or Tags.

5. Use the ⬜ (Rectangle) Draw tool and draw the boundary shown in Figure 9–85. The sheets extend beyond the boundary.

The boundary is highlighted for clarification.

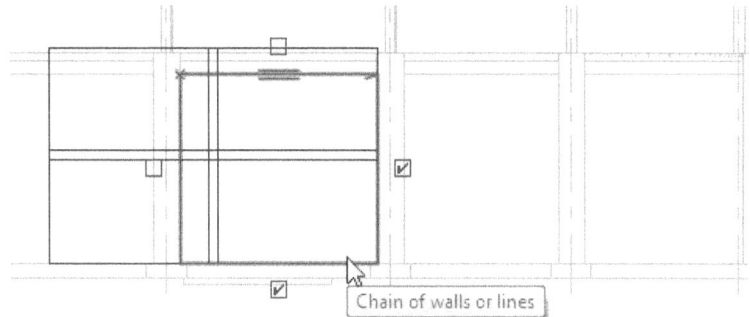

Figure 9–85

6. Select all of the check boxes so that the ending edges are set up, as shown in Figure 9–86.

Figure 9–86

7. Click ✔ (Finish Edit Mode).

8. The fabric sheets display. You can modify the fabric sheet origins to change the fit, if required.

9. Select the same wall and in the *Modify | Walls* tab> Reinforcement panel, click 🗒 (Fabric Sheet).

10. Add individual fabric sheets to the wall area to the right of the previous fabric area reinforcement, as shown in Figure 9–87. You can press <Spacebar> to rotate the sheets as you place them.

Structural Fabric Reinforcement : Fabric Sheet : Fabric Sheet 1

Figure 9–87

11. Open a 3D view and rotate it to display the area where the fabric reinforcement is added, as shown in Figure 9–88.

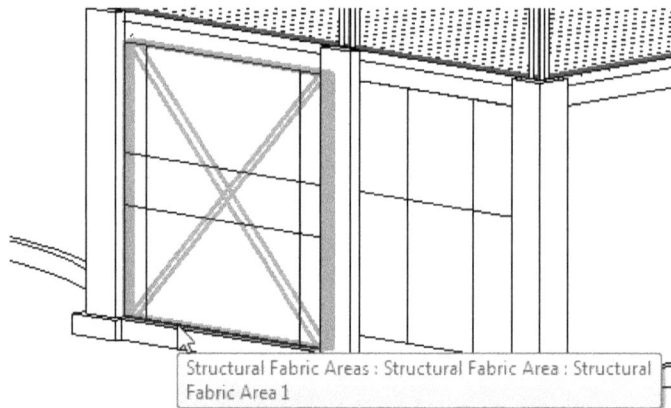

Structural Fabric Areas : Structural Fabric Area : Structural Fabric Area 1

Figure 9–88

12. Save the project.

Chapter Review Questions

1. Which of the following elements can have reinforcement added to it? (Select all that apply.)

   a. Structural walls

   b. Non-structural walls

   c. Foundation walls

   d. Partition walls

2. The settings in the Rebar Cover Settings dialog box, as shown in Figure 9–89, are contained in the host that is being reinforced.

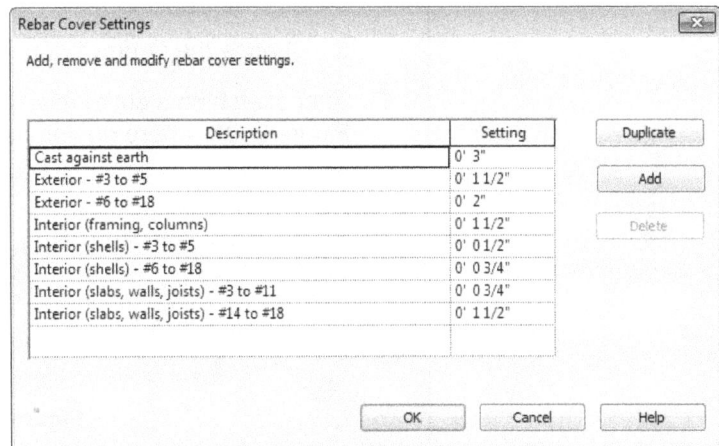

Figure 9–89

   a. True

   b. False

3. How do you load additional reinforcement into your model if it is not already available? (Select all that apply.)

   a. In the Rebar Shape Browser, right-click and select **Load**.

   b. In the *Modify | Place Rebar* tab>Family panel, select **Load Shapes**.

   c. In the *Insert* tab>Load from Library panel, select **Load Family**.

   d. In the Project Browser, in the Families>Structural Rebar section, right-click and select **Load Shapes**.

4. How do you add multiple evenly spaced instances of rebar such as that shown in Figure 9–90?

Structural Rebar : Rebar Bar : #4 : Shape 17A

Figure 9–90

a. Modify the Layout Rule.

b. Use the **Array** command.

c. Edit the Constraints.

d. Change the **Quantity** option.

5. After sketching a custom rebar shape, as shown in Figure 9–91, where do you assign the name?

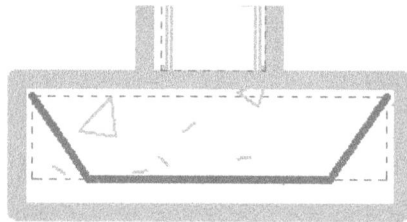

Figure 9–91

a. Right-click on the rebar and select **Rename**.

b. After finishing the sketch type it in the Name dialog box that comes up.

c. In Properties, beside the Shape parameter.

d. In the Project Browser, under Structural Rebar>Rebar Shape.

6. In which type of elements can you add structural area reinforcement as shown in Figure 9–92? (Select all that apply.)

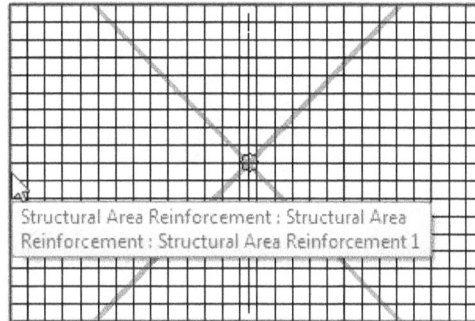

Figure 9–92

a. Foundation slabs

b. Structural floors

c. Structural walls

d. Wall Foundations

7. To display reinforcement in a 3D view, as shown in Figure 9–93, where do you make the modification?

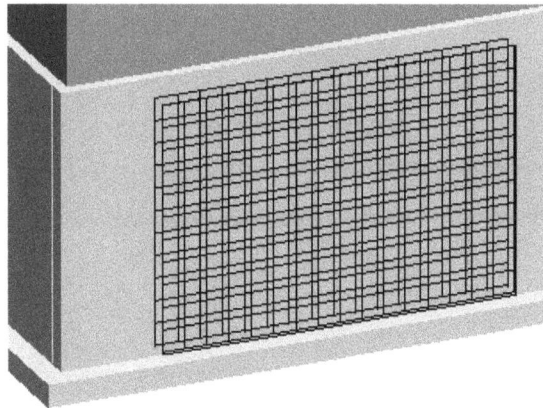

Figure 9–93

a. The Visibility Graphics Overrides dialog box.

b. The View Visibility State in the rebar properties.

c. The 3D View Properties in the view properties.

d. The Visual Style of the view.

Command Summary

Button	Command	Location
Rebar Set Presentation Tools		
	Select	• **Ribbon:** In a plan view with a rebar set selected, *Modify	Structural Rebar* tab> Presentation panel
	Show All	• **Ribbon:** In a plan view with a rebar set selected, *Modify	Structural Rebar* tab> Presentation panel
	Show First and Last	• **Ribbon:** In a plan view with a rebar set selected, *Modify	Structural Rebar* tab> Presentation panel
	Show Middle	• **Ribbon:** In a plan view with a rebar set selected, *Modify	Structural Rebar* tab> Presentation panel
Reinforcement Elements		
	Area	• **Ribbon:** *Structure* tab> Reinforcement panel or with a concrete structural member selected *Modify	contextual* tab>Reinforcement panel
	Fabric Area	• **Ribbon:** *Structure* tab> Reinforcement panel or with a concrete structural member selected *Modify	contextual* tab>Reinforcement panel
	Fabric Sheet	• **Ribbon:** *Structure* tab> Reinforcement panel or with a concrete structural member selected *Modify	contextual* tab>Reinforcement panel
	Path	• **Ribbon:** *Structure* tab> Reinforcement panel or with a concrete structural member selected *Modify	contextual* tab>Reinforcement panel
	Rebar	• **Ribbon:** *Structure* tab> Reinforcement panel or with a concrete structural member selected *Modify	contextual* tab>Reinforcement panel
Reinforcement Tools		
	Cover	• **Ribbon:** *Structure* tab> Reinforcement panel
	Edit Constraints	• **Ribbon:** *Modify	Structural Rebar* tab> Rebar Constraints panel
	Constrained Placement	• **Ribbon:** *Modify	Structural Rebar* tab> Rebar Constraints panel
	Multi-planar	• **Ribbon:** *Modify	Create Rebar Sketch* tab>Reinforcement panel

	Parallel to Work Plane	• **Ribbon:** *Modify	Place Rebar* tab> Placement Orientation panel
	Parallel to Cover	• **Ribbon:** *Modify	Place Rebar* tab> Placement Orientation panel
	Perpendicular to Cover	• **Ribbon:** *Modify	Place Rebar* tab> Placement Orientation panel
	Pick New Host	• **Ribbon:** *Modify	Structural Rebar* tab> Host panel
	Rebar Cover Settings	• **Ribbon:** *Structure* tab> Reinforcement panel
	Reinforcement Settings	• **Ribbon:** *Structure* tab> Reinforcement panel
	Remove Fabric System	• **Ribbon:** with a structural fabric area selected *Modify	contextual* tab> Reinforcement panel
	Sketch Rebar	• **Ribbon:** *Modify	Place Rebar* tab> Placement Methods panel

Structural Analysis

Once all of the framing, foundations, and slabs are in place, you can test the model to ensure that it will stand up to the loads that will be placed upon the building. To do this in the Autodesk® Revit® software, you use the analytical model.

Learning Objectives in this Chapter

- Prepare a model for analysis.
- Display analytical model elements in a view.
- Make adjustments to the structural analytical model elements.
- Set boundary conditions with information about the surrounding environment.
- Add area loads, line loads, and point loads.

10.1 Preparing Projects for Structural Analysis

Although the Autodesk Revit software does not perform the actual calculations, it can provide all of the information required for analysis. In the program, you can set up and create structural settings (such as Load Cases), create analytical views, adjust analytical elements, and add Point Loads, Line Loads, and Area Loads using analytical views as shown in Figure 10–1.

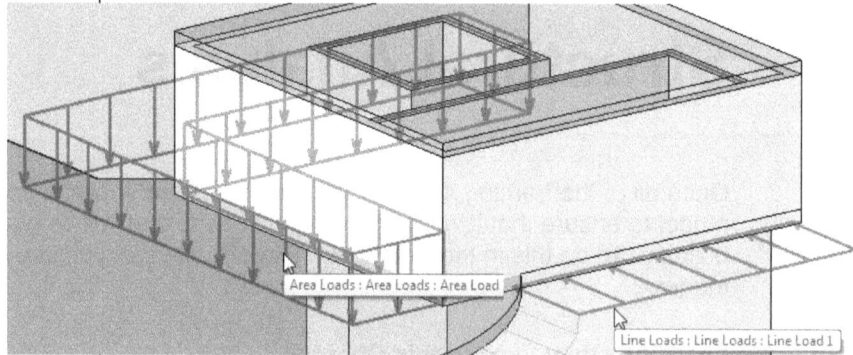

Figure 10–1

- If you have the Autodesk subscription program, you can use the Structural Analysis Toolkit. The toolkit includes additional load options and integration with the Autodesk Robot™ Structural Analysis Professional software for precision structural analysis.

Check your analytical software to ensure that it accepts loads from the Autodesk Revit software.

- Once the loads are in place, the model is exported to your analysis software. After the calculations have been performed, the model is imported back into the Autodesk Revit software.

- During this process, the model does not physically move. This procedure is a flow of data. You do not have to worry about finding an insertion point or ensuring that the model is lined up correctly.

- The actual steps of exporting to and importing from analysis programs depend on the program that you have selected. Some install an add-on to the Autodesk Revit software and others have you export a specific file format.

Structural Settings

The first step in preparing the analytical model is to review the structural settings in the Autodesk Revit software. The Structural Settings dialog box (shown in Figure 10–2) has five tabs containing information for *Symbolic Representation Settings*, *Load Cases*, *Load Combinations*, *Analytical Mode Settings*, and *Boundary Conditions Settings*.

Structural Settings				
Symbolic Representation Settings	Load Cases	Load Combinations	Analytical Model Settings	Boundary Conditions Settings

Symbolic Cutback Distance

Brace: 3/32" Column: 1/16"

Beam/Truss: 3/32"

Brace Symbols

Plan representation:
Parallel Line

Parallel line offset:
3/32"

☑ Show brace above
Symbol:
Connection-Brace-Parallel

☑ Show brace below
Symbol:
Connection-Brace-Parallel

Kicker brace symbol:
Connection-Brace-Kicker

Connection Symbols

Display Symbols for:
Beams and Braces

Connection Type:	Annotation Symbol:
Moment Frame	Connection-Moment-
Cantilever Moment	Connection-Moment-

Load...

OK   Cancel   Help

Figure 10–2

- To open the Structural Settings dialog box, in the *Manage* tab>Settings panel, click 🔲 (Structural Settings) or in the *Structure* tab>Structure panel's title, click ⌄ (Structural Settings) in the lower right corner.

- The Structural Settings dialog box includes all of the structural settings, not just the analytical settings. The *Symbolic Representation Settings* tab (shown in Figure 10–2) contains options that are mainly used for the graphical model and the common defaults.

Load Cases

The *Load Cases* tab (shown in Figure 10–3), enables you to display and modify existing Autodesk Revit load cases and create new ones to suit the code and analysis software with which you are working. For example, you might need a specific load case for an extra large mechanical roof top unit or a special sub-category (nature), such as Residential or Offices for the Live Loads category.

You can also open this dialog box using the ribbon. In the Analyze tab>Loads panel, click

(Load Cases).

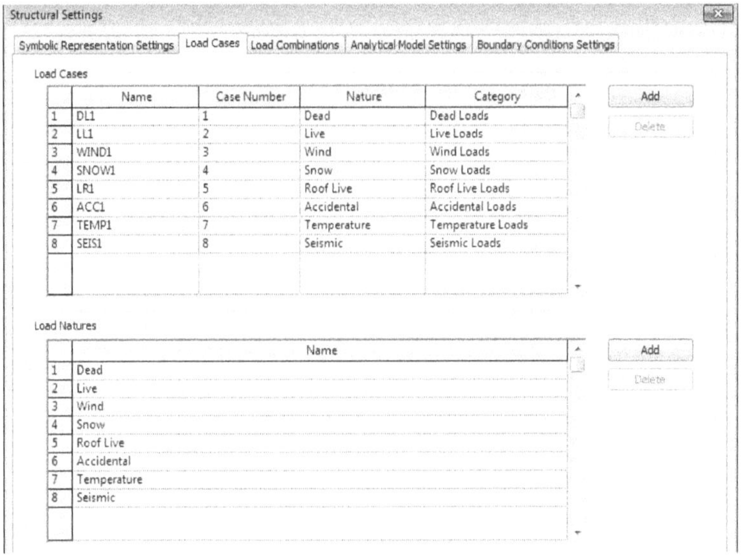

Figure 10–3

- Before you place loads in the model, it is good practice to establish all of the required loads in this dialog box.

How To: Create Load Cases

1. In the Structural Settings dialog box, in the *Load Cases* tab, select a Load Case from the list and click **Duplicate**.
2. A new case is added to the list. Type a new *Name* and select the *Nature* and *Category* from the lists.

- The new load case can be used as an area load and be physically placed in the model.

- To create a new Load Nature, click in the Load Natures table and click **Add**. Type a new *Name* for the Load Nature.

- When you create a new load case or nature, they can be exported as loads into the analysis software you are using.

Load Combinations

In Autodesk Revit, you can create load combinations (as shown in Figure 10–4), by using a formula based on existing loads. You can assign gravity, lateral, or a combination of the two. You can build the load combination and then physically apply it to the model.

You can also open this dialog box using the ribbon. In the Analyze tab>Loads panel, click

(Load Combinations).

Figure 10–4

How To: Create Load Combinations

1. In the Structural Settings dialog box, in the *Load Combinations* tab, in the top right corner of the *Load Combination* field, click **Add**.
2. Enter a name for the new load combination in the *Name* field, such as the example shown in Figure 10–5.

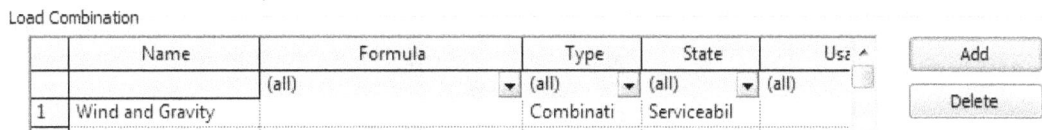

Figure 10–5

3. To create the formula, verify that the new load combination is selected.
4. In the *Edit Selected Formula* area, click **Add** to add the number of cases you want to use.

5. In the *Case or Combination* column, select from the drop-down list.
6. In the *Factor* column, specify the intensity of the case applied as shown in Figure 10–6.

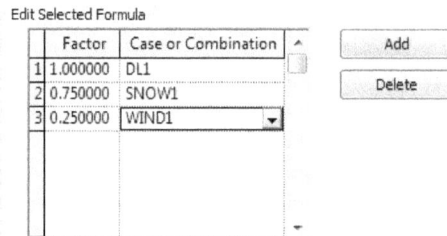

Edit Selected Formula

	Factor	Case or Combination	
1	1.000000	DL1	
2	0.750000	SNOW1	
3	0.250000	WIND1	

Add
Delete

Figure 10–6

The Load Combination Usage is a descriptive field. Keep this naming convention as consistent with your analysis software as possible.

7. In the *Load Combination Usage* area, click **Add**, enter a *Name*, and select the **Set** option (as shown in Figure 10–7) so that it applies to the current Load Combination.

Load Combination Usage

	Set	Name	
1	✓	Large RTUs	

Check All
Check None
Add
Delete

Figure 10–7

8. Back in the *Load Combination* area, select the *Type* from the drop-down list:
   - **Combination:** Provides information for a single combination.
   - **Envelope:** Provides the maximum and minimum results for a group of load combinations.
9. Select the *State* from the drop-down list:
   - **Serviceability:** Categorizes the load based on an expected force (such as wind and gravity) and natural loads (such as snow and even deflection).
   - **Ultimate:** Tests the load against unexpected forces and the overall stability of the structure when pushed to an ultimate state.
10. Click **OK** to close the dialog box. The new load combination is available for use.

Analytical Model Settings

The *Analytical Model Settings* tab (shown in Figure 10–8) is used to check the structural stability of your model as you design. You can customize when warning dialog boxes open if a structural item is placed incorrectly in the model.

You can also open this dialog box using the ribbon. In the Analyze tab>Analytical Model Tools panel's title, click ⌐ (Analytical Model Settings).

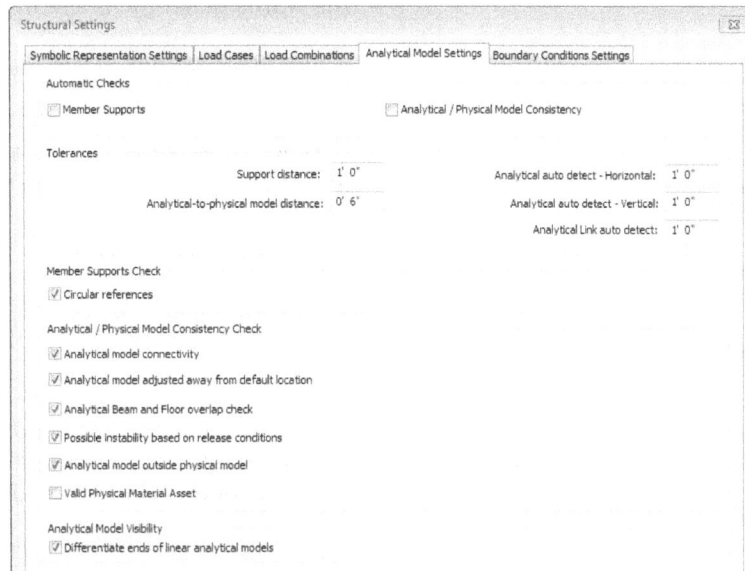

Figure 10–8

In the *Automatic Checks* area, select which relationships you want to check as structural elements are placed in the project. The options include **Member Supports** and **Analytical / Physical Model Consistency**.

- These automatic checks can become cumbersome as you design, therefore these options are rarely used early in the project where many structural members are unsupported. For example, if **Member Supports** is selected and you place a structural column without a bearing footing or pier, a warning prompts you about the structural deficiency.

The *Tolerances* area (as shown in Figure 10–9), enables you to adjust the maximum distances permitted when you use the automatic check options.

Figure 10–9

> **Hint: Reviewing Design Issues**
>
> Instead of running automatic checks as you are designing a project, you can wait and review and check for issues later.
>
> *   In the *Manage* tab>Inquiry panel, click ⁴▣ (Review Warnings). This opens a dialog box containing a list of all of the warnings for the entire model.
>
> *   There are two tools in the *Analyze* tab>Analytical Model Tools panel: ☰ (Check Supports) and ▥ (Consistency Checks). These tools produce warnings based on settings in this dialog box so that you know where to make potential adjustments.

*   In the *Member Supports Check* area, specify if you want to enable checks for **Circular references** during either automatic checks or when you run one of the analysis checking tools.

*   In the *Analytical/Physical Model Consistency Check* area, specify the options you want to check during either automatic checks or when you run one of the analysis checking tools.

*   In the *Analytical Model Visibility* area, select **Differentiate ends of linear analytical models** if you want to see different colors for the start and end of analytical elements, as shown in Figure 10–10.

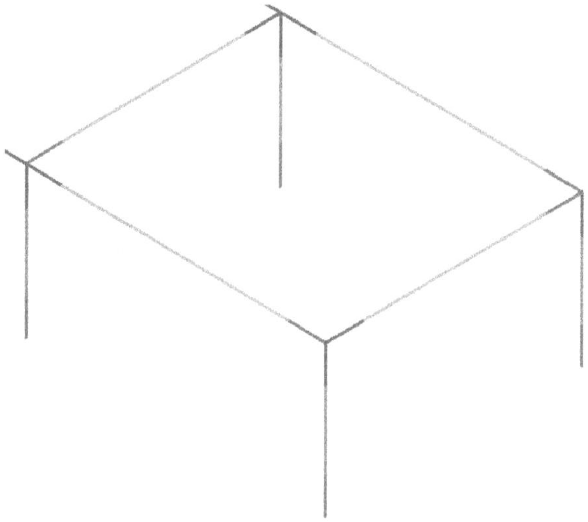

Figure 10–10

Boundary Conditions Settings

Boundary Conditions Settings are applicable if you are defining a condition in which other forces are assumed to support a structural element. A typical boundary condition would be supporting the earth underneath a footing (as shown in Figure 10–11), or a slab on grade. As you physically place a boundary condition in the model, these settings define its appearance.

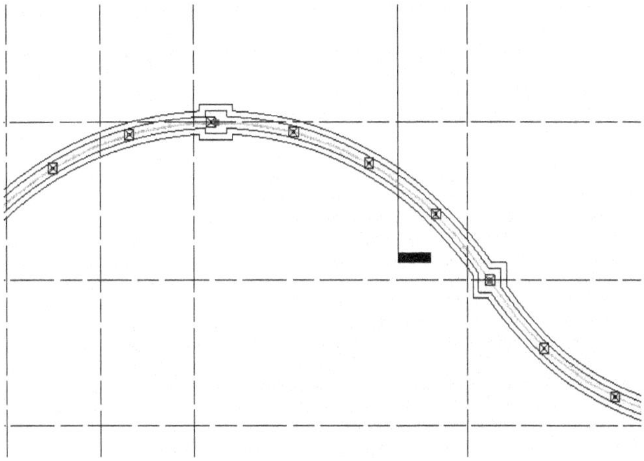

Figure 10–11

You can also open this dialog box using the ribbon. In the Analyze tab>Boundary Conditions panel's title, click ⬝ (Boundary Condition Settings).

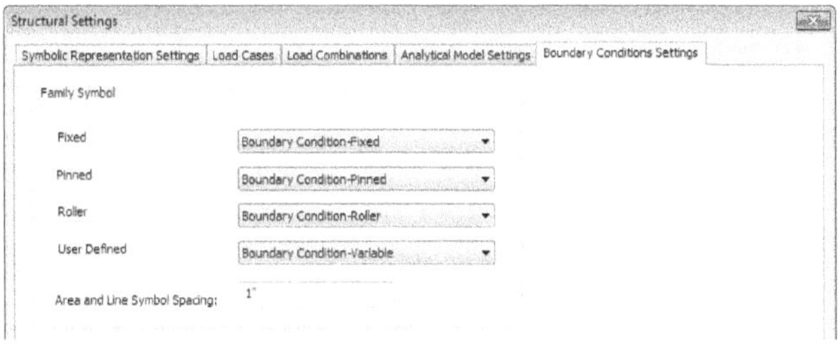

- There are four definable Boundary conditions for the Family symbol: *Fixed*, *Pinned*, *Roller*, and *User Defined*, as shown in Figure 10–12.

Figure 10–12

- It is recommended that you maintain the same family symbol with the condition to avoid confusion.

10.2 Viewing Analytical Models

As structural components are placed into the model, an analytical representation equivalent to the components is added as well. The default structural project template includes Structural Plan analytical views for Level 1 and Level 2 as well as a 3D analytical view. These views do not contain additional information, but instead display the model elements differently. Figure 10–13 shows the visual difference between an analytical model (on the left) and a physical model (on the right).

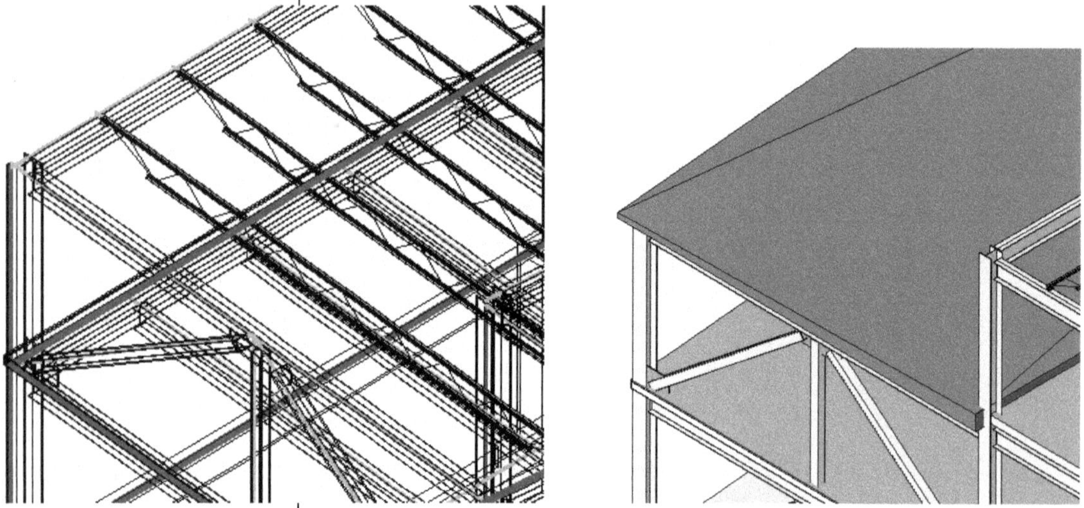

Figure 10–13

- In the View Control Bar you can toggle between ⬚ (Hide Analytical Model) and ⬚ (Show Analytical Model) in any view

- To select the analytical element, use <Tab> to cycle through the options. You can also hide the physical element.

- To establish a view as an analytical view, you can apply a View template to it. In the Project Browser, right-click on the view name and select **Apply Template Properties**. Select the appropriate Analytical view template from the list as shown in Figure 10–14.

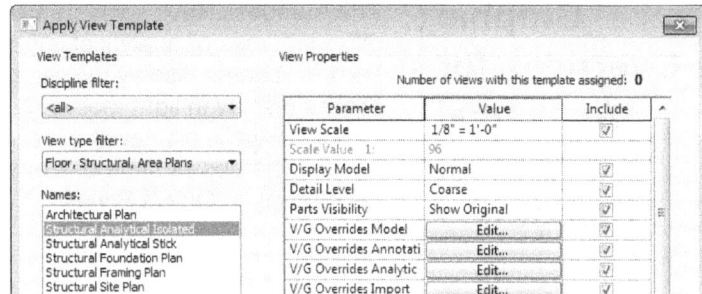

Figure 10–14

- Your company template might provide other options.

- View Templates can be copied from one project to another using Transfer Project Standards.

- You can temporarily override view properties to see the analytical elements or other view template setups. In the View Control Bar, expand ⌗ (Temporary View Properties) and select a View Template, as shown in Figure 10–15. If no recent templates display, select **Temporarily Apply Template Properties...** and in the dialog box select the view template you want to use.

Figure 10–15

- To toggle off Temporary View Properties, in View Control Bar expand ⌗ (Temporary View Properties) and select **Restore View Properties**.

Graphic Overrides for Analytical Model Categories

The Autodesk Revit software uses different colors to indicate the different types of analytical lines. For example, the analytical lines for beams display in orange, columns display in blue, braces display in light mossy green (as shown in Figure 10–16), Structural walls display in cyan, and structural floors display in brown. The appearance of elements in the analytical model are set globally in Object Styles.

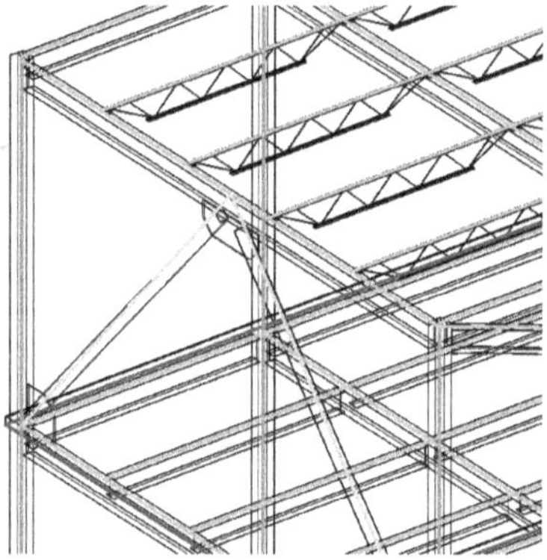

Figure 10–16

- The appearance and visibility of analytical elements can be overridden in a specific view in Visibility/Graphic Overrides, as shown in Figure 10–17.

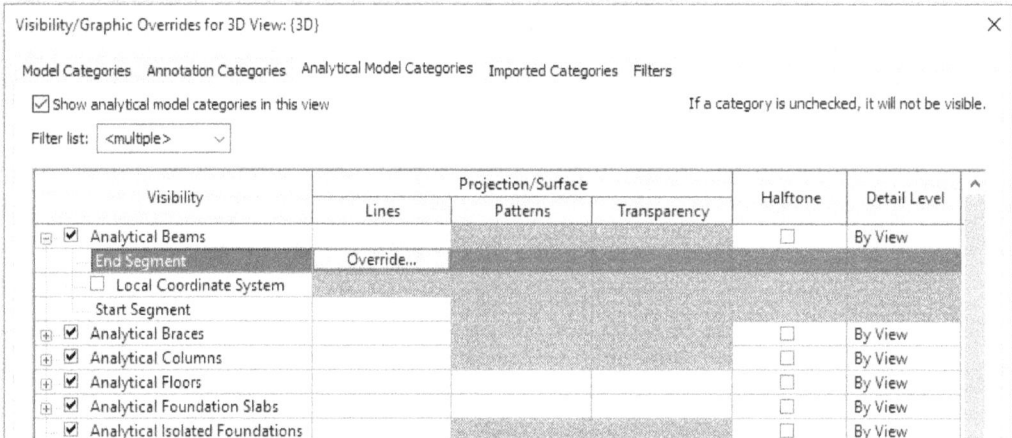

Figure 10–17

- To see the different colors for the End Segment and Start Segment of analytical elements (as shown for a brace in Figure 10–18) in the Structural Settings dialog box, in the *Analytical Model Settings* tab, select **Differentiate ends of linear analytical elements**.

- You can override the default colors in the Visibility/Graphic Overrides dialog box by expanding the category (such as Analytical Beams shown in Figure 10–17) and selecting a color for the End Segment or Start Segment.

Figure 10–18

Displaying the Local Coordinate System

To display the Local Coordinate System (LCS) widget, expand the category (such as Analytical Beams, as shown in Figure 10–17) and select **Local Coordinate System**.

- The widget shows the x-axis (red), y-axis (green), and z-axis (blue) of the LCS, as shown in Figure 10–19 for a beam. It displays on straight and curved beams and walls.

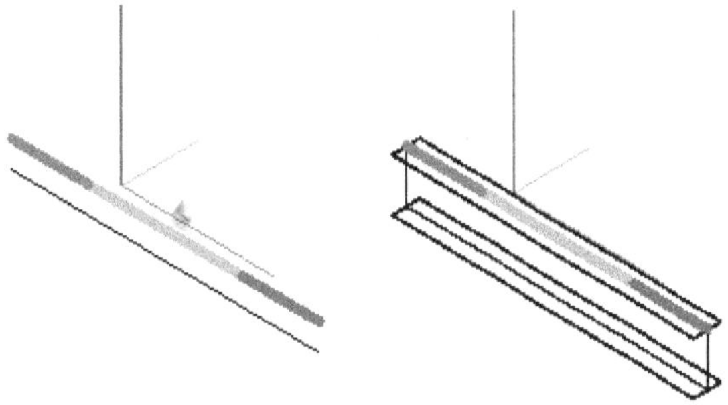

Coarse Detail Level   *Medium/Fine Detail Level*

Figure 10–19

- Analytical beams (shown in Figure 10–19), braces, and columns are oriented with the x-axis from the beginning to the end of the element. The y-axis is the horizontal strong axis, and the z-axis is the vertical weak axis.

- Elements that host the LCS include analytical beams, braces, columns, floors, foundation slabs, and walls.

- Analytical walls (as shown on the left in Figure 10–20) are oriented with the x-axis in the vertical orientation, y-axis perpendicular to the x-axis, and the z-axis from the interior to exterior face.

- Analytical floors and slabs (as shown on the right in Figure 10–20) are oriented with the x-axis following the span direction, y-axis perpendicular to the x-axis, and the z-axis perpendicular to the top surface.

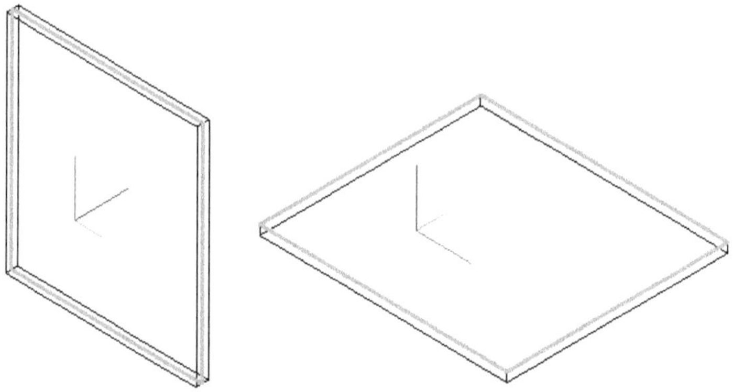

Figure 10–20

Practice 10a | Analytical Settings and Views

Practice Objectives

- Create analytical views and view the analytical model.
- Create Load Cases and Load Combinations.

Estimated time for completion: 15 minutes

In this practice you will create analytical views for a foundation and a roof plan. You will then modify analytical settings to show the start and end of beams and display this in a 3D view. You will also add a Load Case and a Load Combination to the Structural settings for a project, as shown in Figure 10–21. The items set here work in conjunction with the next practice, which involves placing loads into the model.

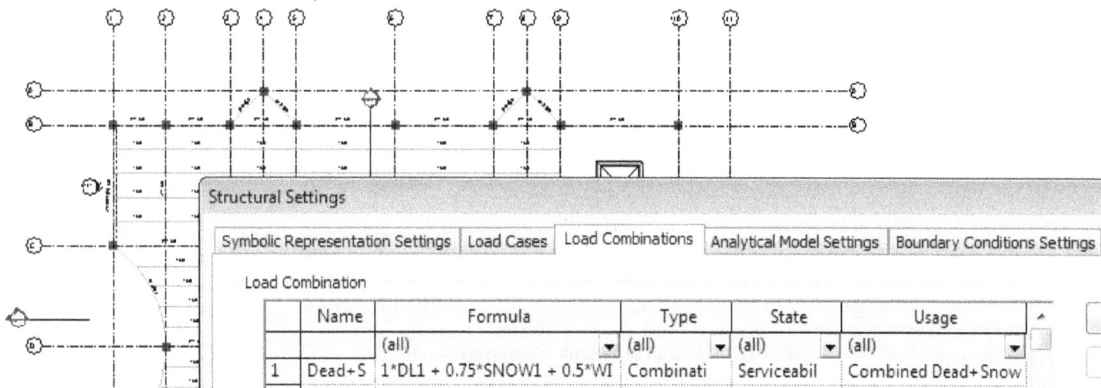

Structural Settings

Symbolic Representation Settings | Load Cases | Load Combinations | Analytical Model Settings | Boundary Conditions Settings

Load Combination

	Name	Formula	Type	State	Usage	
		(all)	(all)	(all)	(all)	
1	Dead+S	1*DL1 + 0.75*SNOW1 + 0.5*WI	Combinati	Serviceabil	Combined Dead+Snow	

Figure 10–21

Task 1 - Create Analytical Views.

1. Open **Syracuse-Suites-Settings.rvt**.

2. In the Project Browser, select the **Structural Plans: T.O. FOOTING** view, right-click, and select **Duplicate View> Duplicate With Detailing**.

3. Right-click on the new view and select **Rename**. Name it **T.O. FOOTING – Analytical** and click **OK**.

4. Right-click on the new view and select **Apply Template Properties...**

5. In the *Names* category, select **Structural Analytical Stick** and click **OK**.

6. Zoom in on the plan to display the analytical view, as shown in Figure 10–22.

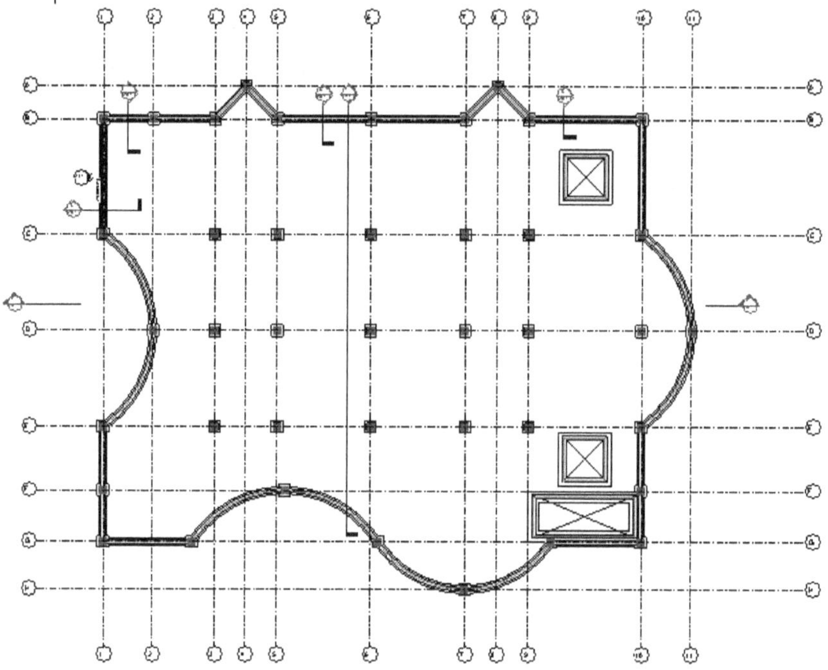

Figure 10–22

7. Duplicate the **Structural Plans: TOS-14 ROOF** view and rename it TOS-**14 ROOF - Analytical**. Apply the **Structural Analytical Stick** template to it as well.

8. Save the project.

Task 2 - Viewing Analytical Models

1. Open the 3D Views>**View 1- Analytical** view.

2. In the View Control Bar, expand 🗔 (Temporary View Properties) and select **Temporarily Apply Template Properties**.

3. In the Temporarily Apply Template Properties dialog box, select **Structural Analytical Isolated-3D** and click **OK**. Only the analytical elements display, as shown in Figure 10–23.

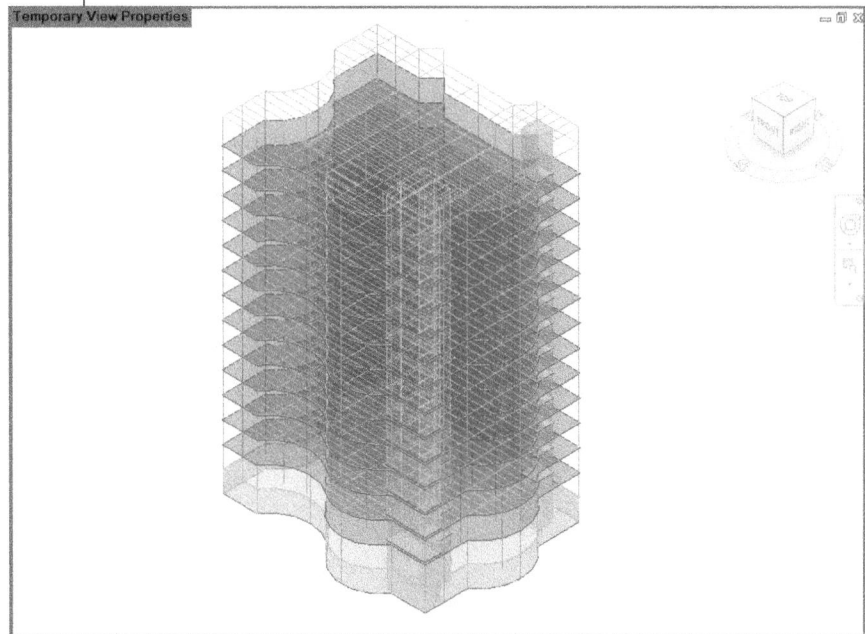

Figure 10–23

4. Zoom in to an intersection of columns and beams.

5. In the *Structure* tab>Structure panel's titlebar, click
   ⌐ (Structural Settings).

6. In the Structural Settings dialog box, select the *Analytical Model Settings* tab.

7. At the bottom of the dialog box, select **Differentiate ends of linear analytical models** and click **OK**.

8. The beam start and end colors now display, as shown in Figure 10–24.

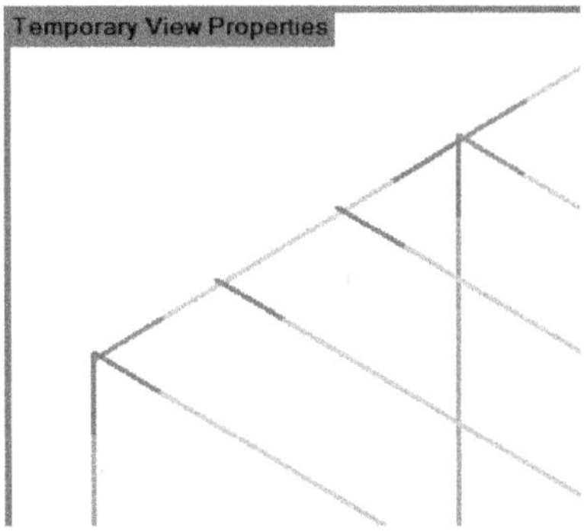

Figure 10–24

9. Open the Visibility/Graphic Overrides dialog box.

10. In the *Analytical Model Categories* tab, expand *Analytical Beams,* select **Local Coordinate System,** and click **OK**.

11. The LCS widget displays on the beams.

12. Save the project.

Task 3 - Create Load Cases and Load Combinations.

The Structural Settings dialog box automatically opens in the Load Cases tab because of the way you selected to open it.

1. In the *Analyze* tab>Loads panel, click 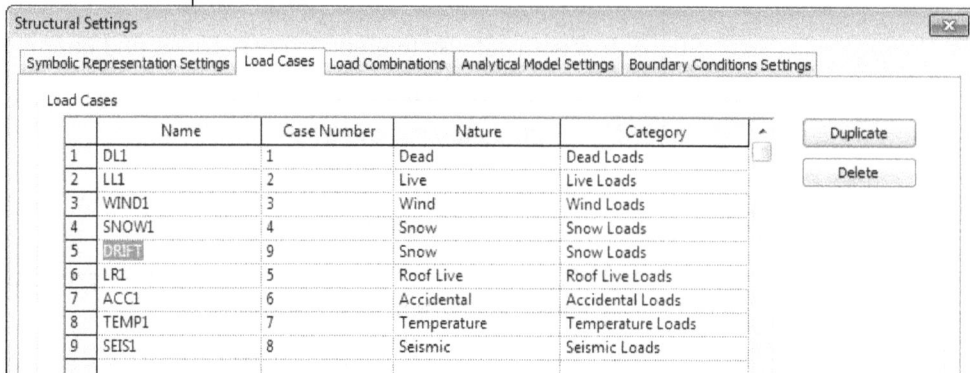 (Load Cases).

2. In the Structural Settings dialog box, in the *Load Cases* tab, in the *Load Cases* area, select the *Name* **SNOW1**.

3. Click **Duplicate**.

4. Click in the new Load Case **SNOW1 (1)** and rename it as **DRIFT**. By duplicating it, the *Nature* and *Category* are already set to **Snow** and **Snow Loads** as shown in Figure 10–25.

	Name	Case Number	Nature	Category	
1	DL1	1	Dead	Dead Loads	
2	LL1	2	Live	Live Loads	
3	WIND1	3	Wind	Wind Loads	
4	SNOW1	4	Snow	Snow Loads	
5	DRIFT	9	Snow	Snow Loads	
6	LR1	5	Roof Live	Roof Live Loads	
7	ACC1	6	Accidental	Accidental Loads	
8	TEMP1	7	Temperature	Temperature Loads	
9	SEIS1	8	Seismic	Seismic Loads	

Figure 10–25

5. Switch to the *Load Combinations* tab.

---

6. In the *Load Combination* area, click **Add**. Name the combination **Dead+Snow+Wind**, as shown in Figure 10–26.

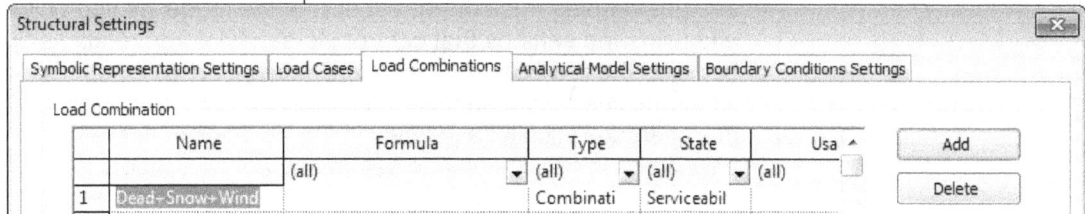

Figure 10–26

7. Select the new name.

8. In the lower left corner, in the *Edit Selected Formula* area, click **Add** three times and then setup the *Factors* and *Case or Combinations* as shown in Figure 10–27. This also displays in the *Formula* area for the Load Combination.

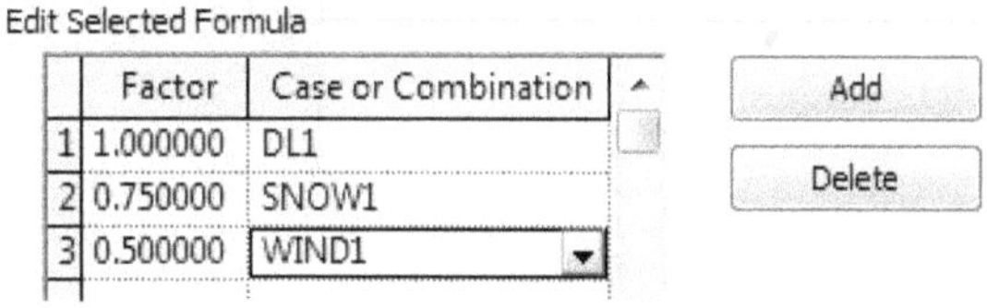

Figure 10–27

9. In the lower right corner, in the *Load Combination Usage* area, click **Add**, *Name* it **Combined Dead+Snow+Wind**, and select the **Set** option as shown in Figure 10–28.

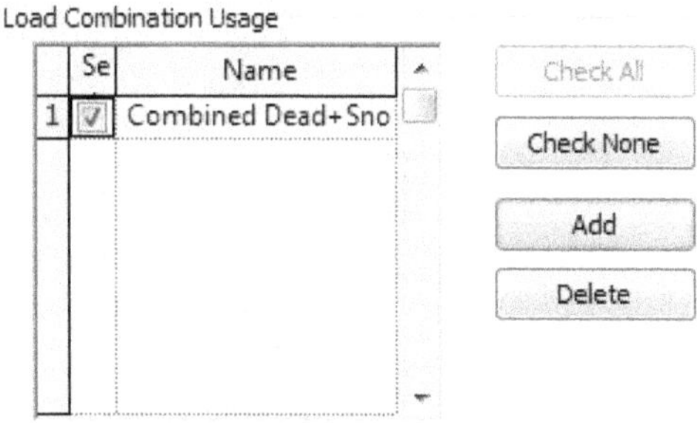

Figure 10–28

10. In the Structural Settings dialog box, click **OK**.

11. Save the project.

10.3 Adjusting Analytical Models

You are keeping track of two aspects of the model as you build and using the settings that control the behavior and relationship between the physical and analytical models. As you model a structure, it is recommended that you study how your model is designed analytically (as shown in Figure 10–29), as well as physically. Taking the time to set up and adjust a model for analysis is beneficial when you need to export the model to an analysis software package.

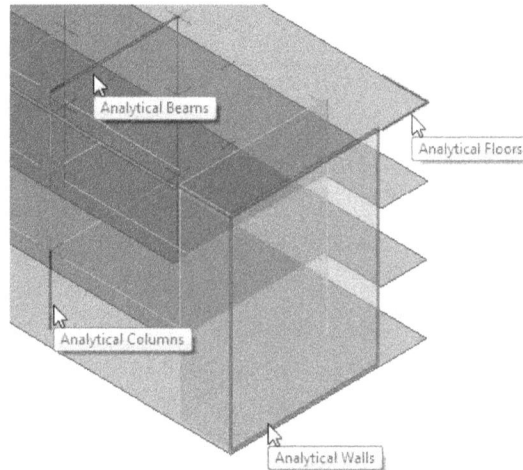

Figure 10–29

- If you do not want to include an analytical element in your analysis you can temporarily disassociate the analytical from the physical model elements. Select the analytical element. In the *Modify | Analytical Element* tab>Analytical Model panel, click (Disable Analytical). When you want to display it again, select the physical model element and, in Properties, select **Enable Analytical Model**, as shown in Figure 10–30.

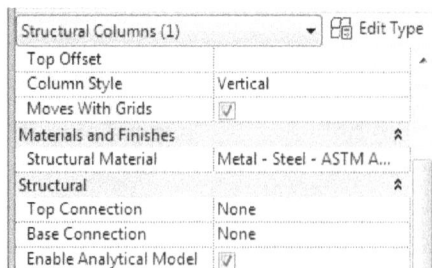

Figure 10–30

Analytical Justifications

To understand what you can change, it helps to have an understanding of the standard justifications for analytical elements. Typically, the analytical lines of a structural elements extend to connect it with the supporting structural element's analytical lines. For example, framing lines extend to columns and joists extend to beams even if these are not at the same elevation.

Columns Beams and Braces

- By default, the analytical line element for beams and braces displays at the top of the physical framing members while the analytical line for columns is centered on the column. This can be changed in the properties of the analytical elements.

- In cases where a beam is attached to columns and supported by braces, the analytical line might stay at the reference level even if the beam is offset below that level.

- Bracing, where the framing is at an angle, is analyzed at a chord centerline that extends into the members it is laterally supporting. The problem occurs when the physical model stops and the analytical plane keeps extending. This starts to influence the analytical model and can force unwanted inconsistencies.

Foundation Slabs and Structural Floors

- If a slab is placed in the model, the default analytical positioning occurs at the top outside edge of the slab system. If the same slab is placed bearing on walls below, the analytical plane adjusts to align with the analytical plane settings in the bearing wall. The slab analytical plane also adjusts to be at the bottom of the slab.

Walls and Footings

- The analytical walls have similar properties to framing in that the analytical model can be dependent on its host related physical geometry, or can be configured to extend to other members regardless of its host's offset from level.

- When a new wall is drawn on top of a foundation wall with the inside face flush (as shown on the left in Figure 10–31), in a 3D Analytical view the analytical plane is aligned with the analytical plane of the bearing wall (as shown on the right in Figure 10–31), although the physical centerlines of these walls do not line up.

Figure 10–31

Analytical Properties

Each type of analytical element includes properties for structural analysis, the element's connection to the model, analytical properties and analytical alignment are shown for an Analytical Column in Figure 10–32.

Press <Tab> to cycle through the elements and select the analytical element, or in the Properties palette, expand the element type and select the analytical element.

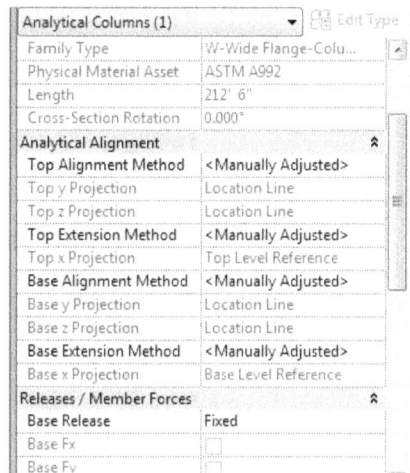

Figure 10–32

Changing Analytical Alignments in Properties

Although setting analytical alignments to **Auto-detect** works well, you sometimes require the projection be set to a specific location in the element. For example, a column can extend beyond a slab to represent a true graphical appearance of column splicing. However, analytically it should be set to the level. This is the required location for analysis when exporting the analytical model.

How To: Change the Analytical Alignment

1. Select the analytical element that you want to modify.
2. In Properties, in the *Analytical Alignment* category, expand the *Alignment* or *Extension Method* for the part of the element that you want to modify, and change it to **Projection**, as shown in Figure 10–33.

Analytical Columns (1)	▼ 🔡 Edit Type
Family Type	W-Wide Flange-Colu...
Physical Material Asset	ASTM A992
Length	212' 6"
Cross-Section Rotation	0.000°
Analytical Alignment	☆
Top Alignment Method	Projection ▼
Top y Projection	Auto-Detect
Top z Projection	Projection
Top Extension Method	<Manually Adjusted>
Top x Projection	Top Level Reference
Base Alignment Method	<Manually Adjusted>

Figure 10–33

3. Once the method has been set to **Projection** you can modify the projections using the drop-down list.

- *Extensions* (vertical) can be set to the levels or top or bottom of the element while *Alignments* (Horizontal) can be set to the justifications of the elements or along a grid line.

- If the analytical projection is beyond an acceptable difference between the physical model and the analytical model, a warning dialog box opens. Some clearance is to be expected, but should be within reason. You can set the tolerances for the analytical representations model in the Structural Settings dialog box, in the *Analytical Model Setting*s tab.

Manually Adjusting the Analytical Model

The **Analytical Adjust** tool enables you to directly manipulate the nodes of beams and columns. It opens the Edit Analytical Model panel and toggles on nodes at the ends of beams and columns as shown in Figure 10–34. You can select nodes and move them individually, either by dragging the node itself or using the 3D control to move the node along specific axes or planes. The tool panel also has a tool to facilitate the adjustment of analytical walls.

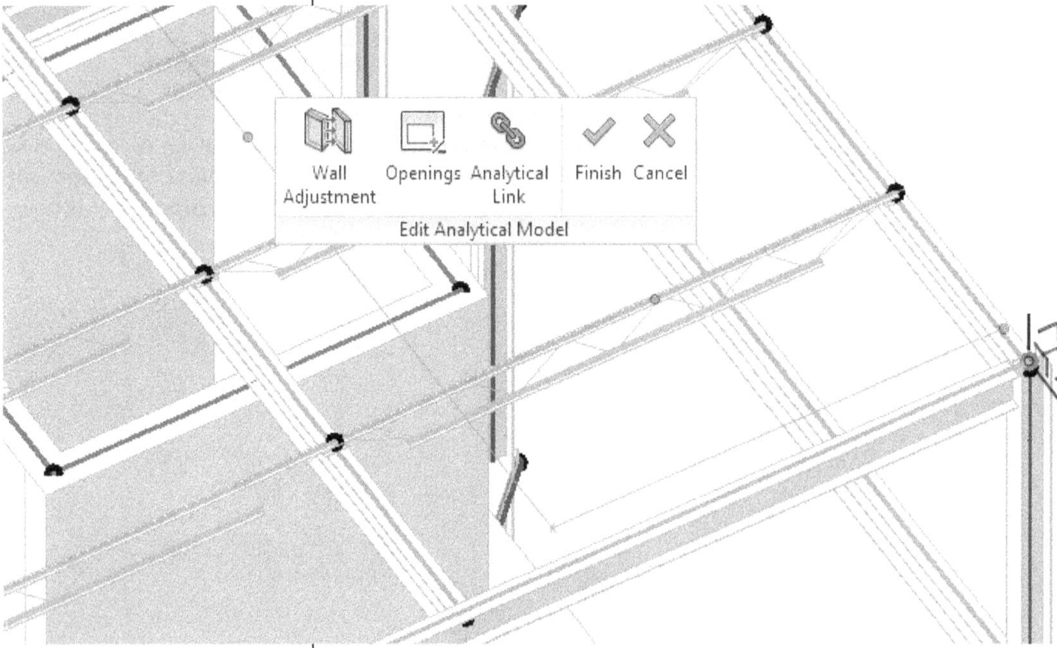

Figure 10–34

How To: Make Manual Adjustments to the Analytical Model

1. In the *Analyze* tab>Analytical Model Tools panel, click (Analytical Adjust).
2. Select the node that you want to modify.
3. Drag the node or use the 3D control to change the location. Press <Spacebar> to toggle the coordinate system of the 3D control between world coordinates and relative coordinates.
4. Repeat with other nodes as required.

5. In the floating Edit Analytical Model panel, click (Finish).

• (Wall Adjustment) enables you to modify the analytical walls in relation to other analytical walls.

- If you want to return to the default alignment methods used with **Auto-detect**, click ⬛ (Analytical Reset). This removes any adjustments made manually or with projection.

Openings

An analytical model with openings in wall and floor structures can be simplified by specifying that specific openings should be excluded from analysis.

How To: Include or exclude openings in the Analytical Model

1. In the *Analyze* tab>Analytical Model Tools panel, click ⬛ (Analytical Adjust).
2. In the Edit Analytical Model floating panel, click ⬛ (Include/Exclude Openings).
3. Checkboxes display in all of the openings, as shown on the left in Figure 10–35. Clear the box for any openings that you want excluded from the analytical model. The analytical surface color fills the opening, as shown on the right in Figure 10–35.

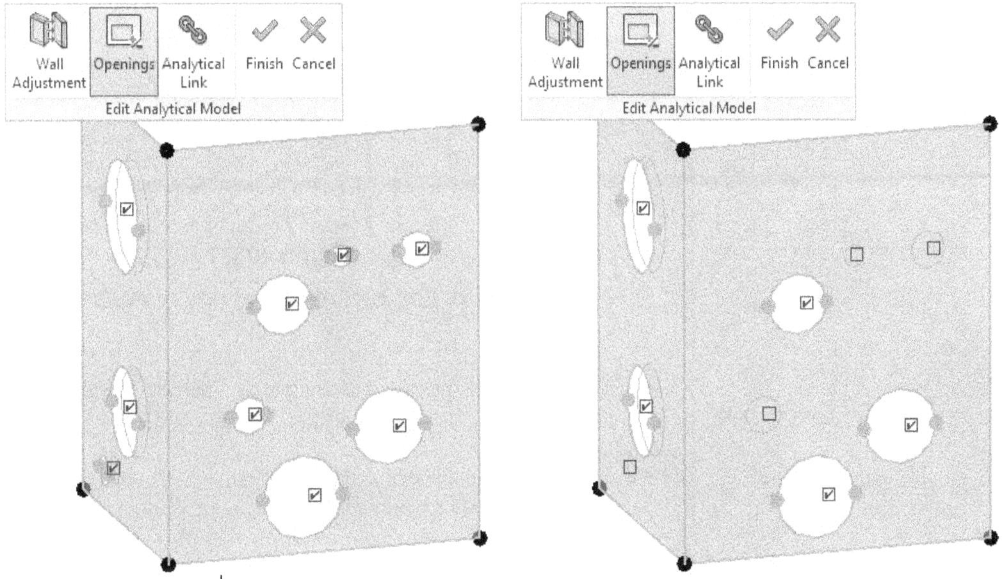

Figure 10–35

4. Click ⬛ (Finish).

- The physical wall has all of its openings as before, but some of the openings do not display in the analytical model, as shown in Figure 10–36.

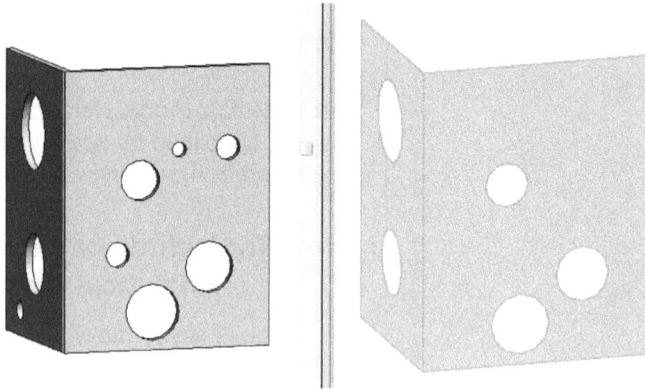

Figure 10–36

Creating Analytical Links

The Autodesk Revit software enables you to manually create analytical links between analytical nodes, which do not have a connection based on a physical structural element at the same location, as seen in Figure 10–37.

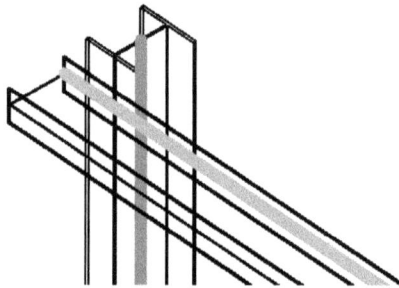

Figure 10–37

- Analytical links can be created in any direction, including vertical.

- The physical model is disregarded when calculating the tolerance for analytical links.

- The tolerance is not calculated along an axis, but as a distance in 3D space.

How To: Create Analytical Links

1. In the *Analyze* tab>Analytical Model Tools panel, click
    (Analytical Adjust).
2. In the Edit Analytical Model floating panel, click
    (Analytical Link).
3. Select the two Analytical Nodes between which you need a link as shown on the left in Figure 10–38. The Autodesk Revit software draws a link between the two nodes as shown on the right in Figure 10–38.

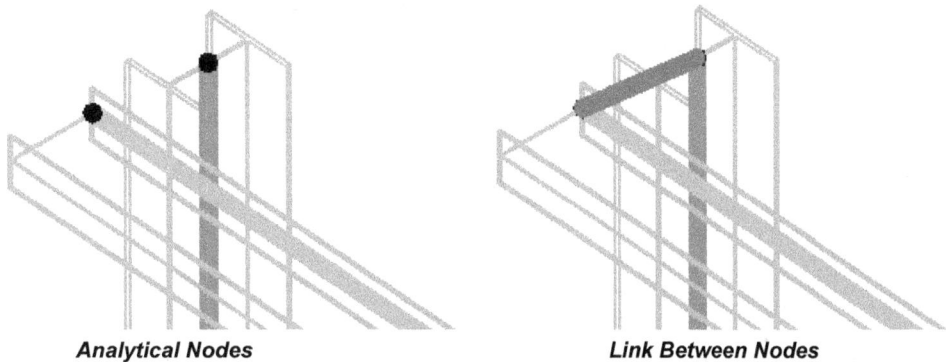

Analytical Nodes   *Link Between Nodes*

Figure 10–38

4. Click   (Finish).

- The rigidity of the links can be set in the Type Properties dialog box. The appearance of the link line is based on the Analytical Link category in Object Styles or Visibility/Graphic Overrides.

10.4 Placing Loads

As you continue to prepare your model to be analyzed you can add loads to the building. These include boundary conditions with information about the surrounding environment, area loads, (as shown in Figure 10–39), line loads, and point loads.

Area Loads : Area Loads : Area Load 1

Figure 10–39

Boundary Conditions

A boundary condition defines the support conditions of the surrounding environment, such as the footing bearing on earth. Although you physically do not have topography, this setting sends the data to your analysis application, indicating that a natural bearing surface is not physically defined in the model. For example, the analytical wall foundations lines around the building are selected, as shown Figure 10–40.

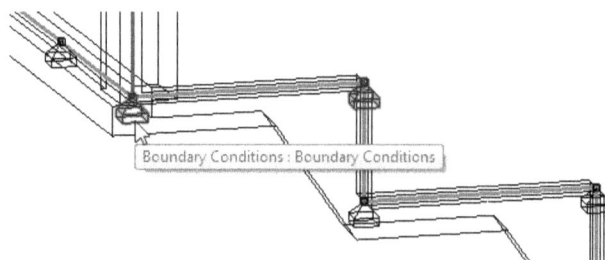

Boundary Conditions : Boundary Conditions

Figure 10–40

How To: Add a boundary condition

1. Open a structural plan or 3D analytical view.
2. In the *Analyze* tab>Boundary Conditions panel, click

    (Boundary Conditions).

3. In the *Modify | Place Boundary Conditions* tab>Boundary Conditions panel, click ⬚ (Point), ⬚ (Line), or ⬚ (Area) depending on the condition being added.

 ⬚	**Point** conditions define the support of the end or join of structural framing elements, such as an isolated footing, column, or beam. The *States* of a Point condition include: **Fixed**, **Pinned**, **Roller**, and **User**.
 ⬚	Line conditions define the support of a linear structural framing element, such as a structural wall or linear footing. The *States* of a Line condition include: **Fixed**, **Pinned**, and **User**.
 ⬚	Area conditions define the support for a structural floor or a foundation slab. The *States* of a Area condition include: **Pinned** and **User**.

4. In the Options Bar (or Properties), select the *State,* as shown in Figure 10–41.

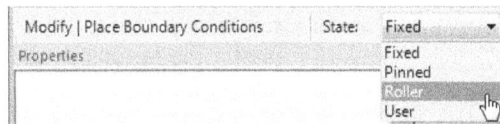

Figure 10–41

- When you select **User,** you need to modify the x, y, and z **Translation in** and **Rotation about** options in Properties. Area conditions do not have **Rotation about** options.

5. In Properties, specify the **Orient to** option. This can be set to **Project** or **Host Local Coordinate System.**
6. Select the appropriate point, line, or area boundary.
7. Ensure that the boundary symbol is attached to the correct analytical line. It helps to be in a 3D Analytical view to display this because it can indicate where potential problems are located, as shown in Figure 10–42.

To fix the problem, in Properties, set the Base Extension of the analytical column so that it touches the foundation. The point boundary condition moves with the analytical column.

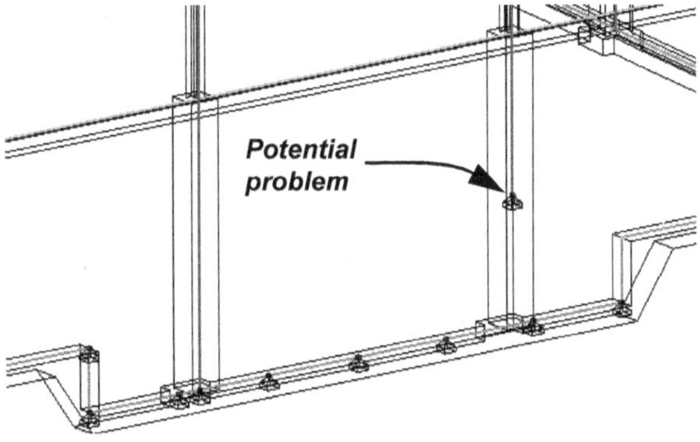

Figure 10–42

Adding Loads

Once you have placed the boundary conditions, you can create the same three kinds of load placements: **Point Loads**, **Line Loads** (as shown in Figure 10–43), and **Area Loads**. These are used by the analysis software to size the structural members.

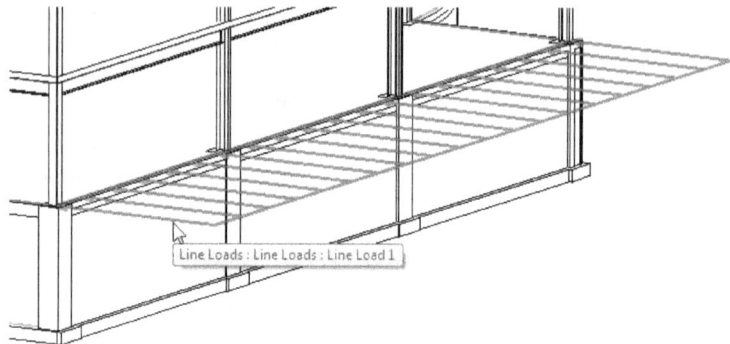

Line Loads : Line Loads : Line Load 1

Figure 10–43

For each of the three types of loads you can place them in a model independently by clicking on the screen or selecting a host. This results in six different options for placing a load as shown in Figure 10–44.

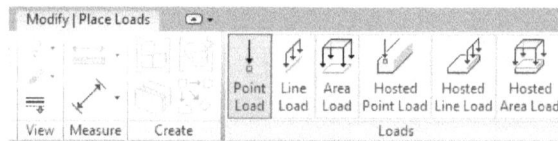

Figure 10–44

For example, if you have a snow load, you can place it into the model as an area load hosted by the roof. If you want to add a drifting snow load, you would sketch the area load, as shown in Figure 10–45.

Placing independent loads requires more work than using hosts, but you still need to assign Load Cases and set the orientation in either method.

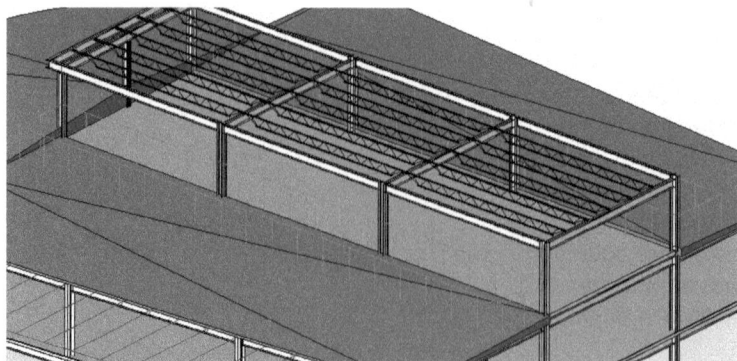

Figure 10–45

- Before placing loads, set up any Load Cases you might need.

  In the *Analyze* tab>Load panel, click ⌐ (Load Cases) or open the Structural Settings dialog box and select the *Load Cases* tab.

Load Types

↓	**Point Load:** Set the *Placement Plane* in the Options Bar before selecting the location for the point.
	Line Load: Draw the line load using the tools in the Draw panel. In the Options Bar, set the *Placement Plane* and whether you want to **Chain** the lines as you draw.
	Area Load: Draw the area load using the tools in the Draw panel. In the Options Bar, set the **Chain** and **Offset** options as required. You can also create a sloped area load using ⌣ (Reference Point) in the Tools panel. You can select **Projected Load** in Properties for the load intensity to be projected along the sloped projection.
	Hosted Point Load: Select an analytical point to host the load. Analytical points are at the ends of structural elements.
	Hosted Line Load: Select an analytical element. The load is assigned along the entire linear edge.
	Hosted Area Load: Select an analytical element. The load is assigned all around the analytical element, such as a slab or wall.

How To: Add Loads

1. Open an analytical view, such as a 3D analytical view.

2. In the *Analyze* tab>Loads panel, click ⊡ (Loads).
3. In the *Modify | Place Loads* tab>Load panel, select the type of load you want to use.
4. For non-hosted loads, in the Options Bar, specify the *Placement Plane*. This can be any datum element, including grids, levels, and reference planes.

5. In Properties, modify the parameters as required.

- **Load Case:** Applies the load case to the load that is added to the model.
- **Orient to:** Specifies the coordinate system for the orientation of the load.
- **Fx, Fy, Fz:** Indicates the direction from which the load is coming.
- **Mx, My, Mz:** Indicates the moment around the axis.
- **Nature:** Shows the user-friendly name for the load setup in the *Load Cases* tab of the Structural Settings dialog box.

6. For non-hosted loads, click the point or use the Draw panel tools to sketch the line or area boundary. When drawing an Area Load, click ✓ (Finish Edit Mode) to complete the boundary and place the load.
For hosted loads, select the host. Figure 10–46 shows a load displayed for a hosted load on an analytical slab.

If you placed boundary conditions, they might be displayed. You can hide these conditions as required.

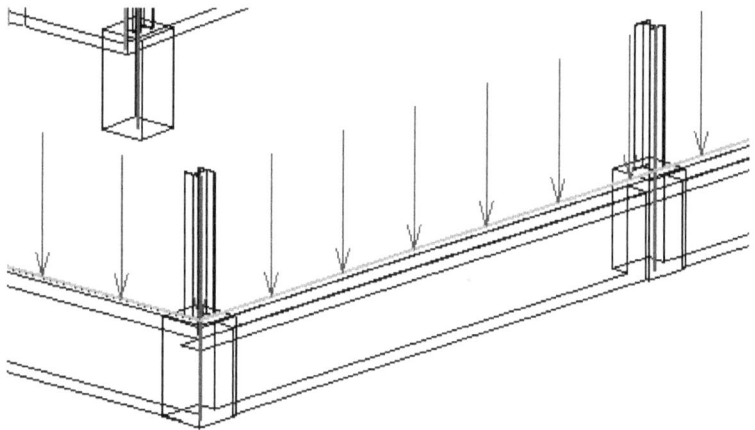

Figure 10–46

Coordinate System Orientation Options

- **Project** - Uses the global coordinate system (x-, y-, z-axis) of the project.

- **Work Plane** - Uses the current work plane as the coordinate system. (This only works with unhosted load.)

- **Host Local Coordinate System** - Uses the LCS of the selected host (This only works with hosted loads).

Setting the Direction

You change the direction of a line load by changing the force direction. In the example shown in Figure 10–47, a line load is placed on a host beam. Then, in Properties, the *Fx1*, *Fy1*, and *Fz1* parameters are set to modify the direction.

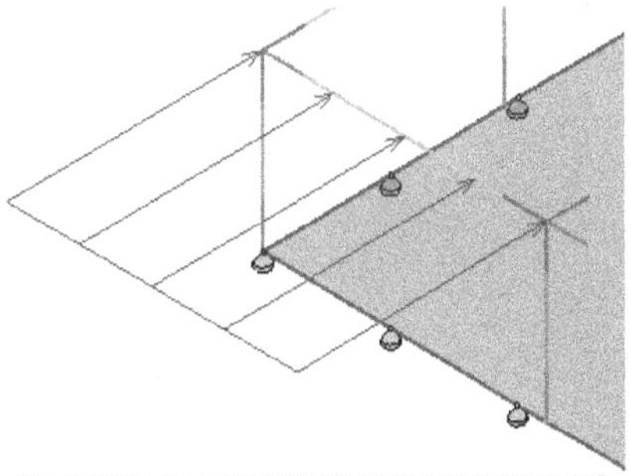

Structural Analysis	⌃
Is Reaction	☐
Load Case	DL1 (1)
Orient to	Host Local Coordinate S...
Fx 1	0.000 kip/ft
Fy 1	1.000 kip/ft
Fz 1	0.000 kip/ft

Figure 10–47

Practice 10b

Place Loads

Practice Objectives

- Place Boundary conditions.
- Place Area Loads and Line Loads.

Estimated time for completion: 20 minutes

In this practice you will add boundary conditions around linear and isolated footings, and place line loads and area loads (as shown in Figure 10–48), on a roof.

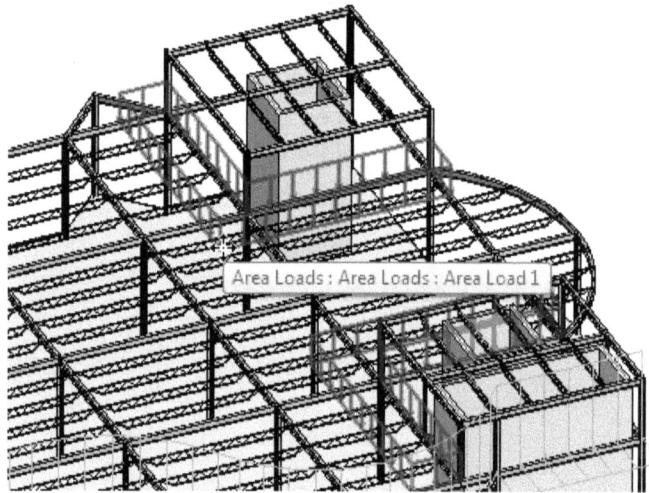

Figure 10–48

Task 1 - Place Boundary Conditions.

1. Open **Syracuse-Suites-Loads.rvt**.

2. Open the **Structural Plans: T.O. FOOTING - Analytical** view.

3. Zoom in on the lower left corner of the building.

4. Select one of the cyan Analytical Walls elements (press <Tab> to cycle through options). Hold <Ctrl> and select one of the foundation walls.

You want to put the boundary conditions on the analytical footings and not on the foundation wall.

5. In the View Control Bar, expand ⌇ (Temporary Hide/Isolate) and select **Hide Category**. All of the foundation walls and their associated analytical walls are temporarily hidden and the dark green analytical lines for the foundation are displayed as shown in Figure 10–49.

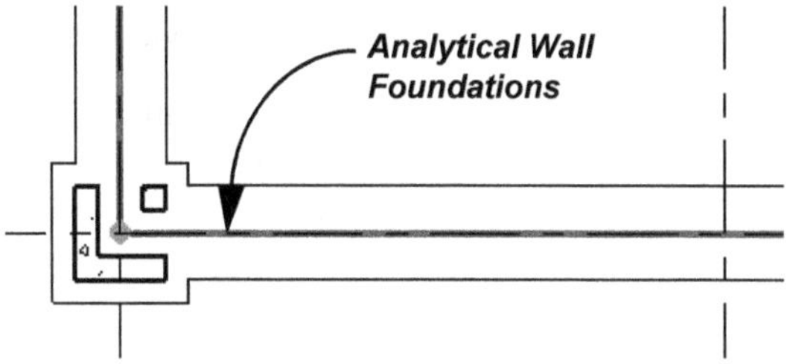

Figure 10–49

6. In the *Analyze* tab>Boundary Conditions panel, click

    ⬚ (Boundary Conditions).

7. In the *Place Boundary Conditions* tab>Boundary Conditions

    panel, click ⬚ (Line).

8. In the Options Bar, set the *State* to **Fixed**.

9. Select the **Analytical Wall Foundations** that define the center of the footings to place the boundary conditions, as shown in Figure 10–50. Continue around the entire perimeter of the building.

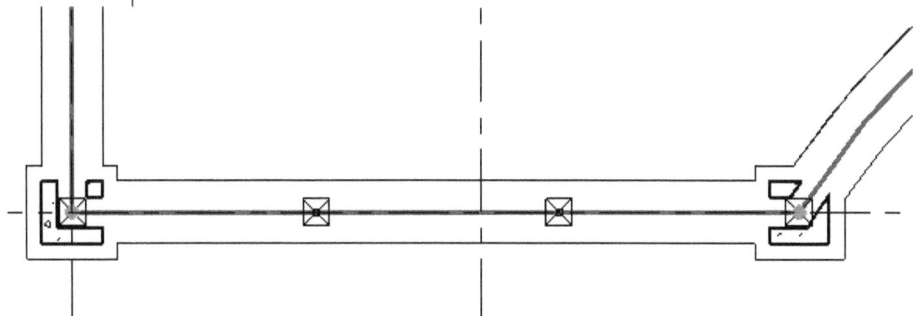

Figure 10–50

10. Open the **3D Views: View 1 - Analytical** view.

11. In the View Control Bar, expand (Temporary View Properties) and select the view template **Structural Analytical Isolated -3D**. (If it does not display in the Recent Templates list, select **Temporarily Apply Template Properties...** and then select the view template.)

12. Rotate the view to display the bottom of the building.

13. Window around the bottom of the building and then Filter out everything except **Analytical Columns**, as shown in Figure 10–51. Click **OK**.

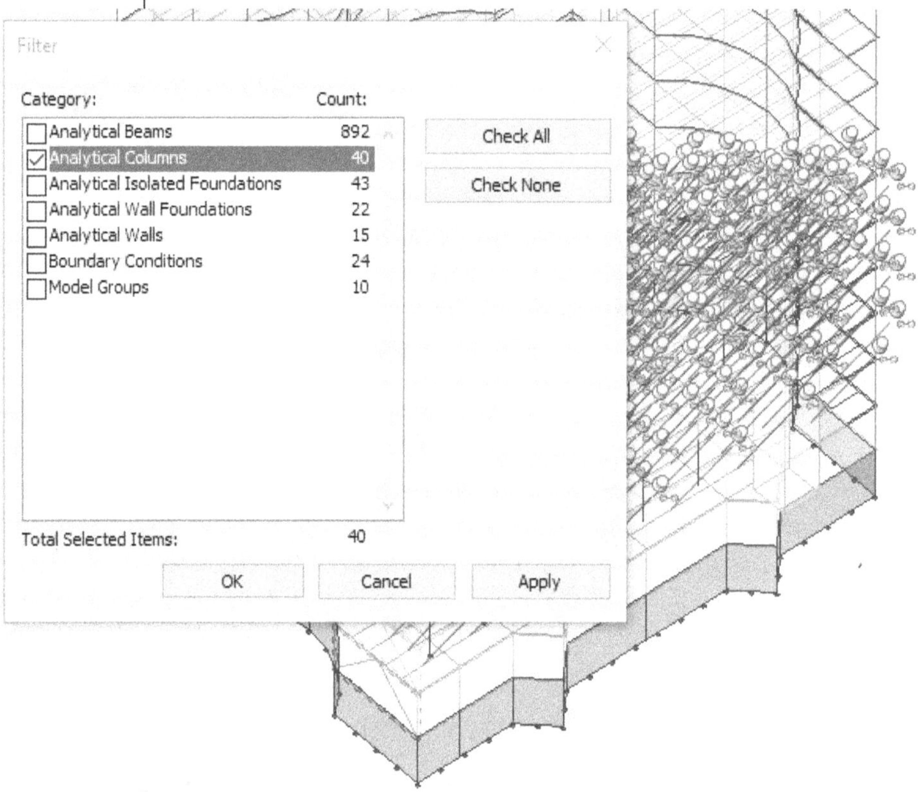

Figure 10–51

14. In the View Control Bar, expand *Temporary Hide/Isolate* and select **Isolate Element**. Note that only the selected columns display and you can apply boundary conditions to them more easily.

15. In the *Analyze* tab>Boundary Conditions panel, click (Boundary Conditions).

16. In the *Modify | Place Boundary Conditions* tab>Boundary Conditions panel, click ⌷ (Point).

17. In the Options Bar, set the *State* to **Fixed**.

18. Click on the bottom of each of the Isolated Footings on which the piers bear.

19. Zoom in as required to select the dots at the bottom of the blue analytical column for each of the Analytical Isolated Footings on which the piers bear, as shown in Figure 10–52.

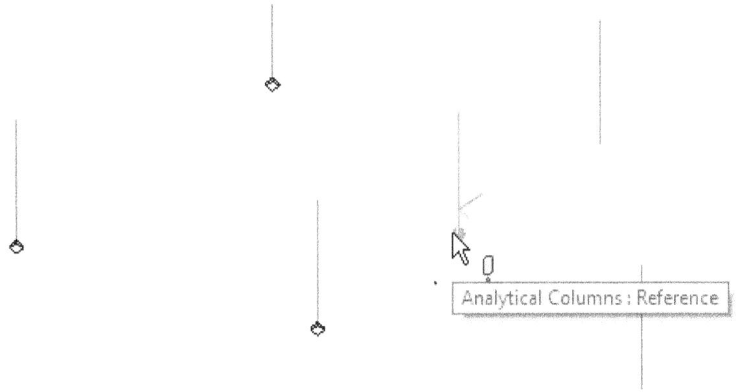

Figure 10–52

20. In the View Control Bar, expand ▣ (Temporary View Properties) and select **Restore View Properties**.

21. Reset Temporary Hide/Isolate.

22. Save the project.

Task 2 - Place Area Loads.

---

1. Open the **Structural Plans: TOS-14 ROOF-Analytical** view.

2. Select one of the structural framing tags and type **VH** to hide all of them in the view.

3. Zoom in on the upper right penthouse area between grids A and C and 8 and 10.

4. In the *Analyze* tab>Loads panel, click ▦ (Loads).

5. In the *Place Loads* tab>Loads panel, click ▦ (Area Load).

6. Draw a sketch of the drift region around the penthouse area, and offset it **8'-0"** from the framing, as shown in Figure 10–53. Ensure that you trim the boundary line to form a complete, closed loop.

Figure 10–53

7. Repeat around the penthouse on the other side between grids E and G and 8 and 10. (You can sketch more than one area in a session, but they each must be closed sketches.)

8. In Properties, in the *Structural Analysis* area, set the *Load Case* to **DRIFT (9)** and verify that *Fz1* is set to (negative) **-0.1000**, as shown in Figure 10–54.

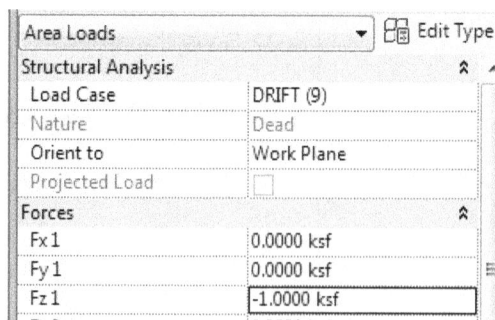

Figure 10–54

9. In the Mode panel, click ✔ (Finish Edit Mode).

10. The model displays as shown in Figure 10–55.

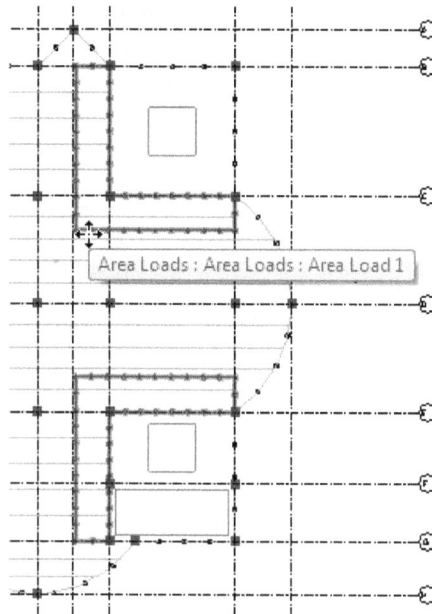

Figure 10–55

11. Save the project.

Task 3 - Place Line Loads.

1. Continue working in the **Structural Plans: TOS-14 ROOF - Analytical** view.

2. Zoom out so to display the south edge of the building.

3. In the *Analyze* tab>Loads panel, click ⊞ (Loads).

4. In the *Modify | Place Loads* tab>Loads panel, click
   ⟋ (Hosted Line Load).

5. In Properties, set the *Load Case* to **WIND1 (3)**, set *Fy1* to **0.500 kip/ft**, and set *Fz1* to **0.00kip/ft**, as shown in Figure 10–56.

Line Loads (1)	▼ Edit Type	
Structural Analysis		≫ ▲
Load Case	WIND1 (3)	
Nature	Wind	
Orient to	Project	
Uniform Load	☑	
Projected Load	☐	
Forces		≫
Fx 1	0.000 kip/ft	☰
Fy 1	0.500 kip/ft	
Fz 1	0.000 kip/ft	

Figure 10–56

6. Select the analytical beam lines on the south edge of the building, as shown in Figure 10–57.

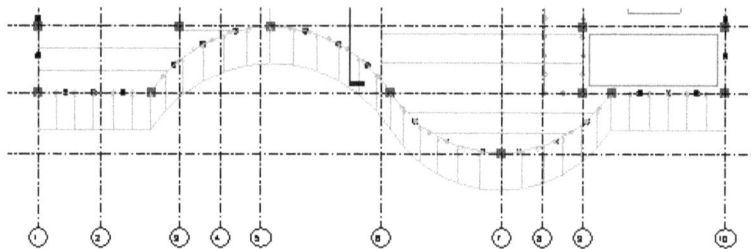

Figure 10–57

7. End the command.

8. Return to the 3D analytical view and rotate it so you can see the loads.

9. Save the project.

Chapter Review Questions

For the first four questions, match the graphics in Figure 10–58 to the correct description of each view.

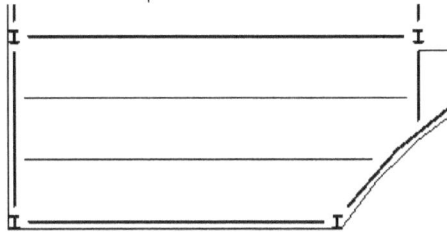

Figure A

Figure B

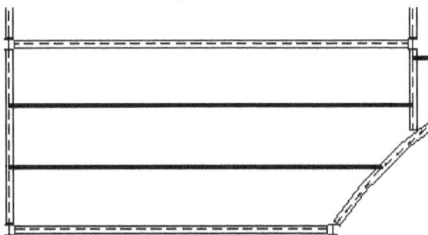

Figure C

Figure D

Figure 10–58

1. Medium/fine level of detail set in the View Control Bar.

    a. Figure A

    b. Figure B

    c. Figure C

    d. Figure D

2. Boundary conditions added to the model.

    a. Figure A

    b. Figure B

    c. Figure C

    d. Figure D

3. Coarse level of detail set in the View Control Bar.

    a. Figure A

    b. Figure B

    c. Figure C

    d. Figure D

4. Analytical Isolated view template applied.

   a. Figure A

   b. Figure B

   c. Figure C

   d. Figure D

5. If you are having a hard time selecting an analytical element in a view, which of the following is a short-term method that would help?

   a. Set the *Detail Level* to **Coarse**.

   b. Use **Temporary Hide/Isolate**.

   c. Apply a Temporary View Properties override.

   d. Toggle off non-analytical elements in Visibility Graphics Overrides.

6. Figure 10–59 is an example of...

	Name	Formula	
		(all)	▾ (a
1	Dead+Snow+Wind	1*DL1 + 0.75*SNOW1 + 0.5*WIND1	C

Figure 10–59

   a. Load Cases

   b. Load Combinations

   c. Boundary Conditions

   d. Analytical Settings

7. Boundary Conditions include information about the surrounding environment, not physical loads on the structure.

   a. True

   b. False

8. Which of the following is NOT a type of load that can be accessed using the **Loads** command as shown in Figure 10–60?

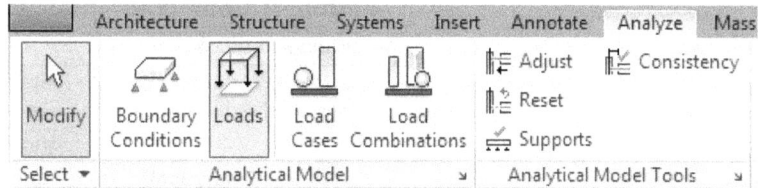

Figure 10–60

   a. Point

   b. Area

   c. Node

   d. Line

9. Which of the following enable you to make manual adjustments to the Analytical Model without changing the physical model?

   a. In the *Analyze* tab, select the **Analytical Adjust** command.

   b. In an Analytical view, select the Analytical line and use the **Move** command in the *Modify* tab.

   c. In the Properties dialog box, select the **Start level** and **End level offset**.

   d. In an Analytical view, select an Analytical line and change its properties.

Command Summary

Button	Command	Location
Adjusting Analytical Models		
	Analytical Adjust	• **Ribbon**: *Analyze* tab>Analytical Model Tools panel • **Shortcut:** AA
	Analytical Link	• **Floating panel**: Edit Analytical Model
	Analytical Reset	• **Ribbon**: *Analyze* tab>Analytical Model Tools panel • **Shortcut:** RA
	Check Supports	• **Ribbon**: *Analyze* tab>Analytical Model Tools panel
	Consistency Checks	• **Ribbon**: *Analyze* tab>Analytical Model Tools panel
	Disable Analytical	• **Ribbon**: *Modify	Analytical Element* tab>Analytical Model panel
	Openings	• **Floating panel**: Edit Analytical Model
	Show/Hide Analytical Model	• **View Control Bar**
	Temporary View Properties	• **View Control Bar**
	Wall Adjustments	• **Floating panel**: Edit Analytical Model
Boundary Conditions		
	Area (Boundary Conditions)	• **Ribbon**: *Modify	Place Boundary Conditions* tab>Boundary Conditions panel
	Boundary Conditions	• **Ribbon**: *Analyze* tab>Boundary Conditions panel
	Boundary Conditions Settings	• **Ribbon**: *Analyze* tab>Boundary Conditions panel's title, click (Boundary Condition Settings)
	Point (Boundary Conditions)	• **Ribbon**: *Modify	Place Boundary Conditions* tab>Boundary Conditions panel

Loads

	Area Load	• **Ribbon**: *Modify	Place Loads* tab> Loads panel
	Hosted Area Load	• **Ribbon**: *Modify	Place Loads* tab> Loads panel
	Hosted Line Load	• **Ribbon**: *Modify	Place Loads* tab> Loads panel
	Hosted Point Load	• **Ribbon**: *Modify	Place Loads* tab> Loads panel
	Line Load	• **Ribbon**: *Modify	Place Loads* tab> Loads panel
	Loads	• **Ribbon**: *Analyze* tab>Loads panel
	Point Load	• **Ribbon**: *Modify	Place Loads* tab> Loads panel

Structural Settings

	Analytical Model Settings	• **Ribbon**: *Analyze* tab>Analytical Model Tools panel's title, click ⌐ (Analytical Model Settings)
	Load Cases (Settings)	• **Ribbon**: *Analyze* tab>Load panel
	Load Combinations (Settings)	• **Ribbon**: *Analyze* tab>Load panel
	Structural Settings	• **Ribbon**: *Manage* tab>Setting panel or *Structure* tab>Structure panel's title, click ⌐ (Structural Settings).

Project - Concrete Structure

This chapter contains a practice project that can be used to gain additional hands-on experience with the topics and commands covered so far in this student guide. This project is intended to be self-guided and does not include step by step information.

Project Objectives in this Chapter

- Start a new project and add datum elements (levels and grids) and concrete columns that establish the base of the concrete structure.
- Create the foundation elements of the building, including walls, wall foundations, and footings under the columns.
- Add beams and beam systems to complete the structural framework and add floors.

11.1 Start a Structural Project

Practice Objectives

- Start a new project based on a template.
- Add Levels and Grids.
- Add structural columns.

Estimated time for completion: 10 minutes

In this practice you will start a new project and add levels, grids, and concrete columns, as shown in Figure 11–1.

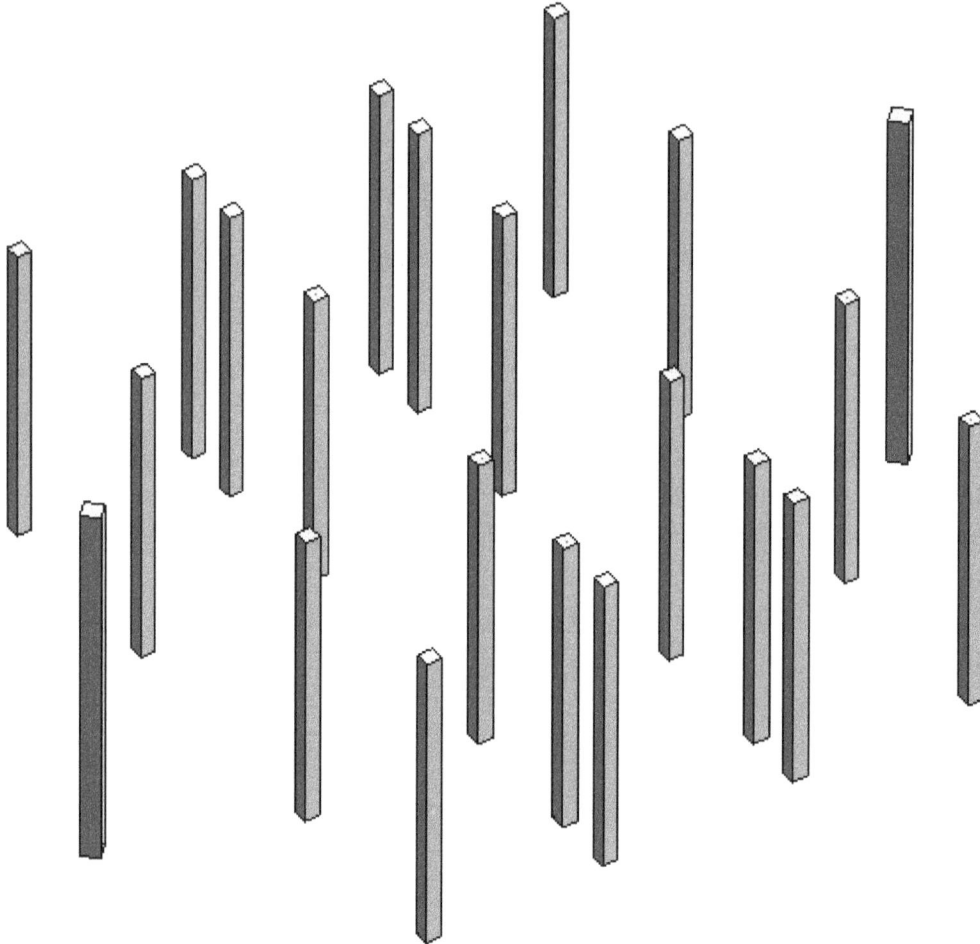

Figure 11–1

Task 1 - Start a new project and add datum elements.

1. Start a new project based on the default **Structural Template**. Save the new project to your practice files folder as **Concrete Structure.rvt**.

2. Open the **Elevations (Building Elevation): South** view.

3. Add the levels shown in Figure 11–2.

Ensure that you create plan views for each level. If you copy them, you need to add the plan views after finishing the levels.

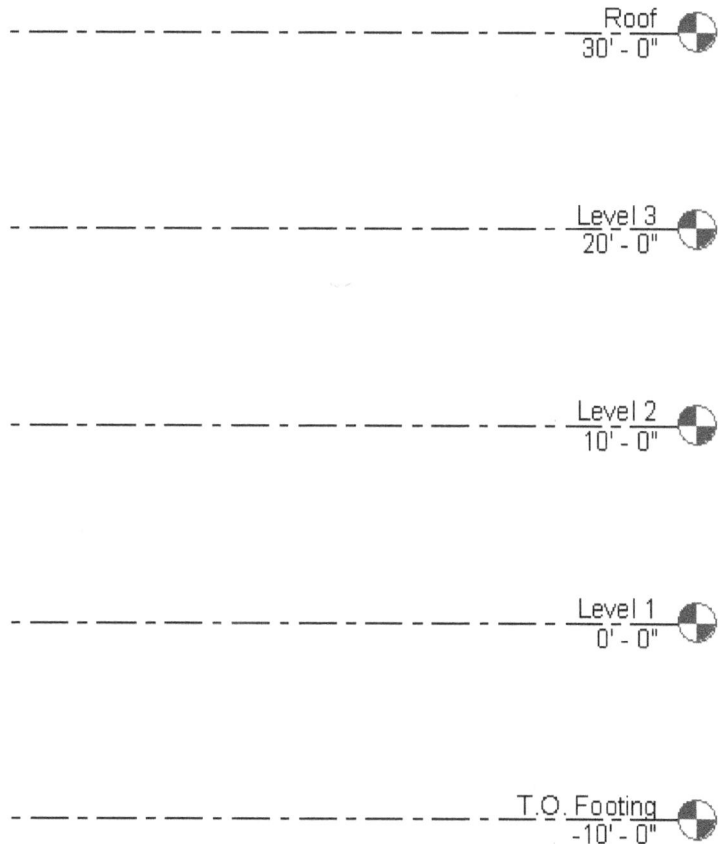

Figure 11–2

4. Open the **Structural Plans: Level 1** view.

5. Add the gridlines that are shown in Figure 11–3. The dimensions are for information only.

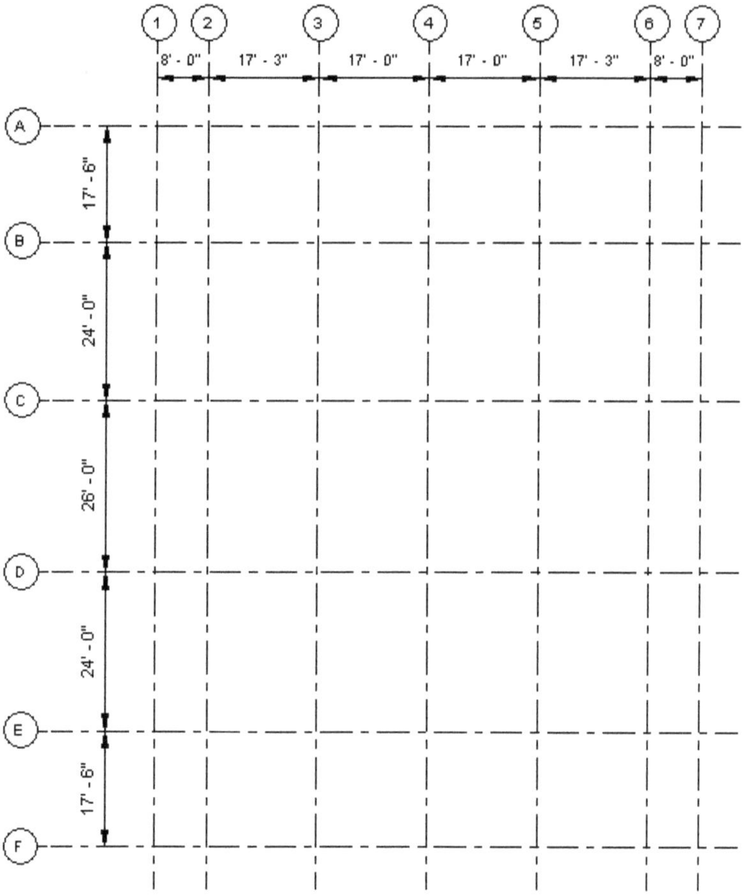

Figure 11–3

6. Save the project.

Task 2 - Add columns

1. Open the **Structural Plans: Level 1** view.

2. Start the ▯ (Structural Column) command. Duplicate one of the Concrete-Rectangular Columns types and create a new 24 x 24 column type.

3. Add Columns that go from the **T.O.Footing** level to the **Roof** level, as shown in Figure 11–4.

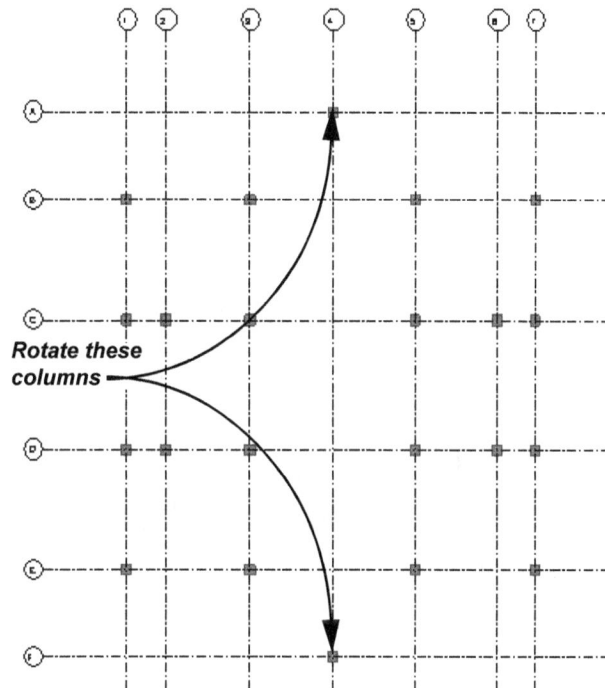

Figure 11–4

4. Rotate the top and bottom columns 45 degrees.

5. Open a 3D view to view the columns.

6. Save the project.

11.2 Create Foundation Elements

Practice Objectives

- Add structural foundation walls.
- Add wall footings and isolated footings.

Estimated time for completion: 10 minutes

In this practice you will add walls, foundation walls, and isolated foundations, as shown in Figure 11–5

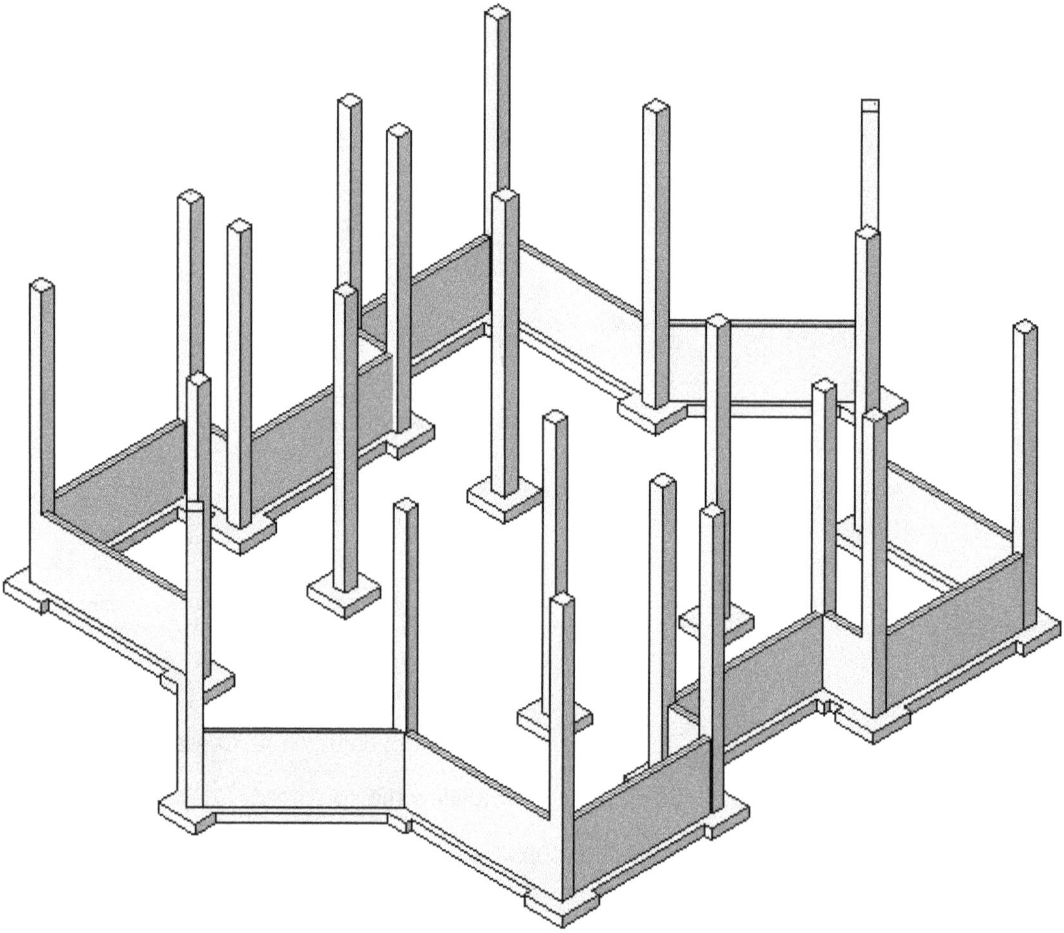

Figure 11–5

Task 1 - Add walls.

1. Open the project **Concrete-Structure-Foundations.rvt**, found in your practice files folder.

2. Open the **Structural Plans: Level 1** view.

3. Draw the walls shown in Figure 11–6 using the following information:

   - *Type:* Basic Wall: **Foundation - 12" Concrete**
   - *Base Constraint:* **Level 1**
   - *Base Offset:* (negative) **-10'-0"**
   - *Top Constraint:* **Up to level: Level 1**
   - *Top Offset:* **0'-0"**

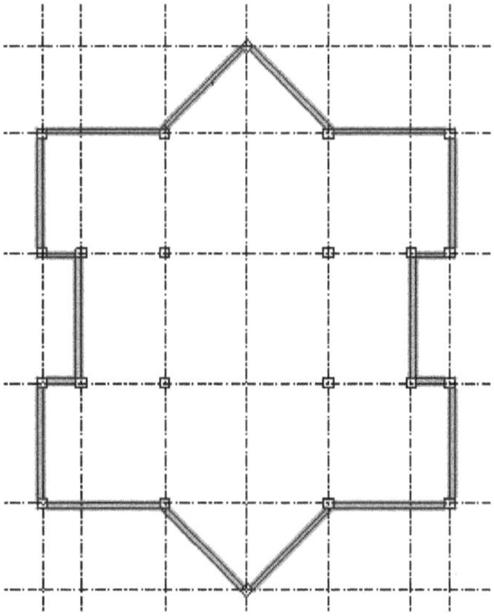

Figure 11–6

   - The outside edge of the walls are aligned to the outside of the columns.

4. Save the project.

Task 2 - Add foundations

1. Open the **Structural Plans: T.O. Footing** view.

2. Add isolated footings under all of the columns. Create a new **Footing-Rectangular: 72" x 72" x 18"** in size.

3. Add wall footings under all of the walls. Create a new **Wall Foundation: Bearing Footing - 36" x 18"** in size. When you are finished, the plan should look like Figure 11–7.

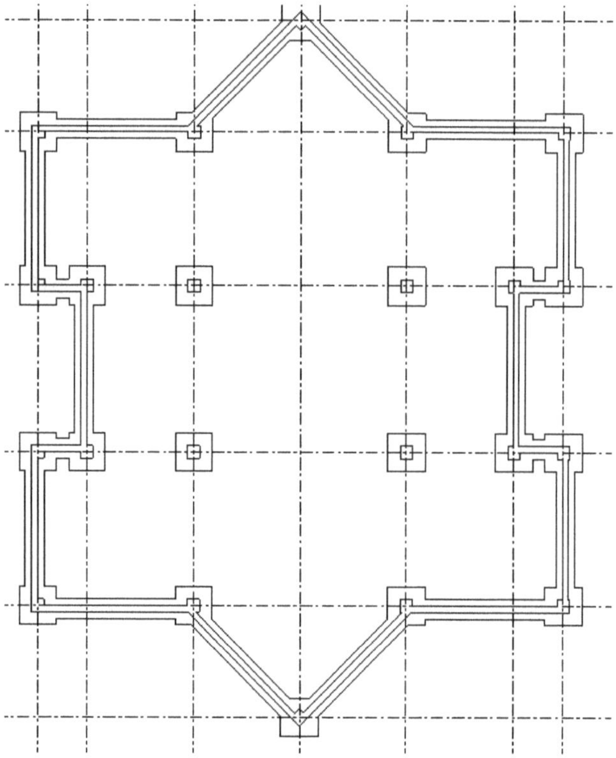

Figure 11–7

4. Save the project.

11.3 Frame a Concrete Structure

Practice Objectives

- Add beams and beam systems.
- Add structural floors.

Estimated time for completion: 30 minutes

In this practice you will frame the concrete structure shown in Figure 11–8. You will add girders using individual beams and joists using beam systems. You will then copy and paste the structural elements to additional floors. Finally you will add a floor and then copy it to other levels as well.

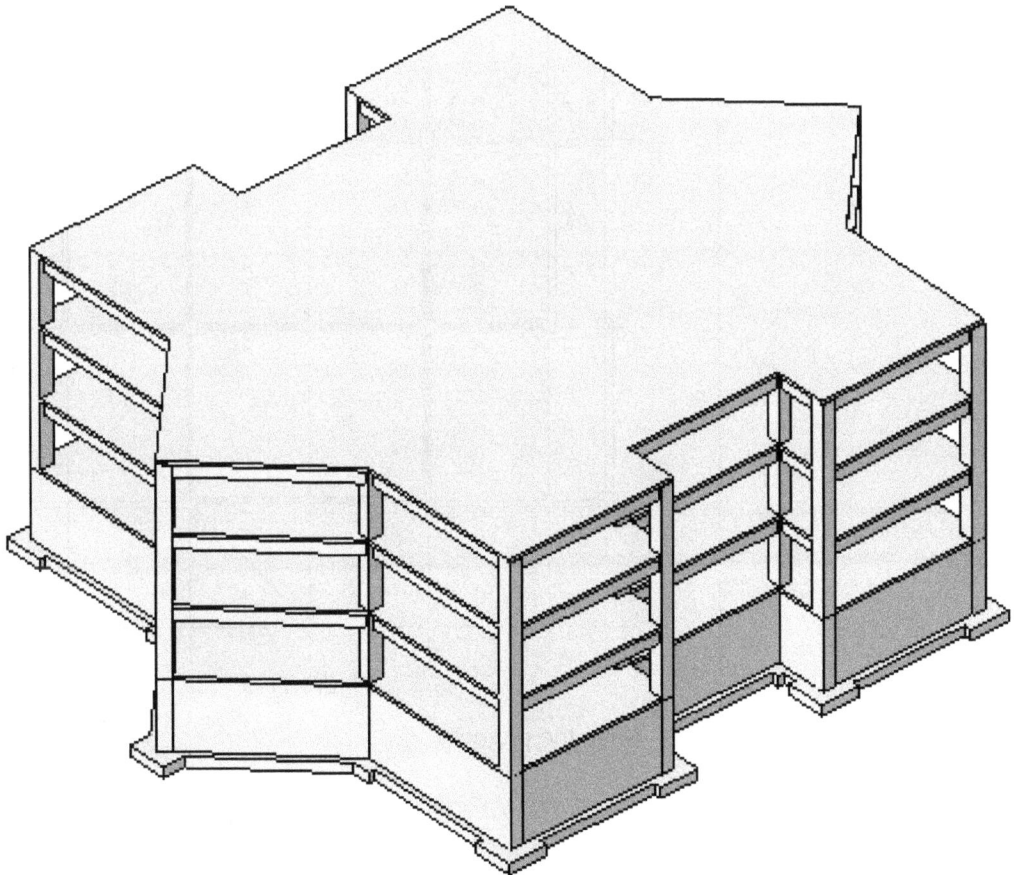

Figure 11–8

Task 1 - Add girders.

1. Open the file **Concrete-Structure-Framing.rvt** in your practice files folder.

2. On Level 1, add beams using the type **Concrete Rectangular Beam: 12x24**, as shown in Figure 11–9.

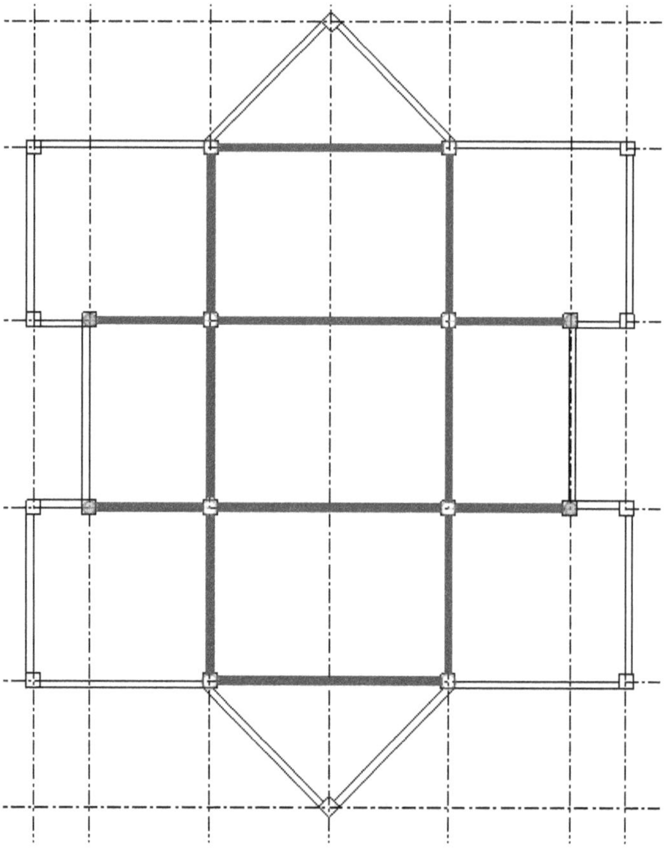

Figure 11–9

3. Save the project.

Task 2 - Add joists using beam systems.

1. Load the **Pan Joist.rfa** family from the Revit Library> *Structural Framing>Concrete* folder.

2. Using the ▥ (Beam System) command and the following parameters, add the joists as shown in Figure 11–10. Where you cannot use **Automatic Beam System**, sketch the beam system.

   - *Elevation:* **4 1/2"**
   - *Layout Rule:* **Maximum Spacing**
   - *Maximum Spacing:* **5'-0"**
   - *Beam Type:* **Pan Joist: 8 x 24**
   - *Tag on Placement:* **off**
   - *Tag new Members in view:* **None (for Sketched)**

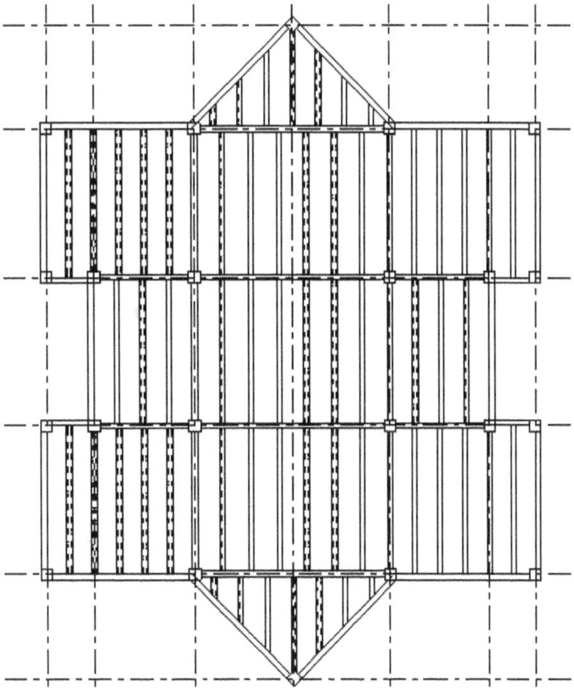

Figure 11–10

3. Save the project

Task 3 - Add beams and beam systems to the other floors.

1. Repeat the process of creating beams and beam systems on Level 2. All girders should be on center (as shown in Figure 11–11), and therefore, all of the beam systems can be placed automatically.

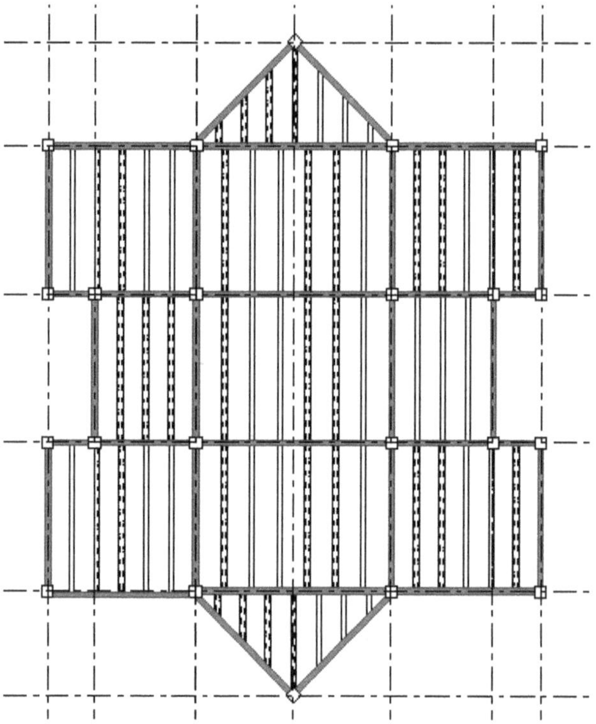

Figure 11–11

- For the angled bays it is easiest to add the beam system using one of the default directions, and then edit the boundary to change the beam direction.

2. Copy (using **Copy to the Clipboard** and **Paste Aligned**) all of the beams and beam systems from Level 2 to Level 3 and the Roof level.

   - Select only the **Structural Framing (Girder)** and **Structural Beam Systems**, not **Structural Framing (Joist)** as they are part of the Beam System.

3. Open a 3D view. The copied beams and beam systems display as shown in Figure 11–12.

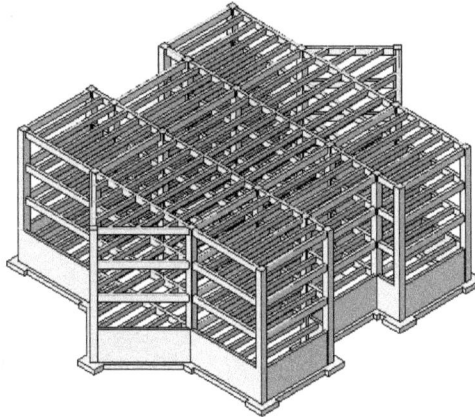

Figure 11–12

4. Save the project.

Task 4 - Adding floors.

1. In the **Level 1** view, add a structural floor using the **Floor: 6" Concrete** type with the *Height Offset from Level* set to **6"**. Select the outside face of the wall for the boundary and attach the walls to the floors.

2. Copy the floor to the other levels above the first floor.

3. The new floors display as shown in Figure 11–13.

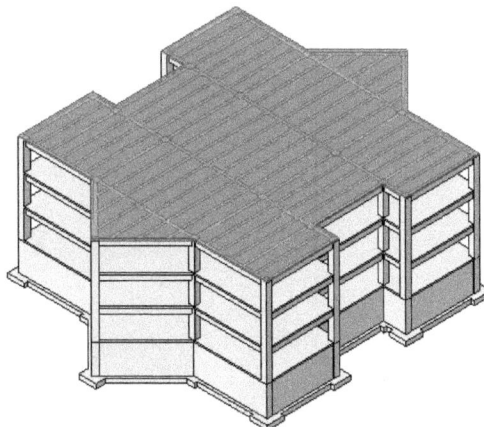

Figure 11–13

4. Save the project.

Chapter

12

Creating Construction Documents

The accurate creation of construction documents in the Autodesk® Revit® software ensures that the design is correctly communicated to downstream users. Construction documents are created primarily in special views call sheets. Knowing how to select titleblocks, assign titleblock information, place views, and print the sheets are essential steps in the construction documentation process.

Learning Objectives in this Chapter

- Add Sheets with titleblocks and views of a project.
- Enter the titleblock information for individual sheets and for an entire project.
- Place and organize views on sheets.
- Print sheets using the default Print dialog box.

12.1 Setting Up Sheets

While you are modeling a project, the foundations of the working drawings are already in progress. Any view (such as a floor plan, section, callout, or schedule) can be placed on a sheet, as shown in Figure 12–1.

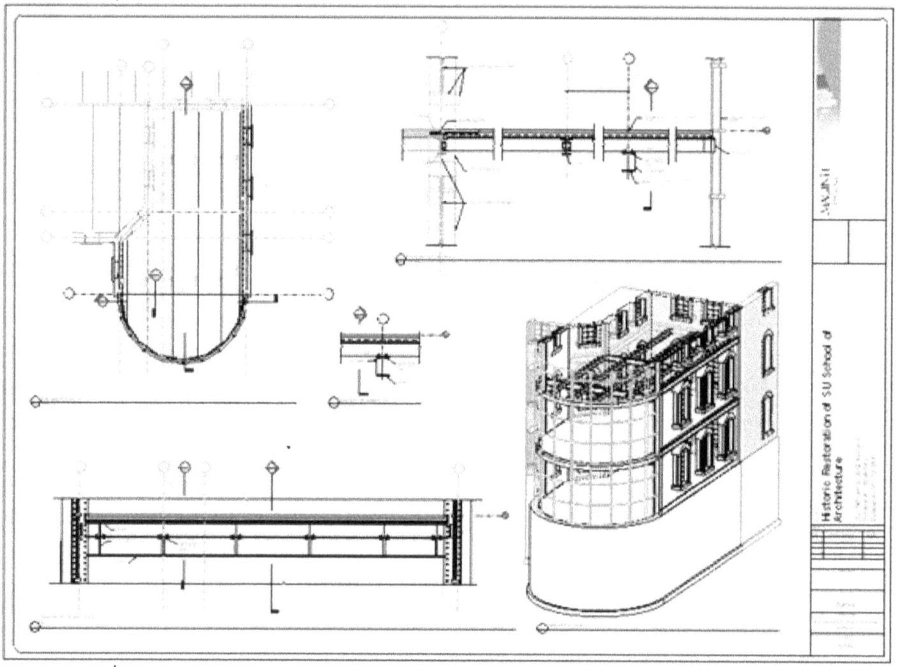

Figure 12–1

- Company templates can be created with standard sheets using the company (or project) titleblock and related views already placed on the sheet.

- The sheet size is based on the selected title block family.

- Sheets are listed in the *Sheets* area in the Project Browser.

- Most information on sheets is included in the views. You can add general notes and other non-model elements directly to the sheet, though it is better to add them using drafting views or legends, as these can be placed on multiple sheets.

How To: Set Up Sheets

1. In the Project Browser, right-click on the *Sheets* area header and select **New Sheet...** or in the *View* tab>Sheet Composition panel, click (Sheet).
2. In the New Sheet dialog box, select a titleblock from the list as shown in Figure 12–2. Alternatively, if there is a list of placeholder sheets, select one or more from the list.

*Click **Load...** to load a sheet from the Library.*

Hold <Ctrl> to select multiple placeholder sheets.

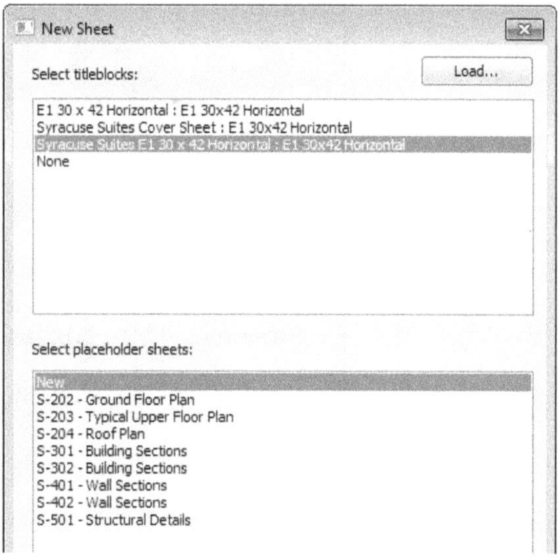

Figure 12–2

3. Click **OK**. A new sheet is created using the preferred title block.
4. Fill out the information in the title block as required.
5. Add views to the sheet.

- When you create sheets, the next sheet is incremented numerically.

- When you change the *Sheet Name* and/or *Number* in the title block, it automatically changes the name and number of the sheet in the Project Browser.

- The plot stamp on the side of the sheet automatically updates according to the current date and time. The format of the display uses the regional settings of your computer.

- The Scale is automatically entered when a view is inserted onto a sheet. If a sheet has multiple views with different scales, the scale displays **As Indicated.**

Sheet (Title Block) Properties

Each new sheet includes a title block. You can change the title block information in Properties, as shown in Figure 12–3 or by selecting any blue label you want to edit (Sheet Name, Sheet Number, Drawn by, etc.), as shown in Figure 12–4.

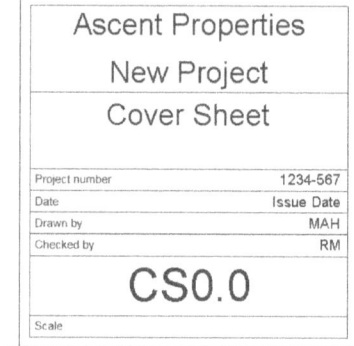

Figure 12–3   Figure 12–4

Properties that apply to all sheets can be entered in the Project Properties dialog box (as shown in Figure 12–5). In the *Manage* tab>Settings panel, click (Project Information).

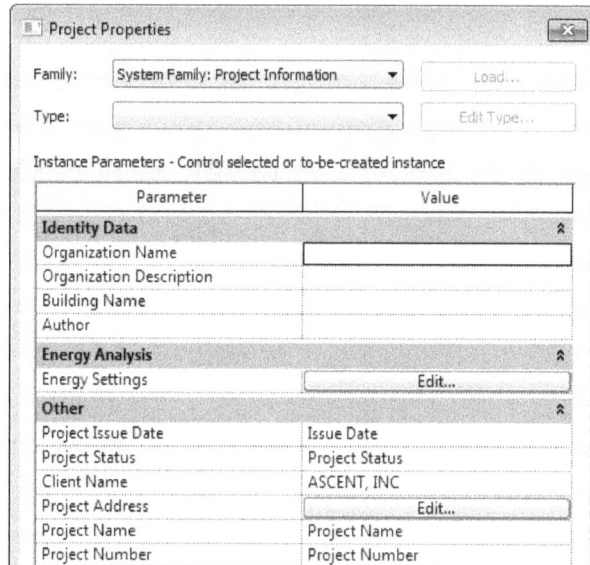

Figure 12–5

12.2 Placing and Modifying Views on Sheets

The process of adding views to a sheet is simple. Drag and drop a view from the Project Browser onto the sheet. The new view on the sheet is displayed at the scale specified in the original view. The view title displays the name, number, and scale of the view, as shown in Figure 12–6.

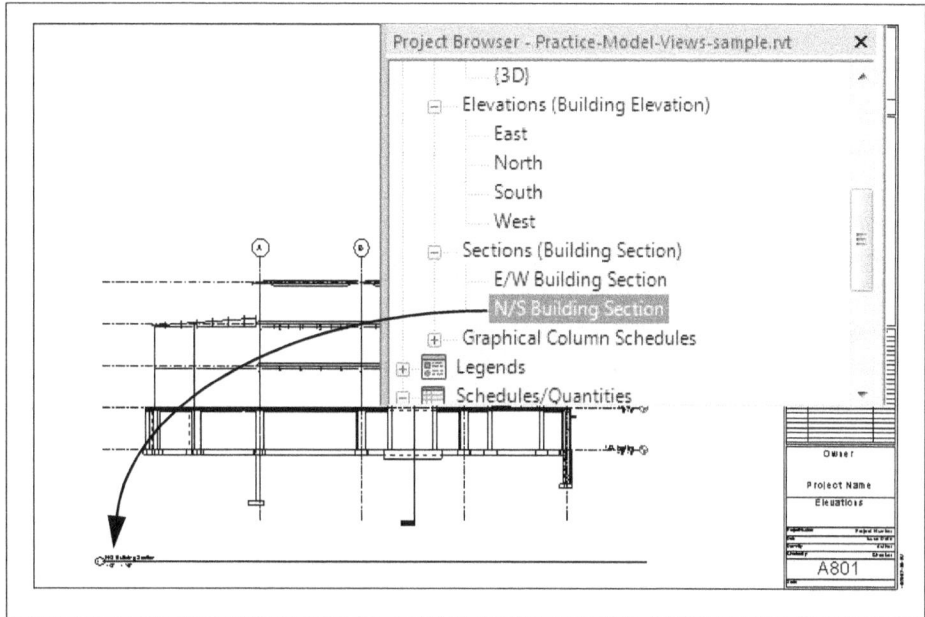

Figure 12–6

How To: Place Views on Sheets

Alignment lines from existing views display to help you place additional views.

1. Set up the view as you want it to display on the sheet, including the scale and visibility of elements.
2. Create or open the sheet where you want to place the view.
3. Select the view in the Project Browser, and drag and drop it onto the sheet.
4. The center of the view is attached to the cursor. Click to place it on the sheet.

Placing Views on Sheets

- Views can only be placed on a sheet once. However, you can duplicate the view and place that copy on a sheet.

- Views on a sheet are associative. They automatically update to reflect changes to the project.

- Each view on a sheet is listed under the sheet name in the Project Browser, as shown in Figure 12–7.

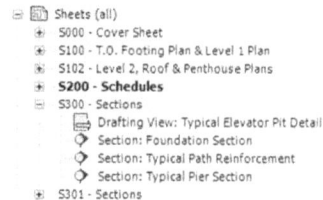

Figure 12–7

- You can also use two other methods to place views on sheets:

  - In the Project Browser, right-click on the sheet name and select **Add View...**
  - In the *View* tab>Sheet Composition panel click (Place View).

  Then, in the Views dialog box (shown in Figure 12–8), select the view you want to use and click **Add View to Sheet.**

This method lists only those views which have not yet been placed on a sheet.

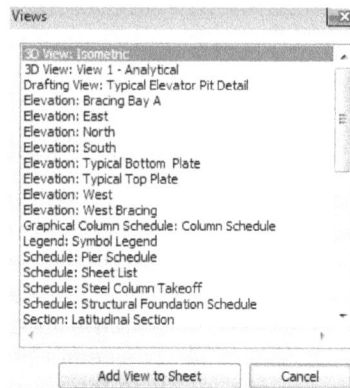

Figure 12–8

- To remove a view from a sheet, select it and press <Delete>. Alternatively, in the Project Browser, expand the individual sheet information to show the views, right-click on the view name and select **Remove From Sheet**.

Hint: Setting up the Project Browser

To view and change the Project Browser's types, select the top level node of the Project Browser (which is set to *Views (all)* by default) and select the type you want to use from the Type Selector. For example, you can set the Browser to only display views that are not on sheets, as shown in Figure 12–9.

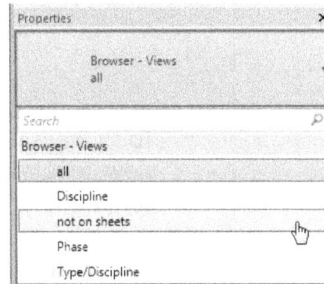

Figure 12–9

Moving Views and View Titles

*You can also use the **Move** command or the arrow keys to move a view.*

- To move a view on a sheet, select the edge of the view and drag it to a new location. The view title moves with the view.

- To move only the view title, select the title and drag it to the new location.

- To modify the length of the line under the title name, select the edge of the view and drag the controls, as shown in Figure 12–10.

North-South Entry
1/8" = 1'-0"

Figure 12–10

- To change the title of a view on a sheet without changing its name in the Project Browser, in Properties, in the *Identity Data* area, type a new title for the *Title on Sheet* parameter, as shown in Figure 12–11.

Identity Data		
View Template	<None>	
View Name	North-South Entry	
Dependency	Independent	
Title on Sheet	First Floor Entrance	
Sheet Number	S.1	

Figure 12–11

Rotating Views

- When creating a vertical sheet, you can rotate the view on the sheet by 90 degrees. Select the view and set the direction of rotation in the Rotation on Sheet drop-down list in the Options Bar, as shown in Figure 12–12.

Figure 12–12

- To rotate a view to an angle other than 90 degrees, open the view, toggle on and select the crop region and use the **Rotate** command to change the angle.

Working Inside Views

To make small changes to a view while working on a sheet:

- Double-click *inside* the view to activate it.
- Double-click *outside* the view to deactivate it.

Only elements in the viewport are available for modification. The rest of the sheet is grayed out, as shown in Figure 12–13.

Only use this method for small changes. Significant changes should be made directly in the view.

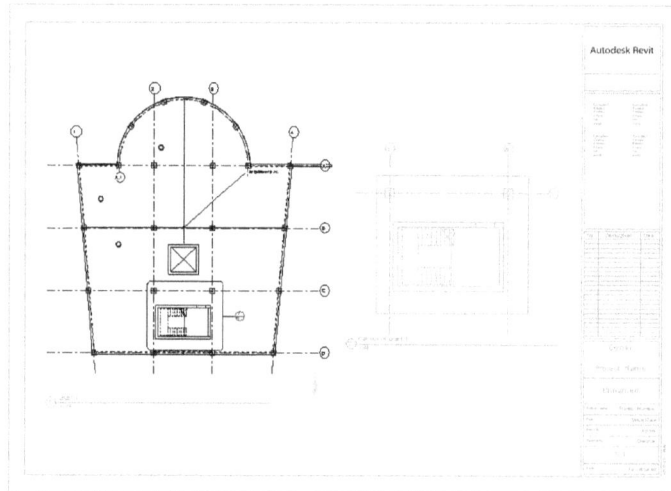

Figure 12–13

- You can activate and deactivate views by right-clicking on the edge of the view or by using the tools found on the *Modify | Viewports* and *Views* tab>Sheet Composition panel.

- Changes you make to elements when a view is activated also display in the original view.

- If you are unsure which sheet a view is on, right-click on the view in the Project Browser and select **Open Sheet**. This item is grayed out if the view has not been placed on a sheet and is not available for schedules and legends which can be placed on more than one sheet.

Resizing Views on Sheets

Each view displays the extents of the model or the elements contained in the crop region. If the view does not fit on a sheet (as shown in Figure 12–14), you might need to crop the view or move the elevation markers closer to the building.

If the extents of the view change dramatically based on a scale change or a crop region, it is easier to delete the view on the sheet and drag it over again.

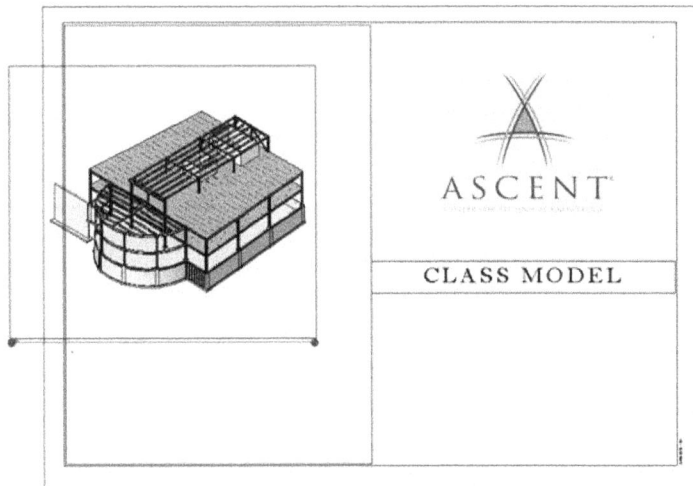

ASCENT

CLASS MODEL

Figure 12–14

Hint: Add an Image to a Sheet

Company logos and renderings saved to image files (such as .JPG and .PNG) can be added directly on a sheet or in a view.

1. In the *Insert* tab>Import panel, click 🖼 (Image).
2. In the Import Image dialog box, select and open the image file. The extents of the image display as shown in Figure 12–15.

Figure 12–15

3. Place the image where you want it.
4. The image is displayed. Pick one of the grips and extend it to modify the size of the image.

- In Properties, you can adjust the height and width and also set the *Draw Layer* to either **Background** or **Foreground**, as shown in Figure 12–16.

Dimensions		⋏
Width	1' 5 185/256"	
Height	1' 1 41/64"	
Horizontal Scale	1.000000	
Vertical Scale	1.000000	
Lock Proportions	☑	
Other		⋏
Draw Layer	Background	

Figure 12–16

- You can select more than one image at a time and move them as a group to the background or foreground.

Practice 12a | Create Construction Documents

Practice Objectives

- Set up project properties.
- Create sheets.
- Place views on sheets.

Estimated time for completion: 15 minutes

In this practice you will complete project information, create a cover sheet, and add views to the sheet. You will then create a foundation plan sheet, as shown in Figure 12–17, and as many other sheets as time permits, modifying the scales as required.

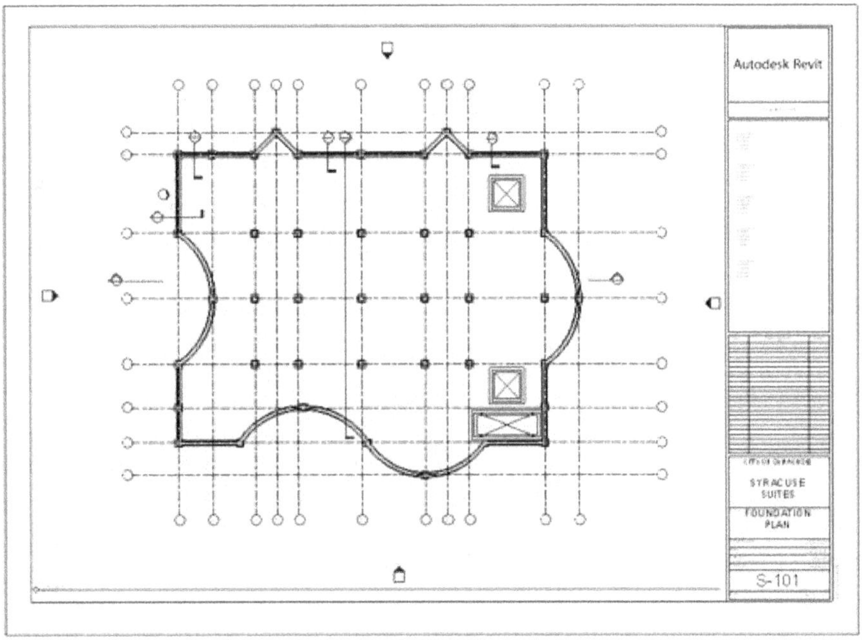

Figure 12–17

Task 1 - Complete the project information.

1. Open **Syracuse-Suites-Sheets.rvt**.

2. In the *Manage* tab>Setting panel, click 🗏 (Project Information).

These properties are used across the entire sheet set and do not need to be entered on each sheet.

3. In the Project Properties dialog box set the following parameters (or use your own information based on your company standards):

   • *Project Issue Date:* current date

   • *Project Status:* **Design Development**

   • *Client Name:* **CITY OF SYRACUSE**

   • *Project Address:* **1234 Clinton St. Syracuse, NY 13066** click **Edit...**

   • *Project Name:* **SYRACUSE SUITES**

   • *Project Number:* **1234-567**

4. Click **OK**.

5. Save the project.

Task 2 - Create a cover sheet.

Some sheets already exist in the project.

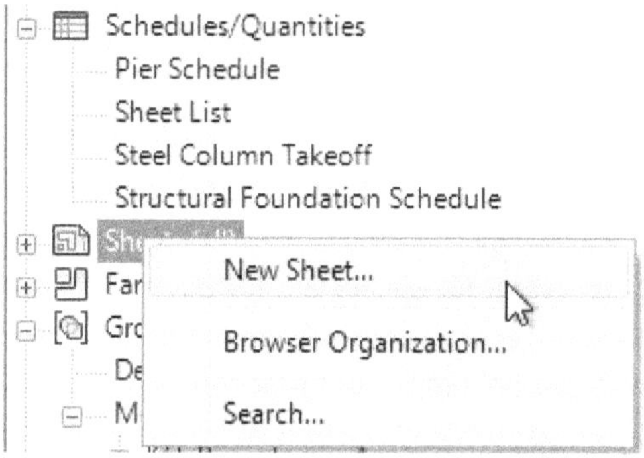

1. In the Project Browser, right-click on *Sheets (all)* and select **New Sheet**, as shown in Figure 12–18, or in the *View* tab> Sheet Composition panel, click ⬜ (New Sheet).

Figure 12–18

2. In the New Sheet dialog box, *Select Titleblocks* area, select **Syracuse Suites Cover Sheet: E1 30x42 Horizontal** and click **OK**.

3. In the Project Browser, *Sheets* category, right-click on new sheet and select **Rename**.

4. In the Sheet Title dialog box, set *Number* to **S-000** and *Name* to **COVER SHEET**, as shown in Figure 12–19.

Sheet Title	
S-000	Number
COVER SHEET	Name

Figure 12–19

5. In the Project Browser, expand **3D Views**.

6. Select the **Isometric** view and drag it to the coversheet.

7. Delete the view because it is too large.

8. Open the **Isometric** view and set the *Scale* to **1/16"=1'-0"**.

9. Switch to the cover sheet and place the view on the sheet.

10. In the *Legends* category, add the Symbol Legend to the sheet as shown in Figure 12–20.

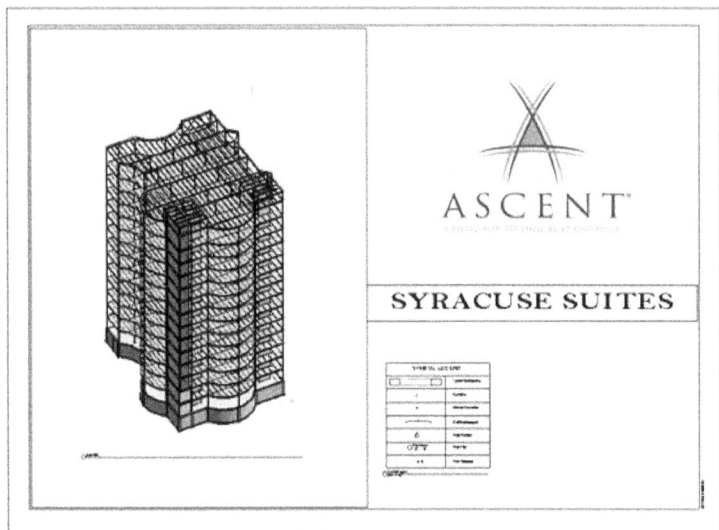

Figure 12–20

Task 3 - Create additional sheets.

1. In the *View* tab>Sheet Composition panel, click (Sheet).

2. In the New Sheet dialog box, select the titleblock **Syracuse Suites E1: 30x42 Horizontal** and click **OK**.

3. In the Project Browser, right-click on **S-001 – Unnamed** and rename it as **S-201: FOUNDATION PLAN**, as shown in Figure 12–21.

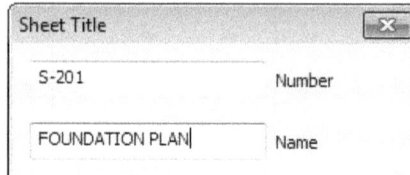

Figure 12–21

4. Click **OK**.

5. In the Project Browser, find the **T.O. FOOTING** structural plan view and drag it onto the sheet, centering it in the view as shown in Figure 12–22.

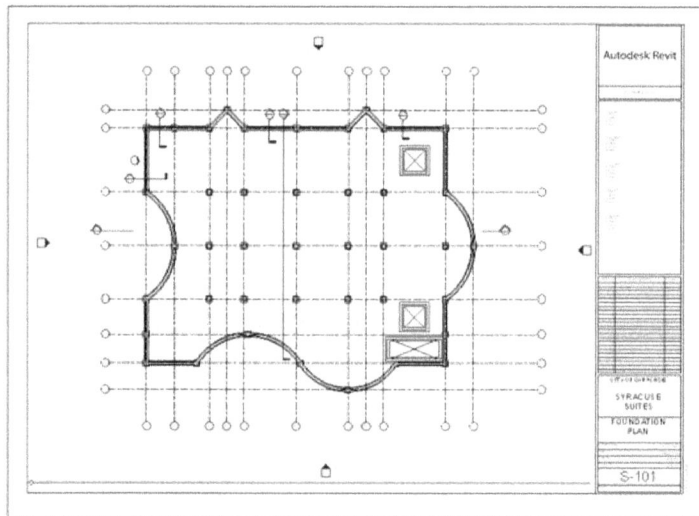

Figure 12–22

6. Several sheets already exist in the project. Place the Structural Plans: **00GROUND FLOOR PLAN** view on the sheet **S-202-Ground Floor Plan.**

7. Zoom in to see the title of the view. It displays as **00 GROUND FLOOR PLAN**, as shown in Figure 12–23.

Figure 12–23

8. In the Project Browser, select the view and then, in Properties, scroll down to the *Identity Data* section. Change the *Title on Sheet* to **GROUND FLOOR - STRUCTURAL PLAN**, as shown in Figure 12–24.

Identity Data	⋩
View Template	<None>
View Name	00 GROUND FLOOR PLAN
Dependency	Independent
Title on Sheet	GROUND FLOOR - STRUCTURAL PLAN
Sheet Number	S-202
Sheet Name	Ground Floor Plan

Figure 12–24

9. Click **Apply**. The title changes on the sheet, as shown in Figure 12–25.

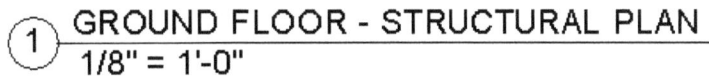

1) **GROUND FLOOR - STRUCTURAL PLAN**
1/8" = 1'-0"

Figure 12–25

10. (Optional) Add views to the other sheets.

- If any views do not fit on the sheet, change the scale.

11. When the sheets have been created, browse through them separately and note that all of the tags are filled out, as shown in Figure 12–26. This enables you to verify whether the tags point to the sheets correctly. If a tag does not display detail and sheet numbers, the view has not been dragged onto a sheet.

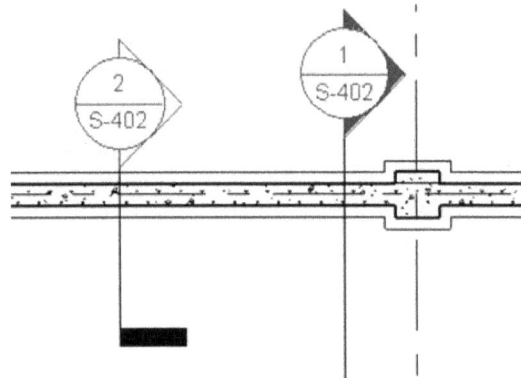

Figure 12–26

12. Save the project.

12.3 Printing Sheets

With the **Print** command, you can print individual sheets or a list of selected sheets. You can also print an individual view or a portion of a view for check prints or presentations. To open the Print dialog box (shown in Figure 12–27), in the *File* tab, click

🖶 (Print).

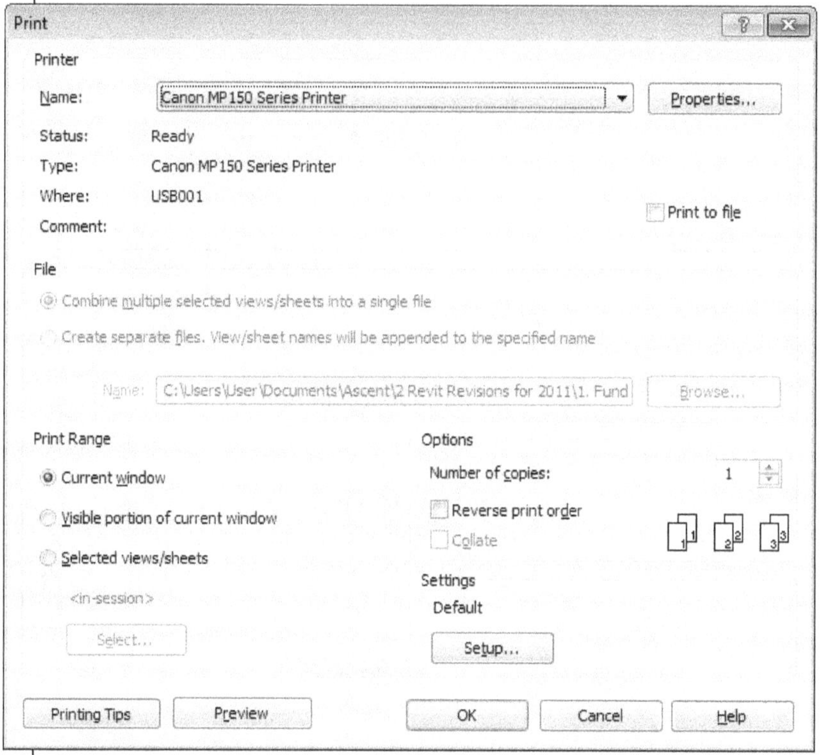

Figure 12–27

Printing Options

The Print dialog box is divided into the following areas: *Printer, File, Print Range, Options*, and *Settings*. Modify them as required to produce the plot you want.

*   **Printing Tips**: Opens Autodesk WikiHelp online, in which you can find help with troubleshooting printing issues.

*   **Preview**: Opens a preview of the print output so that you can see what is going to be printed.

Printer

Select from the list of available printers, as shown in Figure 12–28. Click **Properties...** to adjust the properties of the selected printer. The options vary according to the printer. Select the **Print to file** option to print to a file rather than directly to a printer. You can create .PLT or .PRN files.

You must have a .PDF print driver installed on your system to print to PDF.

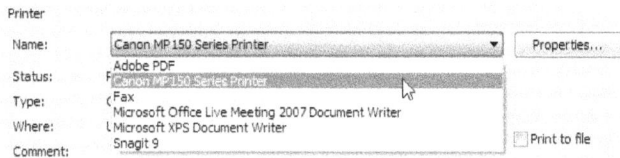

Printer

| Name: | Canon MP150 Series Printer ▼ | Properties... |

Status: | Adobe PDF
| Canon MP150 Series Printer

Type: | Fax
| Microsoft Office Live Meeting 2007 Document Writer

Where: | Microsoft XPS Document Writer

Comment: | Snagit 9

☐ Print to file

Figure 12–28

File

The *File* area is only available if the **Print to file** option has been selected in the *Printer* area or if you are printing to an electronic-only type of printer. You can create one file or multiple files depending on the type of printer you are using, as shown in Figure 12–29. Click **Browse...** to select the file location and name.

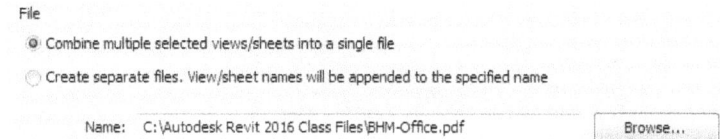

File

◉ Combine multiple selected views/sheets into a single file

○ Create separate files. View/sheet names will be appended to the specified name

Name: C:\Autodesk Revit 2016 Class Files\BHM-Office.pdf   Browse...

Figure 12–29

Print Range

The *Print Range* area enables you to print individual views/sheets or sets of views/sheets, as shown in Figure 12–30.

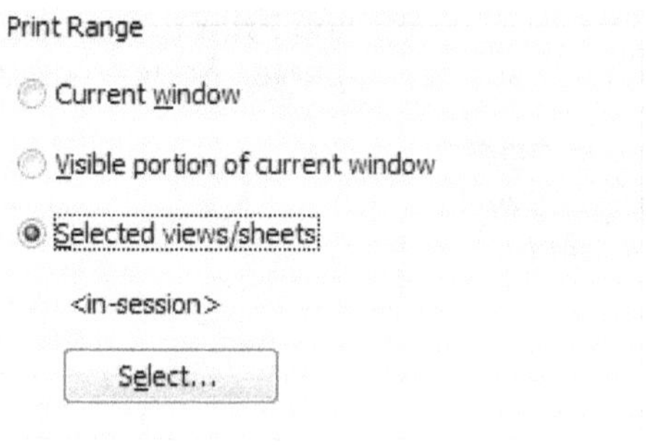

Print Range

○ Current window

○ Visible portion of current window

◉ Selected views/sheets

<in-session>

Select...

Figure 12–30

- **Current window**: Prints the entire current sheet or view you have open.

- **Visible portion of current window**: Prints only what is displayed in the current sheet or view.

- **Selected views/sheets**: Prints multiple views or sheets. Click **Select...** to open the View/Sheet Set dialog box to choose what to include in the print set. You can save these sets by name so that you can more easily print the same group again.

Options

If your printer supports multiple copies, you can specify the number in the *Options* area, as shown in Figure 12–31. You can also reverse the print order or collate your prints. These options are also available in the printer properties.

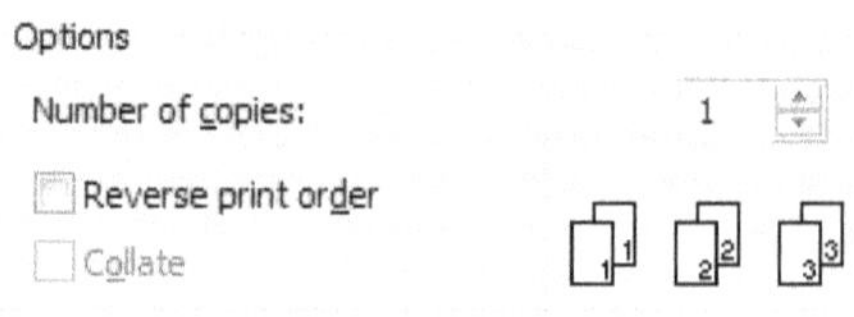

Options

Number of copies: 1

☐ Reverse print order

☐ Collate

Figure 12–31

Settings

Click **Setup**... to open the Print Setup dialog box, as shown in Figure 12–32. Here, you can specify the *Orientation* and *Zoom* settings, among others. You can also save these settings by name.

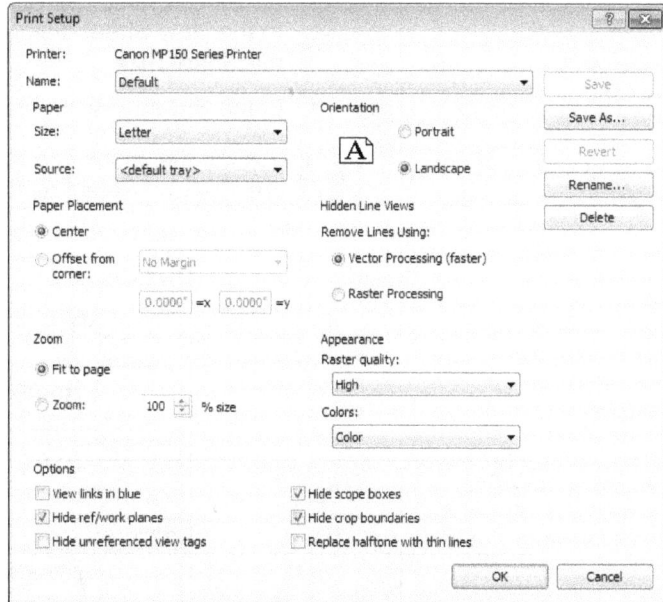

Figure 12–32

- In the *Options* area specify the types of elements you want to print or not print. Unless specified, all of the elements in a view or sheet print.

Chapter Review Questions

1. How do you specify the size of a sheet?

   a. In the Sheet Properties, specify the **Sheet Size**.

   b. In the Options Bar, specify the **Sheet Size**.

   c. In the New Sheet dialog box, select a title block to control the Sheet Size.

   d. In the Sheet view, right-click and select **Sheet Size**.

2. How is the title block information filled in as shown in Figure 12–33? (Select all that apply.)

   ```
   ASCENT Properties
     Office Building

      Cover Sheet
   Project Number          1234.56
   Date                  Issue Date
   Drawn By                  Author
   Checked By               Checker

        CS000
   Scale
   ```

   Figure 12–33

   a. Select the title block and select the label that you want to change.

   b. Select the title block and modify it in Properties.

   c. Right-click on the Sheet in the Project Browser and select **Information**.

   d. Some of the information is filled in automatically.

3. On how many sheets can a floor plan view be placed?

   a. 1

   b. 2-5

   c. 6+

   d. As many as you want.

4. Which of the following is the best method to use if the size of a view is too large for a sheet, as shown in Figure 12–34?

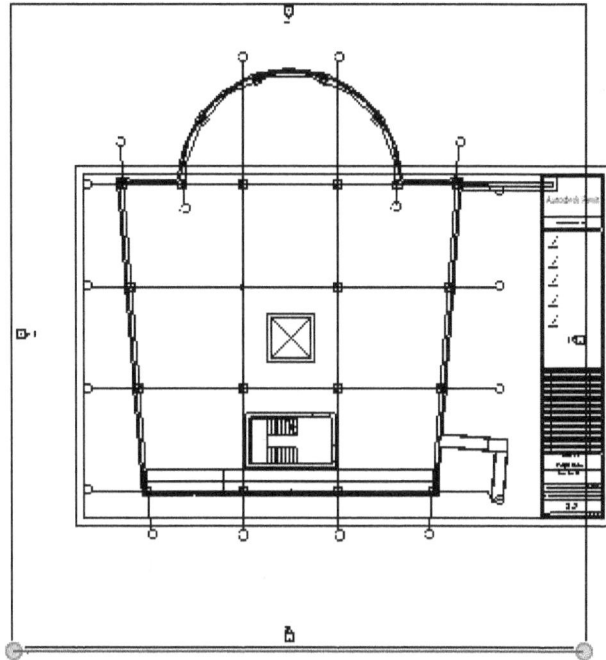

Figure 12–34

a. Delete the view, change the scale and place the view back on the sheet.

b. Activate the view and change the View Scale.

5. How do you set up a view on a sheet that only displays part of a floor plan, as shown in Figure 12–35?

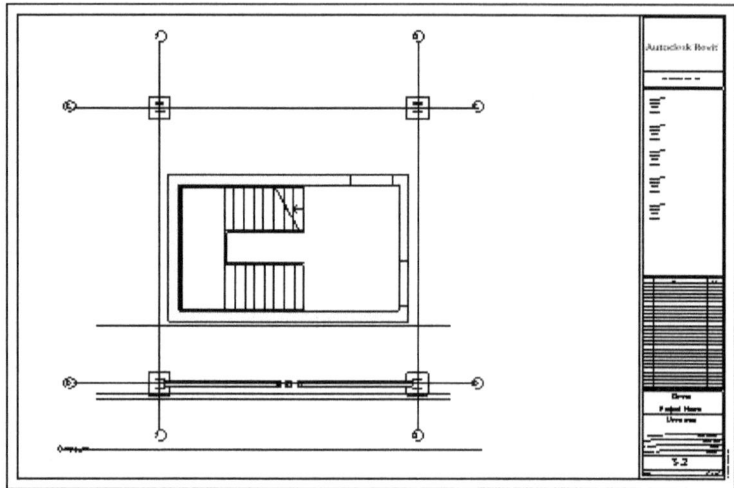

Figure 12–35

a. Drag and drop the view to the sheet and use the crop region to modify it.

b. Activate the view and rescale it.

c. Create a callout view displaying the part that you want to use and place the callout view on the sheet.

d. Open the view in the Project Browser and change the View Scale.

Command Summary

Button	Command	Location
	Activate View	• **Ribbon:** *(select the view) Modify | Viewports* tab>Viewport panel • **Double-click:** *(in viewport)* • **Right-click:** *(on view)* Activate View
	Deactivate View	• **Ribbon:** *View* tab>Sheet Composition panel>expand Viewports • **Double-click:** *(on sheet)* • **Right-click:** *(on view)* Deactivate View
	Place View	• **Ribbon:** *View* tab>Sheet Composition panel
	Print	• **File tab**
	Sheet	• **Ribbon:** *View* tab>Sheet Composition panel

Annotating Construction Documents

When you create construction documents, annotations are required to show the design intent. Annotations such as dimensions and text can be added to views at any time during the creation of a project. Detail lines and symbols can also be added to views as you create the working drawing sheets, while Legends can be created to provide a place to document any symbols that are used in a project

Learning Objectives in this Chapter

- Add dimensions to the model as a part of the working drawings.
- Add text to a view and use leaders to create notes pointing to a specific part of the model.
- Create Text Types using different fonts and sizes to suit your company standards.
- Draw detail lines to further enhance the documentation view.
- Add view-specific annotation symbols for added clarity.
- Create legend views and populate them with symbols of elements in the project.

13.1 Working with Dimensions

You can create permanent dimensions using aligned, linear, angular, radial, diameter, and arc length dimensions. These can be individual or a string of dimensions, as shown in Figure 13–1. With aligned dimensions, you can also dimension entire walls with openings, grid lines, and/or intersecting walls.

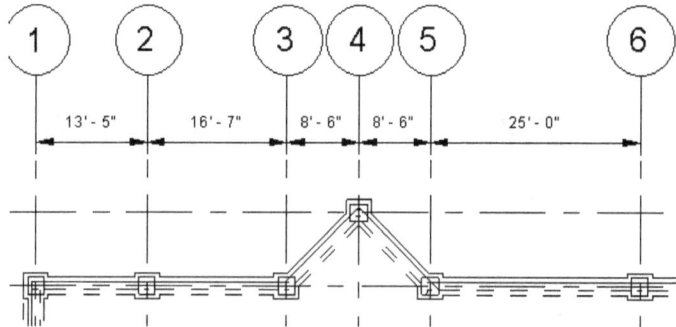

Figure 13–1

- Dimensions referencing model elements must be added to the model in a view. You can dimension on sheets, but only to items added directly on the sheets.

- Dimensions are available in the *Annotate* tab>Dimension panel and the *Modify* tab>Measure panel, as shown in Figure 13–2.

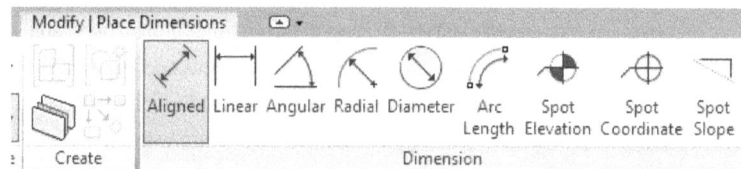

Figure 13–2

How To: Add Aligned Dimensions with Options

1. Start the ✎ (Aligned) command or type **DI**.
2. In the Type Selector, select a dimension style.

✎ *(Aligned) is also located in the Quick Access Toolbar.*

3. In the Options Bar, select the location line of the wall to dimension from, as shown in Figure 13–3.

- This option can be changed as you add dimensions.

Modify | Place Dimensions   Wall centerline ▾   Pick: Individual Reference ▾   Options

Wall centerlines
Wall faces
Center of core
Faces of core

Figure 13–3

4. In the Options Bar, select your preference from the Pick drop-down list:

- **Individual References**: Select the elements in order (as shown in Figure 13–4) and then click in empty space to position the dimension string.

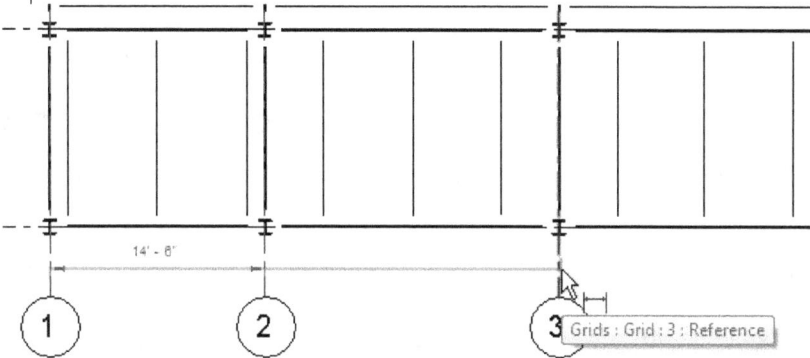

14' - 6"

1   2   3   Grids : Grid : 3 : Reference

Figure 13–4

- **Entire Walls**: Select the wall you want to dimension and then click the cursor to position the dimension string, as shown in Figure 13–5.

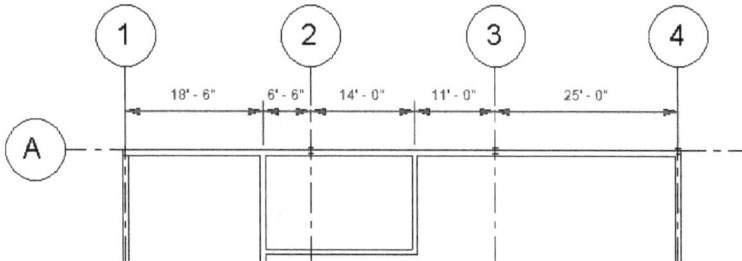

1   2   3   4

18' - 6"   6' - 6"   14' - 0"   11' - 0"   25' - 0"

A

Figure 13–5

- When dimensioning entire walls you can specify how you want *Openings*, *Intersecting Walls*, and *Intersecting Grids* to be treated by the dimension string. In the Options Bar, click **Options**. In the Auto Dimension Options dialog box (shown in Figure 13–6), select the references you want to have automatically dimensioned.

*If the **Entire Wall** option is selected without additional options, it places an overall wall dimension.*

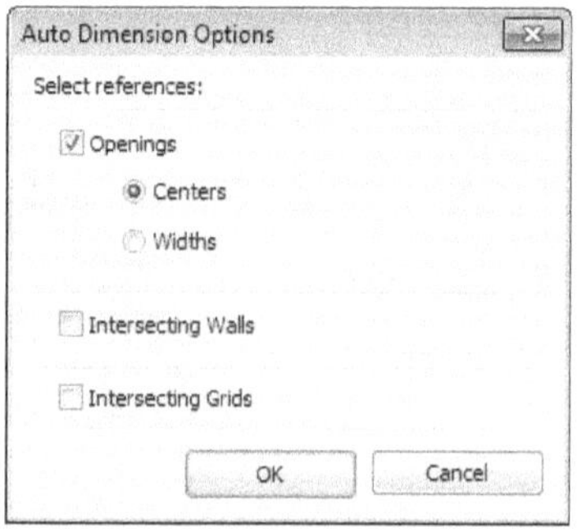

Figure 13–6

How To: Add Other Types of Dimensions

*When the **Dimension** command is active, the dimension methods are also accessible in the Modify | Place Dimensions tab> Dimension panel.*

1. In the *Annotate* tab>Dimension panel, select a dimension method.

	Aligned	Most commonly used dimension type. Select individual elements or entire walls to dimension.
	Linear	Used when you need to specify certain points on elements.
	Angular	Used to dimension the angle between two elements.
	Radial	Used to dimension the radius of circular elements.
	Diameter	Used to dimension the diameter of circular elements.
	Arc Length	Used to dimension the length of the arc of circular elements.

2. In the Type Selector, select the dimension type.
3. Follow the prompts for the selected method.

Modifying Dimensions

When you move elements that are dimensioned, the dimensions automatically update. You can also modify dimensions by selecting a dimension or dimension string and making changes, as shown in Figure 13–7.

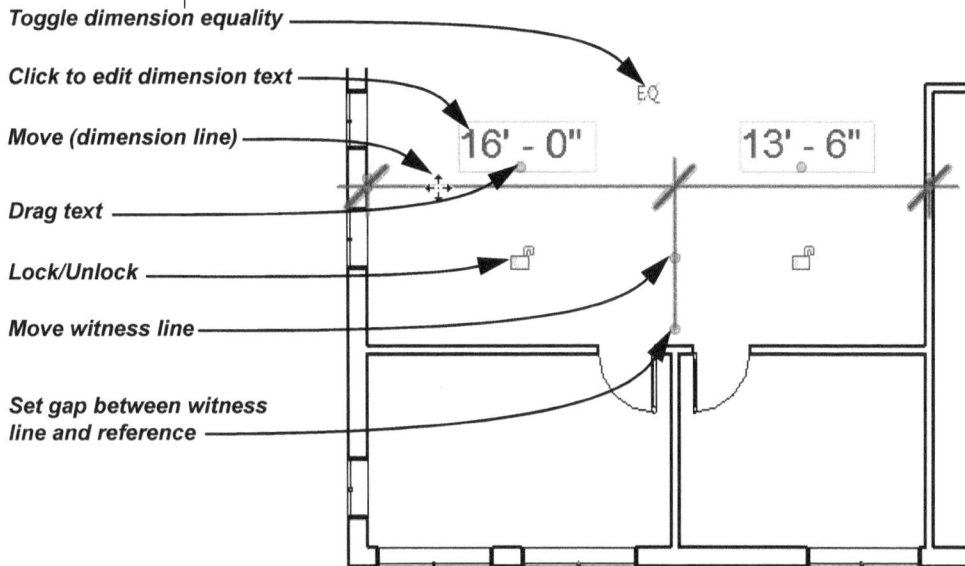

Toggle dimension equality ⎯⎯⎯⎯⎯⎯⎯⎯⎯

Click to edit dimension text ⎯⎯⎯

Move (dimension line) ⎯⎯⎯

Drag text ⎯⎯⎯

Lock/Unlock ⎯⎯⎯

Move witness line ⎯⎯⎯

Set gap between witness line and reference ⎯⎯⎯

Figure 13–7

- To move the dimension text, select the **Drag text** control under the text and drag it to a new location. It automatically creates a leader from the dimension line if you drag it away. The style of the leader (arc or line) depends on the dimension style.

- To move the dimension line (the line parallel to the element being dimensioned) simply drag the line to a new location or select the dimension and drag the ⁺⁺ (Move) control.

- To change the gap between the witness line and the element being dimensioned, drag the control at the end of the witness line.

- To move the witness line (the line perpendicular to the element being dimensioned) to a different element or face of a wall, use the **Move Witness Line** control in the middle of the witness line. Click repeatedly to cycle through the various options. You can also drag this control to move the witness line to a different element, or right-click on the control and select **Move Witness Line**.

Adding and Deleting Dimensions in a String

• To add a witness line to a string of dimensions, select the dimension and, in the *Modify | Dimensions* tab>Witness Lines panel, click ⊢⊣ (Edit Witness Lines). Select the element(s) you want to add to the dimension. Click in space to finish.

• To delete a witness line, drag the **Move Witness Line** control to a nearby element. Alternatively, you can hover the cursor over the control, right-click, and select **Delete Witness Line**.

• To delete one dimension in a string and break the string into two separate dimensions, select the string, hover over the dimension that you want to delete, and press <Tab>. When it highlights (as shown on top in Figure 13–8), pick it and press <Delete>. The selected dimension is deleted and the dimension string is separated into two elements as shown on the bottom in Figure 13–8.

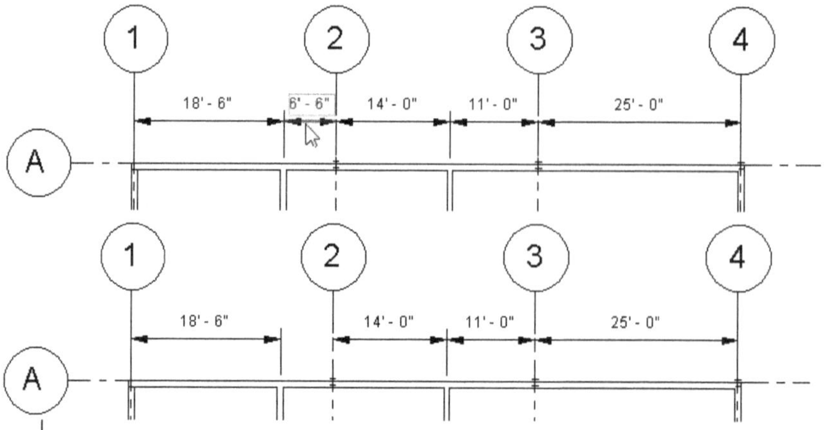

Figure 13–8

Modifying the Dimension Text

Because the Autodesk® Revit® software is parametric, changing the dimension text without changing the elements dimensioned would cause problems throughout the project. These issues could cause problems beyond the model if you use the project model to estimate materials or work with other disciplines.

You can append the text with prefixes and suffixes (as shown in Figure 13–9), which can help you in renovation projects.

Figure 13–9

Double-click on the dimension text to open the Dimension Text dialog box, as shown in Figure 13–10, and make modifications as required.

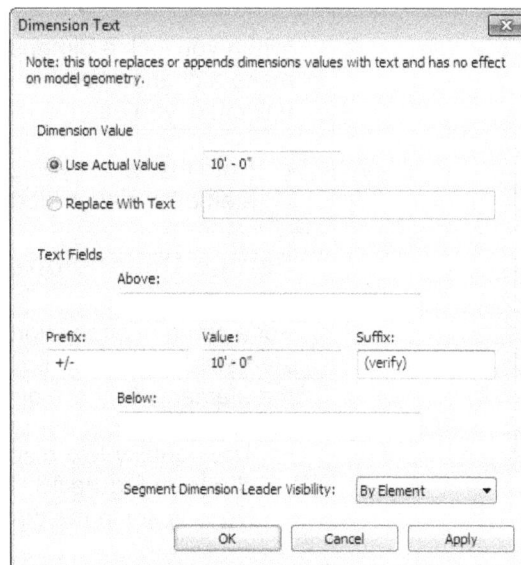

Figure 13–10

Setting Constraints

The three types of constraints that work with dimensions are locks and equal settings, as shown in Figure 13–11, as well as labels.

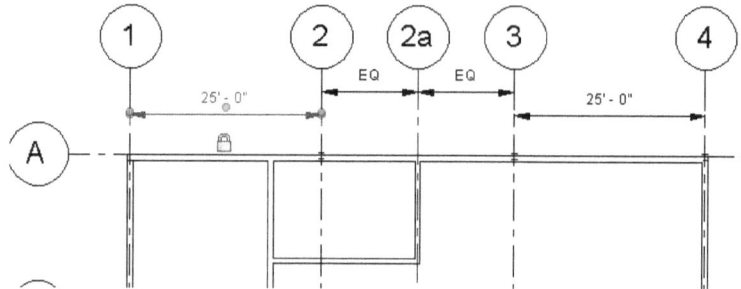

Figure 13–11

Locking Dimensions

When you lock a dimension, the value is set and you cannot make a change between it and the referenced elements. If it is unlocked, you can move it and change its value.

- Note that when you use this and move an element, any elements that are locked to the dimension also move.

Setting Dimensions Equal

For a string of dimensions, select the **EQ** symbol to constrain the elements to be at an equal distance apart. This actually moves the elements that are dimensioned.

- The equality text display can be changed in Properties, as shown in Figure 13–12. The style for each of the display types is set in the dimension type.

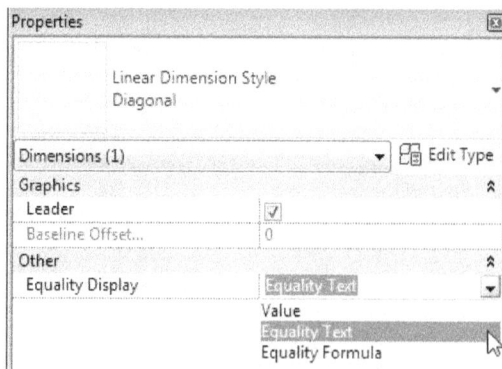

Figure 13–12

Labeling Dimensions

If you have a distance that needs to be repeated multiple times, such as the *Bay Length A* label shown in Figure 13–13, or one where you want to use a formula based on another dimension, you can create and apply a global parameter, also called a label, to the dimension.

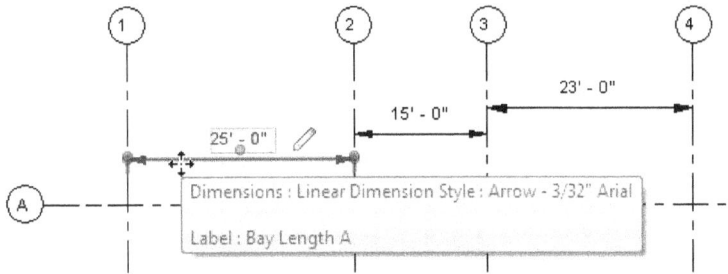

Figure 13–13

- To apply an existing label to a dimension, select the dimension and in the *Modify | Dimension* tab>Label Dimension panel, select the label in the drop-down list, as shown in Figure 13–14.

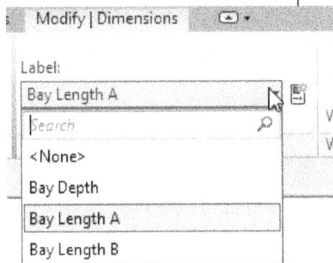

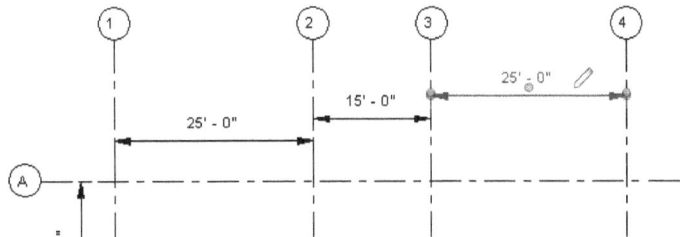

Figure 13–14

How To: Create a Label

1. Select a dimension.
2. In the *Modify | Dimension* tab>Label Dimension panel click

   ▣ (Create Parameter)
3. In the Global Parameter Properties dialog box type in a *Name* as shown in Figure 13–15 and click **OK**.

Figure 13–15

4. The label is applied to the dimension.

How To: Edit the Label Information

1. Select a labeled dimension.
2. Click **Global Parameters**, as shown in Figure 13–16.
3. In the Global Parameters dialog box, in the *Value* column, type the new distance, as shown in Figure 13–17.

Global Parameters

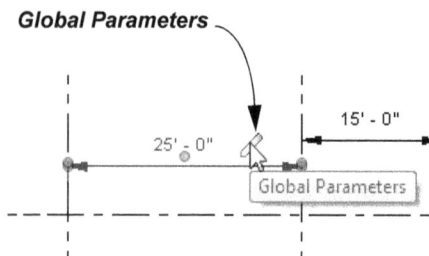

Figure 13–16

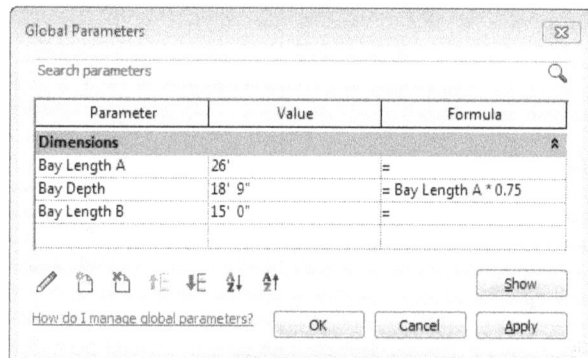

Figure 13–17

4. Click **OK**. The selected dimension and any other dimensions using the same label are updated.

- You can also edit, create, and delete Global Parameters in this dialog box.

Working with Constraints

To find out which elements have constraints applied to them, in the View Control Bar, click ⊬̲ (Reveal Constraints). Constraints display as shown in Figure 13–18.

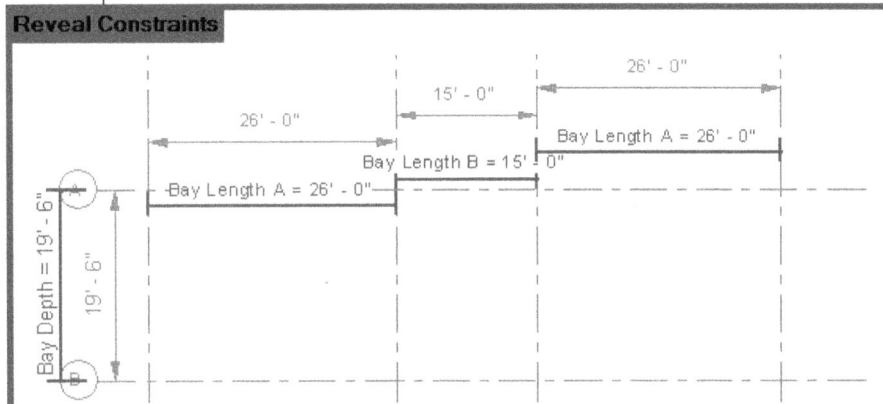

Figure 13–18

- If you try to move the element beyond the appropriate constrains, a warning dialog box displays, as shown in Figure 13–19.

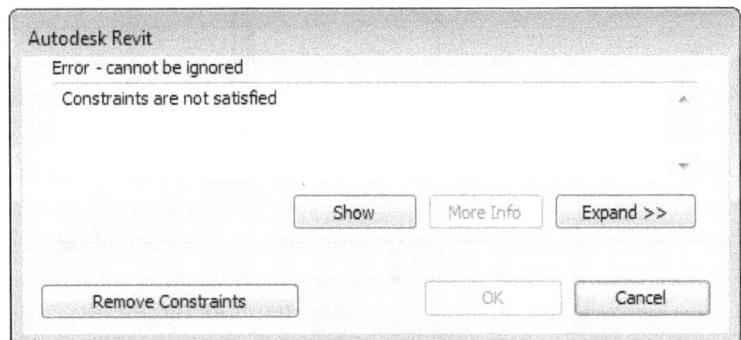

Figure 13–19

- If you delete dimensions that are constrained, a warning dialog box displays, as shown in Figure 13–20. Click **OK** to retain the constraint or **Unconstrain** to remove the constraint.

Autodesk Revit

Warning - can be ignored

A dimension labeled by a parameter is being deleted, but the elements will still be constrained. Push "Unconstrain" to remove the constraints or "OK" to leave elements constrained.

Show   More Info   Expand >>

Figure 13–20

Multi-Rebar Annotation

These annotations only work with rebar created using the multi-rebar layout. This does not work with structural area, path, or fabric reinforcement.

The dimension-like Multi-Rebar Annotation tool dimensions and tags multiple rebar elements based on the parameters from the referenced elements, as shown in Figure 13–21.

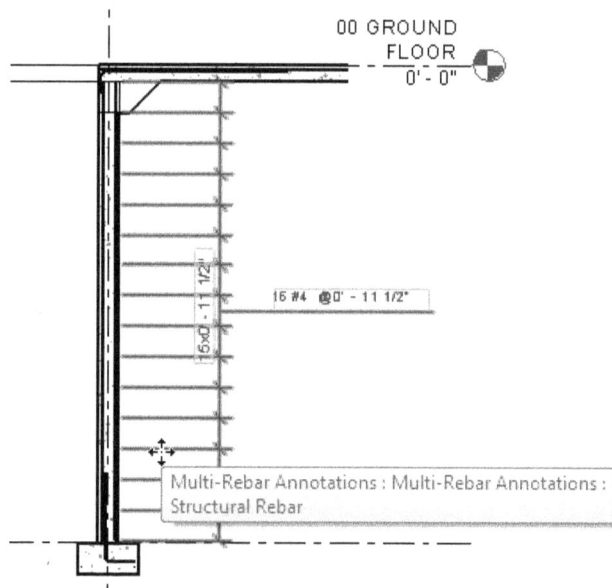

00 GROUND
FLOOR
0' - 0"

16 #4 @0' - 11 1/2"

Multi-Rebar Annotations : Multi-Rebar Annotations : Structural Rebar

Figure 13–21

- There are two different types - aligned (annotations display parallel to the tagged rebar) and linear (annotations are aligned to the horizontal or vertical axis of the view).

- There must be at least two rebar elements in a set for the multiple-rebar dimensions to work.

How To: Add Multi-Rebar Annotation

1. In the *Annotate* tab>Tag panel, expand ✦ (Multi-Rebar Annotation) and select ✦ (Aligned Multi-Rebar Annotation) or ⌐ (Linear Multi-Rebar Annotation).
2. In the Type Selector, select the annotation type you want to use.
3. Select the element to tag.
4. Click to place the dimension string.
5. Click to place the line off the dimension string
6. Click to place the tag (text).
7. Continue placing annotation as required.
8. Click ↖ (Modify) or press <Esc> to finish.

• The dimensions and tags can be modified separately. After you select one of the elements, in the *Modify | Multi-Rebar Annotations* tab>Edit panel, click ▢① (Select Tag) or ⊢ (Select Dimension). Then modify the elements using controls, as shown for a tag in Figure 13–22.

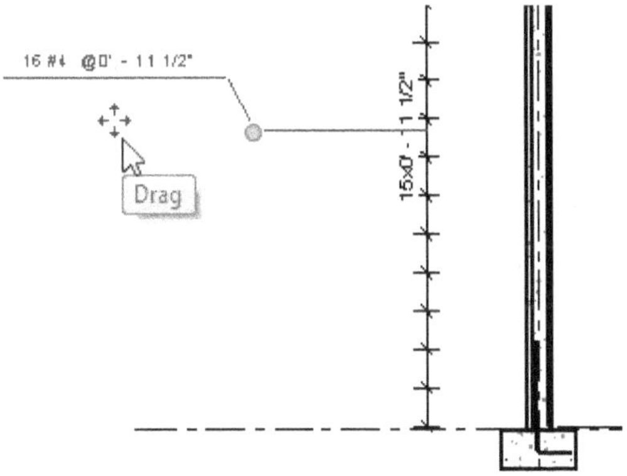

Figure 13–22

• Editing the dimension uses the same controls as other dimension strings.

- The dimensions of the Multi-Rebar Annotation change automatically in relation to the Rebar Presentation style. For example, in Figure 13–23, ☐ (Show First and Last) is shown on the left and ▦ (Show All) on the right. This graphic uses the **Structural Rebar Section** Multi-Rebar Annotations type.

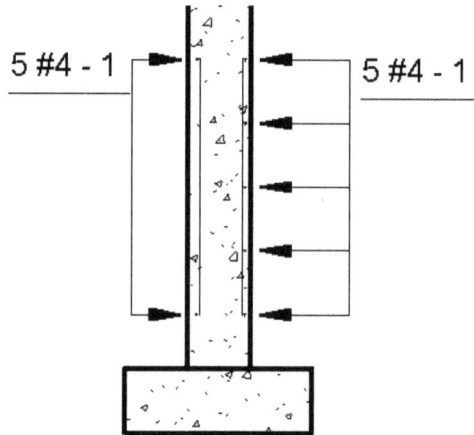

Figure 13–23

Practice 13a | Work with Dimensions

Practice Objectives

- Add aligned and radial dimensions.
- Add multi-rebar annotation

Estimated time for completion: 10 minutes

In this practice you will annotate a floor plan by adding Aligned dimensions for gridline locations and Radial dimensions for curved beams, as shown in Figure 13–24. You will also add text notes to a plan and detail view, and multi-rebar annotation to an elevation callout.

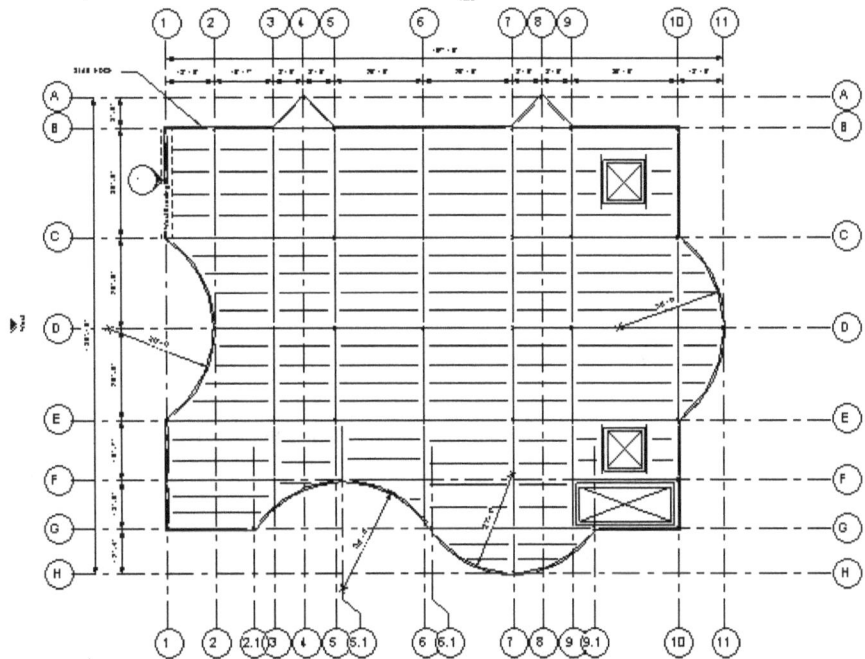

Figure 13–24

Task 1 - Place dimensions.

1. Open **Syracuse-Suites-Dimensions.rvt**.

2. In the Project Browser, right-click on the **Structural Plans: TOS-1ST FLOOR** view and select **Duplicate View> Duplicate**.

3. Rename the new view to **TOS-1ST FLOOR - Dimensioned**.

4. In the View Control Bar, change the *Scale* to **1/16" = 1'-0"**.

5. In the *Annotate* tab>Dimension panel or Quick Access Toolbar, click ⟋ (Aligned).

6. Click on **Grid 1** then **Grid 11** and then out to the right of **Grid 11** to create one overall dimension, as shown across the top in Figure 13–25.

7. You are still in the **Aligned** command. Select **Grid 1** and continue selecting the other grid lines in sequence without stopping until you select **Grid 11**. When you get to the end, select to the right of the string to place the dimensions. as shown below the overall dimension in Figure 13–25.

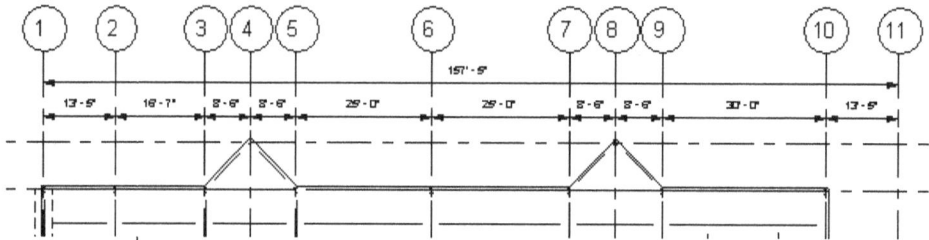

Figure 13–25

8. Add a grid-to-grid dimension vertically from **Grid A** to **Grid H**. and another single dimension from **Grid A** to **Grid H**. Modify the location of the grid markers as required.

9. In the *Modify | Place Dimension* tab>Dimension panel, click ⟋ (Radial) and add radial dimensions to the four circular bays, as shown for one of them in Figure 13–26.

If there is overlapping text, select the text and move it to an open area where it can be read.

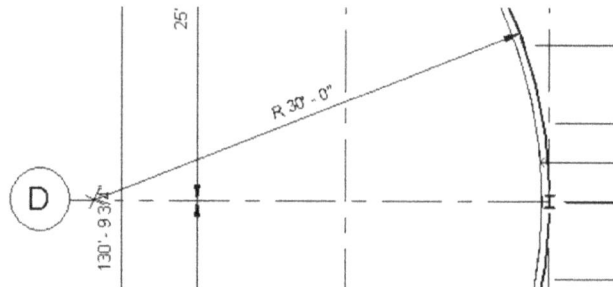

Figure 13–26

10. Save the project.

Task 2 - Add multi-rebar annotation.

1. Open the **Elevations (Building Elevation): North** view.

2. Zoom in on the foundation wall and create a callout of the area between Grids 5 and 7, as shown in Figure 13–27.

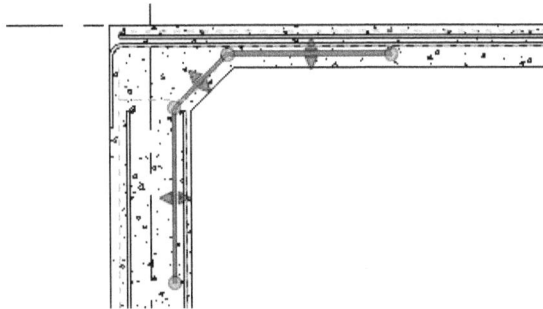

Figure 13–27

3. In the Project Browser, rename the new view to **Foundation Rebar Elevation** and open it. There is no rebar displayed to annotate.

4. Open the **Sections (Wall Section): Typical Foundation Wall Section** view.

5. Select the multi-rebar set, as shown in Figure 13–28.

Figure 13–28

6. In Properties, open the View Visibility States dialog box and select **View unobscured** beside the **Foundation Rebar Elevation** view, as shown in Figure 13–29.

View Type	View Name	View unobscured	View as solid
Elevation	Typical Top Plate	☐	☐
Elevation	Typical Bottom Plate	☐	☐
Elevation	Foundation Rebar Elevat	☑	☐
Section	Typical Foundation Wall	☑	☐
Section	Longitudinal Section	☐	☐

Figure 13–29

7. Click **OK**.

8. Click in the view to release the selection.

9. Return to the **Foundation Rebar Elevation** view. Note that the rebar is now displayed.

10. In the *Annotate* tab>Tag panel, click ✛ (Aligned Multi-Rebar Annotation).

11. Select the rebar set and place the annotation. Every instance in the rebar set is automatically dimensioned, as shown in Figure 13–30.

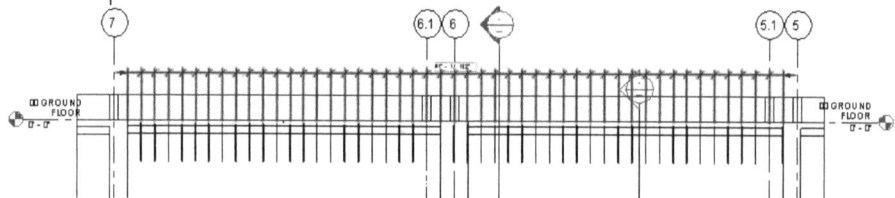

Figure 13–30

12. Click ▷ (Modify) and select the rebar set.

13. In the *Modify | Structural Rebar* tab>Presentation panel, click ☐ (Show First and Last)

14. The dimensions are modified to fit the presentation style, as shown in Figure 13–31.

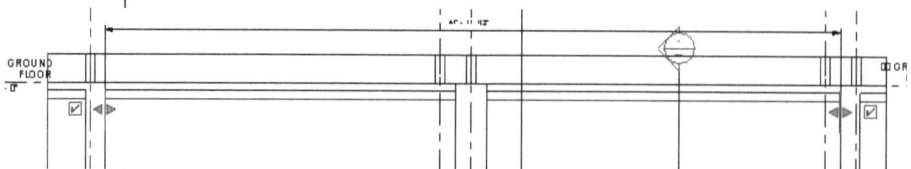

Figure 13–31

15. Save the project.

13.2 Working With Text

The **Text** command enables you to add notes to views or sheets, such as the detail shown in Figure 13–32. The same command is used to create text with or without leaders.

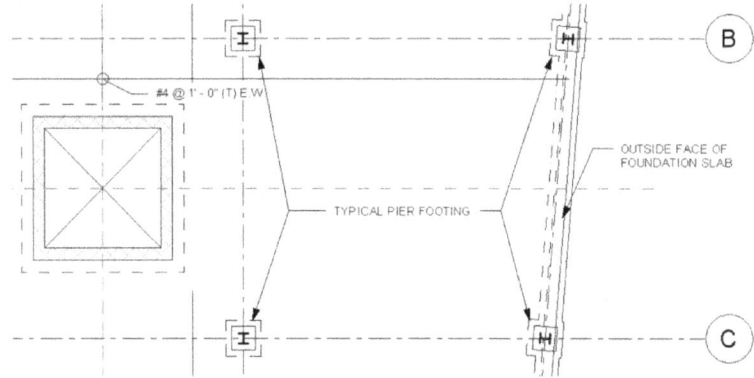

Figure 13–32

The text height is automatically set by the text type in conjunction with the scale of the view (as shown in Figure 13–33, using the same size text type at two different scales). Text types display at the specified height, both in the views and on the sheet.

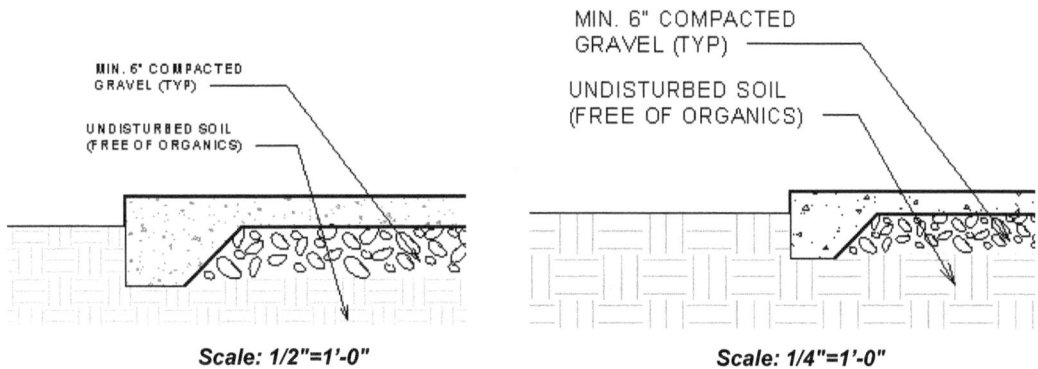

Scale: 1/2"=1'-0"   *Scale: 1/4"=1'-0"*

Figure 13–33

How To: Add Text

1. In the Quick Access Toolbar or *Annotate* tab>Text panel, click

   A (Text).

The text type sets the font and height of the text.

2. In the Type Selector, set the text type.
3. In the *Modify | Place Text* tab>Leader panel, select the method you want to use: A (No Leader), ←A (One Segment), ⟋A (Two Segments), or ⟋A (Curved).
4. In the Paragraph panel, set the overall justification for the text and leader, as shown in Figure 13–34.

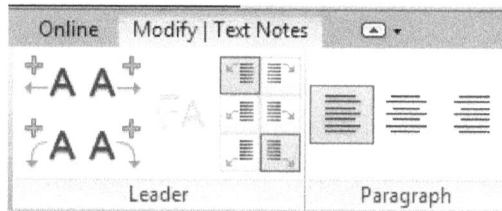

Figure 13–34

Use alignment lines to help you align the text with other text elements.

5. Select the location for the leader and text.
   - If **No leader** is selected, select the start point for the text and begin typing.
   - If using a leader, the first point places the arrow and you then select points for the leader. The text starts at the last leader point.
   - To set a word wrapping distance, click and drag to set the start and end points of the text.
6. Type the required text. In the *Edit Text* tab, specify additional options for the font and paragraph, as shown in Figure 13–35.

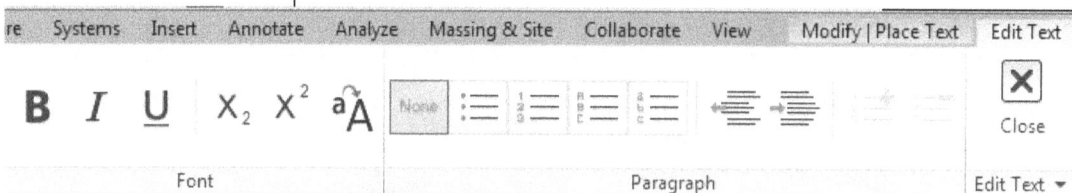

Figure 13–35

7. In the Edit Text tab>Edit Text panel, click ☒ (Close) or click outside the text box to complete the text element.
   - Pressing <Enter> after a line of text starts a new line of text in the same text window.

How To: Add Text Symbols

1. Start the **Text** command and click to place the text.
2. As you are typing text and need to insert a symbol, right-click and select **Symbols** from the shortcut menu. Select from the list of commonly used symbols, as shown in Figure 13–36.

Figure 13–36

3. If the symbol you need is not listed, click **Other**.
4. In the Character Map dialog box, click on a symbol and click **Select**, as shown in Figure 13–37.

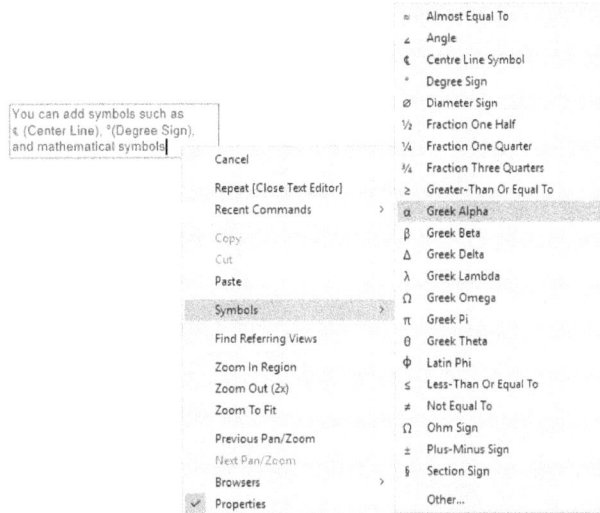

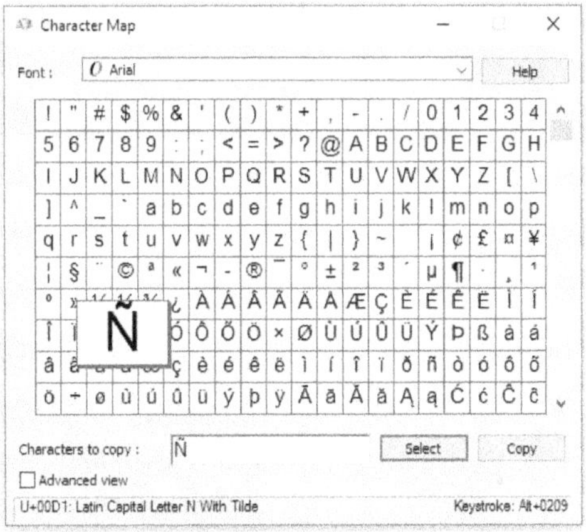

Figure 13–37

5. Click **Copy** to copy the character to the clipboard and paste it into the text box.

• The Font in the Character Map must match the font used by the text type. You cannot use a different font for symbols.

Editing Text

Editing text notes takes place at two levels:

- Modifying the text note, which includes the **Leader** and **Paragraph** styles.

- Editing the text, which includes changes to individual letters, word, and paragraphs in the text note.

Modifying the Text Note

Click once on the text note to modify the text box and leaders using controls, as shown in Figure 13–38, or using the tools in the *Modify | Text Notes* tab.

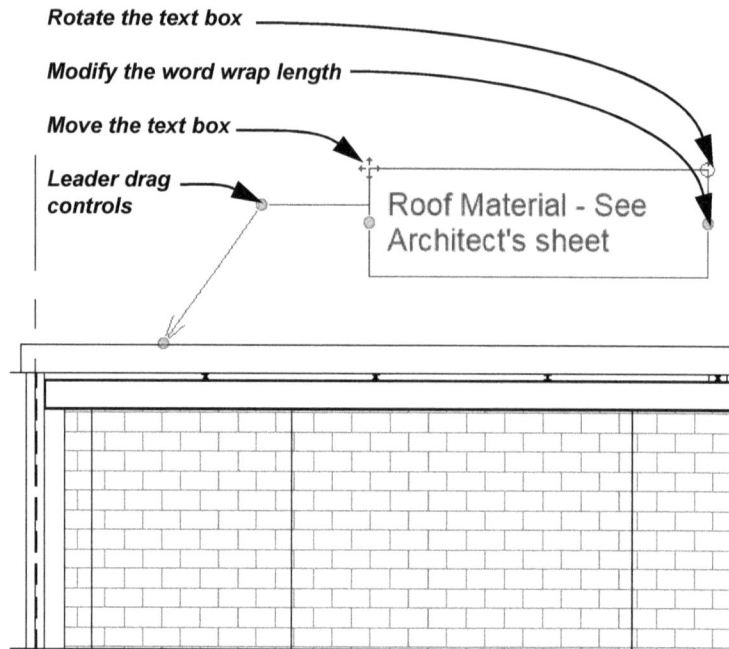

Rotate the text box

Modify the word wrap length

Move the text box

Leader drag controls

Roof Material - See Architect's sheet

Figure 13–38

How To: Add a Leader to Text Notes

1. Select the text note.
2. In the *Modify | Text Notes* tab>Leader panel, select the direction and justification for the new leader, as shown in Figure 13–39.
3. The leader is applied, as shown in Figure 13–40. Use the drag controls to place the arrow as required.

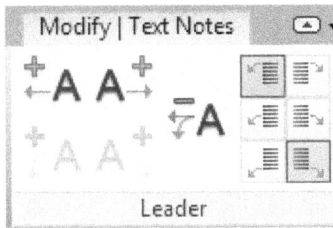

Figure 13–39

Figure 13–40

- You can remove leaders by clicking ⊤A (Remove Last Leader).

Editing the Text

The *Edit Text* tab enables you to make various customizations. These include modifying the font of selected words as well as creating bulleted and numbered lists, as shown in Figure 13–41.

General Notes
1. Notify designer of intention to start construction at least 10 days prior to start of site work.
2. Installer shall provide the following:
   - 24-hour notice of start of construction
   - Inspection of bottom of bed or covering required by state inspector
   - All environmental management inspection sheets must be emailed to designer's office within 24 hours of inspection.

Figure 13–41

- You can **Cut**, **Copy**, and **Paste** text using the clipboard. For example, you can copy text from a document and then paste it into the text editor in Revit.

- To help you see the text better as you are modifying it, in the *Edit Text* tab, expand the Edit Text panel, and select one or both of the options, as shown in Figure 13–42.

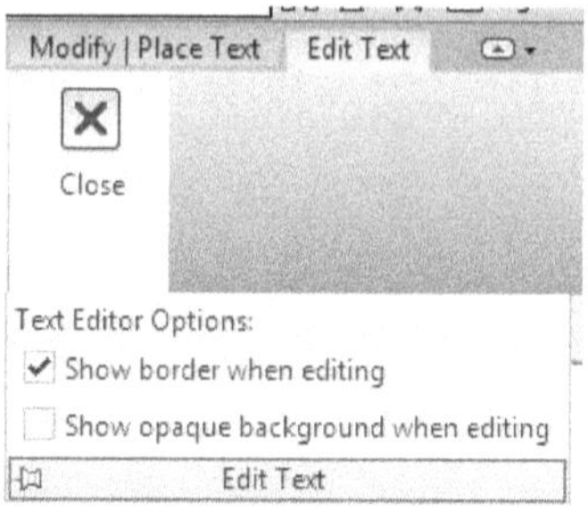

Figure 13–42

How To: Modify the Font

1. Select Individual letters or words.
2. Click on the font modification you want to include:

B (Bold)	X_2 (Subscript)
I (Italic)	X^2 (Superscript)
U̲ (Underline)	ᵃA (All Caps)

- When pasting text from a document outside of Autodesk Revit, font modifications (e.g, Bold, Italic, etc.) are retained.

How To: Create Lists

1. In Edit Text mode, place the cursor in the line where you want to add to a list.
2. In the *Edit Text* tab>Paragraph panel, click the type of list you want to create:

☰ (Bullets)	☰ (Uppercase Letters)
☰ (Numbers)	☰ (Lowercase Letters)

3. As you type, press <Enter> and the next line in the list is incremented.

The indent distance is setup by the Text Type Tab Size.

4. To include sub-lists, at the beginning of the next line, click ☰ (Increase Indent). This indents the line and applies the next level of lists, as shown in Figure 13–43.

> 4. The applicant shall be responsible:
>   A. First Indent
>   a. Second Indent
>   • Third Indent

Figure 13–43

• You can change the type of list after you have applied the first increment. For example, you might want to use a list of bullets instead of letters, as shown in Figure 13–44.

5. Click ☰ (Decrease Indent) to return to the previous list style.

• Press <Shift>+<Enter> to create a blank line in a numbered list.

• To create columns or other separate text boxes that build on a numbering system (as shown in Figure 13–44), create the second text box and list. Then, place the cursor on one of the lines and in the Paragraph panel click ☰ (Increment List Value) until the list matches the next number in the sequence.

General Notes
1. Notify designer of intention to start construction at least 10 days prior to start of site work.
2. Installer shall provide the following:
   • 24-hour notice of start of construction
   • Inspection of bottom of bed or covering required by state inspector
   • All environmental management inspection sheets must be emailed to designer's office within 24 hours of inspection.
3. Site layout and required inspections to be made by designer:
   • Foundations and OWTS location and elevation
   • Inspection of OWTS bottom of trench
4. The applicant shall be responsible for:
   • New Application for redesign.
   • As-built location plans

General Notes (cont.)
5. The installer/applicant shall provide the designer with materials sheets for all construction materiasl prior to designer issuing certificate of construction.
6. The applicant shall furnish the original application to the installer prior to start of constuction

List Incremented

Figure 13–44

6. Click ☰ (Decrement List Value) to move back a number.

> **Hint: Model Text**
>
> Model text is different from annotation text. It is designed to create full-size text on the model itself. For example, you would use model text to create a sign on a door, as shown in Figure 13–45. One model text type is included with the default template. You can create other types as required.
>
>
>
> **Figure 13–45**
>
> * Model text is added from the *Architecture* tab>Model panel, by clicking (Model Text).

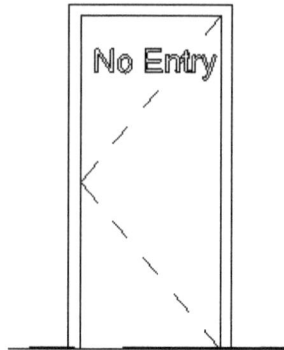

Spell Checking

The Spelling dialog box displays any misspelled words in context and provides several options for changing them, as shown in Figure 13–46.

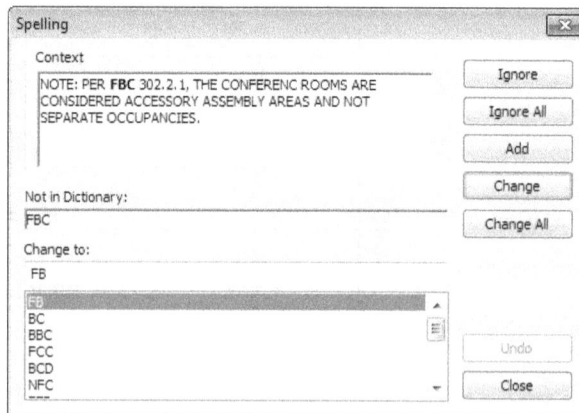

Figure 13–46

- To spell check all text in a view, in the *Annotate* tab>Text panel, click ^{ABC} (Spelling) or press <F7>. As with other spell checkers, you can **Ignore**, **Add**, or **Change** the word.

- You can also check the spelling in selected text. With text selected, in the *Modify | Text Notes* tab>Tools panel, click ^{ABC} (Check Spelling).

Creating Text Types

If you need new text types with a different text size or font (such as for a title or hand-lettering), you can create new ones, as shown in Figure 13–47. It is recommended that you create these in a project template so they are available in future projects.

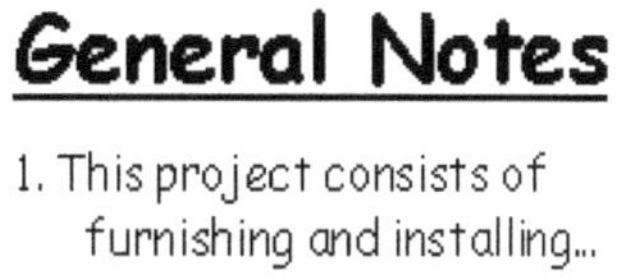

General Notes

1. This project consists of
   furnishing and installing...

Figure 13–47

- You can copy and paste text types from one project to another or use **Transfer Project Standards**.

How To: Create Text Types

1. In the *Annotate* tab>Text panel, click (Text Types).
2. In the Type Properties dialog box, click **Duplicate**.
3. In the Name dialog box, type a new name and click **OK**.

4. Modify the text parameters, as required. The parameters are shown in Figure 13–48.

Parameter	Value
Graphics	⌃
Color	■ Black
Line Weight	1
Background	Opaque
Show Border	☐
Leader/Border Offset	5/64"
Leader Arrowhead	Arrow 30 Degree
Text	⌃
Text Font	Arial
Text Size	1/4"
Tab Size	1/2"
Bold	☐
Italic	☐
Underline	☐
Width Factor	1.000000

Figure 13–48

- The **Background** parameter can be set to **Opaque** or **Transparent**. An opaque background includes a masking region that hides lines or elements beneath the text.

- In the *Text* area, the **Width Factor** parameter controls the width of the lettering, but does not affect the height. A width factor greater than **1** spreads the text out and a width factor less than **1** compresses it.

- The **Show Border** parameter, when selected, includes a rectangle around the text.

5. Click **OK** to close the Type Properties dialog box.

Practice 13b

Work with Text

Practice Objectives

- Add text notes.
- Modify text with lists.

In this practice you will add text into a structural plan view and a framing elevation, as shown in Figure 13–49. You will then copy in a text note and create a numbered list.

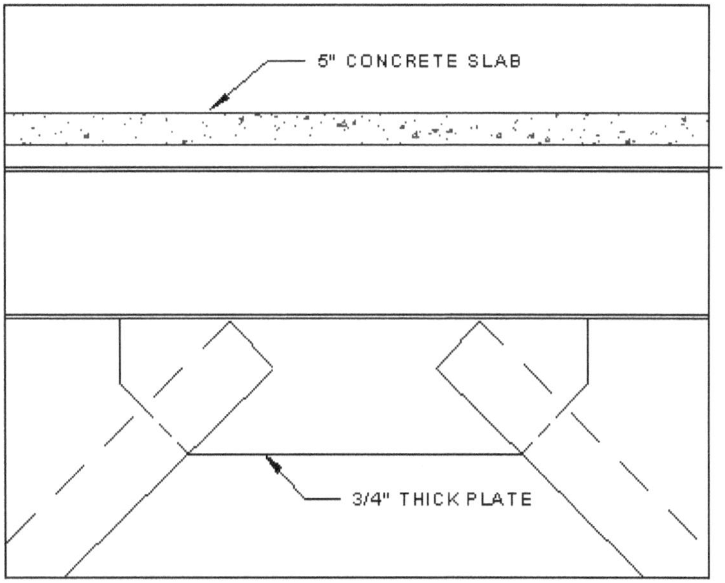

Estimated time for completion: 10 minutes

5" CONCRETE SLAB

3/4" THICK PLATE

Figure 13–49

Task 1 - Add text to a structural plan view.

1. Open **Syracuse-Suites-Text.rvt.**

2. Open the **Structural Plans: TOS-1ST FLOOR - Dimensioned** view.

3. Zoom in on the upper left corner of the plan.

4. In the *Annotate* tab>Text panel, click **A** (Text).

5. In the Type Selector, select **Text: 3/32" Arial**.

6. In the *Modify | Place text* tab>Leader panel, click ⟋ᴬ (Two Segments).

7. Select the first point so that the text points to the slab edge. This is what you are going to label. Select the second point any distance away from the first point.

8. Type **Slab Edge** (in Titlecase) and click ▷ (Modify).

9. Position the text as required.

10. Double click on the text so that the *Edit Text* tab opens.

11. Highlight all of the letters and in the *Edit Text* tab>Font panel, click ᵃÃ (All Caps). The text updates as shown in Figure 13–50. Close the *Edit Text* tab

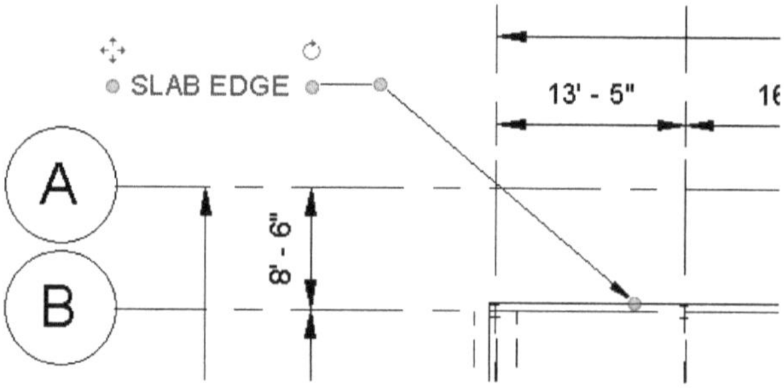

Figure 13–50

12. Zoom out to fit the view.

13. Save the project.

Task 2 - Add text to a framing elevation.

1. Open the **Elevations (Framing Elevation): Typical Top Plate** view.

2. Modify the location of the level markers so that they do not overlap the view.

Do you use uppercase letters for your notes? It is not important anymore because of the clarity of typed in text. Check your office standards.

3. Add the text leaders **3/4" THICK PLATE** and **5" CONCRETE SLAB**, as shown in Figure 13–51.

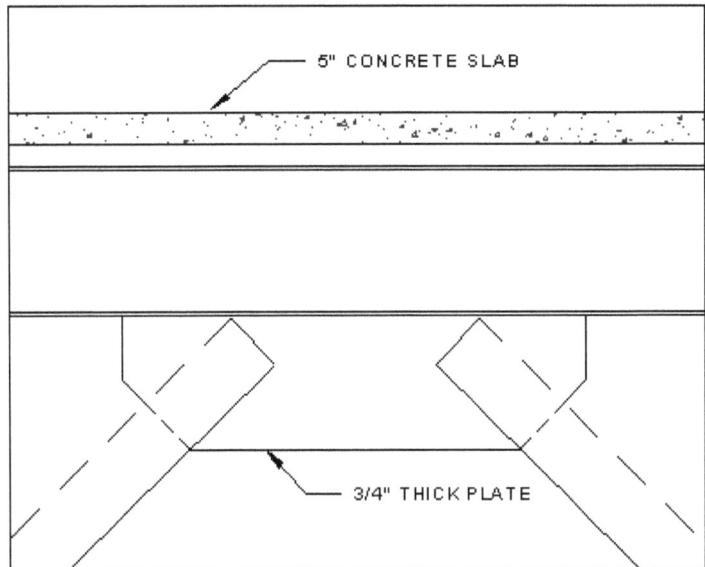

Figure 13–51

4. Save the project.

Task 3 - Add General Notes and create lists.

1. Open the **S-000 - COVER SHEET** view.

2. Zoom in on the area with the Symbol Legend.

3. Start the **Text** command and in the *Modify | Place Text* tab> Leader panel, click **A** (No Leader).

4. In the Type Selector, select **Text: 1/8" Arial**.

5. Click and drag to place a box similar to Figure 13–52.

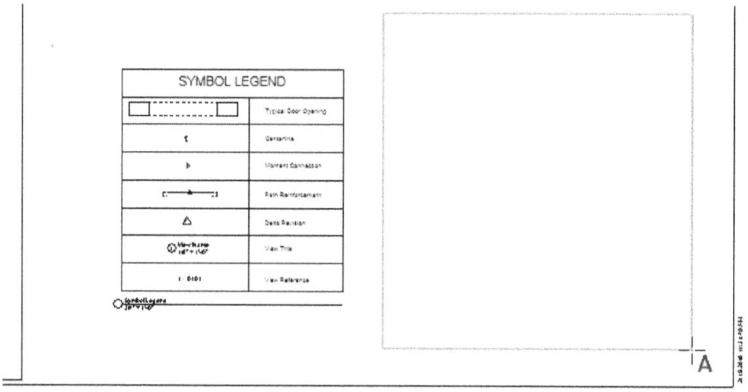

Figure 13–52

6. In Microsoft Word or another text editor, open **Structural Steel Notes.docx** or **Structural Steel Notes.txt**.

7. Select all of the text and copy it to the clipboard (type <Ctrl>+C).

8. Return to Autodesk Revit and in the *Edit Text* tab>Clipboard panel, click (Paste). The text is added as shown in Figure 13–53.

Figure 13–53

9. Zoom in and modify the text so it resembles that in Figure 13–54.

- Select the **Notes** heading and click $^a\widehat{A}$ (All Caps).

- Set the **A. B.** and **C.** headings to **B** (Bold).

- Select each group of text and click ≣ (List: Numbers).

- Change the indented list to ≣ (List: Uppercase Letters).

STRUCTURAL STEEL NOTES

A. CODES AND SPECIFICATIONS
1. ABC BUILDING CODE, 2010.
2. ASCE 7-05. MINIMUM DESIGN LOADS FOR BUILDINGS AND OTHER STRUCTURES.
3. ACI 301-05 SPECIFICATIONS FOR STRUCTURAL CONCRETE FOR BUILDINGS AS MODIFIED BY THE CONSTRUCTION DOCUMENTS.
4. AISC 303-05 CODE OF STANDARD PRACTICE FOR STEEL BUILDINGS AND BRIDGES AS MODIFIED BY THE CONSTRUCTION DOCUMENTS.
5. ANSI/AWS D1.1 STRUCTURAL WELDING CODE - STEEL

B. FOUNDATIONS
1. THE FOUNDATION DESIGN IS BASED UPON THE RECOMMEDATIONS INCLUDED IN THE REPORT OF GEOTECHNICAL EXPLORATION PREPARED BY H.C. NUTTING, DATED MAY 17, 2011.
2. FOUNDATION ELEVATIONS SHOWN ARE ESTIMATED AND ARE FOR BIDDING PURPOSES ONLY. ACTUAL ELEVATIONS MAY VARY TO SUIT SUBSURFACE SOIL CONDITIONS.
3. COLUMN SPREAD FOOTINGS ARE DESIGNED FOR A MAXIMUM BEARING PRESSURE OF 3000 PSF. BASEMENT WALL FOOTING MAXIMUM BEARING PRESSURE 2500 PSF. NON-BASEMENT WALL FOOTINGS MAXIMUM BEARING PRESSURE 2000 PSF. SOILS UNSUITABLE FOR SUPPORTING FOUNDATIONS SHALL BE REMOVED AS DIRECTED BY THE GEOTECHNICAL ENGINEER, AND BACKFILLED TO DESIGN BEARING ELEVATION WITH LEAN CONCRETE.
4. ALL BEARING SURFACES SHALL BE UNDISTURBED, LEVEL (WITHIN 1 IN 12), AND SHALL BE APPROVED BY THE GEOTECHNICAL ENGINEER PRIOR TO PLACING CONCRETE.
5. UNLESS APPROVED OTHERWISE BY THE GEOTECHNICAL ENGINEER AND THE STRUCTURAL ENGINEER, ALL FOOTINGS ARE TO BE POURED NEAT (WITHOUT SIDE FORMS). WHERE EARTH CUTS WILL NOT STAND, SIDES SHALL BE FORMED, SUBJECT TO ENGINEERS' APPROVAL.
6. SET COLUMN DOWELS AND ANCHOR RODS WITH TEMPLATE PRIOR TO CONCRETING.

C. CONCRETE
1. CONCRETE STRENGTHS:
   A. FOOTINGS AND GRADE BEAMS: 3000 PSI
   B. EXTERIOR CONCRETE EXPOSED TO WEATHER: 4500 PSI AE
   C. TYPICAL CONCRETE UNLESS NOTED OTHERWISE: 4000 PSI
   D. INTERIOR CONCRETE SLABS ON METAL DECK: 4000 PSI NORMAL WEIGHT
   E. BACKFILL (LEAN) CONCRETE: 1000 PSI
2. PROVIDE 3/4" BEVELS AT CORNERS OF ALL EXPOSED COLUMNS, EDGES OF EXPOSED BEAMS AND SLABS, AND TOP EDGES AND CORNERS OF EXPOSED WALLS.
3. MAXIMUM LENGTH OF WALL POUR BETWEEN CONSTRUCTION JOINTS SHALL NOT EXCEED 120 FEET. MAXIMUM LENGTH OF SLAB POURS BETWEEN CONSTRUCTION JOINTS SHALL NOT EXCEED 120 FEET. MAXIMUM AREA OF SLAB POURS NOT TO EXCEED 10,000 SF.
4. JOINTS NOT INDICATED ON STRUCTURAL DRAWINGS ARE NOT PERMITTED UNLESS APPROVED BY STRUCTURAL ENGINEER.
5. PLACE NO OPENINGS, SLEEVES, INSERTS, ETC., IN CONCRETE WORK UNLESS CRITERIA INDICATED ON STRUCTURAL DRAWINGS IS MET, OR IS APPROVED IN WRITING BY THE STRUCTURAL ENGINEER.
6. CONCRETE CONSTRUCTION TOLERANCES ARE AS SHOWN IN THE PROJECT SPECIFICATIONS.

Figure 13–54

10. Zoom out to see the full sheet.

11. Save the project.

13.3 Adding Tags

Tags identify elements that are listed in schedules. Some tags are inserted automatically if you use the **Tag on Placement** option when inserting the elements. You can also add them later to specific views as required. Many other types of tags are available in the Autodesk® Revit® software, such as structural column tags and structural framing tags, as shown in Figure 13–55.

Additional tags are stored in the Library in the Annotations folder.

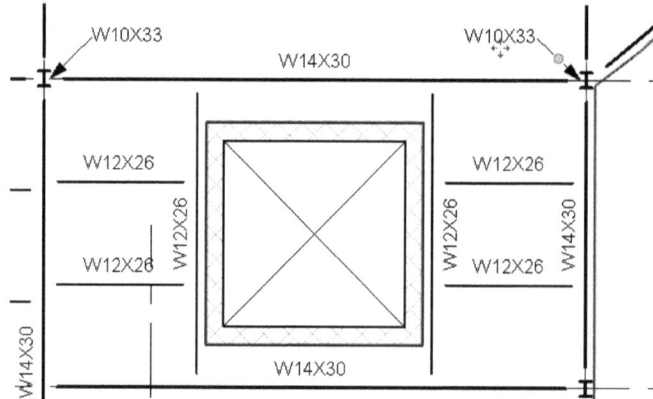

Figure 13–55

- The **Tag by Category** command works for most elements, except for a few that have separate commands.

- Tags can be letters, numbers, or a combination of the two.

You can place three types of tags, as follows:

- (Tag by Category): Tags according to the category of the element. It places column tags on columns and wall tags on walls.

- (Multi-Category): Tags elements belonging to multiple categories. The tags display information from parameters that they have in common.

- (Material): Tags that display the type of material. They are typically used in detailing.

How To: Add Tags

1. In the *Annotate* tab>Tag panel, click ⌐① (Tag by Category), ⌐ (Multi-Category), or ⌐ (Material Tag) depending on the type of tag you want to place.
2. In the Options Bar, set the options as required, as shown in Figure 13–56.

| Modify | Tag | | 🖳 Horizontal ▾ | Tags... | ☑ Leader | Attached End | ▾ | ↦ | 1/2" |

Figure 13–56

3. Select the element you want to tag. If a tag for the selected element is not loaded, you are prompted to load it from the Library.

Tag Options

*   You can set tag options for leaders and tag rotation, as shown in Figure 13–57. You can also press <Spacebar> to toggle the orientation while placing or modifying the tag.

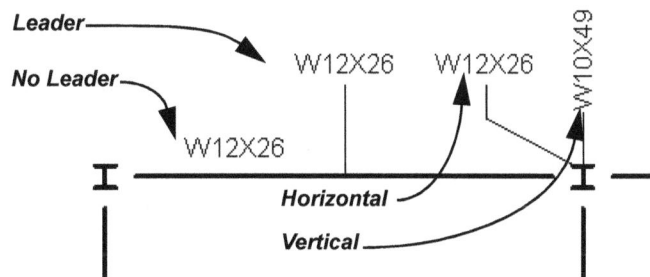

Figure 13–57

*   Leaders can have an **Attached End** or a **Free End**, as shown in Figure 13–58. The attached end must be connected to the element being tagged. A free end has an additional drag control where the leader touches the element.

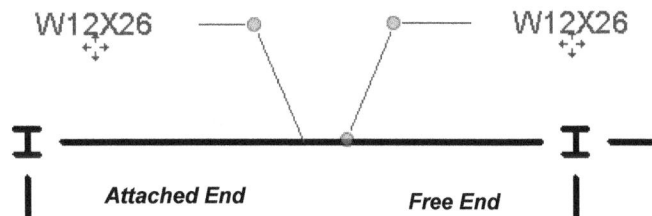

Figure 13–58

- If you change between **Attached End** and **Free End**, the tag does not move and the leader does not change location.

- The **Length** option specifies the length of the leader in plotting units. It is grayed out if **Leader** is not selected or if a **Free End** leader is defined.

- If a tag is not loaded a warning box opens as shown in Figure 13–59. Click **Yes** to open the Load Family dialog box in which you can select the appropriate tag.

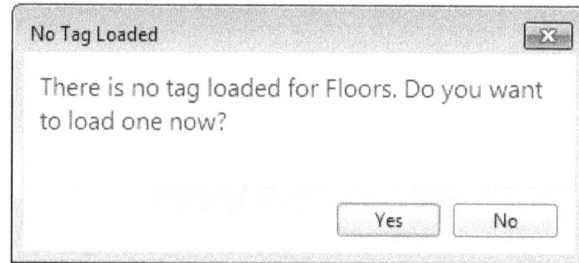

Figure 13–59

- Tags can be pinned to they stay in place if you move the element that is tagged. This is primarily used when tags have leaders.

- Some structural elements (such as Fabric Sheets, Area Reinforcements, etc.), have both tags and symbols, as shown in Figure 13–60.

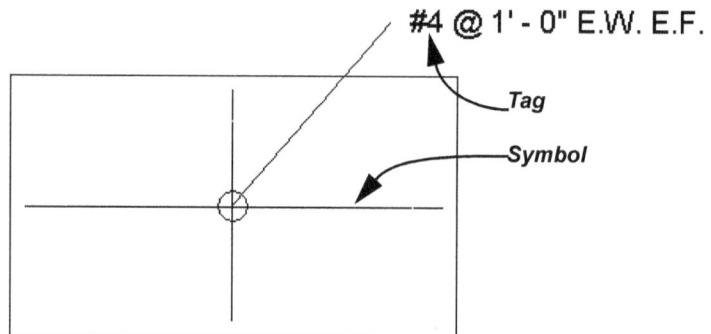

Figure 13–60

How To: Add Multiple Tags

Enhanced
in 2018

1. In the *Annotate* tab>Tag panel, click (Tag All).
2. In the Tag All Not Tagged dialog box (shown in Figure 13–61), select the checkbox beside one or more categories to tag. Selecting the checkbox beside the Category title selects all of the tags.

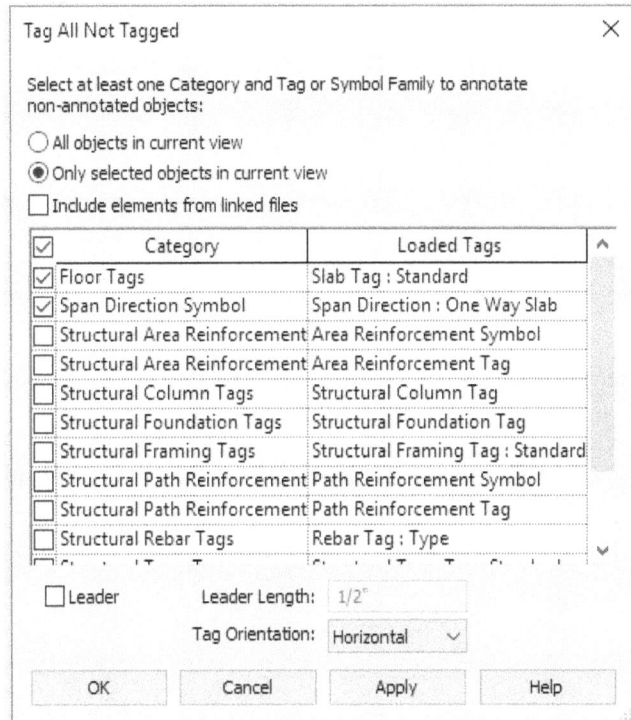

*To tag only some elements, select them before starting this command. In the Tag All Not Tagged dialog box, select **Only selected objects in current view**.*

Tag All Not Tagged   ✕

Select at least one Category and Tag or Symbol Family to annotate
non-annotated objects:

◯ All objects in current view
◉ Only selected objects in current view
☐ Include elements from linked files

☑	Category	Loaded Tags	⌃
☑	Floor Tags	Slab Tag : Standard	
☑	Span Direction Symbol	Span Direction : One Way Slab	
☐	Structural Area Reinforcement	Area Reinforcement Symbol	
☐	Structural Area Reinforcement	Area Reinforcement Tag	
☐	Structural Column Tags	Structural Column Tag	
☐	Structural Foundation Tags	Structural Foundation Tag	
☐	Structural Framing Tags	Structural Framing Tag : Standard	
☐	Structural Path Reinforcement	Path Reinforcement Symbol	
☐	Structural Path Reinforcement	Path Reinforcement Tag	
☐	Structural Rebar Tags	Rebar Tag : Type	⌄

☐ Leader   Leader Length: 1/2"

                  Tag Orientation: Horizontal ⌄

| OK | Cancel | Apply | Help |

Figure 13–61

3. Set the *Leader* and *Tag Orientation* as required.
4. Click **Apply** to apply the tags and stay in the dialog box. Click **OK** to apply the tags and close the dialog box.

• When you select a tag, the properties of that tag display. To display the properties of the tagged element, in the

   Modify | *<contextual>* tab>Host panel click (Select Host).

How To: Load Tags

1. In the *Annotate* tab, expand the Tag panel and click

   (Loaded Tags And Symbols) or, when a Tag command is active, in the Options Bar click **Tags...**
2. In the Loaded Tags And Symbols dialog box (shown in Figure 13–62), click **Load Family...**

Loaded Tags And Symbols		✕

Select an available Tag or Symbol Family for each Family Category listed

Note: Multi-Category Tag Families are not shown below.

Filter list: `<multiple>`   Load Family...

Category	Loaded Tags	Loaded Symbols	^
Supports			
Structural Area...	Area Reinforcement T	Area Reinforcement S	
Structural Bea...	Structural Beam Syste		
Structural Col...	Structural Column Ta		
Structural Con...			
Structural Fabr...			
Structural Fou...	Structural Foundatior		
Structural Fra...	Structural Framing Ta		
⊟ Structural Inter...			
Internal Ar...			
Internal Li...			
Internal Po...			˅

OK   Cancel   Help

Figure 13–62

3. In the Load Family dialog box, navigate to the appropriate *Annotations* folder, select the tag(s) required and click **Open**.
4. The tag is added to the category in the dialog box. Click **OK**.

Instance vs.Type Based Tags

Some elements are tagged in a numbered sequence, with each instance of the element having a separate tag number. Other elements (such as trusses and walls) are tagged by type. Changing the information in one tag changes all instances of that element.

- To modify the number of an instance tag (such as a door or room), double-click directly on the number in the tag and modify it, or, you can modify the *Mark* property. Only that one instance updates.

- To modify the number of a type tag, you can either double-click directly on the number in the tag and modify it, or select the element and, in Properties, click ⊞ (Edit Type). In the Type Properties dialog box, in the *Identity Data* area, modify the *Type Mark*, as shown in Figure 13–63. All instances of this element then update.

Figure 13–63

- When you change a type tag, an alert box opens to warn you that changing a type parameter affects other elements. If you want this tag to modify all other elements of this type, click **Yes**.

- If a type tag displays with a question mark, it means that no Type Mark has been assigned yet.

Hint: Tagging Elements in Detail Views

When you tag elements in a cropped view, the tag is placed at the default location of the element and might not display in the callout. In the View Control Bar, click ⌨ (Do not Crop). Tag the elements, and then move the new tags in the crop window, as shown in Figure 13–64. Click ⌨ (Crop View) to return to the area of the callout view.

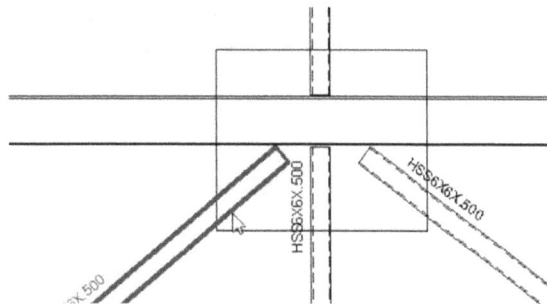

Figure 13–64

Tagging in 3D Views

You can add tags (and some dimensions) to 3D views, as shown in Figure 13–65, as long as the views are locked first. You can only add tags in isometric views.

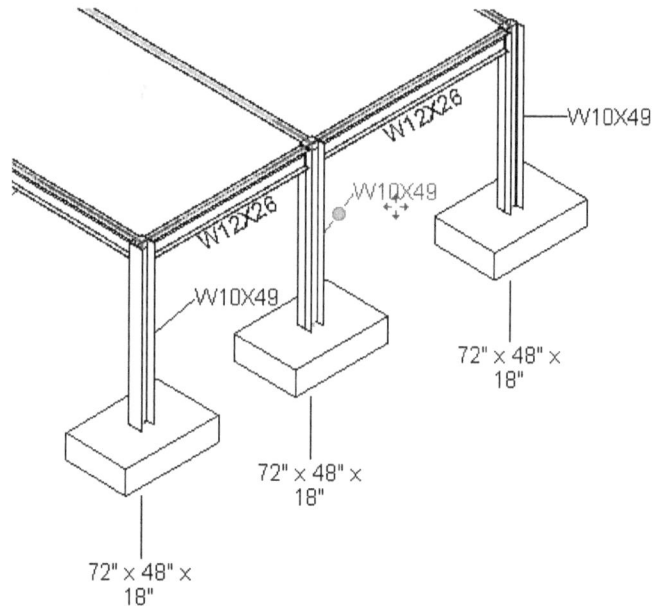

Figure 13–65

- Locked views can be used with perspective views. This enables you to create the view as you want it and then save it from being modified.

How To: Lock a 3D View

1. Open a 3D view and set it up as you want it to display.

2. In the View Control Bar, expand 🏠 (Unlocked 3D View) and click 🏠 (Save Orientation and Lock View).

- If you are using the default 3D view and it has not been saved, you are prompted to name and save the view first.

- You can modify the orientation of the view, expand 🏠 (Locked 3D View) and click 🏠 (Unlock View). This also removes any tags you have applied.

- To return to the previous locked view, expand 🏠 (Unlocked 3D View) and click 🏠 (Restore Orientation and Lock View).

Beam Annotations

The Beam Annotation tools enable you to place beam tags, annotations, and spot elevations to all elements in a view, as shown in Figure 13–66.

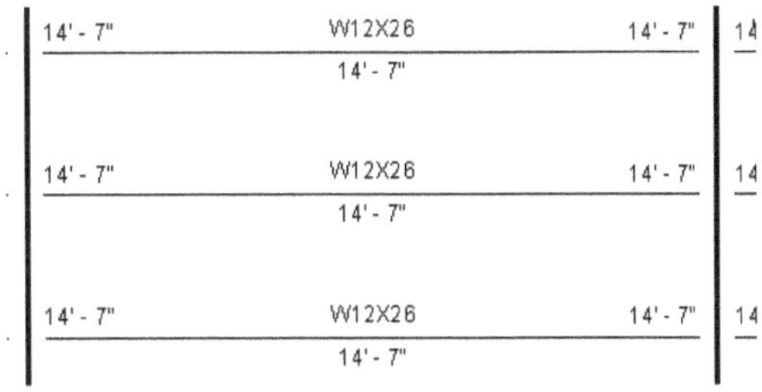

Figure 13–66

- Beam annotations can be put at the end points and midpoints on either side of beams. You can also specify different annotations for level beams and sloped beams.

- To limit the number of beams that are annotated, select them first and then start the command. Otherwise, all of the beams in a view are annotated.

- Beams in linked files can be included.

- You can replace existing annotations or leave them in place without duplicating them.

- You can define values for steel connection parameters, including releases and member forces. These values can be used by the designer, fabricator, and analysis applications. They are available for use in schedules and annotations.

How To: Place Beam Annotations

1. In the *Annotate* tab>Tag panel, click ☷ (Beam Annotations).
2. In the Beam Annotations dialog box, as shown in Figure 13–67, specify the locations of the annotation at which you want them to display on each beam.

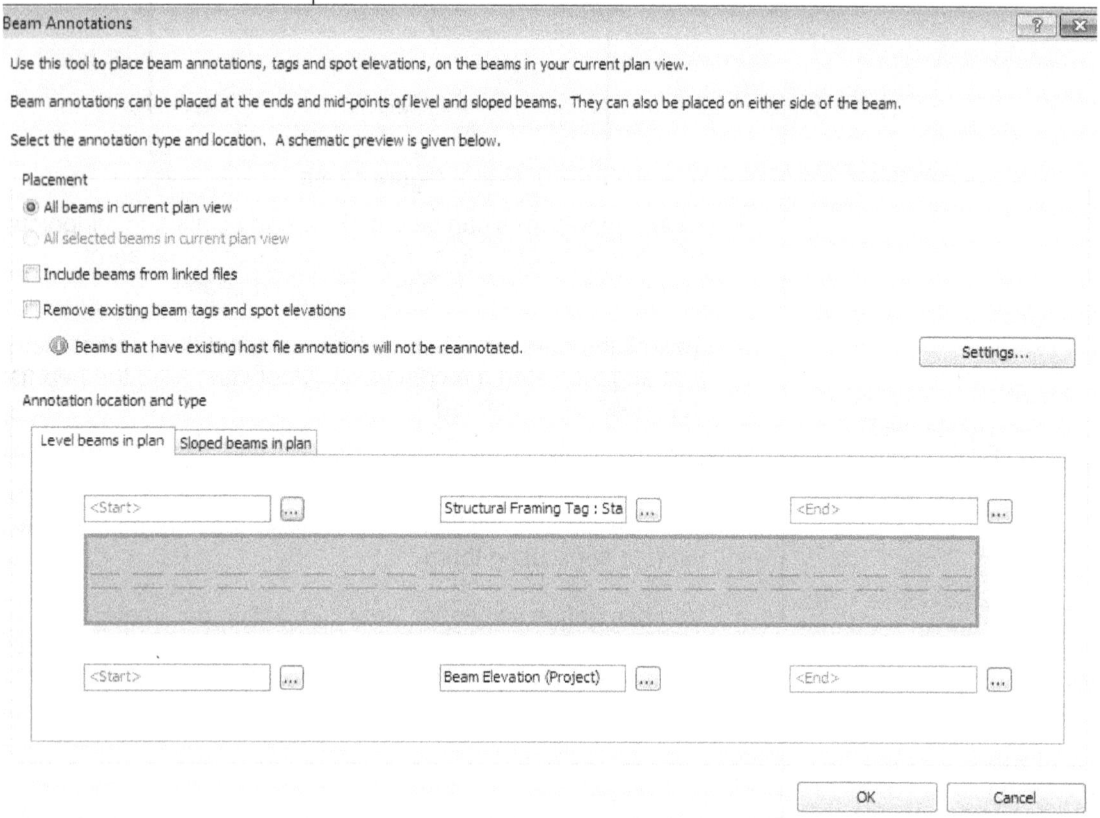

Beam Annotations   ? ✕

Use this tool to place beam annotations, tags and spot elevations, on the beams in your current plan view.

Beam annotations can be placed at the ends and mid-points of level and sloped beams. They can also be placed on either side of the beam.

Select the annotation type and location. A schematic preview is given below.

Placement

◉ All beams in current plan view

◯ All selected beams in current plan view

☐ Include beams from linked files

☐ Remove existing beam tags and spot elevations

ⓘ Beams that have existing host file annotations will not be reannotated.   [Settings...]

Annotation location and type

| Level beams in plan | Sloped beams in plan |

| <Start> | [...] | Structural Framing Tag : Sta | [...] | <End> | [...] |

| <Start> | [...] | Beam Elevation (Project) | [...] | <End> | [...] |

[OK] [Cancel]

Figure 13–67

3. To change the type of annotation at various locations, click

   ⬚ (Browse) next to the edit box to open the Select
   Annotation Type dialog box, shown in Figure 13–68.

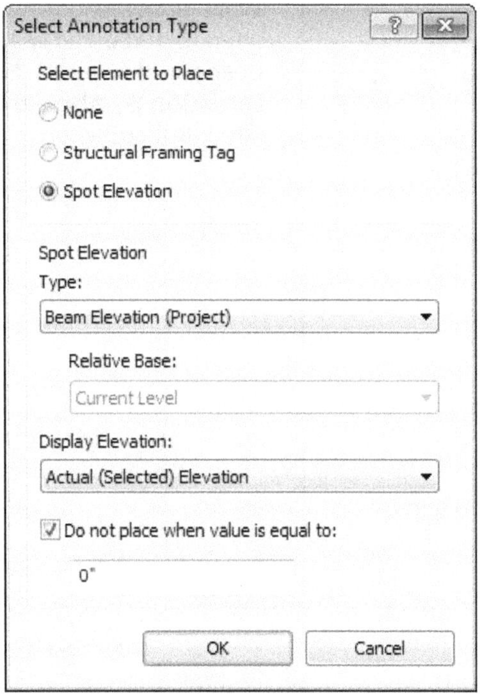

Figure 13–68

4. Specify the options in the dialog box and click **OK**.

5. Click **OK** to place the beam annotations.

13.4 Adding Detail Lines and Symbols

While annotating views for construction documents, you might need to add detail lines and symbols to clarify the design intent or show information. Several symbols, such as the **Span Direction Symbol** (shown in Figure 13–69), are specific to structural projects.

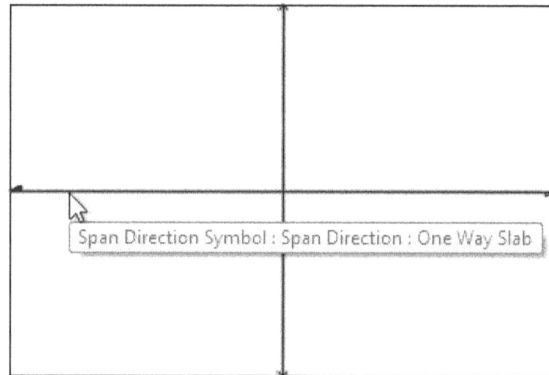

Span Direction Symbol : Span Direction : One Way Slab

Figure 13–69

- Detail lines and symbols are view-specific, which means that they only display in the view in which they were created.

How To: Draw Detail Lines

1. In the *Annotation* tab>Detail panel, click ⬚ (Detail Line).
2. In the *Modify | Place Detail Lines* tab>Line Style panel, select the type of line you want to use, as shown in Figure 13–70.

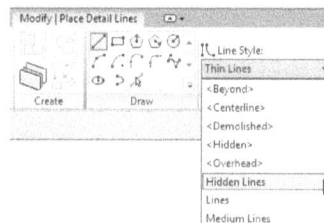

Figure 13–70

3. Use the tools in the Draw panel to create the detail lines.

Using Symbols

Symbols are 2D elements that only display in one view, while components can be in 3D and display in many views.

Many of the annotations used in working drawings are frequently repeated. Several of them have been saved as symbols in the Autodesk Revit software, such as the North Arrow, Center Line, and Graphic Scale annotations as shown in Figure 13–71.

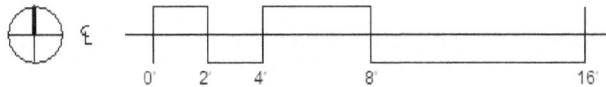

Figure 13–71

- You can also create or load custom annotation symbols.

How To: Place a Symbol

1. In the *Annotate* tab>Symbol panel, click (Symbol).
2. In the Type Selector, select the symbol you want to use.
3. In the *Modify | Place Symbol* tab>Mode panel, click

   (Load Family) if you want to load other symbols.
4. In the Options Bar, as shown in Figure 13–72, set the *Number of Leaders* and select **Rotate after placement** if you want to rotate the symbol as you insert it.

Figure 13–72

5. Place the symbol in the view. Rotate it if you selected the **Rotate after placement** option. If you specified leaders, use the controls to move them into place.

Structural Specific Symbols

Several types of structural elements use symbols or symbols and tags together. If the associated symbols are not applied when you create the element, you can add them later. They are found in the *Annotate* tab>Symbol panel, as shown in Figure 13–73.

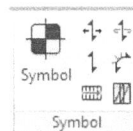

Figure 13–73

- You can also use the **Tag All Not Tagged** command to add symbols to a view.

How To: Add Reinforcement Symbols

1. In the *Annotate* tab>Symbol panel, click the type of symbol you want to use:

   ↑ (Beam System Symbol)

   ↔↑↔ (Span Direction Symbol)

   ⊸↑ (Area Reinforcement Symbol)

   ↱ (Path Reinforcement Symbol)

   ▨ (Fabric Reinforcement Symbol)

2. Select the related reinforcement element (not the individual rebar).

3. Select a location for the symbol. The symbol expands to fit the extents of the beam system, as shown for **Path Reinforcement** in Figure 13–74.

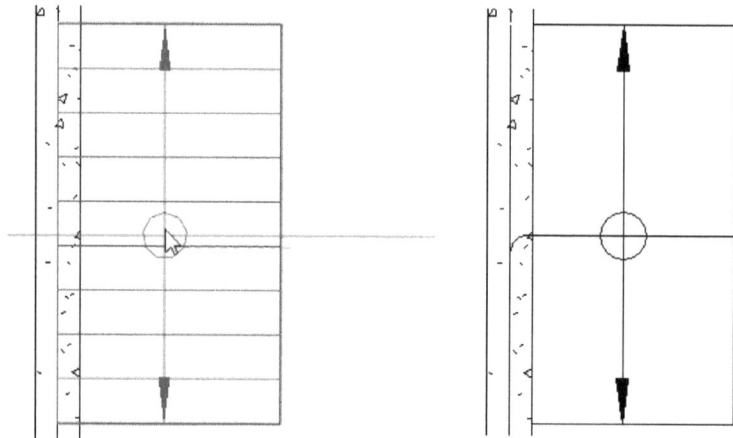

Figure 13–74

4. You can continue selecting similar elements and placing the symbol.

5. When you are finished, click �“ (Modify) or press <Esc> to end the command.

- To add a tag to the reinforcement elements, use the ⌐① (Tag by Category) command.

Changing the Span Direction of Floors and Slabs

By default, span direction symbols are added when you create a structural floor or foundation slab. They can be used to change the span direction of the floor or slab without having to edit the sketch. You can modify the floor span direction symbol once it is in the view through the Type Selector, as shown in Figure 13–75. (Note that Foundation Span Direction Symbols do not have these choices.)

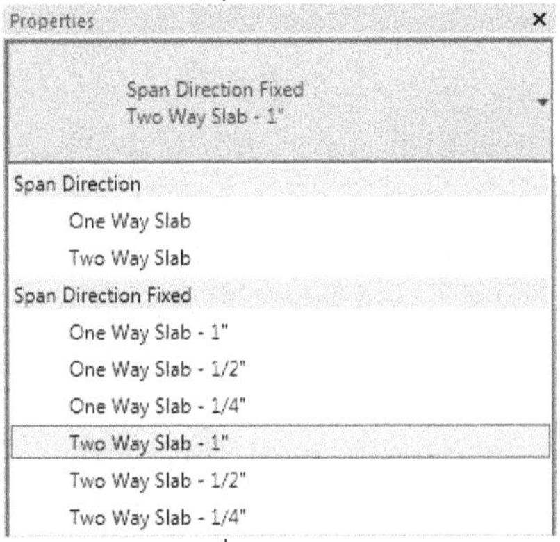

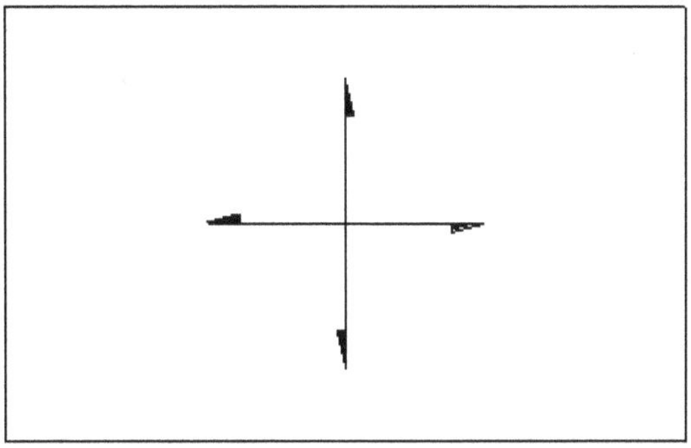

Figure 13–75

How To: Change the Span Direction

1. Select the Span Direction symbol.
2. In the *Modify | Span Direction Symbol* tab>Align Symbol panel, click ⬚ (Align Perpendicular).
3. Select the side of the slab that you want the span to be perpendicular to.
4. The Span Direction Symbol changes direction, as shown in Figure 13–76.

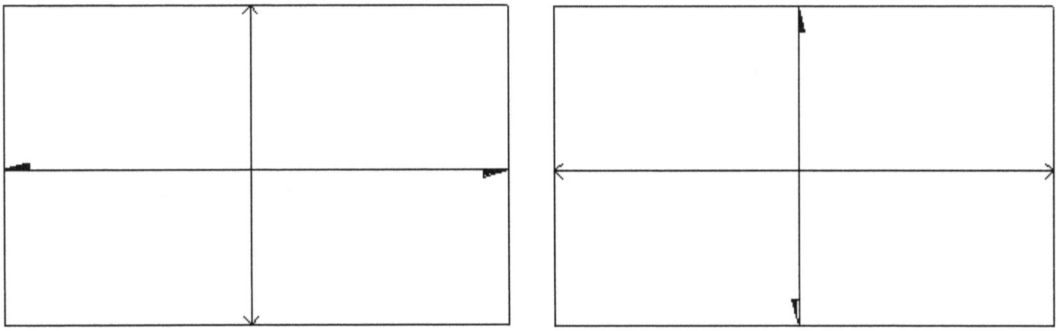

Figure 13–76

Beam System Symbols verses Framing Tags

Beam Systems can be annotated by either tagging each individual beam, or by using a beam system symbol, as shown in Figure 13–77. When placing a beam system, you can select

(Tag on Placement), and in the Options Bar, set the *Tag Style* to either **Framing** or **System**. The *Framing* option tags each beam in the system, while the *System* option applies a beam system symbol.

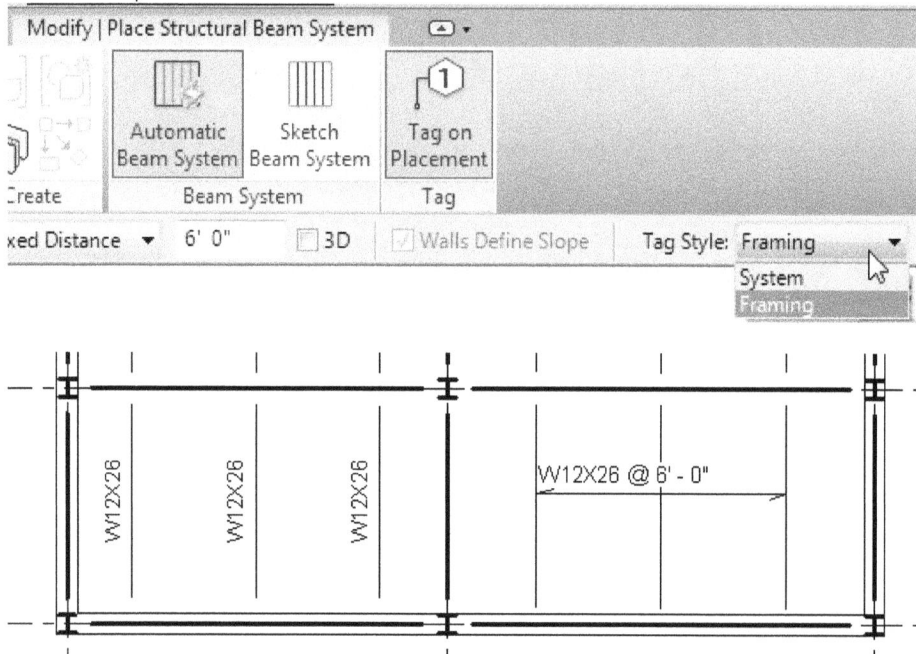

Figure 13–77

- To add the individual framing tags later, use the (Tag by Category) command. To add a Beam System Symbol use the

  (Beam System Symbol) command.

Practice 13c | Add Tags and Symbols

Practice Objectives

- Add tags.
- Place Beam System Symbols.

Estimated time for completion: 10 minutes.

In this practice you will tag some framing elements using the **Tag by Category** command and the **Beam System Symbol.** You will then use **Tag All Not Tagged** to tag the rest of the framing elements. You will then add the rest of the beam system symbols, as shown in Figure 13–78.

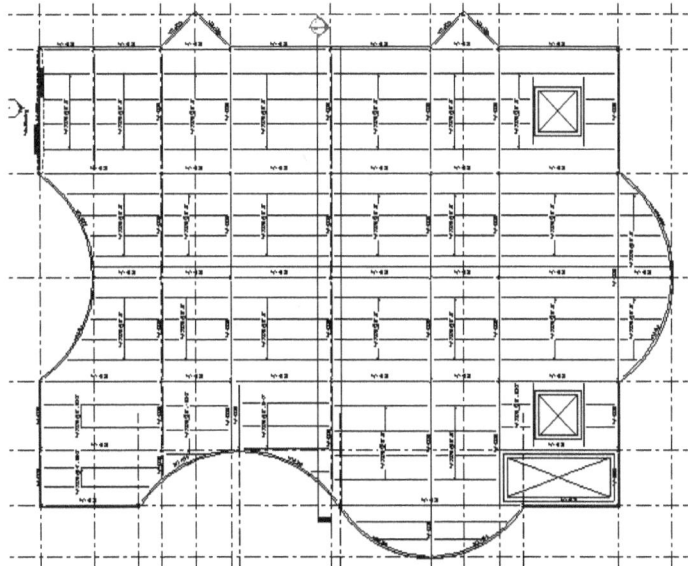

Figure 13–78

Task 1 - Tag framing elements using Tag by Category and Beam System Symbol.

1. Open **Syracuse-Suites-Tags.rvt**.

2. Create a duplicate of the **Structural Plans: TOS-1ST FLOOR** view and name it **TOS-1ST FLOOR - Framing.**

3. In the *Annotate* tab>Tag panel, click ⌐① (Tag by Category).

4. In the Options Bar, ensure that **Leader** is not selected.

5. Tag several of the outside beams, as shown in Figure 13–79.

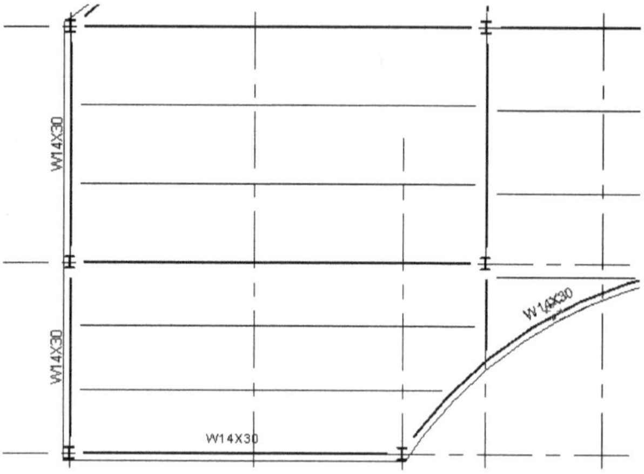

Figure 13–79

6. While still in the command, hover the cursor over the inside beams. Note that you can tag each beam separately.

7. Click � (Modify)

8. In the *Annotate* tab>Symbol panel, click ↑ (Beam System Symbol).

9. Click on a beam system and then click to place the location of the symbol. It automatically fits to the correct size of the beam system, as shown in Figure 13–80.

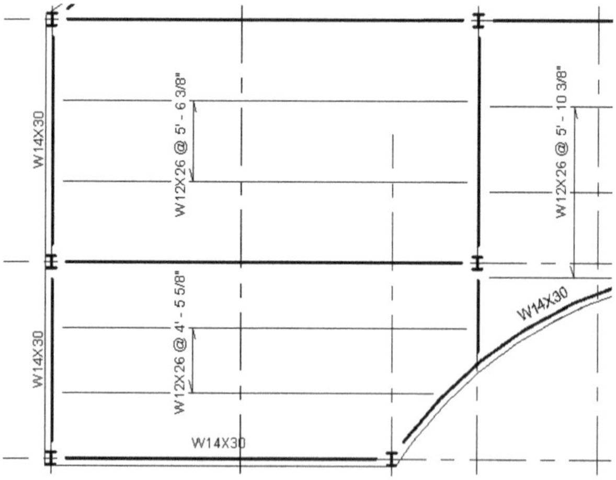

Figure 13–80

10. Save the project.

Task 2 - Tag framing elements that are not tagged.

1. Continue working in the **TOS-1ST FLOOR - Framing** view.

2. In the *Annotate* tab>Tag panel, click 🪧① (Tag All).

3. In the Tagged All Not Tagged dialog box, ensure that **All objects in current view** is selected.

4. Browse to the *Structural Framing* category and select **Structural Framing Tag: Standard**, as shown in Figure 13–81. Click **OK**.

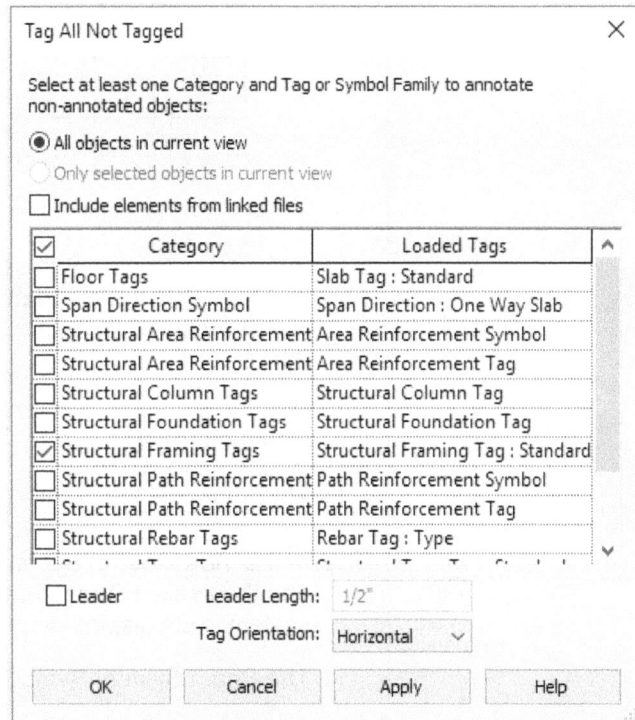

Figure 13–81

5. This tags all of the structural framing elements, including each one of the breams in the beam systems.

6. Undo the tagging.

7. Select one of the beam system joist beams in the framing system.

8. Right-click and select **Select All Instances>Visible in View**. All of the joists that are the same are selected, as shown in Figure 13–82.

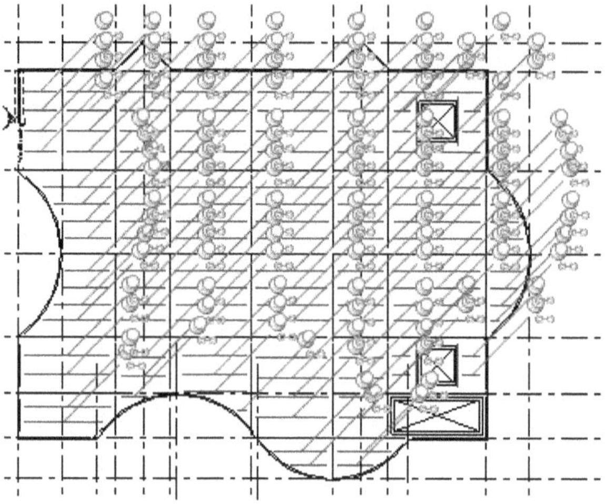

Figure 13–82

9. In the View Control Bar, select ✣ (Temporary Hide/Isolate) and then select **Hide Element**. (Do not hide the category as you still want to be able to tag the rest of the beams.

10. Run the ⬚ (Tag All) command again, selecting the same structural framing tag.

11. This time only the non-joist beams are tagged.

12. In the View Control Bar, select ✣ (Temporary Hide/Isolate) and then select **Reset Temporary Hide/Isolate**. The beam system joists display once again.

13. The Beam System Symbol is not available in **Tag All Not Tagged**, therefore you need to use the ⌐ (Beam System Symbol) to tag the rest of these. Use the alignment lines to help you place the symbols relative to other nearby symbols.

14. Zoom to fit the view.

15. If you have time, you can apply the various reinforcement symbols to other views as applicable.

16. Save the project.

13.5 Creating Legends

A legend is a separate view that can be placed on multiple sheets. Legends can be used to hold installation notes that need to be placed on a sheet with each floor plan, key plans, or any 2D items that need to be repeated. You can also create and list the symbols that are used in your project, and provide explanatory notes next to the, as shown in Figure 13–83.

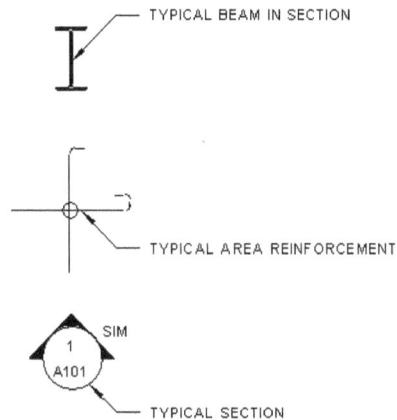

TYPICAL BEAM IN SECTION

TYPICAL AREA REINFORCEMENT

SIM
1
A101

TYPICAL SECTION

Figure 13–83

- You use ⬚ (Detail Lines) and A (Text) to create the table and explanatory notes. Once you have a legend view, you can use commands, such as ⬚ (Legend Component), ⬚ (Detail Component), and ⬚ (Symbol), to place elements in the view.

- Unlike other views, legend views can be attached to more than one sheet.

- You can set a legend's scale in the View Status Bar.

- Elements in legends can be dimensioned.

How To: Create a Legend

1. In the *View* tab>Create panel, expand ⬚ (Legends) and click ⬚ (Legend) or in the Project Browser, right-click on the *Legends* area title and select **New Legend**.

2. In the New Legend View dialog box, enter a name and select a scale for the legend, as shown in Figure 13–84, and click **OK**.

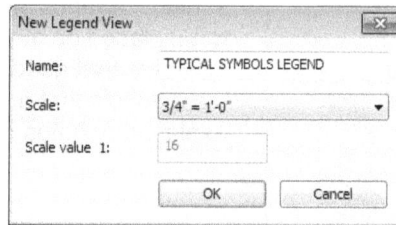

New Legend View	
Name:	TYPICAL SYMBOLS LEGEND
Scale:	3/4" = 1'-0"
Scale value 1:	16
	OK Cancel

Figure 13–84

3. Place the components in the view first, and then sketch the outline of the table when you know the sizes. Use **Ref Planes** to line up the components.

How To: Use Legend Components

1. In the *Annotate* tab>Detail panel, expand ⬜ (Component) and click ▦ (Legend Component).
2. In the Options Bar, select the *Family* type that you want to use, as shown in Figure 13–85.

   • This list contains all of the elements in a project that can be used in a legend.

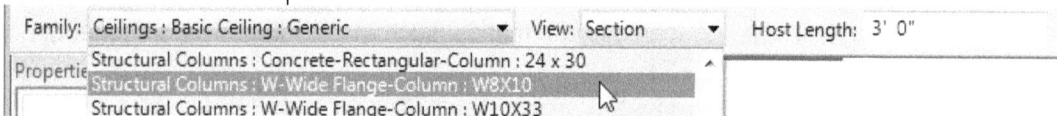

Family: Ceilings : Basic Ceiling : Generic ▼ View: Section ▼ Host Length: 3' 0"

Propertie Structural Columns : Concrete-Rectangular-Column : 24 x 30
Structural Columns : W-Wide Flange-Column : W8X10
Structural Columns : W-Wide Flange-Column : W10X33

Figure 13–85

3. Select the *View* of the element that you want to use. For example, you might want to display the section of the floors, as shown in Figure 13–86.

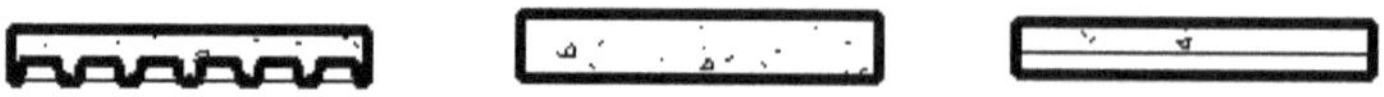

Figure 13–86

4. For section elements (such as walls, floors, and roofs), type a distance for the *Host Length*.

   • Elements that are full size, such as planting components or doors, come in at their full size.

Practice 13d | Create Legends

Practice Objective

- Create legends using legend components and text.

Estimated time for completion: 10 minutes

In this practice you will add a legend and populate it with Legend Components, Symbols, associated text, and detail lines (as shown in Figure 13–87), as well as create a Key Plan for use on multiple sheets.

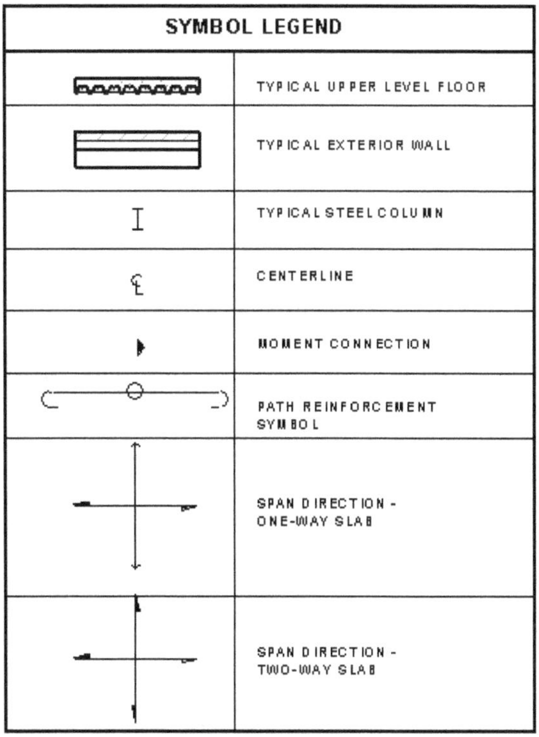

Figure 13–87

Task 1 - .Add a Symbol legend.

1. Open **Syracuse-Suites-Legends.rvt**.

2. In the *View* tab>Create panel, expand (Legends) and click (Legend).

3. In the New Legend View dialog box, set the *Name* to **TYPICAL SYMBOL LEGEND** and set the *Scale* to **3/4" = 1'-0"**, as shown in Figure 13–88.

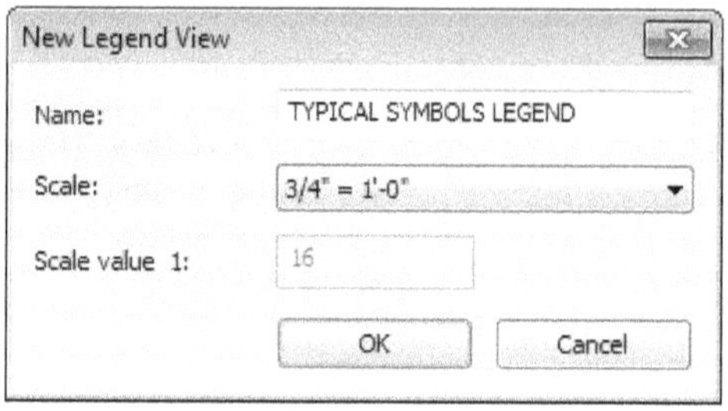

New Legend View	
Name:	TYPICAL SYMBOLS LEGEND
Scale:	3/4" = 1'-0"
Scale value 1:	16
	OK Cancel

Figure 13–88

4. Click **OK**.

5. In the *Annotate* tab>Detail panel, expand ⬚ (Component) and click ⬚ (Legend Component).

6. In the Options Bar, set the following, as shown in Figure 13–89:

   - *Family*: **Floors: Floor: 3" LW Concrete on 2" Composite Metal Deck**
   - *View*: **Section**
   - *Host Length*: **4'-0"**

Family: Floors : Floor : 3" LW Concrete on 2" Composite ▼   View: Section   ▼   Host Length: 4' 0"

Figure 13–89

7. Click to place the floor legend component in the view.

8. Add the text **TYPICAL UPPER LEVEL FLOOR** close to legend, as shown in Figure 13–90.

TYPICAL UPPER LEVEL FLOOR

Figure 13–90

9. Add several other legend components such as a wall in plan view, a column in section view, and add titles beside them.

10. In the *Annotate* tab>Symbol panel, click ⬚ (Symbol).

11. In the Type Selector, select **Centerline**. Place it below the door and add the text **CENTER OF LINE DESIGNATION** next to it.

12. Add another symbol, **Connection - Moment - Filled** and label it **MOMENT CONNECTION**.

13. Add several more elements and label them as required.

14. In the *Annotate* tab>Detail panel, click (Detail Line).

15. Select a Line Style and use (Rectangle) and/or

    (Line) in the Draw panel to draw a frame around the symbols and text as shown in Figure 13–91, and then at the top of the legend, add the text note **SYMBOL LEGEND** as a title.

Your legend will vary according to the symbols you selected to add.

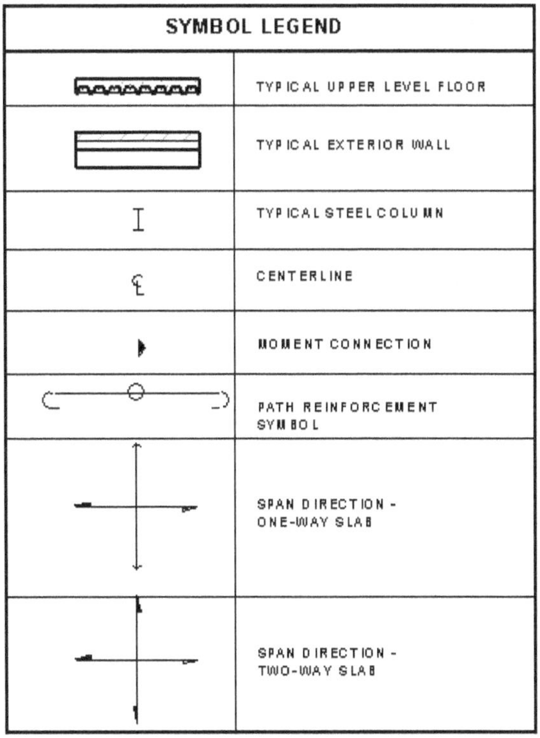

SYMBOL LEGEND	
	TYPICAL UPPER LEVEL FLOOR
	TYPICAL EXTERIOR WALL
I	TYPICAL STEEL COLUMN
₵	CENTERLINE
▶	MOMENT CONNECTION
	PATH REINFORCEMENT SYMBOL
	SPAN DIRECTION - ONE-WAY SLAB
	SPAN DIRECTION - TWO-WAY SLAB

Figure 13–91

16. Save the project.

Task 2 - Create a Key Plan Legend.

1. Open the **Structural Plans: 00 GROUND FLOOR** view.

2. Select the foundation slab and temporarily isolate it. This displays the outline of the building.

3. In the *Annotate* tab>Detail panel, click ⬜ (Detail Line).

4. In the *Modify | Place Detail Lines* tab>Line Styles panel, select the *Line Style*: **Wide Lines**.

5. In the Draw panel, click ⬚ (Pick Lines).

6. Select the lines of the slab all of the way around to establish the key plan outline.

7. Click ⬚ (Modify) to clear the selection of the lines.

8. Select all of the detail lines. (Hint: use Filter.)

9. In the *Modify Lines* tab>Clipboard panel, click ⬚ (Cut to Clipboard). You can also press <Ctrl> + X.

10. In the *View* tab>Create panel, expand ⬚ (Legends) and click ⬚ (Legend).

11. Give the legend a *Name* and *Scale* as shown in Figure 13–92.

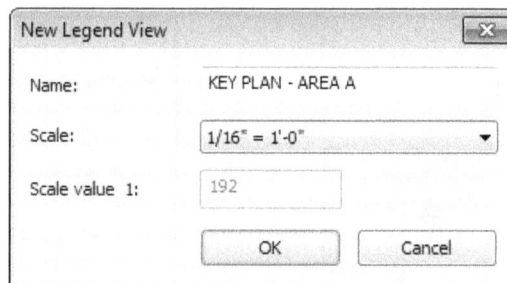

New Legend View		
Name:	KEY PLAN - AREA A	
Scale:	1/16" = 1'-0"	▼
Scale value 1:	192	
	OK	Cancel

Figure 13–92

12. Click **OK**.

13. Press <Ctrl> + V and then click to place the elements.

14. In the *Modify | Detail Groups* tab>Edit Pasted panel, click

    ✓ (Finish).

15. Modify the outline as required to create a useful key plan, as shown in Figure 13–93.

    - Use **Detail Lines** to divide the outline as required.
    - Use **Text** to add information. Create a new text size so it is large enough to see.

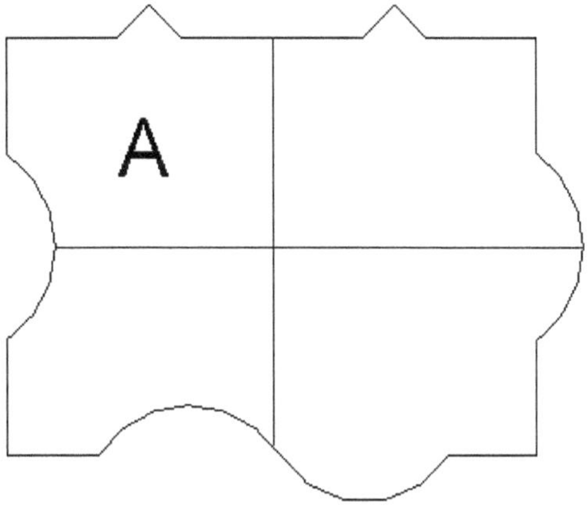

*It is important to use the **Duplicate with Detailing** option as **Detail Lines** and **Text** are detail elements.*

Figure 13–93

16. In the Project Browser, in the *Legends* area, select the **Key Plan** legend view. Right-click and select **Duplicate> Duplicate with Detailing**. This creates a copy of the key plan that you can modify as shown in Figure 13–94.

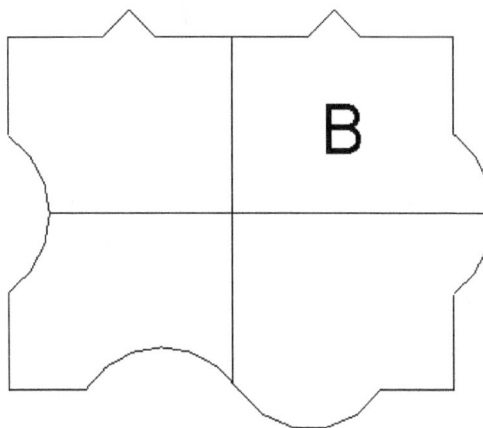

Figure 13–94

17. Save the project.

Chapter Review Questions

1. When a grid is moved (as shown in Figure 13–95), how do you update the dimension?

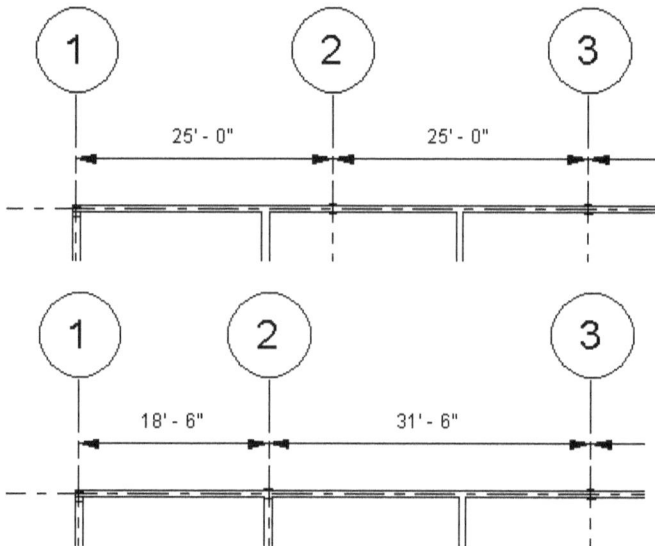

Figure 13–95

a. Edit the dimension and move it over.

b. Select the dimension and then click **Update** in the Options Bar.

c. The dimension automatically updates.

d. Delete the existing dimension and add a new one.

2. How do you create new text styles?

a. Using the **Text Styles** command.

b. Duplicate an existing type.

c. They must be included in a template.

d. Using the **Format Styles** command.

3. When you edit text, how many leaders can be added using the leader tools shown in Figure 13–96?

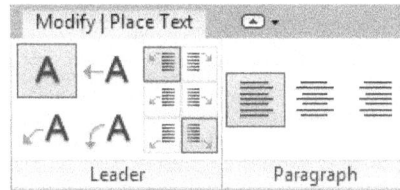

Figure 13–96

a. One

b. One on each end of the text.

c. As many as you want at each end of the text.

4. Detail Lines created in one view also display in the related view.

a. True

b. False

5. Which of the following describes the difference between a symbol and a component?

a. Symbols are 3D and only display in one view. Components are 2D and display in many views.

b. Symbols are 2D and only display in one view. Components are 3D and display in many views.

c. Symbols are 2D and display in many views. Components are 3D and only display in one view.

d. Symbols are 3D and display in many views. Components are 2D and only display in one view.

6. When creating a Legend, which of the following elements cannot be added?

a. Legend Components

b. Tags

c. Rooms

d. Symbols

Command Summary

Button	Command	Location
Dimensions and Text		
	Aligned (Dimension)	• **Ribbon:** *Annotate* tab>Dimension panel or *Modify* tab>Measure panel, expanded drop-down list • **Quick Access Toolbar** • **Shortcut:** DI
	Angular (Dimension)	• **Ribbon:** *Annotate* tab>Dimension panel or *Modify* tab>Measure panel, expanded drop-down list
	Arc Length (Dimension)	• **Ribbon:** *Annotate* tab>Dimension panel or *Modify* tab>Measure panel, expanded drop-down list
	Diameter (Dimension)	• **Ribbon:** *Annotate* tab>Dimension panel or *Modify* tab>Measure panel, expanded drop-down list
	Linear (Dimension)	• **Ribbon:** *Annotate* tab>Dimension panel or *Modify* tab>Measure panel, expanded drop-down list
	Radial (Dimension)	• **Ribbon:** *Annotate* tab>Dimension panel or *Modify* tab>Measure panel, expanded drop-down list
A	Text	• **Ribbon:** *Annotate* tab>Text panel • **Shortcut:** TX
Detail Lines and Symbols		
	Detail Line	• **Ribbon:** *Annotate* tab>Detail panel • **Shortcut:** DL
	Stair Path	• **Ribbon:** *Annotate* tab>Symbol panel
	Symbol	• **Ribbon:** *Annotate* tab>Symbol panel
Legends		
	Legend (View)	• **Ribbon:** *View* tab>Create panel> expand Legends
	Legend Component	• **Ribbon:** *Annotate* tab>Detail panel> expand Component

Creating Details

Creating details is a critical part of the design process, as it is the step where you specify the exact information that is required to build a construction project. The elements that you can add to a model include detail components, detail lines, text, keynotes, tags, symbols, and filled regions for patterning. Details can be created from views in the model, but you can also add 2D details in separate views.

Learning Objectives in this Chapter

- Create drafting views where you can add 2D details.
- Add detail components that show the typical elements in a detail.
- Annotate details using detail lines, text, tags, symbols, and patterns that define materials.

14.1 Setting Up Detail Views

Most of the work you do in the Autodesk® Revit® software is exclusively with *smart* elements that interconnect and work together in the model. However, the software does not automatically display how elements should be built to fit together. For this, you need to create detail drawings, as shown in Figure 14–1.

Details are created either in 2D drafting views, or in callouts from plan, elevation, or section views.

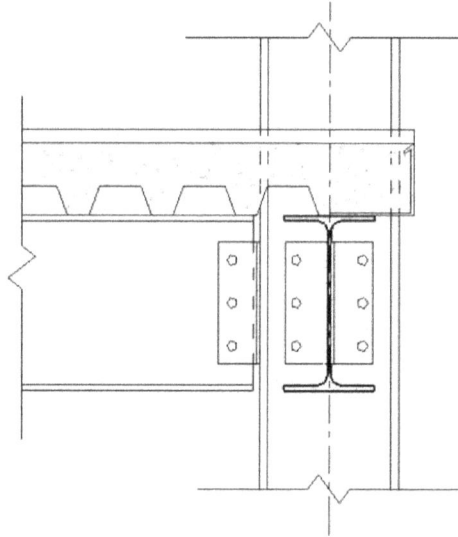

Figure 14–1

How To: Create a Drafting View

1. In the *View* tab>Create panel, click ▭ (Drafting View).
2. In the New Drafting View dialog box, enter a *Name* and set a *Scale*, as shown in Figure 14–2.

Drafting views are listed in their own section in the Project Browser.

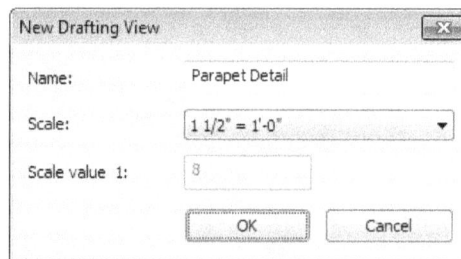

Figure 14–2

3. Click **OK**. A blank view is created with space in which you can sketch the detail.

How To: Create a Detail View from Model Elements

1. Start the **Section** or **Callout** command.
2. In the Type Selector, select the **Detail View: Detail** type.
   - The marker indicates that it is a detail, as shown for a section in Figure 14–3.

Callouts also have a Detail View Type that can be used in the same way.

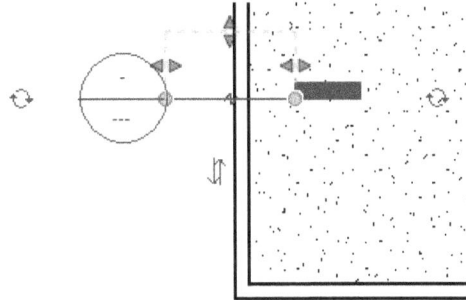

Figure 14–3

3. Place the section or a callout of the area you want to use for the detail.
4. Open the new detail. Use the tools to sketch on top of or add to the building elements.

- In this type of detail view when the building elements change, the detail changes as well, as shown in Figure 14–4.

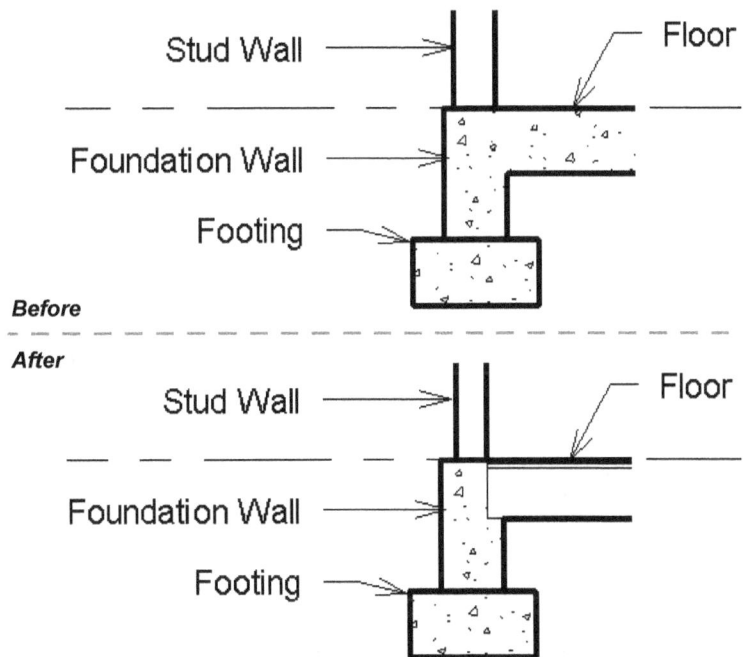

Figure 14–4

- You can create detail elements on top of the model and then toggle the model off so that it does not show in the detail view. In Properties, in the *Graphics* area, change *Display Model* to **Do not display**. You can also set the model to **Halftone**, as shown in Figure 14–5.

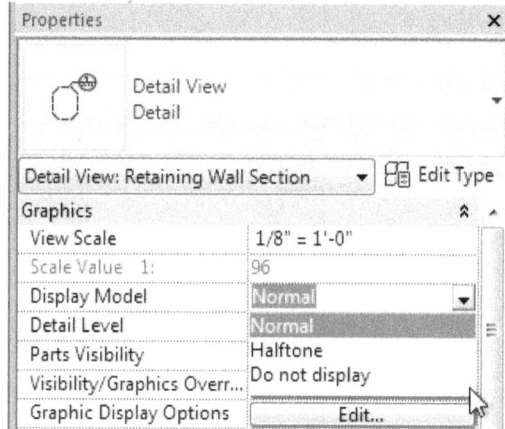

Figure 14–5

Referencing a Drafting View

Once you have created a drafting view, you can reference it in another view (such as a callout, elevation, or section view), as shown in Figure 14–6. For example, in a section view, you might want to reference an existing roof detail. You can reference drafting views, sections, elevations, and callouts.

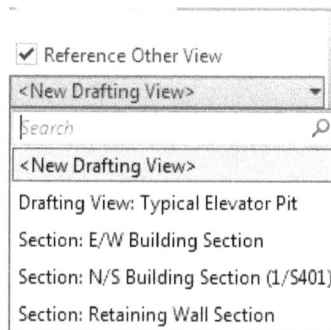

Figure 14–6

- You can use the search feature to limit the information displayed.

How To: Reference a Drafting View

1. Open the view in which you want to place the reference.
2. Start the **Section, Callout,** or **Elevation** command.
3. In the *Modify* | *<contextual>* tab>Reference panel select **Reference Other View**.
4. In the drop-down list, select **<New Drafting View>** or an existing drafting view.
5. Place the view marker.

6. When you place the associated drafting view on a sheet, the marker in this view updates with the appropriate information.

- If you select **<New Drafting View>** from the drop-down list, a new view is created in the *Drafting Views (Detail)* area in the Project Browser. You can rename it as required. The new view does not include any model elements.

- When you create a detail based on a section, elevation, or callout, you do not need to link it to a drafting view.

- You can change a referenced view to a different referenced view. Select the view marker and in the ribbon, select the new view from the list.

Saving Drafting Views

To create a library of standard details, save the non-model specific drafting views to your server. They can then be imported into a project and modified to suit. They are saved as .RVT files.

Drafting views can be saved in two ways:

- Save an individual drafting view to a new file.
- Save all of the drafting views as a group in one new file.

How To: Save One Drafting View to a File

1. In the Project Browser, right-click on the drafting view you want to save and select **Save to New File...**, as shown in Figure 14–7.

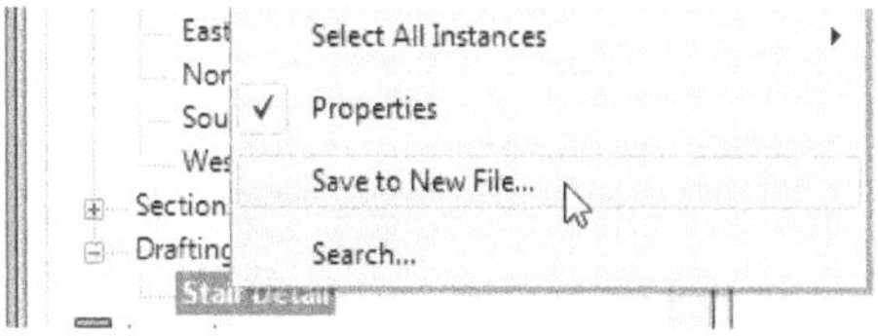

Figure 14–7

2. In the Save As dialog box, specify a name and location for the file and click **Save**.

How To: Save a Group of Drafting Views to a File

You can save sheets, drafting views, model views (floor plans), schedules, and reports.

1. In the *File* tab, expand ⬚ (Save As), expand ⬚ (Library) and then click ⬚ (View).
2. In the Save Views dialog box, in the *Views:* pane, expand the list and select **Show drafting views only**.
3. Select the drafting views that you want to save as shown in Figure 14–8.

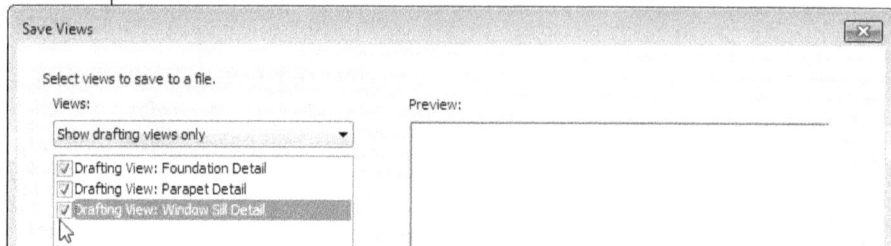

Figure 14–8

4. Click **OK**.
5. In the Save As dialog box, specify a name and location for the file and click **Save**.

How To: Use a Saved Drafting View in another Project

1. Open the project to which you want to add the drafting view.

2. In the *Insert* tab>Import panel, expand ⬚ (Insert from File) and click ⬚ (Insert Views from File).

3. In the Open dialog box, select the project in which you saved the detail and click **Open**.

4. In the Insert Views dialog box, limit the types of views to **Show drafting views only**, as shown in Figure 14–9.

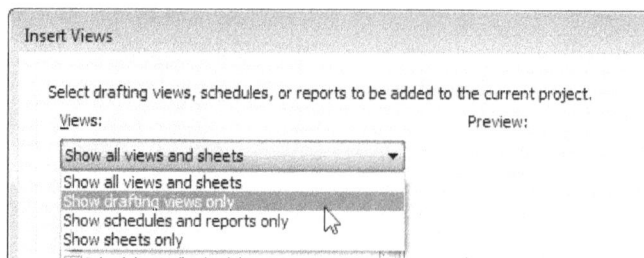

Figure 14–9

5. Select the view(s) that you want to insert and click **OK**.

Hint: Importing Details from Other CAD Software

You might already have a set of standard details created in a different CAD program, such as the AutoCAD® software. You can reuse the details in the Autodesk Revit software by importing them into a temporary project. Once you have imported the detail, it helps to clean it up and save it as a view before bringing it into your active project.

1. In a new project, create a drafting view and make it active.

2. In the *Insert* tab>Import panel, click (Import CAD).

3. In the Import CAD dialog box, select the file to import. Most of the default values are what you need. You might want to change the *Layer/Level colors* to **Black and White**.

4. Click **Open**.

- If you want to modify the detail, select the imported data. In the *Modify | [filename]* tab>Import Instance panel, expand

  (Explode) and click (Partial Explode) or (Full

  Explode). Click (Delete Layers) before you explode the detail. A full explode greatly increases the file size.

- Modify the detail using tools in the Modify panel. Change all the text and line styles to Autodesk Revit specific elements.

14.2 Adding Detail Components

Autodesk Revit elements, such as the casework section shown in Figure 14–10, typically require additional information to ensure that they are constructed correctly. To create details such as the one shown in Figure 14–11, you add detail components, detail lines, and various annotation elements.

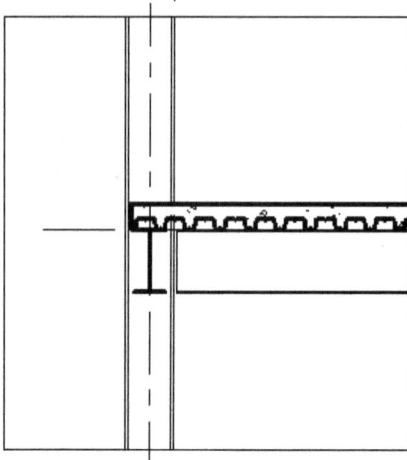

Section
Figure 14–10

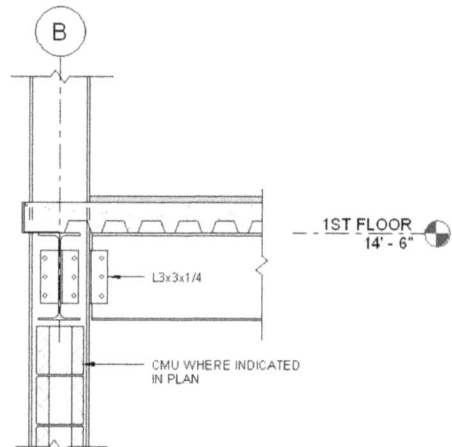

Detail Built on Section
Figure 14–11

- Detail elements are not directly connected to the model, even if model elements display in the view.

Detail Components

Detail components are families made of 2D and annotation elements. Over 500 detail components organized by CSI format are found in the *Detail Items* folder of the library, as shown in Figure 14–12.

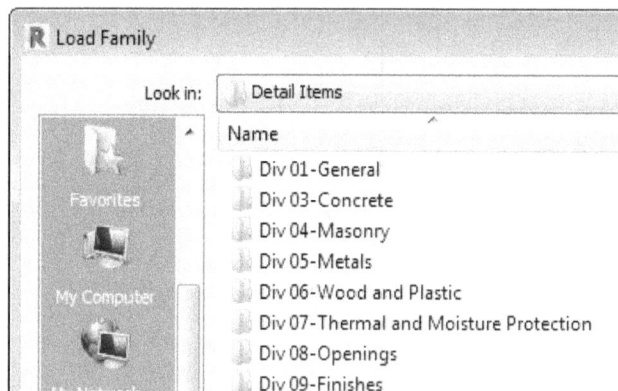

Figure 14–12

How To: Add a Detail Component

1. In the *Annotate* tab>Detail panel, expand ▣ (Component) and click ▣ (Detail Component).
2. In the Type Selector, select the detail component type. You can load additional types from the Library.
3. Many detail components can be rotated as you insert them by pressing <Spacebar>. Alternatively, select **Rotate after placement** in the Options Bar, as shown in Figure 14–13.

☐ Rotate after placement

Figure 14–13

4. Place the component in the view.

Adding Break Lines

The Break Line is a detail component found in the *Detail Items\ Div 01-General* folder. It consists of a rectangular area (shown highlighted in Figure 14–14) which is used to block out elements behind it. You can modify the size of the area that is covered and change the size of the cut line using the controls.

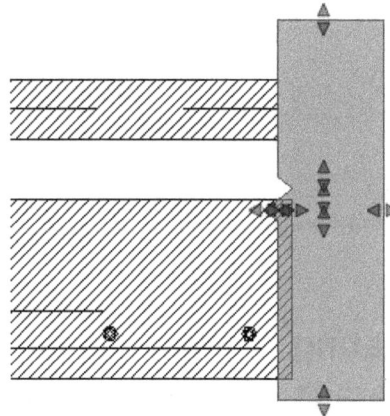

Figure 14–14

Hint: Working with the Draw Order of Details

When you select detail elements in a view, you can change the draw order of the elements in the *Modify | Detail Items* tab> Arrange panel. You can bring elements in front of other elements or place them behind elements, as shown in Figure 14–15.

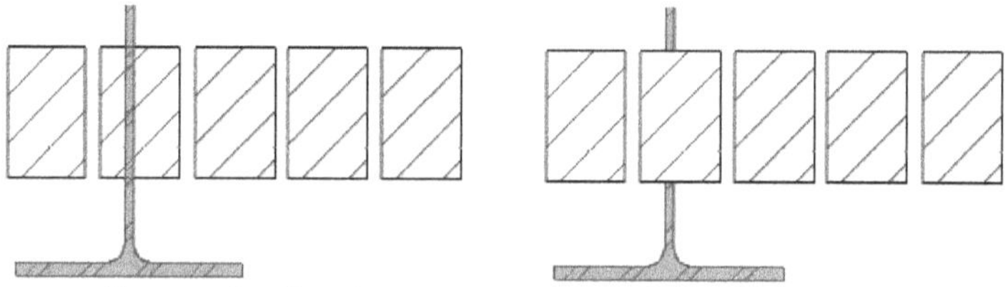

Draw order: front   **Draw order: back**

Figure 14–15

-   **(Bring to Front):** Places element in front of all other elements.

-   **(Send to Back):** Places element behind all other elements.

-   **(Bring Forward):** Moves element one step to the front.

-   **(Send Backward):** Moves element one step to the back.

- You can select multiple detail elements and change the draw order of all of them in one step. They keep the relative order of the original selection.

Repeating Details

Instead of having to insert a component multiple times (such as with a brick or concrete block), you can use (Repeating Detail Component) and create a string of components, as shown in Figure 14–16.

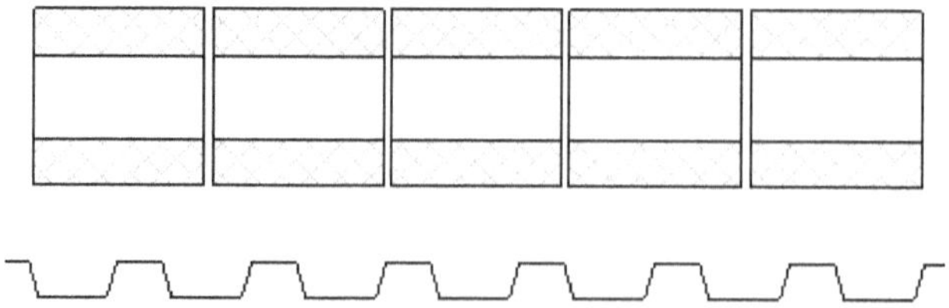

Figure 14–16

How To: Insert a Repeating Detail Component

1. In the *Annotate* tab>Detail panel, expand ⬚ (Component) and click ⬚ (Repeating Detail Component).
2. In the Type Selector, select the detail you want to use.
3. In the Draw panel, click ✓ (Line) or ⬚ (Pick Lines).
4. In the Options Bar, type a value for the *Offset*, if required.
5. The components repeat as required to fit the length of the sketched or selected line, as shown in Figure 14–17. You can lock the components to the line.

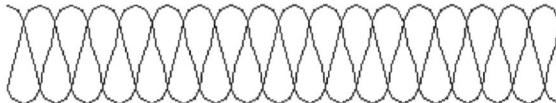

Existing Line ⸺ ⸺ Repeating Detail

Figure 14–17

Hint: ⬚ **(Insulation)**

Adding batt insulation is similar to adding a repeating detail component, but instead of a series of bricks or other elements, it creates the linear batting pattern, shown in Figure 14–18.

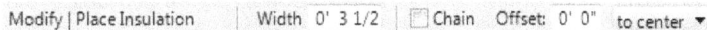

Figure 14–18

Before you place the insulation in the view, specify the *Width* and other options in the Options Bar, as shown in Figure 14–19.

| Modify | Place Insulation | Width 0' 3 1/2 | ☐ Chain | Offset: 0' 0" | to center ▾ |

Figure 14–19

14.3 Annotating Details

After you have added components and sketched detail lines, you need to add annotations to the detail view. You can place text notes and dimensions as shown in Figure 14–20, as well as symbols and tags. Filled regions are used to add hatching or poche.

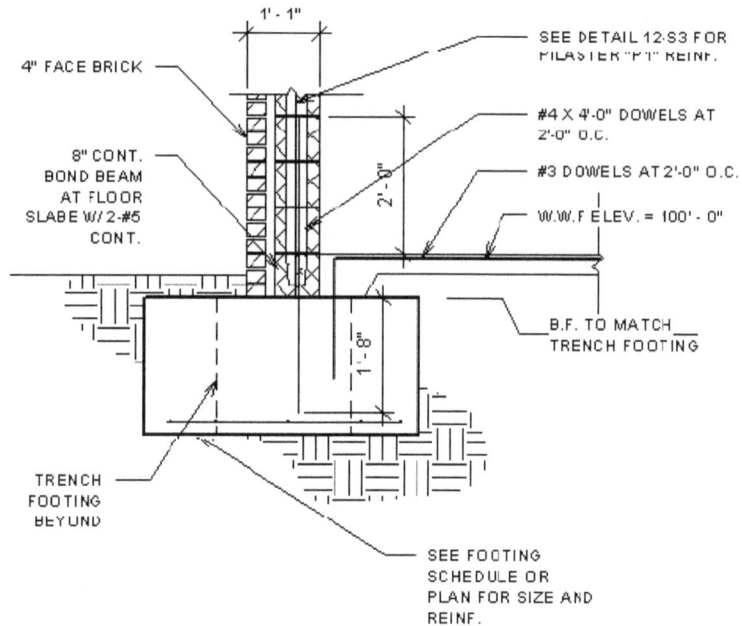

Figure 14–20

Creating Filled Regions

Many elements include material information that displays in plan and section views, while other elements need such details to be added. For example, the concrete wall shown in Figure 14–21 includes material information, while the earth to the left of the wall needs to be added using the **Filled Region** command.

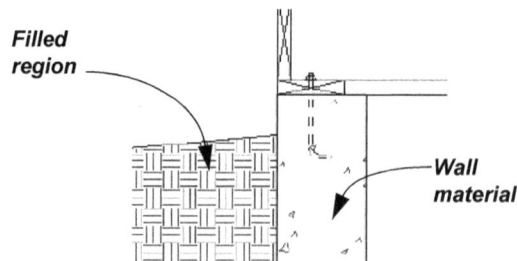

Figure 14–21

The patterns used in details are *drafting patterns*. They are scaled to the view scale and update if you modify it. You can also add full-size *model patterns*, such as a Flemish Bond brick pattern, to the surface of some elements.

How To: Add a Filled Region

1. In the *Annotate* tab>Detail panel, expand ⬚ (Region) and click ⬚ (Filled Region).
2. Create a closed boundary using the Draw tools.
3. In the Line Style panel, select the line style for the outside edge of the boundary. If you do not want the boundary to display, select the <Invisible lines> style.
4. In the Type Selector, select the fill type, as shown in Figure 14–22.

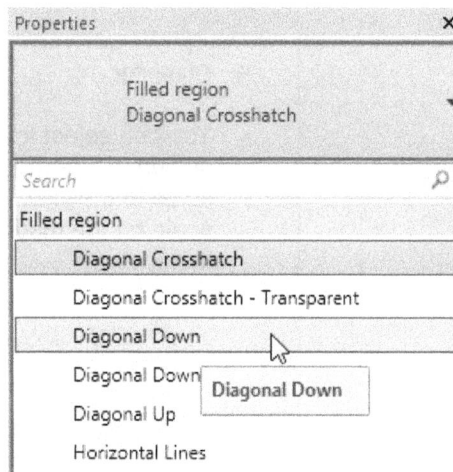

Figure 14–22

5. Click ✓ (Finish Edit Mode).

- You can modify a region by changing the fill type in the Type Selector or by editing the sketch.

- Double-click on the edge of the filled region to edit the sketch.

  If you have the Selection option set to ⬚ (Select elements by face) you can select the pattern.

Hint: Creating a Filled Region Pattern Type

You can create a custom pattern by duplicating and editing an existing pattern type.

1. Select an existing region or create a boundary.
2. In Properties, click ⊞ (Edit Type).
3. In the Type Properties dialog box, click **Duplicate** and name the new pattern.
4. Select a *Fill Pattern*, *Background*, *Line Weight*, and *Color*, as shown in Figure 14–23.

Graphics	⋩
Fill Pattern	Concrete [Drafting] ⋯
Background	Opaque
Line Weight	1
Color	■ Black

Figure 14–23

5. Click **OK**.

• You can select from two types of Fill Patterns: **Drafting**, as shown in Figure 14–24, and **Model**. Drafting fill patterns scale to the view scale factor. Model fill patterns display full scale on the model and are not impacted by the view scale factor.

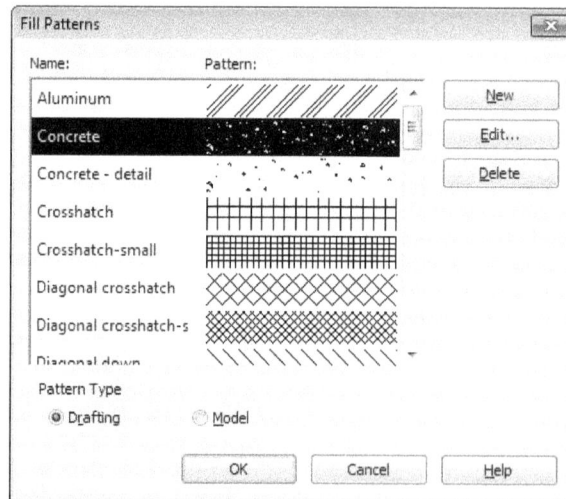

Figure 14–24

Adding Detail Tags

Besides adding text to a detail, you can tag detail components using (Tag By Category). The tag name is set in the Type Parameters for that component, as shown in Figure 14–25. This means that if you have more than one copy of the component in your project, you do not have to rename it each time you place its tag.

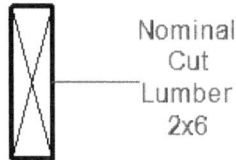

*The **Detail Item Tag.rfa** tag is located in the Annotations folder in the Library.*

Type Parameters

Parameter	Value	
Dimensions		✕
Width	0' 1 1/2"	
Depth	0' 5 1/2"	
Identity Data		✕
Keynote	06110.F4	
Type Comments		
Assembly Description		
Assembly Code		
Type Mark	Nominal Cut Lumber 2x6	
OmniClass Number		

Figure 14–25

Hint: Multiple Dimension Options

If you are creating details that show one element with multiple dimension values, as shown in Figure 14–26, you can easily modify the dimension text.

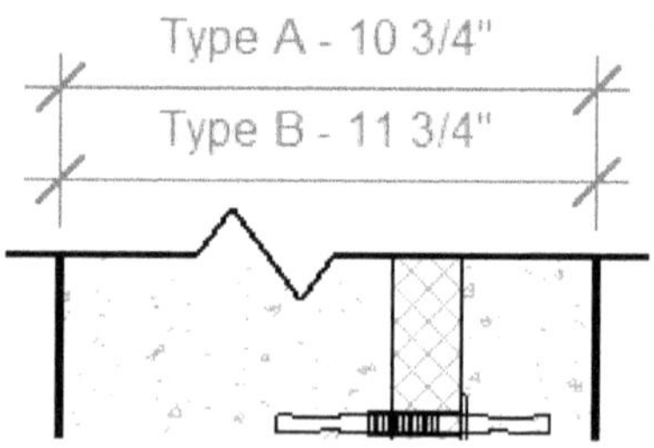

Figure 14–26

Select the dimension and then the dimension text. The Dimension Text dialog box opens. You can replace the text, as shown in Figure 14–27, or add text fields above or below, as well as a prefix or suffix.

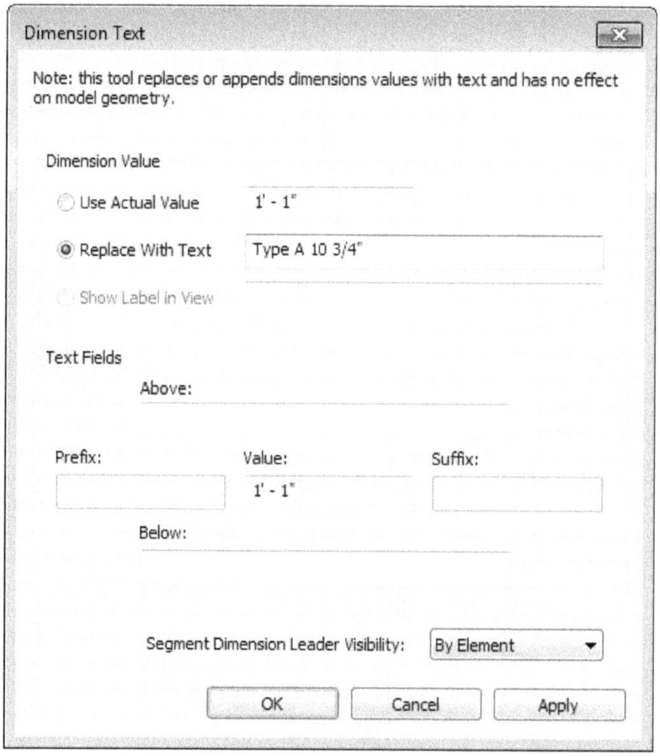

Figure 14–27

- This also works with Equality Text Labels.

Practice 14a

Create a Detail Based on a Section Callout

Practice Objectives

Estimated time for completion: 20 minutes

- Create a detail based on a section.
- Add filled regions, detail components, and annotations.

In this practice you will create an enlarged detail based on a section, modify lineweights, create filled regions, and add detail components, and annotation as shown in Figure 14–28.

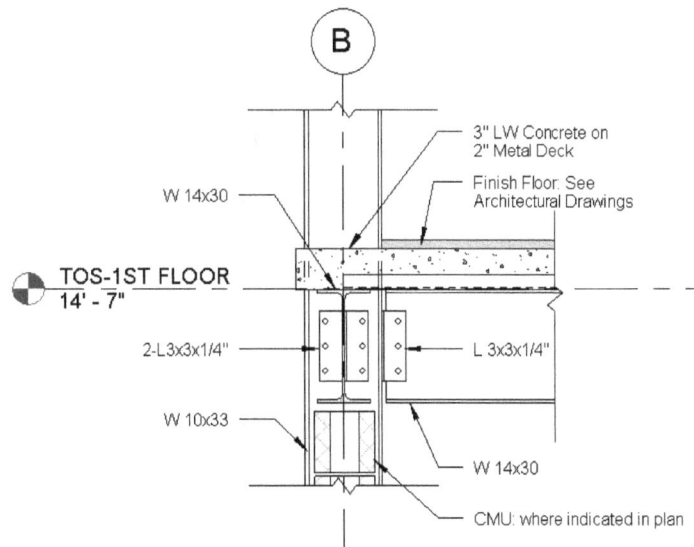

Figure 14–28

Task 1 - Create an enlarged detail.

1. Open **Syracuse-Suites-Detailing.rvt**

2. Open the **Sections (Building Section): North-South Section** view.

3. Zoom in on the intersection of the **TOS-1ST FLOOR** level and **Grid B** (on the left). Adjust the crop region as required.

4. In the *View* tab>Create panel, click ⌖ (Callout).

5. Create a callout as shown in Figure 14–29 and double click on the callout head to open it.

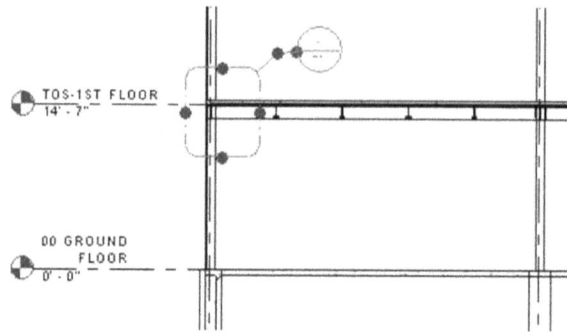

Figure 14–29

Set the Detail Level to ▨ (Fine) if required.

6. In the View Control Bar, set the *Scale* to **3/4"=1'-0"**.

7. Select the **TOS-1ST FLOOR** level datum and use the **Hide Bubble** control to hide the bubble on the right.

8. Zoom in close to the intersection to display the line thicknesses. The slab and beam section cut lines are too heavy.

9. Select the slab. Right-click and select **Override Graphics in View> By Element...**

10. In the View-Specific Element Graphics dialog box, change the *Cut Lines Weight* to **2** as shown in Figure 14–30.

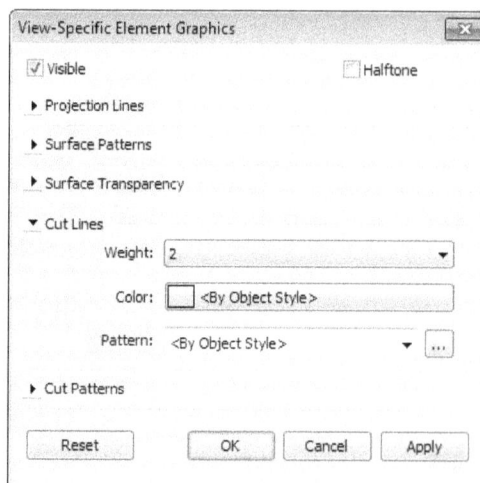

Figure 14–30

11. Click **OK**.

12. Select the beam that is cut in section and change the *Cut Lines Weight* to **3**.

13. Save the project.

Task 2 - Create filled regions to display an architectural floor.

---

1. In the *Annotate* tab>Detail panel, click ⬚ (Filled Region).

2. In the Type Selector, select **Filled Region: Solid Black.**

3. Click ⊞ (Edit Type).

4. In the Type Properties dialog box, click **Duplicate...** and create a new type named **Solid Gray**.

5. In the Type Parameters, change the *Color* to a light gray.

6. Click **OK** to return to the sketch.

7. In the *Modify | Create Filled Region Boundary* tab>Draw panel, use the drawing tools to create a **1"** thick boundary above the floor slab, as shown in Figure 14–31.

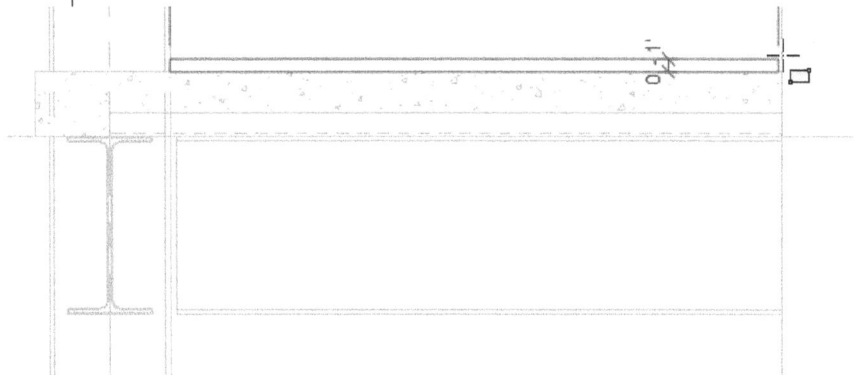

Figure 14–31

8. Click ✓ (Finish Edit Mode) in the Mode panel. The region representing an architectural floor, displays as shown in Figure 14–32.

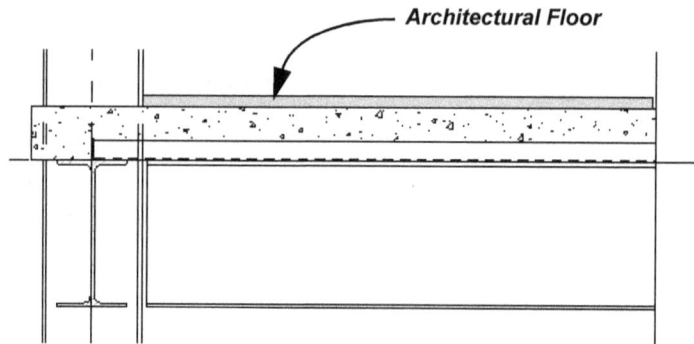

Figure 14–32

Task 3 - Add detail components.

1. In the *Annotate* tab>Detail panel, click ⬜ (Detail Component).

2. In the *Modify | Place Detail Component* tab>Mode panel, click ⬇ (Load Family).

3. Browse to the *Detail Items>Div-05-Metals> 050500-Common Work Results for Metals>050523-Metal Fastenings* folder. Open the files **L-Angle-Bolted Connection-Elevation.rfa** and **L-Angle-Bolted Connection-Section.rfa**. Press <Ctrl> to select both files.

4. In the Type Selector, select **L-Angle-Bolted Connection-Elevation: L3x3x1/4"**.

5. Click ⬛ (Edit Type).

6. In the Type Properties dialog box, change the *Number Of Bolts* to **3**. Click **OK**.

7. Place the component at the intersection of the midpoint on the beam in elevation and the column it frames into as shown in Figure 14–33.

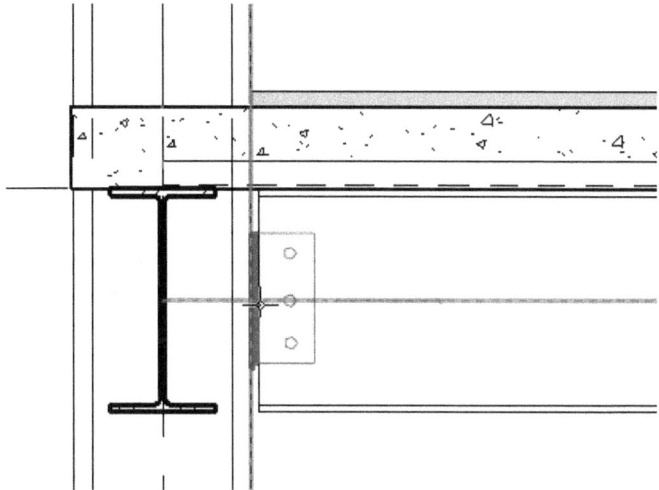

Figure 14–33

8. Repeat the procedure. This time place the **L-Angle-Bolted Connection-Section** on the sectioned beam. After it is placed, select it and stretch the grips ◀ ▶ to be tight around the member as shown in Figure 14–34.

To make it easier to see, toggle on ▤ (Thin Lines) in the Quick Access Toolbar.

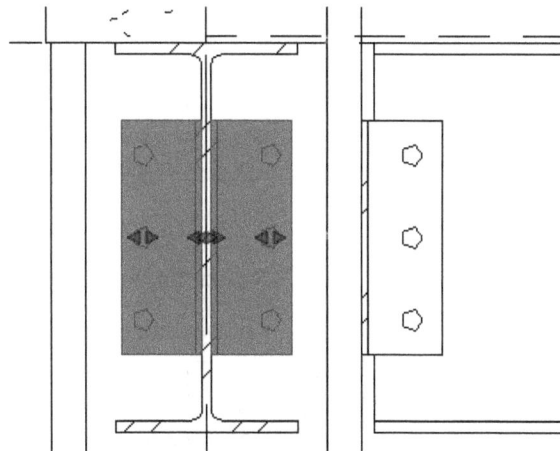

Figure 14–34

9. Save the project.

Task 4 - Add repeating detail components.

1. In the *Annotate* tab>Detail panel, expand Component, and

   click ⬚ (Repeating Detail Component).

2. In the Type Selector, select **Repeating Detail: CMU**.

3. In the Options Bar, set the *Offset* to **0' 3 13/16"**
   (or **=7 5/8" / 2**). (Hint: You can type formulas wherever a
   number can be added.)

4. Select the bottom midpoint of the **W14x30** section and draw a
   line down to display at least 2 CMU blocks, as shown in
   Figure 14–35.

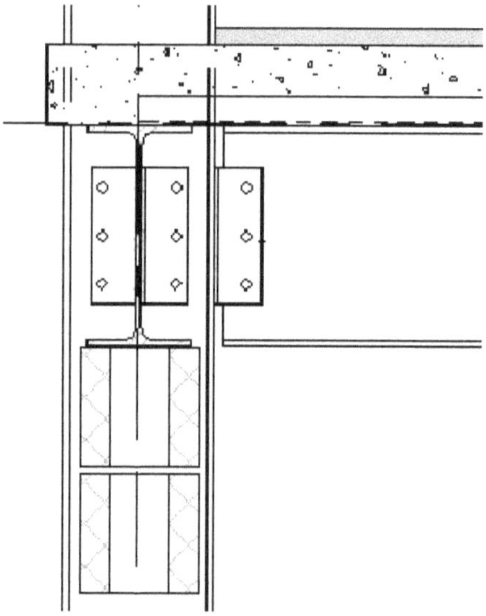

Figure 14–35

5. Select the new CMU wall, and in the *Modify | Detail Items>*
   Arrange tab, click ⬚ (Send to Back).

6. Click ✛ (Move) to move the entire CMU wall down **1"** to
   create space for a bearing plate for the beam.

7. Save the project.

Task 5 - Annotate the detail.

1. In the *Annotate* tab>Detail panel, click ⬚ (Detail Component). Click ⬇ (Load Family) to add a break line.

2. Browse to the *Detail Items>Div 01-General* folder and open the file **Break Line.rfa**.

3. Add break lines to the top, bottom, and right side of the detail as shown in Figure 14–36. Press <Spacebar> to rotate the Break Line as required.

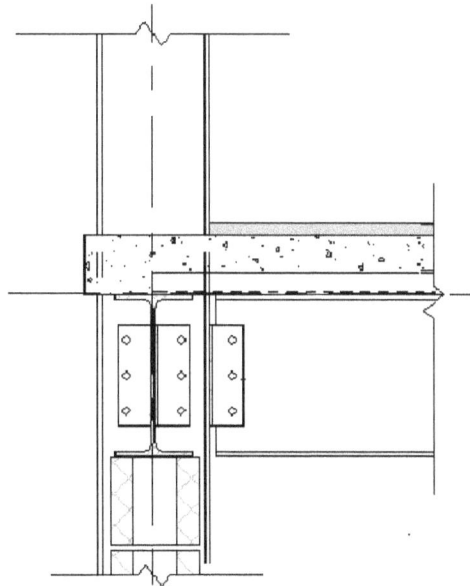

Figure 14–36

Modify the crop region so that excess elements do not display on the outside of the break lines.

4. Leave plenty of room for annotation by making the annotation crop region larger.

5. In the *Annotate* tab>Text panel, click **A** (Text).

6. Add notes to complete the detail as shown in Figure 14–37.

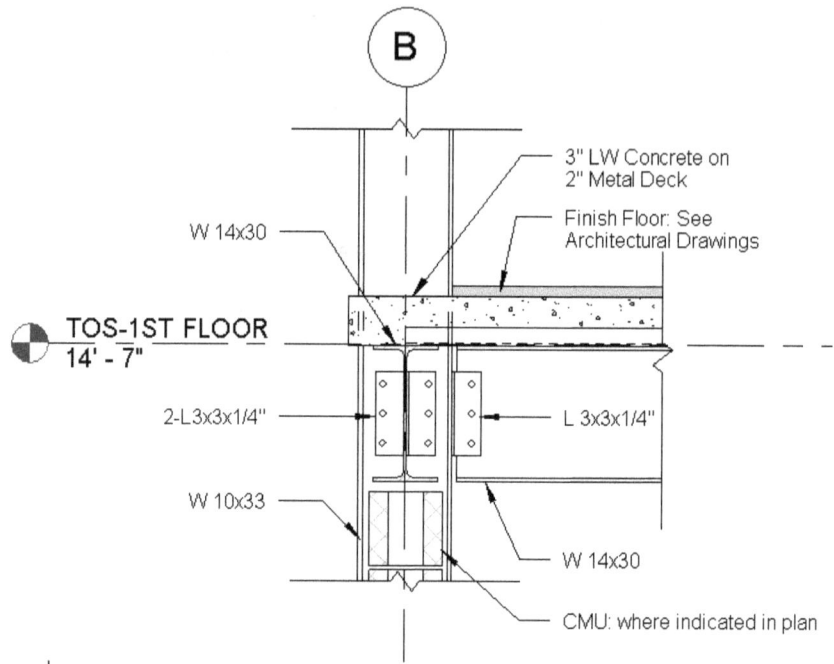

Figure 14–37

7. In the View Control Bar, click ⬛ (Hide Crop Region).

8. Save the project.

Practice 14b

Create a Bracing Detail

Practice Objective

- Create callouts and add tags and details lines.

In this practice you will create a callout of a framing elevation and add tags as well as a detail of a top plate, as shown in Figure 14–38.

Estimated time for completion: 10 minutes.

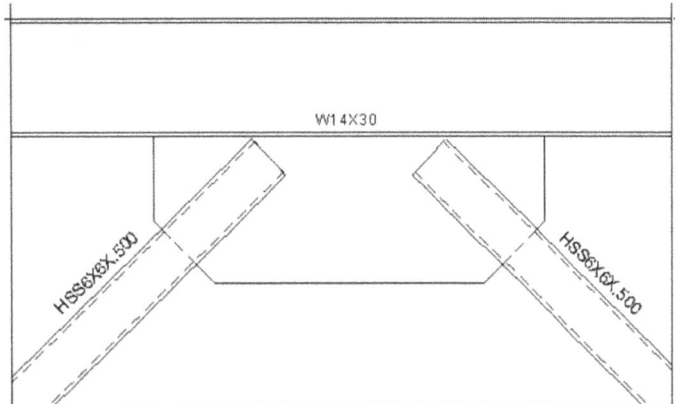

Figure 14–38

Task 1 - Create a bracing detail.

1. Open **Syracuse-Suites-Detailing.rvt**

2. Open the **Elevations (Framing Elevation) West Bracing** view.

3. In the *View* tab>Create panel, click ⌀ (Callout).

4. In the Type Selector, select **Elevation: Framing Elevation**.

5. Draw the callout around the entire bay between the 1st and 2nd floors as shown in Figure 14–39.

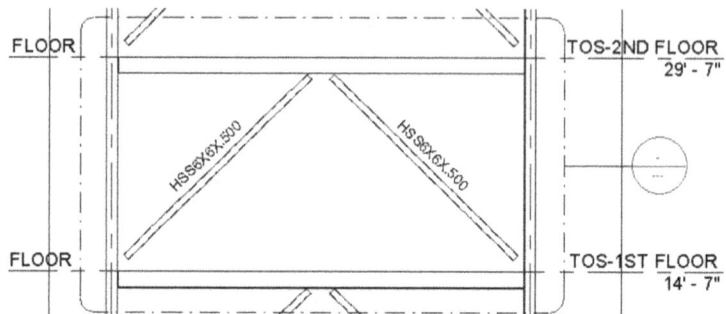

Figure 14–39

6. In the Project Browser, in the *Elevations (Framing Elevation)* area, rename the callout as **Bracing Bay A**.

7. Open the callout.

8. In the Options Bar, set the *Scale* to **1/4"=1'-0"**, if it is not already set.

9. Add tags to the braces.

10. Save the project.

Task 2 - Create a detail of a callout.

1. Create another callout of the area where the top plate should be added.

2. Open it and set the *Scale* to **3/4"=1'-0"**.

3. In the Type Selector, set the type to **Elevation: Framing Elevation**.

4. In the Project Browser, rename the callout **Typical Top Plate**.

5. In the View Control Bar, click 🔲 (Do Not Crop View).

6. Use 🔲 (Tag by Category) without a leader and tag the bracing.It shows outside of the cropped area so you need to move the tags into the crop area. as shown in Figure 14–40.

7. In the View Control Bar, click ⬚ (Crop View) to reapply the cropping.

8. In the *Annotate* tab>Detail panel, click ⬚ (Detail Line).

9. In the *Modify | Place Detail Lines* tab>Line Styles panel, select **Thin Lines**. Use the **Line** command to draw and represent a gusset plate as shown in Figure 14–40.

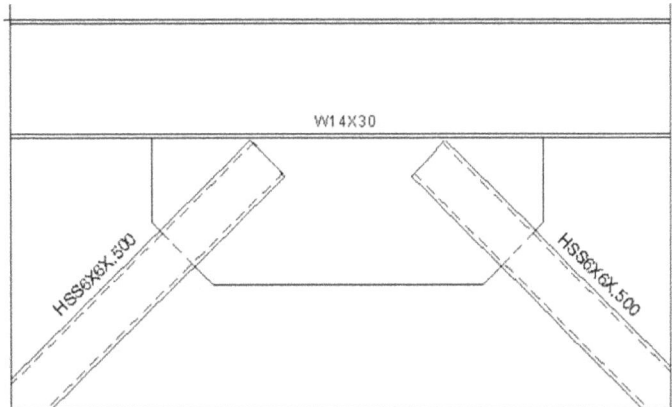

Figure 14–40

10. If time permits create, annotate, and detail a Typical Bottom Plate.

11. Save the project.

Practice 14c | Additional Details

Practice Objective

- Create and annotate details.

In this practice you will create two structural details.

Use the project **Syracuse-Suites-Detailing.rvt** for these details.

Estimated time for completion: 10 minutes each

Task 1 - Foundation detail

Create a new Drafting View and draw the detail shown in Figure 14–41 using the various sketching tools and structural detail components.

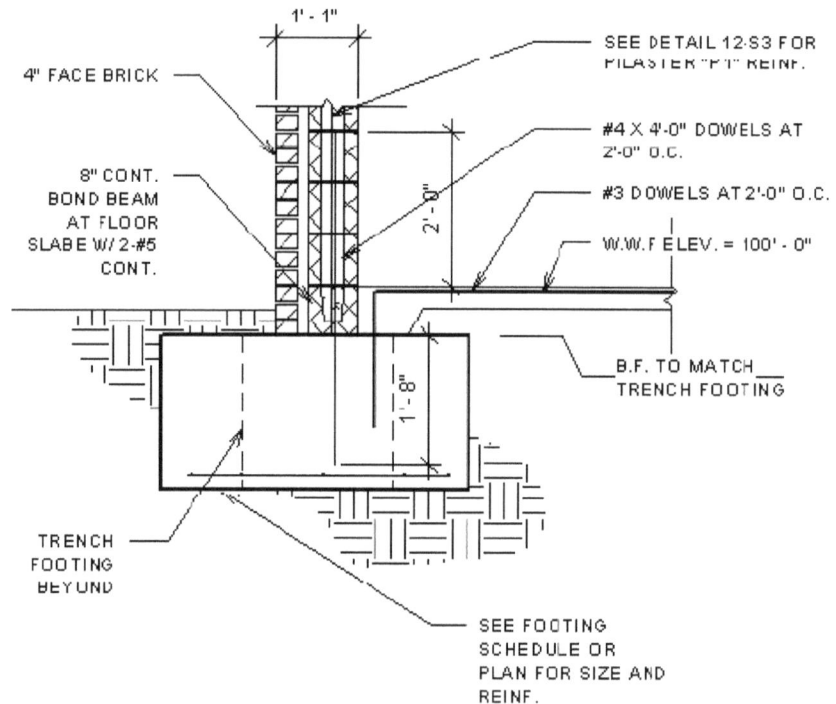

Figure 14–41

- Use the **Invisible lines** line type when you draw the lines for the fill boundary. The curved lines are made with splines.

- Create the Earth pattern type by duplicating an existing type and assigning a new drafting pattern to it.

Task 2 - Typical elevator pit detail

Create a new Drafting View and draw the detail shown in
Figure 14–42 using the various sketching tools, annotation
elements, and filled regions.

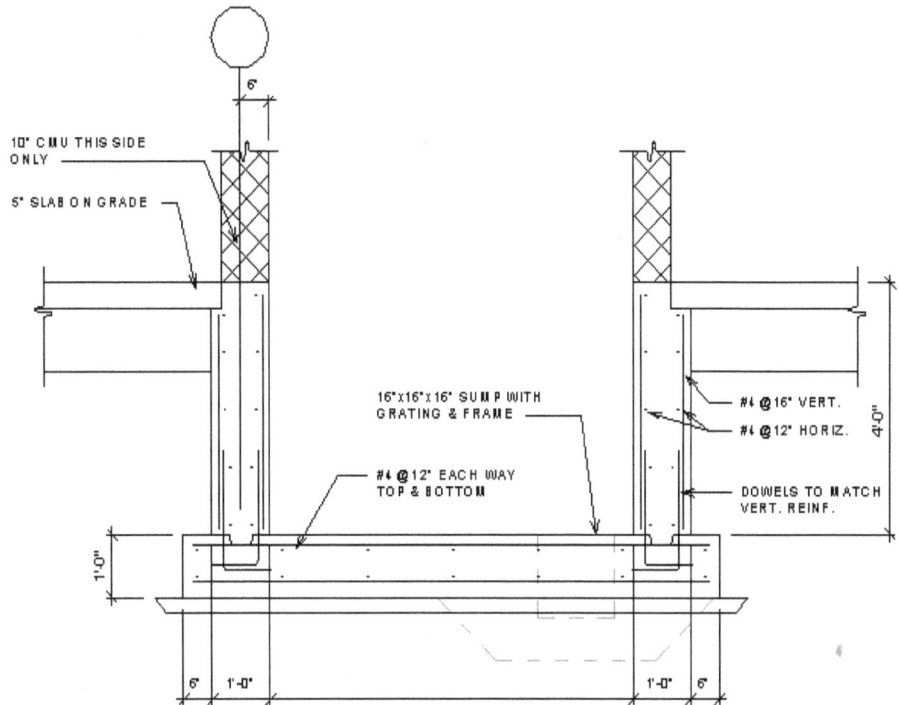

Figure 14–42

Add concrete filled regions as shown in Figure 14–43

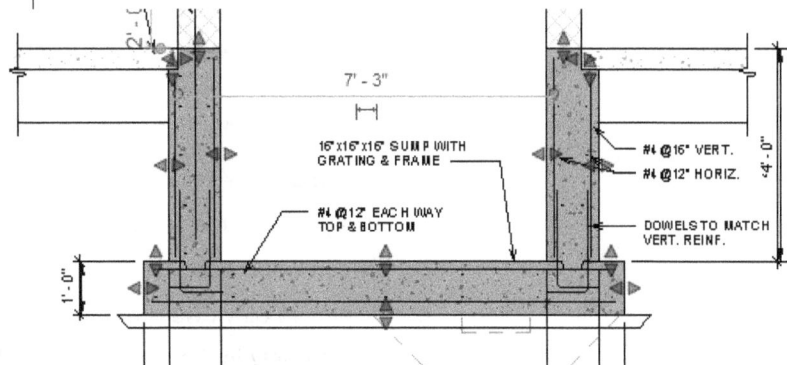

Figure 14–43

Chapter Review Questions

1. Which of the following are ways in which you can create a detail? (Select all that apply.)

   a. Make a callout of a section and sketch over it.

   b. Draw all of the elements from scratch.

   c. Import a CAD detail and modify or sketch over it.

   d. Insert an existing drafting view from another file.

2. In which type of view (access shown in Figure 14–44) can you NOT add detail lines?

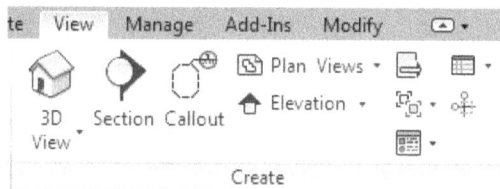

Figure 14–44

   a. Plans

   b. Elevations

   c. 3D views

   d. Legends

3. How are detail components different from building components?

   a. There is no difference.

   b. Detail components are made of 2D lines and annotation only.

   c. Detail components are made of building elements, but only display in detail views.

   d. Detail components are made of 2D and 3D elements.

4. When you sketch detail lines they are...

   a. Always the same width.

   b. Vary in width according to the view.

   c. Display in all views associated with the detail.

   d. Display only in the view in which they were created.

5. Which command do you use to add a pattern (such as concrete or earth as shown in Figure 14–45) to part of a detail?

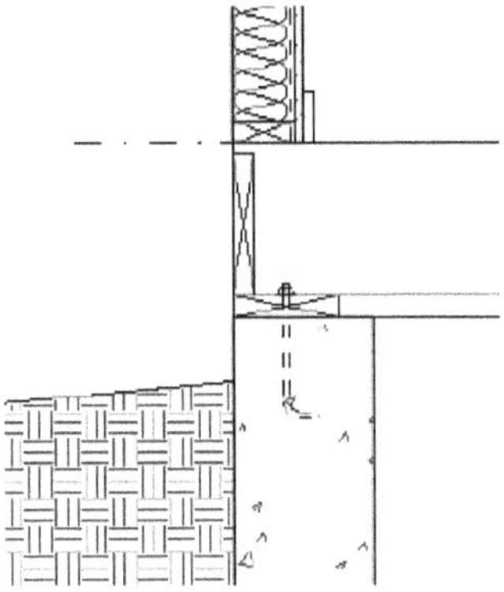

Figure 14–45

a. Region

b. Filled Region

c. Masking Region

d. Pattern Region

Command Summary

Button	Command	Location
CAD Import Tools		
	Delete Layers	• **Ribbon:** *Modify	<imported filename>* tab>Import Instance panel
	Full Explode	• **Ribbon:** *Modify	<imported filename>* tab>Import Instance panel> expand Explode
	Import CAD	• **Ribbon:** *Insert* tab>Import panel
	Partial Explode	• **Ribbon:** *Modify	<imported filename>* tab>Import Instance panel> expand Explode
Detail Tools		
	Detail Component	• **Ribbon:** *Annotate* tab>Detail panel> expand Component
	Detail Line	• **Ribbon:** *Annotate* tab>Detail panel
	Insulation	• **Ribbon:** *Annotate* tab>Detail panel
	Filled Region	• **Ribbon:** *Annotate* tab>Detail panel
	Repeating Detail Component	• **Ribbon:** *Annotate* tab>Detail panel> expand Component
View Tools		
	Bring Forward	• **Ribbon:** *Modify	Detail Items* tab> Arrange panel
	Bring to Front	• **Ribbon:** *Modify	Detail Items* tab> Arrange panel
	Drafting View	• **Ribbon:** *View* tab>Create panel
	Insert from File: Insert Views from File	• **Ribbon:** *Insert* tab>Import panel> expand Insert from File
	Send Backward	• **Ribbon:** *Modify	Detail Items* tab> Arrange panel
	Send to Back	• **Ribbon:** *Modify	Detail Items* tab> Arrange panel

Scheduling

Schedules are used to gather information stored in the various elements in the project and present them in a table format. In Autodesk® Revit®, you can create schedules specifically for structural projects, such as footing schedules, material takeoff schedules, and graphical column schedules. These schedules can then be added to sheets to create construction documentation.

Learning Objectives in this Chapter

- Understand schedules and their use in structural projects.
- Create and modify graphical column schedules that show the number, location, and height of columns.
- Modify schedule content, including the instance and type properties of related elements.
- Add schedules to sheets to create construction documents.

15.1 Structural Schedules

The Autodesk Revit software enables you to quickly create accurate schedules that can otherwise be time-consuming and difficult to maintain accurately throughout the lifecycle of a project. When you add model elements to a project, the schedule automatically updates to include the elements.

There are two types of schedules used specifically with columns: Graphical Column Schedules (as shown in Figure 15–1), and Material Takeoff Schedules. Other schedules can be created as required for a project.

Most schedules should be created in templates so that they can be reused in multiple projects.

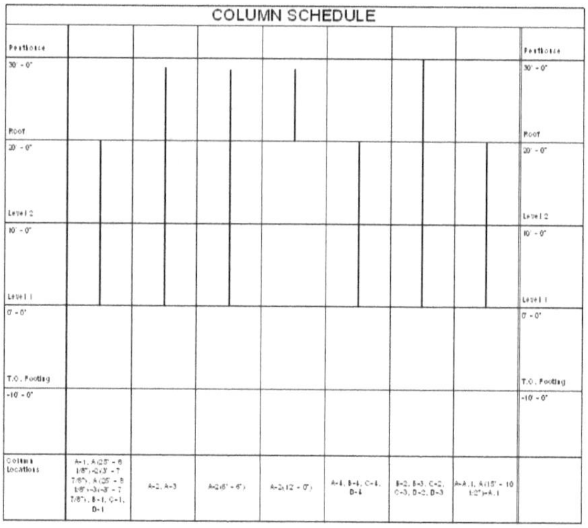

Figure 15–1

- Schedules are the added benefits of using a modeling program. Once data is placed into the model you can automatically retrieve information that previously had to be retrieved manually. If columns are in the model, they are in the schedule. If columns move, change size, length, or are deleted, the schedule updates to accurately reflect these changes.

- You are not required to have actual elements in the model when you are creating schedules. You can schedule information that model elements contain.

- All properties that are stored in the model elements as well as those specified by the user can be added to schedules.

15.2 Graphical Column Schedules

Graphical column schedules are commonly displayed at the end of a set of construction documents. The schedule identifies the type of column, the floors to which the column extends, column locations, and the group to which similar columns belong, as shown in a closeup view in Figure 15–2.

00 GROUND FLOOR			
0' - 0"			
00 T.O. FOOTING			
-15' - 0"			
Column Locations	A-4	A-8	B-1

Figure 15–2

How To: Create a Graphical Column Schedule

1. In the *View* tab>Create panel, expand ▦ (Schedules) and
   click ▦ (Graphical Column Schedule) or in the Project Browser, right-click on the Schedule/Quantities node and select **New Graphical Column Schedule...**
   - A Warning box might open as shown in Figure 15–3, which you can ignore. This can be fixed later.

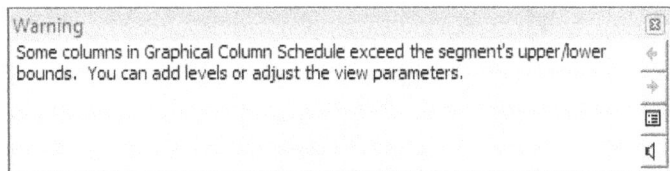

> **Warning**
> Some columns in Graphical Column Schedule exceed the segment's upper/lower bounds. You can add levels or adjust the view parameters.

Figure 15–3

2. A column schedule is created using the columns already placed in the project, as shown in Figure 15–4.

Graphical Column Schedules are located in the Project Browser under Graphical Column Schedules (not under Schedule/Quantities like most other schedules).

Penthouse						
30' - 0"						
Roof						
20' - 0"						
Level 2						
10' - 0"						
Level 1						
0' - 0"						
T.O. Footing						
-10' - 0"						
Column Locations	A-1	A-2	A-2(1 2' - 0")	A-3	A-4	A.

Figure 15–4

Modifying Graphical Column Schedules

Once you have a graphical column schedule in your project, you can adjust the Properties, as shown in Figure 15–5. You can format the schedule and display the information to suit your particular requirements.

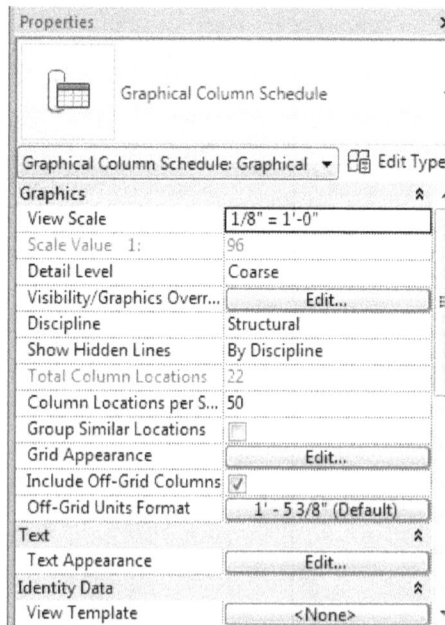

Figure 15–5

- **Group Similar Locations:** Modifies the column layout to only display one type of each column and then lists the applicable columns locations for each type.

- **Grid Appearance:** Opens the Graphical Column Schedule Properties dialog box with the *Grid Appearance* tab selected, as shown in Figure 15–6, with options on how to display the grid.

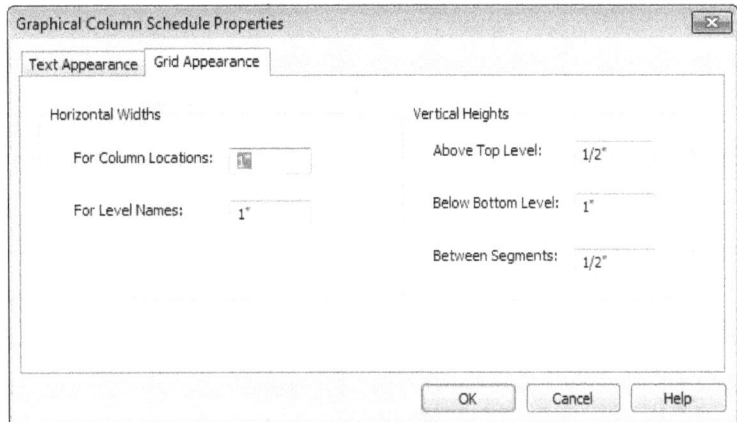

Figure 15–6

- **Include Off-Grid Columns** and **Off-Grid Units Format:** Groups the column with the column designation and adds the offset dimension in the box below the column.

- **Text Appearance:** Opens the Graphical Column Schedule Properties dialog box with the *Text Appearance* tab selected as shown in Figure 15–7. This is where you set up the font style, size, and options for the text in the schedule.

Figure 15–7

In the *Other* area, as shown in Figure 15–8, you can specify the columns, levels, and materials that are displayed.

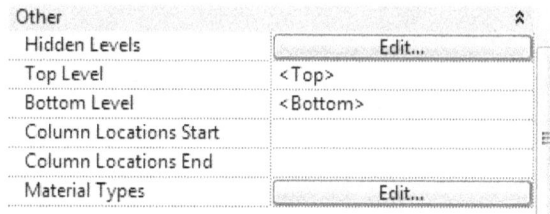

Figure 15–8

- **Hidden Level:** Enables you to remove any arbitrary levels using the Levels Hidden in Graphical Column Schedules dialog box as shown in Figure 15–9.

Figure 15–9

- **Top Level** and **Bottom Level:** Sets where the schedule displays the top and bottom levels. The default is normally used.

- **Column Locations Start** and **Column Locations End:** Specify the locations that are used to start the schedule. Sometimes the start is not logically going to be A1.

- **Material Type:** Enables you to create a filter of columns by materials. For example, if you only want the schedule to display steel columns, select that material in the Structural Material dialog box as shown in Figure 15–10.

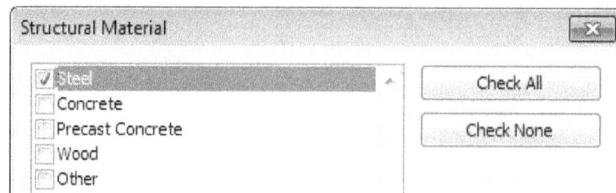

Figure 15–10

Practice 15a | Create a Graphical Column Schedule

Practice Objective

- Create a graphical column schedule.

Estimated time for completion: 10 minutes

In this practice you will create a graphical column schedule that shows only steel columns, as shown in part in Figure 15–11.

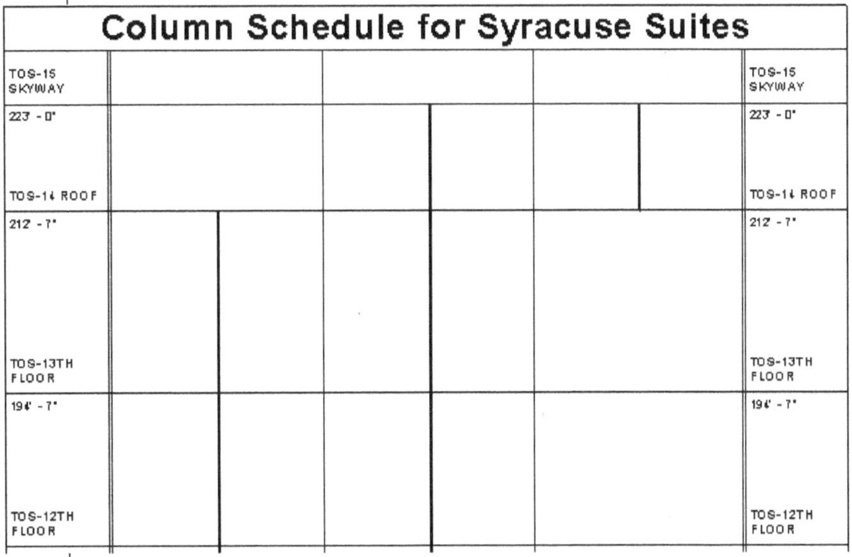

Figure 15–11

Task 1 - Create the graphical column schedule.

1. Open **Syracuse-Suites-Schedule.rvt**.

2. In the *View* tab>Create panel, expand ▦ (Schedules) and click ▦ (Graphical Column Schedule). A Graphical Column Schedule view displays.

---

3. In the Project Browser, expand the *Graphical Column Schedule* category. Right-click on Graphical Column Schedule 1 and rename it as **Steel Column Schedule**, as shown in Figure 15–12.

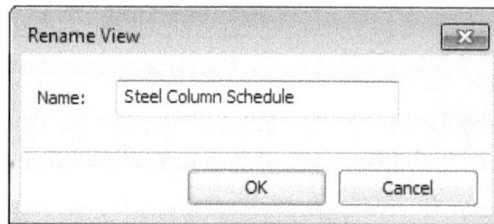

Figure 15–12

4. Click **OK**.

5. In Properties or in the View Control Bar, change the *Scale* to **3/32" = 1'-0"**. In Properties select the *Group Similar Locations* option. The schedule changes to display only one of each type of column.

6. Next to *Grid Appearance*, click **Edit...**.

7. In the Graphical Column Schedule Properties dialog box, *Grid Appearance* tab, set the *Horizontal Widths>For Column Locations* to **2"** and the *Vertical Heights>Below Bottom Level* to **2"**, as shown in Figure 15–13.

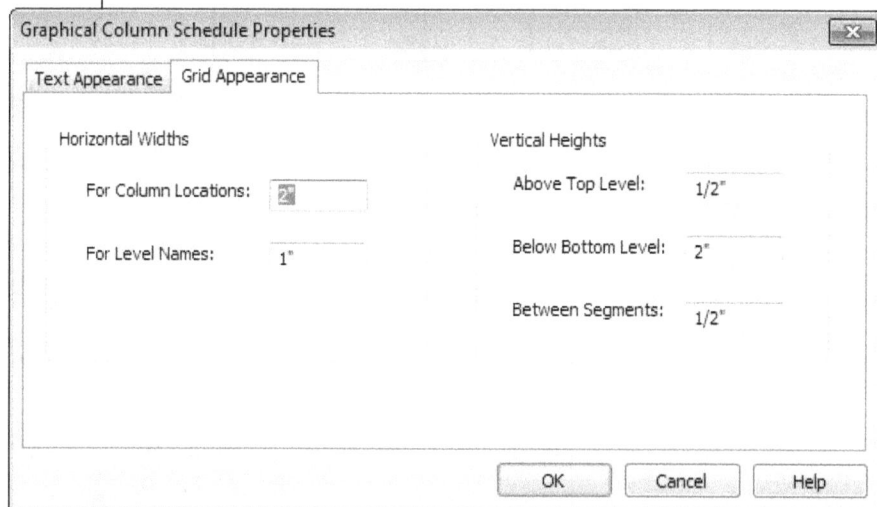

Figure 15–13

8. Switch to the *Text Appearance* tab.

9. Ensure that the *Title text* font is **Arial**, increase the *size* to **1/4"**, and make the text **Bold**, as shown in Figure 15–14.

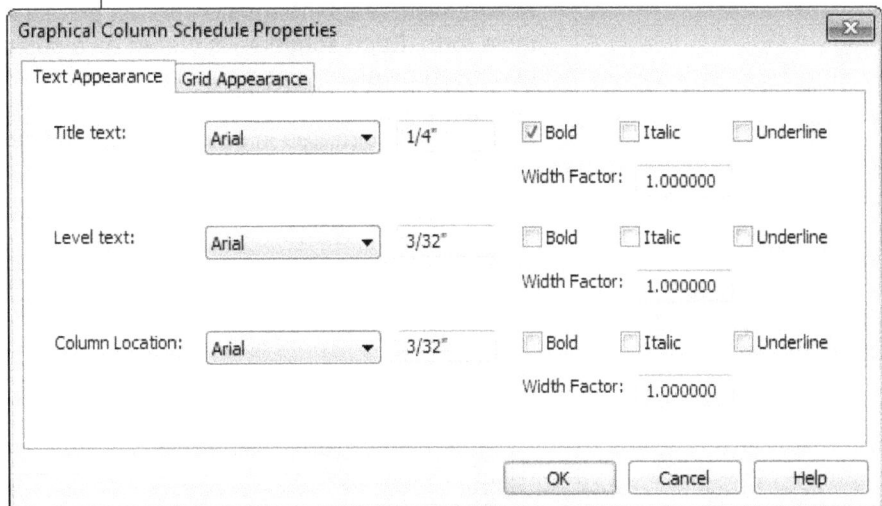

Figure 15–14

10. Click **OK**.

11. In the *Other* area, beside *Material Types,* click **Edit...**.

12. In the Structural Material dialog box, click **Check None** and then select only the **Steel** option, as shown in Figure 15–15.

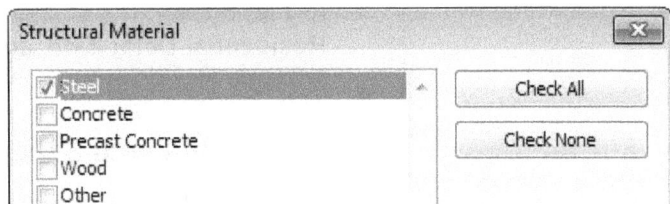

Figure 15–15

13. Click **OK**.

14. Save the project.

15.3 Working with Schedules

Schedules extract information from a project and display it in table form. Each schedule is stored as a separate view and can be placed on sheets, as shown in Figure 15–16. Any changes you make to the project elements that affect the schedules are automatically updated in both views and sheets.

Schedules are typically included in project templates. Ask your BIM Manager for more information about your company's schedules.

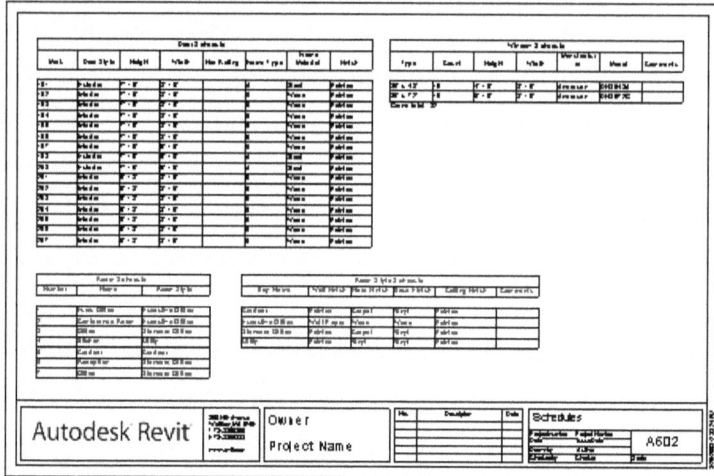

Figure 15–16

• The Architectural Template (**Default.rte**) does not include any schedules. The **Construction-Default.rte**, **Residential-Default.rte**, and **Commercial-Default.rte** template files do include useful schedules.

How To: Work with Schedules

1. In the Project Browser, expand the *Schedules/Quantities* area (as shown in Figure 15–17), and double-click on the schedule you want to open.

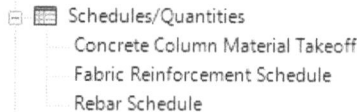

⊟ ▦ Schedules/Quantities
      Concrete Column Material Takeoff
      Fabric Reinforcement Schedule
      Rebar Schedule

Figure 15–17

2. Schedules are automatically filled out with the information stored in the instance and type parameters of related elements that are added to the model.
3. Fill out additional information in either the schedule or Properties.
4. Drag and drop the schedule onto a sheet.

Modifying Schedules

Information in schedules is bi-directional:

- If you make changes to elements, the schedule automatically updates.

- If you change information in the cells of the schedule, it automatically updates the elements in the project.

How To: Modify Schedule Cells

1. Open the schedule view.
2. Select the cell you want to change. Some cells have drop-down lists, as shown in Figure 15–18. Others have edit fields.

If you change a Type Property in the schedule, it applies to all elements of that type. If you change an Instance Property, it only applies to that one element.

A	B	C	D	E
Family and Type	Major Direction Wir	Major Spacing	Minor Direction Wir	Minor Spacing
Fabric Sheet: 6	W4.2	0' - 6"	W4.2	0' - 6"
Fabric Sheet: 6	W4.0	0' - 6"	W4.2	0' - 6"
Fabric Sheet: 6	W4.2	0' - 6"	W4.2	0' - 6"
Fabric Sheet: 6	W4.4	0' - 6"	W4.2	0' - 6"
Fabric Sheet: 6	W4.7	0' - 6"	W4.2	0' - 6"
Fabric Sheet: 6	W7.5	0' - 6"	W4.2	0' - 6"
Fabric Sheet: 6	W8.1	0' - 6"	W4.2	0' - 6"
Fabric Sheet: 6	W8.3	0' - 6"	W4.2	0' - 6"
Fabric Sheet: 6	W4.2	0' - 6"	W4.2	0' - 6"
Fabric Sheet: 6	W4.2	0' - 6"	W4.2	0' - 6"

Figure 15–18

3. Add the new information. The change is reflected in the schedule, on the sheet, and in the elements of the project.

- If you change a *Type Property*, an alert box opens, as shown in Figure 15–19.

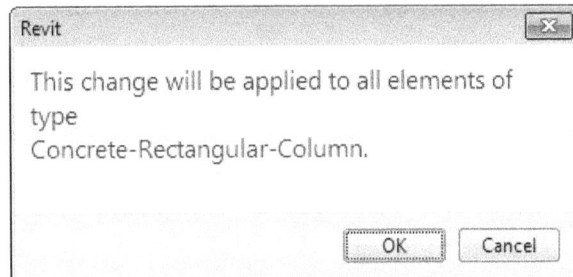

Revit

This change will be applied to all elements of type
Concrete-Rectangular-Column.

OK   Cancel

Figure 15–19

- When you select an element in a schedule, in the *Modify Schedule/Quantities* tab>Element panel, you can click

  (Highlight in Model). This opens a close-up view of the element with the Show Element(s) in View dialog box, as shown in Figure 15–20. Click **Show** to display more views of the element. Click **Close** to finish the command.

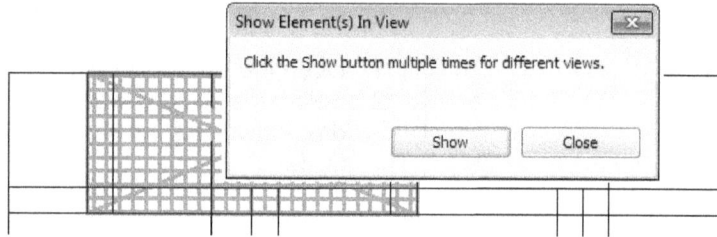

Figure 15–20

Modifying a Schedule on a Sheet

Once you have placed a schedule on a sheet, you can manipulate it to fit the information into the available space. Select the schedule to display the controls that enable you to modify it, as shown in Figure 15–21.

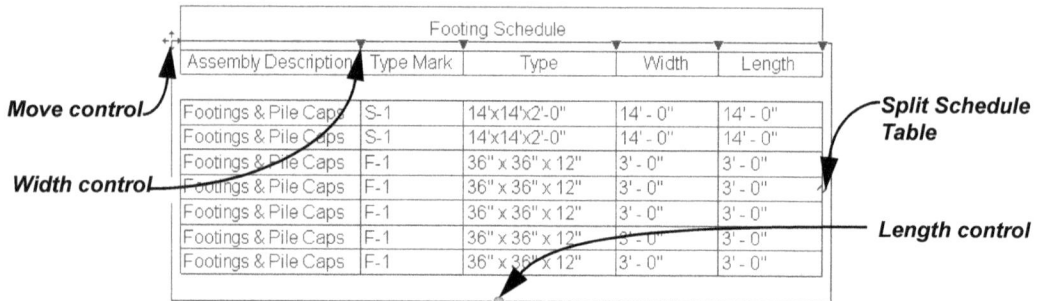

Figure 15–21

- The blue triangles modify the width of each column.

- The break mark splits the schedule into two parts.

- In a split schedule you can use the arrows in the upper left corner to move that portion of the schedule table. The control at the bottom of the first table changes the length of the table and impacts any connected splits, as shown in Figure 15–22.

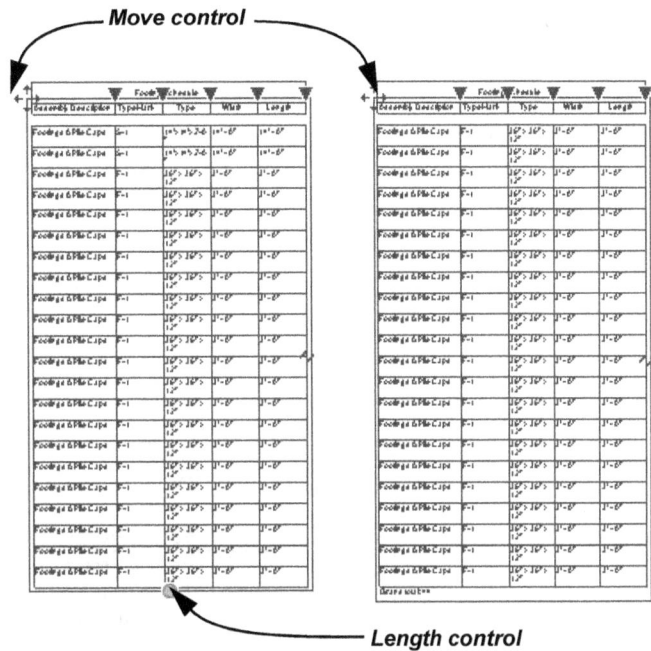

Figure 15–22

- To unsplit a schedule, drag the Move control from the side of the schedule that you want to unsplit back to the original column.

Practice 15b | Work with Schedules

Practice Objectives

- Update schedule information.
- Add a schedule to a sheet.

Estimated time for completion: 10 minutes

In this practice you will add Type Mark information to a structural elements schedule and the elements that are connected to that schedule. You will then place the schedule on a sheet and add elements in the project. The final information displays as shown in Figure 15–23.

Structural Elements Schedule		
Type Mark	Family and Type	Count
Structural Columns		
P-1	Concrete-Rectangular-Column: 24 x 24	43
	W-Wide Flange-Column: W8X10	2
	W-Wide Flange-Column: W10X33	41
Structural Foundations		
	Footing-Rectangular: 14'x14'x2'-0"	2
	Footing-Rectangular: 36" x 36" x 12"	43
	Foundation Slab: 6" Foundation Slab	1
W-1	Wall Foundation: Bearing Footing - 24" x 12"	17
W-2	Wall Foundation: Bearing Footing - 36" x 12"	4
Structural Framing		
	HSS-Hollow Structural Section: HSS6X6X.500	28
	K-Series Bar Joist-Rod Web: 14K6	16
	K-Series Bar Joist-Rod Web: 16K7	100
	W-Wide Flange: W12X26	1558
	W-Wide Flange: W14X30	1023

Figure 15–23

Task 1 - Fill in schedules.

1. Open **Syracuse-Suites-Schedules.rvt.**

2. Open the 3D Views: **3D Foundation** view. This view only displays the foundation elements, including concrete piers, footings, walls, and wall footings.

3. In the Project Browser, expand *Schedules/Quantities*. Note that four schedules have been added to this project.

4. Double-click on **Structural Elements Schedule** to open it. The existing structural elements in the project populate the schedule, as shown in Figure 15–24.

<Structural Elements Schedule>		
A	B	C
Type Mark	Family and Type	Count
Structural Columns		
P-1	Concrete-Rectangular-Column: 24 x 24	42
	W-Wide Flange-Column: W8X10	2
	W-Wide Flange-Column: W10X33	41
Structural Foundations		
	Footing-Rectangular: 14"x14'x2'-0"	2
	Footing-Rectangular: 36" x 36" x 12"	42
	Foundation Slab: 6" Foundation Slab	1
	Wall Foundation: Bearing Footing - 24" x 12"	17
	Wall Foundation: Bearing Footing - 36" x 12"	4
Structural Framing		
	HSS-Hollow Structural Section: HSS6X6X.500	28
	K-Series Bar Joist-Rod Web: 14K6	16
	K-Series Bar Joist-Rod Web: 16K7	100
	W-Wide Flange: W12X26	1558
	W-Wide Flange: W14X30	1023

Figure 15–24

5. Note that only the *Concrete* columns have a **Type Mark**.

6. In the *Type Mark* column beside **Wall Foundation: Bearing Footing - 24" x 12"**, type **W-1.**

7. The warning dialog box shown in Figure 15–25 displays because the element is a type parameter; therefore, you are alerted before you make any changes. Click **OK**.

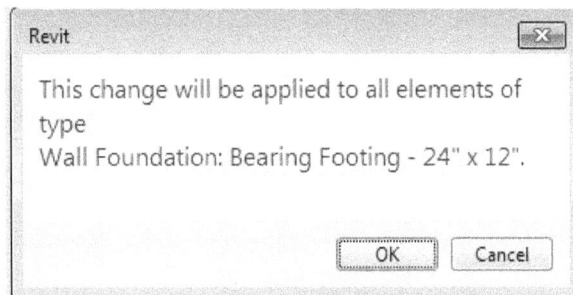

Revit

This change will be applied to all elements of type
Wall Foundation: Bearing Footing - 24" x 12".

OK   Cancel

Figure 15–25

8. Select **Wall Foundation: Bearing Footing - 36" x 12"**. In the *Modify | Schedule/Quantities* tab>Element panel, click (Highlight in Model).

9. In the Show Element(s) in View dialog box, click **Show** until you see a foundation element displayed in the **3D Foundations** view, as shown in Figure 15–26. Click **Close**.

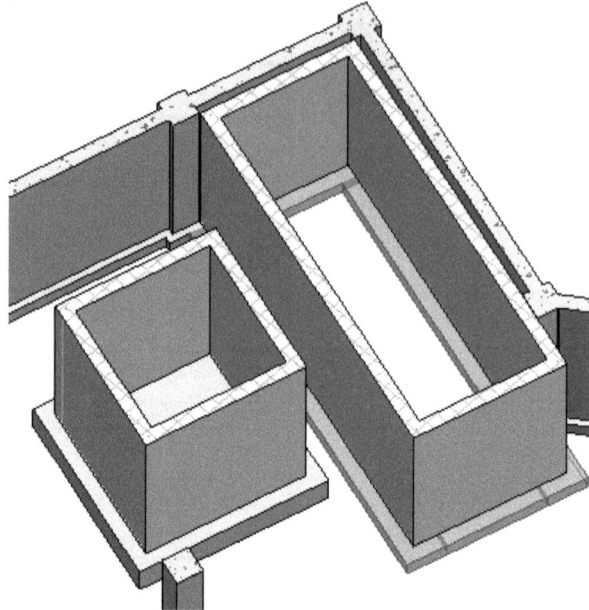

Figure 15–26

10. With the elements highlighted, in Properties, click ⬚ (Edit Type).

11. In the Type Properties dialog box, in the *Identity Data* area, set the *Type Mark* to **W-2**.

12. Click **OK** to finish.

13. Return to the **Structural Elements Schedule** view, as shown in Figure 15–27. The **Type Mark** is now applied.

Remember that you can press <Ctrl>+<Tab> to switch between open windows, as required.

<Structural Elements Schedule>

A	B	C
Type Mark	Family and Type	Count
Structural Columns		
P-1	Concrete-Rectangular-Column: 24 x 24	42
	W-Wide Flange-Column: W8X10	2
	W-Wide Flange-Column: W10X33	41
Structural Foundations		
	Footing-Rectangular: 14'x14'x2'-0"	2
	Footing-Rectangular: 36" x 36" x 12"	42
	Foundation Slab: 6" Foundation Slab	1
W-1	Wall Foundation: Bearing Footing - 24" x 12"	17
W-2	Wall Foundation: Bearing Footing - 36" x 12"	4
Structural Framing		
	HSS-Hollow Structural Section: HSS6X6X.500	28
	K-Series Bar Joist-Rod Web: 14K6	16
	K-Series Bar Joist-Rod Web: 16K7	100
	W-Wide Flange: W12X26	1558
	W-Wide Flange: W14X30	1023

Figure 15–27

14. Open the other schedules and review the information.

15. Save the project.

Task 2 - Add schedules to a sheet.

---

1. In the Project Browser, open the sheet **S8.1 - Schedules**.

2. Drag and drop the **Structural Elements Schedule** view onto the sheet, as shown in Figure 15–28.

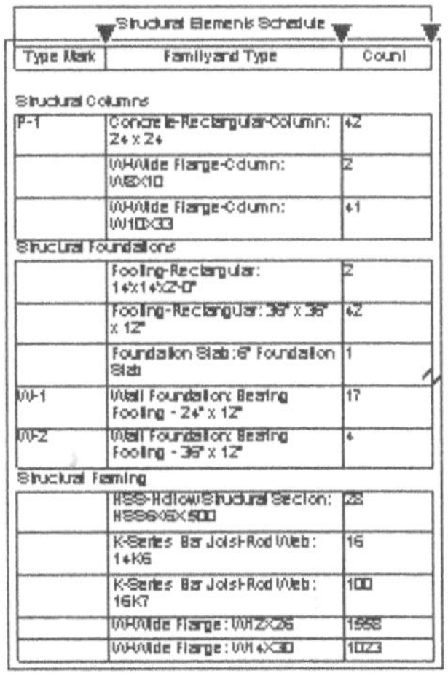

Your schedule may look different then the one shown in Figure 15–28.

Figure 15–28

3. Zoom in and use the arrows at the top of the schedule to modify the width of the columns to ensure that the titles display correctly.

4. In the schedule, note the number of Concrete Columns and their related footings.

5. Open the **00 T.O. Footing** view.

6. Zoom in and copy a concrete column and its footing to a nearby grid location that does not have an existing column, similar to that shown in Figure 15–29.

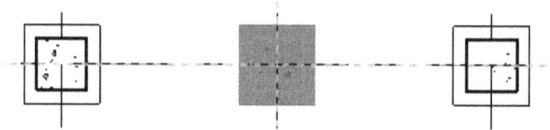

Figure 15–29

7. Switch back to the sheet view. Note that the numbers in the schedule have automatically updated to include the new column.

8. Switch to the **Structural Elements Schedule** view. Note that these column numbers have also been updated.

9. Save the project.

Chapter Review Questions

1. What happens when you delete a column in an Autodesk Revit model, as shown in Figure 15–30?

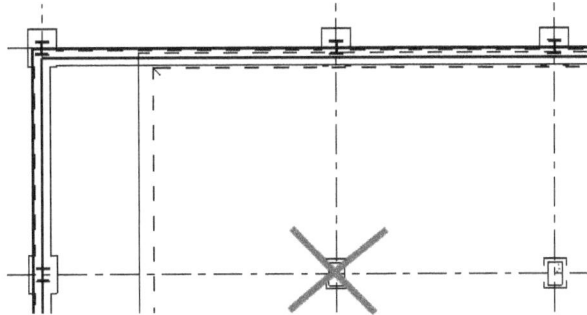

Figure 15–30

   a. You must delete the column on the drawing sheet.

   b. You must delete the column from the schedule.

   c. The column is removed from the model, but not from the schedule.

   d. The column is removed from the model and the schedule.

2. How do you add a column to a Graphical Column Schedule?

   a. Type the *Column Number* into the Column Schedule. The rest of the information is automatically updated.

   b. The column information is added automatically to the schedule when you add the column to the model.

   c. Select **Update** in the schedule view to add the column to the schedule.

   d. Draw the column in the Graphical Column Schedule.

3. In a schedule, if you change type information (such as a **Type Mark**) all instances of that type update with the new information.

   a. True

   b. False

Command Summary

Button	Command	Location
	Graphical Column Schedule	• **Ribbon:** *View* tab>Create panel> expand Schedules

Introduction to Worksets

Worksharing is a workflow used in the Autodesk® Revit® software when multiple people are working on a single project model. The model is broken up into worksets. Individuals open and work on in local files that are synchronized to a central file upon saving.

For more information about establishing and using Worksets, refer to the *Autodesk Revit Collaboration Tools* student guide.

Learning Objectives in this Appendix

- Review worksharing principles.
- Open a local file to make changes to your part of a project.
- Synchronize your local file with the central file, which contains changes from all the local files.

A.1 Introduction to Worksets

When a project becomes too big for one person, it needs to be subdivided so that a team of people can work on it. Since Autodesk Revit projects include the entire building model in one file, the file needs to be separated into logical components, as shown in Figure A–1, without losing the connection to the whole. This process is called *worksharing* and the main components are worksets.

Figure A–1

When worksets are established in a project, there is one **central file** and as many **local files** as required for each person on the team to have a file, as shown in Figure A–2.

*The **central file** is created by the BIM Manager, Project Manager, or Project Lead, and is stored on a server, enabling multiple users to access it. A **local file** is a copy of the central file that is stored on your computer.*

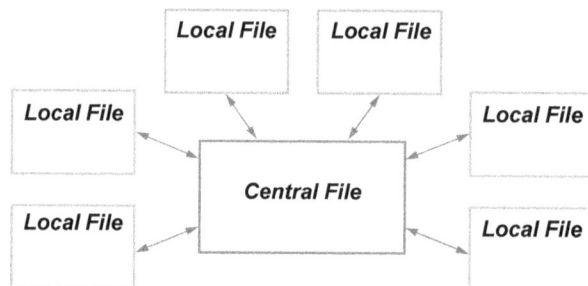

Figure A–2

- All local files are saved back to the central file, and updates to the central file are sent out to the local files. This way, all changes remain in one file, while the project, model, views, and sheets are automatically updated.

How To: Create a Local File

1. In the File tab or Quick Access Toolbar click 📂 (Open). You must use this method to be able to create a local file from the central file.
2. In the Open dialog box, navigate to the central file server location, and select the central file. Do not work in this file. Select **Create New Local**, as shown in Figure A–3.
3. Verify that this option is selected and click **Open**.

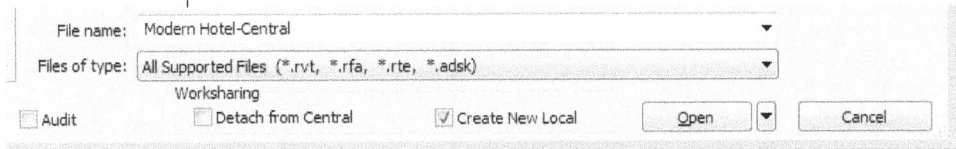

File name:	Modern Hotel-Central	▼
Files of type:	All Supported Files (*.rvt, *.rfa, *.rte, *.adsk)	▼

Worksharing

☐ Audit   ☐ Detach from Central   ☑ Create New Local   Open ▼   Cancel

Figure A–3

User Names can be assigned in Options.

4. A copy of the project is created. It is named the same as the central file, but with your *User Name* added to the end.

- You can save the file using the default name, or use

  💾 (Save As) and name the file according to your office's standard. It should include *Local* in the name to indicate that it is saved on your local computer, or that you are the only one working with that version of the file.

- Delete any old local files to ensure that you are working on the latest version.

How To: Work in a Workset-Related File

1. Open your local file.
2. In the Status Bar, expand the Active Workset drop-down list and select a workset, as shown in Figure A–4. By setting the active workset, other people can work in the project but cannot edit elements that you add to the workset.

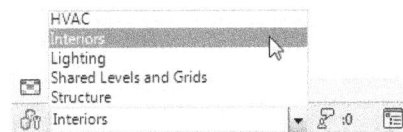

HVAC
Interiors
Lighting
Shared Levels and Grids
Structure

Interiors   ▼ 👤 :0 📋

Figure A–4

3. Work on the project as required.

Saving Workset-Related Files

When you are using a workset-related file, you need to save the file locally and centrally.

- Save the local file frequently (every 15-30 minutes). In the Quick Access Toolbar, click ⊟ (Save) to save the local file just as you would any other project.

- Synchronize the local file with the central file periodically (every hour or two) or after you have made major changes to the project.

Hint: Set up Notifications to Save and Synchronize

You can set up reminders to save and synchronize files to the central file in the Options dialog box, on the *General* pane, as shown in Figure A–5.

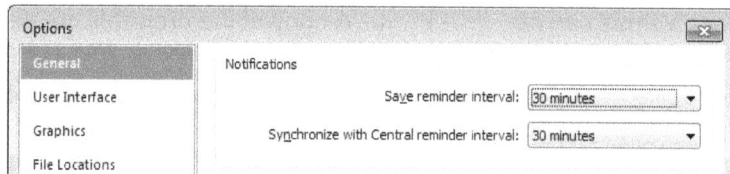

Options		
General	Notifications	
User Interface		Save reminder interval: 30 minutes
Graphics		Synchronize with Central reminder interval: 30 minutes
File Locations		

Figure A–5

Synchronizing to the Central File

There are two methods for synchronizing to the central file. They are located in the Quick Access Toolbar or the *Collaborate* tab> Synchronize panel.

Click ⟳ (Synchronize Now) to update the central file and then the local file with any changes to the central file since the last synchronization. This does not prompt you for any thing. It automatically relinquishes elements borrowed from a workset used by another person, but retains worksets used by the current person.

Click ⬚ (Synchronize and Modify Settings) to open the Synchronize with Central dialog box, as shown in Figure A–6, where you can set the location of the central file, add comments, save the file locally before and after synchronization, and set the options for relinquishing worksets and elements.

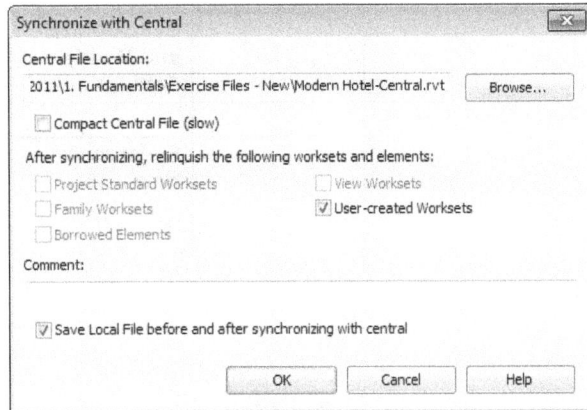

Figure A–6

- Ensure that **Save Local file before and after synchronizing with central** is checked before clicking **OK**. Changes from the central file might have been copied into your file.

- When you close a local file without saving to the central file, you are prompted with options, as shown in Figure A–7.

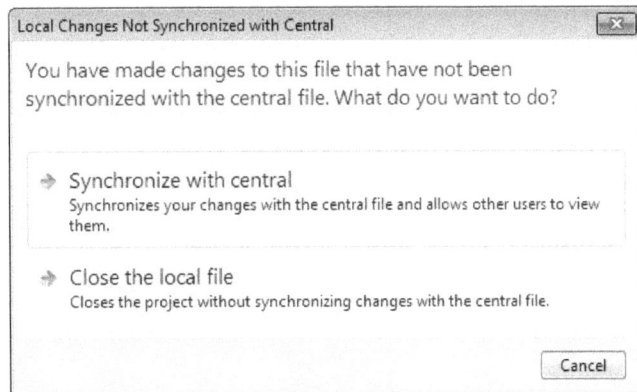

Figure A–7

Command Summary

Button	Command	Location
	Save	• **Quick Access Toolbar** • **File tab:** Save • **Shortcut:** <Ctrl>+<S>
	Synchronize and Modify Settings	• **Quick Access Toolbar** • **Ribbon:** *Collaborate* tab> Synchronize panel>expand Synchronize with Central
	Synchronize Now	• **Quick Access Toolbar** • **Ribbon:** *Collaborate* tab> Synchronize panel>expand Synchronize with Central

Additional Tools

There are many other tools available in the Autodesk® Revit® software that you can use when creating and using models. This appendix provides details about several tools and commands that are related to those covered in this student guide.

Learning Objectives in this Appendix

- Save and use selection sets of multiple building elements.
- Add slanted structural columns.
- Create structural slab types for foundation slabs.
- Create rebar types.
- Edit plan and section profiles.
- Use guide grids to help place views on sheets.
- Add revision clouds, tags, and information.
- Annotate dependent views with matchlines and view references.
- Import and export schedules.
- Create basic building component schedules.
- Create repeating detail types.

B.1 Reusing Selection Sets

When multiple elements types are selected you can save the selection set so that it can be reused. For example, a structural column and an architectural column need to move together. Instead of picking each element, create a selection set that you can quickly access as shown in Figure B–1. You can also edit selection sets to add or remove elements from the set.

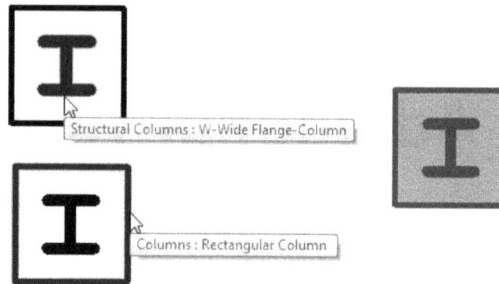

Figure B–1

- Selection sets are a filter of specific elements rather than types of elements.

How To: Save Selection Sets

1. Select the elements that you want to include in the selection set.
2. In the *Modify | Multi-Select* tab>Selection panel, click
   (Save).
3. In the Save Selection dialog box, type a name for the set as shown in Figure B–2, and click **OK**.

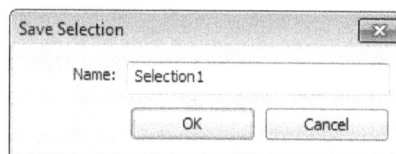

Figure B–2

How To: Retrieve Selection Sets

1. Select any other elements you might want to use. In the

   Modify | Multi-Select tab>Selection panel, click ⬚ (Load). Alternatively, without any other selection, in the *Manage* tab>

   Selection panel, click ⬚ (Load).
2. In the Retrieve Filters dialog box (shown in Figure B–3), select the set that you want to use and click **OK**.

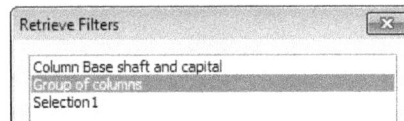

Figure B–3

3. The elements are selected and you can continue to select other elements or use the selection.

How To: Edit Selection Sets

1. If elements are selected, in the *Modify | Multi-Select* tab>

   Selection panel, click ⬚ (Edit). Alternatively, without any selection, in the *Manage* tab>Selection panel, click

   ⬚ (Edit).
2. In the Edit Filters dialog box (shown in Figure B–4), in the **Selection Filters** node, select the set that you want to edit and click **Edit...**.

Rule-based Filters are not selection sets but apply to categories of elements, such as the Interior filter shown in Figure B–4.

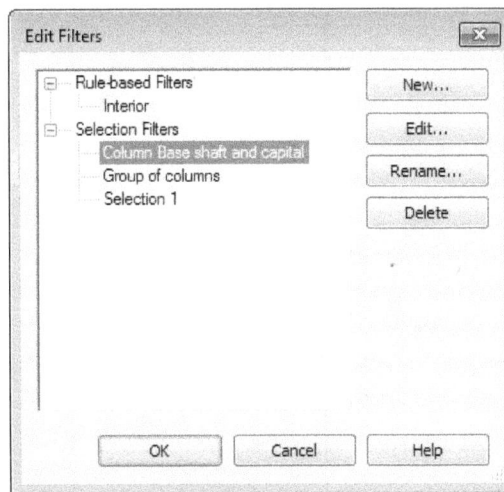

Figure B–4

- If you want to modify the name of the Filter, click **Rename...**.

3. The selection set elements remain black while the rest of the elements are grayed out. The *Edit Selection Set* contextual tab displays as well, as shown in Figure B–5.

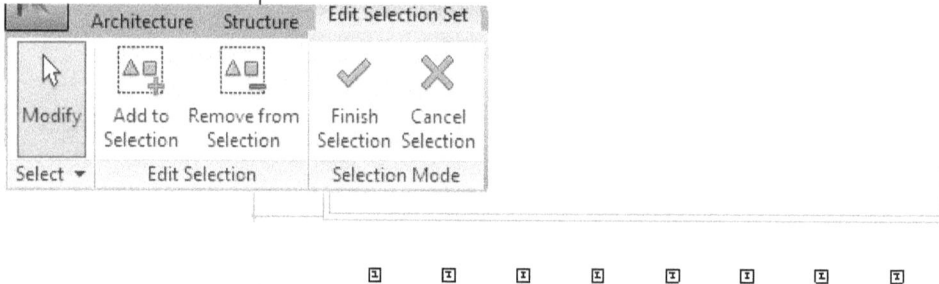

Figure B–5

4. Use ⬛ (Add to Selection) to select additional elements for the set and ⬛ (Remove from Selection) to delete elements from the set.

5. When you have finished editing, click ✓ (Finish Selection).

- In the Filters dialog box, click **OK** to finish.

B.2 Placing Slanted Structural Columns

In today's building designs, it is not uncommon to come across slanted (tilted) structural columns, as shown in Figure B–6. Slanted structural columns can be placed in plan views, elevations, sections, or 3D views.

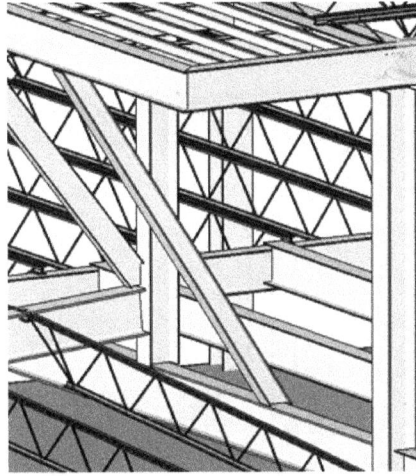

Figure B–6

- Slanted columns are not included in Graphical Column Schedules, but can be included in Building Component Schedules based on structural columns.

How To: Place Slanted Structural Columns in Plan Views

1. In the *Structure* tab>Structure panel, click ⬚ (Column).
2. In the Type Selector, select the required column type.
3. In the *Modify | Place Structural Column* tab>Placement panel, click ⬙ (Slanted Column).
4. In the Options Bar, set the elevation for the *1st Click* and *2nd Click*, as shown in Figure B–7. You can also set the offsets from the elevation.

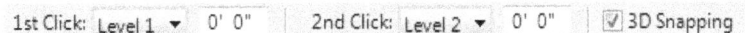

1st Click: Level 1 ▼   0' 0"   2nd Click: Level 2 ▼   0' 0"   ☑ 3D Snapping

Figure B–7

5. Select a point for the *1st Click*.
6. For the *2nd Click* location (with the elevation set in the Options Bar), select a point on any required element or anywhere in the drawing area.

Working in 3D Views

The simplest way to place a slanted column in a 3D view is to set the 3D Snapping option and then select two points anywhere along a structural element or on an endpoint, as shown on the left in Figure B–8.

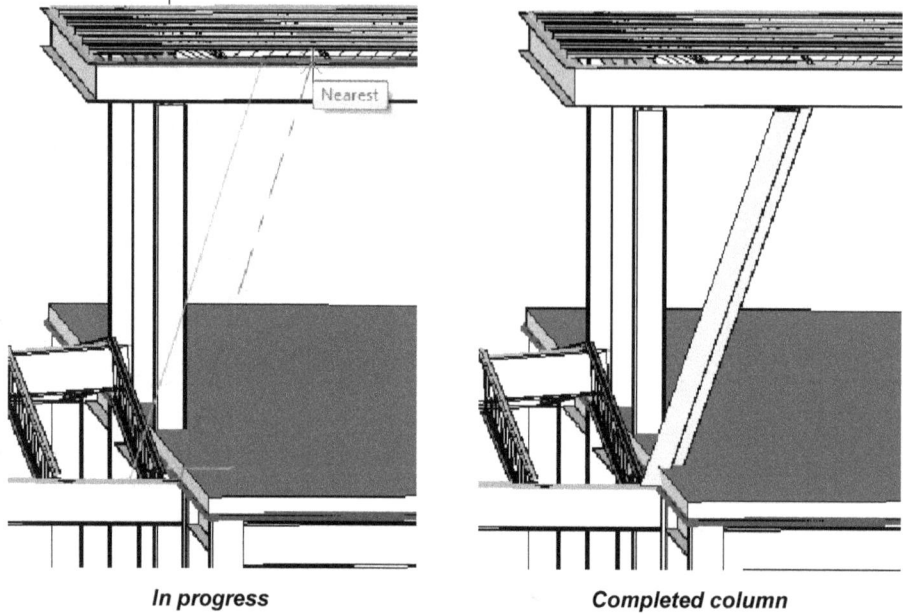

In progress   *Completed column*

Figure B–8

- The selection of structural elements defaults to the structural analysis line. This ensures that the slanted structural column is joined correctly for support and analysis.

Working in Elevations or Sections

While placing a slanted structural column in an elevation or a section view, you want to set the Work Plane along a grid line or named reference plane. This can be done before or during the **Structural Column** command.

- In the Work Plane dialog box, select a work plane from the Name drop-down list, as shown in Figure B–9. Click **OK**.

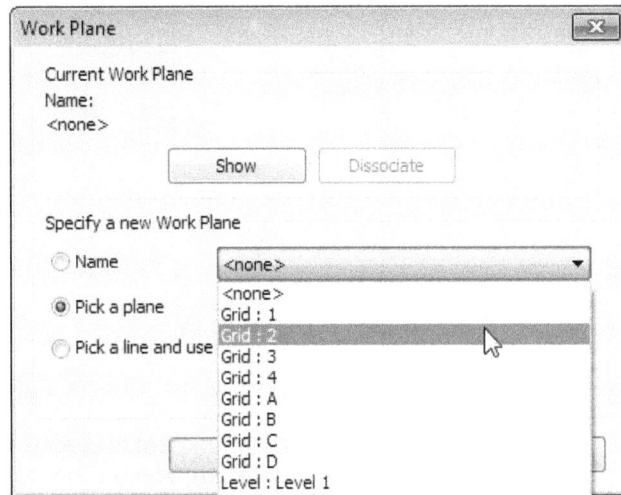

Figure B–9

Modifying Slanted Structural Columns

Several tools enable you to modify slanted structural columns:

- A slanted column can be adjusted along an attached beam and be able to cut the slanted column to an attached structural floor or slab.

- A slanted column can be cut horizontally, vertically, or perpendicularly, even when it is not attached to an element.

- Beam joins automatically adjust when resizing an existing slanted column.

B.3 Creating Slab Types

Several slab types are available in the template files that are included with the software, as shown in Figure B–10. You can also create additional slab types based on the provided types, as required.

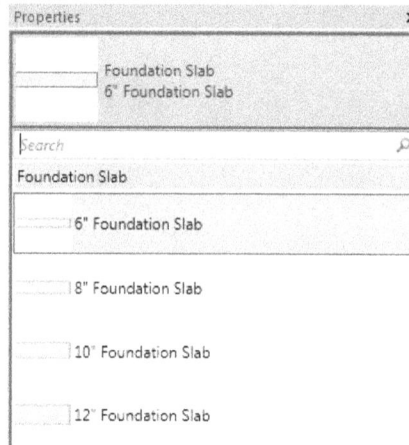

Figure B–10

- Reinforcement is placed in a slab in a separate function. Therefore, you are not required to add it to the slab type.

- The process of creating a structural floor or roof slab type is similar.

How To: Create a Slab Type

1. Start the **Structural Foundation: Slab** command or select an existing slab.
2. In the Type Selector, select a type similar to the one you want to create and in Properties, click ⬚⬚ (Edit Type).
3. In the Type Properties dialog box, click **Duplicate...** and enter a name for the new type.
4. Next to the Structure parameter, click **Edit...**, as shown in Figure B–11.

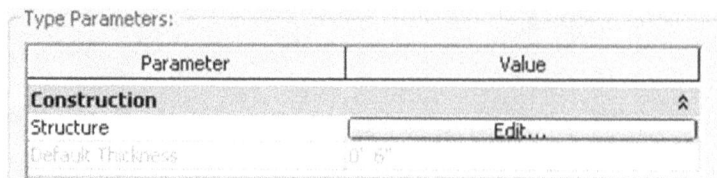

Figure B–11

- You can also set up Graphics, Identity Data, and some Analytical Properties in the Type Properties dialog box.

5. In the Edit Assembly dialog box, as shown with the Preview pane open in Figure B–12, you can change the composition of the slab. When you are finished, click **OK** to close the Edit Assembly dialog box and to close Type Properties.

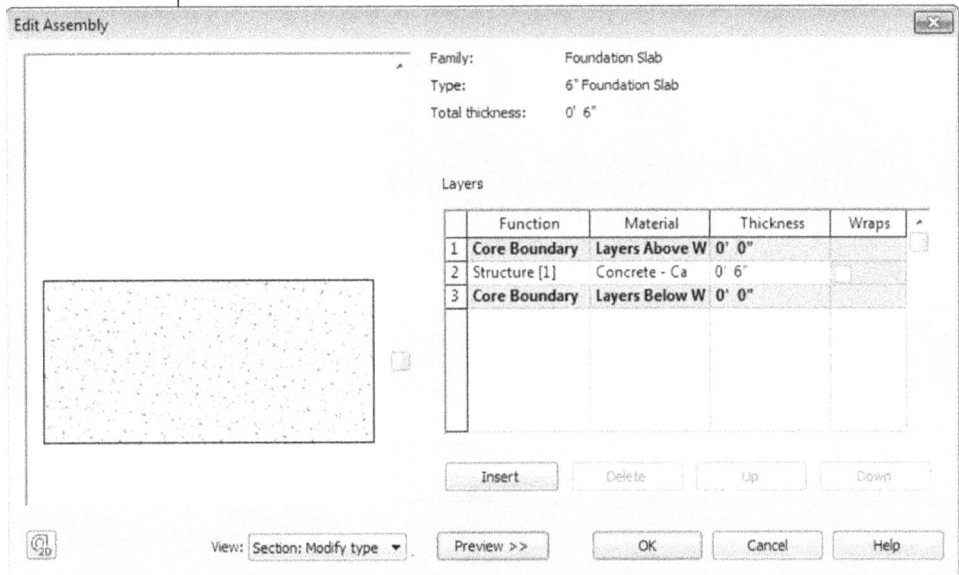

Figure B–12

- When you specify the layers for the compound element, you assign them a *Function*, *Material*, and *Thickness*.

- Use the buttons to insert additional layers and to rearrange them in the layer list. You can also delete layers from the list.

- Core boundaries separate the structural core of the slab assembly from non-structural layers above and below.

- Click **<<Preview** to display the layers of the slab in section. This tool is most useful when the slab is more complex.

B.4 Creating Rebar Types

You can create new Rebar types. When a rebar element is

selected, click ⬚ (Edit Type) in Properties. In the Type Properties dialog box, duplicate an existing type and fill out the rest of the parameters as shown in Figure B–13. Any changes made here impact all other instances of the Rebar Bar type.

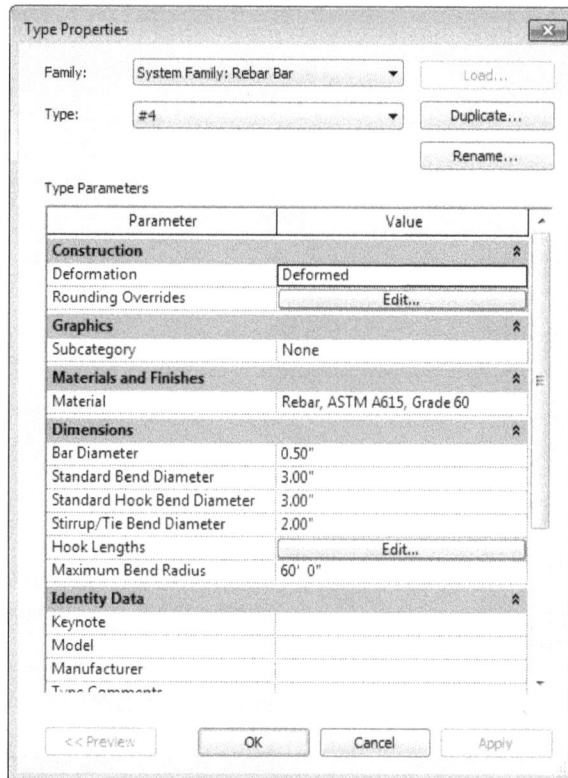

Figure B–13

- You can change the *Hook Lengths* parameter by clicking **Edit...** and using the Rebar Hook Length dialog box, as shown in Figure B–14. Options include *Hook Length*, *Tangent Length*, and *Offset Length*.

Rebar Hook Lengths

Rebar Bar Type:

#4

Rebar Bar Diameter:

0' 0 1/2"

Rebar Hook Length can be automatically calculated based on the Rebar Hook Extension Multiplier property, or the Hook Length can be manually overridden here. The Offset Length is optional and is only used for scheduling

Rebar Hook Type	Auto Calculation	Hook Length	Tangent Length	Offset Length
☑ Standard - 90 deg.	☐	0' 8"	0' 8"	
☑ Standard - 180 deg.	☐	0' 6"	0' 4 129/256"	0' 4"
☑ Stirrup/Tie - 90 deg.	☐	0' 4 1/2"	0' 4 1/2"	
☑ Stirrup/Tie - 135 deg.	☐	0' 4 1/2"	0' 4 71/128"	0' 3 1/16"
☑ Stirrup/Tie Seismic -	☐	0' 4 1/2"	0' 4 71/128"	0' 3 1/16"

OK   Cancel

Figure B–14

Hint: Creating Rebar Hook Types

If you need to add Rebar Hook Types you can duplicate an existing type in the Project Browser, in the *Families>Structural Rebar* category.

Double-click on the new hook type. This opens the Type Properties in which you can modify the *Style*, *Hook Angle*, and *Extension Multiplier,* as shown in Figure B–15.

Parameter	Value
Dimensions	⌄
Style	Standard
Hook Angle	90.000°
Extension Multiplier	12.000000

Type Parameters

Figure B–15

The *Extension Multiplier* value is multiplied by the diameter of the bar and then adds the bend radius to the equation. Therefore, if the bar *Diameter* is **0.5"** and the *Multiplier* is **24**, the actual hook *Length* is **1'-0"**.

B.5 Editing Plan and Section Profiles

In plan and section details, you might need to modify portions of the cut to display the specific intersection of two faces, as shown in Figure B–16. This can be done using **Cut Profile.** The cut profile changes the shape of the elements at their cut plane, but does not modify their 3D information. The cut is only displayed in the view in which it is drawn.

If you are working on a compound face, such as a wall with several layers of information, change the Detail Level to Medium or Fine to display the fill patterns.

Figure B–16

- You can modify the cut of walls, floors, and roofs.

How To: Use Cut Profile

1. In the *View* tab>Graphics panel, click ▦ (Cut Profile).
2. In the Options Bar, select to edit the **Face** or **Boundary between faces** as shown in Figure B–17.

Edit: ○ Face ◉ Boundary between faces

Figure B–17

3. Select the face or boundary that you want to edit.
4. In the *Modify | Create Cut Profile Sketch* tab>Draw panel, use the sketch tools to sketch a new profile as shown in Figure B–18.

Figure B–18

5. Click ✔ (Finish Edit Mode).

- If a Warning box opens, verify that the lines start and end on the same boundary line and that they do not make a closed loop or cross over each other.

B.6 Working with Guide Grids on Sheets

You can use a guide grid to help you place views on a sheet, as shown in Figure B–19. Guide grids can be set up per sheet. You can also create different types with various grid spacings.

When moving a view to a guide grid, only orthogonal datum elements (levels and grids) and reference planes snap to the guide grid.

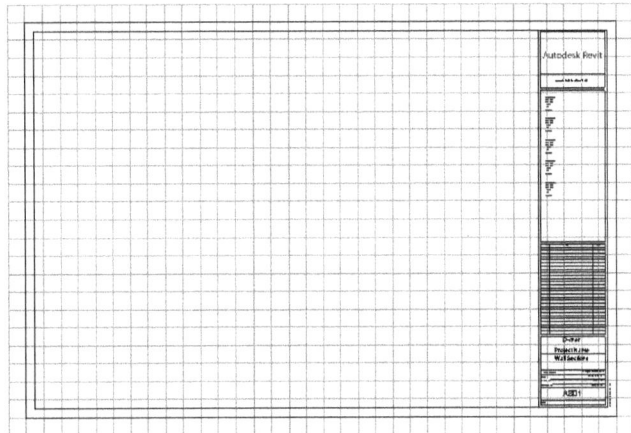

Figure B–19

- You can move guide grids and resize them using controls.

How To: Add A Guide Grid

1. When a sheet is open, in the *View* tab>Sheet Composition panel, click ⊞ (Guide Grid).
2. In the Assign Guide Grid dialog box, select from existing guide grids (as shown in Figure B–20), or create a new one and give it a name.

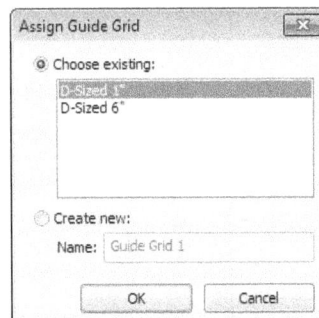

Figure B–20

3. The guide grid displays using the specified sizing.

How To: Modify Guide Grid Sizing

1. If you create a new guide grid you need to update it to the correct size in Properties. Select the edge of the guide grid.
2. In Properties, set the *Guide Spacing*, as shown in Figure B–21.

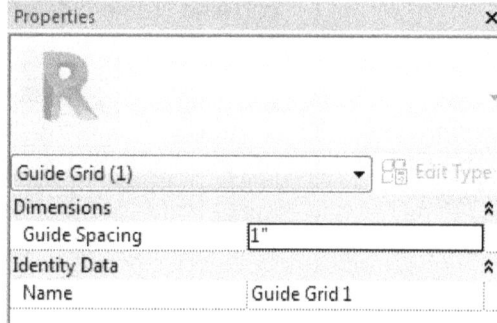

Figure B–21

B.7 Revision Tracking

When a set of working drawings has been put into production, you need to show where changes are made. Typically, these are shown on sheets using revision clouds and tags along with a revision schedule in the title block, as shown in Figure B–22. The revision information is setup in the Sheet Issues/Revisions dialog box.

No.	Description	Date
1	Change in detail due to soil	Date 1
2	Increased load - updated sizes	Date 2

Figure B–22

- More than one revision cloud can be associated with a revision number.

- The title blocks that come with the Autodesk Revit software already have a revision schedule inserted into the title area. It is recommended that you also add a revision schedule to your company title block.

How To: Add Revision Information to the Project

1. In the *View* tab>Sheet Composition panel, click ⬡ (Sheet Issues/Revisions).
2. In the Sheet Issues/Revisions dialog box, set the type of *Numbering* you want to use.
3. Click **Add** to add a new revision.

4. Specify the *Date* and *Description* for the revision, as shown in Figure B–23.

Sequence	Revision Number	Numbering	Date	Description	Issued	Issued to	Issued by	Show
1	1	Numeric	Date 1	Move Door				Cloud and Tag
2	2	Numeric	Date 2	Revise Restroom La				Cloud and Tag
3	3	Numeric	Date 3	Modification to stru				Cloud and Tag

Add
Delete

Numbering
◉ Per Project
○ Per Sheet

Row
Move Up
Move Down
Merge Up
Merge Down

Numbering options
Numeric...
Alphanumeric...

Arc length
0' 0 3/4"

OK   Cancel   Apply

Figure B–23

- Do not modify the *Issued*, *Issued by*, or *Issued to* columns. You should wait to issue revisions until you are ready to print the sheets.

5. Click **OK** when you have finished adding revisions.

- To remove a revision, select its *Sequence* number and click **Delete**.

Revision Options

- *Numbering:* Specify **Per Project** (the numbering sequence is used throughout the project) or **Per Sheet** (the number sequence is per sheet).

- *Row*: To reorganize the revisions, select a row and click **Move Up** and **Move Down**, or use **Merge Up** and **Merge Down** to combine the revisions into one.

- *Numbering Options:* Click **Numeric...** or **Alphanumeric...** to bring up the Customize Numbering Options dialog box where you can specify the numbers or letters used in the sequence as well as any prefix or suffix, as shown for the *Alphanumeric* tab in Figure B–24.

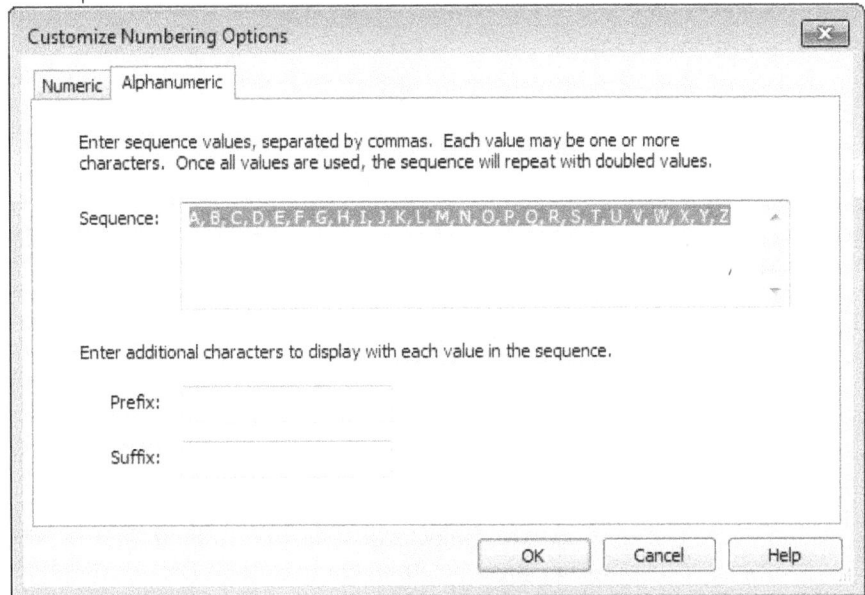

Figure B–24

- *Arc length:* Specify the length of the arcs that form the revision cloud. It is an annotation element and is scaled according to the view scale.

How To: Add Revision Clouds and Tag

1. In the *Annotate* tab>Detail panel, click ⬡ (Revision Cloud).
2. In the *Modify | Create Revision Cloud Sketch* tab>Draw panel, use the draw tools to create the cloud.

3. Click ✔ (Finish Edit Mode).

4. In the Options Bar or Properties, expand the Revision drop-down list and select from the Revision list, as shown in Figure B–25.

If the revision table has not be set up, you can do this at a later date.

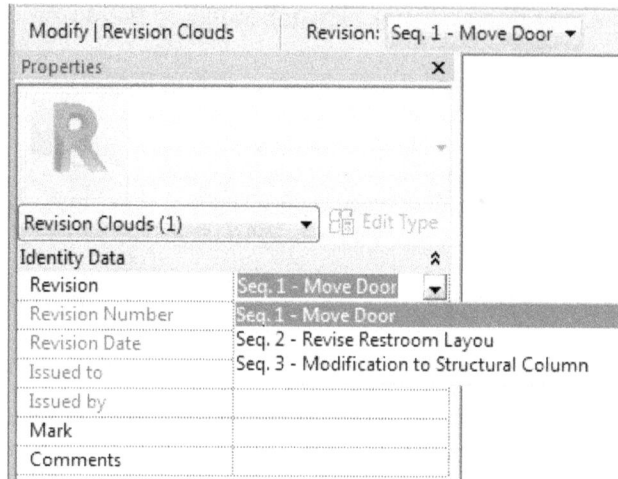

| Modify | Revision Clouds | Revision: Seq. 1 - Move Door ▾ |

Figure B–25

5. In the *Annotate* tab>Tag panel, click (Tag By Category).
6. Select the revision cloud to tag. A tooltip containing the revision number and revision from the cloud properties displays when you hover the cursor over the revision cloud, as shown in Figure B–26.

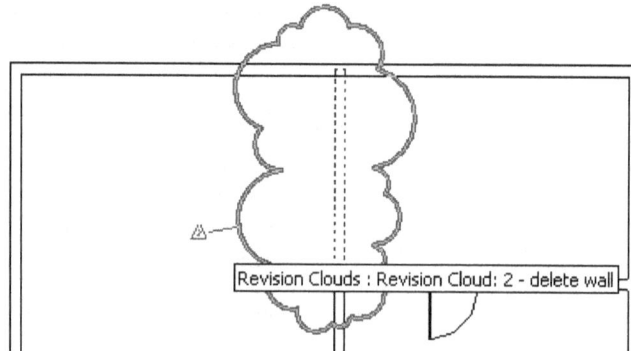

Figure B–26

- If the revision cloud tag is not loaded, load **Revision Tag.rfa** from the *Annotations* folder in the Library.

- The *Revision Number* and *Date* are automatically assigned according to the specifications in the revision table.

- Double-click on the edge of revision cloud to switch to the Edit Sketch mode and modify the size or location of the revision cloud arcs.

- You can create an open cloud (e.g., as a tree line), as shown in Figure B–27.

Figure B–27

Issuing Revisions

When you have completed the revisions and are ready to submit new documents to the field, you should first lock the revision for the record. This is called issuing the revision. An issued revision is noted in the tooltip of a revision cloud, as shown in Figure B–28.

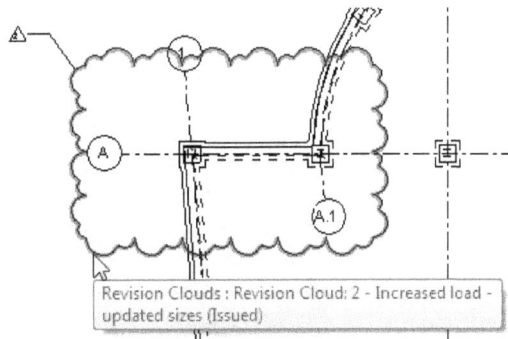

Revision Clouds : Revision Cloud: 2 - Increased load - updated sizes (Issued)

Figure B–28

How To: Issue Revisions

1. In the Sheet Issues/Revisions dialog box, in the row for the revision that you are issuing, type a name in the *Issued to* and *Issued by* fields, as required.
2. In the same row, select **Issued**.
3. Continue issuing any other revisions, as required.
4. Click **OK** to finish.

- Once the **Issued** option is selected, you cannot modify that revision in the Revisions dialog box or by moving the revision cloud(s). The tooltip on the cloud(s) note that it is **Issued**.

- You can unlock the revision by clearing the **Issued** option. Unlocking enables you to modify the revision after it has been locked.

B.8 Annotating Dependent Views

The **Duplicate as a Dependent** command creates a copy of the view and links it to the selected view. Changes made to the original view are also made in the dependent view and vice-versa. Use dependent views when the building model is so large that you are required to split it into separate sheets, as shown in Figure B–29.

Figure B–29

- Using one overall view with several dependent views makes it easier to see changes, such as *to the scale* or *detail level.*

- Dependent views display in the Project Browser under the top-level view, as shown in Figure B–30.

Figure B–30

How To: Duplicate Dependent Views

1. Select the view you want to use as the top-level view.
2. Right-click and select **Duplicate View>Duplicate as a Dependent**.
3. Rename the dependent views as required.
4. Modify the crop region of the dependent view to show the specified portion of the model.

- If you want to separate a dependent view from the original view, right-click on the dependent view and select **Convert to independent view**.

Annotating Views

Annotation Crop Region and Matchlines can be used in any type of view.

To clarify and annotate dependent views, use **Matchlines** and **View References**, as shown in Figure B–31.

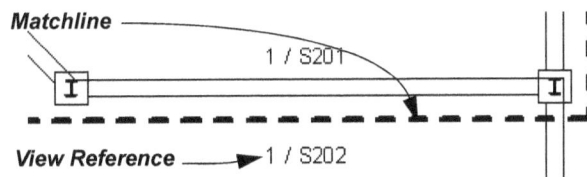

Figure B–31

- Sketch **Matchlines** in the primary view to specify where dependent views separate. They display in all related views and extend through all levels of the project by default.

- **View References** are special tags that display the sheet location of the dependent views.

How To: Add Matchlines

1. In the *View* tab>Sheet Composition panel, click (Matchline).

2. In the Draw panel, click (Line) and draw the location of the matchline.

3. In the Matchline panel, click (Finish Edit Mode) when you are finished.

- To modify an existing matchline, select it and in the *Modify | Matchline* tab>Mode panel, click (Edit Sketch).

- To modify the color and linetype of Matchlines, in the *Manage* tab>Settings panel, click ⊞ (Object Styles). In the Object Styles dialog box that opens, in the *Annotation Objects* tab, you can make changes to Matchline properties.

How To: Add View References

1. In the *View* tab>Sheet Composition panel or *Annotate* tab>Tag panel, click ⚐ (View Reference).
2. In the *Modify | View Reference* tab>View Reference panel, specify the *View Type* and *Target View*, as shown in Figure B–32.

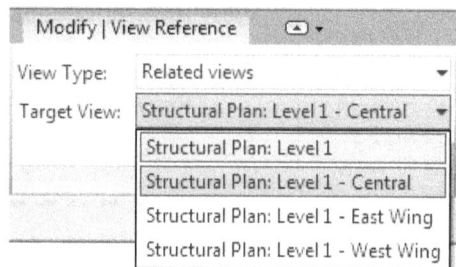

Modify	View Reference	▣ ▾
View Type:	Related views	▾
Target View:	Structural Plan: Level 1 - Central	▾

Structural Plan: Level 1
Structural Plan: Level 1 - Central
Structural Plan: Level 1 - East Wing
Structural Plan: Level 1 - West Wing

Figure B–32

3. Place the tag on the side of the matchline that corresponds to the target view.
4. Select another target view from the list and place the tag on the other side of the matchline.
5. The tags display as empty dashes until the views are placed onto sheets. They then update to include the detail and sheet number, as shown in Figure B–33.

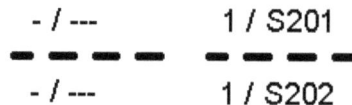

- / ---   1 / S201

- / ---   1 / S202

Figure B–33

- Double-click on the view reference to open the associated view.

- If only a label named **REF** displays when you place a view reference, it means you need to load and update the tag. The **View Reference.rfa** tag is located in the *Annotations* folder. Once you have the tag loaded, in the Type Selector, select one of the view references and, in Properties, click 🔲 (Edit Type). Select the **View Reference** tag in the drop-down list, as shown in Figure B–34, and click **OK** to close the dialog box. The new tag displays.

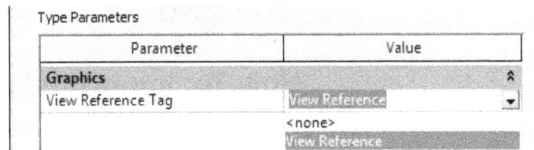

Type Parameters

Parameter	Value
Graphics	⌃
View Reference Tag	View Reference ▾
	<none>
	View Reference

Figure B–34

B.9 Importing and Exporting Schedules

Schedules are views and can be copied into your project from other projects. Only the formatting information is copied; the information about individually scheduled items is not included. That information is automatically added by the project the schedule is copied into. You can also export the schedule information to be used in spreadsheets.

How To: Import Schedules

1. In the *Insert* tab>Import panel, expand ⌕ (Insert from File) and click ⌕ (Insert Views from File).
2. In the Open dialog box, locate the project file containing the schedule you want to use.
3. Select the schedules you want to import, as shown in Figure B–35.

If the referenced project contains many types of views, change Views: to **Show schedules and reports only***.*

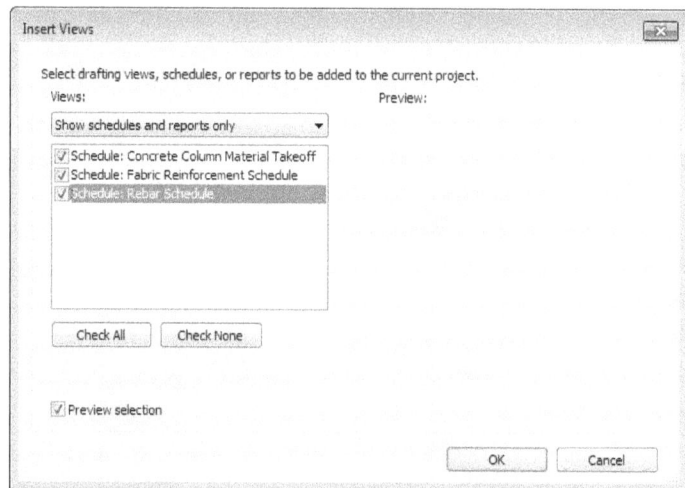

Figure B–35

4. Click **OK**.

How To: Export Schedule Information

1. Switch to the schedule view that you want to export.

2. In the Application Menu, click ⌕ (Export)> ⌕ (Reports)> ⌕ (Schedule).

3. Select a location and name for the text file in the Export Schedule dialog box and click **Save**.
4. In the Export Schedule dialog box, set the options in the *Schedule appearance* and *Output options* areas that best suit your spreadsheet software, as shown in Figure B–36.

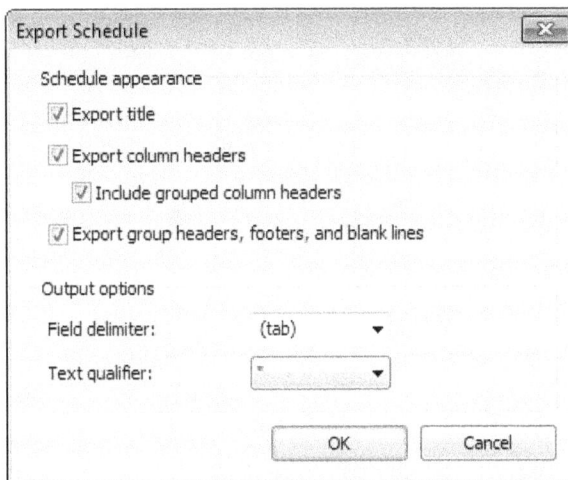

Figure B–36

5. Click **OK**. A new text file is created that you can open in a spreadsheet, as shown in Figure B–37.

Figure B–37

B.10 Creating Building Component Schedules

A Building Component schedule is a table view of the type and instance parameters of a specific element. You can specify the parameters (fields) you want to include in the schedule. All of the parameters found in the type of element you are scheduling are available to use. For example, a concrete column schedule (as shown in Figure B–38) can include instance parameters that are automatically filled in (such as the **Height** and **Width**) and type parameters that might need to have the information assigned in the schedule or element type (such as the **Fire Rating** and **Frame**).

\<Concrete Column Material Takeoff\>

A	B	C	D	E	F
		Diimensions			
Type Mark	Count	Type	Length	Base Level	Material
A	6	12 x 18	10' - 0"	Level 1	Concrete, Cast-in-Place gray
B	6	18 x 24	12' - 0"	T.O. Footing	Concrete, Cast-in-Place gray
C	14	24 x 30	12' - 0"	T.O. Footing	Concrete, Cast-in-Place gray
Grand total: 26					

Figure B–38

How To: Create a Building Component Schedule

1. In the *View* tab>Create panel, expand ⊞ (Schedules) and click ⊞ (Schedule/Quantities) or in the Project Browser, right-click on the Schedule/Quantities node and select **New Schedule/Quantities**.

2. In the New Schedule dialog box, select the type of schedule you want to create (e.g., Doors) from the *Category* list, as shown in Figure B–39.

In the Filter list drop-down list, you can specify the discipline(s) to show only the categories that you want to display.

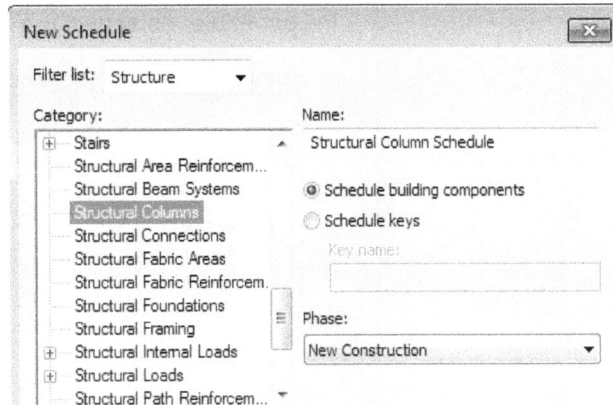

Figure B–39

3. Type a new *Name*, if the default does not suit.
4. Select **Schedule building components.**
5. Specify the *Phase* as required.
6. Click **OK**.
7. Fill out the information in the Schedule Properties dialog box. This includes the information in the *Fields*, *Filter*, *Sorting/Grouping*, *Formatting*, and *Appearance* tabs.
8. Once you have entering the schedule properties, click **OK**. A schedule report is created in its own view.

Schedule Properties – Fields Tab

In the *Fields* tab, you can select from a list of available fields and organize them in the order in which you want them to display in the schedule, as shown in Figure B–40.

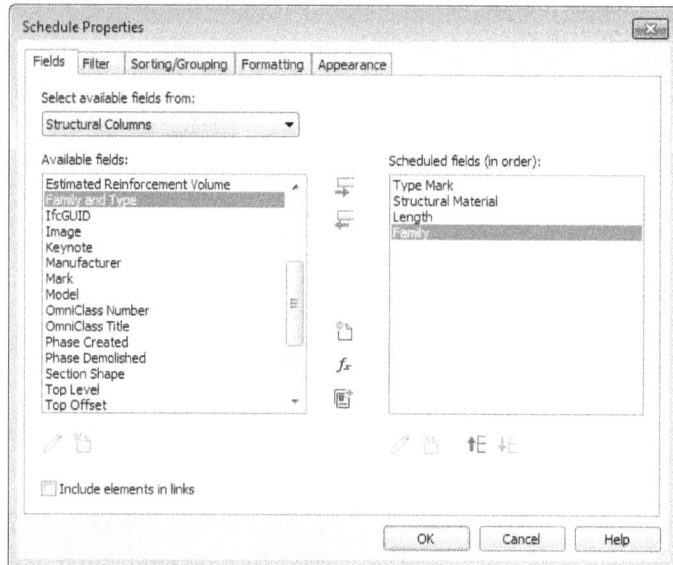

Figure B–40

How To: Fill out the Fields Tab

You can also double-click on a field to move it from the Available fields to the Scheduled fields list.

1. In the *Available fields* area, select one or more fields you

   want to add to the schedule and click ⬇ (Add parameter(s)). The field(s) are placed in the *Scheduled fields (in order)* area.

2. Continue adding fields, as required.

   • Click ⬆ (Remove parameter(s)) to move a field from the *Scheduled fields* area back to the *Available fields* area.

   • Use ↑E (Move parameter up) and ↓E (Move parameter down) to change the order of the scheduled fields.

Other Fields Tab Options

Select available fields from	Enables you to select additional category fields for the specified schedule. The available list of fields depends on the original category of the schedule. Typically, they include room information.
Include elements in links	Includes elements that are in files linked to the current project, so that their elements can be included in the schedule.
⬚ **(New parameter)**	Adds a new field according to your specification. New fields can be placed by instance or by type.
f_x **(Add Calculated parameter)**	Enables you to create a field that uses a formula based on other fields.
⬚ **(Combine parameters)**	Enables you to combine two or more parameters in one column. You can put any fields together even if they are used in another column.
✎ **(Edit parameter)**	Enables you to edit custom fields. This is grayed out if you select a standard field.
⬚ **(Delete parameter)**	Deletes selected custom fields. This is grayed out if you select a standard field.

Schedule Properties – Filter Tab

In the *Filter* tab, you can set up filters so that only elements meeting specific criteria are included in the schedule. For example, you might only want to show information for one level, as shown in Figure B–41. You can create filters for up to eight values. All values must be satisfied for the elements to display.

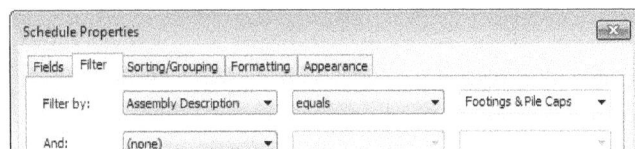

Figure B–41

- The parameter you want to use as a filter must be included in the schedule. You can hide the parameter once you have completed the schedule, if required.

Filter by	Specifies the field to filter. Not all fields are available to be filtered.
Condition	Specifies the condition that must be met. This includes options such as **equal**, **not equal**, **greater than**, and **less than**.
Value	Specifies the value of the element to be filtered. You can select from a drop-down list of appropriate values. For example, if you set *Filter By* to **Level**, it displays the list of levels in the project.

Schedule Properties – Sorting/Grouping Tab

In the *Sorting/Grouping* tab, you can set how you want the information to be sorted, as shown in Figure B–42. For example, you can sort by **Mark** (number) and then **Type**.

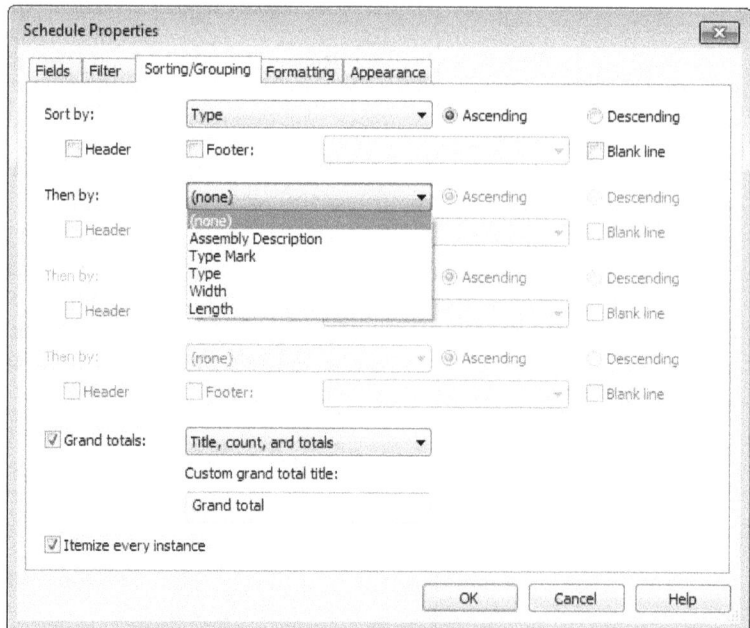

Figure B–42

Sort by	Enables you to select the field(s) you want to sort by. You can select up to four levels of sorting.
Ascending/ Descending	Sorts fields in **Ascending** or **Descending** order.
Header/ Footer	Enables you to group similar information and separate it by a **Header** with a title and/or a **Footer** with quantity information.
Blank line	Adds a blank line between groups.
Grand totals	Selects which totals to display for the entire schedule. You can specify a name to display in the schedule for the Grand total.
Itemize every instance	If selected, displays each instance of the element in the schedule. If not selected, displays only one instance of each type.

Schedule Properties – Formatting Tab

In the *Formatting* tab, you can control how the headers of each field display, as shown in Figure B–43.

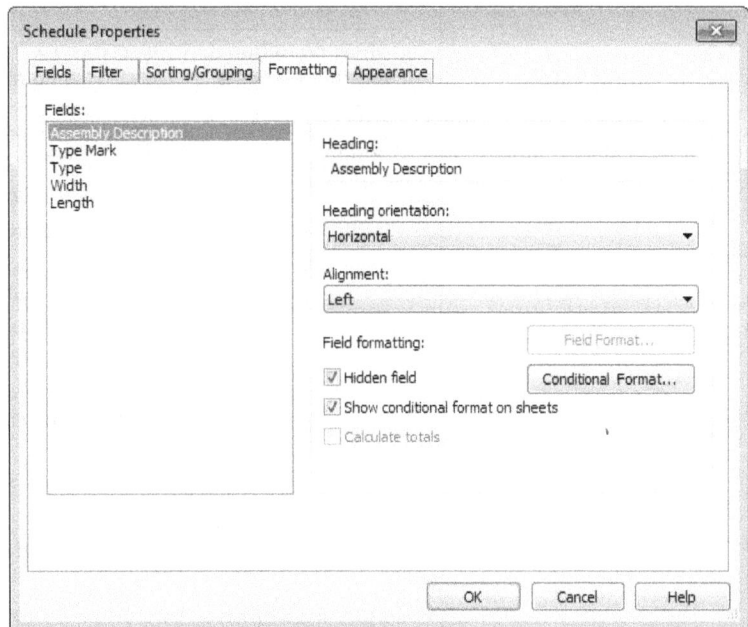

Figure B–43

Fields	Enables you to select the field for which you want to modify the formatting.
Heading	Enables you to change the heading of the field if you want it to be different from the field name. For example, you might want to replace **Mark** (a generic name) with the more specific **Door Number** in a door schedule.
Heading orientation	Enables you to set the heading on sheets to **Horizontal** or **Vertical**. This does not impact the schedule view.
Alignment	Aligns the text in rows under the heading to be **Left**, **Right**, or **Center**.
Field Format...	Sets the units format for the length, area, volume, angle, or number field. By default, this is set to use the project settings.
Conditional Format...	Sets up the schedule to display visual feedback based on the conditions listed.
Hidden field	Enables you to hide a field. For example, you might want to use a field for sorting purposes, but not have it display in the schedule. You can also modify this option in the schedule view later.
Show conditional format on sheets	Select if you want the color code set up in the Conditional Format dialog box to display on sheets.
Calculation options	Select the type of calculation you want to use. All values in a field are: • **Standard** - Calculated separately. • **Calculate totals** - Added together. • **Calculate minimum** - Reviewed and only the smallest amount is displayed. • **Calculate maximum** - Reviewed and only the largest amount is displayed. • **Calculate minimum and maximum** - Reviewed and both the smallest and largest amounts are displayed. • This is often used with rebar sets.

Enhanced
in 2017

Schedule Properties – Appearance Tab

In the *Appearance* tab, you can set the text style and grid options for a schedule, as shown in Figure B–44.

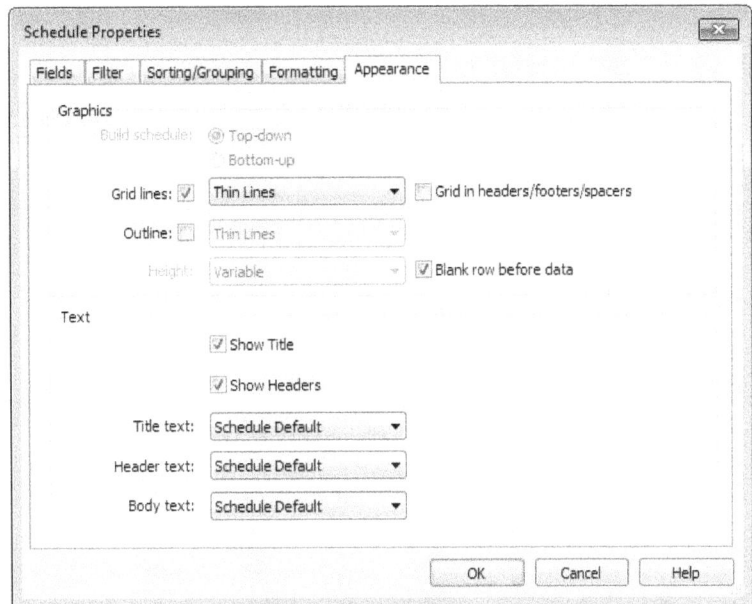

Figure B–44

Grid lines	Displays lines between each instance listed and around the outside of the schedule. Select the style of lines from the drop-down list; this controls all lines for the schedule, unless modified.
Grid in headers/ footers/spacers	Extends the vertical grid lines between the columns.
Outline	Specify a different line type for the outline of the schedule.
Blank row before data	Select this option if you want a blank row to be displayed before the data begins in the schedule.
Show Title/Show Headers	Select these options to include the text in the schedule.
Title text/Header text/Body Text	Select the text style for the title, header, and body text.

Schedule Properties

Schedule views have properties including the *View Name*, *Phases* and methods of returning to the Schedule Properties dialog box as shown in Figure B–45. In the *Other* area, select the button next to the tab that you want to open in the Schedule Properties dialog box. In the dialog box, you can switch from tab to tab and make any required changes to the overall schedule.

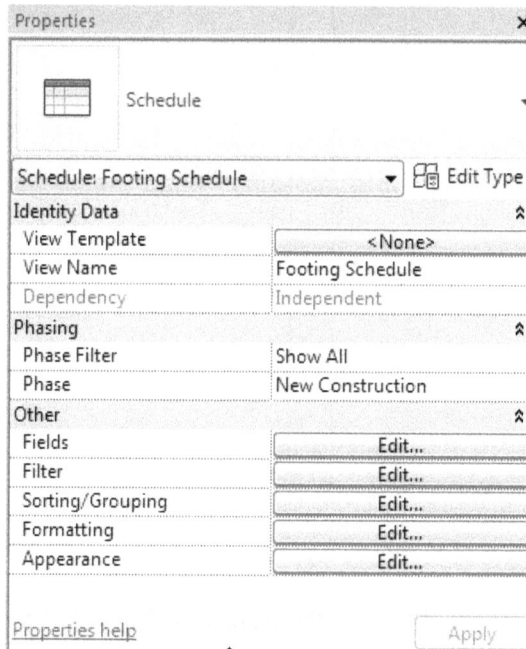

Figure B–45

Material Takeoff Schedules

Material takeoff or count schedules (shown in Figure B–46) are used for material estimates and organization. This type of schedule can be added to a drawing sheet, but is typically intended for project quantities.

<Concrete Column Material Takeoff>

A	B	C		D	E	F
		Diimensions				
Type Mark	Count	Type	Length	Base Level	Material	
A	6	12 x 18	10' - 0"	Level 1	Concrete, Cast-in-Place gray	
B	6	18 x 24	12' - 0"	T.O. Footing	Concrete, Cast-in-Place gray	
C	14	24 x 30	12' - 0"	T.O. Footing	Concrete, Cast-in-Place gray	
Grand total: 26						

Figure B–46

- The procedure for creating material takeoff schedules is the same as building component schedules, except that it uses a different command. In the *View* tab>Create panel, expand

  (Schedules) and click (Material Takeoff). Alternatively, in the Project Browser, right-click on the *Schedule/Quantities* node and select **New Material Takeoff**.

- The available fields include all of the material parameters, as shown in Figure B–47.

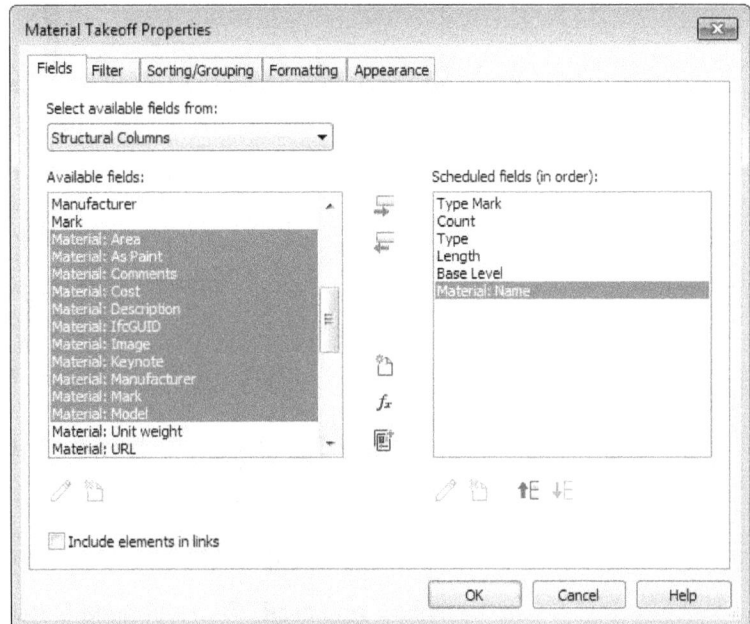

Figure B–47

B.11 Creating a Repeating Detail

Repeating detail components are very useful when working on complex details, such as those that include a brick wall. You can also create a repeating detail using any detail component, such as the glass block shown in Figure B–48.

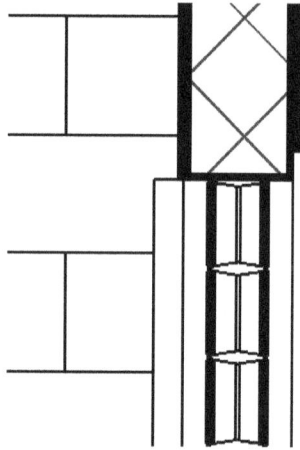

Figure B–48

How To: Create a Repeating Detail

1. Load the detail component that you want to use.

2. In the *Annotate* tab>Detail panel, expand ⬜ (Component) and click ▤ (Repeating Detail Component).

3. In Properties, click ▤ (Edit Type).
4. In the Type Properties dialog box, click **Duplicate...**. Enter a name.
5. Set the *Detail* parameter. This is the component name.
6. Fill out the rest of the parameters, as shown in Figure B–49.

Type Parameters

Parameter	Value
Pattern	⌃
Detail	Brick Standard : Running Section
Layout	Fixed Distance
Inside	☑
Spacing	0' 2 5/8"
Detail Rotation	None

Figure B–49

7. Set the *Layout* to **Fill Available Space**, **Fixed Distance**, **Fixed Number**, or **Maximum Spacing**. Select the **Inside** option if you want all components to be within the specified distance or line. Leaving this option clear causes the first component to start before the first point.

8. Set the *Spacing* between components if you are using **Fixed Distance** or **Maximum Spacing**.

9. Set the *Detail Rotation* as required, and close the dialog box.

Command Summary

Button	Command	Location
Annotations		
	Matchline	• **Ribbon:** *View* tab>Sheet Composition panel
	View Reference	• **Ribbon:** *View* tab>Sheet Composition panel or *Annotate* tab>Tag panel
Slanted Columns		
	Structural Column	• **Ribbon:** *Structure* tab>Create Panel • **Shortcut:** CL
	Slanted Column	• **Ribbon:** *Modify	Place Structural Column*>Placement panel
Revisions		
	Revision Cloud	• **Ribbon:** *Annotate* tab>Detail panel
	Sheet Issues/ Revisions	• **Ribbon:** *Manage* tab>Settings panel> expand Additional Settings
Schedules		
	Schedule/ Quantities	• **Ribbon:** *View* tab>Create panel> expand Schedules • **Project Browser:** right-click on **Schedule/Quantities** node>New Schedule/Quantities...
	Insert Views from File	• **Ribbon**: *Insert* tab>expand Insert from File
n/a	**Schedule (Export)**	• **Application Menu:** expand Export> Reports>Schedule
Selection Sets		
	Edit Selection	• **Ribbon:** *Modify	Multi-Select*> Selection panel
	Load Selection	• **Ribbon:** *Modify	Multi-Select*> Selection panel
	Save Selection	• **Ribbon:** *Modify	Multi-Select*> Selection panel

Appendix

C

Autodesk Revit Structure Certification Exam Objectives

The following table will help you to locate the exam objectives within the chapters of the Autodesk® Revit® student guides to help you prepare for the Autodesk Revit Structure Certified Professional exam.

Exam Topic	Exam Objective	Student Guide	Chapter & Section(s)
Collaboration	Create and modify levels	• Revit Structure Fundamentals	• 3.3
	Create and modify structural grids	• Revit Structure Fundamentals	• 5.1
	Import AutoCAD files into Revit	• Revit Structure Fundamentals	• 3.1
		• Revit Collaboration Tools	• 3.1
	Link Revit models	• Revit Structure Fundamentals	• 3.2
		• Revit Collaboration Tools	• 2.1
	Control the visibility for linked objects	• Revit Collaboration Tools	• 2.2
Documentation	Using temporary dimensions	• Revit Structure Fundamentals	• 2.1
	Annotate beams	• Revit Structure Fundamentals	• 13.3
	Add and modify text annotations	• Revit Structure Fundamentals	• 13.2
	Add and use dimensions and dimension labels	• Revit Structure Fundamentals	• 13.1
	Use detail components	• Revit Structure Fundamentals	• 14.2
	Create and modify column schedules	• Revit Structure Fundamentals	• 15.2

Exam Topic	Exam Objective	Student Guide	Chapter & Section(s)
Documentation (continued)	Create and modify footing schedules	• Revit Structure Fundamentals	• 15.3 • B.8
		• Revit BIM Management	• 2.2
	Create and modify standard sheets	• Revit Structure Fundamentals	• 12.1, 12.2
Modeling	Place and modify structural columns	• Revit Structure Fundamentals	• 5.2
	Place and modify walls	• Revit Structure Fundamentals	• 6.1
	Create custom wall types	• Revit BIM Management	• 3.1
	Place footings	• Revit Structure Fundamentals	• 6.2, 6.4
	Create concrete slabs and/or floors	• Revit Structure Fundamentals	• 8.1
	Create and modify stepped walls in foundations	• Revit Structure Fundamentals	• 6.2
	Place rebar	• Revit Structure Fundamentals	• 9.2
	Add beams	• Revit Structure Fundamentals	• 7.1
	Add beam systems	• Revit Structure Fundamentals	• 7.1
	Add joists	• Revit Structure Fundamentals	• 7.1
	Add cross bracing to joists	• Revit Structure Fundamentals	• 7.1
	Create and use trusses	• Revit Structure Fundamentals	• 7.3
	Create and modify floors	• Revit Structure Fundamentals	• 8.1
	Create and modify custom floors	• Revit BIM Management	• 3.1
	Create and modify sloped floors	• Revit Architecture Fundamentals	• 9.3
	Add floor openings for stairs	• Revit Structure Fundamentals	• 8.2
	Create and modify stairs	• Revit Architecture Fundamentals	• 12.1
	Create and modify ramps	• Revit Architecture Fundamentals	• 12.5
	Model and use roofs	• Revit Structure Fundamentals	• 8.1
		• Revit Architecture Fundamentals	• 11.2, 11.4
Views	Create section views	• Revit Structure Fundamentals	• 4.4
	Create framing elevations	• Revit Structure Fundamentals	• 4.4
	Use callout views	• Revit Structure Fundamentals	• 4.3

Index

* 9 7 8 1 9 4 6 5 7 1 5 4 0 *